I'm certain everyone in the military who gets assigned as a sniper hates the thought that people might think you're an executioner. I'm a shooter. A sniper. Not an executioner. But sometimes, I confess, the certainty that was my best defense mechanism thirty-five years ago evaporates. It happens when I make that turn and wind up in a mental cul-de-sac, going in circles. It happens when I relive my first kill, or my second—a woman—or when I relive shooting four Buddhist monks in the middle of a rubber plantation, watching the blood seep into their saffron robes, hearing the death cries of the one that I didn't kill cleanly.

That's when I have to deal with the knowledge that if I were a fly on the wall, watching what I had done, I would say, "You're an executioner." But the fly isn't there—he's in my head. I can't allow myself to call myself an executioner, however irrational that might sound. It may not even make sense to anyone but me, but that's the way it is.

I just did what I had to do, and it changed my life forever. . . .

"*A Sniper's Journey* is a must read for all who desire to know what it was like to get caught up in one of Vietnam's 'black budget' wars within a war. Gary Mitchell's account is riveting and revealing. And his living with the aftermath is heroic. Simply put, often those who know about these 'wars within' don't tell. Gary is telling. America would be wise to listen!"
—Brig. Gen Ezell Ware, Jr. (CA, Ret.), author of *By Duty Bound*

A SNIPER'S JOURNEY

THE TRUTH ABOUT THE MAN BEHIND THE RIFLE

GARY D. MITCHELL WITH **MICHAEL HIRSH**

FOREWORD BY DOUGLAS VALENTINE

NAL
CALIBER

NAL Caliber

Published by New American Library, a division of
Penguin Group (USA) Inc., 375 Hudson Street,
New York, New York 10014, USA
Penguin Group (Canada), 90 Eglinton Avenue East, Suite 700, Toronto,
Ontario M4P 2Y3, Canada (a division of Pearson Penguin Canada Inc.)
Penguin Books Ltd., 80 Strand, London WC2R 0RL, England
Penguin Ireland, 25 St. Stephen's Green, Dublin 2,
Ireland (a division of Penguin Books Ltd.)
Penguin Group (Australia), 250 Camberwell Road, Camberwell, Victoria 3124,
Australia (a division of Pearson Australia Group Pty. Ltd.)
Penguin Books India Pvt. Ltd., 11 Community Centre, Panchsheel Park,
New Delhi - 110 017, India
Penguin Group (NZ), cnr Airborne and Rosedale Roads, Albany,
Auckland 1310, New Zealand (a division of Pearson New Zealand Ltd.)
Penguin Books (South Africa) (Pty.) Ltd., 24 Sturdee Avenue,
Rosebank, Johannesburg 2196, South Africa

Penguin Books Ltd., Registered Offices:
80 Strand, London WC2R 0RL, England

Published by NAL Caliber, an imprint of New American Library, a division of Penguin Group
(USA) Inc. Previously published in an NAL Caliber hardcover edition.

First NAL Caliber Trade Paperback Printing, January 2007
10 9 8 7 6 5 4 3 2 1

NAL CALIBER and the "C" logo are trademarks of Penguin Group (USA) Inc.

NAL Caliber Trade Paperback ISBN: 978-0-451-22051-6

The Library of Congress has cataloged the hardcover edition of this title as follows:

Mitchell, Gary D. (Gary Don). 1949–
A sniper's journey : the truth about the man behind the rifle/Gary D. Mitchell with
Michael Hirsh.
p. cm.
Includes bibliographical references.
ISBN 0-451-21652-0 (hardcover)
1. Mitchell, Gary D. (Gary Don), 1949—Mental health.   2. Post-traumatic stress
disorder—Patients—United States—Biography.   3. Combat—Psychological aspects.
4. Snipers—United States—Biography.   5. Vietnamese Conflict,
1961–1975—Veterans—United States—Biography.   6. Vietnamese Conflict,
1961–1975—Personal narratives, American.   I. Hirsh, Michael, 1943–   II. Title.
RC552.Pg6M58 2006
616.85'212'0092—dc22   2005019516

Set in Berkley
Designed by Ginger Legato

Printed in the United States of America

For my wife,
Ellen,
who has remained by my side
as I live with the memories that haunt me daily;
and for my parents,
Gladys and Alexander

—Gary D. Mitchell

For my mother,
Essie Hirsh,
and for all the mothers who have known the anguish
of sending their children off to war

—Michael Hirsh

FOREWORD

by Douglas Valentine

Gary Mitchell, at the age of nineteen, became an assassin for the U.S. government, and that experience affected him for the rest of his life. *A Sniper's Journey* is a fascinating and often tragic story about a young man's struggle to survive under perilous circumstances. It's a story of a grown man's quest to find peace of mind.

The drama began in June 1969, when Gary found himself in an infantry outfit in central South Vietnam. The war was raging. Nearly ten thousand GIs were killed that year. It was the second-deadliest year in a war that claimed fifty thousand American lives. The situation was desperate. The people in charge were willing to do anything to win.

Under these dire circumstances, Gary became a sniper and was plunged into a world of deadly intrigues and wrenching emotional conflicts that remain unresolved today. But he wasn't used as infantry snipers are currently being used in Iraq. He wasn't positioned on a rooftop, in radio contact with his commanders, carefully selecting and picking off insurgent snipers in modern "hit-and-run" urban warfare.

As Gary explains, "This was a preplanned assassination, and in comparison to combat, I had plenty of time to think about it, to decide whether it was something I was willing to do."

In Gary's case, anonymous men, probably employed by the CIA, used him to assassinate unsuspecting people from a distance, while he was in hiding. The people he killed never heard the report from his rifle.

The great irony of *A Sniper's Journey* is that Gary Mitchell had no idea whom he was working for on his sniper missions. He didn't know about the Phoenix Program while he was in Vietnam. He didn't learn about it until thirty years later. But it is very likely that Mitchell's sniper missions were part of Phoenix.

Created in 1967 by the CIA, Phoenix was designed to "neutralize" the people in the shadow government that ran the insurgency in South Vietnam. To "neutralize" meant to kill, capture, or make to defect. Robert Komer, the CIA officer initially in charge of Phoenix, imposed a quota of eighteen hundred neutralizations per month on the people running the program in the field. In 1969, Phoenix neutralized 19,534 people. Of those, 4,832 were killed. By the time the war was over, the CIA estimated that Phoenix had killed some twenty thousand people. The Vietnamese put the number at over forty thousand.[1]

The Phoenix Program in 1969 had some six hundred American military men, and fifty CIA officers in Saigon, and at region, province, and district headquarters.[2] They had no forces of their own, but could reach into any unit and grab anyone they needed. If they wanted to "search and destroy" a village that was thought to harbor guerrilla leaders, they could send in a regular army battalion to do the job. They could call in a B-52 attack on a remote village, if that village was thought to harbor an important individual in the shadow government.

But search-and-destroy missions and five-hundred-pound bombs did little to win the hearts and minds of the Vietnamese. So Komer told his Phoenix staff "that he wanted a 'rifle shot' approach—a

1 "Phoenix 1969 End of Year Report" (Saigon, February 28, 1970, Headquarters, United States Military Assistance Command, Civil Operations and Rural Development), p. 6.
2 Hearing on the Nomination of William E. Colby (Committee on Armed Services, U.S. Senate, July 2, 20, 25, 1973), p. 172.

sniper's attack, not a shotgun approach" against the people managing the insurgency.[3]

There you have it from the horse's mouth. The crux of the Phoenix concept was using snipers to assassinate the leaders of the Viet Cong insurgency.

Which is why expert shooters like Gary were in hot demand in 1969.

Understanding Phoenix is essential in putting what Gary Mitchell did in its proper historical context. Otherwise, what you're about to read seems almost unbelievable.

Gary's coauthor, Michael Hirsh, knew that I had written a book about the Phoenix Program, and that Professor Alfred W. McCoy described it as "the definitive account." Published in 1990, it took five years to research. It is based on interviews with the CIA officers who created and ran the program, including the first Phoenix chief, Robert Komer, and his successor, William E. Colby, who managed the program from 1969 to 1971. Colby would serve as director of Central Intelligence from 1973 to 1975.

In simple terms, the Phoenix Program had two tiers: tactical and strategic. On the tactical level—from the 240 districts down to several thousand hamlets—its purpose was the political control of people. To this end, everyone in South Vietnam was registered in a national ID program. Everyone was investigated, and those deemed to be Viet Cong supporters were entered into a computerized blacklist. People who were not actively opposing the VC were considered sympathizers and put on the blacklist, too.

The blacklist enabled the people running Phoenix to conduct a massive dragnet across South Vietnam. This was the purpose of the tactical lower tier.

There were forty-four provinces in Vietnam. A province was like

---

3   Douglas Valentine, *The Phoenix Program* (New York, William Morrow & Company, 1990), p. 131.

a state in the United States. A district was like a county. The CIA ran Phoenix at the province level and above.

If a tactical-level VC suspect was "at large," the Phoenix district adviser notified his CIA boss in the province capital. At this point the CIA sent a counterterror team, often Green Berets or Navy SEALs, to neutralize the suspect. If the VC suspect could not be captured and brought to the Province Interrogation Center, he or she was killed.

Neutralizations at the strategic level required more careful planning and execution than at the tactical level. For example, Buddhists composed the vast majority of the Vietnamese population, and many Buddhists held positions of power in business and government. The Saigon government could not be seen to be repressing Buddhists who opposed U.S. policies, so the CIA neutralized troublesome Buddhists in ways that ensured "plausible deniability."

One way of ensuring plausible deniability was to use expendable army snipers like Gary Mitchell to assassinate important people who were otherwise untouchable.

All CIA assassinations meet this "deniability" criterion. They must be deniable by the expendable people who carry them out, as well as those who plan them.

Phoenix veterans tend to despise the word *assassin,* because many of their targets were not military personnel. People on the blacklist included union organizers, doctors, lawyers, schoolteachers, and even Buddhist monks. Some of these people were secret members of the shadow government that ran the insurgency. Others were nationalists opposed to U.S. policy. Some were victims of mistaken identity, or falsely accused, or targeted by corrupt officials for failing to pay bribes.

The CIA bosses chose the targets, and CIA assassins don't like thinking, as one spook put it, that Phoenix was "the greatest blackmail scheme ever invented: 'If you don't do what I want, you're VC!' "

To admit that Phoenix was an assassination program would mean that the people who created it and ran it, and those who served as its assassins, might someday be labeled war criminals. Which is a powerful enough motive for everyone involved to deny that the program ever assassinated anyone.

But what else do you call a carefully selected "targeted kill" of a key individual by a sniper?

In *A Sniper's Journey,* you will learn about unbelievable things that not only were possible, but routine during the Vietnam War.

Don't be surprised to learn that the same thing is happening today. As reported in *Newsweek,* U.S. Special Operations assassination teams are being deployed in Iraq to effect what they call "the Salvador Option."[4] The Salvador Option was an extrapolation of the Phoenix Program, conceived and often managed by the same people.

Christopher Dickey, in his book *With the Contras,* spoke about the training manual given to the CIA contract officers who ran the death squads in El Salvador. He describes it as "a little book with a cover in the blue and white of the Nicaraguan flag. The graphic motif was rows of heads with large holes through them. Targets. It looked as if they were targets for snipers."[5]

That training manual was created by and for people in the Phoenix Program.

A Sniper's Journey is a complete war story because it acknowledges that the war doesn't always end when your tour of duty is over and you go back to the real world. For some veterans like Gary Mitchell, the war rages on forever, because the realization has surfaced that they did things they weren't supposed to do. And the only way they can find any peace of mind is to tell their story.

Alas, there are many prohibitions against doing that. For a person of conscience, it is hard to write about killing people. In this respect, *A Sniper's Journey* is not just a story of a young man's lost innocence;

---

4   Michael Hirsh and John Barry, "The Salvador Option," *Newsweek,* January 14, 2005.

5   Christopher Dickey, *With the Contras* (New York, Simon & Schuster, 1985), p. 256.

it's about a grown man's endless quest for validation. For no matter where Gary Mitchell journeys in search of a tangible connection to his past, there is no evidence of his ever having been a sniper.

There never will be. Finding documented proof of covert operations is like going to the local Mafia boss for the inside scoop on crime. It's not going to happen.

The military and CIA spend billions of dollars learning how to manipulate people. The process starts with breaking down a young person's personality and rebuilding him as a killing machine. The moral prohibitions the recruits have learned at home, in school, at church, about right and wrong, are replaced with new taboos. It's like being sworn into a secret society and swearing never to reveal its secrets. The soldiers come out of boot camp able to do things that, under normal circumstances, they would never consider.

Initially, a soldier is taught to feel no remorse, so that he functions as part of the machine. Years later, when he finds himself grappling with nightmares and shame, the taboos prevent the soldier from telling what he has done. The skeletons stay in the closet.

But sometimes the machine breaks down, and people like Gary Mitchell emerge from the wreckage to tell their stories. In Gary's case, it's taken more than three decades. Sometimes it happens sooner, as in the case of the whistle-blower among the MPs at Abu Ghraib.

No matter how long it takes, the government is prepared to discredit those who go public, who attempt to puncture the balloon of plausible deniability. Spooks and soldiers who have engaged in similar activities emerge from the shadows to discredit the renegades who speak out or stumble into the public limelight.

Some people will say that Gary Mitchell's story doesn't ring true. Certified snipers will insist that the CIA didn't need to borrow regular army guys. The Green Berets and Navy SEALs who volunteered for assassination missions will be the most vitriolic in their criticism.

FOREWORD

They knew what they were getting into. They signed nondisclosure statements and are subject to fines and imprisonment if they break the code of silence. Their careers and reputations are at stake.

Even if Gary Mitchell were to find the people who guided him on his sniper's journey, they would disavow him. Witness what happened when a Navy SEAL revealed that former Nebraska senator Bob Kerrey had participated in the murder of over a dozen innocent Vietnamese civilians. Witness the criticism heaped upon Hugh Thompson, the man who single-handedly stopped the My Lai massacre. The list goes on and on, but the outcome is always the same: The lone whistle-blower is invariably discredited.

A Sniper's Journey is a warning to Americans that their government is more powerful, more manipulative, and more ruthless than they could ever believe.

Living with this problem is the challenge of Gary Mitchell's life. Writing *A Sniper's Journey* is the cathartic act that sets the record straight. It is a story of self-realization and healing, told without bitterness, about things we need to know.

With the assistance of coauthor Michael Hirsh—who served as an army combat correspondent in Vietnam—Mitchell finds redemption by telling what happened. Mike Hirsh adds his own unique blend of humor, compassion, and experience, and helps Gary tell his story without being apologetic. They tell it with candor and a sense of time and place that turns the unimaginable into a lesson about truth. It is a lesson that helps us understand and cope with the great uncertainties, sorrows, and mysteries of living in such tumultuous times.

Douglas Valentine is the author of *The Hotel Tacloban* (a widely acclaimed account of life in a Japanese POW camp), *The Phoenix Program*, *TDY* (an action/adventure novella about the CIA's involvement in international drug smuggling), and *The Strength of the Wolf*, a nonfiction book about the early years of federal drug law enforcement. A sequel,

FOREWORD

The Strength of the Pack, about the origins of the DEA, is forthcoming in 2006 through the University Press of Kansas. Mr. Valentine is the author of many articles about the war on terror, which are easily accessible on the Internet.

THE RULES

In 1969, the CIA's highest official in South Vietnam, future Director of Central Intelligence William Colby, issued the following "instruction":

The PHOENIX program is one of advice, support and assistance to the GVN (Government Viet Nam) Phuong Hoang program aimed at reducing the influence and effectiveness of the Viet Cong Infrastructure in South Viet Nam. . . .

Operations against the Viet Cong Infrastructure include the collection of intelligence, identifying these members (of the Viet Cong), inducing them to abandon their allegiance to the Viet Cong and rally to the government . . . and, as a final resort, the use of military or police force against them if no other way of preventing them from carrying on their unlawful activities is possible. Our training emphasizes the desirability of obtaining these target individuals alive and of using intelligent and lawful methods of interrogation to obtain the truth of what they know about

other aspects of the Viet Cong Infrastructure. U.S. personnel are under the same legal and moral constraints with respect to the operations of a Phoenix character as they are with respect to regular military operations against enemy units in the field. Thus, *they are specifically not authorized to engage in assassinations* [italics mine] or other violations of the rules of land warfare, but they are entitled to use such reasonable military force as is necessary to obtain the goals of rallying, capturing, or eliminating the Viet Cong Infrastructure in the Republic of Viet Nam.

INTRODUCTION

My wife, Ellen, and I had a rule: Holiday time is ours and ours alone. Call us on the phone—we don't answer. Knock on our door—we're not home. It's been that way almost from the time we got married—second marriages for each of us—back in 1981 when we were both soldiers stationed in Germany. I forget how the tradition started, but it seemed to work for us.

At least I thought it did. But hey, I'm a guy; how am I supposed to know what a woman is thinking? What seemed like the beginning of the end, or maybe it was the end of the beginning of our relationship, happened on Christmas Day in 1996. We were home alone in Los Angeles, and had spent Christmas Eve with Ellen's family. Of course, when we headed for home, it was with a large bag of leftovers—turkey, rolls, stuffing, the works—which we planned to eat while watching a Christmas movie on television.

You're probably wondering what all this has to do with what I've called *A Sniper's Journey*. Trust me and hang in there for a minute; it's all part of the road I'm traveling.

Late in the afternoon Ellen was in the kitchen warming up the leftovers and I came in to help. I had been a little edgy and snapped at her a couple of times over nothing. Nowadays, I would recognize the signs and know what was coming. But at that time—not a clue.

I was trying to open a package of dinner rolls, the kind that's heat-sealed in cellophane, and I just couldn't find the seam. Finally, in frustration and anger, I screamed a couple of expletives and threw the rolls onto the counter.

I'll let Ellen tell it from her perspective, because this book isn't just about me and how the killing I did and the dying I saw affected me. It's about us, our relationship, and how my experiences in the army impacted our marriage.

"I was standing there, watching Gary struggle with the package of rolls. I watched the change begin to show on his face. He was even beginning to sweat a little bit, and then he started cussing, and the entire demeanor of his body went from casually relaxed to tense and stiff in an instant. His face became hard, and then he slammed the rolls onto the counter.

"If you've never seen a transformation like that, or even if you have, it's scary to watch. As soon as he threw the rolls I said, 'Gary, what the hell is the matter with you?' And that did it. That's all it took. He started screaming and yelling at me. What had been the beginning of a very pleasant afternoon had suddenly turned—as it had so many times in the past—into this horrible nightmare. At that point, anything I said or did was just fuel for the fire that was burning inside of him."

I told you her perspective would be worth hearing. Okay, I was completely out of control by that time. There was nothing she could do or say that was going to defuse my rage. I was, for lack of a better term, totally and completely insane at that moment. She told me to calm down, and that was really the wrong thing to say to me. Of course, anything she said would have been the wrong thing. "Calm down, listen to what you're saying, take a deep breath." It was all wrong.

I looked at her and raised my fist like I was going to hit her, and even in the state I was in, I knew better than to actually do it. So I slammed my fist onto the counter so hard that the impact caused a couple of glasses to fall over.

Ellen recalls, "When he made his hand into a fist and actually started to draw back, I thought that he was really going to let me have it. I couldn't even see my Gary in the face that was glaring at me. I took a couple of staggering steps backward just at the time that he slammed his fist into the counter.

"I immediately started to cry, and the tears did what words never could do. It was like throwing a glass of cold water in his face. I could see his face just crumple; all the rage and anger drained out. He reached for me, instantly saying, 'I'm sorry, I'm sorry. Oh, my God, I'm sorry!'

"When he moved toward me, I backed up a couple of more steps and stared at him, wondering who the hell this person is.

"I said, 'That's it! I've had enough! No more! Get some help, *now,* or get a lawyer.'"

When I realized what I had done, scaring Ellen so badly that she broke down into tears, I was shocked and ashamed. Ellen was the light of my life. I honestly believe that if she hadn't come into my world when she did, I might have done what a lot of Vietnam vets have done—killed myself. Ellen has always been willing to talk with me, cry with me, or hold me as I cried. She had never criticized, passed judgment, or withdrawn in horror. But now—this.

At that moment I was scared, angry with myself, and embarrassed; I felt like every bit of the ass that I had been a few moments before. Ellen was just standing there, trembling and crying. The more she cried, the more her body was racked by the sobs. I reached out and she backed away, and at that moment I wanted to die; I really did.

I begged her to forgive me, and she kept backing farther away. All kinds of thoughts went through my mind. *Will she ever kiss me again? Will she ever trust me again? My God, what will I do if she actually gets a lawyer?*

She said, "Please don't touch me." I went outside and sat on the patio. I didn't know what to do. After a while she came outside, and calmly but firmly said, "I'm not kidding. I've had enough. You get some help. This is not open to debate."

At that point, if she'd asked me to shoot myself, I'd have gladly done it. But she said, "Gary, I love you. I've done everything I can, but nothing seems to work. I will not put up with this anymore."

So now you've got some idea of where my story is going. Getting there hasn't been—as they used to say—"half the fun." When I finally saw a psychologist for the first time, she listened as I described the nightmares and episodes of violence, the periods of misery, the inability to leave my war experiences behind. And she asked me to write them down, to write a journal of my memories and nightmares. And that's what *A Sniper's Journey* is—a telling of the events that shaped my life, as I now remember them. The journey began in Granbury, Texas, moved on to Vietnam, where I was used as an always-get-the-job-done sniper, through a twenty-four-year army career that took me from buck private to chief warrant officer with an American advisory group to the Saudi Arabian National Guard in the first Gulf War. It's a journey that continues to this day, because, as those who suffer from it—and those who love them—know all too well, the battle we fight with post-traumatic stress disorder (PTSD) is ongoing. My hope is that the servicemen who are now fighting another war, and the families who will welcome changed men and women home from that war, can learn from my experience and deal with the emotional trauma that war inevitably causes before it tears them and their families apart.

—Gary D. Mitchell
Los Angeles, California
November 11, 2005

CHAPTER ONE

Let's Join Up

In February of 1968 I was eighteen years old, one of eighty-eight kids in the senior class at the only high school in Granbury, Texas, thirty-seven miles southwest of Fort Worth. I had the world by the tail and a tiger in my tank. I was convinced beyond the shadow of any doubt that I was hipper and, quite frankly, much more intelligent than many of those around me, especially my parents. While they hadn't yet reached older-than-dirt status, at sixty-three and fifty-eight, respectively, my father and mother seemed ancient to me. They'd had fourteen children, eight of whom had died in infancy. All that life experience gave my parents the confidence to believe that they knew what was best for me. I was convinced they were wrong.

Granted, this certainty about who I was and what I was capable of deciding for myself was relatively newfound. Like most boys moving into their late teens, I'd been testing the limits; but under the watchful eyes of just about every adult in Granbury, there wasn't a whole lot I could get away with. Talk about taking a village . . . Granbury kids were the poster children for the concept.

Consider our chat about me joining the army. It happened one evening at the dinner table. Our family custom was to watch the *CBS Evening News* with Walter Cronkite and get our nightly measure of combat footage from an obscure little country in Southeast Asia called Vietnam before adjourning to the kitchen for our evening meal.

Before eating, my father would always say a prayer of thanks, which he always concluded with a request to protect America's service members, especially those over in Vietnam. My family was given to honoring our military. Fact is, from World War II forward for half a century, my parents had almost continually had one of their children in the service. My oldest brother, Leon, had been an army infantryman fighting in Europe. Another brother, Harrell, served in the Marine Corps during the Korean War. And another brother, Howard, was on active duty in the air force and was about to retire just as I was signing up. Much to what I'm sure was the relief of my mother, my sisters Barbara and Ruth never entered the service.

I came from a generation that, as children, watched John Wayne, Audie Murphy, Jimmy Stewart, Glenn Ford, and others give fantastic movie performances in which they always died heroically, not suffering terribly from their wounds, and in general, glorifying warfare. We also tuned in to TV series such as *Combat!* with Vic Morrow, and *Twelve O'Clock High* with Robert Lansing that portrayed the heroics of war, but gave little indication of the mental and physical suffering.

So I figured it shouldn't have come as a surprise to Mom and Dad when I said, "I think I'll join the army."

My father didn't miss a beat: "No, you're not, either."

I was eighteen; I was graduating from high school. I thought I should be able to decide my own future. I puffed out my boyish chest and asked, "Why not?"

Dad's answer was simple. "Because I said you're not, that's why—eat your supper."

Rather than heeding his warning, I said, "I'm old enough. I don't have to have your permission to join. I can do it if I want to, and you can't stop me."

My mom looked shocked, but she made no comment. However, the look on her face indicated that the family was going to soon need the services of a good funeral director, because she was quite sure that my father was going to kill me.

He looked at me with his face showing a hurt and anger that parents experience when the children they've raised from infancy begin to assert their independence. But to my surprise, he didn't even raise his voice when he said, "Okay, but you'll be making a mistake, and you'll regret it if you do," and without another comment, he continued to eat his dinner.

For the rest of the evening I couldn't think of anything other than the fact that my dad thought I'd be making a mistake. Surely someone with my level of worldly experience and intelligence could make up his own mind without parental guidance. After all, it wasn't a life-or-death decision—or so it seemed to me then. I was just considering joining the army for three short years. Absurd as it may sound, the fact that the army was smack in the middle of an armed conflict really didn't cross my mind.

Why? Because Granbury, Texas, population three thousand, had been only slightly touched by the war. One young man whose sister-in-law was in my high school class had died, and two others, one of whom was my cousin, had been seriously wounded. The entire town—like much of the country—was still somewhat naive about the growing conflict. The fact that we could see the war nightly on our television screens didn't make it any more real to us than *Gunsmoke*. We had our few who found ways to avoid the draft, but for the most part, the young men being drafted served, and a number elected to volunteer. And with those few exceptions, all returned home safely and resumed their lives.

That night I tossed and turned a lot, awakening in the morning to the realization that I was now even angrier at the comments my father had made than I'd been at dinner. I always drove to school with a friend named Steve, and we usually stopped at a small store and bought a Coke to drink on the way. On this morning, the entire time we were in the store and then on the way to school I groused to him about the way my father had dismissed my decision. I repeated the argument that hadn't had any impact on my dad. "Hey, I'm eighteen. I'm old enough to be drafted. Why shouldn't I join the army? Isn't it the thing you should do, especially during a war?" (Decades later, I can see that this argument was inconsistent with my ability the previous evening to ignore the fact that the army was fighting a war in order to convince my parents—and myself—that a three-year enlistment carried no inordinate risks. The only way to explain it—I was a hormonally driven teenager; logical thinking and deductive reasoning weren't necessarily part of the package.)

I was whipping myself into a fiery rage that can only be experienced by a child on the cusp between adolescence and adulthood. The very idea that I could make a mistake—how dared he? During the remainder of the drive to school, I moaned and groaned about the situation. Just as we pulled up, I said, "Let's skip school. I'm going to join the army!" My friend didn't even turn the car engine off; he simply turned the corner and headed toward Fort Worth.

The recruiter welcomed us warmly—after all, he was getting a gift that all recruiters wished for: a free recruit, a walk-in, a warm body that would be graduating from high school in only three months, and old enough that he didn't need his parents to sign.

I took the tests, passed them without difficulty, and allowed myself—no, demanded—to be scheduled for a physical examination. The following week I skipped school again and went to the Armed Forces Entrance and Examination Station (AFEES). There I took more intelligence and aptitude tests and then faced the battery of medical exams one must pass in order to enter the armed forces.

I passed every test and examination they administered and was sent to see a counselor to select my job in the army. For no reason that I can recall, I wanted to be a truck driver, but according to the counselor, training classes for that MOS (military occupational specialty) were filled. As an alternative, he offered me a job as a mechanic, which I accepted, signed the papers, and then headed back home to Granbury.

Now there was only the little matter of telling my parents that against their best advice I had joined the army. Suffice it to say that the conversation did not go well. My father was infuriated that, in a rebellious state, I would ignore his opinion and enter the military— especially in the midst of an armed conflict. In retrospect, what was weighing on his mind was that he and my mother had been through this twice before, a fact that I didn't bother to take into consideration. Mom didn't say much, but my father went into full lecture mode. He talked about kids rebelling, going against parental wishes, thinking they knew more than the people who raised them from birth.

It was not a pleasant conversation for someone who was under the delusion that he was a grown-up. If I thought I could have gotten away with it, I would have stood up to him and declared my adulthood, but I had to put all my mental energies into shielding myself from the verbal flak that my dad was sending in my direction. The unpleasantries lasted about an hour, and it was pretty much one-way. He was sermonizing from the mountaintop, and I was down below, and you know what they say about what flows downhill.

In the end, he accepted that it was out of his hands and simply said, "You're a man, now; you'd better take care of yourself. It would kill your mama if something happened to you." I understand now that it would have hurt him just as much as it would have hurt my mom.

My high school graduation ceremony took place on May 24, and I had three final weeks of civilian life before I reported for induction in mid-June. There was no point in looking for a three-week job, so I just roamed around town trying to capitalize on the newfound status I was enjoying as a high school grad as well as an incipient man in uniform. Because my father was already drawing his Social Security, I got a small monthly check. It was only about eighteen dollars, but that was a lot more in 1968 than it is now. Gas back then was just thirty-four cents a gallon, a McDonald's burger with fries and a shake was only sixty-three cents, a pack of Marlboros was half a buck, and a ticket to the movies was a dollar. With the money burning a hole in my pocket, I drove around town in my '65 Ford pickup trying to chase girls. My problem was that I was a bit like the dog that liked to chase cars—if he caught one, he probably wouldn't know what to do with it. I'd managed to lose my virginity a few months before graduation, and I was hopeful that it marked the start of a new era in the social life of Gary D. Mitchell. But that comes under the heading of "the best-laid plans of mice and men often go awry." *Unlaid* would be more like it.

Perhaps it's time to change the subject and talk about religion instead.

The last church service I attended in Granbury took place the day before I departed for active duty, and it was especially touching, even for a worldly-wise eighteen-year-old. The pastor talked about my joining the army and how patriotic an act that was. Then he offered a special prayer for my protection in this new endeavor. Protection? Despite the warning my father had given me I still didn't have a clue. But several of the men in the church were WWII and Korea veterans, and we even had one WWI veteran, and they knew what was coming.

The next morning I said good-bye to my parents. Dad was stoic, while Mom shed a few tears. Through it all I was trying not to bawl and squall like a ten-year-old. My friend Steve volunteered to deliver me to the recruiting station on what would be my last morning as a civilian for a couple of dozen years. Neither one of us said much on the hour-long drive. When we finally arrived, we shook hands, I took my little gym bag from the backseat, and he drove away with barely a nod of good-bye.

I reported to the recruiter and he put me, along with several other enlistees, on a bus to Dallas, where we spent the night in the lap of luxury at the Texas Hotel. The following morning we went to the Armed Forces Examination and Entrance Station (AFEES), had a quick medical screening to make sure we were still fit to fight for our country, and then took our oath of enlistment. Then, with a kid who'd taken Junior ROTC in high school acting as our platoon sergeant, we were put on a bus to Fort Polk, Louisiana. Many hours later we arrived at the reception station at Polk, where the pejorative term *trainee* was embedded in my vocabulary forever. It was a term of disrespect that we all grew to hate. By the end of basic training, I would rather have been called a son of a bitch than a trainee.

CHAPTER TWO

Combat

You remember the movie *Private Benjamin* with Goldie Hawn? "There must be some mistake," she said, looking around the basic-training barracks for the first time. "I joined the army with the condos." Somehow I think that Private Benjamin and I must have had the same recruiter, a guy who was willing to fudge the truth and hide the fine print if it would get me to sign on the dotted line.

I wasn't looking for condos; I signed up to be an army mechanic. That's even what they trained me to be, but they also sent me to advanced infantry school. I did get to play with army trucks for a short time in Korea, but there was a war going on, and I was told the infantry couldn't fight it without me. When I got word that I was going to Vietnam to be part of the 1st Air Cavalry Division (Airmobile), I went right down and had a conversation with my first sergeant. What a mistake that was.

I showed him my enlistment contract. He showed me the fine print: ". . . will be trained as a mechanic." "Did we train you as a mechanic?" he asked.

"Yes, First Sergeant."

"Well, what are you complaining about, soldier? We did what we said we were going to do. You're trained." My next stop was the army's Jungle Warfare School on Okinawa.

A month later, there I was, assigned to B Company, 2nd Battalion, 7th Infantry, the famed Garry Owen Battalion, living in a hooch in the general vicinity of Phuoc Vinh in central South Vietnam. And now here I was, ten days after arriving in country, gearing up to go out on my first combat patrol, a night ambush. I was carrying an eighty-pound rucksack, an M-60 machine gun, and several ninety-round belts of ammo, a pretty good load for a now-nineteen-year-old kid who weighed less than 140 pounds dripping wet. And dripping wet was my current condition. Not because it was raining, but because sweat was pouring off me in buckets. Some of it was because I hadn't yet acclimated to the heat and humidity, but mostly it was unadulterated fear on a scale heretofore unimaginable to a kid fresh out of small-town Texas. Until now, my biggest fears fell into two categories: dating related and father related. There had been the possibility of being turned down for a date by a girl I had the hots for in my high school class, or meeting her father if she happened to say yes—both were problematical. Having my father find out from the town cop that he'd caught me with a case of beer in the backseat had once been terrifying. But now all that was kid's stuff. No matter how much my father had yelled at the time, I lived through it.

I couldn't say that about the next few hours in the jungle. Since I hadn't been around long enough to build up the "it just doesn't matter" emotional armor that the old guys seemed to have, all I could do before we headed for the perimeter of the base camp was tote up the things I was afraid of.

I was afraid I might die, or worse, suffer a debilitating wound. I was afraid I might screw up and compromise the mission. I was afraid I might freeze under fire, or show fear. I was afraid I might wet my pants—or worse. Underlying it all, even though I didn't actually understand it yet, was that I was afraid I might let my buddies down. That one doesn't really rise to a conscious level until you've been under fire several times, 'cause it takes a while for you to figure out that what soldiers fight for is not a cause, not an ideology, not even a

country. In a place where a skinny kid named Gary Mitchell has, ab-
surdly, become an instrument of American foreign policy, all a guy
really fights for is his buddies. Someday, if I survive it, I figure that I
can put on a DAV or Legion or VFW or VVA cap and speak about the
nobility of going into battle for my country, but back then, that
wasn't what drove me.

It's not an original thought, but anyone in uniform who's been in
a war comes to that understanding, while those who haven't been
there still talk about glory on the battlefield—a nice concept on a
large scale, but meaningless when death might be one bullet away.
And contrary to popular belief, in a war where both sides are often
shooting at targets they never see, the bullet that gets you doesn't
even need to have your name on it; "to whom it may concern" will
do the job.

As we left the base camp for the spot where we were going to establish an L-shaped ambush, I kept thinking that it didn't make
sense for them to give me, the FNG (military slang for Fucking New
Guy), the machine gun. The guy with the M-60 is the one who needs
the steadiest nerves and who has to be able to maintain fire discipline. Unless the squad gets into a fight where the only way out is for
everyone to let fly in an effort to suppress the enemy, you don't want
to be just blasting away. And truth be told, I didn't know how I'd
handle the weapon if things got ugly.

By the time we arrived at the ambush site and set up, it was so
dark I couldn't see my hand in front of my face. I was dying for a cigarette, but that was out of the question. My head hurt, my mouth
was dry, and I had stomach cramps.

The headache could have been from the weight of the helmet.
The dry mouth could have been because we hadn't had any water for
a while—drinking from a canteen makes noise, and the sound of
swishing water carries a long way in the jungle at night. Or the
cotton-mouth might have been nerves. The stomach cramps could
be a result of the heat, or from not having adjusted to humping all of

that weight, or from the infamous malaria pills that were known to cause diarrhea in the most seasoned guys. Frankly, given how my gut felt, I was praying that the phrase *scared shitless* had some basis in fact, because the alternative could be really ugly.

A thousand questions ran through my mind, all of them unanswerable. The biggest one was, Will we actually end up in a firefight tonight, or will it be a dry run? My squad leader had placed everyone in position, and we all were supposed to know where our squadmates were located, the field of fire we were supposed to cover, and where we were not supposed to fire unless our position was being overrun.

Time seemed to stand still. I glanced at the glow-in-the-dark face on my watch. 2230—10:30 P.M. We had been in position for just over an hour. Without contact, we would remain here until dawn and then hump back to our base camp. The thing everyone seems to worry about on a night ambush is falling asleep, but as frightened as I was, I don't think I could have fallen asleep on a bet. Every sound in the trees caught my attention; my imagination began to play tricks on me. If I could have just spoken to the nearest guy, it would have helped. Or smoked a cigarette, or had something to eat, or a cup of coffee. Not a chance.

We couldn't even slap at the bugs that were munching away at any exposed skin they could find. So much for the army's insect repellent. Well, maybe that's not fair. I figure without it they would have at least chewed off an ear or two. When I had reached the point that I thought I could not be more miserable, it started to rain. Of course, I couldn't move to get my poncho, so I got wet. If I had been any wetter I would have drowned. I remembered my mother saying to me when I was a kid that I didn't have enough sense to come in out of the rain. The thought made me smile for just a second. If she could see me now.

It was about midnight, and time seemed to slow down even more. Pure misery, coupled with fear, was almost more than a nineteen-year-old could stand. And then it happened. The noise came from directly in front of me! It was slowly moving straight at me! I wanted to yell to the guy hidden a few yards away, but I couldn't. I wanted to ask the squad leader what to do, but I couldn't. None of the field problems in advanced infantry training (AIT) had taught me how to deal with a situation like this. I wasn't supposed to talk, and I absolutely wasn't supposed to shoot unless the squad leader gave the signal to fire, but something was coming straight at me. *What do I do? I just can't sit here and wait to die.*

My temples were throbbing so hard I was sure the enemy could hear them. If they couldn't, it was only because my beating heart was so loud it drowned them out. I had to do something! Whatever was out there was getting closer! The other guys had to hear it, but there was no way for me to confirm that. What if they'd fallen asleep? We could get wiped out while I was waiting for the signal to fire. At the very least, could I allow an opportunity for an ambush and squad body count to pass?

I made an instant decision to spray and pray, cutting loose with the M-60. After hours of sitting there in the dark like a blind man, listening to natural sounds like buzzing insects and hard rain, smelling wet jungle smells, the eruption of full automatic fire was a shock to all the senses.

The larger shock came when my squad leader started yelling, "Cease fire, cease fire!"

My training had been very effective. My aim had been true. The problem was, the only body our squad would be counting that night was the water buffalo I had killed. The squad leader figured it was passing through on its way to the stream about two hundred yards behind us.

I had compromised our position. We had to return to our base camp. If I had a tail, it would have been between my legs. But worst of all, the other squad members were really harassing me about my first combat kill. I'd become "Ol' Deadeye Mitch." And just when

I thought it couldn't get any worse, it did. I was going to have to face our platoon sergeant. You've heard about a fate worse than death? Suddenly I understood what that expression meant. Now I was really scared.

Since the squad leader appeared so upset, I could only imagine what the platoon sergeant—or his boss, the lieutenant who was our platoon leader—might do. This could go all the way up to the first sergeant or company commander. I'd disobeyed a direct order not to fire unless instructed to do so. They could court-martial me for that. How would I explain it to my father? All my older brothers had been in the service; but my dad had not been in the service. They'd all been honorably discharged. Now I was going to change all that. Everyone back in Granbury would know. What was that expression—death before dishonor? That's where my head was on the way back into the base camp.

We arrived at base camp about 0430—4:30 A.M.—and my squad leader brought me into the platoon sergeant's tent. For what seemed like hours we endured an ass reaming that covered infractions ranging from incompetence, through wasted time and ammunition, to the danger everyone had been placed in because the enemy could have ambushed us once I revealed our position. I was almost in tears.

All of a sudden the platoon sergeant looked in my direction and burst into the most surprising laughter I've ever heard. My squad leader cracked up, too. I was standing there, red-faced and still unsure of what to do. Finally, the senior NCO said, "Welcome to Vietnam, Mitch. Go get some sleep." Just as I reached the door, he said, "Mitch, this one's on me. Don't let it happen again—understand, soldier?"

I left, cleaned my weapon, restocked my ammunition, and finally had that cigarette and cup of coffee.

It really didn't take long for me to fall into the routine of combat operations. Routine pretty much came to mean boredom punctuated by occasional moments of terror, which is to say that I was still fairly uncomfortable on patrols. I was now a rifleman, but like everyone else, carried a few belts of ammunition for the machine gun.

Early one morning we were returning from an all-night ambush where we'd made no contact, and rather than work our way around the edge of a small rice paddy, someone made the choice to go across it. I'd learned by now that rice paddies were great ambush locations—for us and the enemy—but none of us questioned the decision. Maybe it was the fact that we knew there was a lukewarm meal and dry cots waiting for us that prompted us to take the shortcut. And we almost got away with it.

We were three-quarters of the way across when the first shot rang out, causing us to dive into the water and take cover behind the paddy berms, while blasting the wood line in an effort to keep the bad guys down. What we had to quickly figure out was where the shot came from. It would have been easier if he had sprayed a clip in our direction. But this guy—if there was only one; we couldn't be sure—wasn't a novice. Each time he threw a shot at us, it came from a different location. Because we couldn't find him, we couldn't get up and move.

Then the pace picked up a bit. We now had at least two shooters—one from the front and one from the right flank, and their aim was getting better. One of my squad members was hit, and the medic had to try to get to him. But every time he made a move in the direction of the wounded man, another shot would ring out. After a while it seemed as though the enemy was toying with us, since they never actually hit the medic, just kept him pinned in place.

After a few more minutes, the shooter to our flank got lucky and scored a direct hit on the radio. Now we had no way of communicating, or getting air or artillery support or reinforcements from the base camp, which was less than four kilometers away.

It had become obvious that the shooters were much better than we had initially given them credit for. Their plan was to shoot and move, shoot and move. Without exposing ourselves we could do nothing, and doing nothing was not going to get us out of there. One of the ways you break an ambush is to start firing and run toward the enemy. Not only does it force them to take cover, but it turns static targets—us—into moving ones. The plan our squad leader devised would have us rush the area to our front, where we suspected one of the enemy fighters was still located. While we were doing that, the medic could get to our wounded guy. This would put the medic and his patient in a precarious position, because while the rest of us would be inside the wood line, the two of them would still be fully exposed in the rice paddy.

One negative thing about battle plans is that the bad guys don't have to sign off on them. When we charged the wood line, the two shooters suddenly became many. Two more of my buddies were wounded on the way, but we were able to drag them into the wood line with us. Now we had to do something to pull the enemy's focus from the medic and his patient. My squad leader decided that a couple of us would race back to the medic and help him drag our partner in, while the rest of the squad did all in their power to burn up their weapons with rapid fire.

Lucky me, I was chosen along with a buddy to make the run to the medic. We took off our rucksacks and the extra machine gun ammunition, and waited for the squad members to start firing so we could move. This was one of those moments when I thought my folks might have a shot at collecting on my life insurance. The opposing force had already proven to us that they were a well-coordinated unit that had been professionally trained. They knew what they were doing and how to get the most out of their location. They also had evened the odds by taking out our radio; it was us against them, and would stay that way unless we got very lucky.

On the squad leader's signal, all hell broke loose. Our guys were firing as fast as they could, and we were running as fast as we could, zigging and zagging, trying to provide the least shootable target. The guy with me was slightly wounded. Just a small flesh wound on the shoulder that grazed him more than it hit. Later, he told me it felt like a bee sting. Miraculously, we were still alive when we reached the medic. Our problem now was that any fool would know what the next step was, and we'd long since stopped thinking that the enemy was a fool. The squad was going to start shooting again, and we were going to try to get the medic and our casualty back to the wood line.

That's when we got lucky. While we were waiting for the shooting to start, a Cobra gunship happened to fly over. Of course, they had no idea what was going on. The squad leader fired a red star cluster (a signal pyrotechnic) in the general direction of the aircraft. It wasn't near enough to endanger the bird, but close enough to get the pilot's attention. The most beautiful sight I had ever seen was that of the Cobra banking to check out what was going on.

In its own way, the arrival of the gunship was both good and bad news. If the pilot knew where our lines were, and where the enemy was, no problem. But if he had to guess—big problem. Cobras are equipped with miniguns that are most unforgiving when they start shooting. How did we solve the problem without a radio?

The squad leader yelled that he was going to pop white smoke grenades to mark his location, and he wanted one of us to throw red smoke toward the enemy. That meant we had to toss two grenades, because the medic had seen fire from one area, and the wounded in action (WIA) had seen fire from another.

I yelled back that we'd throw ours as soon as he threw his. Each of us had pulled the pin on a grenade, and held the spoon in place until we saw the white smoke. The only thing that made me think this plan might work was that the Cobra was lazily drifting back and forth, watching us, and waiting. No question that the pilot could see us; he just didn't know where the rest of our guys were at and didn't want to take any chances firing until he was certain.

The instant we saw the white smoke pop, we threw our reds and dropped as deep into the water as we could get without drowning ourselves. The Cobra banked and started a campaign of deforestation all around the red smoke. When the gunship started shooting, the squad also started firing. We jumped up, each grabbed an arm, and began dragging the wounded man to the wood line as fast as we could move. I know it was painful, and he groaned the whole way, but we kept going. It was one of the longest eighty meters I had ever run.

As soon as we got into the woods, we could hear other aircraft coming in our direction, obviously summoned by the gunship pilot. The whole episode was over in minutes. We got our wounded onto a Dustoff that would take them to the nearest medical facility, and we regrouped to move on back to our base camp.

By the time I had been in Vietnam about a month I'd participated in a number of firefights, quite a few ambush patrols, and several reconnaissance-by-force missions that everyone described by the much less politically correct title of *search and destroy*.

Up to that time I had not knowingly taken the life of another human being. Don't get me wrong—I'd fired my share of rounds with every intent to kill as many of the enemy as I could, but I'd never actually seen someone I'd fired at die. On this warm and clear afternoon, that fact, along with my life, was destined to change.

We were preparing to cross a stream, always a dangerous part of any movement. While in the water, you have nowhere to go if you are fired upon. Before the squad crossed, my buddy walking point and the squad leader were watching the opposite bank as well as the surrounding area, attempting to locate anything out of the ordinary. Not seeing anything, they waved us forward. But just as the point man stepped into the stream, the Viet Cong sprang their ambush from the opposite bank. Why the enemy began firing before we were all in the water, I don't know, but their mistake was our good fortune. Maybe it was their turn to have a nervous FNG screw up their ambush. Sometimes you catch a break.

The point immediately jumped out of the stream and into the underbrush uninjured, and all of us began to return fire. During the firefight, one of the VC rose up slightly into a position where I could plainly see him. Since my arrival in country, my shooting skills and instincts had been honed significantly, so without thinking I fired a short burst of three or four rounds from my M-16.

Everything suddenly changed into slow motion. All of the sounds were muffled, as if they were coming from a great distance away. I could see his body twitch with the impact of each round in his torso. It almost appeared that he looked directly at me as he slowly fell backward onto the bank, and then his crumpled body edged into the shallow water, dead. We were so close, I was sure I could see the light in his eyes change when life as we know it departed his body.

The firefight continued for what seemed to be an eternity, although thinking back I know it was just a few short minutes before the VC pulled back and disappeared into the woods. We carefully crossed the stream, passing right next to my first combat kill. I could hear my buddies' enthusiastic praise as I came across the stream. "Damned good," said one. "Right on, Mitch," said another. A third pumped his fist and cut loose with a loud "All riiiiiiight!!" I almost tripped stepping out of the stream because I couldn't take my eyes off of the man lying there. He wasn't just a gook or a slope or a dink or a VC. He was a human being, and I had ended his life. Purposefully and intentionally. I came to Vietnam a kid, and now I was a killer. The squad leader must have gotten a good look at my face, because he grabbed my arm, helped me step out of the stream, and asked, "Mitch, you okay?"

Of course I answered, "Yeah, fine, just missed my step." But on the way back to our base camp I couldn't get out of my mind the sight of the dead man lying in the water where we left him. I kept replaying the firefight in my head. I must have watched myself fire that burst of rounds twenty times. Outwardly I tried acting as if nothing were bothering me, but internally I was wrestling with what soldiers throughout the ages have agonized over. Against everything I'd been taught as a child, I had taken another life. I'd heard other guys in the same circumstances rationalize it with pat phrases like "It don't mean nothing" or the all-purpose "Sorry 'bout that." Maybe for them that stuff worked. But it wasn't doing the job for me.

Once we arrived at the base camp, we cleaned our weapons, restocked our ammunition, and then had some time to eat, rest, and write letters. I remember that the inactivity was horrendous for me. I tried to write but couldn't concentrate, so I didn't finish the letter. After all, how do you tell your parents that you killed someone? I went over to the mess tent and got a cup of coffee, wishing I could drink a few beers, but we were scheduled to go out again shortly after sunset. Finally I walked down to the end of the tents next to a bunker and sat down on the ground. I was staring at the perimeter, looking at absolutely nothing, when I heard a voice say, "Are you all right?"

I looked up and it was my squad leader. I suddenly realized that I had tears running down my cheeks. Having been through it himself, and with other young men in the squad, he knew what I was feeling, the conflicting emotions I was experiencing. His comment was simple. "It won't get any easier, but you will learn to live with it. Nearly everyone goes through the same thing you're going through right now. They just don't admit it. We've gotta move out in about two hours, so you've got a little time to work things out in your mind. If things go right tonight, you might have to do it again. I need to know that you can."

Without another word, he reached into his pocket, took out a pack of cigarettes, shook one loose, and offered it to me. Then he pulled out his Zippo, lit it for me, and walked away, leaving me alone with my despair. I took a deep drag, exhaled, then tossed the smoke on the ground, put my head down on my knees, and silently sobbed. My innocence was gone, lost at the edge of a stream ten thousand miles from home. At that moment, I had no way of knowing what it meant for my future—but I knew that deep inside, I'd changed.

War takes place at the extreme ends of a continuum—it's either dull and boring, or filled with more excitement than one could possibly imagine. And it can go from one extreme to the other faster than the speed of light. There are exceptions to this rule, however, moments where you actually have time to consider that you're being put into a situation where death is a distinct possibility. What's still a mystery to me is that when I was in one of those situations, I chose to move forward rather than play it safe.

Consider a patrol we were on about a week after my first kill. We had been out for a couple of days when the point found the opening to a tunnel. This was very unusual, because they were normally so well camouflaged that unless you knew exactly what you were looking for, you'd almost have to fall through the entrance in order to find it. This led my squad leader to believe that it could be one of only two things: either Charlie had heard us coming and left very quickly, or it was a trap. Personally, I didn't have a clue which it was, but I did know that this would probably lead to a very exciting day for one unlucky SOB.

We called for engineer support because they usually took care of tunnels. No help available. We called for ARVN (Army of the Republic of Vietnam) engineer support. No help available. We couldn't just blow the tunnel entrance and move on, because within hours after we were gone, the VC would have dug it out and it would be fully functional. Tunnels had been known to lead to underground field headquarters, hospitals, supply storage areas, and more. Experience had taught us that tunnels usually provided all kinds of information for our intelligence folks, so we couldn't just leave it without sending someone down.

When the squad leader started looking up and down the squad, I knew what was coming. I weighed less than 140 pounds and was five feet ten inches tall. Unfortunately, I was the smallest guy on the patrol. I willed myself to grow three inches and gain forty pounds, but before my will could win the battle with nature, he looked at me and said, "Mitch, do I have a deal for you." I was volunteered. Eventually I would grow to a height of six feet and weigh two hundred pounds, but the future would do me no favors on this day. Suffice it to say that I was more than a little upset.

Tunnels were terrifying. We'd actually had classes on them where we learned they could hold all kinds of nightmarish things: water traps, ambushes, and explosive booby traps. The only thing certain about going into a VC tunnel was the uncertainty of what you might face.

I stripped off my ruck, took off my fatigue jacket, and, feeling buck-naked wearing just a T-shirt and pants, prepared to go in. In one hand I had a borrowed .45-caliber pistol with one nine-round magazine and one additional round in the chamber. In the other I held a flashlight. I stood silently at the entrance as my larger buddies tied a rope around my waist. If I got myself blown up or shot in an underground firefight, the theory was that they could drag my body out without having to send anyone else down to get what was left of me.

I could see my squad leader keeping his eyes on me as I was preparing for the ordeal, and strangely, it wasn't the first time I'd noticed he was watching me closely. I also had the same feeling I'd had on my first patrol. I was scared shitless and realized that I had absolutely no control over what was about to happen. *Pure terror* is an inadequate term to describe the feelings I was experiencing. At a time like that you're doing about thirty things at once. You pray. You try to plan what you will do if something happens. You hope the medic is as good as you think he is, and you try to show your buddies that you have no fear. All the while they're being helpful and encouraging, you know that deep down, they're relieved that it's you and not them going down that hole.

When I was as prepared as I was going to be, the squad leader radioed command that "we" were ready to proceed. My unspoken question was: *What we? Does he have a mouse in his pocket?* If ever there was an "I" mission, this was it.

Command gave the okay to proceed, and two of us moved about

twenty meters to the tunnel entrance. If I dropped in the hole and it blew up, only my rope handler and I would get blown to pieces. Just before I climbed down, I paused to offer a silent but heartfelt prayer that went something like this: *God, forgive me of all my sins, and have mercy on my soul. God, don't let me die. God, don't let me screw up. God, don't let me be maimed—go ahead and let me die instead. God, don't let me show my fear so much that I pee my pants in front of everybody.* I figured that just about covered all the eventualities, and the rope handler was urging me to get moving. So I did.

As soon as you enter a tunnel, the temperature becomes cooler and the humidity drops noticeably. The smell is musty. You strain to listen, but the only sound is your heart beating so loud you're sure it would keep you from hearing the snap or click of a booby trap. Then again, it might be just as well—at least if you didn't hear it you wouldn't know that you were about to die.

After crawling about twenty feet in, I found the first booby trap. It was one of our own grenades, buried with the pin pulled. It had just enough dirt to hold the spoon in place, but if you crawled over it, your movement would cause it to roll, permitting the spoon to pop. I gently lifted the grenade, ensuring that the spoon did not pop, and backed up to the entrance. I yelled, "Grenade," threw it in the opposite direction of the squad, and dropped back into the hole.

I resumed crawling, passed the spot where I'd found the grenade, and began looking for the next booby trap. The training manuals say that it should be at or near the entrance to a chamber or group of chambers, so as I moved I kept sweeping the walls, floor, and ceiling with my flashlight. Having the light was simultaneously a blessing and a curse. It meant I could see where I was going, but it also meant that if there was anyone else down there, they could easily see me coming. I continued moving the flashlight around and noticed that about fifteen inches in front of my face there was a stick or root hanging from the ceiling of the tunnel. I was just about to stretch my hand out to push it aside, when the root moved!

I froze in place. Roots don't move. When I aimed the light at the thing, I noticed several more just like it, hanging from the ceiling to within about four inches of the floor. Then it hit me: They were snakes! *Dear God, what do I do now?* They were too low to crawl under, and the tunnel was too narrow for me to go around them. A silent but deadly booby trap.

Vietnam was home to a variety of poisonous snakes, including cobras, kraits, and the fabled bamboo vipers, which GIs referred to as "the two-step," because the rumor was that if you're bitten, you'll fall dead before you can take two steps. I'd spent a lot of time in the outdoors growing up in Texas, and never got comfortable with snakes. So to come face-to-face with them in a tunnel where the VC had hung them from the ceiling on very fine threads was, for me, a too-close encounter of the worst kind.

I backed out of the tunnel and reported my findings to the squad leader, who told me to make a cup of coffee while they figured out what to do. We couldn't just toss a grenade into the tunnel, because there'd be no way of knowing that it had killed them all, and the ones that survived might be loose in the dirt. The explosion might also cave in the tunnel, and that wouldn't make the intelligence people very happy.

There really seemed to be only two solutions: Try to burn them out, or get them out by hand. Given that I've always had an uncontrollable fear of snakes, burning them out was my choice. Actually, sending someone else down to deal with the problem was my first choice, but that didn't seem to be an option. Have I mentioned how nice it is to be needed? I was not a happy camper.

Then we began to worry that if I went down there and burned them out it might use up all the oxygen in the tunnel. This brought us back to square one: getting the snakes out by hand. My squad leader said that I could take my time figuring it all out, as long as I was ready as soon as I finished my coffee.

I began running the problem over in my head. There were at least half a dozen snakes down there hanging from the ceiling. Was that all of them? Were there any just crawling around waiting for me? There was only one way to find out. Go back and see.

We got a stick about eighteen inches long and fashioned a loop at the end of it with commo wire. It was a homemade version of something I'd seen on *Wild Kingdom,* but the TV snake wranglers were getting the big bucks for taking chances with poisonous snakes. I never saw anything about this in my recruiting sergeant's office. And there was certainly nothing about it in the papers I signed that guaranteed me training as a mechanic. Maybe someday, if I survived this experience, I'd get to hide under the hood of a deuce-and-a-half. But not right now.

Back down the hole I went, this time maneuvering with a pistol, flashlight, and the snake catcher. I put the loop around the first snake. This was not an easy task, since the snake was wiggling and I was shaking. I tightened the loop, and then the snake really started wiggling. Between its wiggling and my shaking, the string came loose from the ceiling of the tunnel. It was now too late to change my mind. Hoping the snake could not wiggle out of the loop, I started backing out of the tunnel. That's when I realized that I had no plan in the event it got loose. I didn't know whether the species was inclined to attack or flee—and at what speed. Fortunately the noose held, and I made it out of the tunnel with the snake. I released it, and another member of the squad killed it as soon as my loop was clear.

Five more times I made this journey, crawling through the tunnel, lassoing a deadly snake, and then backing out. How long did it all take? Days. Weeks. Months. Not really, but it sure felt like it. Finally, with all the known snakes gone, I had to make one last trip into the tunnel to determine what was in there.

I made it past where the grenade had been, past where the snakes had been, and almost to what, at first, looked like the end of the tunnel. But then it made a ninety-degree turn to the right. What could be next? Another grenade booby trap? More snakes? A couple of VC undercover B-girls on R & R from 100 P Alley in Saigon asking me to buy them Saigon tea?

Would you believe none of the above? The tunnel made that right turn and opened into a large chamber. A large, very empty chamber. No cache of weapons or ammunition. No medical facilities. No sleeping or cooking facilities. No battle plans for the invasion of Saigon. No . . . nothing. I'd crawled over a grenade, handled snakes, and almost died of heart failure to find an empty chamber!

I went back outside and reported to the squad leader that the only thing there was an empty chamber. We blew the tunnel entrance and returned to our base camp, where military intelligence was waiting to speak to us. They kept telling me I had obviously screwed up, that I had missed something. Finally, for the first time but certainly not the last time in my army career, I spoke my mind, suggesting that if they were so certain that there was something of value to be found in that tunnel, they could get off their dead asses and look for it themselves. My squad leader didn't even flinch when I said it.

Thus far I'd managed to come through every combat mission I'd been on without injury. That was a good thing, but I couldn't shake the thought that it was only a matter of time before I got my turn.

About 0600 on a relatively cool morning, I finally got an assignment that was a bit closer to what I'd signed up to do. We were going on a resupply convoy for ammunition, food, repair parts, fuel, and the ten thousand other things that are needed to fight a war and keep the troops going—and based on the fact that I'd driven a truck some while I was in Korea, I was assigned to drive.

We were headed to the giant army base at Long Binh, a three- or four-hour trip down a heavily traveled road that was swept by the engineers every morning for newly planted mines. After driving for about an hour and a half, we stopped for sandwiches and hot coffee. We also got briefed on the fact that our route took us past a rubber plantation where several convoys had recently been ambushed. The intelligence raised the pucker factor, but compared to being on a foot patrol through enemy territory, driving a deuce-and-a-half seemed like a piece of cake. We grew even more confident when the convoy made it completely through the plantation area without incident. But it seems that in a combat zone, even when you're out of the woods, you're not out of the woods.

We were passing a convoy outbound from Long Binh when it happened. A command-detonated mine exploded under one of the last trucks in the oncoming group just as it was passing the vehicle I was driving, which was pretty much in the middle of our convoy. When a huge mine designed to take out a tank or a truck goes off, the explosion consumes all of the oxygen in the immediate area. For a second or two that seems like a lifetime, you can't breathe. You're also being banged around as the energy from the blast throws every-thing outward. Then you get part two of the blast—the implosion, where everything including oxygen gets sucked back in.

I wasn't sure what hit me. Could have been a small piece of shrapnel from the truck they tried to blow up, or a small piece of rock flying out of the hole where the mine had been buried. What-ever it was, it punctured the scalp above my left ear, traveled be-tween the scalp and skull, and exited at the crown of my head. Judging by the amount of blood pouring from the wound, I thought half my head was gone. It didn't compute that I couldn't actually be consciously thinking about how badly I'd been hit, yet have suffered a fatal head wound. I just knew I was dead!

My first instinct was to reach up and touch it, but I was afraid to. Who knew what I'd be dipping my hand into? Would I have to try to push my brain, or at least what was left of it, back into my head? Then it dawned on me that the explosion may just have been the opening shot in a full-scale attack on the convoy. When we were briefed early that morning, we'd been told to keep moving if anything happened. You didn't want to stop and sit in a potential kill zone. I knew that if I paused to deal with my injury, I'd be blocking the trucks behind us, and it would give the enemy a perfect opportunity to wipe us out.

So while constantly smearing away the blood that was pouring down my face, I kept driving, praying that we'd be able to stop before I bled out or ran off the road, whichever came first. About two miles down the road, my prayers were answered when the convoy commander ordered a halt to check for damaged vehicles and wounded personnel.

Remarkably, I was the only one in the entire convoy who'd been injured. The medic checked me over, said I would live, put a pressure bandage on the entrance and exit wounds—and we continued on to Long Binh. I don't think I've ever had a headache like that one.

When we arrived at the staging area, the medic used the convoy commander's jeep to take me to the 120th Medical Evacuation Hospital. They cleaned me up, X-rayed my head, and put a single suture on the exit wound. Then they released me to full duty. I would have never believed that so much blood could come pouring out of such a tiny, relatively minor wound. The only meds they gave me to take were aspirin for the headache, and they told me that if it persisted for more than twenty-four hours, to go see our battalion surgeon.

When we returned to the staging area and reported to the convoy commander that I wouldn't be needing a body bag after all, he took one look at me and made what I thought was a brilliant command decision: On the convoy back to base camp, I'd be riding shotgun. I don't know whether or not he could actually see it, but I was shaking so badly that I'm not sure I could have operated the clutch, so he got no argument from me.

The trip back was uneventful. When we arrived, the medic took me over to the battalion's medical platoon and asked our own doc to look me over. He gave me two days of limited duty, during which I had time to reflect on the irony that thus far, I'd survived jungle firefights without a scratch but nearly managed to get myself blown up while driving a truck, which is pretty close to what I signed up to do.

CHAPTER THREE

Marksmanship School

I'd learned a lot during my first few months in combat, but most of all I learned that just about anything you do, including nothing, can get you killed. Therefore, in the interest of survival, any legitimate opportunity to avoid combat operations is one that should be embraced. Just getting an afternoon off because your congressman is coming to visit is cause for soaring morale. That probably explains the reports that the politicians brought home about how everybody they met was in great spirits. Hell, we get pulled off the line, get clean fatigues, a shower, real food instead of Cs—life is good.

So in early August, when my squad leader takes me to see the platoon sergeant, and this E-7 tells me they're sending me away for a week to attend a specialized marksmanship course, I'm happier than a possum in the middle of a May rainstorm. I actually allow myself to smile when he says he likes what he's been hearing about me, especially that I don't panic under fire like some of the FNGs. But what I'm thinking is, anything that'll make me shoot better will improve my chances of going home to Texas.

Next morning around 0630, when my buddies in B/2/7 were moving out on another operation, I grabbed my M-16 and hauled a duffel bag with enough clothing for a week down to the airstrip. I tried not to seem too impressed when I discovered they'd brought in a Huey just for me. The flight to Long Binh was quick and uneventful, and when we got there, the crew chief pointed to a hole in the fence, and a tent just beyond it.

I checked in and found a bunch of other guys who'd also been selected for the marksmanship training. Eventually there were thirty of us, and they hauled us in trucks to a secluded area—it took a while to get there, so I'm not even sure if it was on the base or not—where we were told to stash our gear quickly and report back to a pair of staff sergeants who would be our instructors.

I could tell that these two guys had been around. And they were old. Okay, so maybe *older* is a better way to put it. I was nineteen; if they were thirty, they looked ancient to me. Looking back, I guess they might have been between thirty and forty, which made them three days older than dirt, and it was God's little joke that they had lived that long. I thought it was odd that they had no unit patch on their fatigues, but they did have U.S. ARMY and a name tag above the pockets, so I didn't think much of it at the time.

Their spiel was in the same vein as the one given to me by my own platoon sergeant. "You've all been selected because you shoot relatively well and you kept your head together under fire." They said their mission was to teach us to become better shooters with our M-16, and that we'd "learn some special things with an M-14." They never once used the term *sniper,* not that first day, nor five days later when I completed their course.

It was almost noon when they finally got started. The first briefing began with a warning: "Anybody who doesn't give a hundred and ten percent, we'll put you on the first bird out of here." There's nothing they could have said that would have motivated me more. It was a matter of self-preservation. If I go back, I go out on patrol; here, I don't have to. They were giving me an excuse not to be dead. I wasn't about to turn them down.

We spent that first afternoon cleaning our own M-16s. We tore them down till there was nothing left to tear down. We cleaned everything, even the outside, because that's what they wanted us to do. I hadn't cared if it was rusty on the outside. The way I looked at it, a little rust made for better camouflage. And as long as the bolt carrier and all the moving parts were moving the way they were supposed to, it wasn't going to jam. We knew that from experience. All thirty of us had been in country for several months, all combat veterans. We were probably equally divided between PFCs and spec 4s, maybe a couple of buck sergeants.

But our experience in the field suddenly wasn't important. The sergeants had their own rules for their own games, and they were serious about them. Even today I still don't understand the meticulous effort to clean the stock and grip, but I didn't want to go on patrol, so I would've spit-shined the thing if they told me to. During the next couple of hours, the sergeants were constantly coming around, making sure that we were doing what we were supposed to do. Finally my rifle parts passed inspection, and one of them said, "Okay, oil it; reassemble it."

We were assuming that since this was a marksmanship school, they'd want to get us onto the firing range as quickly as possible. Once again, that thing about "never assume anything" came into play. Instead of shooting, they had us reading. Everyone received a dog-eared copy of the "Army Marksmanship Manual," and from late afternoon until lights out, they had us in our tents reading it. We were far enough off the beaten path that there were no electric lights in the tents, but they'd thoughtfully provided lanterns. And, of course, there was the usual bitching. "Why are we reading this thing again? I know about a sight picture, and a cheek-stock weld with the 16 and a thumb-cheek weld with the M-14." We all knew about leading a moving target, and that if the wind was blowing perpendicular to the path of the bullet, you had to adjust your sight. These were basics. But, again, if it's a choice between spending an evening reading a training manual or spending it out on ambush, I'll take the book. Hell, I'll take the whole library.

Early the next morning, after a gourmet breakfast of C-rats and coffee, they hauled us out to what turned out to be a pretty decent firing range. They'd used concrete construction pipes set in the ground to simulate foxholes, and beside each hole they'd marked off a prone firing position. We began firing at fixed silhouettes twenty-five meters out. Hitting the target wasn't the object; what they wanted us to do was to try to tighten our shot groupings. It was the kind of precision shooting that nobody bothered with in the field with an M-16. Aiming? Shot group? I vaguely remember that from training. I was used to just squeezing off a few rounds and hoping one hit. So it took me a while to get back in the mode of a Texas rabbit hunt, where hitting a small target with a single shot actually mattered. The instructors kept pacing behind us, chain-smoking like steel-mill chimneys, and saying, "Stabilize your breathing." I don't think any of us knew what they were talking about. Did they want us to hold our breath and shoot? They didn't clarify. Just, "Stabilize your breathing. It makes the weapon shake." I didn't ask, and I don't think anyone else did, either.

Finally I put three shots in the target tight enough that the sergeant's quarter-size metal disk covered them, and I was moved to the fifty-meter targets. Tight shot groups were still the task, and when I succeeded there, I went on to one hundred meters, then two hundred, and finally to 250 meters, still with the M-16.

When they moved us to the drop-down targets three hundred meters out, all they wanted us to do was hit it, where didn't matter. It didn't take long before we discovered that if you could hit the dirt in front of the target, it would kick up and knock it over. But I didn't do that too often, because I found that even at that distance, which is about three football fields plus another ten yards, I was a pretty good shot. They wanted us to be able to hit it consistently—and they defined that as eight rounds out of ten. If you couldn't do that, you were gone, and on that first day a couple of guys got sent home.

We went back to the tents, cleaned our weapons, and enjoyed

a good night's sleep. We had no way of knowing it was the last full night's sleep we were going to get until the course was over.

The next morning everyone was issued a standard M-14, and we started working in teams of two on the twenty-five-meter targets, zeroing our weapons. One guy would take his turn as the shooter, while the other served as spotter, using a scope to give ranges, and to report hits and misses. Then we'd switch. By the end of the day we were back at the three-hundred-meter target. Just before darkness fell, we stopped shooting, ate our C-rations, and did some smoking and joking. Then they took us back out to the twenty-five- and fifty-meter ranges for night fire. When it started raining I remember thinking, *Okay, that's it for tonight*. But it wasn't. We just kept shooting.

When I was with my unit, I'd been in firefights at night and in the rain. But that's a completely different kind of shooting. Spontaneous. Not analytical. On a firing range it's a new experience. The rain and moon create shadows on the target. The targets look different in moonlight than they do in sunlight. The standard military silhouette target looks larger at night; somehow the moonlight magnifies it, especially those sixties-era white targets with black circles. I had expected them to give us some instruction before turning us loose for night firing, but I guess they wanted us to figure out what we could for ourselves.

The next morning was when the sergeants began teaching us technique. I remember them saying that because the targets look larger than they actually are, we have to take this into consideration when aiming. If the downrange target looks two inches tall, it's probably only an inch and three-quarters. That doesn't sound like much of a difference, but at three hundred meters, a quarter of an inch is critical. If you're off by that much, you're either going to miss completely, or it won't be a good hit. It was after that lecture that we were introduced to the scope.

Even though I'd first learned to hunt at the age of twelve, it was always with plain iron sights on the barrel of a rifle. I'd never even looked through a scope. So when they mounted it on my M-14 and handed the rifle back to me, it was a revelation. The target was right there, almost on top of me. They helped us zero the weapons, and that's when shooting became more than just instinct. Suddenly there was math involved. They started with the adjustments that raise or lower the impact point at three hundred meters. Those are little pick marks on vertical lines in the scope. Raise the weapon to put the next pick mark on the target and the bullet will strike two and a half, three inches higher. Once we got that worked out in our heads, they showed us how similar adjustments in aiming moved the strike point left or right. That was more thinking than I was used to doing with a loaded rifle in the bush, and they told us that this was just the beginning, because there were mathematical adjustments we'd have to learn to compensate for distance—shooting five hundred meters with a scope zeroed for three hundred, for example—and for angle—firing uphill or down—as well as over water.

Where I had been used to a solid cheek weld to establish a sight picture through the peep-and-open steel sights, I had to adjust in order to properly use the scope. You didn't want your eye up against the rear element of the scope, because that prevents a full sight picture. Conversely, you didn't want your shooting eye to be so far from the rear of the scope that you're seeing too much space around the scope. It's a matter of trial and error, and yes, experience. The key to the whole thing is a proper thumb-cheek weld that consistently puts your eyeball in the same position behind the scope. That, and the stock placed solidly in the pocket of your shoulder, so that you're physically locked to the weapon. Without that cheek weld, it's possible that when the rifle kicks back, it will move independently of your head, and the scope could smack you right in the eye. With a proper weld when you pull the trigger, you move back as one unit—your body, your cheek against your thumb, and the rifle.

For the remainder of that day, through much of the night, and into the next day, all we were doing was shooting, shooting, and shooting. We left the scopes zeroed at three hundred meters, but were aiming at targets as far as five hundred meters out. They'd given us a little spotter scope that they taught us to use, but since we were shooting at known distances on the range, it wasn't something we came to rely on during the course.

On the final day, the class was down to thirteen guys. Seventeen had already been sent home because they just couldn't do the job. Now they were having us practice on targets seven hundred meters out. Eight hundred meters is half a mile. During all my time in country, there hadn't been an opportunity to engage targets that could be seen that far away. But it never dawned on me that I was being trained to find those types of targets and kill them. I was so naive that I was still invested in the notion that this was marksmanship school, and if it made me a better shooter, it improved my chances of seeing Texas again.

Once the instructor thought I was comfortable shooting at seven-hundred-meter targets with the M-14, he pulled a switch. I got into the foxhole and fired at all the range distances with the scoped 14. Then the instructor would take that rifle and hand us our M-16 with open sights, and have us fire from 50 to 250 meters. And then they'd have us switch again. They were trying to see if we could adjust quickly between the two rifles. It took practice, but I didn't have any real trouble with it.

Next came my final exam. I started with the M-16 and fired on all the ranges, 50, 100, 150, 200, 250, and 300 meters. Then I switched to the M-14. At five hundred meters, you had to have four hits out of four. When I got up to seven hundred meters, the E-6 told me I was expected to have one hit out of two shots. Then he said, "Okay, only one person has hit this target today. Let's make it two." So I fired the first round, and it hit. He reached over and patted me on the back and said, "See if you can do it again." So I fired, and I hit again. He said, "Son, I believe you could shoot a gnat off an elephant's ass without disturbing the elephant. Get off my range. We're through here."

I went back to their little admin tent with my M-14 and my personal M-16, cleaned both weapons, and turned in the 14. The clerk wrote down my name and Social Security number (which had replaced service numbers), and said, "Okay, go back to your unit." That was it. I looked around at the other guys coming off the range and realized the ones who didn't make the cut had only one rifle, the M-16 they brought with them from their unit.

Most nineteen-year-olds aren't terribly introspective. Never during the time I spent at the shooting school did I wonder why I was learning how to hit a target nearly half a mile away, when that kind of opportunity had not presented itself on any of the combat ops I'd been in with the 2/7. It didn't dawn on me that they'd just trained me to become a sniper; during the weeklong school, no one had ever used that term. I guess I was pretty naive and trusting of my superiors. I had been around long enough to become cautious, but not yet cynical about what was being said and done. One thing I was sure of was that as a spec 4 in an infantry squad, it didn't matter why I was being told to do something. Figuring out the reason for it was well above my pay grade. The other thing was that I certainly hadn't been around long enough to comprehend that everything that's done in the military is done for a reason. As an individual, I might not understand the reason if it were explained to me, and chances are, it was never going to be explained to me at all. But there's always a reason, and at that stage in what would turn out to be a twenty-four-year army career, I didn't question it.

When I reported back to my platoon at company headquarters, I walked into the orderly room and the clerk said, "Hey, Mitchell, how you doin'?"

I said, "I got through it; I'm here."

He said, "Yeah, you were gone the whole week, so I know you got through it." And with that, life immediately returned to what we considered normal: guard duty, patrol, this and that detail. Guys in my squad asked where I'd been, and I told them I'd been sent for marksmanship training, to learn how to shoot better. Nobody had told me not to talk about it; there was nothing spooky about it. I came back a better shooter than when I'd left, and that made me feel a bit more confident. For the time being, that was a good thing.

CHAPTER FOUR

The Old Man Wants to See You

Life returned to normal following my return from marksmanship school. We'd go out on patrols, engage the enemy—or not—return to base camp to rest, refit, and recuperate for as long as we could, and then do it all over again.

It was clear that in our area of responsibility in South Vietnam, we were fighting a classic guerrilla enemy. Today the label du jour is *insurgent,* but making any Vietnam-Iraq comparisons tends to get political, so for the moment I'll just tell you about how it was in my first war.

The division's intelligence officers had grown increasingly concerned about a small village not far from the base camp that they believed was hiding, supporting, and sheltering Viet Cong guerrillas who were routinely harassing other villages as well as staging occasional attacks on our troops. Something had to be done about it, and Company B/2/7 got the assignment.

It all began with a daylight patrol in an area about three kilometers from the village. From a grunt's point of view, daylight patrols were not a good thing. We could be seen leaving the base camp by innocent-looking civilians just tending to their rice paddies who could spot us coming and spread the word. There was no stealth involved—and maybe that was part of the plan. I don't know. In

Gary D. Mitchell with Michael Hirsh

fairness, I should hasten to add that we weren't terribly fond of night patrols either, because even with the one or two starlight scopes available to us, we were still out there in the dark. And as I learned on my first one that ended with the unfortunate demise of an enemy water buffalo, sitting quietly in one place, no talking, smoking, eating, laughing, or scratching for hours on end wasn't especially comfortable. I suppose had I been a student of Zen Buddhism I could have profitably used the enforced quiet time to meditate, but I had this crazy thing about not wanting to get killed, so remaining silently overamped on adrenaline was my only real choice.

I should also mention that having now spent more than two months in country, I'd adopted the attitude of the typical infantryman: "It just doesn't matter." That applied to everything related to life and death. See the bodies that your squad killed. It doesn't matter. Watch the medics zip a buddy into a body bag. It doesn't matter. Sure, you get a twinge in your gut, but you have to go on, so you don't even realize that the gut twinge comes from an invisible knife blade being stuck into your psyche and twisted, just a little. Just enough so that you're briefly aware of a pain, but you automatically make it go away. You have to. It's the only way to keep going. You don't let anything affect you, or more correctly, you don't allow anything to affect your job performance. *Xin loi.* Sorry 'bout that. It just doesn't matter.

But back to this daytime patrol. As we crossed the base camp perimeter, the squad leader gave the order to lock and load. We all jammed a magazine into our weapons, chambered a round, and put the rifle on safe. I always had the feeling that my blood pressure went up a few notches as the round slammed home, probably because it meant we were outside the protective womb of the base camp and now had only one another and our radio for support.

In our single-file line I was second, behind the point man. If he went down, my job was to take point and continue leading the patrol. In short order and without incident, we arrived at the area we

• 44 •

were assigned to sweep. Halfway through on our second pass, Charlie made known his objections to our presence. We were ambushed.

It was clear almost from the beginning that the VC attacking us were not prepared for a large-scale fight. We took no incoming mortar rounds, and the sporadic rifle fire aimed our way hit no one. The squad's response was massive firepower, and the VC chose to break contact and run. We trailed them like a posse in hot pursuit of the bad guys, and our running firefight led us right to the edge of the suspect village, where the enemy shooters disappeared.

Even though this was not an out-of-the-ordinary experience for grunts in Vietnam, it was especially difficult because it reminded us that we weren't able to easily distinguish friendlies from enemies at close range. There were no white hats and black hats in our version of the Wild West; face-to-face everyone claimed to be our friend. If I heard "VC numbah ten, GI numbah one" one more time, I swore I'd kill someone. Who knew that I'd soon have the chance to make good on that oath?

By radio we informed the CO what had happened, and he directed other squads to join up with us and surround the village. Once we moved in, the village elders, who told our interpreter that we were obviously mistaken, because there were no Viet Cong in their village, met us formally. "VC numbah ten . . ." I refused to hear it. I could feel my level of hostility climbing in direct proportion to the quantity of bullshit that was being hurled in our direction. I'd get that itchy feeling on the back of my neck, and could tell that it would take more than a couple of Tums to neutralize the acid that was pouring into my stomach. At some point I suppose it dawned on me that deliberately antagonizing a bunch of adrenaline-hyped, homesick, armed-to-the-teeth American teenagers was, at best, an incautious thing for the village elders to do.

But they persisted in claiming that there were no strangers in the village—and we insisted that since we chased VC into the village, if there were no strangers among them, then the village must be VC.

Not understanding Vietnamese as spoken by our interpreter (an ARVN sergeant who seemed like he was on our side), I'm not sure that our argument was presented in such logical fashion. It didn't matter. The elders continued to deny the charge. They really had no other choice.

If it was a VC village, then they fully supported the operations of the local guerrillas, many of whom were probably fathers and sons from this very village, and they couldn't divulge who the VC were or where they were hiding. On the other hand, if it was a village that supported the South Vietnamese government but the local VC were forcing them to provide food and shelter to our enemy, for their own protection they had to deny that the VC were present. For the village, it was a lose-lose situation. No matter how the village elders handled things, they were going to lose. Such was the nature of the war in Vietnam.

With negotiations at a standoff, we withdrew from the village and set up a perimeter around it, and informed command via radio what was going on. About forty-five minutes later they called us back and instructed us to go into the village and speak to the elders one more time. If we still got the same answers, we were told to conduct a Zippo raid.

Zippo lighters were as ubiquitous in Vietnam as P-38s, the tiny can opener issued with C-rations. Often the Zippos were engraved with dates of arrival in country, with unit crests, or with lovable aphorisms such as: KILL 'EM ALL AND LET GOD SORT 'EM OUT. Zippos were incredibly reliable; they'd light time after time after time. They were used for lighting the variety of smoking materials found among military personnel; and they were used to light improvised cooking devices we created to heat a canteen cup of coffee or hot chocolate (take empty C-ration can and cut airholes in the sides near the bottom; fill can with dirt or sand; soak contents with gasoline; light with Zippo).

Zippos were also remarkably effective in burning down a village made up of thatched-roof houses. And when we got the same "No VC here" answer from the elders once again, that's what we did. We proceeded to burn the village to the ground.

At the time it didn't bother me. There were no moral pangs; no conflict between squad members about whether this was the right way to treat people; no philosophical discussion about whether this didn't just make more enemies for us. We got the order to Zippo the place, and that's what we did. Much later, when I remembered the mission, I remembered the anguished look on the villagers' faces as we burned their homes, homes they had lived in since God only knows when. But while we were doing it, no qualms.

We stayed in the area long enough to keep them from putting out the fires. Everything burned to the ground. Homes of young and old, bags of rice, everything we could get our hands on. And we ignored their pleas that they were not VC, that VC were "numbah ten," pointing rifles at them to prevent them from interfering with the process.

When the report went in, it was termed a successful operation, with quantities of enemy matériel and food stocks destroyed. The VC would later try for retribution by mortaring our base camp several nights in a row, but while it scared the crap out of us, the incoming rounds were mostly ineffective.

It was very early in the morning a few days after we burned the village that a messenger came by our tent to tell me that the old man wanted to see me. Once again I got that knot in the pit of my stomach. Had I screwed up? Was something wrong at home?

I reported to the captain in the bunker that served as company headquarters, and waited for the hammer to come down on my head. But all he said was "Mitchell, you did pretty good in the marksmanship training." That caught me off guard, because I expected something else.

I said, "Yes, sir, I guess I did." So he reaches behind his desk and picks up this hard rifle case. He opens it up, and there's an M-14 with a scope. He takes it out, hands it to me, and then gives me two loaded twenty-round magazines. I couldn't be sure if it was the same weapon I fired at the school.

He says, "We've got some people who want you to demonstrate how well you've learned. Go to the landing pad; there's a helicopter waiting on you. They'll take you out, where you'll be given the details on your target."

That was the moment when I realized what had happened. It was instantaneous. I couldn't believe how naive I had been, not figuring out what was going on. I took the rifle, but I just stood there looking at him like a fool. I can't even imagine what the look on my face was like, but he finally said, "Well, what're you waiting on?"

It never even entered my consciousness at that time that I wasn't going to get to zero this rifle—to take it to a range and fire at a fixed distance, adjusting the scope so that the bullet consistently went where I wanted it to go, not a few inches right or left, up or down. I've thought about that a lot, and the only thing that makes sense to me is that all the scopes were the same; all the rifles were the same. When I had turned my rifle in at the school, I knew that my personalized zero setting was three clicks right of center, two clicks south of level, and they had put that in the scope on the weapon the captain had just handed me. As long as I wasn't shooting more than a couple hundred meters, it wasn't critical.

Anyway, I went back to our tent, changed my helmet for a baseball cap, grabbed my web gear with a first-aid kit and canteen, and headed to the helicopter, carrying the rifle with one magazine loaded and the other in a cargo pocket of my fatigues. I was the only passenger on the Huey, a chopper that can easily carry eight combat troops in the back. We flew for maybe fifteen, twenty minutes, and then started circling. I could see we were at a crossroads, and nearby was an armored personnel carrier (APC). Did it make sense that there was a lone APC sitting out in the middle of nowhere? No. Next question.

We landed, and since there was nothing else in sight but the APC, it wasn't necessary for the crew chief to point me in that direction. But he did anyway. As I ducked low and headed toward the armored vehicle, a guy stuck his head out of the rear hatch, waved me in, and told me to sit on the side bench next to another kid from the 1st Cav carrying an M-16. The two men who were about to issue orders that could change our lives—or end them—were Americans. They wore standard jungle fatigues but had nothing on them identifying rank, unit, not even branch of service. Green fatigues, jungle boots. Period. They started talking, and you couldn't tell where they were from. No accent. No nothing. Two white guys with short haircuts, age thirty to forty.

"Okay, we're going to give you each a map. It's going to have two dots on it. One dot is where your target's going to be; the other is where your pickup point is going to be."

Then they handed me a photograph; I think it was a five-by-seven. "Here's your target. If you'll notice, there's a little scar above his eye." They let us study the photo for a minute, and then took it back. As we left the APC, the guy told us, "Don't talk about your units, and don't give full names. Just give your first name or a nickname. And pick up your brass."

They told us to wait outside, so after we exited the APC, I turned to the other kid and said, "My name's Mitch, and I've got seven and a half months left."

And he says, "Well, my name's Wayne, and I've got three months left."

We're standing there talking and smoking when the helicopter comes in. Wayne says, "I guess that's our transportation. I was hoping it wouldn't get here. I was on one of these things one time when we didn't have any transportation, and just waited for a while, and they got me a chopper ride back to my unit."

I said, "You've done this before?"

"Yeah," he says. And that was it. I didn't ask him anything else. I guess I was a perfect candidate for the job. I didn't ask a lot of questions. Got on the helicopter and had about half an hour to think about what was going on. And to be scared.

When we got off, Wayne checked his compass and we went into the wood line. The chopper left us, and there we were. He asked me if I could shoot well enough and run fast enough for us to get out of this alive, and I said, "God, I hope so!"

The two of us walked for about thirty minutes, till we came to a small open area, about a hundred meters long by a hundred meters wide. At the opposite side was a stream. Wayne was checking his map, and then looking at the clearing. We agreed that this must be the place. So I bent down and began looking through the scope. I got right beside one of the large trees, lay down, and could see everything in the clearing from there. And Wayne lay down next to me—not against me, but close enough that if either one of us had stretched our arm out about halfway, we could've touched the other.

About half an hour went by, and six North Vietnamese soldiers came into the open area, looking relaxed, just walking and talking. Then the main body of troops came in, about a dozen of them, and I remember whispering to Wayne, "Do you suppose a flank is going to walk over our asses?" We didn't know if they had a patrol out, protecting their flank.

I was still looking through the scope when I saw the troops talking to our target. I could only assume he was a high-ranking officer. I could distinguish his face, his eyes, and the scar we'd seen in the photo. This was very different from combat. This was hunting, but the target wasn't a deer or a rabbit; it was a man. Nothing in my training had prepared me for the moment when I realized that I had the power of life and death over another human being. If you can be shocked, angered, and in awe at the same time, I was. This was my John Wayne or Gary Cooper moment. They were the movie idols I grew up with. But the differences between being a Hollywood sniper and a real one were instantly clear to me, and I was terrified.

Wayne was looking through his spotter scope, and as soon as he saw the guy with a whole lot of rank on his shoulders and a scar over his eye, he said, "Have you got him?"

I said, "Yes."

And he said, "Okay, it's on you." That was like a line out of the movies. I could imagine the music dropping down till all you could hear was a drumroll. An insistent drumroll, building in volume and intensity, begging to be silenced by a single shot.

At the moment I saw the whole bunch of NVA it hit me that we were expendable, me and Wayne—just so much cannon fodder. Stop the movie scene. Enough of that drumroll. This was real. We'd never been taught sniper-craft. Just had to remember the stuff we learned on regular combat patrols and way back in advanced infantry training (AIT). Set up inside the wood line, well back from the edge. This was OJT—on-the-job training—and I realized that I was dead. I'm dead because there's a whole bunch of them and there's only two of us. I'm dead because I've got only forty rounds of ammunition, and I'm not sure how much Wayne is carrying for his M-16. No grenades; not even a .45. And contrary to what's been written by some military historians about sniper teams never being sent into the bush without a radio to call for reinforcements or for artillery or air support, we had no radio. Officially, I guess, we didn't exist. There wasn't going to be a notation in our 201 file that we'd been lent to the CIA or whoever those spooks were. We were on our own. And we were about to be dead.

I started to pick up a sight picture just as the target stopped at a stream and reached down to get a double handful of water to splash on his face. He had his back to me. He shook the water off his hands to the front, and then he stretched. He was in a crucifixion pose, and I took two breaths. On the second breath, I just let it half out. The reason is that at the shallowest part of your breath, when you've got nothing left in your lungs, there's a tremor. It's imperceptible, but it's there.

And at the top of your breath, when your lungs are full, there's a tremor just before you start exhaling. So you let about half of it out, which is the most stable part of your breathing cycle, and then you hold it.

In AIT they taught us to aim at the center of mass on the silhouette targets. On a man, it's the top of the breastbone. It's a perfect aiming point because if your rifle kicks up a little bit, you'll hit his head. If you drop the barrel a little bit, you're going to hit his heart. If you go left or right, you're going to get a lung. The target's back was to me, but it was still center of mass. He was less than two hundred meters away, so there wasn't going to be a lot of droppage of the round, and it wasn't a far enough distance to worry about the wind causing a deflection. It was just quick, down and dirty.

I held my breath and gently squeezed the trigger. The sound of the single shot in the relatively quiet forest seemed incredibly loud. He went headfirst into the stream, and Wayne said, "Clean." We slid backward; I grabbed the shell casing, and we took off. We'd run for a few minutes when we began hearing rounds whizzing through the underbrush. They sounded like a freight train coming through the air—nothing like the way it sounds on TV. It was a "pffft-*crack!*" So the round was passing before the sound of the shot got to us. And the bullets never stopped coming. They were still shooting at us as we got close to our pickup point.

Both of us could hear the helicopter sitting on the ground.

A brief digression for readers who are sticklers for proper procedure as set forth in various army training manuals: Was it bizarre that a chopper would wait on the ground out in the middle of nowhere, rather than orbit until we were spotted? Yes. The typical procedure for a pickup in a combat area was for the ground unit to pop colored smoke, radio the choppers to tell them what color they'd popped, listen for the pilot to acknowledge that he'd seen the smoke, and then have the Huey come in to make the pickup. There were a couple of reasons why that scenario was not going to work: We had no smoke grenades, and we had no radio. At some point in my sniper career, I recall being told that carrying that stuff would just add weight, it would slow us down, and it might get snagged as we ran through the bush, all of which was undeniably true. The fact that smoke and a radio might save our lives was also undeniable, but as I said earlier, I'd just figured out that we were expendable. I'll plead guilty to being a slow learner.

The briefers had told us that the chopper would sit for only ten minutes—maybe not even that long. If we weren't there, we were going to have to walk back from here, and we had no idea where *here* was. We hadn't been told where we were going to be. The map we'd been given was only about twelve inches by ten inches. It didn't have any border information, didn't have any of the legend. Nothing that really told us exactly where we were. So we had to get to that Huey. Otherwise we were just two more MIAs, and our families would never know that we'd been hung out to die.

Talk about surround sound. From behind us we're hearing automatic weapons fire; to our right and left, at our feet and over our heads, we're hearing the "pfft-*crack*" of rounds just missing; to our front we're hearing the RPMs on the chopper's rotor going up; we know the pilot's bringing the engine to flight idle. In seconds he'll pull pitch and that bird will be gone, leaving us to die.

When we heard the engines accelerating, we didn't say anything; we just looked at each other and started running harder, slamming branches and brush out of the way and tightening the grip we had on our rifles so we wouldn't accidentally drop them and have to stop. We'd given up any hope of camouflaging our movements. All that mattered was catching that helicopter.

Just as we came into the clearing, he lifted off and began to circle around to head back to wherever the hell he'd come from. We were shouting, "We're here, we're here!" We knew instinctively that there was no way he could hear us, but we kept shouting and waving. Desperate people do strange things. Luckily, the crew chief or door gunner must have seen us, because that bird circled back in and set down.

As it touched the ground, we dove in face-first, and we'd barely slammed onto the floor of the slick when the bird took off. We didn't get in the seats or strapped in or anything before we were up and gone. As we circled around, we took some fire—I could hear a "tik-tik-tik." The crew chief shouted at us, "Are you guys all right?"

As I acknowledged that we were, I realized that this was not the same crew that had dropped us off, and it dawned on me that we were part of something that had taken some fairly elaborate planning. What was going through my mind at that moment, however, was not the notion of congratulating the higher-ups on their logistical achievement. I was more wrapped up in practical considerations. *How do I get out of here alive? Am I ever going to see Texas again? What in God's holy name am I doing here?*

I looked at Wayne, and he looked at me, and we were both huffing and puffing. He reached into a pocket and pulled out a pack of cigarettes. They were Kools. I remember that because I didn't like Kools. He pulled out a Zippo and we sat there and smoked. I had no concept of time. All I remember is that we landed and dropped Wayne off, and then we flew back to my base camp—ten, fifteen, maybe twenty minutes. Touched down, I got off, and they were gone.

I took the rifle back to my commander, handed it to him, and left. He didn't ask me anything, and I was still too scared to talk. I returned to my tent and was sitting there when the squad leader stuck his head in. "Are you all right?"

"Yeah."

"Did everything go all right?"

"Yeah, I guess so." And he left. That was my debrief.

That was it. Later on I began to wonder how they knew that I didn't go out, lie in the woods, fire a round, and get on the helicopter. How did they know I'd actually made the kill?

Then I began to dwell on the nature of what I'd just done, examining it from several angles. It was absolutely unlike any combat experience I'd had to that point. In combat you're counting on your buddies and they're counting on you to do what has to be done to get everyone home alive. But getting assigned to kill a specific person? I began trying to figure out what got me through it. That's when I realized that up until the shot was fired, it was pretty mechanical. It was training kicking in. But once the rifle fires, the brain's response is all electrical and chemical. It's as though a little guy in a tux stands up between your ears and shouts, "Let's get ready to rumble," so loud that you're certain the enemy two or three hundred meters away can clearly him.

The instant result is nervous stimulation that causes the center of the adrenal glands that sit atop each of your kidneys to release two of the body's most powerful hormones directly into the bloodstream. The effects of this flood of adrenaline (epinephrine) and noradrenaline (norepinephrine) into the bloodstream are profound and almost instantaneous:

- There's an increase in the rate and strength of the heartbeat that results in increased blood pressure
- Blood is shunted from the skin and internal organs to the skeletal muscles, coronary arteries, liver, and brain
- Blood sugar levels rise
- Clotting time of the blood is reduced
- Metabolic rate increases
- Bronchial tubes dilate
- Pupils dilate
- Goose bumps develop and hairs stand on end

In terms of taking the body from find-and-shoot mode to get-me-the-hell-out-of-here mode, that all makes a lot of sense. Except for the goose bumps. As near as I can figure, the only useful function they perform is to help you confirm that at that precise moment you are so scared that if you had to think to breathe, you'd suffocate.

From that first shooting experience, I knew that getting real-time confirmation of that fact was not an issue. There was that momentary pause between the sound of the rifle firing and my spotter telling me it was a good hit. Then we instantly went into flight mode—I know it's usually called "flight or fight"—but trust me on this one; we weren't interested in any option other than *di-di*'ing out of there a lot faster than ASAP. We had to get up, get out, and survive the run to our helicopter. Someone once told me that adrenaline is the most powerful drug known to man. We were freakin' high on adrenaline, and we didn't really come down until we were safely out of the area. That's when I could begin rethinking what I'd just been through. And after that first shoot, all I could think was, *What have I gotten myself into? Can I do this? I don't have anybody to blame it on but myself.*

That night I cornered the squad leader. "Why didn't you tell me you were having me trained as a sniper?"

And his answer was "Oh, y'know, I've got all the confidence in the world that you can do whatever needs to be done, and that you've got the initiative and the know-how and the skills."

My response was a little hostile. "Well, thanks a lot, asshole. Why me?"

"We have our reasons," he said. And that was the only answer he'd ever give. I found out later that this was his second tour in Vietnam, and he'd been a sniper during his first tour. The guys who volunteer and are selected to go to sniper school in today's military are given batteries of psychological tests and examinations to see if they match a sniper profile that's been developed. Back in the Vietnam era, they didn't have me or any of the guys I trained with at marksmanship school examined by a shrink to determine our fitness for the job, so it seems to make sense that they would have turned to former snipers in the infantry and asked them to identify soldiers who had what it takes. But that's just supposition; since there's no paperwork, no notations in my records, I can only guess.

It sounds unbelievable that somebody could be as naive as I was and not ask questions before following orders to undertake an out-of-the-ordinary mission, but that was the army back then. You didn't ask a lot of questions. It was "do what you're told and do it well enough to get by, keep the sergeant off your ass, and survive." Later in my career it was a lot different. "I beg your pardon? Excuse me? Which one of us is crazy? One of us is on narcotics—I'll pee in a bottle right now, okay? What the hell do you mean, go off by ourselves, just the two of us?" But that was years later, after the country lost its innocence, after the revelations of the Pentagon Papers, after Nixon and Watergate, after Reagan, Ollie North, and Iran-Contra. Even those of us who had military careers learned that there were occasions when it was essential to question authority—although we never put the bumper sticker on our Hummers.

CHAPTER FIVE

The Woman Is Your Target

I'd been in Vietnam about three months and had knowingly killed two people. The first one had been in a combat situation, and even though it had obviously affected me, I didn't have to work too hard to rationalize it. We'd been ambushed, my buddies were under fire, and I could do something about it. So I did.

What happened to me on that operation is precisely what every sergeant I came in contact with in basic and AIT worked hard to achieve. When the right circumstances presented themselves, that fresh-faced kid from Granbury, Texas, who worried that his father would invoke capital punishment—or at least corporal punishment—if he got caught misbehaving, would kill.

In his Pulitzer Prize–nominated book, *On Killing: The Psychological Cost of Learning to Kill in War and Society,* former West Point psychologist Dave Grossman (who also happens to be a retired lieutenant colonel and Army Ranger) writes: "When faced with a living, breathing opponent, a significant majority of soldiers revert to a posturing mode in which they fire over their enemy's heads." He adds that soldiers must be trained intensively to overcome the natural reluctance to kill other people.

Based on my responses under fire, I can only guess that the reluctance threshold of some soldiers is lower than that of others. My first sniper killing is a whole different ball game, and I still don't understand my response.

I accepted an assignment that had me hunting a man like I used to hunt deer. Find a hide, lie in wait, confirm the target, kill him. What was there about me that I could do it? What did the army know about me that led them to choose me?

First, the squad leader says that I'm being sent to marksmanship school because of all his guys, I'm the one who keeps his head in a tough situation. He liked the way I handled myself. (When he said it the first time, I didn't know he'd been a sniper on a previous tour in Vietnam.) And I liked that he said it. I was flattered that he thought I was exceptional.

Second, the instructors never let on that we were being taught to operate in anything but a combat environment, with our unit. No one ever asks why we'd have to knock off a target seven hundred meters out during a unit operation in the jungles or mountains of Vietnam. I'd been on infantry operations for a couple of months, and I was never—not even once—in a situation where being able to hit a target more than seven football fields away would have come in handy. Yet it never dawned on me to raise my hand and ask the question.

Third, when the captain sent me out on the first mission, was he that smooth that he had me on the chopper before it even crossed my mind to ask what he was getting me into? I'm a nineteen-year-old kid who enlisted to be a truck mechanic. I had been taught all my life not just to trust authority, but also to obey it without question. My parents. My teachers. The neighbors. The local cop. And then my drill sergeants, who made it clear that if I paid attention to what they could teach me, I might actually survive the war. And once I got to Vietnam, my squad leader, platoon sergeant, first sergeant, and the company commander. I thought they were all supposed to be interested in keeping me alive. No one sent up a flare and said, "Sorry, Mitchell. New game plan."

Finally, there were the two spooks in the APC. The shit they laid on me was so slick I didn't even feel myself sliding down the slippery slope. I don't even know whether they knew it was my first time, but they certainly didn't leave any room in their spiel for me to say, "Uh, let's slow this thing down and talk about it. You want me to go where and do what?"

So what does it come down to with that first mission? I'll tell you. It's a five-word sentence that causes chills, because it has an ugly provenance: I was only following orders.

And now that they knew I'd done it once, they could pretty much count on the fact that I'd do it again.

If there is a joy to being with a combat unit in the military, it's found in the camaraderie you have with your buddies. While you may not be close with your entire squad, there are usually a couple of guys whom you enjoy hanging with, guys you feel comfortable talking to about anything. The problem I had was that after my first shoot, I didn't have anyone I could confide in.

I didn't want to discuss it in the squad because I didn't know how they'd react. I wasn't about to talk to my squad leader about it, because he was the one who got me into this mess in the first place, so he really wasn't high on my buddy list. All I could do was wonder when—or if—they'd be coming to get me again. Unfortunately, I had to wait only about a week.

The charge of quarters (CQ) woke me at about 2:30 in the morning and told me the company commander wanted to see me as soon as I could get there. Again, at that time, I thought that there were only two reasons the CO would want to see someone: Either you were in trouble or there was an emergency of some type at home. Since it was the middle of the night, which was not when discipline for minor infractions was meted out, I opted to believe something was wrong back in the States. What else could have gotten the CO out of his rack at that hour?

I dressed quickly, put on my web gear, and went to the bunker that served as the orderly room, hoping someone would be there to tell me what to expect before I saw the old man, but the CQ was the only one around. There was no opportunity for us to talk. He said the commander was waiting and I should report immediately. I knocked on the partition that separated his office from the rest of the bunker, and he called me in.

Sitting on his desk was a rifle case. The sight of it caused three things to occur instantaneously: complete relief at the realization that there was nothing wrong at home, understanding that I had again been selected for a shoot, and instant fear.

The last time had shown me that I really didn't want to be out in the jungle alongside only one other person, with the very strong possibility of someone chasing the two of us. Now it was apparent that it was going to happen again.

It seemed more than a bit odd to go through the formal "Specialist Mitchell reporting as ordered, sir" in the middle of the night, but I did it anyway. He told me there was a helicopter waiting for me at the airfield, so I'd better hurry. I saluted, took the rifle from the case, and left his office. I stepped out into the night and started for the airfield. I wanted to go back to my tent for a couple of things but thought better of it.

When I arrived at the airfield, the helicopter was sitting there running. The doors were open. I guess, since I was the only one who showed up with an M-14, they assumed that I was the guy they were waiting for. I climbed aboard and we lifted off into the pitch-black sky almost before I could get my seat belt fastened.

We flew north for a couple of hours. Just as dawn broke, we started down. Knowing that this was the most dangerous time of the day in Vietnam, I began to tense up somewhat. Once again, we landed near an armored personnel carrier. I grabbed my gear and started toward the APC when a guy stepped out and told me to take a smoke break in front of the vehicle. This was one of the same briefers whom I had met on the first mission.

I went around the track, sat down and lit a cigarette, making sure that I kept the cherry cupped in my hand. After what seemed ages, a second helicopter landed, and two GIs left the APC and got on the aircraft. One was carrying a rifle similar to mine. *This is going to be an interesting day,* I thought. At least two teams working simultaneously. I'd jumped to the conclusion on the first mission that only one of these operations was taking place at a time. Apparently I was wrong.

After about ten minutes another helicopter landed and dropped off a single passenger. Since I had the special rifle and he was carrying an M-16A1, it was a pretty good bet that he was my second. A few minutes later we were called inside the track and the briefing began much as before. Again, the briefers wore nothing to indicate rank, unit, or even branch of service. No preliminaries, no "good morning," just right down to business.

We quickly discovered that for us, this was to be an entirely different kind of shoot. We had barely sat down on one of the benches inside the APC when they handed us a piece of a map, and a photograph.

"Okay, there's two people in the picture. Look at the woman. Note the scar over one eyebrow. She's your target." Well, I looked at the guy who was with me, and I looked back at the picture. It was clear that we were stunned. The spook said, "Okay, we've noted your reaction. If you don't think you want to do this, let us know now so we can task somebody else." And then he moved right along so quickly that we didn't have a chance to say anything.

I was aware from the combat ops I'd been on that the VC actively recruited and used women, but to this point I'd not knowingly encountered one. It seemed as though that was about to change, in a very chilling way.

We were dismissed and stepped outside of the carrier. No helicopter was on the ground, and we didn't hear an inbound Huey, so we stepped over to the edge of the wood line and squatted down and lit a cigarette.

My spotter sighed. "A woman."

"Damn," I responded.

Clearly we were both taken aback by the mission, but there was no discussion between us. Finishing our smokes, we got up and strolled back over to the carrier and asked if they had any coffee left. They poured us some in, of all things, a paper cup. I hadn't seen a paper cup in quite a while. These guys knew how to live.

We stood in front of the carrier, drank our coffee, and smoked another cigarette. I should have been nervous about standing in the middle of nowhere, but somehow I was confident there was heavy security around the perimeter. I didn't think anyone with the authority that these folks seemed to have would be running around without it.

A few minutes later one of the spooks came out of the track and was looking around at nothing in particular, but you could tell he was seeing everything. I offered him a cigarette and he surprised me by accepting it. We all stood there just looking around, waiting.

Then I realized why he had come out. He was looking for our aircraft and at the same time checking on us, probably to evaluate our mental state. After about five minutes or so he stubbed out the cigarette and went back inside the carrier.

We just grinned at each other, and my spotter muttered something about the REMF (Rear Echelon Motherfucker) being a little jittery. We both laughed and smoked another cigarette. My partner wondered aloud if we should impose on them for another cup of coffee. "Why not?" I asked. But when we ambled over to the open rear hatch, one of the spooks said the coffee was gone and they were getting ready to depart.

For a second I wondered what they were going to do with us, but then, off in the distance, we could hear an inbound Huey. Problem solved. We took off on yet another green helicopter with no unit markings, manned by an American crew whose origins were equally mysterious, and flew south for about an hour and a half, which by my calculations put us only about a half hour north of Phuoc Vinh, near where this mission had begun in the middle of the night. It didn't make any sense. So what else was new?

The landing was more of a combat insertion than a passenger drop-off. No sooner had our boots hit the ground than the pilot pulled pitch and was out of there. Not a good sign, as far as I was concerned. We oriented our ground position with the map, located the two dots that told us how far we'd have to run once we'd taken out the target, and began what looked to be a six-hour mission on the ground.

We had been dropped about four kilometers from our scheduled firing position, and it took almost two hours to get there because the underbrush was so thick. When we arrived at the first dot, we found ourselves on the crest of a small hill overlooking the village. Now all we had to do was identify the target, which required that she show herself. We hadn't been instructed to go hooch to hooch trying to find her, which was a good thing, because it wasn't something I was interested in doing.

We lay there in hiding for about an hour, all the time regretting the coffee we had drunk earlier. There is an obvious and quite simple solution to that problem, but with memories of childhood unpleasantness in our heads, and not having had special operations training during which deliberately peeing in one's pants is taught as a sign of dedication to duty, honor, and mission, we opted to just lie there and suffer rather than wetting our pants.

Time began to get critical—for both the mission and our bladders. Our helo was due in three hours, and if we had no interference it was a two-hour walk to the pickup point on the map. Still, there was no movement at all around the village. Something was going to have to happen pretty quickly, or we would have to abort the shoot.

Our briefers had told us if something went wrong on any shoot, we could abort, but we had no idea what would happen if we did. In the military, there are always consequences—often bad ones—when lower-ranking soldiers start thinking for themselves. We were more worried about what our superiors would do to us if we called off the shoot than we were about whether we were going to miss our pickup. It's classic drama—we might have to choose not between a good solution and a bad one, but between two bad ones: potential punishment or being abandoned in Indian country by ourselves.

We really didn't know what to do, but sometimes the best choice is to do nothing, and that worked for us that day. Because about half an hour later, we began to hear noises to the east of the village. The villagers were returning from wherever they had been. We had no idea if they had been in their rice fields, visiting another village, or what. We were just extremely relieved that they had returned.

I eased into a comfortable shooting position, turned my baseball cap around backward, looked through the scope, and began to gently sweep across the village and villagers trying to find our target. I'd made a couple of passes when the second whispered, "Contact, two o'clock." Gently easing the rifle to the area he had pointed out, I saw two ladies standing talking to each other. The one on the right had the small scar on her forehead that we had been instructed to look for. She was the target!

The range was very short. It was about 250 meters, downhill. Not the best shooting angle. When you shoot downhill, you can misjudge distance easily. But it would have been worse if we had to also shoot over water. During my week at school, I'd learned that the movement of water causes some air turbulence, and that can affect the trajectory of the round.

I swept the area around her to see if anyone else was in my line of fire if the shot went astray, but the only other person who could be in danger was the woman the target was talking to. Glancing at my watch, I realized there was not a lot of time to wait and see if the second woman would leave, giving me a little more margin for error. Thinking like that was clearly nerves at work, because shooting with a scope at this range in bright sunlight, even downhill, did not require me to be Carlos Hathcock, the Marine Corps gunnery sergeant with ninety-three confirmed kills. If I could settle myself down, it would be an easy shot.

Out of the corner of my eye I saw my spotter looking over at me, nodding, and then looking back at the target. There was no point in putting it off any longer. I took a couple of deep breaths. On the second one I let half of the breath out and held, focusing intently on the sight picture. At 250 meters, the crosshairs were positioned right on the center of mass. I was perspiring profusely, but since it wasn't dripping into my eyes, it wasn't a real problem.

The object in this type of shooting is to actually surprise yourself when the weapon fires. That means the tip of your trigger finger moves imperceptively, first taking up the slack, then continuing to apply gentle pressure until the pad of tissue at the tip of the index finger is, itself, compressed. You keep squeezing until suddenly you feel the recoil, and as your entire body moves back with the rifle, then resettles, you see the gas from the round obscuring the sight picture for a second. With a muzzle velocity of about 855 meters per second, there's no question that by the time you comprehend that the weapon has fired, the bullet should have struck the target.

But even with a relatively close target like this one, there's still that moment of uncertainty when my view is obscured, when I don't really *know* whether or not I've hit the target, and if I have, whether it has been a killing shot. It seemed like an eternity, just lying there, neither of us moving. But it couldn't have been more than a second until my spotter simply whispered, "Target," so I knew even before the scope cleared that it had been a successful shoot.

Suddenly both of us realized that we were still lying in the same position. My memory here is a bit hazy, but I seem to recall hearing the phrase "Let's get the fuck out of here." I don't think I could have agreed more or phrased it more eloquently. As my partner began to scoot backward, I frantically looked to my right side, spotted the spent brass cartridge shell, and as I, too, scooted backward, grabbed it on the fly. When we had backed farther into the brush, we stood up, and, even though we couldn't see it, looked back toward the village as though we expected to see half the North Vietnamese Army coming after us.

The impulse, of course, is to run, but in a relatively quiet, forested area, two men running make more noise than a Texas twister tearing through a trailer park. We started off at a brisk walk, which seemed to get brisker by the moment because we had no idea if the village had a defense system in place or not. To tell the truth, I really didn't want to know. I just wanted to get out of there as fast as I could.

After about forty-five minutes, we stopped for a quick breather, and I wondered aloud if we were being followed, or if this was going to be an easy escape. My answer came in the form of a round zipping past us. We took off at a dead run, hoping that we were quick enough to outrun them, but knowing we couldn't outrun the rounds they were firing in our direction. After what seemed like forever we slowed to a fast walk, and I wondered aloud if they were still after us. As an afterthought, I asked my partner if we were still on course to our extraction site. Time was running short, and our margin for error was thin.

According to our calculations, we were about four hundred meters from a stream. If we were on course, there would be a bend just downstream from where we would cross. When we got to the stream it was flowing straight. The question was elementary: Were we above or below the bend we were looking for, and how far off were we? We had no success at all trying to find some sort of landmark we could orient with. We could see only about a hundred meters in any direction, so orienting to the map was pretty much out of the question.

We really had no choice other than to keep moving, hoping that we were not completely disoriented, and that we were still moving in the proper general direction. Hoping for that kind of good fortune in a combat zone is a recipe for disaster, but what choice did we have? Once again, we came face-to-face with the notion that we were expendable. With more than five hundred American GIs dying in combat each month in the summer of '69, who would notice two more? Who would even wonder what we were doing out by ourselves when they found our bodies—*if* they found our bodies?

Strangely, considering what the two of us had been conned into doing, we did spend some time talking about what would happen if we died. Not while we were trying to make sure it didn't happen, mind you, but while we were hanging out around the APC, waiting to go on this mission. It was important to me that my partner agree to try to carry my body to the helicopter. I didn't want to be abandoned in the jungle, left there to be picked over by the enemy, the animals, and the bugs. It just didn't seem right. It wasn't how I was brought up. A man should have a fitting burial, especially a man who dies for his country.

With luck, however, neither one of us was going to have to worry about bringing his buddy's body back. We apparently had managed to outrun our pursuers, but while there were no more bullets whizzing past us, we still didn't know where we were or which way we were supposed to head. Within minutes we came across a trail, but that did nothing to help orient us. Carefully examining our map fragment, neither one of us could see the trail. It meant that it either wasn't shown on the map, or we were going in the wrong direction. We were hoping for the former, but had no way of being certain until we finally came across a large stream that was on the map.

Turns out we had drifted about two kilometers off course, and were now about three klicks from our pickup point, with just over ninety minutes to get there. It doesn't sound like a problem—just over 1.8 miles to travel and an hour and a half to do it in. But we weren't running on a track; we were trying to race through heavy jungle carrying rifles, concerned that the enemy might be right behind us, and that our ride home could leave without us if we didn't make it.

We ignored almost everything we had ever been taught. We went in a straight line with no zigging or zagging. We went as directly and as fast as we could. When we were about a kilometer from the pickup point, we heard the aircraft approaching. We'd been told he would wait no longer than ten minutes for us once he was on the ground. What we had no way of knowing was how much longer till he landed and began counting down those ten minutes of ground time.

The sound of a helicopter is very indistinct in flight. You can hear it, but unless you can actually see it, you really can't make a decent guess at distance or speed. Our only choice was to run as though our lives depended on it, so we hit the trail that led to that magical dot on the map and ran like hell.

We were down to what we later calculated was about seven hundred meters when we heard the aircraft idle down. Time was running out, and we were both certainly running out of energy. I was hurting all over, scared I would hear the aircraft engine pitch change and trying not to start yelling. It wouldn't have done any good, because they wouldn't have been able to hear us anyway.

Suddenly we could see the bird. Again we strained to use any energy left in us to make it to the chopper. When we were about fifty meters away, but still in heavy jungle, we heard the pitch of the engine begin to change. Our lungs were about to burst, but that sound just about broke my heart. We were close to making it to safety, but close counts only in horseshoes, hand grenades, and nuclear weapons. Close wouldn't keep us alive. Just as we broke through the edge of the tree line, the Huey lifted off, pitched nose down, and began to turn and climb. We didn't know what to do. I was afraid because I knew that I was going to die right there at the crossing of two trails.

As the aircraft began to pick up altitude it circled back over the clearing, and the crew chief saw us waving desperately. For a second we couldn't be sure whether they were going to come down for us or not, but the pilot pulled his ship into a tight turn and dropped down. It didn't take more than three seconds for us to throw ourselves through the open door, grab hold of one of the seat stanchions, and find ourselves airborne.

Sitting on the cabin floor soaked with sweat that was quickly evaporating in the cooler air about fifteen hundred feet up, I had my first opportunity to reflect on what I'd just done. All my life I'd been raised to respect women. I had a difficult time putting a woman—even a Vietnamese woman—in the same category as a male enemy soldier. Yes, I knew that the Viet Cong were using not only women, but also children, to attack American troops. But that didn't mean I'd find it easy to kill them. Sure, if it were a heated moment, my unit under attack, a true us-or-them situation, I wouldn't have any qualms about doing what had to be done. But this—this planned, calculated shooting of a specific woman who was no immediate threat to me or my buddies—was something completely different. And I knew at that moment on the helicopter that I'd be dealing with this event in my young life for some time to come.

We flew for a while, those thoughts pounding in my head to the "whap-whap-whap" of the Huey's rotors, then landed in what seemed to be the middle of nowhere. Couldn't tell where we were, or if we'd been there before. The crew chief signaled for us to get off, which we did. They pulled pitch and left us standing in the middle of an open field—not a good place to be when you have no clue whether you're still in Indian country.

But before the sounds of our departing bird faded out, two Hueys circled in. We each got on a helicopter, and as we lifted off I could see my partner waving at me. I returned his wave and settled back in my uncomfortable seat for the trip to my base camp, and what I hoped would be a more normal combat assignment.

CHAPTER SIX

The Little Girl

Since my second sniper mission a few weeks earlier, I'd been out on some relatively routine patrols, but nothing out of the ordinary. Then we got tasked for something slightly different.

Our intelligence folks knew that the VC were collecting taxes from several villages within a few kilometers of our base camp near Phuoc Vinh, and the powers that be wanted us to do something about it.

Company B of the 2/7 got the assignment, and we worked in platoon sectors within the general area of the operation. There were a couple of small firefights, each lasting only a few minutes, but nothing significant. The VC would engage us briefly, and then withdraw.

On the last skirmish, one of our guys was hit, and from a blood trail that we found, we knew that at least one of the VC had taken a bullet. We lost time while waiting for a Dustoff to pull our wounded buddy out, and then we began tracking the enemy, knowing that we were at least fifteen minutes behind them.

The trail led to a village that was known to be loyal to the Saigon government. Our intel folks said that the village elders had provided sound intelligence for us on a couple of occasions, and that they'd denied support to the VC.

When we got into the village, we found that the enemy force we were trailing had, indeed, been there, and a little girl of three or four years had paid the price. The VC had asked for taxes and/or sanctuary from the elders, and when they were refused, they grabbed the girl and hacked off one leg about two inches above the knee with a machete. When we got to her she was in agony, and our medic said she could die soon from shock and loss of blood.

Our platoon sergeant put security around the village, notified command and called for a medical helicopter, then detailed me to help the medic. I would have rather gone out on the perimeter.

I'd seen dead bodies, both ours and theirs; I'd helped with our wounded; I'd watched guys die. It all comes along with being a grunt, and you learn how to handle it—or convince yourself that you've learned. That's what the GI mantra "It don't mean nothing" was all about—learning how to numb yourself to the horror that might confront you on a regular basis. But this was more than I wanted to be involved with.

I had to hold the little girl, who was writhing in pain, while the medic used a tourniquet to get the bleeding stopped and started an IV. We had to get her lower extremities higher than her head to try to keep as much blood flow as possible to her brain and major organs. Since her skin felt cold and clammy to the touch, we also had to try to keep her warm. She was in pain; she was scared—and now these strange-looking men were handling her in ways that her young mind couldn't comprehend.

All the while we were trying to treat her and keep her calmed down, her mother was screaming hysterically and trying to get her baby away from us. It took another guy from the platoon to restrain her. At the time we were doing it, the logic of keeping the mother away from her daughter made sense, but years later, rolling the incident around in my head, I found myself questioning what we did. As a parent, I know there's no way anyone could keep me from my child's side if he were critically hurt. How could we have done that to a poor Vietnamese mother who had no way of being sure that what we were doing to her daughter was an effort to help save her life? Frankly, I'm surprised she didn't try to kill us.

When the Dustoff arrived, we had another problem: There was no place for them to land. They had to lower a litter on a cable, and as it came down, the platoon sergeant warned everyone not to touch it. As soon as it was within reach, he whacked it with a steel rod that the medic carried to dissipate the static electricity that could knock you on your butt if you weren't careful.

While the Vietnamese trackers stood there shaking, with tears in their eyes, I placed the little girl in the basket as gently as I could. She had continued to cry, and occasionally scream, which made it that much more difficult for us American tough guys to deal with it. Once we had her strapped in, the aircrew lifted the basket and pulled it inside the aircraft.

As the Huey banked and started away, the mother suddenly realized that they were not going to wait for her. She became even more hysterical, attacking the medic and the platoon sergeant. Ultimately, the only way we could deal with her was to have the medic inject a sedative to calm her down.

After explaining to the village elders where the girl was being taken, and telling them that the mother would recover from the effects of the tranquilizer in a couple of hours, the classic tougher-than-nails platoon sergeant looked at the trackers and through tears in his eyes told them that we were not going to return to our base camp until we found the sons of bitches who did this.

By this time we were about an hour behind them, and the medic and I were covered in the little girl's blood. I was crying and felt sick to my stomach, and the doc, a guy who had a reputation for being calm and collected no matter what kind of hell was going on around him, had tears running down his cheeks.

It didn't take a genius to know what every guy in that platoon was thinking as we set out after the VC bastards who'd done this. The trackers were performing as they had never performed before, and they kept telling us that we were getting closer. I thought it was a miracle that they could follow the trail, because the jungle canopy was getting thicker, and even though it was only midafternoon, at ground level it was getting darker.

We continued to move, never stopping for a break. No one complained, not even the guys who were usually the first ones to ask when we were going back to base camp. I've never seen any group in my life that was more determined for revenge.

Right around nightfall one of the trackers lifted his arm in a signal for us to halt. We dropped to our knees and waited for the platoon sergeant to move up front to hear what the trackers had to say. It took just a second for him to turn around and give us the thumbs-up: We'd found them.

As quickly as possible, we deployed in squads to surround them. Once we were in position, one of the trackers shouted in Vietnamese that they were surrounded, and that we were going to take them prisoner.

It was clear that they had no idea we'd been on their trail, because when I was able to get in close I could see that they'd been sitting around a small fire, cooking rice. Their reaction to the tracker was unfortunate—for them. They made a couple of mistakes: First, they didn't immediately raise their hands in surrender, and second, they reached for their weapons.

Our platoon sergeant knew in an instant what was going to happen and tried to stop it. He really did want to take them alive, to haul them back to the village for interrogation. But his shout came a moment too late. Twenty rifles spoke as one.

Twenty riflemen of different marksmanship capabilities suddenly learned to aim true. Either that or the rifles were on fully automatic, in which case, you really don't need to be a good marksman. Just aim in the general direction and the recoil will give you a pretty good spread of your rounds.

Five VC all entered the hereafter simultaneously. The shooting lasted about three seconds. Personally, I emptied an eighteen-round magazine and wanted to shoot more, but it was over.

Since it was too dark to head back to the village with the bodies, we set up camp, put out security, and stayed for the night. The next morning we pulled, dragged, and carried the bodies back to the village and dropped them at the feet of the village elders.

When we arrived back at the base camp, we learned that the little girl would live. Her mother, along with a couple of the villagers, had walked roughly fifteen kilometers to the hospital, where the base commander had made arrangements for her to stay with her daughter.

Nowadays, when they talk about civilian casualties, they refer to it as "collateral damage." That makes it sound too clean and clinical. For my buddies and me that afternoon, it was about as ugly as war can get. That child had no control over whether her village paid taxes to the VC or supported the South Vietnamese government. She didn't have a say in whether her village furnished intelligence information to the U.S. military. She was innocent. And there wasn't one of us who made it through that mission who could toss off an "It don't mean nothing" with any degree of authority. All of us who'd been there for a while pretty much felt that our hearts had hardened to stone, that we'd seen so much awfulness that we couldn't feel any more.

That little girl proved that we were wrong. And you know something? That was probably a good thing.

CHAPTER SEVEN

Michelin Man

I was raised in a religious family. We attended the First Assembly of God Church in Granbury, Texas, went every Sunday morning, and also on Wednesday nights. I went because my family went, not because I was so religious. I really didn't have a lot of choice in the matter. If I wanted to get along with my parents, I'd go to church with them. I'm not even sure at what level I believed in God then, but how many eighteen-year-olds really do? You believe in your friends, you believe in girls, and you believe in cars. It was an *American Graffiti* life; even the news reports from Vietnam, the body counts, the assassinations of Martin Luther King and Bobby Kennedy, the antiwar demonstrations didn't make a significant impact.

Sitting in a hooch almost ten thousand miles from Granbury tends to give you a different perspective on what's important in life. With my second sniper assignment behind me, my life had radically changed. First, the two mystery men pop my cherry by having me kill an NVA officer. That must have been my test. Too bad I passed it. The next assignment they give me is to kill a woman. And I do it, no questions asked. That's gotta be as bad as it can get.

Mitchell, you dumb shit, you're wrong again.

We'd been out on patrol for forty-eight hours. Forty-eight miserable, stinking, wet, unproductive, monsoon rain–filled hours, and the entire squad was looking forward to a chance to get into some clean clothes, eat some hot chow, and just kick back. We were almost at the base camp when the radioman walked past me, up to the squad leader, and gave him the handset. He listened a bit, then came back to me, placed his hand on my shoulder, and said that the platoon sergeant wanted to see me when we got back in.

When you're living like we were in Vietnam, small pleasures can make your day, like using a three-holer instead of doing a squat-and-dump in the bush; showering with lukewarm water; putting on a pair of dry socks; or getting a cup of coffee out of a pot in the mess hall rather than having to make it yourself from the C-ration amenities packet. When it appears that for no good reason you have been singled out to be denied one or more of these pleasures, exasperation can set in.

I was irritated. I'd already jumped to the conclusion that the captain was going to hand me my special rifle and send me someplace where I would probably die. It was a good bet that helicopters weren't going to be flying in this weather, so I figured any travel would be by road, which meant I was going to be wet, uncomfortable, and extremely vulnerable. I asked the squad leader if I had time to change clothes and get a cup of coffee. He had no objections. In weather like this, he said, another thirty or forty minutes probably wouldn't make any difference.

I was sitting in the mess hall, enjoying a cigarette with my coffee, when the company clerk came in, sat down with me, and offhandedly mentioned, "The old man is not happy waiting for you." I may have been unhappy, but getting my company commander pissed off at me would definitely not have a positive impact on my situation, so I double-timed it over to the orderly room.

When I walked in, the captain handed me the rifle and told me there was a jeep waiting at the west gate. Great. I slogged through the deluge all the way across the compound, where I found the vehicle. In it were the same two smug anonymous guys who gave me my assignment on the last two missions. As we drove off, I felt a little confused. Was I the second? The spotter rather than the shooter? Where were we picking up the other guy? I was curious because it would give me a chance to see where he was based, even if I didn't know precisely what unit he was in. It's not that it mattered, just that I'd begun connecting the dots and trying to figure out what was going on, and I saw an opportunity here to gather some personal intel.

As we rolled down the road in the pouring rain, the guy behind the wheel started the briefing, and I noticed how nervous his partner seemed to be. Then the lightbulb went off and I understood: He was going to be the second on this mission. I tapped him on the shoulder and said, "Make sure you listen close." He just gave me a dirty look, and the driver laughed. I was right. The other guy was going with me on this one, and he wasn't happy about it.

Lighting a cigarette in the pouring rain was a trick and a half. Even though the canvas top was up, the jeep had no doors, and the poncho I had on was hardly keeping me dry. I kept waiting for the usual information about the target, but the driver just danced all around it, which did nothing to lower my anxiety level. I'd figured out after the first mission that these guys didn't care whether I lived or died. They weren't ugly about it; it's just that on their to-do list, making sure Gary Mitchell was upright when he went home to Texas was somewhat less than a high priority. The fact that one of them was going to put his ass on the line right next to mine was almost enough to make me smile.

We stopped at a compound to fill the jeep's gas tank, then got back on the road heading for the giant U.S. Army base at Long Binh, about twenty miles northeast of central Saigon, and just three or four miles from the U.S. Air Force base at Bien Hoa. I'd been on operations in the rubber plantations in this area, and wasn't thrilled about driving through them in a lone jeep. But after almost two hours on the road, we made it to the base without any problem, ending up at transient billeting. The briefer handed me a plastic bag and said

I had a bunk reserved. He'd keep the rifle and they'd pick me up the following morning. Before I could even get out of the rain, the two spooks had pulled away.

I was assigned a bunk, and after I found it I opened my plastic bag of goodies. A razor, shaving cream, deodorant, soap, and a towel, all new. I guess these guys wanted their snipers smelling springtime fresh. (I know, the notion of a sniper using any scented personal-hygiene product doesn't smell right. In today's army, they wouldn't allow it; they don't even accept smokers into sniper training now. But this is now and that was then, and I always had the feeling that they were making a lot of the rules up and ignoring all of the existing rules as they went along.) There were also ten dollars in military payment certificates (MPC) in the bag. This was the currency issued to our armed forces in order to keep greenbacks off the black market. I took my first really hot shower in a couple of months, dressed, and, since the rain had finally stopped, decided to look around.

The army in Vietnam served three types of rations. Cs were small cans packed in a cardboard box—one box was one full meal for one GI. Bs were essentially Cs, but in unit-sized containers, and mostly had to be reconstituted in a central kitchen. As were the meals we dreamed about. Fresh meat. Fresh vegetables. And wonder of wonders, fresh milk. This is what they were serving in the mess hall at Long Binh, and I wasn't shy about taking advantage of the opportunity. After downing at least half a steer and more fresh milk than I ever thought a guy could drink at one sitting, I decided to take in a movie.

Hard to believe that the guys stationed at Long Binh were in the same army I was. We called them REMFs, and in Vietnam there were roughly ten of them for every guy in the bush. That night, I joined the REMFs at the movies. They were showing a Western starring Gary Cooper; they had a popcorn machine. For almost two hours I was able to forget why I was in Long Binh and what I was going to be doing the next day.

When the movie ended, I went to the Enlisted Men's Club and was tempted to have a cold beer. You know those beer commercials that play on TV, the ones that show a close-up of an ice-cold, sweating bottle of beer, with drops of moisture dripping slowly down the side? That's how tempting the beer was at the club. But I didn't know what was in store for me in the morning, so I opted for a Coke. Didn't want anything cluttering up my thought processes. I was hoping to survive the next day and wanted to do what little I could to increase my odds. Yeah, I knew that Coke has caffeine in it, but by now you probably realize that I'm a heavy coffee drinker—definitely not decaf—so I wasn't concerned about the effect of a little more caffeine from the Coke.

Every so often I'd reflect back on what my life had been like just a little more than a year earlier, when I'd been a relatively carefree kid in Texas. That kid was gone, and I was no longer sure who I really was, what I'd become—and why, and what kind of future I might have.

They woke me at 0500 the next morning. I took another hot shower, shaved, and tried not to drown in the rainstorm as I walked to the mess hall for breakfast. I've always been blessed with a good appetite, and the mission ahead of me didn't change that. When I finished, I went back to the transient billeting area to wait for the people I had begun to call superspooks.

Shortly after noon they pulled up in the jeep and I climbed in. The rain that had started again during the night still hadn't let up, and we could barely see out the windshield. I knew we were heading south out of Long Binh, probably on the Vung Tau cutoff, past the village of Bear Cat. Three or four miles southeast is the town of Long Thanh, and between the two on the northeast side of the road is nothing but rubber plantations at least three miles deep.

When we reached the plantation area, the driver slowed to a crawl. He was obviously looking for something or someone. When he spotted a tiny road, he turned in. Now I was really unhappy. The rubber plantations were a living reminder of the French Colonial era—some of the largest still carried the Michelin name—and it was no secret that the Viet Cong had tunneled beneath many of them. My unit had fought battles in a number of the plantations, and in the end, the VC always managed to just disappear as though they'd evaporated. It was uncanny and never failed to unnerve us. Taking a slow jeep ride through one of these plantations without additional security was stupid—hell, I was the only one with a rifle, and even though the spooks were carrying sidearms, I had no confidence that they knew how to use them.

When we got about a quarter mile off the main highway, we came to a Buddhist monastery in the middle of a large clearing. "This is where you get off," said the briefer. He'd already given us a map, but it showed only one single dot. Missing was the second dot that on the two previous missions had designated the pickup point. The weather was so bad that helicopters probably weren't flying, so maybe there was no point in designating the extraction point. But its absence was definitely not a confidence builder.

I looked at the briefer and asked again about the target and the pickup. I'd already figured out that I was expendable, and I didn't think I could question the assignment, but if they were going to cut my head off, I had no intention of stretching my neck for them. I'd come to believe that the army owed me a chance to make it out alive. The driver pointed to an elderly, lone monk wearing a traditional saffron robe who was approaching us, and said that he would show us the target and where we would be picked up. "Trust him," the chief spook said. "He's loyal to the South. He and the others have been providing intelligence for years, and they've never been wrong. Just do what they say, when they say it."

With that the jeep drove off, and the monk beckoned my newbie second and me to follow him into an outlying building, where he pulled back a carpet and opened a well-concealed tunnel entrance in the wooden floor. I'd been down a tunnel before and could recall nothing pleasant about the experience. This assignment was getting worse by the moment.

The spook looked down, just sort of shrugged his shoulders, and jumped into the tunnel. There was a wooden ladder but we really didn't need it going down.

As I jumped in, I remember thinking, *Okay, we're all gonna die anyway*.

It was a large tunnel—much larger than the one I'd had to crawl through. There were probably still a couple inches of headroom when I stood straight up. We walked for about twenty yards and then the tunnel made a ninety-degree right turn, went another few yards, and made a left turn. There were two more turns and we entered a chamber about a third the size of a cheap motel room.

The room was lit by electric lights and stocked with C-rations, water, a couple of cots, and a civilian radio that the spook was able to tune to Armed Force Radio Vietnam (AFVN). It looked like the U.S. government had prepared the whole setup. I don't know where the air came from—I couldn't see any vents—but oxygen didn't seem to be a problem.

The monk said, "Wait here, and I'll come back and get you." That was a bad moment. We were in the rubber plantation, underground in a hostile area, and he was just going to go away and leave us? Now wouldn't that irritate the warts off of a toad's ass?

I finally drank some water, ate some Cs, and tried to pry information out of my second. "What's the deal with no target?" I asked. He didn't respond. What I'm thinking is that we're not coming back from this mission. I know it's beginning to sound like an obsession, but consider the circumstances and cut me some slack, okay? We've got one dot on the map where the kill is supposed to happen, and nothing to indicate transportation home. It says to me, "Mitchell, you're on a one-way ticket." But I didn't raise hell 'cause I was too scared and didn't want to rock the boat. Later in my career I'd have said, "It's my fucking boat; I'll turn this son of a bitch over if I want to. Let's get some answers." But most nineteen-year-olds don't mouth off like that, which is why they send nineteen-year-olds to war. So I did what GIs do under circumstances like this: I went to sleep. At least I could be well rested for my crossing of the River Jordan.

About four in the morning, the same monk came back. He told us that we must move very quietly so as not to disturb the sleep of the other monks, making it clear that not all of them were as loyal to the South as he was. He assured us that he and the other loyal monks knew which ones had to be watched, and they were very careful about it.

Great, I thought. *I'm underground in an area that's controlled by the VC, inside a monastery that may have VC posing as monks, or monks who are actually loyal to the cause of the VC, and now I'm supposed to go for a walk.*

Had I been more politically aware, I might have been able to figure out what was going on. But that would have required that I followed the politics of America's involvement in Vietnam, and even though my rifle and I were the physical embodiment of American foreign policy, like most kids my age I had no interest in international politics. I didn't pay attention to the changes of government in Saigon, and the active role the United States had played. And I didn't know anything about the Buddhists who were opposed to the war and our involvement in it. I just wanted to go home.

When a seventy-three-year-old monk named Thich Quang Duc assumed the lotus position in a busy Saigon intersection in 1963, had gasoline poured over his saffron robes, and then struck a match, immolating himself, I was still in grade school. The monk's very public suicide was the first of many demonstrations Vietnam's Buddhists held against the Catholic-run government and its principal backer, the United States. Six years after Quang Duc's death, Buddhist monks were still a thorn in the side of the Saigon government, and had I been paying attention, I could have figured out what I was doing there with my sniper rifle listening to one monk tell me there were others in this monastery who were not loyal to the South.

While I hadn't figured out the politics, I had concluded that this was my last mission, because there was no way to escape. The fact that I'd survived my first two killing assignments was no comfort. I had one rifle with two twenty-round magazines, but this time my second didn't have an M-16. Once again, we had no grenades, no radio, no signal flares. Was I scared? You couldn't have driven a straight pin up my ass with a ten-pound sledgehammer.

The three of us retraced our steps back to the trapdoor and climbed the ladder. The monk led us around the outside of the monastery and said we had to follow him in the darkness through the rubber plantation. Now this was not wise. I was sure of that. The VC moved at night; that was when army units set up ambushes. This monk might know what was going on inside his monastery, but he couldn't possibly know what VC units in the area were doing. Nevertheless, like a sheep going to slaughter, I followed him.

We walked in silence for about forty minutes until we reached the base of a huge rubber tree that concealed the opening to yet another tunnel. Down we went. We traveled underground for a pretty good distance before we came to the end of the tunnel and emerged next to another large tree. In the morning twilight I could make out that our position overlooked a relatively small, open area. Mercifully it wasn't raining, and we could see down a well-used trail on the other side. The monk told us to wait for him there. He said it might be a couple of hours, but we should wait patiently—and no smoking. The smell would attract any VC in the area and lead them right to us.

We sat down on the ground and waited for a very tense hour. I nearly launched into orbit when the monk suddenly spoke to us. He'd managed to return without making a sound. I have no idea where he came from; he was just there. He told us that in about another hour, five monks would be coming past our location. They would be wearing their bright orange robes with hoods over their heads.

"You must kill the other four," he told us.

"The other four?" I asked.

"Yes, we're all monks."

It took a second for it to sink in. This monk was going to be coming down the trail with four other monks; all dressed alike, all wearing hoods. I was to kill the other four.

"But what if I can't tell which one you are?" I asked.

"Shoot all of us. We will be coming down the trail."

At that moment it didn't register that this monk who was loyal to our government had just told me that, if it appeared that I had no other choice, I should kill him. Even if it had registered, I'm not sure that I would have argued with him. There was no time.

Then he calmly told us that after the shooting, we should go due west for about one and a half kilometers, to a clearing. We should wait there for a helicopter to pick us up. Checking our map, I could see that there was, indeed, a clearing precisely a klick and a half to the west. We would have to cross a stream to get there, but it should be a quick trip.

I was not very receptive to the idea of shooting monks. It would be like walking through the town where I now live and going to the Catholic church to get the priest. Then you go over to the Assembly of God church and you get the minister. And you go to the Episcopal church and you get their priest. And you go down the road to the synagogue and get the rabbi, and you take them all out and shoot them. I was having an even harder time dealing with the fact that the monk who had guided and protected us said that if we couldn't positively identify him, we should shoot them all. I flashed back to that engraved Zippo someone had shown me, the one that said SHOOT 'EM ALL AND LET GOD SORT 'EM OUT. At this moment, that seemed like a very bad joke.

My mind was reeling with all sorts of thoughts—most of them

ugly. Foremost was the notion that somebody in command, somewhere, didn't care whether or not I came back alive. A sniper's survival depends on his ability to fire one shot, make the kill, and move. While the people you're shooting at may be able to ascertain the general direction a single shot came from, they can't be sure where you are. Firing a second shot is tantamount to waving a red flag and yelling, "Hey, asshole, we're over here!" Firing four shots—maybe more if I missed on one of them—is suicidal. Then there was the matter of deliberately killing this man who was on our side. How could I do that? I panicked, my brain racing. I had to figure something out right this second. I looked at my spotter. Here's a guy who has to be making the big bucks. He's supposed to have the big picture. "You got any ideas?" It was not so much a question as a plea. He shook his head. No help there. I looked back at the monk, examining him from head to toe. Nothing. Not a single thing that would distinguish him from his brothers through my scope.

Then it dawned on me. Not a perfect solution, but one that increased his chances of living another day. "If my first shot isn't you, throw your hood off and run like hell and we'll try to pick you out." He smiled at us and walked back down the trail.

I turned to my second and said, "Did he just tell us that if we can't identify him, to kill all of them?"

And he said somberly, "I believe he did."

"I guess that proves that some people think that there are some things worth dying for," I responded. Still hoping that the spook had figured out something better, I asked, "Do you think you'll be able to spot our guy?"

My question was a waste of good breath. "We'll have to wait and see," he said.

It was beginning to dawn on me why the chief spook hadn't given me my target when he picked me up. If I'd had twelve hours to dwell on what I was being asked to do, maybe he thought I might refuse. But we were already in the middle of the rubber plantation, definitely Indian country, and I didn't have much of a choice. The trick now was to figure out how to accomplish the mission, and get out alive.

I checked my rifle for the thousandth time, popping out the magazine, clearing the round from the chamber, loading it back into the mag, then ramming the magazine back in, and listening as it stripped the round off the top and seated it back in the chamber. Still no rain, although the skies looked like they could open up at any moment. The shooting distance was relatively close, perhaps 150 meters. Concealment wasn't going to be an issue because we weren't going to di-di after just one round. My second was showing a lot more deference than he had when he'd been handing out the assignments on my first two missions. "What're you gonna do?" he asked.

"I'm gonna start with the guy in the back and hope it's not our guy."

"When are you gonna do it?"

"We'll wait until they get off the trail and out into the clearing."

I'd decided to start at the rear because when they fall, it's not as much of an alarm to the other people. Yeah, they'll all hear the shot, but it's like if you're hunting ducks. You shoot the one in the rear; the ones in the front don't necessarily know that the one in the rear is down. I also knew that I wanted them to take off running, not lie down or trip and fall over a body in front of them. On the ground they'd make a real small target to shoot at. An upright target—even one that's running—is easier to hit. While it may not sound like brilliant reasoning now, it made sense to this kid from Granbury who was hiding in the middle of a rubber plantation in Vietnam. The suddenly deferential spook certainly didn't have any better suggestions.

A few minutes later we began to hear faint chanting. They were coming. I lay down in a comfortable firing position. This was going to take either four or five shots, as quickly as I could get them off.

I was terrified. Scared that I wasn't up to the shoot. They were monks, after all. I was concerned we might not be able to spot the friendly monk. It was bad enough killing like this, but to kill someone who protected you, who helped you—how could I live with myself after that?

As they came into sight, I was watching through my scope, moving it from the face of the monk at the rear of the procession, quickly to number four, then three, two, and one. But the shadows thrown by the hoods prevented me from seeing their faces. Desperately I worked my way back to number five. No luck. I took my eye away from the scope and looked at my second. He had his scope up and was also scanning the monks.

"Yes?" I asked hopefully.

"No. They all look the same."

I couldn't wait a second longer. I leaned into the scope, put the crosshairs on the chest of number five, and squeezed the trigger. Feeling the recoil and sensing the spent cartridge automatically ejecting as the next round was seated, I moved the rifle slightly and saw that the rearmost monk was down. Out of the corner of my eye I saw number two throw his hood back. Even before he could break into a run, my second said, "Do you have him?"

I mumbled a yes as I swung the rifle to the right, putting the crosshairs on the chest of number one, and almost instantly pulled the trigger. He went down and our monk went running past him. By this time they were all running, squealing, yelling incomprehensibly. I picked up another target, number four, and shot again. A miss. The spook said nothing. I mumbled to myself, "Calm down, asshole! Just do it so we can get out of here!" Following number four through the scope, I led him just a bit and squeezed. He went down.

One more to go. I fired and as he went down our friend ran by us. He was crying. There were horrific sounds coming from the clearing. I looked back and saw that the second monk I'd shot—number one in the procession—was on the ground, twitching like a dog that had been hit by a car. It hadn't been a solid hit. It slammed him down, but he just lay there, shuddering and making an agonizing, hideous death rattle. For a second as I took in the scene, I imagined that I was seeing my pastor from Granbury lying there, writhing in pain, and the sick feeling that passed over me is indescribable.

The amazing thing was that in the heat of the moment, I could take it all in, all of it. See it and hear it. Even smell it. On some missions things went into extreme slow motion, and sometimes they went into warp speed. This whole shoot couldn't have taken five seconds, but it felt like an hour in slow-mo. We needed to give our guy a chance to get away so it wasn't just "bang-bang-bang-bang." It was "bang-bang, pause, bang-bang." And in the rubber plantations, sound seems to echo; it's magnified. Anyone within a couple of miles would have heard the shots. We had to hope that they'd have trouble figuring out what direction they were coming from.

Then there was the blood. It has its own smell. Some say it's like copper. It's distinctive, and we could smell it, almost taste it.

I should have been up and running, but for a small eternity everything just stopped. Then the second said, "Four for four," confirming that the wounded monk had died. I snapped out of my brief stupor and we took off running due west, wondering if our monk was waiting for us somewhere down the trail.

We had traveled about two hundred meters when we saw him. He was sitting with his knees drawn up and his arms wrapped around them, his head pressed to the left side of his knees, rocking back and forth with tears rolling down his cheeks. It was obvious that he was horrified at what he'd done. Everything that had just happened flew in the face of his Buddhist precepts. *Avoid killing any living thing. All tremble at violence. Life is dear to all. In times of war give rise in yourself to the mind of compassion, helping living beings abandon the will to fight.*

He looked up at us and gave a slight nod, and then stood and started down the trail. I had assumed he was elderly, but I had a hard time keeping up with him. He moved quickly, with long strides, and instinctively we found ourselves stepping in his footprints. For one thing, the maneuver conceals the number of people in a group.

For another, if he stepped there and didn't set off a mine or booby trap, it must be safe.

I'd barely noticed that rain was now coming down with a vengeance. It was so heavy we could hardly see ahead of us, which was why we suddenly broke out into the clearing where our ride was supposed to be waiting. Despite the weather, a Huey was there. The monk turned around and sort of bowed to us, and he was gone.

I'd learned during my relatively short time in country that you're not out of the woods till you're out of the woods. One look at the pilots told me that getting off the ground and safely back to base in this weather was not going to be a slam dunk. They looked as frightened as we were, and if they were scared, I just knew I should be terrified. Conditions were absolutely below acceptable minimums for flying, visibility was zero, and clouds were down to the ground. As they cranked the engines up and lifted off, it was a certainty that they were flying blind. How the aviators navigated back to Long Binh is something I don't even want to know. When we landed, the senior spook met us at the airfield. He took the rifle and gave me another plastic bag, and then the two of them drove me back to the transient billets. The last thing he said to me was, "I'll pick you up tomorrow morning." That was it. No questions, no comments.

I dropped my stuff on a bunk and went over to the EM Club, where I sat alone and drank several beers. Didn't talk to anyone. Just drank and thought about what I'd done. I knew right then that I'd remember, until I drew my last breath, the cries of anguish from the monk who had guided us. The four that I killed had different political opinions, but they were still his brethren. And I guess it would've been like taking four members of my own squad and setting them up to be killed. What kind of person can do that? You've got to be dedicated to a cause. That cause has to mean more to you than your very life. It's still amazing to me.

But just as I question how the monk could do what he did, I know there are people who will question how I could do what I did. And it all goes back to the standard answer: "Training, training, training." A psychologist might call it: "Conditioning, conditioning, conditioning." You're taught from the first day you're in the military to respond, and respond immediately, especially in a combat situation, because you don't have time to ask questions and get answers. It's got to be an instantaneous, automatic response without question. So that's what I did. They said, "Do it," and I did it. True, this wasn't the kind of killing that they prepare you for in a pitched battle, where you don't have any time to think about it. This was a preplanned assassination, and in comparison to combat I had plenty of time to think about it, to decide whether it was something I was willing to do. But that same conditioning took over. I'd been given an assignment; I had to carry it out.

I didn't even think about why I would do something so horrendous. And no one cautioned me that decades later I'd be paying a price for that decision, that I'd be second-guessing my actions.

I'm certain that everyone in the military who gets assigned as a sniper hates the thought that people might think you're an executioner. I'm a shooter. A sniper. Not an executioner. But sometimes, I confess, the certainty that was my best defense mechanism thirty-five years ago evaporates. It happens when I make that turn and wind up in a mental cul-de-sac, going in circles. It happens when I relive shooting four Buddhist monks in the middle of a rubber plantation, watching the blood seep onto their saffron robes, hearing the death cries of the one who I didn't kill cleanly. That's when I have to deal with the knowledge that if I were the fly on the wall, watching what I had done, I would say, "You're an executioner." But the fly isn't here—he's in my head. I can't allow myself to call myself an executioner, however irrational that may sound. It may not even make sense to anyone but me, but that's the way it is. I just did what I had to do, and it changed my life forever.

CHAPTER EIGHT

Recovery from the A Shau

Talk about contrasts. I'd spent a little over three months in an infantry platoon, humping through the jungle on search-and-destroy missions, vulnerable to everything and anything the enemy could throw at me, with only a helmet, flak jacket, my buddies, and my M-16 for protection.

Then they transferred me to Phu Bai, promoted me to spec 5, and made me the commander of an M-88 armored recovery vehicle. Now when I go outside the wire I'm surrounded by about fifty-six tons of cast and rolled armor in a twenty-eight-foot-long tracked vehicle powered by a 980-horsepower, 1790-cubic-inch, twelve-cylinder, air-cooled gasoline engine. I wouldn't be so bold as to say the thing was indestructible but . . . it sure was a contrast to the way I had been fighting the war.

Our unit at Phu Bai was responsible for direct support of a variety of units—medical, transport, signal, and supply to mention a few—and, of course, a number of artillery fire support bases (FSB) strung out from the South China Sea almost all the way to Vietnam's western border with Laos.

Without the front lines common to the large unit warfare of WWII and Korea, the American military needed to find a way to have artillery support constantly out in the field to protect infantry units that could be inserted quickly, anywhere, under the somewhat newly developed airmobile concept. The accepted solution to this problem was to secure fire support bases—sometimes just called firebases—in strategic positions throughout the country.

In I Corps, the northernmost sector of South Vietnam, there were many of these, most often secured after significant battles with entrenched North Vietnamese Army units. The 101st Airborne Division headquartered at Camp Eagle, nine kilometers west of Phu Bai, had various units, among them the 1/83rd Artillery, more or less permanently based at FSBs Birmingham, Bastogne, and Blaze.

In July 1969, a few months before I was transferred to Phu Bai, Blaze was turned into a forward supply point for the 3rd Brigade of the 101st. Our maintenance unit was designated as the backup repair facility for armor and tracked artillery vehicles at Blaze, which was roughly twenty-seven kilometers—about seventeen miles from Phu Bai as the Huey flies. I don't remember what the road mileage was; suffice it to say it was longer, slower, and more dangerous than hopping a helo at the Phu Bai–Hue Airfield.

The firebases we supported were in territory that included the dreaded A Shau Valley, well-known as an entry point for North Vietnamese units, troops, and supplies being infiltrated from the north. Each firebase usually had several artillery batteries, firing cannons ranging from the small 105mm Howitzers, which could fire close to the base, to the much-longer-range guns, such as the 155mms and 175mms responsible for supporting ground units operating in its area of responsibility, which might be up to twenty-two miles out. To provide perimeter defense for the artillery, each firebase had a platoon of at least five tanks, as well as an infantry company that was part of a full battalion working the area nearby. The infantry unit, most often from the 101st Airborne, would rotate the companies between the field and the FSB. In addition, each firebase had at least a squad of combat engineers whose sole mission was to keep the jungle a reasonable distance from the perimeter, which was without question a full-time task. The good news for me was that my unit wasn't required to stay out on one of the fire support bases—we went in and out as required.

That's why I was less than thrilled, shortly after being made the commander of one of our M-88s, to be given the assignment of hauling out to Firebase Blaze and bringing back a disabled M-60 tank with a blown engine.

The whole thing about being in charge made me uncomfortable. Not because I didn't think I could do the job, but because I realized that if I made a mistake, made a bad decision, one of my men, one of my friends, could be injured or killed, and what bothered me even more was that I knew a couple of them were married and had children. I was haunted by the notion that my decisions, often made in split seconds, had a direct effect, for good or for bad, on people that I had never met up to that time, and still haven't met some thirty-five years later. For an old man of twenty, this was an awesome responsibility, one that would keep me awake at night.

Departure preparation from Phu Bai was the standard procedure. We made sure we had fuel—the beast was always refueled after returning from a mission, but we double-checked anyway. We made certain that all ammunition had been replenished, oil levels were at the correct levels, and extra oil was stored on the vehicle, and we did a full radio check from each position—commander, driver, mechanic, and rigger. Two of us tended to the .50-caliber heavy machine gun that I'd likely be manning if we got hit, making sure that the head space and timing were properly set. The consequences of improper settings are not pleasant: The gun can be damaged, the gunner can be damaged, or the thing won't fire on full automatic when it's needed the most. We've learned that it pays to take the time to do it right.

Finally, everyone went to the latrine, because pit stops on the road to any of the firebases were not recommended, although given the nature of gastrointestinal systems under extreme stress, sometimes they couldn't be avoided.

We rolled out of the Phu Bai cantonment area by ourselves, no other vehicles, no accompanying escort. Just a long trip on a dirt road that offered numerous opportunities for the enemy to pay us a visit. I guess the theory was that if we got in trouble, air support would be available. At least, I like to think that someone in charge had given some thought to the matter.

As we passed out of the gate, I inserted the ammunition belt into the .50-caliber gun and half cocked it. In order to fire the first round, a .50 has to have the charging handle pulled twice. We rode with it pulled once. If something happened, we had to pull only one more time, which could be done in the blink of an eye.

The M-88 has a maximum speed of roughly twenty-five miles per hour, so if a mission is uneventful—and we always hoped it would be—there's lots of time for one's mind to wander. In my case, as we drove out to Blaze I found myself thinking about life in Granbury, which, from the perspective of being in the middle of a war zone, more and more resembled Mayberry. At one point I found myself almost laughing out loud as I recalled the terror that had torn through my guts when the local Barney Fife pulled me over and made me think that life as I knew it was about to come to a complete halt because I was underage and had a case of Pearl beer in a cooler on the backseat. The perspective check that confronted most of us every day was the surgeon general's warning on the side of every package of cigarettes we smoked. There wasn't one of us chain-smokers who didn't wish that we'd be given the opportunity to live long enough to die of lung cancer.

When we arrived at FSB Blaze, I told the crew that we wanted this to be a quick turnaround. There shouldn't have been any problem getting back home to Phu Bai before dark, but there was no point in lollygagging and tempting fate. I'm a firm believer that Murphy never rests. If it can go wrong, it will, at the worst possible time, and towing a broken-down tank for hours down a dirt road offers lots of opportunities for Murphy to ply his craft.

In less than an hour, my crew had refueled the M-88, prepared the tank for towing, and hooked everything up. The maintenance sergeant signed off on the paperwork, took my receipt for his tank, and we were out of there. With luck, we'd be back in Phu Bai by 1300 hours, in plenty of time to hit the mess hall before it closed. We had a final cup of coffee, and started the trip back.

Everything went fine until we got to the first of a series of hills we had to climb in order to get out of the A Shau Valley. That's when the notion of being back in time for lunch began to diminish. The problem was simple: It had rained the night before, the road was slippery red clay, and with a combined weight of 116 tons (56 for the loaded M-88 and 60 for the Patton tank), our recovery vehicle was running at full RPM and getting no traction. The tracks were simply spinning, which is not a good thing when you're on a narrow road with jungle on both sides. Actually, it wouldn't even be a good thing if we were on Interstate 5 climbing the Grapevine on the highway from Los Angeles to Bakersfield, near where I now live, because once those tracks start spinning, steering and braking control are minimal, and in some cases nonexistent. It tends to get really uncomfortable for the guy who is supposed to be in charge and keep these things from happening.

What I opted to do was back ourselves down to the bottom of the incline, where we took a break in order to try to figure out how to proceed. I called the firebase on the radio and told them we were having problems, and the maintenance sergeant said they'd be right out to help.

I was so focused on the spinning tracks that I hadn't given much thought to security and, just as on the outbound leg of this mission, we had no escort vehicles, no infantry on the ground looking out for us. I knew there was a reason the guys with lots of stripes on their sleeves got the big bucks, because when the sergeant from the firebase arrived, he'd brought a full squad of infantrymen to provide security for us while we worked.

What we decided to do was disconnect the tank from the M-88, drive my vehicle to the top of the incline, and then try to winch the tank up the hill. Setting up for an operation like this sounds simple, but keep in mind that the main winch cable on an M-88 is 1.25 inches in diameter and not that easy for guys on slippery ground to move around. We got the cable on the tank, but before we could back the M-88 up the hill, paying cable out the front, the tow truck from AAA arrived. Okay, so it wasn't from AAA. Just checking to see if you're paying attention. It was a dozer from the combat engineers based at Blaze. After some discussion they maneuvered around and hooked the front of their vehicle to the back of ours.

When we were ready to try it, I had everyone in my crew drop down inside and close the armored hatches over our heads—just in case the cable snapped. The dozer pulled forward, and my driver applied power in reverse, putting tension on the cable. Our combined weight at this point was 138 tons, roughly the takeoff weight of a Boeing 757-200, if you're into meaningless comparisons.

As the dozer accelerated, so did we, and our little-engine-that-could began to pull the tank up the hill. I was quite nervous, especially since we were barely moving and both towing vehicles were putting out as much torque as they safely could. The engineers had the dozer at full acceleration; my driver was giving the M-88 as much gas as possible without losing traction.

We began creeping up the hill, the steel cables fore and aft singing from the stress of the pull. We were moving so slowly that the grunts could leisurely stroll along beside us, perhaps unaware that they were in the danger zone should one of the cables snap.

At some point during this little parade it struck me that we were at the edge of the dreaded A Shau Valley, violating the number one rule for convoys: No matter what happens, keep moving. The top speed we could achieve towing the tank and safely maintaining control was eighteen to twenty miles per hour, reasonably fast for our combined weight, but not so fast that we wouldn't be an easy target if Charlie or the NVA wanted to cause trouble.

My crew was buttoned up inside a vehicle with armor plating that was supposed to stop everything from bullets to rocket-propelled grenades (RPGs). Unfortunately, I was standing in the commander's hatch with the ring mount of the .50-caliber machine gun loosened, so I could spin 360 degrees if necessary, but unlike with the newer M-88s, and even the old M-113 armored personnel carriers, I didn't have any sort of armor-plated cupola to protect me.

While I wasn't exactly comfortable with my own exposure, I realized that if we were attacked, the option was there for me to drop down and button up the hatch. The dozer driver, on the other hand, was sitting out in the open with only a steel cage to protect him from a broken cable.

All this anxiety over the possibility of being ambushed appeared to be wasted, however, when we got to the top of the hill unscathed. My rigger hopped down to help unhook us from the dozer, then jumped back up on the M-88 and dropped into his hatch. As soon as the dozer cleared the road, my driver put the pedal to the metal and we were off. ETA back at Phu Bai had slipped to 1500. So we miss lunch, but we're first in line for dinner.

Or so we thought. Fifteen miles farther down the road, we began having problems again. The tank was not trailing properly and my driver was having a hard time keeping us on the road. He had a very small, oblong steering wheel that controls the treads. Trying to keep us on the road towing the wayward tank is similar to driving a pickup truck on a freeway while towing a trailer that's got a flat tire. Except, of course, we were on a dirt road in Vietnam, not on a freeway, we weighed about fifty times more than the pickup-trailer combination, and, generally speaking, it's unlikely bad guys with guns would be stalking the pickup truck on the Golden State Freeway. Or maybe not.

I asked my driver if he thought we could make it another couple of miles, which would put us near Firebase Bastogne. I told him it would make me feel a whole lot better about dismounting and checking things out if we had a few hundred guys keeping an eye on us, rather than doing it by our lonesome out on the road. He said he'd try, and to his credit, he got us there.

That was when we discovered that one of the final drive shafts on the tank had slipped a bit, making one track drag slightly. As is often the case with sixty-ton tanks or the family car, the diagnosis took longer than the repair, but once we figured it out, we fixed it and got back on our way.

But just as we began climbing the last little hill out of the A Shau, our visions of an early dinner were shattered when we were ambushed from both sides of the road. As the sound of pinging rounds striking the sides of the M-88 and the tank echoed, and richochets were flying in every direction, my driver and crew mechanic dropped down, buttoned up, and, using the periscopes to watch the road, jammed on the gas. While our top speed dragging a tank is twenty miles per hour, you don't get that going uphill. You crawl, and at that moment we were crawling through the kill zone of a well-prepared NVA or VC ambush at a narrowing of the road, where the jungle closed in on both sides.

I was firing to one side with the .50-caliber, and my rigger was firing to the other with the light machine gun. Both of us were doing everything within our power to burn up the barrels when a hand grenade landed on the top deck of the M-88, rolling around between the mounts and various attachments. You might think that with all the gunfire, there'd be no way to hear the grenade, but trust me on this one—you hear it. It's a sickening, metal-on-metal clunk that instantly gets your attention. And when it starts rolling around, you can't help but keep your eyes on it.

Both my rigger and I saw it and yelled, "Grenade!" simultaneously. He dropped inside the crew compartment. I took a fraction of a second to decide that I had to try to get the grenade off the vehicle. It was a foolish decision that someone with the experience I'd had in combat shouldn't have made. But experience just improves the chances that you'll make the right choice under duress; it doesn't guarantee it. It's realistic, not cynical, to say that bad decisions that turn out well often make heroes. The ones that don't turn out well make widows.

I should have done the same thing my rigger did when we saw the grenade: dropped down inside the armored vehicle. The grenade would have exploded within seconds, doing no damage of any consequence, and I could have just popped back up and resumed firing the machine gun. But I didn't.

Arming a grenade is usually a two-step process. The grenade has a spoonlike device that is held in place by the pin. Generally, if you're going to throw one, you'll hold the spoon against the grenade while pulling the pin with your other hand. (Only movie stars are allowed—and are able—to pull a pin using their teeth. Ordinary mortals have to pull it by hand.) Once you pull the pin, you have two choices: You can just throw the thing at the enemy, which, given that the fuse on a U.S. grenade is supposed to burn for eight seconds, might allow time for him to throw it back at you before it blows up; or you can let the spoon fly off into space and count to three before tossing it. This gives the enemy a lot less time to try to toss it back to you.

In this instance, however, I lost the coin toss, and the opposition had decided that I would receive. I had no idea what the NVA or VC field manual for grenades taught them to do, or whether the guy who threw it at us was following the rules, or whether this was a factory-made Chinese Communist version or a homemade job that might have a fuse of arbitrary length. As a result, I had no way of calculating how much time I had before the thing blew up. I can tell you that it was long enough for my life to flash in front of my eyes, but at age twenty, that doesn't take very long.

As I started to reach for it, I could see that the grenade had hung up between the deck of the M-88 and the A-frame lifting boom. There was no way I could get to it with enough time left to get rid of it, so I changed plans, turned, and had started to drop into the hatch when it detonated.

The sound of the explosion was nothing compared to the hot, searing pain I felt on the back of my right shoulder. My first reaction was that I was going to die. I'm not sure whether or not I actually said the words out loud, but the words my mind composed were *Dear God, I'm going to die!*

Very quickly I realized that I'd survived the blast, and the logical part of my brain that had started to function again was telling me that my three crew members were safe, protected from the blast by the heavy armor of our vehicle. I could feel blood running down my back and right arm, but there was no time to stop and evaluate the extent of my wounds. Since I could still move my arms and head, I figured I'd be able to shoot, so the rigger and I popped back up, grabbed the machine guns, and began firing. The only good news at that moment was that the driver was still doing his best to get us out of there. I could tell from the sound of the engine that he had not released the accelerator in the slightest—not even when the grenade went off.

We finally made it to the top of the hill and out of the kill zone, and began to pick up speed. I could hear the difference in the pitch of the engine. That was when the rigger told my crew that I'd been hit. He and the mechanic pulled me down inside the crew compartment to check me out. The rigger ripped my shirt off, and the mechanic climbed up into my hatch to man the .50-caliber gun.

As soon as the mechanic got my shirt off, he could see that my shoulder had taken a lot of shrapnel from the grenade. I could hear the mechanic—who was second in command just for eventualities like this—calling for a medical helicopter. He gave them our position, and told them we were going to keep moving toward Phu Bai.

Since they'd be coming from that direction, we might cut a couple of minutes off the time it would take to get me off the track and on the way to a hospital.

It seemed like hours but was probably only minutes before I sensed more than felt the driver backing off the accelerator and beginning to brake. The instant we stopped, the driver and rigger jumped off the M-88 with their M-3 grease guns to provide what little security they could for the chopper.

The mechanic stayed with me, all the while maintaining radio contact with the incoming aircraft. Once it landed, he crawled around inside the vehicle and popped open the side door, calling for the medic. As soon as he got to us, I crawled out of the vehicle and began walking to the chopper. Given all the blood that was pouring out of my back, I was justified in thinking that the wounds were more severe than they actually were. The medic had given me a cursory check, and when he saw that I could walk, he decided that I was one patient who was going to make it to the hospital alive and repairable. He, of course, was trained to make those judgments. I wasn't—and I was the guy oozing blood. The distinction clearly affected my outlook on life at that moment.

By the time they got me on the Dustoff, the pain had subsided some—or maybe I was a little numb—and the bleeding had pretty much stopped. In circumstances like this, most people tend to fear what they don't know or haven't previously experienced. I'd survived the head wound on the convoy earlier in my tour, and had actually kept driving. But this was completely different. I was sure that I was going to die, and if that didn't happen, then I would never be able to use my arm again. Or they might just take it off. Optimism has never been my strong suit, so for the duration of the entire fifteen-minute ride to the 85th Evacuation Hospital in Phu Bai, I assumed the worst.

My fears were unfounded and luck was with me, because when the medic got me inside the hospital, I had the entire emergency staff to myself: a couple of nurses, one doctor, and several medics. They washed me, put me facedown on a gurney, and wheeled me over to X-ray.

While we were waiting for the film to be developed, the doctor did his best to make me feel better by telling me that he was pretty sure this was not a "million-dollar wound." That's one that's serious enough to get you evacuated to a hospital outside Vietnam, most likely in Japan, and from there back to a military hospital in the States. When the X-rays arrived, they confirmed his judgment. My back might look like raw meat, and I might be in a lot of pain, but it wasn't enough to send me home. If my sense of humor had been intact, I would have said, "Doc, you call that good news?"

What I didn't realize was that the fun hadn't even begun. The doc had to get the little tiny pieces of shrapnel out of my shoulder, and I'm not sure what medical school he went to, but what they taught him was the Braille method of fragment removal. The first step is to send the guy who usually administers anesthetic to do his laundry or see a movie. Then, when there's no chance that someone is going to be available to put me under for the procedure, the doc tells me that he's going to start sticking a probe into the holes in my back, and it's my job to tell him when he's found a chunk of metal. As the doc soon discovered, I speak Texan, broken English, and fluent profanity.

For the next couple of hours I was demonstrating my multilingual proficiency, occasionally at very high decibels, often indicating a familiarity with the doctor's mother and his parents' marital status. When it was all over, there were thirty-two tiny pieces of shrapnel in a basin. Then, in an imitation of every bad TV commercial he'd ever seen, the doc said, "But wait, there's more." Actually, that's not what he said. He just quietly told me that as time passed, more shrapnel would move around in my back, and he'd have to go in and get it.

So on subsequent days, the doc and I had a ritual we'd go through. He'd come in and ask how I was feeling. I'd say, "Fine," and he'd say something along the lines of "Let's see if we can change that." Even though he was proud of his bedside manner, comedy was definitely not his strong suit. Then the doc and his torture team would start the process all over again: X-rays, followed by probing, and then pulling shrapnel out of my back.

At the end of each session, the doctor would tell me that everything was going to be fine. Then the nurses or medics would bandage me, and after they left I'd walk down the hall to the latrine, go into a stall, shut the door, and cry. I became convinced that these painful sessions would end only when the doc felt I couldn't take any more.

Finally, the shrapnel count was up to eighty-one, and my doc made the surprising announcement that he was done with me. "The rest," he said, "will have to work their way out by themselves." Upon hearing this statement, I embarrassed myself by breaking down and crying in front of everyone. The pain in my back was still intense, but the knowledge that they weren't going to put me through the extraction procedure again was just more than I could emotionally handle.

One of the nurses—I wish I could remember her name to thank her properly—walked me back to my bed, put her arms around me, and let me cry on her shoulder. She didn't have to do it; she just did it. That hug did me more good than she will ever know. Or maybe she did know.

About a week later they released me from the hospital, telling me to return every couple of days for physical therapy. The movement in my right shoulder was slow to come back. I healed, but I never did get my entire range of motion back. The holes were so small that there wasn't much scarring, and by now most of them have gone away completely. The doc later told me that if he'd knocked me out and taken me into surgery to remove the shrapnel, it would have left scars that would have never gone away and would have caused additional damage to the tissue. After about two months, I was back to full duty, once again riding the M-88.

CHAPTER NINE

Faces I've Seen

Talk about shitty duty.

Until one has had the pleasure of spending several hours of a beautiful blue-sky morning pouring diesel fuel into the half barrels that serve as collection devices beneath our two- and three-holers, stirring with a paddle until it's thoroughly mixed with an abundance of organically reprocessed B- and C-rations, igniting the concoction, and then tending to its purification by fire, one has not had the shittiest job in this man's army.

Even when I attempt to speed up the procedure by using jet fuel instead of diesel, the nature of the job doesn't improve. Actually, it just turns potentially lethal. I'm not going to go into great detail here, but I ignored the Vietnamese local who'd been hired by our unit and who'd become a pro at the job, and despite his warning shouts of "GI, you dinky-dau, beaucoup dinky-dau" (loose translation: "You're freakin' nuts"), I torched the mixture with my ever-faithful Zippo. He ran fast enough; I didn't. Moments later, as the two of us were extinguishing globs of burning crap that had spread across the landscape, I had a vision of the headline in my hometown newspaper:

LOCAL MAN KILLED IN VIETNAM
BY EXPLODING SHITCAN

How, I wondered, would my parents live that down?

Yes, that had to be the worst job in the United States Army. At least, that's how I thought at the time. That all changed when my section chief at the service and evacuation platoon in the direct support maintenance company to which I'd been transferred at Phu Bai told me that I'd been selected for a special detail. "Report to the company commander," he said. I wasn't happy about this. I had thought that when I moved from the infantry to driving an M-88 recovery vehicle, there'd be no more special assignments from my CO.

I reported to the captain, expecting him to hand me the rifle and tell me that I was to go to the airfield. Instead, he told me that due to heavy combat activity in the area, the Graves Registration section in Da Nang was overworked and underpaid, and I was among a select few from our unit who had volunteered (strange—I failed to recall having volunteered—obviously I was confused) to give them a little help.

Later that morning, three of us boarded a truck, each lugging a duffel bag with enough clothing for a week, and we were off on a two-hour drive to Da Nang. Shortly after lunch we arrived at Graves Registration HQ, and were welcomed by the first sergeant, who had his clerk help us draw linens and get bunks assigned. For a brief moment this TDY was looking good: The beds at Da Nang were larger and more comfortable than the cots we had at Phu Bai.

We were turned over to an E-7, who actually thanked us for coming and said we were really needed. The three of us piled into his jeep and took off on the fifteen-minute ride to the morgue. One of my buddies asked him what we'd be doing there. He just grinned and said, "Anything that's needed."

We pulled up in front of a group of semipermanent buildings that were painted a sterile white. There was a single large sign with one word printed in large black letters:

MORGUE

What the hell am I doing here? I wondered. *Send me back to the infantry. I've got no business or desire to be messing with any dead people.* But here I was, and I was scheduled to be here for an entire week. My mom had always taught me to make the best out of any opportunity I was presented with. Somehow I'm sure she had no concept of this particular possibility.

We were led into the administration area, which didn't look that unusual, just an office space with desks, phones, files, and the like. Why was everyone looking at us and grinning?

Probably because they could see that that the three of us were terrified, and had absolutely no idea what to expect or what might be expected of us. It pissed me off that they were enjoying our discomfort. Then I remembered how we used to treat FNGs about to go out on their first patrol with us. Payback is a bitch.

The E-7 ordered a spec 4 to give us a tour. He didn't seem particularly happy about playing tour guide. He explained that in the office, all the data on each corpse was collected from the various sections and merged into a single file: insurance forms, next-of-kin notification, mortician's report, death certificate, finance and personnel records, shipping instructions, escort requirements, receiving funeral home info if available—everything that it took to receive, prepare, and ship remains to Hawaii, where final preparations would be completed before the shipment to the soldier's or marine's hometown.

From there he took us to supply. I had been in supply areas before, but nothing like this. Body bags, shipping containers, embalming supplies, and shelf after shelf of United States flags.

Next came the personal-effects area. I don't know whether our guide was taking the shortest route through the entire facility, or was deliberately postponing the inevitable, but the longer we could avoid seeing bodies, the happier we would all be. Personal effects is where everything that was on the body at the time of death or hospitalization was collected. The items were inspected to ensure that nothing was government property, nothing was classified, and nothing was pornographic. The remaining effects would go to Hawaii, where they would be packaged with the effects that the deceased's unit sent directly there, and one shipment would then be sent to the next of kin.

We continued on to the Receiving and Identification Branch, where we got our first glimpse of death on a wholesale scale. Here the remains were received from the hospitals, from battalion aid stations, from anywhere that had a dead body to be sent home. There was a helipad to receive bodies being flown in, and loading docks for those being brought by ambulance or truck. This was where unit identification took place. A squad leader, platoon sergeant, or someone else from the guy's unit would physically look at the remains and verify the identification. Fingerprints were also taken and forwarded somewhere to be matched with official records to confirm the ID. Everything possible was done to ensure that a death notification was not sent in error.

My first impression was that there must have been twenty tables in the receiving area, and they were all occupied, with more bodies lying on gurneys outside, waiting their turn. One of my buddies became very ill at this point, ran out the door, and lost his lunch. I was just shocked by the whole scene, but did what I usually do under grossly unpleasant circumstances in which I'm forced to participate—just held it inside.

I'd been on patrols where guys had been killed, but I had never considered the clinical manner in which these things had to be taken care of. There were so many details, major and minor, before a body was sent home. At age twenty, I was getting one more lesson I never wanted in the facts of war.

Next we went to the preparation rooms, where embalming was taking place on a massive scale. I'd never seen anything like it before, but managed to survive the visit without embarrassing myself. In retrospect, that was probably a mistake.

In the shipping area, each prepared body was placed in a body bag, and then into one of the shipping containers. Each body had a tag with ID information that was also entered on a shipping document attached to the outside of the container. Then the container was placed in a cooler to await shipment. Once flight arrangements to Hawaii were made, the container would be removed from the cooler and respectfully covered with one of the flags we'd seen earlier in supply.

Our guide told us that in Hawaii, another ID process would take place; the body would be dressed in the appropriate uniform and placed in a military casket. It, in turn, would be draped with the flag, and the honor escort would then accompany the remains home, while the shipping container would be sanitized and recycled back to Vietnam for further use.

At the conclusion of our tour we went back to the sergeant's office. He looked at the spec 4 and asked him what he thought. That's when I realized that the purpose of the tour was twofold: to show us what went on in the morgue, while assessing our ability to cope with it. His judgment was quick and ruthless. Send my buddy who puked his guts out back to his unit. Send my other buddy who demonstrated serious discomfort in the prep room to work in admin, supply, or shipping.

Then he looked at me, and said I could handle receiving or prep because I didn't get sick and didn't need a babysitter. Had I only figured out their scheme before the tour ended, I could have deliberately lost my lunch, been put on a truck, and been back at Phu Bai in time for dinner.

We were told that new guys started on the night shift, working from six in the evening until four in the morning, with a break for lunch at midnight. To give us a decent shot at adjusting to the overnight work, we were allowed that first night off, and told to stay up as late as possible so we'd be able to sleep the next day in preparation for our first shift in the morgue.

How do you kill time when you're deliberately trying to stay awake? We're Americans. We go to the movies. And what do Americans in a combat zone watch? A comedy? Don't be silly. That night's flick was *The Alamo,* starring celluloid war hero John Wayne. After the movie we shot pool, and then took a ten-minute walk to a club on the base. By one in the morning I couldn't take it anymore. It had been too much of a day, and I was as exhausted as I'd ever been after a forty-eight-hour patrol.

I was up at noon the next day, woke my buddy, had lunch, killed time comparing notes on life and love (he had a girlfriend; I had barely lost my virginity before I enlisted). Then we forced ourselves to eat dinner before reporting to the morgue at 1800 hours.

A spec 5 from Receiving and Identification collected me, and off we went. All of the tables were still full, and I wondered aloud if they were the same bodies I had seen the day before. He sort of laughed, and then told me that bodies were only there for four hours each. "Figure it out," he said. "There are eighteen tables, and there've been two full ten-hour shifts since you were here yesterday. Twenty hours, five bodies per table. Eighteen tables, ninety bodies."

"Ninety bodies?" I repeated incredulously.

"Well, actually things slowed down and there were only about fifty," he acknowledged. My TDY (temporary duty) at the morgue was taking place right around the Vietnamese Tet holiday celebrating the lunar new year, and while fighting in the area had been heavy, it was nothing like the battles throughout South Vietnam during Tet 1968.

I recall being stunned. Fifty is still a lot of dead GIs. But he didn't give me time to worry about it. My assignment that first night, he told me, would be "the easy job. Help unload bodies from vehicles or aircraft and get them on gurneys. Then move bodies from the table to prep, and from the holding area into R and I."

He took me to supply, where they gave me a pair of knee-high rubber boots, a long wraparound rubber apron, and a pair of thick rubber gloves that reached to my elbows. Strangely, I hadn't really noticed what the workers were wearing during my tour of the place, so I wasn't prepared for it.

I spent that entire night moving bodies; we received more than twenty before midnight, another ten before my shift ended at 0400.

On my second night in the morgue they sent me to the prep room. There I was taught how to give each body two baths—one before preparation, and one afterward. Rather than being repulsed by the whole process, I found myself intrigued by what the embalming technicians were able to do. There were guys who were burned, maimed, with large and small holes and every other condition of bodily destruction and deterioration that I might imagine in my worst nightmare. When the bodies came into the morgue, they were often in shocking condition. But the embalmers were able to make them look more like they were asleep than in pain or distress. When all was said and done, in many cases the remains that left the Da Nang morgue were viewable by family and friends. I suppose that's one of the things that made working at the morgue tolerable—the thought that you weren't just mechanically preparing a body to go from point A to point B, where it would be buried, but making it possible for a family to conduct what was considered to be the standard American funeral, complete with open casket, and take what comfort they could in the experience.

By the end of that second night, I had developed an interest in how it was done, and for the next three nights I worked in the prep room, learning more and more. But I also learned something about what man was capable of doing to man, realizing that I'd been trained in, and was successful at, doing some of these very things; now I was seeing the hideous results of someone else's training.

At the end of the week I was more than ready to go back to my unit and drive a recovery vehicle, back to the infantry and ambush patrols in the jungle, or anywhere else in the country that didn't require me to handle dead bodies. I went by the orderly room on the afternoon prior to my final shift and asked how I was going to get back to Phu Bai in the morning. That was when I received the bad news: I'd done such a good job I wouldn't be going back for a while. My assistance in the morgue had been requested for another two weeks. You'd think I would have learned a lesson from what happened following my success at sniper training. But it never crossed my mind to deliberately screw up, even though it would have saved me a lot of agony. This work ethic is a character flaw that I should probably work on.

By the end of my second week, I was handling the less difficult cases under the watchful eye of one of the embalmers. They'd seen that I had both an interest and a talent for the work, and were happy to have the help. A week later I was doing a large number of all but the most difficult cases alone. You guessed it. They wanted me to stay, but I managed to convince them that my company commander and first sergeant were getting annoyed that I hadn't been returned to regular duty at my unit, so they let me go.

During my three weeks in the Da Nang morgue, I learned more about war than I learned from everything I'd done before and after in the military. I can still see the faces, some young, others older, all of them frozen in death. I don't know their names, where they were from, whether they were single or married, with or without kids, but I can still see each one of them when I shut my eyes. Their injuries, the grotesque positions in which some breathed their last breath, even the color and smell of death. Yes, the smell was sometimes almost more than I could stand, and the odors of the prep room are embedded in my sense memory. For years after my morgue experience

I couldn't eat ham. There was something about the smell that triggered a flashback to my TDY in Da Nang.

I found myself thinking the same kinds of thoughts about the men I helped prepare that I had after each of my sniper missions. But I could relate to these men more, because they were like me: They wore the same uniform I did, spoke the same language I did. None of them would ever again walk down a street in the sunshine, never have children or grandchildren. They'd never kiss a girl, laugh with a friend, drive a car, or see a movie. They'd never be any more than they were on the day they died. It didn't matter whether they had died quickly or slowly, in the field or in a hospital, feeling horrific pain or not. For them it was over. They were just dead.

In my mind's eye I can still see the faces of more than a hundred men, all races, probably all religions. Some died as heroes; some were just in the wrong place at the wrong time, but they were all equal in death. I believed they were all mourned by those they left behind: mothers and fathers, wives, sons and daughters, brothers and sisters, friends and colleagues, who deep down—outward appearances and patriotic statements notwithstanding—would wonder if their loved one's death had real meaning. Because without it, I wondered, can there be any solace?

CHAPTER TEN

My Decision

It was another hot day when my M-88 crew drew the assignment to head out to Firebase Blaze and bring in a self-propelled artillery piece that needed a new gun tube and a new engine. The artillery boys at Blaze had actually blown the engine on the 155 a couple of days earlier, but since the gun tube still had some rounds remaining before it had to be changed, the decision was made to finish the tube off and then send it in to have all the work done at one time.

I'd been working with the same crew since I arrived at Phu Bai. There was our driver, Bill, from New York, married with one child. We were about the same age, but he weighed a lot more than the 135 pounds I carried soaking wet.

The mechanic on our M-88 was also named Bill. He was tall and slender with blond hair, also married. Our rigger was Dave, from either Kentucky or Tennessee. He was strong as a bull ox, but quiet, with a great sense of humor.

My platoon leader's plan for our day was an ambitious one. We were supposed to get an early start, get out to FB Blaze, rig the gun for towing, drag it back to Phu Bai, where mechanics would change the engine and the gun tube, and then we were to tow it back to the firebase before dark. It's not that they needed to use it that night—it's just that no one with good sense would want to be ambling down the road outside of an American base perimeter after dark.

Murphy must have been off duty when we were driving out to Blaze, because nothing at all went wrong: The M-88 drove the way it was supposed to; the enemy didn't have any en route surprises for us; even the weather cooperated. We made excellent time getting out there, and when we arrived they had the gun ready for us to tow. All we had to do was refuel, hook up, grab some coffee, and start back. We typically never had any security escort for these missions. There might be a tow truck or even an M-578 light recovery vehicle with us, but nothing with any real firepower. Everybody was equipped with radios and guns, so I guess the theory was that we could call for help and fight off the bad guys while waiting for it to arrive.

We were about halfway back to Phu Bai when the scariest thing in the world happened. We hit a land mine!

For a split second I couldn't breathe. I don't know whether the explosion just sort of instantly sucked up all the air, leaving us in this vacuum, or whether I was so scared that I just forgot to breathe. The explosion was deafening. For a few moments—I couldn't honestly say whether it was seconds or a couple of minutes—I know I was deaf, and it took a while for my hearing to return to normal. I remember it ramping up slowly, as though someone were turning up the volume on a radio. (Actually, my hearing never did return to the way it was before the explosion; it's a problem that I'm dealing with decades after Vietnam.)

It seemed as though my vehicle and crew were in a huge bubble—or maybe it was just the dust cloud from the blast. We were wearing dust goggles that somehow managed to stay on when the mine went off. If they hadn't, who knows what would have happened to us? I was suddenly struck with the realization that we'd been blown up by a command-detonated mine. That might not have been the case, but since we were immediately attacked after the explosion, it seemed to be a reasonable conclusion to draw. Sure, it could have been your basic pressure-detonated mine that they had planted and just waited for a piece of equipment to run right over it, but at the time that didn't make as much sense as thinking that someone had waited for just the right moment to hit the switch and try to blow us to kingdom come. In any event, a fraction of a second after I'd decided it was a command-detonated mine, we were being raked with rifle and machine gun fire. There we were, in the kill zone of a single-side ambush.

The first thing that happens is panic. It feels like the world is coming to an end. At age twenty, I was experiencing fear that can be understood only by a person who has experienced combat. All kinds of things go through your mind. Am I going to die? Am I going to be wounded? Am I going to screw up? What do I do now? All of that is instantaneous—then, out of reflex/training, you begin to do all of the things you need to do without even thinking, because consciously you don't know whether to shit or go blind, or maybe both.

Sometimes things go into superspeed, and other times they slow down in a slow motion that is so precise that you can see each and every movement. While Dave and I were returning fire, the other two guys had dropped into the vehicle, with our driver trying to do what he could to make the beast move. If it's possible to pray and curse at the same time, I did. Or maybe I alternated between the two. I'm sure God could figure out which words were intended for him and which for the bastards who were trying to kill us at that moment, so I wasn't going to worry about it.

Once I had the panic under control, I tried to figure out where the enemy was, while at the same time screaming into the open hatch for Bill to get us out of there. Talk about multitasking. Even as I was shouting at him, another part of my brain was processing the fact that one of the sounds I heard was our own engine at full acceleration. But there was another, really ugly sound of links from our right track slapping the metal hull. The mine had broken the track, and we weren't going anywhere under our own power.

I had automatically grabbed the butterfly handles on the .50-caliber machine gun, spun around in the cupola, and begun firing into the wood line where our attackers were hiding. A quick glance to my right and I could see that Dave was manning the light machine gun, and it dawned on me that neither of us had been hit. I yelled at the guys inside to get us more ammunition, not realizing that our mechanic was already breaking open the metal ammunition boxes. As the last rounds in the belt were fired, he was already handing up the lead end of a new belt for the .50, and then doing the same for Dave's M-60 machine gun.

Describing it makes it seem as though everything were neat, ordered, and sequential, but that's not the way it is. It's all happening at once. Every single one of my senses was firing on full automatic. I could see it, hear it, touch it, taste it, and smell it simultaneously, and my brain was on overload. I knew for sure from my time with the cav that there were no atheists in foxholes. At that moment I wasn't sure if prayer would help, but I also knew that I had to chance that it did. Praying in a circumstance like that wasn't something I *decided* to do; I just did it while I was firing the .50. Must've been that religious upbringing that my folks gave me as I was growing up. Truth be told, I was a terrified kid who, until that moment, had convinced himself that he was a man.

It took an event like this one for me to understand the song lyric that goes "Praise the Lord and pass the ammunition," because I think we were all doing both.

Dave and I were burning through ammunition as fast as the two Bills could hand it to us. What you hope is that you're knocking them dead, but you can't see anything because the wood line comes almost right up to the edge of the dirt road. Unfortunately, there must have been a lot more of them than our two guns could handle, because they began advancing toward us. They had intermittent cover and were advancing to our side. I kept looking to see if any of the attackers would break cover and run onto the road in front of or behind us, but they didn't.

When we could catch a glimpse of them, we saw they were wearing traditional Vietnamese peasant clothing, not uniforms. Some had rifles and one or two had AK-47s. While we felt as though an entire division were there, intent on shooting us to pieces, there were probably only ten or twelve of them. Some of the time they would shoot as they advanced, and other times they would shoot from behind a tree or in a depression. I saw at least one go down, but I couldn't tell if it was Dave or me who hit him, not that it matters under those circumstances. What I can tell you is that someone figured out that the American military in Vietnam fired fifty thousand bullets for every enemy soldier killed. On that day we did nothing to help lower the ratio. We fired continuously, reloading as fast as humanly possible and burning our way through another belt of ammo. As I moved the gun onto the deck of the M-88, the brass was dropping all around, down through the hatch, sometimes hitting me as it sprayed from the gun and bounced around. I didn't have time to worry about whether I was getting burned, because that would have been the least of my problems.

We were clearly outnumbered. The enemy had at least a dozen guys firing weapons; we had two, and I felt a sense of panic rising in me like acid roiling out of my stomach and up into my throat. Despite the fire Dave and I were pouring at them, one of the enemy popped up right at the side of the M-88 and began firing right at us with his AK-47.

Dave was hit in the chest by a couple of rounds and dropped down into the rigger's compartment. The mechanic who had been passing ammunition jumped up and grabbed the M-60, while Bill, the driver, took over the task of both opening ammunition cans and passing the belts up to the two of us.

We just needed to end this thing in order to be able to try to keep Dave alive, and the enemy was definitely not cooperating. I could see more of them moving toward us through the wood line, and I spun the .50 around and cut loose. When a .50-caliber bullet hits a human, it is devastating. Not only do you see the hole punched into living flesh; you see the target fly backward from the impact. A .50-cal is a half inch in diameter; it's a huge round. If it doesn't kill you, it will certainly make you wish you were dead. At some time during the skirmish, I'm sure I thought about the fact that I was killing or wounding someone, but I can't be positive—maybe this is just another little demon that plays with me in my older years.

My heart was beating so hard I swear I could hear it over the spitting of the machine gun. I used to wonder how soldiers could function in the middle of a battle like this. Now I realize that it's not a choice. Not a real one, anyway, because the self-preservation instinct is impossible to overcome. You can keep fighting, or give up and die. Remember what General Patton said to his troops—a line made famous, coincidentally, in the movie that was released in February 1970, somewhere around the time I found myself under attack in the M-88: "No bastard ever won a war by dying for his country. He won it by making the other poor dumb bastard die for his country."

I didn't think about winning the Vietnam War while I was hanging on to that .50-caliber, but I sure hoped and prayed that I was going to make a bunch of Charlies die for their country; and I guess that at some point they decided that the cost of killing Gary and friends was going to be too high on this day, or they knew that they had screwed with us enough, so they fell back.

The instant that happened, we checked our ammunition, and both Bills dragged Dave up onto the deck, where they could better administer first aid. While they were doing what they could for him, I grabbed the radio and desperately tried to contact Phu Bai Dustoff. If Dave was going to make it we needed a medevac, and we needed it now. Fortunately, the intensity of my message got through, and if they didn't already have a chopper in the air, it must have been sitting on the pad at the 85th Evac with rotors turning, because the guy at the other end gave me an ETA of no more than ten minutes—we were only about fourteen kilometers away.

After I made the radio call, I had our driver come up and man the .50-caliber so I could help with Dave. He had a classic sucking chest wound, and we were using every trick we'd been taught to try to seal the entrance and exit wounds, stop the bleeding, and encourage him to hang on—all at the same time. Even while I was putting pressure on the foil that I hoped would stop air from bubbling out of the wound, I was able to maintain radio contact with the Dustoff. While the radio itself is inside the vehicle, it can be keyed by a switch on the right side of the combat vehicle crewman's (CVC) helmet we all wore. Earphones inside the helmet and a boom microphone attached to the right side make its operation almost hands-free.

When they told me they were only two minutes out, I yelled for Bill to switch places with me, and I went back to the machine gun, grabbing a smoke grenade from just inside the vehicle. I told the pilot that the best landing area was on the road behind the artillery piece we were towing, and then I popped a purple smoke grenade and asked if he could identify it.

"Identify Goofy Grape," he responded.

"Goofy Grape is beautiful," I replied, and he started his descent.

We continued to work on Dave, preparing to move him off the deck of the vehicle as soon as the bird landed, and the medic got to us with a stretcher. I could see Dave looking at me and everyone else with panic in his eyes. You can't keep a guy who's been shot in the chest from knowing how serious his wound is.

Then, just as the Dustoff flared for a landing on the road behind us, the enemy began shooting at us again. I jumped over to the machine gun, swung it around, and began firing, but as I did so, I hit the transmit key on my radio.

"Pull out. Pull out. We're taking heavy fire again."

I had no other choice. When Dave heard the change of pitch in the aircraft rotors, he knew what I'd done. He looked at me with confusion and fear. I don't think I saw anger in his face—but saying that doesn't necessarily make it so. It's one of those things you say to make yourself feel better under impossible circumstances like this.

We finally managed to suppress the enemy fire—I'm not even sure whether it took more than two minutes. The helo landed and they ended up taking Dave away in a body bag. He died before we could get help for him.

Not that it matters to Dave, but I know I made the right decision in telling the pilot to pull out. Intellectually I know that it was the right thing to do, the only responsible thing to do. Do you sacrifice the lives of four men on the Dustoff to save one guy whose chances of making it are iffy, at best? But that doesn't keep me from seeing the look on Dave's face when he heard the aircraft start to lift. The look was almost more than I could bear, and I still see it today, thirty-five years later. He was my buddy, and he was confused, hurt, and scared. He knew he didn't have much time. And I'm the one who made the decision that sealed his fate. As I said, intellectually I know I made the right decision, but emotionally—now that's a completely different side of the story.

"Sorry 'bout that" doesn't cut it. The Vietnam GI's declaration of numbness in battle—"It don't mean nothing"—is a lie. Maybe it just takes a few years away from the war for the anesthetic of combat to wear off and for you to figure out that it means a lot to lose a buddy, and that unless you're sometimes less than a complete human being, the loss is going to be with you for a lifetime.

By the time the Dustoff landed and we got Dave on the stretcher, he was gone. All we could do at that point was help carry him to the helicopter, put him aboard, and go back and see if we could repair the track enough to make the few miles back to Phu Bai.

The three of us worked in silence for about an hour. We took the spare track off the storage rack, and while one person manned the gun, the other two changed it out. It meant removing two damaged track blocks and replacing them, then putting the track back on.

When we were nearly finished, a truck came by and the guys offered to help us out, but by then the heavy lifting was done. We routed the track over the idler wheel at the front and reconnected things. Then we tightened the track just enough to get us out of there, driving back to Phu Bai on our own power. It seemed like a million miles and many hours away, but the trip was actually fairly quick and, fortunately, uneventful.

I'd been dreading being asked to go in and make the formal identification of Dave's body, but another guy in the unit volunteered. I sat down that night to write a letter home to the folks back in Granbury, and told them—nothing.

CHAPTER ELEVEN

Phu Bai Sniper

If you do something often enough, you'd expect it would become routine. But that didn't hold true in Vietnam. Your last ambush could be more exciting than your first, today's combat assault more electrifying than yesterday's.

It was the same with my sniping assignments. No matter how many times I got called to go see the old man, got handed my special rifle, and headed out, it never got to be ordinary. Just the anticipation was enough to make my palms sweat and my pulse rate increase. I've read about some snipers with extremely high kill counts for whom it was all in a day's work; apparently it was work they enjoyed, and they never broke a sweat. Maybe they never even thought about it again.

But that wasn't me. Hell, that *isn't* me. I found myself dwelling on the fact that the people I shot would never see their families again; never know the joy of holding a child, of taking a spouse, of making love. Of course, it's a lot easier to pull the trigger if you can dehumanize what you're seeing through the scope, and that's the way the army has taught killing for decades. "Just another gook" is a much easier kill than Major Truong, Mrs. Nguyen, or a monk named Thich An Danh.

Pretty much anyone who's known the joy of military life in Vietnam, which was long before air-conditioned tents were more common than armored Hummers, is familiar with waking up in the early morning already coated with a sheen of perspiration from the absolute humidity coupled with unbearable heat. If you wake up in all but the cooler mountainous regions of the country and your sheets aren't soaked with sweat, odds are it's not yet time to roll out of the sack.

And that's exactly what happened in the small hours of the night early in 1970 at Phu Bai. We had no assigned missions for our M-88, and I'd expected to spend the day in the motor pool, doing preventive maintenance on the beast one of my crew had given the unwieldy name *I'm a Stranger Here, Lord.* A runner rolled me out of the rack and said the commander wanted to see me. It sparked the usual surge of adrenaline, the natural concern that something bad had happened at home, to the point that when I walked into the orderly room and saw the rifle, I was almost relieved.

The instructions were the customary ones, and when I got to the airfield there was only one Huey sitting there with rotors turning. It had to be my ride and, as usual on the outbound flight, I was the solo passenger.

When we arrived at the armored personnel carrier where the two mysterious men were waiting to brief me, I took a close look to see if there were any identifying marks—we called them "USA numbers," like 4J13283 as an example. But there were none.

I've since learned from other Vietnam vets that it wasn't all that unusual to occasionally see army-looking helicopters with no numbers carrying a strange collection of people on board and being given priority access to facilities and supplies at the bases where they turned up. Bottom line on this: There was no shortage of spooks or spook-driven activity in the war zone.

When I was out there with the briefers in the APC, I also never saw any security, but could only guess that anyone with the kind of authority the two briefers exercised must have had some sort of protection. I mean, APCs are APCs, but they're not impenetrable. They're just made of aircraft-quality aluminum—hell, they can float—so if Charlie had the right weapon, he could easily obliterate it. The only way to avoid that was to keep Charlie out of firing range. As a footnote, I would add that the APC was never fired on, at least when I was around.

On this mission, as in the past, the briefers—the same two guys who had sent me out several times before—wore sterile jungle fatigues, no insignia, no rank, no markings of any kind. By the time I arrived my spotter was already there. We got our briefing, took a look at a photograph of the intended target, were handed our map, and were told that on the way to the site we'd ride in one Huey, but on the way back there'd be two choppers waiting. Mine would be the one in front. The assumption was that if we didn't screw up and get on the wrong helicopter, the pilots would deliver us to our proper homes. It was a strange change in the way we'd been operating that didn't seem to make sense because it just made the coordination of the mission that much more difficult. But I didn't ask about it. Even if I had, the sense I got was that the briefers held nothing but disdain for the troops they were sending out to do the wet work and that they wouldn't have responded anyway.

After a relatively short flight, we were dropped off in a clearing. We had six hours to find and eliminate the target and get back to our pickup point. It was a much longer time than I'd ever been allotted before, and the only reason for that, as near as I could figure, was that our handlers weren't certain exactly what time the target would arrive. What that meant from a practical standpoint was that we were either going to have to wait an excessive amount of time before the shoot, or hide for an equally long time afterward. Neither was near the top of my hit parade of ways I wanted to while away the hours in the Vietnamese countryside.

The area we had to move through was characterized by low hills and valleys. The mission planners—whoever they were—determined that we could be dropped off just a couple of klicks from the village where we'd find our target, because the terrain would prevent anyone there from hearing or seeing our Huey land and then take off. The result was that we had a lot of time to move a relatively short distance through the woods.

Thinking back on missions like this, trying to remember every aspect of them, I realize there are some things that just aren't in the memory bank. It would be nice to be able to describe the sounds in the woods or jungle, the birdcalls or the buzzing of insects, or even the noise that rain makes falling through the canopy. But here's the truth: Early in my tour I learned to completely tune that stuff out and focus only on sounds that served to warn us of danger, things like the rustling of leaves in a way that you know it's not the wind, or sudden cries of alarm from birds, rather than ordinary chirping and calling.

I do remember that the instant we hit the wood line, the bugs began feasting on their daily dose of GI blood. There were times I'd swear that the little plastic squeeze bottles of jungle juice that most guys carried on their helmets just attracted insects, because even though I used the stuff religiously, it didn't take long in country to have bites on your bites.

I had hoped when I moved from down south and the cav up to Phu Bai that my sniper days were over. When I learned that they weren't, I began hoping that we might be sent out on those missions better equipped, especially for communications. Never happen, GI. We still had no radio, no smoke grenades, and no firepower beyond a couple of magazines each for my M-14 and my spotter's M-16. We weren't even supposed to take rations to the field, but occasionally I'd manage to stuff a few cans in my cargo pockets.

We still wore a boonie hat or baseball cap, because a helmet in the woods looks like . . . a helmet in the woods. No flak jackets—they'd just heat us up and slow us down. The truth is that we were the sacrificial lambs of someone else's mission, and we never knew whose mission it really was. We were out there feeling very much alone and very, very scared. It's difficult to explain the level or intensity of fear that you experience when you are so alone in the woods or jungle, no radio, no way of communicating with any person or group that could assist you in any way. Not even a way to talk with the aviators who were assigned to pick us up. If we had met with an unfortunate end, the pilots wouldn't have known. They would have just reported that their scheduled passengers didn't show. It's more than thirty-five years later, and I still want to know who I can curse out for putting me in that position. But I digress. . . .

We made our way through the woods until we reached an embankment across a small creek from the village where our target was supposed to be. As villages go, it was a small one, with probably six or seven thatch-roofed hooches in a semicircle. We could see a path that went down to the stream, so it was a good guess that it, rather than a well, was their source of water.

If there's anything more difficult than running from a shoot, it's waiting before one. In this case, we were there for at least two, maybe three hours, waiting for the target to arrive. We just lay there without moving. Obviously we couldn't smoke or talk. Didn't eat, didn't move around. It was almost like we were set up in an ambush point, waiting for the enemy to wander by.

Finally we saw three people coming into the village, and both of us were able to identify our target as one of the three. I looked around the village a bit, and then picked up a sight picture with the scope. My spotter whispered to me, "You got 'im?"

I mouthed more than said yes, then took in a breath, let it halfway out and held it, took up the slack in the trigger, and continued pulling with my fingertip. It always surprised me when the rifle went off, but that's the way it's supposed to be. The spotter said something to indicate it was a clean hit, and as soon as the scope cleared I could see that the target had flown backward before sinking to the ground. The two guys who were with him had dropped and were now low-crawling to a house sitting just beside the stream.

That was enough sightseeing for us. We crawled back a bit, and I picked up the expended cartridge; then we went down the hill and headed back to the same field we'd been dropped off in hours earlier. It was the only time I could remember that drop-off and pickup were in pretty much the same location.

Our wait for the helicopter seemed to take forever. We just lay on the ground next to a tree and willed ourselves to become invisible and not to emit a smell that was detectable. No water, no smoking, no movement of any kind that might draw attention to us. You think about the little things that can get you killed. Did the GI-issue insect repellent serve as a warning to any VC approaching? I couldn't tell if they could smell it, because I couldn't smell it myself—but that didn't mean I didn't reek of it. Think about wearing aftershave. Once you've had it on for a few minutes, no matter how much you slapped on your face, you don't really smell it anymore, right? Same problem with the jungle juice. So that problem builds and builds and builds inside your mind. And you can't turn to your buddy and ask him, because he's wearing it, too. Even if he weren't, you couldn't ask him, because neither one of you dares to breathe a word.

It's very strange, because you're really alone, even though you're with another person and he's within reach. You begin rethinking everything that has happened in the past few hours and dwelling on everything that could happen in the next few. The introspection becomes simplified in the extreme. *I could have died today, but I didn't. Oh, wait. The day's not over. There's still time.*

Introspection is not something that nineteen- or twenty-year-olds in Vietnam are terribly good at unless fortified by copious quantities of something like the pride of Singapore, Tiger Beer, which had almost twice the alcoholic content of the Schlitz or Budweiser sold at the club. Inside my head I relived the day's mission in stark terms. *The shoot was successful; it was actually a pretty good shot; can we get out of here alive?* At this stage in my life I still wasn't questioning what I'd done. There was no regret, no remorse, no concern that in my head I'd still be going on these missions decades from now. I certainly didn't feel sorrow for having taken a life in the coldest, most calculating way possible.

Despite our having two or three hours to wait, there was no time for deep thinking, because reality would always intrude. Was the helicopter we could hear the one we were waiting for? Not possible; it was still too early. Was my heart beating as loudly as I thought it was? Because if it was, I was dead meat. Charlie had to be able to hear it, and if he could, I'd never hear him coming, because the sound of my heart would drown him out. I didn't say the thoughts were rational, but I was in the middle of a year's worth of irrational.

I've often said that I was scared only one time while I was in Vietnam—that would be from the time I got there till the time I left. Of course, the level of that fear could, and did, vary significantly, depending upon what events were taking place at the moment. And since at the moment I was in the prone position, concealed near the edge of an open field, not knowing if I'd live long enough to board the helicopter that we hoped would be coming for us, the fear level was higher than the audience at a Grateful Dead concert.

Fear makes you wonder if the men who were with our target are right behind us or running away from us. It makes you wonder how many bad guys heard the report of the rifle, and what action they're taking.

Anything and everything goes through your mind. You think about the guys back at the base and how they'll react if you don't come back. You think about how you'll look on one of those tables at the Da Nang morgue, and whether they'll be able to make you look good enough for an open-casket funeral. That, of course, forces you to imagine what you'd look like lying there in your class-A greens, your face waxy with the stuff embalmers use to fool the next of kin into thinking that you died a peaceful, pleasant death. You think about home, the letter you should have written, but didn't, telling your parents how much you love and appreciate them. You wonder if you'll ever get back to Texas again, alive. For a few seconds you think of the girls back home, of some good times you had in your pickup truck at the drive-in, and you wonder if you'll ever see them again.

The fact that you haven't had anything to eat or drink for hours begins to play in your mind, and you wonder if you'll ever again sit in a restaurant or café and have a Coke poured from a bottle, a cup of coffee, or a burger. And that leads you to begin listing the food you miss the most, the dishes Mom made every week, not just for the holidays. *Will I ever again have a chicken-fried steak with cream gravy?*

Before I could come to any conclusions about the likelihood of ever again eating meals that could result in the Heart Association's picketing Mom's kitchen, we heard our helicopter coming in. We knew the approach would be low and fast, especially since we had no way of warning the pilots if the LZ was hot.

They bounced the Huey down, and I don't think it sat on the ground for ten seconds before we dove in. The pilot pulled pitch, put her in a nose-down attitude, and di-di'ed out of there. The flight was short; within minutes they brought the ship down at the intersection of two roads, and the crew chief motioned my spotter and me to jump off.

We did, that helo left, and a short time later two other aircraft came into sight and landed. Per the instructions we'd been given that morning, I jumped in the first one and my buddy climbed into the second. Less than half an hour later I was on the ground at Phu Bai, walking back to my unit.

There was no way I could recognize how much I'd changed in the months I'd been in Vietnam. When everyone around you stinks, you don't know how bad you smell. One thing is certain: I never thought about whether I'd fit in back home in Granbury; all I knew was that I wanted to get there. Would it happen? It probably depended on how many more assignments like this one I'd get, because I knew that the longer I kept rolling the dice, the better the odds were that I'd crap out.

CHAPTER TWELVE

Free-Fire Zone

It was February or March of 1970, and I had three or four months remaining on my one-year tour when, early one morning just as I was about ready to start pulling maintenance on my recovery vehicle, I was summoned to the company commander's office. My body's response was both unpleasant and predictable. My heart raced, and my mind went through the usual list of potential reasons for the call, ranging from an emergency at home to another damned mission with the rifle.

When I entered his office and saw the rifle, it was a classic good news–bad news situation. The good news was that nothing untoward had occurred with my family; the bad news was that someone wanted me to put my life on the line and go kill someone—again.

I was instructed to go across the base at Phu Bai to the XXIV Corps Artillery headquarters. Next to the headquarters was a temporary office building that almost looked like a small mobile home or mobile office from the outside. Parked outside were two unmarked jeeps.

I went inside and found the two anonymous briefers sitting there, waiting. The other half of my team hadn't yet arrived, so we all sat around in silence. There were a lot of questions I would have liked to ask the spooks, starting off with an admittedly selfish one: Why me? When they'd satisfactorily answered that one, my fantasy had me inquiring whether or not it bothered them that the conditions they sent us out under were not necessarily conducive to our getting out alive, for we had no radio, no backup, and no alternative for evacuation if trouble arose and we missed our pickup.

Why didn't that bother them? And I suppose if I really got belligerent, I could suggest that since they were getting the big bucks, they might want to explain why they weren't taking the chances, but passing the hazardous work on to a couple of low-ranking enlisted men who hadn't joined the army to be shooters. Much later I learned that the infantry troops had a nickname for snipers—all of them, not just the ones doing the wet work for anonymous spooks. They called us "Murder, Incorporated," and to say that I resented it is an understatement. In all of my nightmares since Vietnam, I've never considered myself a murderer!

But instead of getting into it with them, I just sat there quietly and waited. After about fifteen minutes my second arrived. He introduced himself as Smitty; I told him I was Mitch, and without any preface the briefing began.

We were given the usual information about transportation, schedule, and extraction location, but for only the second time since I began this orchestrated killing, I wasn't given a specific target. Since the other time this had happened was when I was ordered to kill four Buddhist monks, the omission of the target details seriously concerned me.

When I questioned the two spooks, they somewhat reluctantly told us that there would not be a specific target. After we were inserted, our job was to find someone, anyone, and kill them. The impression we were given was, the more, the merrier. We both realized at that point that we were being sent to a free-fire zone.

A free-fire zone is somewhat unnatural. Its boundaries are limited by both geography and time, according to the rules established by the powers that be—and for reasons you're about to hear, I have to assume that those powers were at least as high as the commanding general of the Military Assistance Command Vietnam (MACV), but possibly much higher and residing in an office not on the banks of the Mekong River, but the Potomac. Why? Because the concept of a free-fire zone most likely violates international law, and when that occurs as a matter of policy, it's a good bet that someone a lot higher than a battalion commander came up with the idea.

In a free-fire zone, anyone that moves between a specific start time and a specific end time within the physical boundaries is considered to be the enemy, and is therefore both an acceptable and viable target. Translation: Shoot anyone that moves. Military or civilian. In uniform or out. Male or female. Old or young. If they're there, you can and should kill them.

I didn't know it at the time—and even if I had, I'm not sure what I would have done differently—but just the concept of a free-fire zone violates the letter and the spirit of the Geneva Conventions, because they prohibit indiscriminate attacks on civilians.

According to Protocol I, Article 51, Section 4, "Indiscriminate attacks are those which are not directed at a specific military objective or those which use a method of attack that cannot be directed at or limited to a specific military objective." I'm not an international human rights lawyer, but that makes it pretty clear that whacking a peasant who happens to wander through the area with his water buffalo is somewhat verboten. So is firing an artillery barrage into an area without making certain that any humans who happen to be in the impact zone are bona fide enemy combatants. That's covered under Section 5a, which says that "area bombardment, where a number of clearly separated military objectives are treated as a single military objective, and where there is a similar concentration of civilians or civilian objects" is proscribed. Finally, with respect to what the American forces called free-fire zones, there's Article 57, which says, "If it becomes apparent that an objective in an attack is not a military one, or if that attack could cause incidental loss of civilian life or damage to civilian objects, then the attack must be called off."

On my other shoots where the assigned targets were apparently civilians, I suppose it's possible that whoever picked the people I was to kill had evidence that they were not innocent civilians, but were agents of the Viet Cong or the North Vietnamese Army. I would have no way of knowing if that were the case, but it is one possibility. However, when I'm told to set up in an area at a specific time and blast away indiscriminately at anyone who happens to come by, not even Johnnie Cochran could have made that one look righteous.

But no matter how much I disliked the assignment or felt I was being misused, I wasn't inclined to object, or to take that step into the abyss of military justice and refuse what some judge advocate general—the military version of a prosecutor—could and most certainly would construe as a lawful order. Truth be told, I'd rather do the killing than have Leavenworth, Kansas, 66048, become my mailing address for the foreseeable future.

So my second took the map and I shouldered my rifle and we climbed into one of the unmarked jeeps for a short ride to the airfield. En route, the spook picked a flashlight with a red lens off the floorboard and handed it to the second, saying, "When the aircraft lands to pick you up, flash it twice so the crew will know it's you. After all, you don't want one of the crewmen shooting at you, now, do you?" Clearly we were dealing with a first-class prick whose concern for our well-being was somewhat less than sincere. Looking back, it was almost as if he wanted the aircrewmen to make the mistake.

Had I known one little fact then that I know now, I would have been more than a bit alarmed at his comment about getting shot by the gunners on the helo coming in to get us. In documents made public long after the Vietnam War ended, it was noted that at one point, orders had been given to eliminate some of the U.S. military personnel involved in the CIA's campaign of murder and assassination of civilians.

My second and I boarded the Huey, which immediately took off and headed west, flying us past Camp Eagle, firebases Bastogne and Birmingham, and finally set us down just inside the infamous A Shau Valley. The A Shau, dubbed the A Shit Valley by the Americans sent there to fight, is located near the Laotian border in the Thua Thien province of I Corps, the northernmost of the four corps areas into which the military had divided South Vietnam. Actually composed of several valleys and mountains, the A Shau was one of the principal entry points of the Ho Chi Minh Trail, down which the North Vietnamese Army sent supplies and additional troops.

The area we were being dropped into was critical to the North Vietnamese Army and Viet Cong units operating in I Corps. That's why it had been the target of several major operations, many of which were conducted by the 101st Airborne Division, the most infamous of these having taken place in May and June of 1969, approximately eight or nine months earlier. Officially, it was Operation Apache Snow, but it quickly became known as the battle of Hamburger Hill.

The purpose of the operation was to cut off the North Vietnamese and prevent them from mounting an attack on the coastal provinces. A year earlier the NVA had launched its Tet attack on the city of Hue from the A Shau. After an eleven-day battle that involved ten infantry assaults by elements of the 101st Airborne Division and the 9th Marine Regiment, Ap Bia Mountain was taken. But the cost was horrific. The U.S. reported 56 killed and 420 wounded. North Vietnamese dead were put at 597, but it was always assumed, since it was their standard practice, that the retreating NVA forces took many additional dead along with their wounded across the border into Laos. Because the operation was not intended to hold territory but rather to keep the North Vietnamese Army off balance, the mountain was abandoned soon after the battle and occupied by the North Vietnamese a month later.

American public outrage over what appeared to be a senseless loss of American lives was exacerbated by the publication in *LIFE* magazine of the pictures of the 241 U.S. soldiers killed the week of the Hamburger Hill battle. It was reported that shortly after Hamburger Hill, MACV commander Gen. Creighton Abrams was ordered by the White House to avoid major battles that would produce heavy casualties. That apparently began the shift to Vietnamization of the war, a policy designed to hand responsibility for the fighting over to the South Vietnamese.

That policy didn't have any bearing on the mission my second and I were now embarked upon, because there we were, alone, in the A Shau. Exiting the aircraft at a run, we dashed into the wood line and waited for the helicopter to take off. We sat there for a couple of moments to catch our breath—or was it to get up our nerve?—and then walked about halfway down the hill to where we could see down a trail.

Our briefers told us we could shoot after 1400 hours (two p.m.), so we had about an hour before we could begin firing. Since our ride home was scheduled to meet us at 2000 hours (eight p.m.) in the same location where we were dropped off, we would have about six hours to locate, engage, and eliminate as many targets as possible, and still get to the pickup point, alive and hopefully unwounded.

We moved uphill another hundred meters along the trail we'd found, staying within the wood line in order to minimize the likelihood of our being seen. We elected to go up the trail so that on our way out, when we had to move quickly, we would be going downhill.

The shooting location we found gave us a view both ways up and down the trail, but we could see only about forty meters up and another twenty-five or thirty meters down. The good thing was that we would be shooting from a small rise and could drop back behind it and be quickly out of sight once I'd fired a shot.

The shooting on this mission was going to be different from on previous occasions. There would be no time for hesitation, because the targets would be on the move. The scope really wasn't necessary, because either one of us could have thrown a rock and hit anyone on the trail. I would have to shoot from the sitting position, rather than the prone. Sitting allows a greater opportunity to make a last-minute adjustment in the direction you're shooting. This was important, because we didn't know from which direction any potential target would come.

We were all set and ready to begin at 1330 hours (one thirty p.m.), which gave us half an hour to relax. When the start time came and went with no one on the trail, we were surprised. I really don't know what we expected. I suppose we thought that at the start time, people would just begin moving up or down the trail for our convenience, but it didn't happen.

Finally, after we'd been in position for nearly two hours, we heard someone coming up the trail. It was clearly a woman's voice, and she was speaking to someone. I pulled the rifle into my shoulder and assumed a firing position, thinking that if I were quick enough, I could get at least two. Besides, the second had an M-16, so if necessary he could take out one or two also.

For a second I flashed back on the second sniper killing I'd done. Months earlier, I'd felt twinges of something—maybe guilt, maybe not—when I shot and killed a woman. Now I was about to do it again. This time, I don't recall even thinking about it as something special. It was like they said, "It don't mean nothin'." Had I become one of those soulless killers with the thousand-yard stare? That's way too much introspection for a hot, sticky day in Vietnam—or so I thought.

I settled into position and began to stabilize my breathing. As soon as she rounded the little crook in the trail, I almost fired, because she came right into the sight picture. Then I saw movement to her left side and realized that she was leading a small child. Slowly I lowered the rifle. Both my second and I passed on the hit—not in front of her child. And even though I'd seen what the VC would deliberately do to a youngster, even though I'd already done things for my spook handlers that I wouldn't ever have thought I'd do, there was no way I'd consider shooting the child. Vietnam may have torn my soul, but I refused to allow it to be ripped from my body.

After a period of time we saw a lone man coming down the trail. He was dressed in the usual Vietnamese garb, so I had to assume he was a civilian, or possibly a guerrilla, but not NVA. I quickly pulled the rifle into my shoulder again and fired. I don't think he ever knew we were there, and if he did we gave him no time to react. One moment he was walking down the path, and the next moment his body had been knocked completely off the other side of the trail.

We quickly grabbed the empty casing and slid off the small rise out of sight, and then sat for a moment intently listening to see if we could hear anyone else moving. Hearing nothing, we moved down the trail to the bottom of the hill, where another trail intersected the one we were on. We watched all four directions to ensure that no one else was in the area and then crossed, continuing on the same trail we'd come down.

Eventually it took us up the relatively steep side of another hill, and after we'd traveled a total of about 450 meters from the first firing position, we located another position that we could shoot from. From this vantage point we could see about eighty meters down the hill, but only about ten or fifteen meters up the hill. It meant I'd be forced to shoot downhill, irrespective of which direction the target was walking.

Around 1700 (five p.m.) we heard someone coming down the trail. I snugged the rifle into the pocket of my shoulder and waited. It was another man dressed similarly to our first target, walking down the hill with a bundle balanced on his left shoulder.

Wondering what was in the bundle, I hesitated a second or two and then feathered the trigger. He flew forward, tumbling farther down the hill, his bundle rolling after him, spilling its cargo of some kind of rather large green leaves.

We quickly moved back into the wood line and sat for a moment. I can't say for sure what my second was doing, but I was trying to control my breathing, and I was probably doing a little praying, too. It wasn't that this shoot was more difficult than the first, or that I suddenly felt more threatened by where we were and what we were doing. It's just that while I may have lost my naïveté in Vietnam, I hadn't yet lost my conscience. For me, taking another human life was never an easy thing to do, and to do it methodically, even mechanically, twice in a few hours and still have time left to do it again made me think about what I'd become—and the thoughts were not especially attractive.

The two of us scampered down the hill, staying off the trail. The foliage was somewhat light, definitely not thick enough to make it difficult to walk, but we were probably making enough noise to lead anyone directly to us. When we came to the trail that we had crossed earlier, we turned to our right, still staying near, but not on the trail.

After what seemed like an eternity, we stopped and sat down, just looking at each other. Both of us were wet with sweat and breathing heavily. We drank from our canteens, and probably violated recommended procedure by not emptying them. We knew that water sloshing around inside a half-full canteen could give us away, but I guess we figured that considering what we were doing out there, it wasn't a big deal.

Within a short time we had regained control of our breathing, so we stood up and started walking. We carefully crossed the trail and found a position, settled in, and waited. We estimated that this position was only about five hundred meters from our scheduled pickup point.

For the rest of the afternoon and as dusk began to fall, we waited. Finally, about 1900 hours, the second said, "I've had all the fun I can stand. Let's get the hell out of here." He got no objections from me. A half hour later we were in position, watching the pickup point and listening for an aircraft. We were at the same LZ we'd dropped into earlier in the day. It was a relatively small natural clearing. Neither one of us questioned the logic of drop-off and pickup being in the same location. How about that for being malleable? It was pretty much, *You know, whatever, I'm gonna die anyway, so what difference does it make?*

After what seemed like a lifetime and a half, we finally heard an inbound Huey. As it settled onto the ground the second flashed the red light twice in the direction of the aircraft. Without waiting for any confirmation—because we hadn't been told to expect any—we started toward the aircraft at a run.

Obviously the aircrew was as unhappy about being in the A Shau Valley as we were, because as soon as we dove through the door they lifted off again and headed east, low and fast. Every once in a while during the flight, my second and I would look at each other, but of course, we couldn't talk without yelling. Anyway, we probably didn't need words to communicate what we were feeling and thinking. *We're alive! We're not wounded! Did you see that gook tumble when the round hit? What the fuck am I doing here? I'll sure be glad to get back home!* After flying for about thirty or forty-five minutes, we landed at the Phu Bai airfield, where the two briefers were waiting for us, one in each unmarked jeep. I climbed into one, the second mounted the other, and with a small wave toward each other, we were on our way back to our respective units. We'd never see each other again.

A postscript: The area we were sent into remained an NVA stronghold for the remainder of the war. A few months after our mission, another element of the 101st Airborne (B/1/327th) was combat-assaulted to Hill 882 on a search-and-destroy operation and ran into a sapper base camp. What they didn't know at the time is that they were facing a full North Vietnamese Army division that was preparing to attack Fire Support Base Ripcord in a plan to keep forces away from the A Shau for much of the summer of 1970.

CHAPTER THIRTEEN

Getting Short

Everyone in Vietnam had a short-timer's calendar. If not an actual physical device—a paper calendar or a stick into which you carved notches—it was a mental countdown clock, so that you always knew how many days you had left on your tour. Unlike our current war in Iraq, where a sequence of morale-dumping surprise extensions of time in the war zone have rendered short-timer calendars essentially meaningless, the promise that army troops would spend no more than a year in the war zone and marines no more than thirteen months was inviolate. The war was unpopular enough at home; the politicians running it certainly didn't want to do the one thing guaranteed to bring the wrath of military families down on their heads. Therefore, the only way a person stayed more than the standard tour of duty was if they voluntarily extended. There were no extensions, no "stop loss."

From the day I arrived in country, I knew that I could count on boarding a Freedom Bird home no later than June 12, 1970. Of course, newbies didn't talk about their rotation date home—way too depressing. That was left for the guys who were truly short to do. And the shorter they were, the more they relished making those of us who were still looking at more than half our tour to go miserable. The rules of short-timer calendars were simple: You didn't count today, and you didn't count your departure day, which was the "wake-up," as in, "I have twelve days and a wake-up to go."

We all hoped to live long enough to inflict that delicious misery on anyone who wasn't as short as we were. And make no mistake about it, the infliction of misery was absolutely intentional, in part because it even allowed us to stick it to those who outranked us—the senior NCOs and officers.

"Hey, Mitch, how short are you?"

"I'm so short I have to look up to see a snake's belly."

"I'm so short I can't see over the toes of my boots."

"I'm so short I can sit on a dime and swing my legs."

"I'm so short I have to reach up to tie my boots."

"I'm so short I can do backflips under my cot."

"I'm so short I can limbo under the door."

"I'm so short I have to cuff my underwear."

"I'm so short I can work as a teller at a piggy bank."

"I'm so short, the only way I can piss is up."

Eventually, "I'm so short . . ." morphed into "I'm too short . . ." as in "I'm too short to do laundry" or "I'm too short to give a shit" or "I'm too short to worry."

But the truth of the matter was that until you were safely out of Vietnamese airspace, you weren't too short to die, which is why the shorter we got, the more careful we got, sometimes to the point of what in the real world might be considered paranoia, but in Vietnam was just the exercise of common sense. All we were really doing was taking to an extreme the notion that anything you do in a combat zone can get you killed, including nothing.

That's why it was common practice in many units to give short-timers the privilege of hanging out in the base camp rather than continuing to go on operations where, if one played the odds, the chances of getting hurt—or worse—were considerably greater. At Phu Bai, the deal I had with the platoon sergeant was that when I got down to thirty days, he'd take me off recovery missions. That would allow me to spend my last weeks in Vietnam in relative safety, while leisurely going through the convoluted paperwork involved in out-processing. I knew some guys who were so psycho during their last month that they refused to go anywhere in the base camp without a helmet and flak jacket. And some guys were so frightened of the possibility of a relatively routine mortar attack that they decided where they'd go—and where they wouldn't go—based on how far the route took them from a bunker. A friend of mine decided that he would be way too exposed going from his hooch to the mess hall, so for his last two weeks in country he never went to eat. We brought food back to the hooch for him, or he lived on C-rations or care packages from home, just so he could stay close to a bunker. I'd have to agree that his theory was sound: There wasn't anything they served in the mess hall that was worth dying for.

By April 12, 1970, I was getting short. I still had another thirty days on the road to survive before I'd get to kick back and enjoy life in the office for my last month in country, but I was feeling cautiously optimistic about surviving Vietnam. That was until my platoon sergeant, Hook Soo Yung, came by my hooch and said, "Mitchell, the first sergeant wants to see you. What the hell have you done?"

Even though I'd made spec 5, the equivalent in pay grade of a three-stripe buck sergeant, there was still no more feared man in uniform than my first sergeant. It's almost impossible to explain if you haven't been in the service, but try imagining if the dean of discipline at your high school possessed the power of life or death over you, and you begin to approach the authority of a first sergeant. This was clearly a man who could make your life miserable in ways you were unable even to imagine. First sergeants had the capacity to be offended by anything. Early in my military career I had a first sergeant who took a dislike to me because I gave him "a case of the ass." To this day, I still don't know what "a case of the ass" is, but I know that whatever it is, it was bad enough to cost me several weekends of freedom.

So when I was told to report to the first sergeant, I went through a mental checklist of the reasons I might be in trouble. I'd pulled all the duty I was supposed to, so it wasn't that. There was still the rifle, which I'd last used two weeks earlier, but when I'd been called to pick it up it was always the company commander who gave me the assignment. That left the possibility that always came to mind: Something was wrong at home.

I began to move out, but SFC Yung said, "Wait, I gotta go with you." Well, that made it even more serious. Having to see the first sergeant is bad, but if your platoon sergeant has to go with you, you've got a real problem on your hands.

We walked into the top's office and he looked up and said, "Well, it took you long enough to get here." He paused long enough to allow my life to flash before my eyes, then added, "Mitchell, what in the hell did you do?" I didn't know what to say because I didn't know what I'd done. Then he went into a real rant. "I got a damned company to run here, and here I am escorting pantywaist bird sergeants around. Now I've gotta take you to battalion headquarters, as if I don't have *important* shit to do."

Suddenly I found myself being marched to battalion HQ by both my platoon sergeant and my first sergeant, and, suffice it to say, I was freaking out. They marched me into the Personnel Services NCO's office, and the guy was expecting me. "Well, my, my, my, Specialist Mitchell. I haven't seen you since you made E-5." I didn't know where this was going, but I was certain it wasn't anywhere good.

"When do you leave?" he asked me, but before I could tell him, he said, "Anybody want coffee?" The two senior sergeants declined, but I jumped on the opportunity to delay whatever bad shit was about to rain down on my sorry ass. I got some coffee, adding milk and sugar to the paper cup.

When I was back in front of his desk, he asked me again, "How long do you have left in country?"

"Fifty-eight and a wake-up, Sergeant."

"Are you sure?" he asked me. Now there were a lot of things that happened to me in Vietnam that I wasn't sure about, but the one thing I was positive about was how many days I had left in this vacation paradise. But he was an E-7, a sergeant first class, so it wasn't going to be in my best interests to say, "Well, you asshole, if I know anything, it's how short I am."

So I just began to mumble, "Yes, Sergeant, that's—"

But he interrupts me like he's not interested in anything I have to say, and while he's digging through papers on his desk, he says, "Well, I don't think that's right. Let me check here." He picks up some papers and looks at them real close, then looks up at my first sergeant and at Sergeant Yung, and, dead seriously, says, "I thought you guys told me this was a good troop. That he's honest. That you could always depend on him."

At this point, I remembered that when shit hits the fan, it *never* spreads evenly. Clearly, before this session was over, I was likely to be the only one in the office neck-deep in crap. I'm ready to crawl in a hole, even a VC tunnel, just to get out of there, but there is no escape. The first sergeant, Rudy Bureau, said, "Well, he's never given us cause to question him before now. Of course, he's pulled some bullshit stunts, but nothing serious." My platoon sergeant just shrugs. It becomes very apparent that there is no way he's going to save my sorry ass.

Then the PSNCO says, "Mitchell, you're lying to me." I turn five shades of white. The tan I've developed over the past ten months just up and disappears.

He waves the papers in front of my face and says, "Specialist, you certainly do not have fifty-eight and a wake-up; you have three days—I don't know why or how, but you got a fifty-six-day drop!"

By that time I'm shaking so bad, when he says "drop," I do just that with the cup of coffee. All I can say is "Holy shit!"

All three of the senior NCOs break up laughing, and as the PSNCO hands me my orders, he says, "It looks like you're going to Fort Hood."

I say, "Fort Hood, I'm going to Fort Hood. I live close to there," still not believing what's happening to me.

The first sergeant says, "You'd better get over to my orderly room and see the clerk to get your clearing papers. If you've only got three days left, you don't have time to waste."

I took off like I'd been shot from a gun, ran all the way to the company orderly room, and ran inside, only to find Captain Gluth standing there. "Mitchell, what the hell are you doing running in my orderly room?" he asked. Had I looked closely, I probably would have noticed that he was fighting hard to conceal a grin. But I was in "don't know whether to shit or go blind" mode, and not exactly absorbing the subtleties of the moment.

Besides, I was puffing so hard that I could barely catch my breath. All I could manage to blurt out was "I got a drop. I'm going home."

The captain then broke out into a smile, handed me a fistful of papers, and said, "Well, I think everybody ought to do that once in a while. Here's your clearing papers." These were the orders that were going to get me from Phu Bai to Da Nang, from Da Nang to Cam Ranh Bay, then onto a Freedom Bird heading to the Continental United States, and on to my new assignment at Fort Hood. Before I could get on my way to start packing, Captain Gluth said, "We have one little detail that we need taken care of before you leave. Come with me."

We went into his office, where I saw the rifle sitting on his desk in the case. He shut the door and said, "You need to clean that." It was the quickest cleaning job I'd ever done on a weapon. Then he had me wrap it in Cosmoline paper, which is what you package a rifle in that's going to be stored for a period of time. When I finished, I put it back in the case and closed it. He gave me a little metal seal—I still remember the number. It was 06652. And I put the seal on—it had a ball on one part and you pushed the wire back into the ball and it latched. He checked to make sure it was secured, then said, "Now get out of here. Take my jeep and get your clearing done."

It didn't cross my mind at that moment to wonder whether the fifty-six-day drop and the off-the-books sniper assignments were linked. When I looked at the paperwork, I saw that the clerk had already gotten most of the signatures needed before I could leave. I had to turn in some gear at supply, sign an authorization for the supply sergeant to ship my nonaccompanying baggage home in my footlocker, pick up my medical, dental, finance, and personnel records, and stop at the mailroom to give them a copy of my orders so they could forward mail to me stateside. Then I had to go to the repair shop, where they had me inventory the weapons on the M-88. Finally, I packed the bag that I was going to carry with me. All you're allowed on the plane is sixty-six pounds, and it doesn't take much to reach that limit. A couple sets of jungle fatigues, some underwear, an extra pair of boots, my shaving kit, and I was good to go. All the photographs I had I put in the footlocker that would be shipped to me.

The rushed process left me no more than fifteen minutes to say my farewells to guys I'd served with for many months. I ran through the section and said, "I'm gone, bye, have a good one, take care of yourself, I'll see you back in the world." I wasn't leaving Vietnam for three days, but I had to be out of Phu Bai in fifteen minutes. Someone ran me down to the airfield in the jeep, where I hooked up with another guy from my unit, Stanley Coutu from Chicago, who was also going home. We caught a ride on a C-130 that would take us to Da Nang.

Years later I'd reflect on the fact that there were guys I should have said good-bye to, but didn't have the chance. There were guys whose home addresses I should have gotten, but never did. There were people I had grown closer to than my own family, but I would never write to them, never see them again. Unlike veterans from World War II, who went home as a unit on board troop ships where they could decompress together, who stayed in touch, who joined VFW and Legion posts to keep the connection, Vietnam vets rarely did, and we were the worse for it. Maybe we thought that when our war was over, we really wanted it to be over, with all ties to it severed. Or if we didn't consciously think it, we acted as though we did. What I had no way of knowing as I rushed to get the chopper for the first leg of the journey home was that while I may have been finished with the war, it wasn't finished with me. By the time I realized that it might help if I could find the guys who lived through it with me, they weren't there to be found, and I had no idea how to find them.

Stan and I spent an uneventful night in the transient tents in Da Nang, if you don't count sirens going off because there was supposedly an enemy probe of the perimeter. The FNGs who were in the tent with us were so green they were still peeing stateside water. When the permanent party NCOs began screaming for everyone to hit the bunkers, the newbies ran as though their lives depended on it. Outwardly, I took a more blasé approach to the situation, which pissed off the NCOs who would be the ones to write up the paperwork if something happened to us while we were in their tents. Truth be told, if a medic had put a blood pressure cuff on me just then, he would have slammed me in the hospital right quick. All I could think was *This close to home, and I'm gonna die.*

When the all-clear sounded a few minutes later, I got back in bed, but wasn't able to sleep. It's like I always said: You're not out of the woods till you're out of the woods, and I still had another twenty-four hours in country before I'd be on that outbound Freedom Bird.

Early the next morning Stan and I got on another C-130 and flew to Cam Ranh Bay, where we reported to the holding area and turned in a copy of our orders. After a while, they ordered everyone into a formation so they could explain the procedure. Calling it a "formation" is giving it much more dignity than it's entitled to. Imagine a couple of hundred guys who are so short, they've already had their last wake-up. Motivating us to do anything other than board the plane was nearly impossible.

"Okay, we got an airplane leaving here this afternoon, so we're going to call your name off. When you hear your name, get your bag; take it over there. You have to go through customs to make sure you're not taking back any bombs, bullets, hand grenades, or other toys." The MPs were set up to go through it all, and they had dogs sniffing everything and everybody to make sure we weren't taking any drugs on the plane.

When they called, "Mitchell, Gary D.," I answered loud enough to wake up the dead. I wanted to make sure there was no doubt that I was there, present and accounted for, and ready to board. After we cleared customs and threw our tagged bags on a truck, I had my last and final strange Vietnam experience.

They put us on a bus with only two ways out: an emergency door in the back that's locked, and the entrance door in the front. The windows were down, but there was wire mesh over the openings so Charlie couldn't toss in a grenade as a parting gift. None of us had weapons, but we were going on a ride that took us past a lot of Vietnamese civilians. It was the longest fifteen-minute ride of my life, and it was absolutely uneventful.

Once we got close to the ramp area we could see a United Airlines stretch DC-8 waiting for us. This was our Freedom Bird. Once again they called the roll, and I think I must've run up those boarding steps two at a time. Within minutes the pilot came on the intercom and said, "Welcome aboard. We're number four in the takeoff sequence. Got a cargo plane, a sortie of two fighters that's our escort out of here, another cargo plane, and then it's our turn."

We began to taxi, and minutes later the pilot said, "Stewardesses"— don't forget, this is ancient history and that's what they were called back then—"we've been cleared for takeoff," and those girls went running for their seats. I guess they'd done this a few times, because the pilot didn't stop, lock the brakes, and wind the engines up. He just turned the corner onto the active runway, throttled up, and we were gone. It was the most wonderful feeling in the world to feel that surge of power push you back into the seat.

When he rotated, gained a bit of altitude, and raised the landing gear, everybody clapped and cheered. If we hadn't been strapped in, we would have jumped up and down. It was a very steep climb out, and after about ten minutes or so, he said, "If you look out the window you can wave good-bye to our escorts." We all watched the fighters waggle their wings and turn back to Vietnam, while we continued on our way back home.

After hopscotching across the Pacific, with one stop in Hawaii, where they let us off the plane while it was serviced, we finally arrived back in the world, the land of the big PX. To the cheers of everyone on board, the plane touched down at McCord Air Force Base adjacent to the army's Fort Lewis in Washington, south of Seattle.

We were bused to an in-processing center, where we got fitted for dress green uniforms, got paid in cash, and were fed unlimited quantities of steak, mashed potatoes, ice cream, pie, and—miracle of miracles—real whole milk. Then it was a bus ride to the Seattle-Tacoma International Airport, where we swarmed the airline counters. Since I was going to Dallas Love Field, I targeted Braniff, and managed to buy a seat on a plane leaving later that evening.

With time to kill, I went into the airport restaurant and ordered a cup of coffee. While I was sitting there, a young man walked up and started staring at me. I hadn't been warned what to expect, or if I had, in my euphoria at getting back home I wasn't paying attention. I looked up and said, "Hi, how're you doing?"

"Well, well, well," he said. "The conquering hero returns."

I didn't understand.

"How many babies did you have to kill to get here?" And then he spit on my brand-spanking-new uniform.

Believe it or not, it still didn't compute that I had just taken center stage in an anti–Vietnam War protest, but it sure made an impression on three older guys sitting at a nearby table. As it turned out, two of them were World War II vets, and the third had served in Korea. They sort of invited the guy and all his friends to leave the coffee shop. In fact, one of them suggested less than politely, "If you come back in here again, I'll whip your ass and pay the fine with a smile." All the while that confrontation was playing out, the waitress was wiping the spittle off my uniform, and I was wondering what the hell had just happened.

Bottom line—the protester left, and the three vets informed the waitress that my money was no good. They would pay for whatever I wanted. So I had a piece of pie and another cup of coffee, and as I was getting ready to go, and the waitress was wiping my uniform off again, I found out that her husband was in Vietnam with about ninety days left.

The red-eye flight home to Texas was as unexciting as you'd want it to be. We landed at about 5:30 in the morning. I came down the ramp and didn't see my mother and sister there to meet me until they slammed me into a wall. I was the baby of the family, and I'm sure that I never realized how much of a strain it was on the whole family, and my mother in particular, to have me in Vietnam. My mom was crying her eyes out, and my sister was saying, "Thank God, thank God he made it." They had no idea.

We got in the car and drove to the filling station that my folks owned. As we pulled in, I remember seeing my dad putting gas in a car, and he just stopped and ran and grabbed me and wrapped his arms around me and wouldn't let go. I think that was when I really began to understand what it meant to my folks to have a child in the service. Between 1943, when one of my brothers joined the army, until 1992, when I retired, my mother always had at least one son on active duty. That's just shy of fifty years of having a family member in uniform. And what none of us knew that morning in Dallas was that even once you were out of uniform, it wasn't over when it was over.

CHAPTER FOURTEEN

Maybe You Can't Go Home Again

I hadn't been home forty-eight hours when I had my first night-mare. The pillow and sheets were soaked with sweat; I'd tossed the blankets onto the floor, and had probably been screaming. I say "probably," because no one came and woke me up. But it was clear that my parents knew something was wrong.

My mother, rest her soul, said that I went to Vietnam her little boy, and I came back somebody she didn't recognize. She always said she loved me, loved me dearly, but moms have a way of knowing the truth, even if they don't speak it. I could tell by the way she looked at me that she knew I wasn't the same sweet, innocent, naive boy that she watched enter the army and go off to war.

No one warned me before I enlisted that the army would change me. Hell, I'd just graduated from high school, the future was tomor-row, and the distant future was next week. I'm not even sure that I consciously realized that by joining the army in 1968, the odds were that I'd be going to Vietnam.

And while I was in Vietnam, following orders and doing what I had to do to stay alive, I certainly didn't contemplate the fact that though I had within me the capacity to kill, to do so would haunt me for the rest of my life. Every bullet I fired that took a life hit me as well. My wounds may not bleed, but they are at least as painful as, and sometimes more so than, the ones that do. For a normal person—and by that I mean someone like me who takes no pleasure in killing—pain and guilt are the legacy of success in war.

My first month home after Vietnam I did my best to pick up with life in Granbury where I had left it. But it was clear pretty quickly that I no longer fit in. I went over a nineteen-year-old kid and came back a twenty-year-old who needed geriatric care. I was an old man. My outlook on life had changed.

Even though I was home in Texas, I still felt responsible for my crew and my friends that were still in Vietnam. Was it survivor's guilt? I'm not sure, but I suppose it could have been. The last person on my M-88 crew was due to rotate in September 1970. Even though I didn't have contact with them—something I regret now—I was concerned about them. On more than one occasion I tossed and turned thinking about what they might still be going through, trying to figure out if I'd trained them well enough to survive.

During that thirty-day home leave, I got together with a bunch of kids I had gone to school with. It was a Saturday night and we were talking about going to the movies. I remember them debating what we were going to see like it was so important. I said, "C'mon, guys, be realistic. This is Granbury, Texas. It's summer. We've got one drive-in with one screen. We can either watch the early picture, or wait and go to the late movie. Unless we drive to Fort Worth, that's the choice."

The truth was, I couldn't even believe I was in the middle of this discussion, and I told them so. "It's just not important, y'know? It doesn't mean anything; it just doesn't mean anything." Clearly they didn't get it. Or possibly I was the one who didn't get it.

I was thinking, *We're going to a movie, or we're not. We're going on a date with a girl, or we're not. She's going to give it up or she's not. C'mon, folks; nobody's dying over this. It doesn't make any difference. If you don't go tonight, you go tomorrow night. If she doesn't give it up tonight, she'll give it up tomorrow night. Or maybe she won't give it up at all. Who cares?* I just knew that nothing that mattered to my friends made any difference to me anymore. Coming home after surviving Vietnam didn't make me a hero; it made me a stranger, and no one I knew was prepared to deal with me on those terms.

My brother-in-law Denver nearly paid the ultimate price for not paying attention to my little mental souvenirs of the war. While I was home on leave he kept insisting that I go out hunting with him. When I was growing up, and especially while I was in high school, we'd gone hunting together quite a bit. Deer, rabbits, varmints—everything that kids growing up in rural or small-town Texas got their marksmanship training on. But Denver didn't sense the change that had taken place in me during my time in Vietnam, and he kept giving me these verbal pokes in the shoulder, the way brothers can do to each other, to get me to relive the good old days.

Finally I relented, and we took our .22 rifles—mine was a semiautomatic—and drove out of town, parked the car along the road, and began hiking in the brush looking for rabbits or squirrels. I'd warned him several times during the drive out of town, and again when we began walking, that he couldn't fire a shot without first letting me know that he was going to shoot. I don't know whether he thought I was kidding, whether he thought he'd have some fun with me, or whether he just plain forgot when he flushed the rabbit or bird or whatever out of the underbrush. Fortunately for him, he was only about thirty feet away from me, because he didn't bother shouting before he shouldered the rifle and fired, and I didn't bother shouting before I dropped to the ground and pumped out several shots in his general direction before I got a grip on myself and stopped squeezing the trigger. He started yelling, skipping and jumping, and even cursing a little bit. He looked like he wanted to cry but he sort of laughed instead. His only comment was "Damn, son, let's go home. I've had enough hunting for one day."

I slowly got up and just looked at him, realizing, more so than he, how close I had come to killing him. That was also the last time I ever went hunting.

We didn't talk about the incident when we returned home; in fact, we never discussed it then or at any of the family gatherings in years to come. The way I felt or reacted was something I could never have explained to my family. I just knew it would be futile to try. Maybe that was one of the reasons I would opt to stay in the army. In the service I knew there were a lot of guys just like me, guys who had done things in Vietnam that they couldn't—or wouldn't—tell anybody about at home. If we had so much to be proud about, why were we afraid to talk about our feelings? Why were we carrying all this guilt?

A month after I got back to Granbury, I packed my bags and reported to Fort Hood, sixty miles north of Austin, Texas, and a three-hour drive from home. I signed in at the replacement company, turned in my records, did the usual in-processing, and spent the next two or three days making sure that lawns were mowed to regulation height and that the grounds, as well as areas under the old WWII-vintage barracks, were free of offending cigarette butts.

Most of the guys coming through were just back from Vietnam, and since we were assigned to the replacement depot and couldn't wander off, we tended to sort ourselves out based on what we'd done in the war—the grunts hung around over here, the cannon cockers over there. So we'd sit on the steps outside these old WWII barracks and smoke and talk, or we'd wander off to the dayroom and shoot pool. Right across the street from the reception center was a little snack bar, which, of course, was off-limits to us for reasons that must have made sense to someone who had nothing better to do than think up ways to annoy people, but that didn't stop us from sneaking over there every so often to buy some of the 3.2 beer they sold.

After a couple of days of this Mickey Mouse, I was assigned as a recovery specialist in E Company, 123rd Maintenance Battalion of the First Armored Division. I got settled into life at a stateside army post, and got married.

Her name was Alinda Francis. I'd gone to high school with her, and we'd been on a couple of dates before I went to Vietnam, but it was nothing serious. When I returned to Granbury I began seeing her again. She was seventeen and I was twenty, and I guess we were in love. She had already left school when we got married, and we moved into a three-bedroom house off post that cost me $90 a month—furnished.

Shortly after that I reenlisted, but it wasn't because I liked the food. What I actually enjoyed was the regimentation. There were very few decisions that I had to make. They told me what to wear, what to eat, where to be, and how to get there, and even though I'd had some horrible experiences in Vietnam, I still thought the army was a great place for this kid from Granbury.

Okay, so the reenlistment bonus helped. What they'd come up with was a variable reenlistment bonus based on how critical your MOS (military occupational specialty) was. I had a reasonably high variable, so when I signed up for six years, I got about ten thousand dollars. That's in 1970 dollars. We bought a new car, a mobile home; we thought we had money to throw in the wind. Of course, we were also pregnant with twins, but we didn't know that until the first one was born and the doctor surprised us. The boys were born just ten months after we got married.

My first few months back in the world were a whirlwind. I returned from Vietnam in April of '70 and reenlisted less than ninety days later, in June, right around the time I got married. Then came a real kick in the head: A month later I came down on a levy to go back to Vietnam.

I'm not one to piss and moan about the unfairness of life, but if ever there was a time to see the chaplain and get my TS (tough shit) card punched, this was it. Instead, I took a shot with the divisional personnel center, where I whimpered and cried, "Oh, wait, guys, I've only been back ninety days. It's not my turn."

Fortunately, the captain I spoke with agreed. "Well, y'know, Mitchell, I guess you're right. It's probably not your turn. There are too many other guys here who haven't been."

Assuming my problem had been fixed, I said, "Good!" Should've remembered what my drill sergeant in basic taught us about "assuming makes an ass of U and me." In August I came down on the Vietnam levy again.

I went back and saw the same captain again. "Y'know, I'm only back a hundred and twenty days, and I'm married, she's pregnant, and, like I said, I've only been back a hundred and twenty days. Seems like we oughta share the wealth of these tours!"

He looked up. "She's pregnant?" He took care of me again.

In 1971 the 1st Armored Division was moved to Germany, and the 1st Cavalry Division was rotated back to the United States from Vietnam for the first time since the Korean conflict. So now, here I was back in the 1st Cavalry Division, but this time I wasn't an infantryman. The unit structure changed, and as part of that realignment I was assigned to B Company, 315th Composite Support Battalion (provisional), and I was still a recovery specialist. Things were actually going pretty well, when fourteen months after my last Vietnam scare, the phone rang again.

They called me and said, "You're on a levy. Go to the orderly room." I was thinking, "Oh, man, I've been back over a year. There's nothing that's going to keep them from shipping me back to the war." I was thinking about Alinda and imagining her trying to deal with the two babies by herself. I was thinking that it was only by the grace of God that I survived the first tour over there; the likelihood of making it through another tour when the North Vietnamese had a much stronger foothold in the country was not good. A lot of things go through your mind, including whether I could give up Budweiser in favor of Molson or Labatt's. I knew it wasn't just draft dodgers who'd gone to Canada; there'd been lots of newspaper stories about deserters being welcomed up there, and even in Sweden. Surprisingly, it turned out the levy wasn't for the war. They were sending me to Germany, which had the reputation of being really good duty for Americans in uniform.

Despite the positive things that had been happening in my life to this point, the demons remained with me, paying regular but unscheduled visits. I still had nightmares, still woke up with cold sweats that drenched the linens. There was no way to hide it from Alinda, because she could see and hear what was going on, but even though she asked questions, I was not inclined to give any kind of detailed answers. I'd just tell her not to touch me. At the risk of sounding like I'm putting words in her mouth, I think she was hoping that if she ignored it, it would go away. She probably thought, *He hasn't been back long; the war is still fresh in his mind.* Her dad was a World War II vet, a Seabee in the Pacific. I never knew whether he came home with any problems. Somehow, although I never asked Alinda, I have the feeling that she may have talked to her mother about it—but I don't really know.

Then there were the other PTSD symptoms I had—even though my condition had yet to be labeled. I had a startle response that was second to none, and when you consider all the armor and artillery units that were assigned, trained, and maneuvered at Fort Hood, I recall spending a lot of time trying to hide my jumpiness so no one would know. After all, I was a man, right? The Fourth of July was no treat for me, especially in Texas, where any fool could buy fireworks from a roadside stand. It took a while for the people I worked with to learn not to come from behind and touch me without first speaking to me. I needed to know they were there before I heard them. After a while I just told 'em flat out, "Don't do that, because it might not be a pleasant experience for you, and it's certainly not going to be a pleasant experience for me when it's over, because I'm going to be saying, 'Oh, shit, what have I done?'"

I wasn't like a lot of vets who got out of the army; the sound of helicopters didn't bother me that much. Fort Hood was home to a corps headquarters and two combat divisions, so there were choppers flying night and day. When we went to the field and they'd come in flying nap-of-the-earth, you could tell which aviators had been to Vietnam and which hadn't just by watching them fly. A low pass over my head did tend to get my attention, however.

One time Alinda and I had gone to a department store in Killeen, and she was trying on a dress while I wandered between the racks, looking for something I thought she might like. Everything was just fine until two women walked behind me and started conversing in Vietnamese. Talk about a chill down your spine. I didn't say anything, and I consciously had to keep myself from an overt physical reaction—like diving under the clothes racks. Because just like that—boom!—I was somewhere else. This happened at a time when I wasn't sleeping well, anyhow, and the sudden mental trip back to the war didn't help.

But then we were off to Erlangen, Germany, where I became a recovery NCO with 3/37th Armor of the 1st Armored Division, and in less than a year that assignment morphed into my becoming the assistant motor sergeant of the newly redesignated 3/37—it became the 2/81st Armor of the 1st Armored Division.

Three years after the twins, Doug and Don, were born, our youngest son, Kevin, came along. Having three young children at home was difficult, and the fact that I was given to mood swings and awful displays of temper didn't help my relationship with Alinda. The nightmares were still with me, and there were times I literally thought that my Vietnam demons were sitting on my shoulder, talking to me.

There were several that paid me regular visits: the woman whom I killed on my second sniper assignment; the four Buddhist monks on my third; my buddy Dave, who died after I waved off the medevac helicopter coming to get him; and my rigger, Bill, whose brain was splattered all over me when an enemy sniper picked him off the back of our M-88.

Bill's death was one of those dumb things that happen in war. Who knew a guy could die because he drank too much coffee? We were on the road to one of the fire bases to pull a gun back to Phu

Bai for repair, when Bill told me we needed to stop so he could take a leak. So at the top of the next rise, we stopped. He got down, took care of business, and climbed back up, taking the mechanic's position in the right front hatch.

Just as we started to move, a single shot range out, hitting Bill in the head, spraying gore everywhere. Frantically, we tried to locate the shooter, but my sniper experience taught me that if you only fire one shot, the odds of being spotted are slim.

I remember calling for a Dustoff to evacuate his body, and then reaching inside the track to find a towel so I could wipe myself off. Strange what you remember years later. When I got back to Phu Bai, I recall that I was almost hysterical trying to get the organic splatter that had been part of my buddy off of me. I couldn't get it done fast enough.

I was not given to a lot of daytime flashbacks. Most of the time I had nightmares. I knew some people who had only flashbacks, and some had both nightmares and flashbacks. In my case the little demons would share my pillow and whisper in my ear. I would wake up in a cold sweat, breathing very fast, and sometimes crying. It always seemed to take place within the first half hour of sleep. I would start tossing and turning, talking in my sleep. Your heart races, you break out into a sweat, your respiration rate is really high, like you have just run three or four races back-to-back without a rest period. You are confused about where you are and what you are doing. It takes a few minutes for you to settle down enough to cry.

Alinda and I made it through another year in Germany, but it was clear to her that our future together was destined to be rocky. She was unhappy living with a person who was obviously miserable. After a period of time she took the kids and left Germany. It was a real blow to my pride, an "I can't hold on to my woman" kind of thing.

Just before Christmas 1974, my dad was hospitalized and I was given emergency leave to go home, and then four months later, when Dad died, I got a compassionate reassignment back to Fort Hood as a recovery NCO with the 1/7th Armored Cavalry of the 1st Cav. Somehow Alinda and I got back together. A year and a half later we found ourselves living in air force housing at Vance Air Force Base when I was assigned to a two-man recruiting station in Enid, Oklahoma.

It marked the beginning of the end of our marriage. I'd begun drinking heavily, and I was still unable to control my temper. I believe the appropriate description of me at the time was "flaming asshole." You know the kind. If assholes were jets, I would have outrun the shuttle.

In June 1978, I was reassigned as motor sergeant of C Battery, 1/333rd Field Artillery, a Lance missile outfit, stationed in Wiesbaden, Germany. It was supposed to be a two-year tour, and we'd decided that Alinda and the boys would remain in the United States. I hadn't been there two months when I got a long brown envelope.

Getting served with divorce papers was devastating, but looking back, I'm not sure if it was because I was in love with her, or because it was an affront to my male ego. I was hurt and angry at the same time. The impact on me was something that I would not wish on my worst enemy. In addition to the PTSD, now I had a "failure as a man" kind of thing going on. The loss of my sons, who were eight and five years old, was devastating, but I really didn't go out of my way to avoid terminal damage to my relationship with the three boys.

I stayed in Germany another three and a half years, seeing the boys only once or twice each year. I don't know which is the chicken and which is the egg here, but they felt I had deserted them and we grew apart.

I now have a relationship with one son, and would like to reestablish a relationship with the other two, but to this point—and it's probably my fault—that has not happened.

CHAPTER FIFTEEN

I Can't Dance; Don't Ask Me

I was truly shitfaced.

It was a Friday evening in June 1980, and my unit at Camp Pieri near the big air force base at Wiesbaden, Germany, had just come through an IG inspection with a rating of 97 percent. We had our outbrief in midafternoon, and by three thirty we all headed to the club for country night. By eight o'clock I was feeling no pain. In fact, I wasn't feeling much of anything when a friend of mine, also a Vietnam vet, named Michael Shively came over and said, "C'mon over; I've got this girl I want you to meet."

I said, "Okay, but let me finish my drink first." I was drinking pretty heavily then, but I don't think it was because of the marriage breakup. I'd been self-medicating before my marriage to Alinda fell apart, and it had continued. I'd figured out that after a night of binge drinking, when I went to sleep I didn't have the dreams—or at least I didn't wake up and remember them. While it wasn't a long-term solution to the problem, it worked for a while.

When Shively invited me to meet this girl, I was already half in the bag. Or maybe farther. I guess I finished the drink; I don't know. I don't remember. But I went across the club to where Shively was sitting and he introduced me to Ellen, who had the biggest blue eyes

I'd ever seen in my life. She had a big smile and was wearing a green blouse and green pants with heels.

Ellen remembers the event that ultimately led to our marriage in a bit more detail. "I saw a fairly drunk, very happy, pretty good-looking guy about my age come staggering over to meet me. He was, y'know, kind of 'real glad to meetcha' kind of thing. He had a real nice Texas accent, and it was clear that he was trying to really maintain. He could still walk, but even that was getting a little iffy."

She's telling the truth—sort of. The fact is that I was just struck dumb by her. I sat down at the table and looked at her. I'm not sure how long it took me to speak, but the first thing I said was "I'm sorry, what was your name again?"

Actually, I must have asked for her name at least five times. Based on my performance at the club that night, I'm surprised that she wanted to see me again. But Ellen says there was just something about me that hooked her. "He was sweet and kind and polite. If I went to stand up, even as inebriated as he was, he'd stand up, clumsily, and pull my chair out for me. Guys just don't do that that often. He just made me feel good."

The other thing that was going on is that my buddy Shively had set me up by telling Ellen that I really like to dance. Truth? I can't dance; don't ask me. But when I came back from the bathroom and once more said, "I'm sorry. What was your name again?" she told me, but added, "I hear you really love to dance."

Even if sober, I would have been just as confused. "You did? I do?"

"Yeah," she said, "that's what Mike tells me. So do you want to dance?"

I did what any red-blooded American male would do under these circumstances. I said, "Uh, sure. But it has to be a slow one."

When the band started playing "Blue Eyes Cryin' in the Rain," Willie Nelson's number one hit and Grammy winner from a few years earlier, we got up, and it was like we had been dancing together all of our lives, her head on my shoulder, my arms holding her close, and the lyrics of a sad song about lost love.

If I hadn't known better, I'd swear it was a setup. Here I am, drunk out of my mind, but on the dance floor holding on to a woman with blue eyes to rival Bo Derek's, and I still couldn't remember her name. I don't even remember leaving the club. I woke up the next morning, opened my eyes and looked around, and thought, *This is not my room.* I raised my head up, looked around some more, and realized that I was in somebody's government quarters, and I said, "My God, what have I done?" followed immediately by "More important, who have I done it with?"

It turned out I was sleeping on a couch covered by a sheet. I lifted it up, took a look, and figured that I must have been good, because I still had my clothes on. My car keys were on the coffee table and my shoes were sitting there. Amazingly, awake now, I did remember Ellen's name. I got up, crept over to the window, and looked out. My car was sitting there. Okay, that was a good sign. So I slipped on my shoes, opened the door, and left. To this day I cannot tell you whose quarters I was in, how I got there, what I did, if anything, after I got there, or who it might have been with. I went back to my own room and went to sleep. The odd thing is, no one ever mentioned it, which was totally out of character for my friends, who must have known.

Once I recovered from the evening's excesses, I began questioning Shively about Ellen. He didn't know all that much. She was a private, just arrived in Germany from Lance missile training school at Fort Sill, Oklahoma. She'd gotten married when she was nineteen, separated five years later, and finally divorced at twenty-seven, just before she enlisted.

I wanted to see her again, but thought I may have killed that possibility with my liquor-induced behavior at the club. Since I had no recollection of our parting that night, I didn't know whether she'd left the possibility open for a second encounter. But I decided to take a shot. A group of us were going to Luxembourg for the Fourth of July, and I asked her to go with us.

Sometimes I think a good case could be made that men and women are actually representatives of different species. I thought that by inviting her on the trip, I was including her in what should be a fun outing. She didn't quite see it that way.

"I wasn't impressed at all. I mean, really—one girl, Gary, and a bunch of other guys? I told him, 'No, thank you very much.' And I didn't speak to him again for about three weeks. Then he asked me out again."

I tried to have a simple date with her at the Eagle's Nest, the little club on post. But she lived in a coed barracks, and one of the guys decided she needed his company wherever she went, including on what I had hoped would be our first date. For whatever reason, Ellen couldn't keep him from coming along. It wasn't a good sign. There we were, the three of us together. Not quite what I'd hoped for. I knew I had to do something, or Miss Blue Eyes and I would have no future worth speaking of.

At long last, the third wheel got up to go to the bathroom, and I leaned over and said, "Y'know, if you can get rid of your bodyguard, why don't we do this again tomorrow night?" She agreed, and the next night Ellen literally had to sneak out of the barracks. We went to the same club and just sat there and talked about all sorts of things.

She says, "I learned that he was a Vietnam veteran and was waiting to be promoted to E-7, sergeant first class. I found out our ages were really close—he was thirty and I was twenty-seven. It made him a little nervous that I was an E-nothing, and he was soon to be promoted to E-7, which would make him a senior NCO. Talk about the appearance of fraternization. The good thing was that he was the motor pool sergeant and not in my Lance missile battery. I learned that he was the youngest of fourteen children, and was a Texas boy through and through—grits, greens, and fried green tomatoes, while I was from Southern California."

It was fairly obvious that I was attracted to her, and I was quite nervous about dealing with some of the heavy stuff in my life. I'd been divorced for two years and had three kids whom I didn't have much contact with. I had no idea how she'd deal with that. But she said it wasn't a problem; she was also divorced. Truth is, it took a while before I was comfortable enough to share the details of why my marriage had fallen apart, and by the time I did, we were engaged.

Actually, I proposed to Ellen on the second date we had without the bodyguard. I walked her back to her barracks and said, "Let's just sit here on the steps." We were about halfway down the stairway to the arms room, just sitting there and talking, when I proposed to her. Actually, I think I made a statement that we were going to get married rather than asking her. It was probably a bigger shock to me than it was to her. I'd told my mother after the divorce that I'd never get married again, and she'd said to me, "Now, son, one of these days a woman's going to come along and sweep you right off your feet, and you will get married again."

I remember saying to her, "She'd better have a damned big broom."

And that was what I said to Ellen—that she had a damned big broom. I wanted her to say yes, but had no idea what her response would be. She thought for a moment, and then said, "I'm flattered. But I don't think I'm going to say yes or no at this point. Let's give it a year and we'll see how things work out."

It wasn't a week later that Ellen got to see a sample of what I'd been living with since I came back from Vietnam. She was spending the night in my room and witnessed me having nightmares firsthand.

Ellen describes it like this. "Gary would wake up every night, three and four times a night, screaming. He'd wake me up, first calling out call signs, and then telling somebody to be careful. And then he started yelling, 'You gotta move! You gotta move now!' It was just awful.

"And then he would wake up; it would be like a springboard action. He'd spring forward and be stiff as a board in a cold sweat.

I couldn't bend an arm or anything. The sweat would pour off of him, and he didn't know where he was. In his mind he'd woken up in Vietnam, so I had to be real careful around him. He never hit me, but I knew that was a possibility.

"I would start talking to him immediately, telling him, 'Honey, it's okay, you're here, you're not in Vietnam. I'm sitting right here beside you,' and I'd take his hand and start to rub it a little bit. And his breathing would go from being labored to shallow and panting. It was terrible. It would take a good five minutes for him to come back around."

Ellen asked me what I was dreaming, but there was no way I could tell her. There was no way she could understand. So all I'd say was "I can't tell you that. It's awful and I can't tell you."

At the same time she was seeing me have the nightmares, Ellen was also getting the sense that I had a drinking problem. I had my own stool at the club. If I came in and somebody else was sitting there, the bartender would make him move. And by the time I got from the door to the bar, my first drink would be sitting there waiting for me. Coupled with the drinking, I also had anger-management issues. Anything could trigger a tirade; it didn't matter whether it was a family issue at home or a job-related situation on the base. When you add up the nightmares, the drinking, and the anger problems, it should have been clear that something wasn't quite right with me and I needed help. But this was 1980. The army wasn't all that supportive of troops with emotional or mental issues, so walking into the docs and asking for help would not have been a good career move.

Even for Vietnam vets who were no longer in the service, getting help with post-traumatic stress disorder was problematic. The first vet center (more formally, the Veterans Readjustment Counseling Center) wasn't established until late in 1979 after a full ten years of political debate about the need for the services they would provide. And when Public Law 96-22 was finally passed, it still didn't deal with the situation realistically. The VA opened ninety-one centers nationwide in 1980, but the law that funded them mandated one year of buildup, one year of operation, and one year of wind-down. The assumption was that the need for services would be met in those three years. What it said to vets was that the government really didn't take our condition seriously, because there's no other explanation for such a wham-bam-thank-you-ma'am approach to mental health care. And if you want to put this all in the context of the times, the nation's first acknowledgment that Vietnam veterans deserved national recognition, the dedication of the Vietnam Memorial on the Mall in Washington, didn't take place until 1982.

Anyway, there I was in Germany, a package of raw nerve endings wrapped up in an army uniform, trying to be loving and lovable while drunk, angry, and, at times, terrified. I knew that my problems had already cost me one marriage, and the loss of the marriage eventually cost me a relationship with my three sons. The problems were exacerbated by the fact that I was halfway around the world, and seldom got to see them. Now that I'd found someone who thought that I was, if not wonderful, at least redeemable, I feared losing her if she found out the source of my problems. So every time Ellen asked me about my nightmares, I declined to tell her.

About the sixth or seventh time it happened and I refused to answer her questions, she'd had enough. She asked me directly, "What were you dreaming?"

I said, "I can't tell you that. It's awful, and I just can't tell you."

"Nope," she said to me, "that's not going to work anymore. Obviously there's something really wrong here. Have you ever talked to anyone about your experiences in Vietnam?"

I said, "No."

And she said, "Well, you're going to tonight, and we're going to start right now, and I don't care how long it takes. I don't care what you tell me. I just want you to start from the beginning and go to the end and just tell me."

So the two of us sat there on my little single bed in the small barracks room, and I told her about Vietnam. What she didn't know
was that I didn't tell her all of it. There was no way I felt she was prepared to hear some of the things I'd done.

Ellen remembers the night precisely. "He starts telling me different
stories from Vietnam, and some of them were horrendous. Some of
them were funny—but most were horrendous. And as I learned years
later, he wasn't telling me the sniper stories. He was holding back.

"I think Gary saw a chance to be able to tell somebody something,
but he was so convinced that if anybody knew what he had done in
the military, he'd be a pariah. But he did tell me about his best friend
being hit—that was Dave. And about another buddy being hit and
his brain matter splattering all over him. That was one of the most
horrific experiences that he had."

That conversation went on for more than three hours. We talked,
and I cried, and we talked some more, and I cried some more. She
never interrupted, never asked for clarification. She just let me talk.
But I was holding back on the stuff that I thought would make her
hate me and cause her to leave, and it hurt because I couldn't let her
know that there was more to tell. Even so, over the course of time I
felt different. The nightmares didn't stop immediately, but their frequency diminished. Instead of five and six a night, I'd have maybe
three a night, and then two, and then one, until it got down to one a
week. That was a huge improvement.

Three months later things seemed to be working out between us,
and she said, "Okay, we can consider ourselves engaged. I accept
your proposal." We went right down to the PX at Wiesbaden and
picked out an engagement ring together.

When word got around, I got called into my commander's office
and received a lecture about fraternization. I'd been promoted to E-7
and Ellen was still a private. Technically we weren't violating any
regs, because I wasn't her supervisor. But my CO advised me to not
make things look so obvious on post—not to go around kissing and

holding hands. Camp Pieri was small—very small. So we had to be more than a little circumspect.

In the meantime, of course, Ellen was getting the word on me from my so-called friends. The highlight, or maybe lowlight, was their description of me jumping from windows when husbands were coming home. It's just the sort of thing you want your fiancée to hear.

It was about three months after we got engaged that we revisited my Vietnam experiences. I'd sewn on my E-7 stripes and moved into the place they called Amelia Earhart, a military hotel that had three floors dedicated as the senior NCO billeting facility. I was transferred to a combat aviation helicopter unit at Lindsey Air Station, and the sergeant major from that outfit was retiring. The timing was bad for me to go to a party and get loaded, because Ellen was going through a cancer scare. She'd had a bad Pap smear, and the doctors were talking about uterine cancer. She got the results—thankfully negative—the day of the party.

Instead of being with her waiting for the results, I went to the retirement dinner and came back late at night, commode hugging, nonwalking drunk, without even remembering that she was supposed to get the results of the tests that day. When I walked into the room after having vomited all over myself, I found a very angry woman waiting for me. Realizing that I was in no condition to discuss my shortcomings as a concerned fiancé, she told me to sleep it off, and left.

When Ellen returned to confront me, she was still very angry, but she saw that I was distraught. Ellen recalls having read: "A lot of people go to war and do what they have to do, and they're able to compartmentalize everything. 'This was war, so therefore it was okay, and it doesn't need to interfere when you return to a normal life.' But it turns out that like many people, Gary wasn't able to do that. In his case, I think it was his religious upbringing: It's a sin to kill, period. And there's no compartmentalization there. You're doing it because you're told to do it, and you're in the army, so it has to happen. But there's nowhere to put it to make it okay. It just floats around and bings around in their brain, somewhat like a Ping-Pong ball with no real place to settle, and it does horrible things.

"One of the things Gary would do when he was very angry at himself—he didn't even know why he'd do some of these things—he would hit himself, hard, in the face, in the chest, on the arms, on the legs, in the stomach, with a clenched fist.

"When I confronted him with his behavior—coming back drunk as he was, and not being there for me on a very scary day—this was his way of dealing with it. Punching himself everywhere he could. And that was scary. But I just knew that a lot of this had to be tied somehow to Vietnam. Nobody had ever mentioned PTSD; that was not anything that was even discussed. But his bizarre behavior just seemed to pop out in heavily stress-laden circumstances. There was nothing normal about it, and he knew it.

"So once he got through that particular episode, I said to him, 'Okay, there have to be other things that you didn't tell me. Let's do it now. Just sit down and start telling me.'"

Without saying it, Ellen was offering me a choice between calling off the engagement or spilling my guts about Vietnam. Not much of a choice when I'd already lost one wife and my kids over it. I didn't know how to explain to her that I was so angry that I had to hit something—and I didn't want it to be her. So I hit myself, sometimes until there were some very ugly bruises.

So while I wasn't ready to tell her everything, I had to share some of what I'd done in Vietnam. I told her that I'd been in country for a short time when they sent me to a sniper training school and taught me how to shoot under every condition imaginable. Then I told her that I went back to my unit, and from there I was sent on quite a few sniper missions where I killed people. I never got specific, but made it clear that killing unsuspecting people on assignment is different from killing in combat, where it's kill or be killed.

I remember Ellen sitting there and listening, and not acting as though what I'd told her was shocking. Years later she let me know that she had been shocked, but she said, "It wasn't like you'd done something horrible. You had no choice. You couldn't go to your company commander and say, 'Excuse me, I don't think so.'"

Ellen would go through a conversation like that with me, telling me that I did what I was told and that was my only course of action at the time, and I'd sit there nodding my head in agreement. If it made her feel better to think she was making me feel better by saying that stuff, what the hell? I had to keep in mind where she was coming from. She was relatively new to the army and was still showing the effects of the indoctrination a recruit receives in basic and advanced training. She also didn't have any rank on her sleeve that would allow her to attempt to even negotiate what she felt was a bad order. As for me, I knew that had I been an E-7 in Vietnam instead of an E-4 when I got assignments that were problematic, I might have had some tools to better deal with the situation.

Ellen was right when she said that back in Vietnam, the thought that I could say no didn't cross my mind. I never thought I had a freakin' choice to turn down any order I received there. The people giving the orders weren't concerned with my future mental health or how the assignments they were giving me were colliding head-on with my moral compass. Hell, I'm certain that some of those people, especially the anonymous ones who handed out orders from an unmarked armored personnel carrier, really weren't concerned with my future at all—or whether I had one beyond the next few hours.

We were trained to follow orders immediately, without question, because actions or lack of actions could have cost someone his life, or at the very least, been responsible for setting him up for a life of agony.

On November 6, 1981, Ellen and I got married in Mission Hills, California, a suburb in the San Fernando Valley. We'd flown from Germany to Texas to see my family, then on to California for the wedding. My mom and my one surviving brother, Howard, attended. Out of my thirteen brothers and sisters, I had only the one brother and two sisters left at that point, and there's only one sister still with us now.

We had three days for a honeymoon, and spent it at Universal Studios in Hollywood. Then we boarded a Lufthansa flight back to Germany, where we had secured government housing, quarters that were provided for married soldiers and their families. At this point in our lives—even though both of us had been down the aisle before—we were like newlyweds. Hell, we were newlyweds, filled with nothing but optimism and hope for an endless future together. Neither one of us sensed there was a time bomb ticking that could doom our relationship.

CHAPTER SIXTEEN

Another War

In January 1983 I was reassigned to Fort Sill, Oklahoma, where I eventually became the S 2/3 Operations NCO with the 100th Service and Supply Battalion. In 1984, Ellen got out of the army.

About four years after I made sergeant first class (E-7), I took the opportunity to apply for warrant officer school. I'd been in the service for seventeen years, and making the change was not done casually. Ellen and I looked at the positives and negatives, and decided that the significantly larger retirement benefits would make it worthwhile for me to apply.

After I'd been a senior NCO, warrant officer school at Aberdeen Proving Ground, Maryland, was a shock. Perhaps as much of a shock as someone going from being a civilian into basic training as a private E-nothing. But I persevered, went through six months of grief and aggravation, and graduated as "Mr. Mitchell."

The training had been intense and time-consuming—imagine basic training that lasts half a year instead of a couple of months. I did have some of my Vietnam nightmares during this period, which were exacerbated by the fact that we were living in the old WWII-style open-bay barracks.

Once we were newly minted as a warrant officer, the army sent us back to Germany. This time it was Bamberg, where I held down a variety of assignments with the 504th Maintenance Company of the 87th Maintenance Battalion. Four years later it was back to Aberdeen, where I joined the Wheeled Vehicle Department at the U.S. Army Ordnance Center, becoming a branch chief, instructor-writer, and an instructor in the Officer Basic Course. I was in charge of basic knowledge and skills (BKS)—the basics for new mechanics: This is a screwdriver; this is electricity; these are gears and their flow of power.

Life was good and we were happy, which probably is what ensured the likelihood that the army would find something different for me to do. I was sitting at Aberdeen, minding my own business, with twenty-nine instructors working for me. I had a wife, on-post housing, a new car and a new truck, a TV with cable. Oh, Lord, I had forty channels on TV, and someone said, "The boss wants to see you."

I went down and reported to the major, and she said, "I got a deal for you." I knew I was in trouble.

"What kind of deal?"

She said, "You know this thing they're calling Desert Shield? Well, you're going to be part of it."

I tried to tell her that I'd already had my turn in a war, so someone else could go, but she wasn't having any of it. So I went, but I flew over there with a feeling of dread. I had made this flight before, and was not the happiest GI on the airplane among the eleven of us who were on our way to join the American advisory group based near Riyadh. From the time I had come home from Vietnam, I'd managed to keep my commanders from being aware that I had any problems related to my service in a combat zone. I had no way of knowing how being in the line of fire once more might affect me—and there was no way I could discuss that concern with anyone.

The Iraqis had invaded Kuwait on August 2, 1990. On the fifth of September, I was in Saudi Arabia as part of OPM-SANG—acronymese for Office of the Program Manager, Saudi Arabian National Guard Modernization Program. I was one of what would become about 150

Americans officially based in the U.S. military compound in Riyadh, but farmed out to appropriate SANG units in the desert in an effort to improve their war-fighting ability.

My specialty was maintenance, and I was assigned to the maintenance company, part of the Logistics Support Battalion, King Abdul Azziz Brigade (2nd Brigade). The unit was bivouacked just outside the city of Al Khafji, which is on the Persian Gulf just a couple of miles south of the Kuwaiti–Saudi Arabian border. I shared a tent with three U.S. Army captains: two combat engineers, Everett Mc-Daniel and Steve Zeltner; and a quartermaster, Keith Nelson.

From the day I arrived, I knew that it was inevitable that I was once again going to be involved in a shooting war. The only question was when. Actually, that wasn't the only question. Sitting in the tent at night, drinking pot after pot of coffee with our tentmates, we pondered questions like "What happens to us Americans when the war starts? What if we're taken prisoner by the Iraqis? Are we expected to stay with our SANG unit no matter what happens?" Frankly, we were overwhelmed by their lack of fighting ability, but we worked to try to improve it on a daily basis, although at times it seemed as if they resisted our attempts to provide training similar to what American army units do.

The average training day went something like this. We would get up between five and six, drink a pot of coffee, and then make tapes or write home. Around seven thirty I would make contact with the commander of the maintenance company. He and I spent time nearly every day discussing such things as forward support, unit defense, deployment, and maintenance on the move.

His troops would be having breakfast about that time and would have already prayed earlier in the morning—they would get up in the predawn hours to pray, and then go back to sleep. Around eight they would be in their work area and remain there until a little after noon, when they would pray again, and then rest during the intense heat of the day. In midafternoon they would go back to work, and then close down around five or five thirty. A few of the Saudi guards-men were willing, and in fact wanted, to learn how the "American" would do it, and would not rest in the afternoon.

All of us taught classes. Because I'm a maintenance guy, my over-riding concern was to train the Saudi maintenance people to keep their equipment functioning in the midst of battle. The general heading was "battlefield damage assessment and repair," but it's a lot more creative than the manual might make it sound. I actually taught them how to use black pepper in a leaking radiator, how a uniform belt can replace a broken fan belt, and how to drive on a flat tire. We dealt with combat recovery, which meant towing a vehicle out of an ongoing firefight in order to repair it and get it back into service, and taught them how to check a vehicle for booby traps if it had been deserted for a short period of time where the enemy might have had access to it. There's an exact science to performing this task, but our mandate was to teach them what to do while the battle was still raging, so what we showed them to do with the potentially booby-trapped vehicle was to hook a cable to it and jerk it with the towing vehicle. If it exploded, it was booby-trapped. If it didn't, it wasn't. Hey, I never said it was rocket science, but unless someone teaches you these little field expedients, how would you know? We also taught defense against chemical weapons, and testing to deter-mine whether you were under chemical attack. Those were critically important topics because no one knew whether or not the Iraqis would use chemical agents.

Generally, the Saudis we were training had an aversion to live fire exercises, which wasn't surprising when you learn that each soldier was expected to account for every bullet he fired, bringing the brass back to a collection point. We looked upon it as rather lackluster preparation for battle. We also had some questions as to whether sol-diers and officers in the SANG unit would stay and fight, especially if the Iraqi army carried out the threats that Saddam Hussein had made and fired missiles into Israel. Such an act would confuse the situation exponentially, because Israel was the enemy of all the Arab nations. If Saddam attacked Israel—even while his forces were occupying Kuwait—and Israel fired back, the Saudis' natural response would be to ally with Iraq and start shooting at the Israelis. You can see the problem: On one front the Saudis could be fighting side by side with Iraq against the Jewish state, and on another front they could be going toe-to-toe with Saddam's forces.

Given that potential for battlefield confusion, we were more than a little concerned that the day would probably come when our lives were going to be on the line, and we weren't even supposed to have "offensive" weapons with which to fight. Each of us had a sidearm, which wouldn't do much good in an infantry or tank battle in the desert. Actually, the sidearm did have one function that we avoided discussing: We knew that if worse came to worst, we each had one 9mm bullet that we'd saved for ourselves. Being captured by the Iraqis, infamous for their death squads and treatment of prisoners, was not an option for me.

After a day of working with our assigned units, the four of us would meet back at our tent to compare notes on our work and our lives. We did all kinds of things that you normally do in your home. We talked about our families, we played cards and dominoes, we laughed and joked, we listened to the radio station that was owned and operated by ARAMCO, formerly the Arabian American Oil Company, and, of course, we argued, though the disagreements were few and far between. In effect, we became a close-knit family. In our own way we became as close as flesh-and-blood brothers are, and any one of us would have done anything we could for another.

All four of us had become members of the "I shit my pants in the field" club, resulting from severe cases of diarrhea. We even joked about the fact that all of us had donated a pair of "dirty" underwear to our shrine, the field latrine. Our intestinal problems could probably be blamed on CNN. No, this is not another knock on the media by a military guy. Actually, just the opposite. We didn't have a television set in our tent, so each evening we would go next door to the maintenance company commander's tent and watch CNN while drinking tea. In the pre–Al Jazeera era, the Arabs really enjoyed America's Cable News Network, especially when honey-haired, blue-eyed Bobbie Batista was in the anchor chair.

Every time we were there, the commander, Captain Ahmed, tried to convince us to stay and eat. Dinner was served Arab-style, which means sans utensils. Aside from the fact that freshly killed goat is not my favorite meal, eating goat or lamb, or occasionally a chicken, solely with my right hand might satisfy the Arabian Miss Manners, but it doesn't do much for me. Consider the technique: Using just your right hand, you strip meat from the carcass that's sitting on a big tray in the center of the table, and eat it. If the piece is too big to swallow in one bite, you have to hold the rest of it in your hand until you finish it. There's no individual plate in front of you where you can set it down. Also on the communal tray are rice and sliced vegetables like cucumber and tomato, all of which must be picked up by hand and shoved into your mouth. And everyone is picking and shoving from the same tray.

Imagine going to Sizzler and watching people help themselves at the salad bar with their hands—no tongs, no forks, no spoons. Just reaching in, grabbing a handful, shoving it into their mouths, and then reaching back in for more. Get the picture? And you thought double-dipping into the chip dip was ugly. Our American digestive systems staged a minirevolt, and more than once we came to the conclusion that a pork MRE was just what the doctor ordered.

While food was a major quality-of-life item and we'd do what we could to see that we ate what we liked as often as possible, frequently going into town to shop at local markets, there were other things we did to make life in a difficult environment more livable. Consider bathing. To do so regularly required that we avail ourselves of—how shall I put this?—unorthodox supply channels.

If there's one thing army veterans are good at, it's scrounging.

I was shocked recently to learn that some soldiers—officers and enlisted—had been court-martialed for scrounging abandoned army vehicles in Kuwait, to better equip their own vehicles when they finally drove into Iraq to participate in the occupation. Stealing government property? You've got to be kidding me. If it's sitting there, and no one is using it, and no one is claiming it, and no one is guarding it, then if my guys need it, we take it. If scrounging is a crime, they'd better build a lot more barracks at Leavenworth, because the entire senior NCO corps in the army, air force, navy, and marines are guilty as charged. Actually, in my humble opinion, it isn't stealing; it's just redistributing government property, and I don't believe any number of courts-martial will change that fact. But I digress.

While we were waiting for the first Gulf War to begin, we decided that what was missing from our daily lives was a hot shower. So we took my pickup truck and visited a U.S. unit that was set up south of us and liberated a field shower. We returned to our area, set it up, and borrowed a large propane burner—actually, a goat cooker—from the Arabs. Then we negotiated a deal with the Arab commander: In return for the privilege of using the shower, he ensured us that his water truck would always keep the tank filled, and that we had at least one extra propane cylinder on hand to heat the water.

January 15, 1991, dawned bright and cool in the kingdom of Saudi Arabia. We all knew that this was the final date that the United Nations resolution had set for the withdrawal from Kuwait by the Iraqi forces. But from our position in the desert outside Al Khafji, there didn't appear to be anything or anyone moving.

Our U.S. adviser element kept a few hotel rooms reserved in Al Khafji so that we could make calls, take a shower, or just "get away from it all" for a short period of time.

The rooms were not fancy, and the decor was so loud that you couldn't have slept in the room. If memory serves me correctly, the bedspreads were white with bright—and I do mean bright—blue stripes. The blue was so bright that it would almost blind you.

The walls were yellow, and hanging on them was the standard hotel-type artwork. The great thing about the rooms was the Western toilet, not just a hole in the floor with a water hose. Everyone did his best to make it into Khafji at least once a week to "crap on porcelain." This is life in a combat unit; we take our pleasures when and where we can.

We received a radio call from the senior American logistics adviser, who reminded us of the date and advised us, "If you can possibly make it into Khafji, you might want to go take a real shower." It sounded as though it might be our last opportunity to experience civilization for quite some time, so we immediately rearranged our schedules in order to scramble into town.

When we got into Khafji, it was apparent that everyone was acutely aware of the date. You could almost taste the tension in the air as we drove through the city. The residents were watching us very closely to see what we were doing or what we were going to do. We had been into Al Khafji enough times since the fall of 1990 that everyone in town recognized our vehicles and knew that we were Americans, living and working in the desert not far out of their town.

As a matter of practice, when we went into town, the little group of logistics advisers whom I was with would stop at a market and pick up some fresh vegetables and, at times, some chicken or beef to use in the preparation of our meal that evening. If you purchased chicken, you picked a live one, and the store employees slaughtered and plucked it for you while you waited. Beef, on the other hand, was frozen and usually imported from Argentina.

On this day we didn't get any meat, just vegetables, because we had decided to eat in the hotel restaurant while we were there; the meal was to be one last treat for ourselves. Saudis owned the stores, but the employees were third-country nationals, normally Filipinos.

I developed a great respect for the Filipinos. They didn't make more than about a hundred dollars a month, but they could speak Arabic as well as English. The English they spoke was not always formal English, but we could communicate with very little difficulty, and they kept the stores pretty well stocked. When we stopped on that day, we couldn't move around the store without being followed very closely by the Filipinos and the Arabs who were there.

The Filipinos liked us because we always treated them with the respect due anyone. Usually the Arabs ignored us because we were foreigners and nonbelievers. But this day was quite different. They weren't really sure what to expect from us. They had children and families whom they were justifiably concerned about. All of them were asking us when the war was going to start. They wanted to know, since Khafji was just about a kilometer from the border of Kuwait. The only thing we could tell them was the truth: We didn't know when the war was going to start. Of course, if we had known we couldn't have told them.

After the final shopping trip, we went on to the hotel, called home, and took our showers. It was while I was enjoying that last shower in the hotel in Khafji that I had a fleeting memory of Vietnam. It was just a momentary vision of monks falling. It took a couple of seconds for me to get my breath back, but that was it. I trembled for a few minutes. Fortunately I was in the shower, so none of my buddies were aware that it had occurred, and I certainly wasn't going to mention it.

Freshly showered, we went to a restaurant for what would prove to be our last meal in Khafji. One of the guys ordered a steak and, being the typical American, I said, "Make that two." We were waiting for our meal when one of the guys noted that the server had given me a very strange look when I placed my order. Sure enough, when he brought the meals, he had taken me literally and brought two complete steak dinners—steak, vegetables, and baked potatoes. All we did was thank him for the great service and give him a great big smile until he left—and then we cracked up.

As we were leaving, the servers, and even the cooks, came out and asked us when the war was going to start. They wanted to know when to get out of town. It was the same question when we turned the room keys in at the desk. As we drove out of town, there were four of us in three vehicles—my four-door, three-quarter-ton, four-wheel-drive Chevrolet pickup, and a pair of Chevys—a Suburban and a Blazer. As our little convoy drove past clusters of Saudis on the street, they'd watch us go by as though they might learn something important. I can't prove it, but I think they had figured out that this was going to be our last trip into town.

When my three roommates and I got back to our tent, it was clear that we were ready to get the show on the road. The old military doctrine of "hurry up and wait" had been in effect for weeks, and we were almost insane. In letters, tapes, and occasional phone calls, we tried to keep our wives and families from knowing that we were ready to get it over with, one way or the other. Either go north or go home, and at that point I don't think we were overly concerned about which direction our travel was to be. We just wanted to travel.

We had been waiting since mid-September 1990. Early in the evening of January 17, 1991 (in the USA), it started. That was about four thirty a.m., January 18, 1991, Saudi Arabian time. It was a shock, but at the same time a relief. On that night our "home away from home" changed.

During the initial attacks, coalition force aircraft had eliminated the electronic ability of Saddam Hussein to see what was happening in Saudi Arabia. They destroyed most of his radars that could "see south." From that point on, he had to use people on the ground to determine what we—or rather, all of the coalition forces—were doing.

Within hours of the initial bombing runs, the ground forces that had been massed in the kingdom of Saudi Arabia started moving north to staging areas for the push into Iraq and Kuwait. These units waited for weeks in the staging areas while attacks on the Iraqis were carried out by aircraft and naval forces. We didn't have to move, because the SANG units were already just a few short kilometers from the Kuwaiti border.

When the American advisers were notified by the senior logistics adviser, Lieutenant Colonel Ward, that the initial attacks in Iraq had taken place, it fell to me to awaken the Saudi maintenance company commander to inform him that Desert Shield had become Desert Storm and coalition forces were on the offensive. I knocked on the flap of his tent and called his name until he responded. He stuck his head out of the door, and I simply said, "The war has started. We are bombing Iraq." He said for us to come over and we would watch CNN, but first he needed to check in with his commander. He used radio, field phones, and runners to awaken his company. The entire encampment instantly came to life. You could see small cookers being lit as the Arab soldiers started heating water to make tea. You could also see the blue glow of television sets (the task force had many) as they tuned in to CNN to watch Peter Arnett's reporting on the bombing of Baghdad. I'm not sure about the technology involved in picking up the CNN signal, but most of the Saudi troops had their TV sets hooked to antennae like you used to see on houses before cable. In some cases, they just used rabbit ears.

Throughout the day the SANG units had staff meetings, and we attended a meeting of our adviser group. Our concerns were many. Would we move, how long before we would move, where would we move to, but most important, would the coalition stay together? Saddam Hussein had threatened to launch Scud missiles into Israel should he be attacked. We did not know how the Arabs would react if that happened. Would they remain in the coalition or would they decide that they could not fight against their "Arab brother"? If the latter, we would be in a somewhat uncomfortable position, there being only about 150 of us American advisers scattered throughout the area.

In planning for the possible dissolution of the Arab Task Force, rendezvous points were identified. All of us programmed the rendezvous points into the ground positioning systems that were mounted in our vehicles so we could travel more quickly. We had two types scattered across the advisory group: Loran, commonly used by ships at that time that used beacons; and Magellan, a satellite GPS. My pickup had both mounted in it.

Periodically throughout the day, my tentmates would contact one another via radio, and on various channels we could hear other advisers also contacting one another. Everyone seemed to understand the critical nature of our position and was understandably concerned about the people we had lived with for the past few months. The tone of conversation was quite subdued.

Each of us found some time during the day to write or make a tape home. We all knew that our wives and families were now the ones going crazy. At this point the wait for us was over. For our families the wait had changed and become even more terrifying. They, and we, always had the hope that we would return home without having had to go into Iraq or Kuwait, but now that hope was gone.

That evening, we ate and then had pot after pot of coffee. All of the coffee as well as the situation had us running around like sugared-up ten-year-olds at a sleepover. Late in the evening we settled down and began to talk.

I was the only one in the group who had been in a combat zone before. To say the least, I was not the happiest camper in the tent. One of the guys asked me if I was as scared that day as I was in Vietnam. And I said that the difference was, when I was in Vietnam I was nineteen, twenty years old. And I was just sure in my own mind then that I was indestructible. In Desert Storm I was forty years old, married with three kids, and I knew that I was an old man. I couldn't run as fast as I used to. I knew that I had a low threshold of pain, I cried easily, and I just had a completely different outlook on life. All of these are things that a grown, married person thinks about that a kid doesn't. Do I have enough life insurance? Is Ellen going to have enough money to continue or start a new life? Have I taken care of the kids like I should with the will? Am I going to be killed? Am I going to be captured? Am I going to survive the captivity? The Iraqis had killer teams that were sent down from Baghdad—*infiltrated* was the word we used, because they were put into the regular army squads that were out. And their job was, You start to surrender—no, you don't. So we knew they were there. All of us had been briefed on or had heard from CNN about the "death squads" that were being sent into the Iraqi forces across the border. Were they going to take kindly to us if they captured us?

Our concerns were somewhat simple. We had confidence in ourselves and in the people we were serving with. But there were several lingering concerns. No, they were fears that each of us was trying to deal with individually and within the group. Would we be wounded, would we be captured, would we be killed? And a question that was discussed at length was whether we would surrender if forced to, or would we go down fighting, so to speak? At this point, we had no idea how the Iraqis would treat prisoners or if they would be summarily executed.

We were all concerned about our families and how they were reacting to the start of hostilities (it would be over a week before we received our first letter or tape from home).

Our families back in the States had become close, if only telephonically, since we had been in Southwest Asia. If I told my wife something, I was telling all of the wives. If the others told their wives something, all of the wives would know within a few short hours. At times we were sure they had a better information network than we did.

We talked a great deal among us about our fears. We confessed things to one another that at any other time would have been taboo. We spoke of our wives and our love for them. We wondered aloud if we had invested in enough life insurance—would they have enough money to set themselves up in a "life after death"? How would we conduct ourselves in combat? Would we freeze or react properly? We discussed the fact that we were advisers and were supposed to carry only self-defense weapons, which meant a 9mm automatic sidearm.

The maintenance commander and I had reached an agreement during that day: Screw the rules—he was going to "loan" a rifle, magazines, and ammunition to me.

We also took a closer look at the supplies and equipment that we kept loaded in our vehicles at all times. We increased the quantity of water and rations. We opted to keep all of our clothes in our vehicles and remove them only when we changed, putting the worn clothes back into the vehicles. At that time I was still a smoker, and like all smokers in that moment, I was concerned about how many cartons of cigarettes I needed to stockpile in order to make it through the war or until I could resupply. Two of us had Chevrolet Blazers, one had a Chevrolet Suburban, and I had a Chevrolet pickup (long wheel base with four doors). We each had a teapot and a propane stove with extra fuel tanks so that we could heat water for instant coffee or tea. In a moment of weakness or overcompensation on the preparedness level, we requested extra first-aid kits from the rear for each of us. We discussed our interpreters and what we would do if they declined to go into Kuwait with us because they were civilians and did not have to go if they did not want to.

We decided that we should have one last pot of coffee, and then go to bed. Each of us, without saying anything to the others, took our pistols out of the holsters and began to disassemble and clean them. We even took all of the rounds out of the magazine and blew the magazines out and wiped the ammunition off.

Finally one of the captains brought up faith, a subject that we had not discussed before. He was curious, since he was the only one who went to church services regularly, whether we believed in God. We assured him that, at that moment, all of us were fervent believers. He asked if he could say a prayer for us and for our families. We immediately agreed. All four of us then joined hands and bowed our heads, and he prayed that each of us received guidance and protection if it was in the divine plan, but mostly he prayed for the comfort of our families, whatever the future outcome.

Then, each of us deep in his own thoughts and without another word to one another, we went to bed, knowing that our futures were changed at best and unsure at worst. All of us slept restlessly, even though it was almost midnight when we went to bed, and we were all up drinking coffee again by four o'clock or four thirty in the morning.

I do not recall our speaking of that night again, but I assure you that it was one of the most intimate joining of soldiers that one can imagine.

During the battle fought at Al Khafji, the Logistics Support Battalion commander, Lt. Col. Abdul Rachman Mughem, opted to employ some of the forward support concepts that we as advisers, and the contracted civilian company the Vinnell Corporation, working with the brigade, had been providing training on. When the support element moved forward, I had the distinct honor of moving with them, driving my Chevy pickup as the trail vehicle in the convoy. This battle took place several days after the start of hostilities, but well before the coalition forces began the ground attack against the Iraqis.

We set up in an area near a deserted school just on the outskirts of the city, close enough to see laundry hanging from the balconies of apartment buildings inside Khafji, which meant we were also close enough to hear small arms and heavy weapons from the infantry battalions that were involved in urban warfare.

The forward support team (FST) was almost ready to start evacuating equipment from the streets of the city to the FST area in order to begin repairs or cannibalize equipment that was damaged beyond repair. The object was to recover the equipment, repair it, and get it back to the using unit as quickly as possible under the theory that a gun in the shop is a gun that is useless.

I moved my truck to the south side of the FST (away from the town) and fired up the small two-burner propane stove to heat some water for a cup of instant coffee for myself and tea for my interpreter. Before the water was ready, I saw the unit's officers talking in very excited tones. I was unable to understand Arabic, but my interpreter quickly said that the FST was under fire from the city.

The question was, did we stay or move? After discussion with the battalion HQ, the decision was made to move back. The unit clearly did not have the personnel or weapons to mount a successful defense of the area they presently occupied.

The intensity of fire, along with the level of my blood pressure, had increased significantly. I do not know how many rounds were fired at us—all were small arms—before we moved the support element a little farther away from the city.

The Saudi soldiers were calm, or at least not panicked, as they were tearing down and loading. I helped one soldier load a couple of oxygen and acetylene cylinders onto his truck. Within moments we loaded the bottles, and the interpreter and I were running back to our truck when a round struck the truck we had just loaded the cylinders on. None of us was injured, and none of the equipment on the truck was damaged enough to hinder movement, so we pulled out quickly. Again, I was the last vehicle in the convoy.

Ultimately, U.S. Marines and the Saudi National Guard drove the Iraqis out of Khafji, and back across the border into Kuwait.

After the battle at Al Khafji, things more or less settled down to some semblance of "normalcy." The Saudis held decoration ceremonies, and they did have some genuine heroes to reward.

Once the ground war started, it was over in about one hundred hours. As the coalition forces moved forward, the Logistics Support Battalion, or at least elements of the battalion, moved forward supporting the combat elements. At age forty, I was more than uncomfortable; I was scared out of my wits. I can't speak for the other advisers, but I was not a happy guy. I thought back to Vietnam, and how things had happened there, and realized that each and every war, or even each individual firefight or battle, is different. Each person reacts differently each time.

As the war moved across the border into Kuwait, elements of the battalion moved forward rearming and repairing without much rest, just as did all members of the coalition forces. There was very little, if any, sleep for anyone. The combat units fought and captured a large number of the Iraqi forces, although I'm not sure the Iraqis really had the heart to fight. I was told that in interrogation the Iraqis said that they had not been paid in months, their officers had departed unannounced, leaving them alone, and their water and rations were at a premium. They were demoralized and hungry. They also had the same fears that we had: How would they be treated as prisoners of war? They had been told they would be killed or that any number of horrible things would happen to them if they surrendered.

Finally we received word that it was all over. After looking myself over to make sure that I didn't have any new orifices in my body, I said a prayer of thanks.

However, in Vietnam I learned that it's never over until it's over. Or you're not out of the woods till you're out of the woods. I should have remembered those lessons for Desert Storm. Because just when we thought it was over, my buddies and I were given an assignment that could easily have gotten us blown to kingdom come: We were told to take ground positioning equipment and map the precise coordinates of the massive minefields the Iraqis had laid in Kuwait.

This was not in my contract! Over twenty years in the army, a couple of wars—and now they wanted me to walk and drive around a minefield? Whose bright idea was this? I guess I understand the need to trace the minefield, but I wasn't enamored with the selection of personnel to do it: a couple of engineer captains and yours truly to assist.

When the Iraqis laid the minefields, it had been done quickly, and many of the mines had not been well camouflaged. For us, that was a good thing. But it had rained heavily over the last couple of weeks, and we wondered if the mines had been moved or covered completely with all of that water and sand washing around.

The thought of the mines made for an uneasy trip across the desert. We traveled two in the lead vehicle and one in the trail vehicle. When we got to where the minefield started on the road, we flipped a coin to see who would walk, who would drive the marker vehicle, and who would drive the trail vehicle to start. We'd agreed on half-hour shifts. The guy walking had to physically walk along the edge of the minefield to keep the vehicle from drifting one way or the other and crossing into the minefield. The marker vehicle had a ground positioning system in it that would give ten-digit military grid coordinates.

We were dealing with a variety of mines. There were the little toe poppers, just a couple of inches across, that weren't meant to kill you—just screw you up. Then there were other mines that were twelve and fourteen inches in diameter. And there were also the big thirty-three-inch Russian antitank mines.

The Iraqis also used something like the Bouncing Betty that Americans had faced in Vietnam, but they laid them in sequences of five. If you set off a trip wire over here, the charge would blow that mine about waist-high into the air, and then the main charge would explode at a height designed to tear a soldier apart. But when the first mine blew into the air it pulled a trip wire on the second mine in the chain, and that kept going until all five of them had blown.

We would walk and drive, listing the grid coordinates every time the minefield border changed directions. At the end of the minefield, or at the end of the day, we would list the coordinates again. By the end of it all we had precise points and directions that the minefield traveled that could be shown on a map for intelligence purposes.

We started off and went about a half a kilometer west, and then the minefield took a ninety-degree turn to the south. We followed it south for a ways, and then it turned west again. This went on for almost half a day, turning one way and then another. We were tired, pissed off, and, more important, terrified. We had been out here doing this for nearly four hours and we hadn't reached the end of one side yet. How big was this thing, anyway?

We stopped and had a great MRE meal with Kool-Aid and coffee.

Then we started again, keeping our eyes on a storm cloud slowly heading in our direction. When it began to sprinkle forty minutes later, we recorded the last coordinate of the day and started back to the highway. All of us were shocked to discover that we'd plotted minefield coordinates that stretched almost ten kilometers before we had to stop.

It had been made clear that we needed to finish the assignment, no matter how long it took or what the weather was doing, but we didn't dare go back out there until it had dried up some. We didn't want to get stuck in our vehicles, but more important, we wanted to give the earth time to settle before we started the trek again.

We would make three more trips to the minefield before we completed the trace. When all was said and done, the minefield was about forty kilometers long and ranged in depth from about a hundred meters to a kilometer. It was a sight to see once it was plotted and marked on the map.

At the end of each day we'd sit and drink coffee, wish for something a little stronger, and silently thank God in our own way for another safe trip through the minefield and another safe day.

When it was all over and I was due to leave, I had one ceremonial task that I took care of all by myself. I'd saved a 9mm round from the first day of Desert Storm, kept it in my pocket. That one was for me if worse really came to worst. Would I have had nerve enough to use it? I can't tell you. I don't know. Fortunately it never reached that point. But just before I left for home I walked out into the desert and shot that round. That one wasn't going to be turned in. Was there something symbolic about the act, or was I just acting the fool? I don't know. But after walking the edge of a minefield for days on end, I figured I was entitled.

CHAPTER SEVENTEEN

Get a Lawyer or Get a Shrink

The only real clues I'd given Ellen about what was going on in Desert Storm were vague ones in audiocassettes that I mailed home. Lines like "We had some pretty tense times." My fear— aside from not wanting to alarm her—was that I didn't want specific details to fall into the wrong hands. It's a war zone; stuff happens. But by not letting her know that it wasn't a walk in the park for those of us involved in the battle for Al Khafji, I didn't give her any reason to prepare for the fact that I might be seriously stressed-out when I got back home. I was also dealing with the notion that my homecoming was just going to be temporary.

When the powers that be no longer had any immediate tasks for me to perform, they said I could go back home to Aberdeen Proving Ground. But it was sort of like playing Monopoly—the "Gary" marker was "just visiting." OPM-SANG wasn't ready to release me back to Maryland. I came home just long enough to clear quarters, clear my unit, and then I was going back to Saudi Arabia, only this time Ellen would be permitted to go with me. But first we had to adjust to being back together, and to hear her tell it, that didn't go so well.

"I went to Baltimore/Washington International Airport to pick him up in a limo with champagne. But I could tell immediately that he wasn't comfortable at all. He came out of the terminal wearing his desert camouflage uniform, and he was a different man. He wasn't the Gary that I was in love with.

"I could tell right off the bat that he'd changed. He was really quiet, not really saying a whole lot. At first I thought it had to do with my expectations. You pick someone up at the airport, you expect they're going to be all exuberant. 'Oh, I'm so excited, I'm home!' Y'know? And he wasn't that way. It wasn't that he was upset to see me; it just wasn't the reaction I expected. So I just tried to put it aside—best-laid plans. 'Oh, well, that's just the way it is.' I'd never met my husband after he'd just gone through a war, so everything was brand-new.

"Gary had lost quite a bit of weight in the desert. He'd gone back to his rail-thin self. But he just didn't react to anything the way he had in the past. His sense of humor was gone. He rarely smiled. I'd ask him a question and get two-word answers. He was very pensive, somewhat morose all of the time. I figured I'd give it some time, but after about a week I could see that the behavior was just continuing, not smiling, not joking, not really there. And the aberrant behaviors were starting back up.

"He wasn't hitting himself like he'd done during that period of time in Germany. But he would hit the wall, or he'd throw something across the room. He'd pick up whatever he could get his hands on—a can of food, his keys, fruit, it didn't make any difference. If he was angry and upset, that's what he'd do.

"So I knew we were starting over from scratch. This war had just screwed him up again, but we had no time to try to deal with it because we had to clear quarters, he had to clear his unit, we had to get the household packed up. There are a lot of things that you just kind of let go because you can only deal with so many things on your plate at one time. And then we flew home to see my family in California and his in Texas before flying to Saudi Arabia."

I was blissfully unaware that Ellen had figured out that our old problems were cropping up again. Nevertheless, we both looked forward to my next assignment in the Middle East as a shared adventure.

We were booked on Saudi Arabian Airlines for the flight to Riyadh, and every few hours during the flight the Muslim passengers would check the compass in the cabin that pointed toward Mecca, spread their prayer rugs in the aisle, and pray. But that was just the beginning of a very foreign odyssey.

Being an American in Saudi Arabia after the war was undoubtedly more difficult for Ellen than for me. The notion of living in the fairyland of *Arabian Nights* wore off in a couple of weeks, and whenever we would venture outside the American compound in Riyadh, the medieval treatment of women tended to make life unbearable. Immediately after the war, many of the *Muttawah*—the religious police—had not yet returned to Riyadh, so the rules weren't as strict off post. Ellen wore what the wives called a "paki" outfit—probably because they were imported from Pakistan—which are big, baggy pants that are tight around the ankles and waist, but loose everywhere else. The paki top had a high collar and long sleeves. It also was long enough that it hung almost to the knees. The sides had slits to facilitate movement. On her feet she wore sandals.

But then the *Muttawah* came back, and as a way to reassert their authority and enforce the radical *Wahhabi* form of Islam, they went nuts. She was no longer allowed to wear the paki outfit in public, because women were not supposed to reveal that they had breasts. So they required American women off the compound to wear a black abaya that covered them from the neck down to the ankles, with long sleeves, and a scarf over the head because no hair could be showing.

Ellen was allowed to show her face for the oddest of reasons—because only whores could show their faces, and they considered non-Muslim women to be whores. You could tell they wanted to call her that on the streets of Riyadh. And one time when we were on R & R in Bahrain, a member of the royal family of Saudi Arabia (there are thousands of them) thought nothing of offering a million dollars to take her up to his room. She was a light-haired, non-Muslim female and, therefore, for sale. The fact that she was sitting with her husband didn't stop him; he was ignoring my presence. When she rejected the offer, he returned to hypocritically sipping his liquor through a straw so as not to violate the Koran's dictate that alcohol not touch his lips.

The *Muttawah,* whose official organization is known as the Authority for the Promotion of Virtue and Prevention of Vice, carried heavy camel quirts on the streets, and when they encountered someone who offended them—irrespective of nationality—they'd beat them. One day we'd gone shopping with another American couple in the gold souk of Riyadh. My friend's wife, who was Puerto Rican and darker skinned than Ellen, wasn't feeling well, and remained in the truck by herself. Because of her skin color, the *Muttawah* took her to be a Saudi woman—I guess they chose to ignore the license plates that identified us as foreigners—and began beating on the truck with their sticks, trying to force her to get out of the vehicle. As you can imagine, she was terrified. When we got there, her husband stepped into the fray, and as they usually do when a man is involved, they backed down. But it was an ugly scene.

During prayer call, everything stops. If you're in a restaurant they turn off the lights and pull metal gates down in front of the windows, and you just have to sit there and wait about forty-five minutes, locked in the place, until they're allowed to reopen. One time I had stopped my truck when the call to prayer was made, but I got out and stood there smoking a cigarette, which I shouldn't have done. The *Muttawah* decided he was going to make an issue of it. He came up to me and raised his stick, and I said, "You hit me with that stick, old man, and I'll take it away from you and stick it up your ass! When I do, they're going to take me down to the mosque and cut my head off, but you're still gonna have that stick up your ass." I'm not sure why, but he chose not to pursue the issue any further.

After an incident involving a Canadian woman, men from the Canadian embassy went *Muttawah* hunting and severely beat the ones that they could find in retaliation for the attack on that particular woman and other attacks that had taken place on Western women and men.

Just getting used to the calls to prayer was difficult for Ellen. At first the sounds were exotic, but after a week, five times a day, it was just a pain in the butt. It's loud and intrusive, and you just want to scream, "Shut up!"

Adjusting to the manner in which the Saudi women were treated was also an ordeal. The American military referred to them as BMOs—black moving objects, or "moving eggplants." The only outfit they were permitted to wear was the abaya, with a heavy black veil that completely covered their heads, a mask over their eyes and mouths, black elbow-length gloves, and black socks with sandals. And the temperature, without exaggeration, was 140 degrees.

There was a Baskin-Robbins ice-cream store that had an air-conditioned room for men to go to eat their cones, but women had to order from an outside window and sit on the curb. They'd pull out their veil and shove the ice-cream cone underneath it, sitting on the curb in 140-degree weather.

Our tour in Saudi Arabia lasted a very long year. When I was passed over for CWO-3 a second time, Ellen and I decided that we were going to get out of the army on our own terms, rather than wait for a letter telling me my services were no longer needed—after all, I had already given them twenty-four years. While my officer evaluation reports were top-notch and recommended me for promotion, mentioning my performance under fire with the SANG during the war, what I couldn't overcome was my age. I was forty-two, and with a flood of younger warrant officers moving up, they just didn't need a dinosaur like me. Had I gone to warrant officer school when I was an E-5 rather than an aging E-7, the story might have been different.

In July 1992, after a year in Saudi following the end of the war, I retired from the service. What to do next? The choice I made was the same one that a lot of retirees made: I got myself a job with a company that contracts to the military. I joined the Vinnell Corporation. While Ellen was working for the Bradley program during our tour in Riyadh, a former battalion commander of mine showed up for a scheduled meeting with the Bradley program manager in Saudi Arabia. He recognized Ellen from our days in Germany and started talking to her about me. She told him that I had submitted my retirement paperwork, and he immediately invited us out to dinner that evening. That's when I was recruited for Vinnell in Saudi Arabia. They had a program with the Saudi military involving the Bradley Fighting Vehicle, and while Ellen settled in California with family, I spent two years working for Vinnell in Tabuk, north of Jidda, assisting with and training soldiers for their maintenance program.

The advantage of working for Vinnell is that it was kind of like being in the army. Nearly everyone working there was retired military, and was used to a very structured way of life. So that sort of cushioned the blow of returning to civilian life. But when I finally came back to the States, I went through culture shock. For almost a quarter of a century, everyone around me had been like family. There was always someone around to help if you needed them, for any kind of circumstance.

As a civilian I felt like I'd been thrown to the wolves, and retiring to California it was even worse. Southern California is a place where you don't know your next-door neighbor, and they don't want to know you. That's not the kind of environment I was coming from. Ellen used to say that all of the military is just like living in the South, where everybody's a neighbor and everybody helps one another. So to be out of the military, and in the LA area to boot, was a double blow. It was a lot to get used to.

We experienced quite a bit of shifting around. I'd start one job, be there awhile, and then go somewhere else. What I was trying to do was find my footing and figure out exactly how civilian life worked. In the army, if you did A, you'd get B and C. Rewards or punishments for deeds done or not done were structured; there were no surprises. There was no such promise in civilian life. For me, it was very confusing and difficult to handle, and I clearly had problems with authority figures whose rules I didn't understand. Ellen had a better perspective on what was going on with me than I did.

"I think Gary's difficulties adjusting triggered everything. All the issues he'd been able to kind of put aside to some degree while he was in the military and his time with Vinnell came tumbling out. He went from rarely having outbursts to always having them. The Vietnam nightmares started to come back. He'd wake up in the middle of the night soaking wet with sweat, as though he'd just been through the war in Vietnam all over again. His pillows weren't lasting three months.

"It was like having a cocked gun around; you never knew when he was going to go off. We could be having a perfectly lovely day, and I'd say one thing that somehow set him off. We'd be driving down the street and talking about what we were going to do that night—a perfectly innocent conversation. And things would escalate out of control.

"He might ask me what restaurant I wanted to go to, and I'd make a suggestion, and he'd say, 'Well, that sounds really good.' We'd be laughing and talking, and I'd notice that the stoplight was yellow, ready to turn red. And by the time he'd go through it, it would be red, and I'd say, 'Honey, you just ran through a red light,' and that did it. Now he'd turn the car into a weapon. He'd slam his foot on the gas pedal and shoot forward, and I was taken aback.

"'What're you doing?' I'd say, and that made him madder, and he'd start swinging in and out of lanes. 'You wanna drive the fucking car?' he'd scream. That sort of thing, until he'd finally calm down. He was the poster boy for road rage—but it didn't even take another driver to set him off. It was just awful.

"As the months went on, things got worse and worse and worse. He'd mostly quit drinking, so that wasn't the problem. Alcohol didn't add to or take away from the rage. It was the same intensity, whether or not he was drinking. And he was having one of these episodes every three or four days."

Ellen talked to me until she was blue in the face, crying, yelling, pounding her fist on the table. I remember her screaming at me, saying, "You've got to hear what you're saying. Can't you hear what you're saying?" But I didn't want to talk about it. I really didn't want to talk about anything. She told me that anger was the only form of expression I had. And she was right. It wasn't about anything concrete; it was just anger for the sake of being angry. I'd be like a race car, going from zero to one hundred in one second. That's how it would go.

By Christmas Day in 1996, Ellen was at her wits' end. She'd tried everything to the point that she was feeling as though she were going crazy, wondering if she was the one doing something to cause my violent mood swings. We'd moved to Azusa, a suburb of Los Angeles, and I was working for Waste Management, doing truck maintenance, when I really snapped. The nightmares had come back full force, and I just wasn't fit to live with. On Christmas Day—a pretty crappy time to act a fool—I started in on her, and it was the straw that broke the camel's back. When I went a little bit nuts because I couldn't easily open the cellophane-wrapped package of dinner rolls, she'd had enough.

She *couldn't* take it anymore, and she'd finally decided she *wouldn't* take it anymore. She told me, "You either get some help now, or you get a lawyer. It's as simple as that. I'm not putting up with it anymore, none of it. You get yourself some help, and if you don't want that, then you can find yourself a new wife."

It was like throwing a glass of cold water in my face. For the first time she said something that actually sank in and got my attention. It took my breath away, and I broke down and started to cry.

The next day when I went into work, I talked to the human resources people and signed up for their employee-assistance program. It would get me only six visits with a psychologist, but it was a start.

A couple of weeks later I showed up at the office of Phoebe Cervantes, a Ph.D. psychologist in West Covina, where my employee-assistance program had referred me. Dr. Cervantes was waiting to get my age, description, etc. I walked in and sat on a couch, while she took a chair off to one side, so as not to block the path between me and the door. I later found out that this was standard shrink operating procedure.

"I know that you're a self-referral through your EAP, so tell me what's going on," she said.

And I began, "Well, my wife thinks I've got a—" And I caught myself, stopped, and started again. "Well, not just my wife. I've got a problem." I began giving her a description of what had been going on, but she interrupted me, and asked me to tell her about myself.

"I work a night shift. I run the maintenance shop for a trash company." She stopped me again.

"I need to know that, but let's go back a ways." By the time the end of the fifty-minute session rolled around, she told me that she was prepared to say tentatively that I was suffering from post-traumatic stress disorder.

I was horrified. Not just because I suddenly had a label, but because I was still seeing things on the news about guys—vets—who couldn't work, didn't work, wouldn't work. They were burdens on society. They were insane. And I was terrified at the thought of being *insane*—that's my word for it, definitely not Dr. Cervantes's. And now I was being told that I'd been insane for years, and didn't know it.

At that first session on the couch I hadn't really gone into the details of what I'd done, or discussed the specifics of what I was reliving in my nightmares. I spent a lot of time talking about my anger-management problem, because I knew that in order not to lose Ellen, that's what I had to fix.

I had no idea of what to expect from a psychologist. What I wanted from her was a miracle. I wanted her to wave the magical psychological wand and say, "Heal," and it would be over. I didn't know if she would send me to a psychiatrist for drugs, or what was going to happen. I was on the verge of losing the woman whom I truly loved, and still do love. I was willing to crawl naked through downtown LA if that was what it took to save our marriage. Did I think it would be a quick fix? Probably so. What I found was the beginning of a journey that is still in progress today.

Toward the end of that first session, Dr. Cervantes asked, "Have you ever written anything about your experiences or dreams?"

The only thing I'd written in the army were reports and evaluations, that sort of thing. I didn't think that was what she meant, so I told her that I hadn't.

She said, "Okay, every time you have a dream or a flashback, I want you to immediately—right then, while it's fresh in your memory—sit down and write about it. Don't worry about spelling; don't worry about grammar. Just let it go. Then bring that back here and we'll go over it together."

I had no idea what she meant by us going over it together. I was still a little bit stunned by the assignment. I'd never really told anyone the whole story. Even when Ellen sat me down in Germany, when our relationship was just starting, I pretty much self-censored. And while I'd swapped war stories with my buddies in the army, those sessions weren't intended to be introspective. Even in that first session with the psychologist, I'd held back; I'd understated things. And she caught me. She said, "Are you being honest with me?" And I knew that I wasn't telling her everything; I was holding back.

At that first session I told her about Dave's death, and how I waved off the Dustoff because we'd started taking fire again. If I recall correctly, I told the story in a pretty mechanical way. "By the time the helicopter came back in, he was already dead." Period. End of discussion. But she didn't go for it. Again, she asked me not only if I was being honest, but if I was being honest with myself.

She told me that I tend to "talk around" incidents, and I didn't really comprehend what she was saying. So she threw my words back at me; she said, "You 'take care of things,' or you 'did the deed,' or you 'took the appropriate action.' What does that mean?"

And I said, "I killed someone." And that was the first time I had said it like that. It had been almost twenty-five years, and I had never really said it out loud, just like that. And I thought, *Okay, I'm gonna write about it, I'll bring it back here, and we'll go over it together.* In my mind, she was going to read it while I sat there looking out the window. I didn't know that wasn't the way she played this game.

I remember coming home and telling Ellen that the shrink wanted me to start writing down my nightmares. We talked about it a little bit, and I told her it scared me. It would've been okay to write it down if nobody were ever going to see it, but now all these things I'd held inside of me, things I'd never really told anyone, were going to be on paper for someone else to actually read.

The next time I had a nightmare, I got up, went to the computer, and wrote it out stream-of-consciousness style. The experience wasn't nearly as bad as I thought it might be, and eventually I would just come home from work, sit down, and begin writing more of the nightmares and memories from Vietnam.

On my second appointment, I walked into Dr. Cervantes's office and handed her a three-ring binder with my writings. She opened it up and began paging through it while I just sat there watching her. For a minute it looked as though she were just going to read it with me sitting there, but then she stopped, looked at me, closed the binder, and handed it back to me. She said, "Why don't you pick one and read it to me?"

It was a terrifying moment. It's one thing to write it. It's one thing to see it in the privacy of your own mind. But it's another thing to

share it and read it with a complete outsider. We had no relationship, and I knew that this therapy with her was not going to be a
long-term thing. The company paid for six sessions, and this was the
second.

I flipped through the pages of the binder and chose to read her
my memories of how my buddy Dave had died before I could get a
Dustoff in. I don't recall deliberately avoiding reading one of the
sniper missions to her, but it's a pretty good bet that it was a sub-
conscious decision not to go there—at least not yet.

I tried watching her face while I was reading my memory of what
happened to Dave. I was looking for a reaction. Let me tell you, I
wouldn't want to play poker with that woman. She didn't show any
emotion at all. In fact, the only time she showed any emotion was at
the end of our last session, when I was leaving. She asked me if she
could make a copy of what I'd written so she could share it with the
other members of her staff.

Anyway, I finished reading to her and sat there waiting for a reaction. She said, "Have you ever told your wife anything?"

"Not really," I said, knowing that when Ellen had made me talk in
Germany about the nightmares, I'd kept a lot of the truth from her.

Cervantes was pretty blunt, saying, "Well, she's hung around for
all these years. Don't you think she has a right to know? These things
helped form the person whom she fell in love with and married, and
has been with, and put up with. You should let her read it."

At first I was dumbstruck with that notion. And then panic began
to set in. I'd been keeping this stuff from Ellen for almost twenty
years, and now there would be no way to maintain my secrecy any
longer. But I was caught between the classic rock and a hard place.
Sharing my memories with her was difficult, but the alternative was
that if I didn't do what my therapist was asking me to do, the consequences of that choice were even worse. Because if Ellen saw that I
wasn't taking the therapy seriously, I'd be sitting in a lawyer's office
right quick.

The first story I gave her to read was about me shooting the water buffalo. But it was really about me being scared stiff. We were living in a house in Azusa at the time, and I didn't want to be around her while she was reading. So she took the binder and went out and sat by the pool. Ellen says, "It was funny and poignant at the same time. He'd never told me that before. But I could feel what it was like for him to be brand-new in country, out on his first patrol, and terrified. From reading it, I could sense what it was like to hear that strange sound coming toward him in the dark, with no one else making any noise, and the fog is settling in, and he's thinking that everybody around him has been slaughtered and he's the only one left to deal with it. It's easy to laugh about it now—too easy. But it began to give me some insight into what was going on in Gary's head.

"After the water buffalo story, I kept right on reading, and that's when I got into the bad stuff—one of the sniper stories, and then the tunnel story, then another sniper story. When we talked about them, he said something about feeling like a Mafia hit man, standing up there, not really in any danger yourself. And there for the purpose of killing a specific person. That was really hard for him to deal with, and it was difficult for me to figure out how I felt about it.

"When I read about his second mission, killing the woman, I knew that for Gary, that cut him more than anything. I know my husband, and deliberately hurting women or children was something that would be virtually impossible for him to do. I saw how he reacted to the mistreatment of women in Saudi Arabia. I honestly would have thought that he'd be incapable of deliberately killing a woman.

"But it was war, and you just don't have the choice. I know that from my own time in the army. The only choice that he would have had was to say no, and then be court-martialed. And I don't believe that as a nineteen-year-old kid he thought he could do that. We've talked about it, and I believe that once he got the training, it never entered his mind to say, 'I'm not going to do it.' He wasn't happy when he found out what he'd been sent to school for. When he was there, he just thought it was a good time. 'Oh, boy, they're teaching me how to shoot better.' They didn't slap him upside the head and say, 'Boy, this is what you're going to school to learn how to do.'

"At nineteen, you're just a stupid kid who's expected to be an adult. That's the problem. I think guys like my Gary were rushed out of childhood so fast and into a weird kind of adulthood, that I don't know that the rest of your psyche catches up with you. And now, much later, we see that it has taken an awful toll."

After she'd had a chance to read what I'd written, Ellen and I sat down to talk. She told me that what she'd read hadn't changed her feelings for me one bit. I cried when she said it. I'd been terrified that reading my journal would make her hate me.

The following week I went back to see Dr. Cervantes. She said, "Okay, did you let Ellen read it?"

"Yes."

"Well, what was her reaction?"

I sort of grinned and said, "Well, she's still here." She didn't push me more for Ellen's reaction. She did something that, at the time, I thought was worse.

"Well," she said, "I think it's time to share it with someone else. Pick a couple other people in your family and let them read it, too."

That was one of the hardest things I ever had to do. I knew Ellen loved me, and I had a sense that she wouldn't throw things at me after she read it. But I couldn't be sure about anyone else. I discussed it with Ellen, and together we picked her mother and her younger sister. I was terrified, literally terrified, because up until that time I had just been Gary, the guy Ellen married who had dragged her all over the world. I didn't know how they were going to react, what it was going to do to my relationship with them or theirs with me. Was it going to change their perception of me, because perceptions are real? It may not make sense, but I was probably more scared of that than I was of giving it to Ellen to read. Ellen had been there when I was having the nightmares; she'd experienced the temper tantrums—nobody else had.

"But he truly was horrified at the notion of giving the journal to my mother and my sister, for them to know what kind of monster he thought he was. It was probably the bravest thing he's ever done. I think he would've rather faced a firing squad."

My fears turned out to be unfounded. Ellen's family reacted with support and loving kindness, and when I finally gave it to my own sister to read, she was loving and supportive as well. As a footnote, I would add that my mother and father both went to their graves without ever knowing about their "baby boy." I really don't think my mother would have been surprised, because I remember that when I was home during my thirty-day leave after Vietnam, she made a point of telling me that I'd changed. I guess mothers really do have a sixth sense, an intuition about their children.

By the end of my sixth and final session with Dr. Cervantes, I was not a happy camper. I didn't think that we had the money to continue paying for therapy on my own, so it was over, and I didn't know what other resources were available. Additionally, I was on my way to Alabama for a job interview. I really didn't have a good grasp on how what happened to me and what I had done in Vietnam related to my anger-management problems twenty-five years later. I just knew it wasn't a straight line. Besides that, I felt like I had met my promise to Ellen to get some help. Dredging up, writing about, and sharing what I felt was "my hurt" was not something that I really wanted to do any more than I was absolutely forced to do.

Dr. Cervantes gave me some education about PTSD when she first diagnosed it in me. The way I recall it, she said that when a person is exposed to a traumatic event—whether it's a car wreck, a family member being kidnapped or murdered, witnessing the death of a child—PTSD can result. Everyone reacts differently to these traumatizing events. Some people aren't bothered, other people get bothered a little bit, and some people end up with a lifelong disability.

(See the appendix for a series of information sheets provided by the VA explaining PTSD, its symptoms, diagnosis, and treatment, as well as where to go for help.)

Cervantes said, "You've got a very mild case of PTSD," and I'm thinking, *If this is mild—my God . . .* because by that time I had realized that my problems with anger control, the temper tantrums, nightmares, and just being an ass were a result of my trying to manipulate myself. In other words, it's a way of escaping the problems that I have, while trying to convince myself and those around me that I am as normal as everyone else—nothing that has happened has had an effect or has changed me.

Even though I had only half a dozen sessions with Dr. Cervantes, I feel that I got a lot out of it. My instant reaction to her diagnosis was that it meant I was insane. She took the time to tell me that I wasn't. She basically said, "This is what the problem is; we may not be able to cure it, but there are tools to help you manage it."

In retrospect, what I should have done was figure out a way to stay in therapy. Instead, I opted for a change of scenery. An opportunity had arisen to move to Huntsville, Alabama, and work for a company that a guy I'd been in the service with was starting. Both Ellen and I wanted out of California, and this seemed like the perfect move. I promised her that once we got to Alabama, I'd find a way to continue therapy—but I didn't.

We loved Huntsville, but the startup company didn't expand or progress as fast as they expected it to, so I was laid off. And unless you're a farmer or a rocket scientist, it's hard to find a job there. We struggled for six or eight months and nothing developed, so we moved back to California, and I went back to work for the same company I'd been working for when we left. Once again, Ellen and I had problems. My anger was out of control.

She says, "We got to the same point again where I had to threaten him with divorce in order to get him to seek help. And that's when he went to the Vet Center in Sepulveda and got himself into a group."

Even though the group wasn't run by a licensed therapist, he was a trained readjustment counselor. In the beginning I felt like I was getting help from the group therapy sessions. A little later I realized that a core group of guys wanted to spend the entire session talking about the great drugs they'd done during the war. Others just bitched and moaned and griped and complained about the same damn things over and over and over again. I put up with it for nearly a year, hoping that my complaints to the group's facilitator would result in constructive change. Unfortunately nothing improved. It seemed that some members of the group felt that the army was responsible for their use of drugs, alcohol, or whatever they chose to use in their efforts to relieve the pain—some mental, some physical.

One night, after what I felt was another useless group session, Ellen and I went online and found a Web site dedicated to Vietnam veterans, where families could leave notes on a message board. A typical note said, "Could someone from my dad's unit please contact me?" And they'd give the unit. "We'd like to know what my dad did in Vietnam. He would never talk about it."

And that phrase echoed. "Never talk about it, never talk about it, never talk about it." That's what they all seemed to say. And almost every dad, brother, or husband on that list had either died of cancer or suicide or drug- or alcohol-related overdoses. But the suicides far outnumbered everything else, and Ellen and I were looking at the screen as I was scrolling through it, and it's "committed suicide, committed suicide, committed suicide." So many of them. And then there were the guys who died of cancer from Agent Orange.

Ellen recalled the moment we found that Web site. "It was so horrifying that they're still killing themselves over a war that's been over for so many years. The number of people they say were killed in Vietnam—the 58,000-plus whose names are on the Wall—is so far off because they're still being killed, and they're still dying because of Vietnam.

"It was so upsetting, we both just broke down into tears and sobbed for about half an hour, just going through that list and seeing how hopeless it could be. And I believe that was a huge turning point for Gary. It's when he realized that he had to get a grip on what had happened to him, on what was happening to him, and try to understand that there were things he could do to control his feelings, his responses to triggers that were way out of proportion to whatever was going on at the moment."

Over the past few years I've tried everything from food supplements to hypnotherapy to help control the outbursts. And they seem to have helped. I've spent more time just feeling normal again—normal like before I went to Vietnam. Frankly, I'd forgotten what that was like, because the craziness had become my new normal, and that clearly wasn't conducive to a happy, ordinary life.

And that's basically where I am right now. I told you at the start that this was the story of my journey. I'm still on the road, still finding my way, occasionally stumbling, but much more optimistic than I've been in years. I still haven't reconciled with all three of my sons, although I have hope that they will one day find time in their lives to forgive me for not being there when needed. To this point, I've still not spoken to them about the things that have happened. Maybe this writing will be, in some small way, an explanation. I hope so.

Ellen and I are still together, still planning on being together forever. I can't forget that my road to recovery really started when she told me to get some help. That was like a slap in the face, warning me that I was getting ready to lose the best thing that had ever happened to me if I didn't make some changes.

I think that in a way it's like alcoholism: Even though it is never cured, you simply have to learn how to coexist with it. First you have to admit you have a problem before you realize that you need help. Since I stood up and said, "Hi, my name is Gary," Ellen has been right there with me. She's laughed with me, cried with me, fussed at me, and put up with my fussing at her. She's always realized that I didn't choose to become the way I am; it's just something that happened. Although she has never condescended to or withdrawn from my pain, she also has never let me off the hook. She made me face who I was, made me see the value in trying to change, and helped me try to use the tools that I have learned to try to get through it. What more could I ask of her?

The following fact sheets are adapted from the Web site of the National Center for Post-Traumatic Stress Disorder of the Department of Veterans Affairs.

For additional information:
- Visit http://www.ncptsd.org/facts/index.html. References and research citations for the information reprinted here may be found at the Web site.
- Call the PTSD Information Line at (802) 296-6300
- Send e-mail to ncptsd@ncptsd.org

What Is Post-traumatic Stress Disorder?

Post-traumatic stress disorder, or PTSD, is a psychiatric disorder that can occur following the experience or witnessing of life-threatening events such as military combat, natural disasters, terrorist incidents, serious accidents, or violent personal assaults like rape. People who suffer from PTSD often relive the experience through nightmares and flashbacks, have difficulty sleeping, and feel detached or estranged, and these symptoms can be severe enough and last long enough to significantly impair the person's daily life.

PTSD is marked by clear biological changes as well as psychological symptoms. PTSD is complicated by the fact that it frequently occurs in conjunction with related disorders such as depression, substance abuse, problems of memory and cognition, and other problems of physical and mental health. The disorder is also associated with impairment of the person's ability to function in social or family life, including occupational instability, marital problems and divorces, family discord, and difficulties in parenting.

Understanding PTSD

PTSD is not a new disorder. There are written accounts of similar symptoms that go back to ancient times, and there is clear documentation in the historical medical literature starting with the Civil War, when a PTSD-like disorder was known as "Da Costa's Syndrome." There are particularly good descriptions of post-traumatic stress symptoms in the medical literature on combat veterans of World War II and on Holocaust survivors.

Careful research and documentation of PTSD began in earnest after the Vietnam War. The National Vietnam Veterans Readjustment Study estimated in 1988 that the prevalence of PTSD in that group was 15.2 percent at that time, and that 30 percent had experienced the disorder at some point since returning from Vietnam.

PTSD has subsequently been observed in all veteran populations that have been studied, including World War II, the Korean conflict, and the Persian Gulf populations, and in United Nations peacekeeping forces deployed to other war zones around the world. There are remarkably similar findings of PTSD in military veterans in other countries. For example, Australian Vietnam veterans experience many of the same symptoms that American Vietnam veterans experience.

PTSD is not only a problem for veterans, however. Although there are unique cultural- and gender-based aspects of the disorder, it occurs in men and women, adults and children, Western and non-Western cultural groups, and all socioeconomic strata. A national study of

APPENDIX

American civilians conducted in 1995 estimated that the lifetime prevalence of PTSD was 5 percent in men and 10 percent in women.

How Does PTSD Develop?

Most people who are exposed to a traumatic, stressful event experience some of the symptoms of PTSD in the days and weeks following exposure. Available data suggest that about 8 percent of men and 20 percent of women go on to develop PTSD, and roughly 30 percent of these individuals develop a chronic form that persists throughout their lifetimes.

The course of chronic PTSD usually involves periods of symptom increase followed by remission or decrease, although some individuals may experience symptoms that are unremitting and severe. Some older veterans, who report a lifetime of only mild symptoms, experience significant increases in symptoms following retirement, severe medical illness in themselves or their spouses, or reminders of their military service (such as reunions or media broadcasts of the anniversaries of war events).

How Is PTSD Assessed?

In recent years, a great deal of research has been aimed at developing and testing reliable assessment tools. It is generally thought that the best way to diagnose PTSD—or any psychiatric disorder, for that matter—is to combine findings from structured interviews and questionnaires with physiological assessments. A multimethod approach especially helps address concerns that some patients might be either denying or exaggerating their symptoms.

How Common Is PTSD?

An estimated 7.8 percent of Americans will experience PTSD at some point in their lives, with women (10.4 percent) twice as likely as men (5 percent) to develop PTSD. About 3.6 percent of U.S. adults aged 18 to 54 (5.2 million people) have PTSD during the course of a given year. This represents a small portion of those who have experienced at least one traumatic event; 60.7 percent of men and 51.2 percent of women reported at least one traumatic event. The traumatic events most often associated with PTSD for men are rape, combat exposure, childhood neglect, and childhood physical abuse. The most traumatic events for women are rape, sexual molestation, physical attack, being threatened with a weapon, and childhood physical abuse.

About 30 percent of the men and women who have spent time in war zones experience PTSD. An additional 20 to 25 percent have had partial PTSD at some point in their lives. More than half of all male Vietnam veterans and almost half of all female Vietnam veterans have experienced "clinically serious stress reaction symptoms." PTSD has also been detected among veterans of the Gulf War, with some estimates running as high as 8 percent.

Who Is Most Likely to Develop PTSD?

1. Those who experience greater stressor magnitude and intensity, unpredictability, uncontrollability, sexual (as opposed to nonsexual) victimization, real or perceived responsibility, and betrayal.
2. Those with prior vulnerability factors such as genetics, early age of onset and longer-lasting childhood trauma, lack of functional social support, and concurrent stressful life events.
3. Those who report greater perceived threat or danger, suffering, upset, terror, and horror or fear.
4. Those with a social environment that produces shame, guilt, stigmatization, or self-hatred.

What Are the Consequences Associated with PTSD?

PTSD is associated with a number of distinctive neurobiological and physiological changes. PTSD may be associated with stable neurobiological alterations in both the central and autonomic nervous systems, such as altered brain-wave activity, decreased volume of the hippocampus, and abnormal activation of the amygdala. Both the hippocampus and the amygdala are involved in the processing and integration of memory. The amygdala has also been found to be involved in coordinating the body's fear response.

Psychophysiological alterations associated with PTSD include hyperarousal of the sympathetic nervous system, increased sensitivity of the startle reflex, and sleep abnormalities.

People with PTSD tend to have abnormal levels of key hormones involved in the body's response to stress. Thyroid function also seems to be enhanced in people with PTSD. Some studies have shown that cortisol levels in those with PTSD are lower than normal, and epinephrine and norepinephrine levels are higher than normal. People with PTSD also continue to produce higher-than-normal levels of natural opiates after the trauma has passed. An important finding is that the neurohormonal changes seen in PTSD are distinct from, and actually opposite to, those seen in major depression. The distinctive profile associated with PTSD is also seen in individuals who have both PTSD and depression.

PTSD is associated with the increased likelihood of co-occurring psychiatric disorders. In a large-scale study, 88 percent of men and 79 percent of women with PTSD met criteria for another psychiatric disorder. The co-occurring disorders most prevalent for men with PTSD were alcohol abuse or dependence (51.9 percent), major depressive episodes (47.9 percent), conduct disorders (43.3 percent), and drug abuse and dependence (34.5 percent). The disorders most frequently comorbid with PTSD among women were major depressive disorders (48.5 percent), simple phobias (29 percent), social phobias (28.4 percent), and alcohol abuse/dependence (27.9 percent).

PTSD also significantly impacts psychosocial functioning, independent of comorbid conditions. For instance, Vietnam veterans with PTSD were found to have profound and pervasive problems in their daily lives. These included problems in family and other inter-personal relationships, problems with employment, and involvement with the criminal justice system.

Headaches, gastrointestinal complaints, immune system problems, dizziness, chest pain, and discomfort in other parts of the body are common in people with PTSD. Often medical doctors treat the symptoms without being aware that they stem from PTSD.

How Is PTSD Treated?

PTSD is treated by a variety of forms of psychotherapy and drug therapy. There is no definitive treatment, and no cure, but some treatments appear to be quite promising, especially cognitive-behavioral therapy, group therapy, and exposure therapy. Exposure therapy involves having the patient repeatedly relive the frightening experience under controlled conditions to help him or her work through the trauma. Studies have also shown that medications help ease associated symptoms of depression and anxiety and help with sleep. The most widely used drug treatments for PTSD are the selective serotonin reuptake inhibitors, such as Prozac and Zoloft. At present, cognitive-behavioral therapy appears to be somewhat more effective than drug therapy. However, it would be premature to conclude that drug therapy is less effective overall, since drug trials for PTSD are at a very early stage. Drug therapy appears to be highly effective for some individuals and is helpful for many more. In addition, the recent findings on the biological changes associated with PTSD have spurred new research into drugs that target these biological changes, which may lead to much increased efficacy.

Help for Veterans with PTSD and Help for Their Families

Veterans experiencing the symptoms of post-traumatic stress disorder (PTSD) often request several types of assistance, as do their families. As a research and education organization, the National Center for PTSD cannot provide this assistance, but we can refer you to the people who can provide assistance. Here are the answers to some questions about PTSD and service-connected disability that are frequently asked by veterans and their families.

Do I Have PTSD?

A natural first question is whether the symptoms really are due to PTSD. Stress symptoms are not always due to PTSD, and it is helpful to know if they are specifically the result of psychological trauma and if they are the full condition of PTSD. Such symptoms may be due to other conditions created by stressors other than trauma (for example, work or financial pressures), medical problems (such as heart conditions or diabetes), or other psychological conditions (such as depression or anxiety).

Resources

The VA Medical Center system's specialized PTSD clinics and programs can provide to eligible veterans educational information and diagnostic evaluations concerning PTSD. The Readjustment Counseling Service's community-based Vet Centers can provide educational information and diagnostic evaluations concerning PTSD to any veteran who served in a war zone or in a military conflict (such as in Panama, Grenada, or Somalia).

If I Have Other Stress, Medical, or Psychological Problems, Do I Also Have PTSD?

Veterans with PTSD often have other types of stress, medical, or psychological problems in addition to PTSD. Sometimes PTSD is unintentionally overlooked when other problems seem particularly pressing, and it can be helpful to know if PTSD also needs to be treated.

Resources

VA Medical Center specialized PTSD programs and VA Readjustment Counseling Service Vet Centers.

APPENDIX

What Kinds of Education and Treatment Can Help Me (or My Veteran Family Member)?

There are several types of education and treatment for PTSD that have proven helpful to veterans and their family members. These include classes on dealing with PTSD symptoms, stress, anger, sleep, and personal relationships. Individual, group, and family counseling and selected medications have also been helpful.

Resources

You may wish to begin by reviewing the general information on PTSD provided on our Web site. For specific options for education and treatment in your local area, contact the closest VA Medical Center specialized PTSD program or VA Readjustment Counseling Service Vet Center.

How Can I Establish That I Am Disabled Due to PTSD Caused by Military Service?

A determination of service-connected disability for PTSD is made by the Compensation and Pension Service, an arm of VA's Veterans Benefits Administration. The clinicians who provide care for veterans in VA's specialized PTSD clinics and Vet Centers do not make this decision. A formal request (claim) must be filed by the veteran using forms provided by the VA's Veterans Benefits Administration. After all the forms are submitted, the veteran must complete interviews concerning her or his social history (a review of family, work, and educational experiences before, during, and after military service) and psychiatric status (a review of past and current psychological symptoms and of traumatic experiences during military service). The forms and information about the application process can be obtained by benefits officers at any VA medical center, outpatient clinic, or regional office.

The process of applying for a VA disability for PTSD can take several months and can be both complicated and quite stressful. The Veterans Service Organizations provide service officers at no cost to help veterans and family members pursue VA disability claims. Service officers are familiar with every step in the application and interview process and can provide both technical guidance and moral support. In addition, some service officers particularly specialize in assisting veterans with PTSD disability claims. Even if a veteran has not been a member of a specific veterans service organization, the veteran still can request the assistance of a service officer working for that organization. In order to get representation by a qualified and helpful service officer, you can directly contact the local office of any veterans service organization. You may also wish to ask for recommendations from other veterans who have applied for VA disability or from a PTSD specialist at a VA PTSD clinic or a Vet Center.

My Claim for a VA PTSD Disability Has Been Turned Down by the Benefits Office, but I Believe I Have PTSD Due to Military Service. What Can I Do?

Contact a veterans service officer, who can explain how to file an appeal and who can help you gather the information necessary to make a successful appeal. You may want to contact a service officer who has extensive experience in helping veterans file and appeal claims specifically for PTSD.

I Can't Get Records from the Military That I Need for My Disability Claim. What Can I Do?

Veterans service officers can help you file the specific paperwork required to obtain your military records. If your service officer is not able to help you get necessary records, ask him or her to refer you to another service officer who has more experience in getting records.

Partners of Veterans with PTSD: Caregiver Burden and Related Problems

By Jennifer L. Price, Ph.D., and Susan P. Stevens, Psy.D.

Introduction

A number of studies have found that veterans' PTSD symptoms can negatively impact family relationships and that family relationships may exacerbate or ameliorate a veteran's PTSD and comorbid conditions. This fact sheet provides information about the common problems experienced in relationships in which one (or both) of the partners has PTSD. This sheet also provides recommendations for how one can cope with these difficulties. The majority of this research involved female partners (typically wives) of male veterans; however, there is much clinical and anecdotal evidence to suggest that these problems also exist for couples where the identified PTSD patient is female.

What Are Common Problems in Relationships with PTSD-Diagnosed Veterans?

Research that has examined the effect of PTSD on intimate relationships reveals severe and pervasive negative effects on marital adjustment, general family functioning, and the mental health of partners. These negative effects result in such problems as compromised parenting, family violence, divorce, sexual problems, aggression, and caregiver burden.

- *Marital adjustment and divorce rates.* Male veterans with PTSD are more likely to report marital or relationship problems, higher levels of parenting problems, and generally poorer family adjustment than veterans without PTSD. Research has shown that veterans with PTSD are less self-disclosing and expressive with their partners than veterans without PTSD. PTSD veterans and their wives have also reported a greater sense of anxiety around intimacy. Sexual dysfunction also tends to be higher in combat veterans with PTSD than in veterans without PTSD. It has been posited that diminished sexual interest contributes to decreased couple satisfaction and adjustment.

Related to impaired relationship functioning, a high rate of separation and divorce exists in the veteran population (those with PTSD and those without PTSD). Approximately 38 percent of Vietnam veteran marriages failed within six months of the veteran's return from Southeast Asia (President's Commission on Mental Health, 1978). The overall divorce rate among Vietnam veterans is significantly higher than for the general population, and rates of divorce are even higher for veterans with PTSD. The National Vietnam Veterans Readjustment Study (NVVRS) found that both male and female veterans without PTSD tended to have longer-lasting relationships with their partners than their counterparts with PTSD. Rates of divorce for veterans with PTSD were two times greater than for veterans without PTSD. Moreover, veterans with PTSD were three times more likely than veterans without PTSD to divorce two or more times.

- *Interpersonal violence.* Studies have found that, in addition to more general relationship problems, families of veterans with PTSD have more family violence, more physical and verbal aggression, and more instances of violence against a partner. In these studies, female partners of veterans with PTSD also self-reported higher rates of perpetrating family violence than did the partners of veterans without PTSD. In fact, these female partners of veterans with PTSD reported perpetrating more acts of family violence during the previous year than did their partner veteran with PTSD.

  Similarly, Byrne and Riggs (1996) found that 42 percent of the fifty Vietnam veterans in their study had engaged in at least one act of violence against their partner during the preceding year, and 92 percent had committed at least one act of verbal aggression in the preceding year. The severity of the veteran's PTSD symptoms was directly related to the severity of relationship problems and physical and verbal aggression against the partner.

- *Mental health of partners*. PTSD can also affect the mental health and life satisfaction of a veteran's partner. Numerous studies have found that partners of veterans with PTSD or other combat stress reactions have a greater likelihood of developing their own mental health problems compared to partners of veterans without these stress reactions. For example, wives of Israeli veterans with PTSD have been found to report more mental health symptoms and more impaired and unsatisfying social relations compared to wives of veterans without PTSD. In at least two studies, partners of Vietnam veterans with PTSD reported lower levels of happiness, markedly reduced satisfaction in their lives, and more demoralization compared to partners of Vietnam veterans not diagnosed with PTSD. About half of the partners of veterans with PTSD indicated that they had felt "on the verge of a nervous breakdown." In addition, male partners of female Vietnam veterans with PTSD reported poorer subjective well-being and more social isolation than partners of female veterans without PTSD.

Nelson and Wright (1996) indicate that partners of PTSD-diagnosed veterans often describe difficulty coping with their partner's PTSD symptoms, describe stress because their needs are unmet, and describe experiences of physical and emotional violence. These difficulties may be explained as secondary traumatization, which is the indirect impact of trauma on those in close contact with victims. Alternatively, the partner's mental health symptoms may be a result of his or her own experiences of trauma, related to living with a veteran with PTSD (e.g., increased risk of domestic violence) or related to a prior trauma.

- *Caregiver burden*. Limited empirical research exists that details the specific relationship challenges that couples must face when one of the partners has PTSD. However, clinical reports indicate that significant others are presented with a wide variety of challenges related to their veteran partner's PTSD. Wives of PTSD-diagnosed veterans tend to assume greater responsibility for household tasks (e.g., finances, time management, house upkeep) and the maintenance of relationships (e.g., children, extended family). Partners feel compelled to care for the veteran and to attend closely to the veteran's problems. Partners are keenly aware of cues that precipitate symptoms of PTSD, and partners take an active role in managing and minimizing the effects of these precipitants. *Caregiver burden* is one construct used to categorize the types of difficulties associated with caring for someone with a chronic illness, such as PTSD. Caregiver burden includes the objective difficulties of this work (e.g., financial strain) as well as the subjective problems associated with caregiver demands (e.g., emotional strain).

Why Are These Problems So Common?

Because of the dearth of research that examines the connection between PTSD symptoms and intimate-relationship problems, it is difficult to discern the exact correspondence between them. Some symptoms, like anger, irritability, and emotional numbing, may be direct pathways to relationship dissatisfaction. For example, a veteran who cannot feel love or happiness (emotional numbing) may have difficulty feeling loving toward a spouse. Alternatively, the relationship discord itself may facilitate the development or exacerbate the course of PTSD. Perhaps the lack of communication, or combative communication, in discordant relationships impedes self-disclosure and the emotional processing of traumatic material, which leads to the onset or maintenance of PTSD.

What Are the Treatment Options for Partners of Veterans with PTSD?

The first step for partners of veterans with PTSD is to gain a better understanding of PTSD and the impact on families by gathering information. Resources on the National Center for PTSD Web site (http://www.ncptsd.org) and in the reference list for this fact sheet may be useful. Particularly helpful are the National Center for PTSD fact sheets about the definition of PTSD, effects of traumatic experiences, and frequently asked questions relevant to veterans and their families. Fact sheets on PTSD and the family and PTSD and relationships may also be useful.

With regard to specific treatment strategies, Nelson and Wright (1996) suggest, "[E]ffective treatment should involve family psychoeducation, support groups for both partners and veterans, concurrent individual treatment, and couple or family therapy." Psychoeducational groups teach coping strategies and educate veterans and their partners about the effects of trauma on individuals and families. Often these groups function as self-help support groups for partners of veterans. Preliminary research offers encouragement for the use of group treatment for female partners of Vietnam veterans. Individual therapy for both the veteran and his or her partner is an important treatment component, especially when PTSD symptoms are prominent in both individuals. Couples or family therapy may also be highly effective treatment for individuals' symptoms and problems within the family system. Several researchers have begun exploring the benefits of family or couples therapy for both the veteran and other family members. In light of the recent research on the negative impact of PTSD on families, Veterans Affairs PTSD programs

APPENDIX

(http://www.va.gov) and Vet Centers (http://www.va.gov/rcs/) across the country are beginning to offer group, couples, and individual programs for families of veterans.

Overall, it seems that the most important message for partners is that relationship difficulties and social and emotional struggles are common when living with a traumatized veteran. The treatment options listed earlier are but a few of the available approaches that partners may find useful in their search for improved family relationships and mental health.

Additional Resources

Vietnam Veteran Wives (VVW http://www.vietnamveteranwives.com), established in 1996, is an organization designed to meet the needs of veterans and their families. The specific and primary purpose of VVW is the advancement of research and the distribution of information about PTSD, Agent Orange, and Gulf War diseases. VVW publishes a variety of literature, including newspapers, magazines, and brochures. VVW provides PTSD counseling, safe retreats for wives during times of crisis, a national hotline, and assistance to the families of incarcerated veterans. Membership is open to all family members and significant others of anyone that served in the military during any period.

Avoidance

by Laura E. Gibson, Ph.D., The University of Vermont

Why Have a Fact Sheet on Avoidance?

Avoidance is a common reaction to trauma, and it can interfere with emotional recovery and healing. It is understandable that individuals who have experienced stressful events want to avoid thinking about or feeling emotions related to those events. Research with a wide variety of populations (e.g., survivors of sexual abuse, rape, assault, and motor vehicle accidents) indicates that those individuals who try to cope with their trauma by avoiding thoughts and feelings about it tend to have more severe psychological symptoms. Because the research clearly suggests that avoidance can interfere with recovery and healing, this fact sheet provides an overview of this common reaction to trauma.

What Does Emotional Avoidance Mean?

Emotional avoidance in the context of trauma refers to people's tendency to avoid thinking or having feelings about a traumatic event. For example, a rape survivor may try to suppress thoughts about her rape by forcing herself to think about other things whenever the thoughts arise, or by simply trying to push away thoughts about the rape. She may use emotional avoidance by stopping herself every time she begins to feel sadness about the rape, or by bringing her attention to something that makes her feel less sad. She may say things to herself like "Don't go there" or "Don't think about it."

What Does Behavioral Avoidance Mean?

Behavioral avoidance generally refers to avoiding reminders of a trauma. An extreme example of behavioral avoidance would be for someone who lived in Manhattan to move out of the city after the 9/11 terrorist attacks to avoid reminders of the trauma. Less extreme examples might involve remaining in Manhattan but making sure to avoid Ground Zero to avoid difficult emotional reminders. Other examples would include individuals who try to avoid driving after they have been in car accidents, or assault survivors who go out of their way to avoid the scene of their attack.

Doesn't Avoidance Help People Cope with Trauma?

Not when it is extreme or when it is the primary coping strategy. Many people were raised hearing advice like "Just try not to think about it," "Try to think about positive things," or "Don't dwell on it." These suggestions seem very logical—especially if you grew up hearing them regularly. However, although the desire to turn one's attention away from painful thoughts and feelings is completely natural, research indicates that the more people avoid their thoughts and feelings about difficult life stressors, the more their distress seems to increase and the less likely they are to be able to move on with their lives.

Is All Avoidance Bad?

No, not all avoidance is bad. If you have experienced a traumatic event in your life, it can be extremely useful to learn ways to focus your thoughts and feelings on things that are not related to the trauma. This is typically referred to as "distraction." Distraction is a useful and necessary skill that allows us to get on with our daily routines even when we are feeling very distressed. If it weren't for our ability to distract ourselves, we would have difficulty getting on with our lives after traumatic life events. Our ability to use distraction skills allows us to go to school or work, buy groceries, etc.—even in the face of difficult life events.

While distraction and avoidance can be very useful in the short term, they become problematic when they are the primary means of coping with trauma. When we caution against the use of avoidance, we are really cautioning against the use of avoidance or distraction as the primary means of coping with a trauma. If an individual were to avoid thinking about or having feelings about a trauma all of the time, they would likely have a much harder time recovering from the trauma.

"But If I Let Myself Experience My Emotions, I Would Be Overwhelmed by Them. . . ."

One common reaction to the suggestion that people should allow themselves to feel difficult emotions is a fear that those emotions will overwhelm them. Sometimes people are afraid that if they start crying, they'll cry forever. Other people worry that if they let themselves experience the anger inside them, they will lose control. Attending therapy with someone who is knowledgeable about trauma can be very useful for individuals who harbor these fears. For suggestions on how to locate a therapist in your area, go to the FAQ page at http://neptsd.org. This page contains information about contacting specialists and support groups for PTSD.

Nightmares

by Laura E. Gibson, Ph.D., The University of Vermont

What Are Nightmares?

Nightmares refer to elaborate dreams that cause high levels of anxiety or terror. In general, the content of nightmares revolves around imminent harm being caused to the individual (e.g., being chased, threatened, injured, etc.). When nightmares occur in the context of post-traumatic stress disorder (PTSD), they tend to involve the original threatening or horrifying set of circumstances that was involved during the traumatic event. For example, someone who was in the Twin Towers on September 11, 2001, might experience frightening dreams involving terrorists, airplane crashes, collapsing buildings, fires, people jumping from buildings, etc. A rape survivor might experience disturbing dreams about the rape itself or some aspect of the experience that was particularly frightening (e.g., being held at knifepoint).

Nightmares can occur multiple times in a given night, or one might experience them very rarely. Individuals may experience the same dream repeatedly, or they may experience different dreams with a similar theme. When individuals awaken from nightmares, they can typically remember them in detail. Upon awakening from a nightmare, individuals typically report feelings of alertness, fear, and anxiety. Nightmares occur almost exclusively during rapid eye movement (REM) sleep. Although REM sleep occurs on and off throughout the night, REM sleep periods become longer and dreaming tends to become more intense in the second half of the

APPENDIX

night. As a result, nightmares are more likely to occur during this time.

How Common Are Nightmares?

The prevalence of nightmares varies by age group and by gender. Nightmares are reportedly first experienced between the ages of three and six years. From 10 percent to 50 percent of children between the ages of three and five have nightmares that are severe enough to cause their parents concern. This does not mean that children with nightmares necessarily have a psychological disorder. In fact, children who develop nightmares in the absence of traumatic events typically grow out of them as they get older. Approximately 50 percent of adults report having at least an occasional nightmare. Estimates suggest that between 6.9 percent and 8.1 percent of the adult population suffer from chronic nightmares.

Women report having nightmares more often than men do. Women report two to four nightmares for every one nightmare reported by men. It is unclear at this point whether men and women actually experience different rates of nightmares, or whether women are simply more likely to report them.

Nightmares and Cultural Differences

The interpretation of and significance given to nightmares varies tremendously by culture. While some cultures view nightmares as indicators of mental health problems, others view them as related to supernatural or spiritual phenomena. Clinicians should keep this in mind during their assessments of the impact that nightmares have on clients.

How Are Nightmares Related to PTSD?

Nightmares are one of seventeen possible symptoms of PTSD. One does not have to experience nightmares in order to have PTSD. However, nightmares are one of the most common of the "reexperiencing"

APPENDIX

symptoms of PTSD, seen in approximately 60 percent of individuals with PTSD. A recent study of nightmares in female sexual assault survivors found that a higher frequency of nightmares was related to increased severity of PTSD symptoms. Little is known about the typical frequency or duration of nightmares in individuals with PTSD.

Are There Any Effective Treatments for Nightmares?

Yes. There are both psychological treatments (involving changing thoughts and behaviors) and psychopharmacological treatments (involving medicine) that have been found to be effective in reducing nightmares.

Psychological Treatment

In recent years, Barry Krakow and his colleagues at the University of New Mexico have conducted numerous studies regarding a promising psychological treatment for nightmares. This research group found positive results in applying this treatment to individuals suffering from nightmares in the context of PTSD. Krakow and colleagues found that crime victims and sexual assault survivors with PTSD who received this treatment showed fewer nightmares and better sleep quality after three group-treatment sessions. Another group of researchers applied the treatment to Vietnam combat veterans and found similarly promising results in a small pilot study.

The treatment studied at the University of New Mexico is called "Imagery Rehearsal Therapy" and is classified as a cognitive-behavioral treatment. It does not involve the use of medications. In brief, the treatment involves helping the clients change the endings of their nightmares, while they are awake, so that the ending is no longer upsetting. The client is then instructed to rehearse the new, nonthreatening images associated with the changed dream. Imagery Rehearsal Therapy also typically involves other components designed to help clients with problems associated with nightmares, such as insomnia. For example, clients are taught basic strategies that may help them to improve the quality of their sleep, such as refraining from caffeine during the afternoon, having a consistent evening wind-down ritual, or refraining from watching TV in bed.

Psychologists who use cognitive-behavioral techniques may be familiar with Imagery Rehearsal Therapy, or may have access to research literature describing it. If you need help locating a cognitive-behavioral therapist in your area, try using the clinical referral directory of the Association for the Advancement of Behavior Therapy.

Psychopharmacological Treatment

Researchers have also conducted studies of medications for the treatment of nightmares. However, it should be noted that the research findings in support of these treatments are more tentative than findings from studies of Imagery Rehearsal Therapy. Part of the reason for this is simply that fewer studies have been conducted with medications at this point in time. Also, the studies that have been conducted with medications have generally been small and have not included a comparison control group (that did not receive medication). This makes it difficult to know for sure whether the medication is responsible for reducing nightmares, or whether the patient's belief or confidence that the medication will work was responsible for the positive changes (a.k.a., a placebo effect).

Some medications that have been studied for treatment of PTSD-related nightmares and may be effective in reducing nightmares include topiramate, prazosin, nefazodone, trazodone, and gabapentin. Because medications typically have side effects, many patients choose to try a behavioral treatment first. If that does not help improve their symptoms, they may choose to try medication.

What Happens If Nightmares Are Left Untreated?

Nightmares can be a chronic mental health problem for some individuals, but it is not yet clear why they plague some people and not others. One thing that is clear is that nightmares are common in the early phases after a traumatic experience. However, research suggests that most people who have PTSD symptoms (including nightmares) just after a trauma will recover without treatment. This typically occurs by about the third month after a trauma. However, if PTSD symptoms (including nightmares) have not decreased substantially by about the third month, these symptoms can become chronic. If you have been suffering from nightmares for more than three months, you are encouraged to contact a mental health professional and discuss with him or her the behavioral treatments described above.

Sleep and Post-Traumatic Stress Disorder
By Pamela Swales, Ph.D.

Many people suffer from problems with their sleep. This can be especially true for those who have witnessed or experienced one or more traumatic events such as rape, military combat, natural disasters, beatings, or neighborhood violence. Some individuals exposed to traumatic physical or psychological events develop a condition known as post-traumatic stress disorder (PTSD). It is well-known that a problem with sleep is one of many problems for those with PTSD. Sleep problems, such as difficulty falling asleep, waking frequently, and having distressing dreams or nightmares, are common to those with PTSD. In fact, sleep disturbance can be a normal response to past trauma or anticipated threat.

What Are the Major Reasons Why People with PTSD Have Problems with Sleep?

Severe psychological or physical trauma can cause changes in a person's basic biological functioning. As a result of being traumatized, a person with PTSD may be constantly hypervigilant, or "on the look-out," to protect him- or herself from danger. It is difficult to have restful sleep when you feel the need to be always alert.

What Are Some Sleep Problems Commonly Associated with PTSD?
Difficulty Falling Asleep
- **Basic Biological Changes**: Actual biological changes may occur as a result of trauma, making it difficult to fall asleep. In addition, a continued state of hyperarousal or watchfulness is usually present. It is very hard for people to fall asleep if they think and feel that they need to stay awake and alert to protect themselves (and possibly others) from danger.
- **Medical Problems**: There are medical conditions commonly associated with PTSD. They can make going to sleep difficult. Such problems include: chronic pain, stomach and intestinal problems, and pelvic-area problems (in women).
- **Your Thoughts**: A person's thoughts can also contribute to problems with sleep. For example, thinking about the traumatic event, thinking about general worries and problems, or just thinking, "Here we go again, another night, another terrible night's sleep," may make it difficult to fall asleep.
- **Use of Drugs or Alcohol**: These substances are often associated with difficulty going to sleep.

Difficulty Staying Asleep
- **Distressing Dreams or Nightmares**: Nightmares are typical for people with PTSD. Usually the nightmares tend to be about the traumatic event or some aspect of it. For example, in Vietnam veterans, nightmares are usually about traumatic things that happened in combat. In dreams, the person with

PTSD may also attempt to express the dominant emotions of the traumatic event; these are usually fear and terror. For example, it is not uncommon to dream about being overwhelmed by a tidal wave or swept up by a whirlwind.

- **Night Terrors**: These are events such as screaming or shaking while asleep. The person may appear awake to an observer, but he or she is not responsive.
- **Thrashing Movements**: Because of overall hyperarousal, active movements of the arms or legs during bad dreams or nightmares may cause awakening. For example, if one were having a dream about fleeing an aggressor, one might wake up because of the physical movements of trying to run away.
- **Anxiety (Panic) Attacks**: Attacks of anxiety or outright panic may interrupt sleep. Symptoms of such attacks may include:

  - Feeling your heart beating very fast
  - Feeling that your heart is "skipping a beat"
  - Feeling light-headed or dizzy
  - Having difficulty breathing (e.g., tight chest, pressure on chest)
  - Sweating
  - Feeling really hot ("hot flashes")
  - Feeling really cold (cold sweat)
  - Feeling fearful
  - Feeling disoriented or confused
  - Fearing that you may die (as a result of these symptoms)
  - Thinking and feeling that you may be "going crazy"
  - Thinking and feeling that you may "lose control"

- **Hearing the Slightest Sound and Waking Up to Check for Safety**: Many people with PTSD, especially combat veterans, wake up frequently during the night. This can be for various reasons. However, once awake, a "perimeter check," or a check of the area, is often made. For example, a vet may get up, check the sleeping area, check the locks on windows and doors, and even go outside and walk around to check for danger. Then the vet may stay awake and vigilant and "stand guard;" he (or she) may not return to sleep that night.

What Can You Do If You Have Problems Sleeping Due to PTSD?

Talk to Your Doctor

Let your doctor know that you have trouble sleeping. Tell your doctor exactly what the problems are; he or she can help you best if you share this information about yourself.

Let your doctor know that you have (or think you have) PTSD. It is not your fault that you have these symptoms. Tell your doctor exactly what they are.

Let your doctor know about any physical problems that you think are contributing to your sleep problems. For example, chronic pain associated with traumatic injuries can make it difficult to sleep.

Let your doctor know about any other emotional problems you have—these may also be contributing to your sleep problems. For example, depression or panic attacks can make it hard to fall asleep or to stay asleep.

There are a number of medications that are helpful for sleep problems in PTSD. Depending on your sleep symptoms and other factors, your doctor may prescribe some medication for you.

Your doctor may recommend that you work with a therapist skilled in dealing with emotional and behavioral problems. Psychologists, social workers, and psychiatrists fall into this category. They can help you take a closer look at, and possibly change, the variety of factors that may be preventing you from sleeping well. They can help you with PTSD and other problems.

Do Not Use Alcohol or Other Drugs

These substances disturb a variety of bodily processes. They impair a person's ability to get a good night's sleep. For example, alcohol may help a person fall asleep, but it interferes with one's ability to stay asleep.

If you are dependent on drugs or alcohol, let your doctor know, and seek assistance for this problem.

Other Strategies

- Limit substances that contain caffeine (e.g., soda, coffee, some over-the-counter medicines).
- Try to set a regular sleep/wake schedule:
  A consistent sleep schedule helps to regulate and set the body's "internal clock," which tells us when we are tired and when it is time to sleep, among other things.
- Make your sleeping area as free from distractions as possible:
  Aim for quiet surroundings; keep the room darkened; keep the television out of the bedroom.
- Consider a light nighttime snack:
  A light snack after dinner may prevent hunger from waking you up in the middle of the night.
- Avoid overarousal for at least two to three hours prior to going to sleep:
  Try not to get your body and mind in "arousal mode." Things that may tend to do this are: heavy meals, strenuous exercise, heated arguments, paying bills, and action-packed movies.
- Don't worry that you can't sleep:
  Remember, there may be a number of reasons for your sleep problems. The first step is to talk to your doctor.

The information on this Web site is presented for educational purposes only. It is not a substitute for informed medical advice or training.

APPENDIX

Do not use this information to diagnose or treat a mental health problem without consulting a qualified health professional.

Self-Harm
by Laura E. Gibson, Ph.D., The University of Vermont

What Is Self-Harm?

"Self-harm" refers to the deliberate, direct destruction of body tissue that results in tissue damage. When someone engages in self-harm, they may have a variety of intentions. However, the person's intention is *not* to kill themselves. You may have heard self-harm referred to as "parasuicide," "self-mutilation," "self-injury," "self-abuse," "cutting," "self-inflicted violence," and so on.

How Common Is Self-Harm?

Self-harm is not well understood and has not yet been extensively studied. The rates of self-harm revealed through research vary tremendously depending on how researchers pose their questions about this behavior. One widely cited estimate of the incidence of impulsive self-injury is that it occurs in at least one person per one thousand annually. A recent study of psychiatric outpatients found that 33 percent reported engaging in self-harm in the previous three months. A recent study of college undergraduates asked study participants about specific self-harm behaviors and found alarmingly high rates. Although the high rates may have been due in part to the broad spectrum of self-harm behaviors that were assessed (e.g., severe scratching and interfering with the healing of wounds were included), the numbers are certainly cause for concern:

- 18 percent reported having harmed themselves more than ten times in the past,

- 10 percent reported having harmed themselves more than a hundred times in the past, and
- 38 percent endorsed a history of deliberate self-harm.
- The most frequently reported self-harm behaviors were needle sticking, skin cutting, and scratching, endorsed by 16 percent, 15 percent, and 14 percent of the participants, respectively.

It is important to note that research on self-harm is still in the early stages, and these rates may change as researchers begin to utilize more consistent definitions of self-harm and more studies are completed.

Who Engages in Self-Harm?

Only a handful of empirical studies have examined self-harm in a systematic, sound manner. Self-harm appears to be more common in females than in males, and it tends to begin in adolescence or early adulthood. While some people may engage in self-harm a few times and then stop, others engage in it frequently and have great difficulty stopping the behavior. Several studies have found that individuals who engage in self-harm report unusually high rates of histories of:

- Childhood sexual abuse
- Childhood physical abuse
- Emotional neglect
- Insecure attachment
- Prolonged separation from caregivers

At least two studies have attempted to determine whether particular characteristics of childhood sexual abuse place individuals at greater risk for engaging in self-harm as adults. Both studies reported that more severe, more frequent, or a longer duration of sexual abuse was associated with an increased risk of engaging in self-harm in one's adult years.

Also, individuals who self-harm appear to have higher rates of the following psychological problems.

- High levels of dissociation
- Borderline personality disorder
- Substance abuse disorders
- Post-traumatic stress disorder
- Intermittent explosive disorder
- Antisocial personality
- Eating disorders

Why Do People Engage in Self-Harm?

While there are many theories about why individuals harm themselves, the answer to this question varies from individual to individual.

Some Reasons Why People Engage in Self-Harm:

- To distract themselves from emotional pain by causing physical pain
- To punish themselves
- To relieve tension
- To feel real by feeling pain or seeing evidence of injury
- To feel numb, zoned out, calm, or at peace
- To experience euphoric feelings (associated with release of endorphins)
- To communicate their pain, anger, or other emotions to others
- To nurture themselves (through the process of healing the wounds)

APPENDIX

How Is Self-Harm Treated?

Self-harm is a problem that many people are embarrassed or ashamed to discuss. Often, individuals try to hide their self-harm behaviors and are very reluctant to seek needed psychological or even medical treatment.

Psychological Treatments

Because self-harm is often associated with other psychological problems, it tends to be treated under the umbrella of a co-occurring disorder like a substance abuse problem or an eating disorder. Sometimes the underlying feelings that cause the self-harm are the same as those that cause the co-occurring disorder. For example, a person's underlying feelings of shame may cause them to abuse drugs *and* cut themselves. Often the self-harm can be addressed in the context of therapy for an associated problem. For example, if people can learn healthy coping skills to help them deal with their urges to abuse substances, they may be able to apply these same skills to their urges to harm themselves.

There are also some treatments that specifically focus on stopping the self-harm. A good example of this is Dialectical Behavior Therapy (DBT), a treatment that involves individual therapy and group skills training. DBT is a therapy approach that was originally developed for individuals with borderline personality disorder who engage in self-harm or "parasuicidal behaviors." Now the treatment is also being used for self-harming individuals with a wide variety of other psychological problems, including eating disorders and substance dependence. The theory behind DBT is that individuals tend to engage in self-harm in an attempt to regulate or control their strong emotions. DBT teaches clients alternative ways of managing their emotions and tolerating distress. Research has shown that DBT is helpful in reducing self-harm. To learn more about DBT, or to locate a DBT therapist in your area, go to: http://www.behavioraltech.com/basics.html.

APPENDIX

Pharmacological Treatments

It is possible that psychopharmacological treatments would be helpful in reducing self-harm behaviors, but this has not yet been rigorously studied. As yet, there is no consensus regarding whether or not psychiatric medications should be used in relation to self-harm behaviors. This is a complicated issue to study because self-harm can occur in many different populations and co-occur with many different kinds of psychological problems. If you are wondering about the use of medications for the emotions related to your self-harm behaviors, we recommend that you discuss this with your doctor or psychiatrist.

How to Find a Qualified Psychologist or Psychiatrist

If you are trying to find a psychologist or psychiatrist, we advise you to ask them whether they are familiar with self-harm. Consider which issues are important to you, and make sure you can talk to the potential therapist about them. Remember that you are the consumer—you have the right to interview therapists until you find someone with whom you feel comfortable. You may want to ask trusted friends or medical professionals for referrals to psychologists or psychiatrists. Consider asking your potential provider questions such as:

- How do you treat self-harm?
- What do you think causes self-harm?
- Do you have experience in treating self-harm?

For tips on communicating with medical providers in a medical context (including communicating with professionals in an emergency room), go to http://www.palace.net/~llama/psych/injury.html, click the icon on the left side of the screen that reads "first aid," and then click the icon "what to expect in the emergency room." For more ideas on finding a therapist who is familiar with the treatment

· 253 ·

of self-harm, go to http://www.palace.net/~llama/psych/injury.html, and then click on "offline resources" on the left side of the screen.

Self-Help Resources

There are a variety of self-help books on the market for people who engage in self-harm. Most of these provide practical advice, support, and coping skills that may be helpful to individuals who engage in self-harm. These approaches have not been studied in research trials, so it is not known how effective they are for individuals who self-harm.

My Friend or Relative Self-Harms. What Should I Do to Be Supportive?

If you have a friend or relative who engages in self-harm, it can be very distressing and confusing for you. You may feel guilty, angry, scared, powerless, or any number of things. Some general guidelines are:

- Take the self-harm seriously by expressing concern and encouraging the individual to seek professional help.
- Don't get into a power struggle with the individual—ultimately they need to make the choice to stop the behavior. You cannot force them to stop.
- Don't blame yourself. The individual who is self-harming initiated this behavior and needs to take responsibility for stopping it.
- If the individual who is self-harming is a child or adolescent, make sure the parent or a trusted adult has been informed and is seeking professional help for them.
- If the individual who is engaging in self-harm does not want professional help because he or she doesn't think the behavior

is a problem, inform them that a professional is the best person to make this determination. Suggest that a professional is a neutral third party who will not be emotionally invested in the situation and so will be able to make the soundest recommendations.

Why Seek Help for PTSD?

Most people experience considerable distress and avoidance after being exposed to a severely traumatic experience. This is a normal and adaptive response and often includes reliving the event in thoughts, images, and dreams. This initial rumination of the event may in fact contribute to the healing process and provide a way of achieving mastery over the event. For most people, these symptoms usually become less severe and gradually disappear over time. For others, the symptoms persist and become chronic, leading to PTSD. About 8 percent of men and 20 percent of women develop PTSD after experiencing a traumatic event, and roughly 30 percent of these individuals develop a chronic form that persists throughout their lifetimes.

The symptoms and problems associated with PTSD can interfere with a person's life and become difficult to manage. Turning to someone for help is the first step in addressing the impact of PTSD in your life. Psychologists and other appropriate mental-health providers help educate people about reactions to extreme stress and ways of processing the event and dealing with the emotional impact.

With children, continual and aggressive emotional outbursts, serious problems at school, preoccupation with the traumatic event, continued and extreme withdrawal, and other signs of intense anxiety or emotional difficulties all point to the need for professional assistance. A qualified mental-health professional can help such children and their parents understand and deal with thoughts, feelings, and behaviors that result from trauma.

APPENDIX

Knowing what kind of help is available, where to look for help, and what kind of questions to ask might make the process of seeking help easier and lead to more successful outcomes.

How Is PTSD Assessed and Treated?

In recent years, a great deal of attention has been aimed at developing reliable assessment tools to aid in the diagnosis of PTSD. Today there is a range of available measures that clinicians can use to diagnose PTSD.

PTSD is treated with a variety of forms of psychotherapy and medication. Today there are some promising treatments that include cognitive-behavioral interventions such as cognitive restructuring and exposure.

How Do I Get an Evaluation?

While it may be tempting to identify PTSD for yourself or someone you know, the diagnosis generally is made by a mental-health professional. This will usually involve a formal evaluation by a psychiatrist, psychologist, or clinical social worker specifically trained to assess psychological problems.

What Can I Expect from an Evaluation for PTSD?

The nature of an evaluation for PTSD can vary widely, depending on how the evaluation will be used and the training of the professional evaluator. As part of a screening, an interviewer may take as little as fifteen minutes to get a sense of your traumatic experiences and its effects. On the other hand, a specialized PTSD assessment can last several hours and involve detailed, structured interviews and questionnaires. Whatever the particulars of your situation, you should always be able to find out in advance from the professional conducting the evaluation what the assessment will involve and what information they will be looking for to determine a diagnosis.

How Is PTSD Treated?

The many therapeutic approaches offered to PTSD patients are presented in Foa, Keane, and Friedman's (2000) comprehensive book on treatment. The most successful interventions are cognitive-behavioral therapy (CBT) and medication. Excellent results have been obtained with some CBT combinations of exposure therapy and cognitive restructuring, especially with female victims of childhood or adult sexual trauma. Sertraline (Zoloft) and Paroxetine (Paxil) are selective serotonin reuptake inhibitors (SSRI) that are the first medications to have received FDA approval as indicated treatments for PTSD. Success has also been reported with Eye Movement Desensitization and Reprocessing (EMDR), although rigorous scientific data are lacking and it is unclear whether this approach is as effective as CBT.

What Is Psychotherapy and How Can It Help Treat PTSD?

Psychotherapy is meant to help with a person's emotional, behavioral, or mental distress. In practice, psychotherapy is the relationship between a professional psychotherapist and a client who work together to make changes in the client's thoughts, feelings, and behaviors. How the psychotherapist goes about helping a client will depend upon the client's goals and the therapist's training and theoretical orientation. Theoretical underpinnings can determine what techniques a therapist uses and the focus of therapy, and they can affect the psychotherapist's style of interaction.

However, sometimes a person's diagnosis will influence the decision about what type of therapeutic orientation the person should engage in. PTSD is a good example of this type of diagnosis, because there are many psychotherapeutic treatments that have been designed specifically to treat PTSD. A client's response to treatment will have a lot to do with the unique values, hopes, and personality factors of that individual, but there are some treatments that have been rigorously studied and shown to be helpful for PTSD.

Who Is Available to Provide Psychotherapy?

There are many different types of professionals qualified to practice psychotherapy. These types can be divided into three basic groups: clinical psychologists, clinical social workers, and psychiatrists.

Clinical Psychologists

Clinical psychologists have doctoral degrees (Ph.D., Psy.D., Ed.D.) from graduate programs that specialize in the study of clinical, research, and educational psychology. Programs that are approved by the American Psychological Association (APA) must meet specific teaching and training requirements that adhere to ethical, academic, and clinical standards. In addition to four years of course work, clinical psychologists must complete one year of supervised clinical training. After the fifth year of training, clinical psychologists must have another one to two years of supervised clinical experience to be eligible for licensure. Licensure is granted after passing an examination given by the American Board of Professional Psychology. Licensure allows the psychologist to practice psychotherapy without formal supervision. Although psychologists are doctors, they cannot prescribe medications.

Clinical Social Workers

Certified social workers have a master's degree or doctoral degree in social work (MSW, DSW, or Ph.D.). Graduate training for the master's level requires at least two years of schooling beyond the four years necessary for the undergraduate degree. To be licensed, clinical social workers must pass an exam given by the Academy of Certified Social Workers (ACSW).

Psychiatrists

Psychiatrists attend medical school and have a medical degree (MD). As with other medical specialties, psychiatrists participate in a three- to four-year residency training in psychiatry after they complete four years of medical school. Child psychiatrists must complete at least one year of concentrated clinical experience with children. Board-certified psychiatrists have also passed a written and oral examination given by the American Board of Psychiatry and Neurology. Psychiatrists, like medical doctors, prescribe medications. Some also provide psychotherapy.

Psychotherapeutic Approaches Commonly Used to Treat PTSD

There are a number of different therapeutic approaches used to treat PTSD. We will briefly explain some of the more effective approaches.

Cognitive-Behavioral Treatment (CBT)

Cognitive-behavioral strategies have been the most frequently studied and most effective form of psychotherapy treatment for PTSD. The essential feature in all cognitive therapies is an understanding of PTSD in terms of the workings of the mind. Implicit in this approach is the idea that PTSD is, in part, caused by the way we think. CBT helps people understand the connection between their thoughts and feelings. CBT can help change the way we think ("cognitive restructuring") by exploring alternative explanations, and assessing the accuracy of our thoughts. Even if we are not able to change the situation, we can change the way we think about a situation.

APPENDIX

CBT is based on the understanding that many of our emotional and behavioral reactions to situations are learned. The goal of therapy is to unlearn the unhelpful reactions to certain events and situations and learn new ways of responding. CBT relies on evaluating thoughts to see whether they are based on fact or on assumptions. Often we get upset because we think something is occurring when it is not. CBT encourages us to look at our thoughts as hypotheses to be questioned and tested. CBT for trauma includes strategies for processing thoughts about the event and challenging negative or unhelpful thinking patterns.

Exposure Therapy

Exposure is one form of CBT. Exposure uses careful, repeated, detailed imagining of the trauma (exposure) in a safe, controlled context to help the survivor face and gain control of the fear and distress that was overwhelming during the trauma. In some cases, trauma memories or reminders can be confronted all at once ("flooding"). For other individuals or traumas, it is preferable to work up to the most severe trauma gradually by using relaxation techniques and by starting with less upsetting life stresses or by taking the trauma one piece at a time ("desensitization"). When exposure is conducted by having the person imagine the trauma (such as a rape), it is called "imaginal exposure." When it is done in real life, such as having the person go into a feared situation such as a crowded place, it is called "in vivo exposure." In most cases, both forms of exposure are used.

CBT often involves reading assignments and homework so that clients can practice on their own the techniques they have learned in therapy.

Pharmacotherapy (Medication)

Medications can reduce the anxiety, depression, and insomnia often experienced with PTSD, and in some cases they may help relieve the distress and emotional numbness caused by trauma memories.

Several kinds of antidepressant drugs have contributed to patient improvement in most (but not all) clinical trials, and some other classes of drugs have shown promise. The FDA has approved two medications, paroxetine and sertraline, for use in the treatment of PTSD. Although no medication has been proven to cure PTSD, medications are clearly useful for symptom relief, which makes it possible for survivors to participate in psychotherapy.

Eye Movement Desensitization and Reprocessing (EMDR)
EMDR is a relatively new treatment for traumatic memories that involves elements of exposure therapy and CBT combined with techniques (eye movements, hand taps, sounds) that create an alternation of attention back and forth across the person's midline. While the theory and research are still evolving for this form of treatment, evidence suggests that it is the exposure and cognitive components of EMDR that make it effective, rather than the attentional alternation.

Group Treatment
Group therapy is often an ideal therapeutic setting because trauma survivors are able to share traumatic material within the safety, cohesion, and empathy of other survivors. In such a setting, the PTSD patient can discuss traumatic memories, PTSD symptoms, and functional deficits with others who have had similar experiences. As group members achieve greater understanding and resolution of their individual traumas, they often feel more confident and able to trust. As they discuss and share how they cope with trauma-related shame, guilt, rage, fear, doubt, and self-condemnation, they prepare themselves to focus on the present rather than the past. Telling one's story (the "trauma narrative") and directly facing the grief, anxiety, and guilt related to trauma enables many survivors to cope with their symptoms, memories, and other aspects of their lives.

How Can I Tell If Therapy Is Working Well?

When you begin psychotherapy, you and your therapist should decide together what goals you hope to reach in therapy. Not every person with PTSD will have the same treatment goals. For instance, not all people with PTSD are concerned with lessening their symptoms. Some people want to learn instead the best way to live with existing symptoms and how to cope with other problems associated with PTSD. Perhaps you want to lessen your feelings of guilt and sadness. Perhaps you would like to work on more tangible aspects of your distress, like your relationships at work, or communication issues with your friends and family. Your therapist should help you decide which of these goals seem most important to you, and he or she should discuss with you which goals might take a long time to achieve.

Your therapist should also provide you with a good rationale for the therapy. That is, you should understand why your therapist is choosing a specific treatment for you, how long they expect the therapy to last, and how they will evaluate its effectiveness. The two of you should agree at the outset that this plan makes sense for you and what you will do if it does not seem to be working. If you have any questions about the treatment your therapist should be able to answer them.

Another aspect important to the course of good therapy is the relationship you have with your therapist. If you feel comfortable with your therapist and feel you are working as a team to tackle your problems, it is likely that the therapy will go well. If you have concerns about your therapist, or concerns about the therapy, you should speak with your therapist about them. Therapy is not easy. It can be difficult to talk about painful situations in your life, or about traumatic experiences that you have had. Feelings that emerge during therapy can be frightening and challenging. Talking with your therapist about the process of therapy, and about your hopes and fears in regards to therapy, will help make therapy successful.

APPENDIX

If you have concerns about your therapy or concerns about your therapist that have not been successfully worked out with your therapist, it might be helpful to consult another professional. It is recommended, however, that you let your therapist know you are seeking a second opinion.

How Do I Find a Qualified Therapist?

Selecting a therapist is a highly personal matter. A professional who works very well with one individual may not be a good choice for another person. There are several ways to get referrals to qualified therapists such as licensed psychologists.

Listed below are some ways to find help. When you call, tell whomever you speak to that you are trying to find a mental-health provider who specializes in helping people who have been through traumatic events. Check the National Center for Post-Traumatic Stress Disorder Web site (http://ncptsd.org) regularly for updated information on how to get help. We will be listing more ways to get help as they become available.

For Veterans

VA medical centers and Vet Centers provide veterans with mental-health services that health insurance will cover or that cost little or nothing, according to a veteran's ability to pay. VA medical centers and Vet Centers are listed in the phone book in the blue Government pages. Under "United States Government Offices," look in the section for "Veterans Affairs, Dept. of." In that section look for VA Medical Centers and Clinics listed under "Medical Care" and for "Vet Centers—Counseling and Guidance," and call the one nearest to where you live. On the Internet, go to http://www.va.gov/ and look for the VHA Facilities Locator link under "Health Benefits and Services," or go to www.va.gov/rcs.

For more information see Specialized PTSD Treatment Programs in the U.S. Department of Veterans Affairs.

APPENDIX

For Nonveterans

Some local mental-health services are listed in the phone book in the blue Government pages. In the "County Government Offices" section for the county where you live, look for a "Health Services, Dept. of" or "Department of Health Services" section. In that section, look for listings under "Mental Health." In the Yellow Pages, services and mental-health professionals are listed under "counseling," "psychologists," "social workers," "psychotherapists," "social and human services," or "mental health." Health insurance may pay for mental-health services, and some are available at low cost according to your ability to pay.

For Anyone

Call your doctor's office or ask friends if they can recommend any mental-health providers.

If you work for a large company or organization, call the human resources or personnel office to find out if they provide mental-health services or make referrals.

If you are a member of a Health Maintenance Organization (HMO), call to find out if mental-health services are available.

Call the National Center for Victims of Crime's toll-free information and referral service at 1-800-FYI-CALL. This is a comprehensive database of more than 6,700 community service agencies throughout the country that directly support victims of crime.

Contact your local mental-health agencies or family physician.

Online Resources

The Anxiety Disorders Association of America offers a referral network of professional therapists, as well as a self-help group network.

The Association for Advancement of Behavior Therapy (AABT) is a professional organization that maintains a database of CBT therapists at https://aabt.org/members/Directory/Clinical_Directory.cfm.

The National Institute of Mental Health Anxiety Disorders has

APPENDIX

published an extensive list of mental health organizations to help the consumer find more information about anxiety disorders and related issues, as well as to obtain referrals for specialists in different geographical areas.

The National Alliance for Mental Illness (NAMI) has a Web site (http://www.nami.org) with information on advocacy for those with mental illness, including affiliates who provide family support groups in different states.

About.com's trauma resource page (http://mentalhealth.about .com/od/traumaptsd)offers a comprehensive listing of information, resources, links, and support groups on a wide array of topics related to trauma, particularly incest and child abuse.

Facts for Health (http://www.factsforhealth.org) offers a referral database for clinicians based on clinicians who have completed a continuing-education course on PTSD or clinicians who have been identified by the directors of the Madison Institute of Medicine as being specialists in PTSD.

The Holistic Health Yellow Pages (http://www.findhealer.com) offer a referral network of holistic practitioners.

For more information call the PTSD Information Line at (802) 296-6300, or send e-mail to ncptsd@ncptsd.org.

ACKNOWLEDGMENTS

We wish to thank our agent, Matt Bialer, at Sanford J. Greenburger Associates, for his creative support, business acumen, and assistance in nurturing our collaboration. Matt's assistant, Anna Bierhaus, also deserves acknowledgment for handling our anxious phone calls with aplomb.

Our appreciation also goes to the editor at New American Library who bought *A Sniper's Journey,* Doug Grad, and the editor who saw it to completion, Mark Chait, and their assistant, Brent Howard.

The unsung heroes in bringing *A Sniper's Journey* to the bookshelves are NAL associate managing editor Sally Franklin and copy editor Tiffany Yates, who has a *really* annoying eye for inconsistencies, echoed words and substandard English. But we *really* do thank her for making our book more readable. The cover design, unique for its avoidance of sniper clichés, is by NAL's chief of graphic design, Anthony Ramondo. We're grateful for his creativity.

The subtext of this book deals with the mental health of those who are called upon to fight our nation's wars, and the emotional price they can pay for following the orders they're given. For the insight they've provided during the writing of *A Sniper's Journey,* the authors are grateful to Elizabeth Heron, Ph.D., whose work with the air force is aimed at preventing emotional trauma in troops about to be deployed in combat, and Roger Melton, MFCC, a therapist and Vietnam veteran who has specialized in the treatment of PTSD.

Debra Johnson Knox at MilitaryUSA.com (and author of *How to Locate Anyone Who Is or Has Been in the Military*) graciously assisted in our attempt to locate service members with whom Gary Mitchell served.

Former army snipers in Vietnam Howard Kramer, Neil Korbas, Deano Miller, Chester Clarke, and Brian K. Sain, founder of American-Snipers.org, provided insight and assistance. No matter what your position on the wars our troops are currently committed to, all agree that asking soldiers to do their job without enough of the right equipment is wrong. AmericanSnipers.org has raised hundreds of thousands of dollars to purchase equipment requested by sniper units in Iraq and Afghanistan, equipment that is unavailable on a timely basis through regular supply channels.

While we consulted a number of books about Vietnam and the Gulf War in writing *A Sniper's Journey,* one unique volume is worth a special mention: *Where We Were in Vietnam* by Michael P. Kelley is the definitive reference work for anyone who served in that war and who might still be wondering where he or she really was. Michael also took the time to share considerable information about rifle ranges not necessarily belonging to American forces where sniper training such as Gary Mitchell underwent may have taken place.

It's always useful to have writer friends who are willing to be brutally honest. In this case, thanks go to John Corcoran and Ira Furman for their moral support, and their time and energy in critiquing the work in progress. Kathy Kirkland typed the interview transcripts, and was first to provide valuable feedback on their content.

Finally, thanks to our wives, Ellen Mitchell and Karen Hirsh, for their unflagging support during this uphill marathon.

Gary D. Mitchell entered the U.S. Army in 1968 and retired in 1992. He served a combat tour in Vietnam from 1969 to 1970. He also participated in Operation Desert Shield and Operation Desert Storm, where he was an adviser to the Saudi Arabian National Guard and fought in the battle of Al Khafji. During his twenty-four-year career, he was stationed in Korea, Vietnam, Germany, and Saudi Arabia, as well as numerous installations in the continental United States. Starting as a private, he retired as a chief warrant officer. He and his wife, Ellen, reside in California.

Michael Hirsh was a combat correspondent with the 25th Infantry Division at Cu Chi, Vietnam, in 1966, where he earned the CIB. In 2002 he was embedded with Air Force Combat Search and Rescue forces in Operation Enduring Freedom on bases in Afghanistan, Pakistan, and Uzbekistan to write *None Braver: U.S. Air Force Pararescuemen in the War on Terrorism*. He is also the author of *Your Other Left: Punch Lines from the Front Lines*. Hirsh is a George Foster Peabody Award and Writers Guild Award winner, as well as an Emmy Award–winning television documentary producer and investigative reporter. He lives in Punta Gorda, Florida.

DOMIOAOIIIRE
DEPORTVGAL

INSIGHT
GUIDES

PORTUGAL

Directed and Designed by Hans Höfer
Edited by Alison Friesinger Hill
Photography by Tony Aruzza

A P A
PUBLICATIONS

PORTUGAL

First Edition (3rd Reprint)
© **1991 APA PUBLICATIONS (HK) LTD**
All Rights Reserved
Printed in Singapore by Höfer Press Pte. Ltd

ABOUT THIS BOOK

Portugal was long one of those countries beloved by a small group of visitors and foreign residents who hoped to keep the country's special charms as secret as possible. Now a healthy democracy and new member of the European Common Market, Portugal is rapidly gaining new friends and devotees.

With a history as rich as any in Europe and a tradition of sending intrepid explorers around the world in search of spices, silks and empire, Portugal is an ideal subject for the kind of serious travel writing for which the Insight Guides have gained international recognition. These books combine fine writing, history in depth and current factual information and outstanding photographs. The books are dedicated to the concept of making travel a truly memorable experience.

This concept was originated in 1970 by **Hans Höfer**, founder and publisher of Apa Publications. A native of West Germany, Höfer was trained in the Bauhaus tradition, combining education in book design, production and photography. His first book, *Insight Guide: Bali*, published in 1970, won international honors and set the pattern for the large library of books that has followed from Apa headquarters in Singapore.

Following his usual procedure, Höfer assigned to a single project coordinator the responsibility for gathering the best available group of writers and photographers qualified to write about the book's subject. In this case, he turned to **Alison Friesinger Hill** who first wrote on Portugal with her husband for *McCall's* Magazine.

Hill has been writing and editing since receiving her degree in English Language and Literature from Harvard College. As a freelancer, she worked for many publications, including *The New York Times Book Review*, *American Health*, *New Woman*, and *Spy*. She and her husband have co-written a humor book called *Otherwise Engaged*. Hill was also the editor of *Insight Guide: Lisbon*. She has traveled in the United States, Switzerland, Greece and Italy.

Tony Arruza, based in West Palm Beach, Florida, already had thousands of photographs of Portugal in his collection. However, he spent months capturing new impressions of a country he loves – dawns in tiny fishing villages, late nights in city nightclubs, perfect shots caught along highways and in the mountains. Arruza is particularly adept at that most elusive subject of photography: people. In the pages that follow, the reader can truly get to know the Portuguese, thanks to Arruza's skill. His work was also featured in *Inside Guide: Barbados*.

Thomas Hill, Alison's husband, wrote the section on Portugal's history and the article "The Portuguese". Holding a degree from Harvard in History and Literature, Hill has had extensive writing experience.

For the section on Lisbon and its environs, and the section on the most important wine provinces, editor Hill turned to **Marvine Howe**. After graduating from Rutgers Journalism School, she covered the African independence movements as a stringer for *The New York Times*. In 1962, she discovered Portugal and made Lisbon her base. Her many years there has led to her great fondness for the country and made her an expert on Portugal. She is now part of *Times'* staff.

Sharon Behn, who contributed the article on the Algarve and also the feature on the

A.F. Hill

Arruza

T. Hill

Howe

pousada and manor-house system of inns, is another serious, well-traveled journalist. Born in Peru, she has lived in the U.S., England, Brazil, and of course, Portugal. Her travel history is endless, and she has written for publications which include *The Los Angeles Times* and Britain's *Independent*. She now freelances and is a stringer at the UPI wire service's Lisbon bureau.

The long article on the Alentejo was written by **Deborah Brammer**, a freelance writer who lives in Lisbon. A native of England, she first ventured out of England at the age of 18, and has had a case of the travel bug ever since. She and her Portuguese husband satisfy this with domestic explorations into the hidden corners of Portugal in their jeep.

Jeremy Boultbee, who wrote about Portugal's most remote sections, Trás-os-Montes and the Beiras, was born in Canada. He lives in Sintra, Portugal, where he pursues careers as ceramicist, canocist and actor, as well as a writer. He formerly worked as a correspondent for Canada's *Maclean's* magazine.

Jenny Wittner wrote the sections on Coimbra and its surrounding areas, as well as compiling the very informative Travel Tips. As an undergraduate at Harvard College, she worked on the *Let's Go* travel series. She later moved to Coimbra and now lives in Lisbon, where she teaches English.

The feature on Portuguese art and architecture was lovingly written by **Ruth Rosengarten**, an artist herself who lives in Lisbon. Born in Israel, Rosengarten received her B.A. in Johannesburg and her M.A. in London, and has been teaching and practicing art since then.

Peter Wise wrote "Trees of the Alentejo" and "Fishing Communities". Until 1974, he and his Portuguese wife were living in England, but after the Revolution they decided to return to her native country. Wise, who is also an expert on the complex subject of Portuguese politics, is currently a stringer for the AP wire service and has written articles for *The Washington Post, The Boston Globe*, and many other publications.

To write about Portugal's stunning wines, Hill recruited an experienced New York City sommelier. **Scott Carney**, of Gotham restaurant, already knew about Portugese wines when he honeymooned there a number of years ago; he just wanted to see and taste for himself. It surpassed his high expectations, and since then Carney has kept up-to-date by constant reading – and sampling.

Jean Anderson probably has written more about Portugal's food than anyone in the U.S. Her book, *The Food of Portugal*, is just one of many cookbooks and magazine articles she has authored. The article she wrote for this guide is a lively introduction to the savory eating found in Portugal.

The author of "Travelers to Portugal", **Katherine Barrett Swett**, is no stranger to Insight Guides, having edited *Insight Guide: Italy*. She has also contributed travel articles to several magazines.

The pseudonymous **Antonio Dos Santos**, who contributed the article "Saints, Miracles and Shrines", is a Portuguese academic.

Among those who helped in many other ways, Hill would like to thank **Antonio Madeira, Evelyn Heyward, Pam Brown** and **Al de Sousa**.

–APA Publications

Brammer   *Wise*   *Anderson*

CONTENTS

SIGHTS

FEATURES

MAPS

TRAVEL TIPS

PORTUGAL BECKONS

Portugal has always been the land on the edge, caught between traditional ways of living—fishing and farming—and the technology and integration that makes the world today so small. It is a cozy country, 34,332 square miles (88,944 square km) in total size and with a population of under 10 million. And it unquestionably has been blessed with some of the most beautiful landscapes in the world—endless beaches, like the Dona Ana near Lagos; craggy mountain ranges, including the Serra da Estrela with its top peak of 6,532 feet (1,991 meters); and the stark open plains of the southern central area, dotted with cork trees. All are crowned by stunning blue skies. It is a temperate country, both in weather and in mood; its people are gentle and warm, and generally an optimistic bunch.

The traveler is welcome in every corner of this marvelous land, from the *boites* in Lisbon, open for dancing until 4 a.m., to the most obscure village in Trás-os-Montes, with its simple ways of baking, spinning and farming. Sample whatever is to your taste—perhaps a little of it all.

This guide will start you off with a thorough lesson in Portugal's long and fascinating history, followed by a brief introduction to its people, insofar as it is possible to sum up any nation of individuals. Next, the Places section will take you on a tour of the entire country. The last section, features, will familiarize you with Portugal's foods and wines, with its wonderful *pousada* and manor house inns, and with its glorious art and architecture. Waste no more time here; read on to discover Portugal!

Preceding pages, the brilliant Serpa light; boat-watching at Cascais; the Alentejo plains; laundry day in Lisbon. Left, the god Bacchus in 17th-century *azulejos*

1147

1227

1497

176

1385

1834

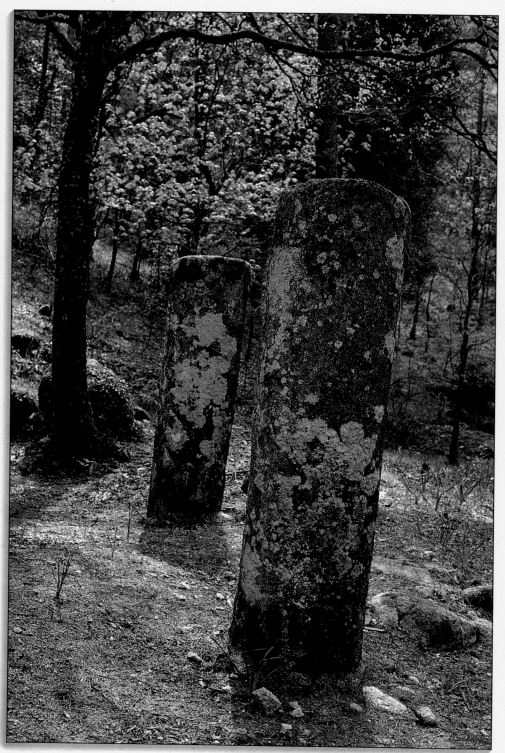

ANCIENT LUSITANIA

Portugal is something of an anomaly on the map of Western Europe. Not separated from neighboring Spain by any natural frontiers nor by a distinctive clime, the country's independence flaunts the dictates of geographical destiny. Each region of Portugal—the only exception being Lisbon's bay and its alluvial plains—corresponds closely to a region across the border. The northern Minho district is similar to Spanish Galicia; the southern Algarve and Alentejo districts to Andalusia and so on. The Tagus and Douro Rivers and the mountains of Beira Baixa extend into Spain. In fact, the natural division of the Iberian peninsula would divide not east from west, but north from south, the Atlantic culture and climate from the Mediterranean.

Yet Portugal exists, wholly an individual, politically and culturally. In fact, as its borders were established in the 13th century, it is one of the oldest nations in Europe. It has discovered and lost an empire, lost and regained its cherished autonomy and, in the last 25 years, stubbornly held and finally lost its last imperial colonies in Africa and the Indies.

A rich prehistoric culture has left its archaeological traces throughout Portugal. There is evidence of the earliest stages of human evolution and a large number of megalithic sites. The variety and quantity of these finds have led many scholars to a theory of maritime irradiation, supposing that cultural diffusion came primarily from overseas. Opponents of this notion point out that most of the megalithic sites are far from the coastline. They think the population grew via natural land routes of settlement which, not surprisingly, correspond to the paths invaders have taken throughout Portugal's history: across the Minho river from the north and over the Alentejo flatlands from the south.

In any case, by the second millennium B.C., the social organization was composed of scattered *castros*, garrisoned hilltop villages that suggest warfare between tribes. The people subsisted on goat-herding and primitive agriculture, and clad themselves in woolen cloaks. Some of their constructions are still standing, for example, at the Citânia de Briteiros near Guimarães. In the south, tribes came under the influence of ninth-century Phoenician and sixth-century Greek trade settlements. These early visitors made their presence felt throughout the south, both on the coast and in-

land, where metals were mined. Interestingly, it is only at this late point that there is evidence of a significant fishing economy among the indigenous people. Perhaps before then the rough-hewn and storm-beaten Atlantic coast was too intimidating for their small boats. During the 5th century B.C., the Carthaginians wrested control of the Iberian peninsula from these earlier traders, but lost it to the Roman Empire in the Second Punic War.

Wars of Conquests: The Romans called the peninsula **Hispania Ulterior**. Here, as elsewhere in the Empire, they combined their economic exploitation with cultural upheaval. They were not traders, after all, but conquerors, who quickly went to the business of founding cities, building roads, and reorganizing territories. They also implemented governmental and judicial systems. There was resistance among the inhabitants. The largest and most intransigent group were the Lusitani, who lived north of the Tagus, and after whom the area that is now Portugal was called Lusitania. Bitter guerrilla fighting was intermittent for two centuries. The most renowned rebel was a shepherd named Viriathus. He led uprisings until he was assassinated in 139 B.C. by three traiterous comrades who had been bribed by the Romans. It was during these wars of conquest that Roman troops are said to have refused to cross the Lima river, believing it to be the Lethe, the mythological river of forgetfulness. Their commander had to cross the river alone, then call each soldier by name to prove that the dip had not affected his memory.

Beginning in 60 B.C., Julius Caesar governed the province from the capital established at Olisipo (Lisbon). Cities were established and colonized at modern day Évora, Beja, Santarém, and elsewhere. Roads linked the north and south, aiding commerce and hastening the homogeneity of the area. Before the decline and fall, the Romans had infused the area with their language, legal systems, currency, agriculture, and eventually, with Christianity. The organization, of *latifundia* was particularly significant, it brought large-scale farming to the area for the first time, particularly in the south. The centers and routes the Romans chose have waxed and waned in importance, but today many are still geographic focal points. The most significant example, of course, is Lisbon.

With the conversion of the late Roman Emperors, the tenets and organizations of Christianity were spread throughout the fading empire. Bishoprics were established in a number of cities, notably Braga and Évora. As the church expanded it drew upon and later usurped the administrative power that had been developed by the Empire. Situated at the edge of Christian expansion, indeed, on the edge of the known world, pre-Portugal was susceptible to frontier rebellions against dogma. Heretical Christian doctrines held sway in Portugal during the 3rd and 4th centuries. In the early 5th century various groups of barbarians occupied the land. The Alani and Vandals each settled in for a short time, but by 419 the Suevi were in sole, if not steady possession of Galicia, and from there they conquered Lusitania and most of the Iberian Peninsula. The Suevi apparently assimilated easily with the existing Hispano-Roman population. But the tide turned on them in the form of the Visigoths. For the next 50 years, military conquest meant religious conversion. In 448, Rechiarius, king of a diminished

of Portugal was now a part of Moslem Spain, loosely organized underneath the Cordoba caliph. To them, this country was *Al-Gharb*, (the West), a term from which was derived the modern name of Algarve. The Moors soon ruled all of Portugal—Christianity was forced north of the Minho where it lay gathering strength for the *Reconquista*.

For centuries, the Moors ruled tolerantly, living in relative tranquility with Jews and Christians. They contributed new methods and crops to agriculture, including fruit orchards and rice fields. In 868, the first significant efforts to break from Spain began. A revolt was staged by a rich landowner nicknamed "The Galician," because he was a native of Spain whose family had converted to Islam. After three failed rebellions, he succeeded in founding a semi-independent state,

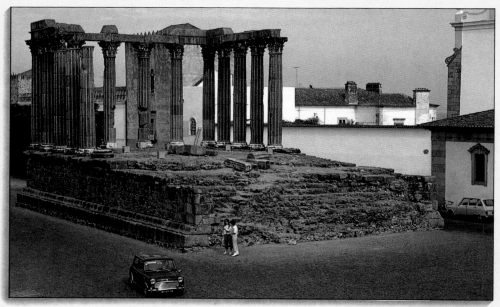

Suevi empire, converted to Catholicism, perhaps hoping to elicit aid from Rome in battling the Visigoths who were Christian but clung to the heretical Arianism. Rechiarius was killed in 457, but the Suevi kingdom survived, led by Masdra. In 465, Masdra's son Recchismundus converted to Arianism, probably to appease the Visigoths. By 550, the growing power of the Catholic Church led to a new round of conversions led by St. Martin of Dume, and apparently the Visigoths had finally had enough. The remnants of the Suevi were politically extinguished in 585.

Invaders from the South: Visigoth rule, an elective monarchy that soon bred internal dissension, was not seriously challenged until the Moors, who had arrived on the southern coast in 711, began their expansion northward. The south

in 885. His son took over after his death, but showed less fortitude, losing it all back to the caliph by 930.

Over the next decade, the overarching authority of the caliph decayed, and small kingdoms, *taifas*, took over. The decentralization naturally led to internal dissension, partly caused by the rise of a religious sect called Sufi. Sufism was a subversive and heretical brand of mysticism that grew popular in reaction to the formalism and rationalism of Islam. Its significance was twofold: just as it allowed Christian forces to push the frontier lines downward from the north, it also allowed for radical Moslem military groups like the Almoravid and the Almohad to rise to power quickly.

The Almoravids, who had built an empire in

Africa, came north. After helping the Islamic rulers to force the Christians back, they decided to take over, to unify the *taifas* under them. By 1095 the Almoravids had succeeded, installing an austere military system and harsh government. As if that weren't enough, they were soon followed by the still more fanatical Almohads. The simmering Reconquista took on the aspect of a Holy War for both Christians and Moslems.

The stormy frontier in the center of Portugal that so threatened the Moslems had been gathering momentum for centuries. The first serious blows for a Christian return were struck in the mid-eigth century by marauders from Asturias-León (northern Spain). All of northern Portugal became a battleground. Slowly towns fell before the Christian armies. Oporto in 868, Coimbra in 878, and by 955, the king of León, Ordona III,

9th century, the area between the Lima and Douro Rivers was made into a separate territory named for its capital city, Portucale. The area was variously divided under the unstable feudal states. Stability came with a dynasty of *duces*, beginning with Gonçalo Mendes, so that the province was held by one family for a century beginning in 950. It was still under the supreme control of the Kingdom of León, but unlike León's other provinces, the power and autonomy of Portucale were on the rise.

Self-proclaimed Emperor: Fernando I of León was the great consolidating force of northern Spain during the 11th century. As part of his policy of centralizing authority, he tried to dismantle Portugal, dividing it into different provinces under separate governors. None of these efforts made a lasting difference. When

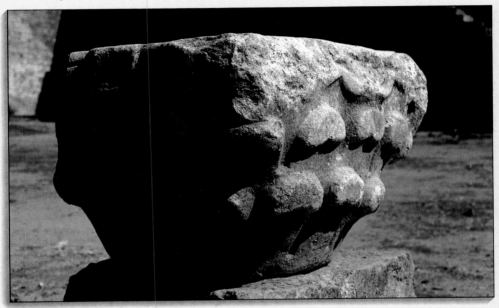

engineered a raid of Lisbon. Most of the victories below the Douro, however, amounted to nothing more than raids, as the territory was seldom held for more than a season or two.

Portugal's independence has been attributed to various causes, including the indigenous megalithic cultures whose borders were accepted by Rome and the resistance that the Suevi offered to the Visigoth hordes. However, it was during the Christian Reconquest of Iberia that Portugal first truly asserted its independent status and its leaders took on a sense of national destiny. Late in the

Left, the Roman temple in Évora, possibly dedicated to the goddess Diana, recently cordoned off to the public. Above, remnants of Visigothic pillar in Serpa

Fernando's successor Alfonso VI took upon himself the title of Emperor, it was over the kingdoms of León, Castile, Galicia and Portugal. "Emperor" was a bit of a stretch at this point, given the unstable ties of vassalage between the various players of the period, but it was an important claim because an emperor logically rules over kings. It was the lure of the title "king" that would inspire Afonso Henriques to battle, deal and connive for the autonomy of his particular *terra*, Portugal.

Afonso Henriques was the son of Henri of Burgundy and his wife Teresa. Henri was among a number of French knights who had arrived in the late 11th century to fight the infidels. They were mostly second and third sons, who, in the feudal system, were left with no real inheritance.

If they wanted land and riches, they usually had to travel abroad to win them. Henri's cousin Raymond, like Henri a fourth son, also came south. After proving his heroism in battle, Raymond married Alfonso VI's daughter Urraca, and was granted the territories of Galicia and Coimbra. With Henri's marriage to Teresa, who was Alfonso's favorite, though illegitimate daughter, he was given the territory of Portugal. With the death of Raymond and Alfonso VI, Urraca inherited that crown, but her second marriage, to another Alfonso, this one known as Alfonso I of Aragon, also set off a complex round of civil wars.

During this period, Henri made significant strides toward the autonomy of the state of Portugal. The most important of these was the support he offered to the archbishops of Braga in an

some of the nobility and her son. Continuing Henri's policies, Teresa schemed successfully to maintain Portugal's independence for awhile, but in 1127 she submitted to Alfonso VII's dominion after her army was defeated. It was in 1128 that the 18-year-old Afonso Henriques led his first rebellion, toppling his mother's rule at the battle of São Mamede, near their castle in Guimarães.

A King is Crowned: Over the next decade, Afonso Henriques vied with his cousin the emperor for ultimate control of Portugal. After a brilliant military conquest over the Moors in the Battle of Ourique, in 1139, he began to refer to himself as king. In 1143, the Treaty of Zamora was signed between them wherein Alfonso VII gave Afonso Henriques the title of King of Portugal in exchange for the usual feudal ties of mili-

ecclesiastical dispute with those of Toledo. Essentially, this rift was parallel to the growing political conflict. The Pope had granted the archbishop of Toledo dominion over all of the Christian Iberian Peninsula. The archbishop at Braga resisted the Roman decree, claiming a traditional right to autonomy, based on ancient ecclesiastical divisions. Henri's support served to solidify Braga's rights for practical purposes, and more importantly, served his own ends: to further solidify the political borders of Portugal.

In 1126 Urraca died and her son, Alfonso Raimundez, became the Emperor Alfonso VII. Henri had died and Teresa had retained Portugal as regent for her son, Afonso Henriques. Without wasting much time in mourning, she took a Galician count, Fernão Peres, as a lover, displeasing

tary aid and loyalty.

Though it was a victory, Afonso Henriques sought to fix the title more firmly by seeking recognition from Rome. Pope Lucius II refused, keeping to a policy of supporting Iberian union in order to better stem the tide of Islam. It was not until 1179 that Pope Alexander III, in exchange for a yearly tribute and various other privileges, finally granted recognition of the Portuguese kingdom to Afonso Henriques, who was by then nearly 70 years old.

By that late date, papal acceptance only served to formalize an entity that was not only well-established but growing. Afonso Henriques had enlisted the aid of crusaders and led the Reconquest over the Moors, adding his conquests to the emerging nation. Santarém and Lisbon were both taken in 1147; the first by surprise attack, the second in a siege that was supported by French, English, Flemish and German crusaders who were passing through Portugal on their way to the Holy Land. The inestimable assistance of these 164 ships of men was entirely fortuitous, and very nearly fell through when Afonso Henriques pronounced that he expected them to fight only for Christianity and not for earthly rewards. The English and Germans walked out; the king quickly rescinded, offering loot and land grants all around.

The Western Crusade: The bishop also added his aid here, providing theological assurance that these were the very same enemy that would be found in the Holy Land. However, this philosophical conundrum apparently plagued Afonso Henriques at times. His confessor questioned the

the Church that the "western crusade" was just as valuable as that to be found in Palestine. Another important development of the Reconquest was the founding of military-religious organizations like the Knights Templar and the Hospitalers. These groups were rewarded with land grants in exchange for chasing out the Moors. Both groups grew wealthy and powerful—uncomfortably so, for some later kings.

In 1170 Afonso Henriques fought his last battle, at Badajoz. The powerful Almohads had enlisted the aid of Fernando II of León, who felt that the Portuguese were recapturing not only the Moorish land, but land that was by right a part of León. The most renowned of Afonso Henriques' military cohorts was Geraldo Geraldes, a local adventurer who was dubbed *O Sem Pavor* (the Fearless) for his brilliant raids into Moslem terri-

diversion of troops from the Crusade, and legend has it that on the way to Santarém—with crusaders in tow—the King was besieged by guilt and anxiety because of the Moorish stronghold's reputation of impregnability. To soothe his torment, he vowed to St. Bernard that he would build the Abbey at Alcobaça in the Virgin's honor if the battle was successful. The battle was won: the Abbey still stands.

Convincing crusaders that one batch of infidel was as good as another was crucial to the Reconquista. Portuguese kings naturally argued with

Left, two depictions of Afonso Henriques, first king of Portugal. Above, an 18th-century engraving of Afonso rallying his troops at the conquest of Lisbon in 1147

tory. This national hero had taken a string of epic victories, but at Badajoz, the combination of Moorish and Leónese forces was too much for Geraldes and his king. The aging Afonso Henriques broke his leg in the midst of the battle and was captured. His release came only after he had surrendered the castles and the territories to both enemy parties. His retreat allowed the Moors to entrench along the battle zone. The founding king of Portugal's days of victory were over, with the final triumph of the Reconquista still a century away. Yet, with Afonso Henriques' monarchy a country was born, and whether this achievement was truly an act of political will or simply a matter of historical confluence, the independence and individuality of the Portuguese nation was forever determined.

A NATION IS BORN

For a century after the death of Afonso Henriques in 1285, the first order of business was the slow riddance of the remaining, and still feisty, Moors. The *Reconquista*, now as good as sanctioned by the Church with various Papal bulls and indulgences as a "western crusade," was still very much underway.

The Knights Templar had arrived in Portugal with the crusaders stopping on their way to Palestine in 1128. They were soon followed by other military-religious orders: Hospitalers, Calatrava, and Santiago. These groups clung to the religious justification for their war-mongering and for their massive accumulation of land and loot. Still, the western crusade remained an awkward idea. Unlike Palestine, where the dividing line between Christians and infidels was clearly drawn, the south of Iberia had intermingled Moslem, Christian, and Jewish peoples in economic, cultural, and even political spheres. In 1197, papal indulgences were even promised in a war against Alfonso IX of Leon, a Christian, though at that time an ally of the Moslems. In truth, the *Reconquista* was, from the beginning, a matter of inheritance as much as religion. The Christians traced their ancestry, and their claims to the land, back to the age of Visigoth rule. They fought for the cities of man, not the City of God.

The frontier war proceeded steadily, if somewhat slowly. The first kings of the Burgundian line after Afonso Henriques continued to press the borders southward. Under Sancho II, the eastern Algarve and Alentejo were incorporated into the burgeoning nation. Under Afonso III, the western Algarve and Faro had fallen by 1249. The latter ruler also moved the capital south from Coimbra to Lisbon in 1256. These boundaries—essentially the ones that exist today—were officially and finally recognized by Castile in the Treaty of Alcañices in 1297. Thus, Portugal is one of the oldest countries in Europe.

Along with political settlement, the *Reconquista* brought Portugal fundamental social transformations. Having reclaimed the lands of the south, they now needed to recolonize and populate them. To do this, the Burgundian kings needed to balance their centralized, essentially military power with popular support. The need for popular and financial support forced kings to consult with *cortes*, local assemblies of nobles,

clergy, and, somewhat later, mercantile classes. At the *cortes* of Leiria (1254), Afonso III conceded the right of municipal representation in questions of taxation and other economic issues. For the most part, the *cortes* were gathered whenever the king needed to raise money. João I would make particular political use of them. When later monarchs used trade and their own military orders to reap great and independent profits, the *cortes* fell into disuse.

Another result of the *Reconquista*, with the expansion of properties and the need for laborers who were willing to resettle, was an increase in social mobility among the lower classes. Distinctions fell away among the various levels of serfs as farm workers became a scarcer and so a more valuable commodity. Another, more general effect of the *Reconquista* was the beginning of amalgamation of the divergent cultures of north and south. The south was still marked by refinement and urbanity; it was a culture with a tradition of tolerance. In contrast, the northern culture had a rough arrogance, the attitude of invaders. They were, though they may have traced their lineages back to pre-Moslem Iberia, an emigrant nobility. Though the cultures of north and south would meld, differences remain even now.

The Church, naturally, rode the *Reconquista* to riches. The various orders were granted vast areas of land by the kings in return for their military aid. The church and clergy were also free of taxation, and were granted the right to collect their own "tenths" from the population. Their power was such that it soon threatened the monarchy. Afonso II was the first ruler of Portugal to defy the Church in attempting to curb its voracious acquisition of property. His efforts generally failed, as did those of his successor, Sancho II, who was finally excommunicated and dethroned in 1245 for his insistence on royal prerogatives.

It was the reign of Dinis, who was known as both the farmer king and the poet king, that truly cemented Portuguese independence, and at the core of independence, the power of the monarchy. It was his foresight and administrative genius that brought the nation into a new era. After briefly joining the nation of Aragon in war against Castile, Dinis ushered in a long period of peace and progress. Dinis encouraged learning and literature, establishing the first Portuguese university in 1288, first in Lisbon and later transferred to Coimbra. Portuguese, having distinguished itself from its Latin roots and from Castilian (which would become Spanish), established itself as the language of the troubadour culture, and the official language of law and state.

Left, Dom Dinis, whose reign saw the foundation of castles, forests, and the University of Lisbon, represented in a 17th-century screen made in China

The troubadour culture—poetry and music spread by peripatetic minstrels—was greatly influential, more so than the official Church teachings of the University. Drawing upon the French tradition, and upon Moorish influences of, the Portuguese troubadours created a unique native literature. These song-poems of love and satire were often written by nobles, among them Dinis the "poet king", of course, and Sancho I as well. The singers were Moors, Jews, some lower nobles, and villeins, members of the free peasant class of the feudal hierarchy. Other forms of literary expression lagged far behind poetry. Neither history nor prose would offer any memorable achievements before the 15th century.

Dinis's rule also brought political progress. Landmark agreements were made to seal peace with Castile (the Treaty of Alcañices, 1297) and finally began to shift the population center of the nation from north to south.

By now a monetary economy was well established, not only for international trade, but internally. Agricultural production was more and more geared toward markets, though self-sufficient farming did not disappear. Dinis encouraged the expansion of the economic system with fairs, large chartered trading centers that encouraged internal trade and thus allowed for greater specialization. Dinis was responsible for chartering 48 of these fairs, more than all the other Portuguese kings combined. The concentration of trade into fairs also, not coincidentally, allowed for a more systematic taxation.

The only section of the Portuguese economy to lag during this period was industrial production. In this case Dinis, and later kings, were counter-

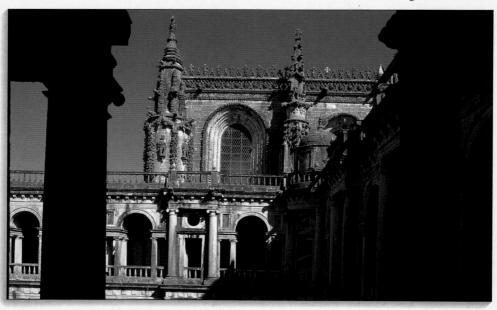

the clergy (the Concordat of 1289). The latter agreement was a major victory for royal jurisdiction in matters of property. During his reign, Dinis fortified the frontier by supporting and sometimes financing the construction of 50 castles. He organized the first national maritime organization, hiring skilled Genoese sailors for the task. In 1308 he signed the original pact of friendship with England that has been reconfirmed and expanded many times since. The "farmer king" also reformed the national agriculture, establishing forest plantations and other programs that soon allowed the export of grain, olive oil, wine and other foodstuffs. Portugal also profited from illicit trade with Islamic countries, acting as intermediary between them and the northern countries. These coastal developments

productive in their resistance to the idea of corporations. Craftsmen tended to work on their own, and thus confined themselves to local markets and limited quantities. There was a bit of goldsmithing, shipbuilding, and pottery done in commercial quantities, but for the most part craftsmen worked alone.

Perhaps the most significant of all of Dinis's accomplishments was his management of the disbanding of the Knights of Templar in 1312. The order was under fire throughout Europe; their demise was imminent. Dinis's triumph was to retain their great wealth within the country and to prevent the Church or any other order from taking over the material and land holdings for themselves. In 1317 he founded a new organization, the Order of Our Lord Jesus Christ. The Order

101 CASTLES

It is said that there are 101 castles in Portugal, most of which were built or rebuilt between the 12th and 14th centuries. King Dinis (1279-1325) began building or expanding more than 50 fortresses during his reign. His labors can be seen throughout Portugal, but the *Ribacoa*, a narrow strip of land along Portugal's eastern boundary, was where he concentrated his efforts. He strengthened the towns of Guarda, Penedo, Penamacor, Castelo Mendo, Pinhel and others, attempting to secure the area from the threat of Castile. He was rewarded: The Treaty of Alcanices, signed in 1297, gave Portugal the Ribacoa.

were on the sites of earlier forts: Morrish, Visiothic, Roman, or earlier. It is interesting to note developments in warfare that were reflected in physical features of Portugal's castles. Long verandas of wood, for example were in early days attached to the castles' walls. Later these were covered with animal hides so they could not be burned easily by flaming arrow, but were abandoned at the end of the 13th century. By then, the carved stone balconies, were used for the same purpose, with the added detail of the machicolation, which allowed defenders to repel attackers as they attempted to scale the castle wall. But the

Dinis provided the money for the castles, and even the exact measurements of the walls and towers. The castles of King Dinis were of a particularly fine construction, with decorations and designs not found on other buildings. Some of the towers were slender and elegant; many balconies elaborate, with detailed machicolations. Dinis often gave certain character or grandness to the structures, as in the 15 towers, he had built at Numao, or the delightful Torre do Galo, "Rooster Tower," at Freixo de Espada a Cinta, with its unusual and beautiful seven faces.

Many castles—built by Dinis and others—

Left, the Convent of Christ in Tomar, built by the Knights Templar and inherited by the Order of Christ. Above, the castle at Almourol.

most significant change came, with the advent of gunpowder and the artillery it brought. The heavy cannons required thicker walls to be built, sloped to resist the more powerful projectiles. Another reason for the thicker walls was so that the ramparts, running along the tops of the walls, could be wider. Earlier only men and their bows stood here, now the castles' heavy artillery was perched. Arrow slits, a common feature in castles, first became round to accommodate the new artillery, but were abandoned as impractical.

The sight of Portugal's charming castles will delight. Several of note are **Almeida**, east of Guarda; **Almourol**, perhaps the most romantic of all, set on its own small craggy island in the Tagus River and surrounded by myths; and, of course, **Guimaraes**, birthplace of Portugal's first king.

was granted all the former possessions of the Knights of Templar, but under royal, not papal control. It was as Grand Master of this Order of Christ that Prince Henry the Navigator would later have the resources to initiate and lead his renowned maritime trading and exploration.

Economic crises: Afonso IV succeeded Dinis. His administration was less sure, and hostilities with Castile waxed and waned. More significantly, his reign was burdened with the Black Plague. The first bout with the disease decimated the country, particularly the urban centers in 1348-9. Throughout the next century the pestilence would return again and again, causing both depopulation and despondency. Concurrently, various demographic and economic crises were beginning to undermine the nation. The attraction of the urban centers left the interior underpopu-

committed to maintaining total independence, and this, coupled with general social unrest, caused turbulence for Pedro I and his son Fernando, and finally brought down the House of Burgundy.

Betrothed to a Spanish princess, Pedro I instead fell madly in love with her alluring lady-in-waiting, Inês de Castro. It was not long before their dalliance became an open affair, much to the disgruntlement of his father, Afonso IV and powerful members of the court. Inês was no peasant though, in fact she was from a powerful Castilian family, and according to some, was manipulating Pedro for political ends.

Inês was banished in 1340, but upon the death of the princess Constanza in 1345, she returned to her lover. She lived in Coimbra with her children, secretly married to Pedro. The threat of a Castil-

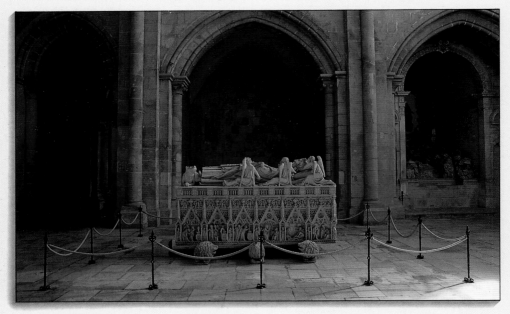

lated. There was insufficient agricultural labor, leaving fields uncultivated and causing inflation in food prices. The kings tried to regulate the movements of the population to thwart migration to the cities, but their methods were ineffectual, based more on toothless coercion than on any persuasive economic motivation. The economic stagnation, whose dreary influence extended to literature, religion, and every element of daily life, would not truly end until the beginnings of the maritime empire.

Politics of this period, despite the independence of Portugal so well established under Dinis, were motivated largely by fear of Castilian domination. In fact, continual intermarriage between the two royal families did keep the possibility of unification open. But the Portuguese were

ian heir was intolerable to Afonso, who finally sanctioned her brutal assassination in 1355.

After being rebuffed in a brief civil war, Pedro, later known as "the Cruel" for his half-mad administration of justice and government, waited patiently for his revenge. He assumed the throne upon his father's death in 1357 and quickly tracked down his lover's assassins. They were brought before the king, who ordered their hearts torn out. In 1361, more than five years after her burial, Pedro ordered Inês to be exhumed, dressed in royal robes and crown, and placed next to him on the throne. Each member of the court was then forced to pay homage by kissing the dead queen's decomposed hand.

Aside from its immediate political consequences, this gruesome tale also later proved to be inspirational for historical dramas, romantic chronicles and poems. Adapted by writers such as Camões (in *Os Lusiadas*) and Antonio Ferreira (in *Castro*), the legend became a central legend for the Portuguese literary imagination. Today, the tombs of Inês de Castro and Pedro I, both in intricately detailed Gothic style, can be seen in the Santa Maria Monastery in Alcobaça.

Despite the instability of the monarch himself, the reign of Pedro I was marked by peaceful coexistence with Castile. Social and political growth was seen as the country recovered from the convulsions of the plague. However, the growing power of the nobles, the clergy and the emergent bourgeoisie, all represented in the cortes, would break loose in active social discontent during the reign of his son and successor, Fernando I.

Fernando tried to unite Portugal and Castile under his rule, engaging the country in a series of unpopular and unsuccessful wars with its neighbor. Even more disastrously, the wars provided a way for France and England to join the turmoil, using the Iberian peninsula as a theater of the Hundred Years' War. In 1373, Enrique II of Castile attacked Lisbon, burning and pillaging the city and forcing Fernando to pledge his alliance. To add to the confusion, the "Great Schism" divided the Catholic Church under opposing popes beginning in 1378, and Fernando alternated his loyalties frequently. The wars had ravaged the whole country, leaving the populace both tired of war and angry at the nobility they blamed for causing it.

Fernando had further alienated his subjects with his unpopular marriage to Leonor Teles, who was perceived to represent the landed gentry. Riots broke out at the marriage and again in 1383 when Fernando died, leaving his widow (with her lover, the Galician count, João Fernandez Andeiro) to rule as Queen-Mother.

Andeiro was assassinated within weeks by João, the illegitimate son of Pedro I and the Master of Avis, one of the national military-religious orders. In the ensuing civil war for the throne, Leonor had the support of most of the nobles and clergy, while João relied upon the support of the middle class. He depended upon the deepening resentment the people now felt toward Castile—Leonor had fled to Juan I of Castile after Andeiro's death—and rode this growing wave to victory. The final military conflict was the Battle of Aljubarrota, a decisive victory for João's troops, despite being outnumbered—thanks in large part to the contribution of a squadron of English archers.

Left, Dom Pedro I waits the Day of Judgement in his tomb at Santa Maria Monastery in Alcobaça. Above, the portal to the unfinished chapels at Batalha

A number of stories and legends surround this battle. The "Holy Constable" Nuno Álvares Pereira was captain of João's small squadron. As he valiantly led his charges in the battle, Nuno was agonizingly thirsty, with no water to be had anywhere on the plain. He swore that no traveler would ever go thirsty here again, and since 1385 a small pitcher of water has been daily placed in a niche of the Aljubarrota chapel of São Jorge. João, too, made a vow. Seeing that his army was vastly outnumbered he felt that victory would require a miracle, he swore to build a great church in the Virgin Mary's honor if his cause won the day. As the Castilian army turned tail and fled, João hurled his lance into the air to choose the place for the construction that would be the great Monastery of Batalha. If the story is true, João had a real good arm, because the battlefield is

some 10 miles from the Monastery.

The rule of João I, founder of the House of Avis, represented a new political beginning. The disputes with Castile continued, but they were winding down. The unsteady Anglo-Portuguese alliance was cemented by the Treaty of Windsor in 1386, a document which has been called to account as recently as World War II, when Britain invoked it to gain fueling way stations for airplanes and seacraft in the Azores.

João I brought stability, but the change of order could not be mistaken for a social revolution. New political representation was established by the mercantile class, but in time it was clear that only the names had changed among the landed aristocracy who still held real power. The new dynasty was much like the old.

EMPIRE BUILDING

João I ruled from 1385 to 1433, fending off the demands of a resurgent nobility by installing his sons Duarte, Pedro, Henry, Fernão, and João in powerful positions as the leaders of military-religious orders. Henry the Navigator, for example, was made Master of the Order of Christ. It was under João I that Portugal first began to look across the seas for solutions to their internal economic and political problems. Trade and exploration would serve both to occupy the nobility and to boost commerce. João's successor, King Duarte, initially continued with overseas expansion, but drew back after a disastrous failed attack on Tangiers. In 1438, Duarte died, setting off a brief civil war to determine who would be regent to his young son Afonso V. Pedro, relying on the support of the bourgeoisie and lower classes, defeated Queen Leonor (yes, another scheming Leonor, this one Duarte's widow) and her noble backers, for a time seemed to have effected a political turn of sorts. When Afonso V came of age, however, he gave his allegiance to the parties that had opposed Pedro. In one last futile attempt, Pedro fought the King at Alfarrobeira, in 1449, and Pedro and most of his followers were killed.

Two of Afonso's uncles were particularly trusted advisors, and stand as symbols of the ideals Afonso held throughout his reign: Henry the Navigator, leader of conquest, and Fernão, the Duke of Bragança and leader of the newly strengthened nobility. Each was granted a large share of independent power. For himself, King Afonso held the honor of his position, remaining above the fray of administration. He did not rule ineptly, but he was a chivalric soul, a debonair leader in an era where politics had been sullied and complicated by the growing power of mercantilists and low nobility. He concerned himself largely with martial glory, which he found crusading in North Africa. In 1471 he took Tangiers. Another of his accomplishment was the minting of the first *cruzado*, the gold coin that became a symbol of the wealth flowing in from the voyages. Unlike many coinages of the era, the *cruzado* was a remarkably stable currency, becoming a form of propaganda for Portuguese domination of world markets.

In 1475, there was civil discord in Castile because of a dispute for the crown. Afonso decided to marry Juana, one of the claimants, and

Left, detail of a Japanese screen (ca. 1593) commemorating the arrival of Portuguese traders. Above, a statue of the Infante D. Henrique in Lagos.

thus unite Portugal and Castile under his monarchy. He invaded in support of her claims, occupied León, but failed to hold his ground. He tried to enlist the aid of King Louis XI of France in support of his claims to the Castilian throne, traveling to France to make a personal plea. He arrived in the midst of Louis XI's tumultuous rivalry with the Duke of Burgundy and proved to be a hapless diplomat, quickly alienating both sides. Frustrated, he abdicated his throne to go on a pilgrimage to the Holy Land, but even this quixotic voyage was thwarted. Louis prevented the Portuguese monarch from embarking, virtu-

ally arresting him, and the despondent Afonso was deported to his homeland. His son, the future João II, stepped down from the throne, letting Afonso resume his nominal position, though thenceforth the rule was shared.

Under these kings, the overseas expansion began in earnest. It began, but no one prepared or knew how to prepare for the empire that was to come. It is important to remember that the discoveries were never systematic: they were sporadic, unplanned and limited. The little policy that existed was a strange mix of crusading ideals, romantic curiosity, and profit motive. Charting the world was always a secondary matter. It was less important, for example, than the search for the odd figure known as Prester John.

A mythical priest and king, Prester John was

supposed to have been the leader of a vast and powerful Christian empire located somewhere in the African interior. His legend was elaborated with tales of a kingdom that was an earthly paradise peopled with a bizarre menagerie of chimeras and mythical characters. Strange as it seems, this tale had an enormous influence on early exploration of Africa. In fact in 1455, after the Portuguese had established their dominance all along the northern coast, a Papal bull granted them the sole right to discovery and conquest of all of Africa except those parts ruled by Prester John. It was only later, by the early 16th century that Portugal's explorers began to realize that spice and gold were more accessible goals, and the voyages in and around Ethiopia were replaced with more profitable itineraries.

Another goal of seafarers was the still-popular

to be a debilitating obsession, diverting attention from surer if less spectacular sources of profit. These lesser goals were nevertheless an impetus for exploration from the start. Fishing ships had circled further and further out in search of richer waters. Moroccan grain, sugar, dyestuffs, and slaves were all found in Africa. These were eventually joined by the spices and rare woods of India and the Orient.

Preliminary to any exploration, of course, the technical aspects of navigation had to be discovered and mastered. Shipbuilding in Portugal took lessons from the Moslems and Italians, refining and strengthening their central-ruddered ships. They soon developed the wide-hulled *caravela* that was ideal for long-voyages with cargo. Key inventions like the compass and portulan chart (a kind of atlas) had vastly improved sailors' ability

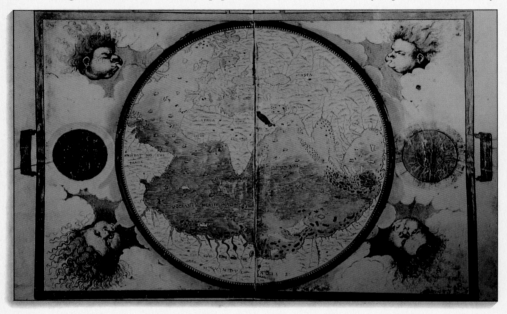

slaughter of the infidel. Attacking Moslems wherever they could be found gave the voyages all the benefits of a crusade: the effort was legitimized, and the church lent its financial resources, to some extent, along with spiritual support, in the form of indulgences and martyrdoms. The sanctions of Rome, like the Bull of 1455, would become an important factor when maritime competition intensified.

Economic and social needs undoubtedly lay at the base of the voyages, but it is difficult to precisely unravel these motivations. Certainly there was a shortage of gold all over Europe. Without it, coinage was severely debased and the growth of commerce was retarded. Gold from Africa, America, and India eventually did find its way into the coffers of Lisbon, but it also proved

to plot and keep a course. Map-making was advancing, although some discoveries were jealously guarded. It is speculated that the Portuguese knew about Brazil some time before Cabral blew off course and officially noticed it in 1500.

Henry the Navigator is often credited with leading the discoveries, masterminding them while surrounded by expert astronomers and shipbuilders at his school of navigation in Sagres. The truth is more humble. His financial sponsorships and enthusiasm made him a definite influence, but discovering the world was beyond the scope of any one man.

With many hands at the tillers, the enterprise was not well-coordinated. Of course, no one knew exactly where they were headed in the first place. The main goal was to press the crusade forward and eventually to reconquer Jerusalem. Obviously, they had other goals as well. Maps were accurate enough to suggest that getting to Jerusalem via Brazil was definitely the scenic route. So Portugal took the world as it came, never quite planning what to do with it all.

Prince Henry's main goal was actually the taming of the North African coast, which meant the banishment of the Moors. He never traveled further than Morocco himself, although some of his brothers did. Records show that he devoted most of his time to squeezing profits out of his various tithes, monopolies and privilege revenues. Apparently, the income generated by the Order of Christ was a pinch; his household spendings and military expeditions to Africa consumed every cent he obtained. Only later in life, with increasing reports of wondrous and far-off places

benefit of their homeland.

Of course, popular history also makes some dubious claims for Portugal's heroes, for example, that they were the first to discover America. Afonso Sanches, blown off course on a trip to the East Indies, is said to have landed on an uncharted western coast, and on his return, shared the log of his misadventure with a certain Genoese navigator named Columbus.

Perhaps the first indisputable hero of the discoveries was Gil Eanes. Madeira and the Azores, along with the north of Africa, had been charted. The islands had begun to be colonized. The fabulous tales of the edge of the world and the various horrors of the south seas were soon connected with the stormy promontory of Cape Bojador, on the west coast of Africa. It became the boundary. Finally, in 1434, Gil Eanes, a pilot commissioned

to inspire him, did Henry give the discoveries his full attention. When he did, it was with the possibilities of early profit firmly in mind.

Epic heroes: It is easy to see why popular history might accord undue credit to an individual like Henry. The Age of Discovery was a time for heroes and adventurers, and also a time for the rebirth of knightly ideals. Fearless mariners sailed off into the unknown realms of sea monsters and cannibals. Their voyages were imbued with noble intentions: for the greater glory of the Church, in the service of knowledge, and for the

Left, the four winds blow hard and steady for the Portuguese Discoverers in this unusual 1519 map. Above, Cabral happens upon Brazil.

by Henry the Navigator, broke the barrier. He found more coast and safe water behind. He returned to Portugal triumphant, bringing wild roses plucked from the land beyond as proof, dubitable as it may have been, of his accomplishment. The next year he led voyages further down Africa's coast, and the way was open for the many who followed. They searched primarily for the legendary *Rio do Ouro* (River of Gold). Some of that precious ore was found, and the trips soon became profitable.

In 1482, Portuguese ships explored the mouth of the Congo River. In 1487, Bartolomeu Dias rounded the Cape of Good Hope. In 1494, Papal intervention in the growing competition between Spain and Portugal resulted in the famous Treaty of Tordesillas, which divided the newly discovered, as well as the still unknown lands between the two countries. This treaty granted Portugal the lands east of a line of demarcation 370 miles (592 km) west of the Azores. This put Brazil within Portugal's sphere. In 1497-99, Vasco da Gama sailed to Calicut in India and back, immediately throwing Portugal into competition with Moslem and Venetian spice traders. In 1500, Cabral officially discovered Brazil. In 1519-22, Ferdinand Magellan, a Portuguese in the service of Spain, led the first voyage to circumnavigate the globe, though he died before the journey was completed.

The expeditions opened the seaways, but there were battles to be fought to establish trading posts in the Indies. Arabs, protecting their own trade interests, fought the Portuguese wherever they could. The Portuguese, of course, were still intent

on eradicating such infidels from the face of the earth. So although Portugal had no intentions of land conquest, by simply striving to establish and maintain a monopoly of the high seas, they were constantly at war.

Succession of conquests: The great leader of these campaigns was Governor-General Afonso de Albuquerque, a brilliant strategist and, in essence, the founding father of the empire in Asia. His victories allowed garrisoned ports and fortresses to be built in key locations. Goa, in India, conquered in 1510, became the center for all operations. Malacca fell in 1511 and served as the East Indies hub, while Ormuz came under Portuguese control in 1515, proving the ideal seat from which to dominate the Persian Gulf. Later, in 1557, Macão was established on a kind of perma-

nent lease with China, extending Portugal's reach to the Far East.

Albuquerque administered these new holdings with a basic policy of colonization rather than exploitation. All the major cities, Goa in particular, were converted by architecture and government into European towns. Interracial marriages were encouraged and Catholic missions established.

The growth of Goa was extraordinary. By 1540 there were 10,000 European-descended households and the town was the seat of a bishopric. However, these few altered cities and the battles of the Indies were in marked contrast to the general policy of peaceful coexistence that Portugal used wherever it could. In Africa, Brazil, and the various islands and archipelagos, they tried to set up trade stations without interfering with local customs or politics.

It is, however, the exceptions that proved the most interesting: in the Congo, for example, where a number of missions were sent. The people of the kingdom there were quite taken with their European visitors, though they could provide little of interest to the tranders. The Portuguese had begun by overestimating the political and cultural sophistication of these people, and once the Congolese were exposed to certain Western practices, they embraced them. They took to Christianity, if their own version of it, and imitated the manners and fashions of the Portuguese. Their first Christian monarch dropped the unwieldy "*Nzinga a Nkuwu*" and renamed himself João I. His son took the name Afonso, and from that point into the 17th century the land was ruled by a succession of native Henriques, Pedros, and Franciscos.

The Congo, though it did provide both ivory and slaves, was not of central economic importance. The Portuguese *caravelas* were too busy reaping bounty elsewhere to pay much attention to cultural matters: spices were carried from the Indies, gold was found in the Sudan and other parts of Africa, sugar and wine was brought from Madeira, sugar and dyestuffs came from Brazil.

The wealth reaped overseas made for a stable economy, but it did not make Portugal rich. Individuals and the monarchy—taking its royal fifth of all trade revenues—became rich, but even they eventually found it difficult to hold or build their fortunes. Neither the relatively sudden rise, nor the long fall of the Portuguese trade empire is easy to encapsulate. There are many points of debate. Still, certain influences may be safely outlined.

At its beginning, the "empire" demanded little

Above, Vasco da Gama stands tall in Sines, the town where he was born. Right, Afonso de Albuquerque in a portrait (ca. 1509) by an unknown artist.

from its diminutive fatherland. Like other small trading centers in Italy and like the later Dutch empire, organization and central authority were more important than mere size. Furthermore, the early expeditions required little manpower. It was only later, when they found themselves trying to enforce their worldwide trade monopoly, that Portugal's small population began to tell. It has been suggested that a crucial deficiency was Portugal's lack of a middle class—quashed by royal and noble dominance of commerce—a group that might have provided qualified and educated planners, pilots and administrators.

In explaining the empire's failure, some have pointed to widespread corruption or to the foreign control of profits garnered from Portuguese expeditions. How great an effect they had is arguable. Certainly the religious efforts that went hand in

hand with Portuguese voyages did not make the wheels of commerce spin any more freely. Whether fighting Moslems with whom they had once peacefully coexisted, or trying to force Christianity down the throats of local populations, the Portuguese lost time and focus from the business of business. Whatever the causes, it is clear that the potential benefits of the burgeoning overseas trade were not being reaped by Portugal. Deflation in Europe stifled trade. Domestic agricultural production, hampered by a lack of manpower, lagged, occasionally causing serious shortages of meat and grain. Even the Crown was in debt, as the cost of the trading empire was, surprisingly, more than its revenues.

It was, of course, many years before these flaws and inabilities truly sank the empire. Trade

continued for several centuries, although it steadily deteriorated. Portugal eventually turned away from the Indies and poured their efforts to maintaining Brazil.

Before the slide began, the lively age of empire did bring sufficient peace and prosperity for Portugal to fortify truly great eras of artistic and humanist achievement. João II had taken over from the flighty Afonso V in 1481. Revitalizing the throne, he managed to take up where Henry the Navigator, who died in 1460, had left off. João turned away from the nobility, minimizing their rights and calling upon the *cortes* for support. A conspiracy soon gathered against the king, but he learned of the central traitors soon enough to strike back. In 1484, the Duke of Bragança was briefly tried and beheaded. When other members of the nobility fled the country for their lives, their titles and holdings reverted to the crown. The Duke of Viseu unwisely mounted a second plot, and was stabbed by the king himself. Another group fled the country, and João II was in the catbird's seat.

The prestige and authority that these fierce, Machiavellian tactics had given to the monarchy would stand undiminished for centuries. However, João's successor, Manuel I had to steer a course between the ferocity of his predecessor and the idealistic nobility of Afonso V. This was accomplished with diplomatic and farsighted administration. The estates of the noble families were largely restored, though this did not restore their political power. Judicial and tax reforms worked to bring authority to government on both the national and local levels. The postal system was instituted. Public services like hospitals were centralized. And essentially, Manuel lifted the power of the monarchy above both the nobles and the *cortes* , launching the first era of enlightened absolutism.

Importance of education: Manuel also fostered contacts with the Renaissance humanism then spreading throughout Europe. There were many trade, religious and cultural contacts with Italy, in particular, and young Portuguese men began to seek educations abroad, at the universities in France or Spain. In fact, Manuel actually tried to buy Paris's renowned Saint Barbara College. Though he failed, it became a center for Portuguese students. By 1487 a printing press had been established in Lisbon. Portugal entered the 16th century with a rush of new cultural currents.

New colleges and educational reforms at home were fundamental elements of the next century's progress. Teaching methods were modernized and curriculum expanded. There was more opportunity for specialization and dialectic. The students were drawn from a larger pool, now including aristocrats and wealthy bourgeois in addition to the young members from the religious orders.

CAMÕES

Luís de Camões did not live to reap the celebrity of his poetry. He began and ended life poor, though he did find romance and adventure in between.

After attending the University at Coimbra, the young poet's prospects were good. However, many twists of fate lay ahead. An affair with one of the Queen's ladies-in-waiting caused his banishment to North Africa, where he lost an eye in military service. Returning to Lisbon, Camões was involved in a skirmish that wounded a magistrate. He ended up in prison and then was banished again, in 1553, this time to Goa in India. It was 1570 before he returned to Lisbon. Having written poetry and plays for many years with some success, he published *Os Lusíadas* in 1572. The poem's worth was recognized immediately, and as a reward Camões received a small royal pension. His final illness, however, was spent in a public hospital. When he died, in 1580, he was buried in a common grave.

The title *Os Lusíadas* means the sons of Lusus, the mythical founder of Portugal: poetically, then, it means "the Portuguese." Echoing classical models, the poem chronicled the voyages of Vasco da Gama, before a panorama of strangely mixed Christian and pagan images.

Os Lusíadas has been hailed throughout Europe (Lope de Vega and Montesquieu were early admirers) sometimes to the detriment of Portugal's other literature, Portugal's one masterpiece. Under Salazar, *Os Lusíadas* became an icon of Portuguese nationalism. Speeches and propaganda were peppered with quotes drawn from the great book, providing a mythos for imperialism, without reflection upon the differences between the 16th and 20th centuries.

The 18th-century verse translation by W. J. Mickle, quoted below, though tinged with the lyrical romanticism of that era, captures the proud spirit of the poem from the opening lines:

Arms and the heroes, who from Lisbon's shore,
Thro' seas where sail was never spread before,
Beyond where Ceylon lifts her spicy breast,
And waves her woods above the watery waste,
With prowess more than human forc'd their way
To the fair kingdoms of the rising day.

In the second canto the treacherous Moslems—"faithless race"—*prepare to attack:*
On shore the truthless monarch arms his bands,

Left, the library at the University of Coimbra, decorated with baroque gilt and chinoiserie japanning. Above, a bust of Camões that once graced a ship's bow.

And for the flee's approach impatient stand:
That soon as anchor'd in the port they rode
Brave Gama's decks might reek with Lusian blood:
Thus weening to revenge Mozambique's fate,
And give full surfeit to the Moorish hate...

In the world of the discoverers, the enemy forces take their strength from the netherworld:

As when the whirlwinds, sudden bursting, bear
Th' autumnal leaves high floating through the air;
So rose the legions of th' infernal state,
Dark Fraud, base Art, fierce Rage, and burning

Hate:
Wing'd by the Furies to the Indian strand
They bend; the Demon leads the dreadful band,
And in the bosoms of the raging Moors
All their collected living strength he pours.

At Vasco da Gama's request, the chronicler aboard the ship retells Portugal's history, and, in this section, recounts the "glad assistance" brought by the crusaders who helped take Lisbon from the Moors.

Their vows were holy, and the cause the same,
To blot from Europe's shores the Moorish name.
In Sancho's cause the gallant navy joins,
And royal Sylves to their force resigns.
Thus sent by heaven a foreign naval band
Gave Lisboa's ramparts to the Sire's command.

The purposes and potential of these changes was not without its crises. The University of Lisbon had a cultural and political influence that was threatening to the crown. It was difficult to impinge upon their traditional autonomy, but Manuel, as part of his general process of centralization, tried to force change through economic and legal pressure.

Finding great resistance, he turned to the idea of founding a new University elsewhere, without success. João III continued these efforts and finally more or less quashed the University, shifting it to Coimbra, and sapping its political strength in the process. Later in the 16th century this conflict culminated in João III's giving control of national education to the Jesuits. It was a victory for the monarchy. There would be no university in Lisbon again until 1911.

Nonetheless, the century inspired a broad-ranging intellectual vigor, a fitting counterpart to the great voyages of discovery. Some of the works produced were directly attributable to the expeditions. Travel books, of both scientific and cultural themes, were a rich vein of literature. Tomé Pires wrote *Suma Oriental* (1550), which described his voyages in the East. Many of these wandering writers were Jesuit missionaries, whose concerns with converting the natives led them to make careful sociological and ethnological observations. The most renowned traveler, the Marco Polo of Portugal, was Fernão Mendes Pinto, whose *Peregrinaçam* (Pilgramage) brought imagination and lively style to the form. Among the historians of this period, who adopted modern concern for accuracy and some

measure of objectivity, were Fernão Lopes, who wrote a history of João I's reign, and João de Barros, who chronicled the conquests in Asia.

The courtly verses typical of King Dinis's reign were still very popular, but the strong influence of the Italian Renaissance broadened the themes of poetry. Out of the troubadour tradition, but going far beyond it, was Gil Vicente, the founder of the Portuguese theater, who wrote scores of satirical and comic one-act plays. Vicente began life as a goldsmith, and in *Farsa dos Almocreves* he writes himself into a farce about an impoverished nobleman who can never pay his entourage or creditors. When the goldsmith asks, eloquently, for long overdue payment, the nobleman procrastinates:

"How most cunningly inlaid
And enamelled is each word!
I rejoice not to have paid
For the sake of having heard
Phrases with such skill arrayed."
(A.F.G. Bell translation)

In the second half of the 16th century, a new group of writers emerged, including António Ferreira, Diogo Bernardes, and, the most renowned of all, Luís de Camões. *Os Lusiadas* Camões's masterpiece, is an epic national poem celebrating the discoveries that was first published in 1572. It is rightfully renowned as a classic of world literature. (See box story.)

However, these great writers aside, Portugal's main contributions to the intellectual ferment of the Renaissance were in science, particularly (and naturally) in navigation, astronomy, math, and geography. Their contribution was not the mere accumulation of facts from foreign places. New methods amounted to a kind of skepticism, a science based on experience rather than recorded facts. Having disproved a dozen theories of the shape, limits, and contours of the earth, the Portuguese felt free to question the other dogmas of antiquity.

Yet even as new writers and new sciences were coming to the fore, a Counter-Reformation (though there had been no real Reformation, the Portuguese Catholics having an essential antipathy to the simplifying and icon-destroying Germanic philosophies) was casting a pall of religious conformism over learning and creativity. In addition, the political threat to Portuguese autonomy—the future union with Spain was already an undercurrent—hung over all these achievements. In fact, Camões, Vicente and many of the others actually wrote as much as half their works in Castilian, the rest in their native Portuguese.

Portuguese Inquisition: João III ruled from 1521-1557. He continued Manuel's expansion of the trade empire and royal authority. Perhaps his most significant act was the establishment of the Inquisition in Portugal. The Inquisition was intended to be a tool of the monarchy, and for a time it was. Eventually, however, it took on a direction and authority of its own. The Papacy knew that there was no real need for the Inquisition, no menaces to the unity of faith in Portugal, so it was resisted for many years. João III used every diplomatic intrigue at his disposal and finally won approval for a greatly limited version of the Inquisition in 1536. In 1547 those restrictions were lifted.

With this turn of events the rule of João III turned, too—away from the humanist influences of Europe and toward religious fanaticism. The bureaucracy of the Inquisition expanded quickly, its main target being the converted Jews known as New Christians. The victimized group was persecuted as much for their role as middle-class mercantilists as for religious deviation. The power of the Inquisition grew quickly, with the

The ascension of King Sebastião in 1568 only exacerbated these excesses. His regency, from 1557-1568, was a period of stability, though marked by signs of trouble to come. The Inquisition grew in power. The *Casa da India*, the national trade corporation, went bankrupt in 1560. Then the 14-year-old Sebastião took the throne. An unstable and idealistic king, with a dangerous streak of chivalry like Afonso V, he took upon himself the crusade against the Moors of North Africa. A lack of funds prevented him from undertaking the task for many years. In the meantime he surrounded himself with cohorts no older and no more sensible than himself, dismissing the warnings of older, more prudent statesmen. Finally sensing that the time was right, he spent every *cruzado* he could raise on mercenaries and outfitting his troops. He set sail for Mo-

inquisitor-generals taking orders only from Rome. The inquisitor-generals also carried the right of excommunication, and utilizing the public and spectacular *autos-da-fé*, soon had an influence far beyond their legal authority. The influence of the Inquisition, with its rigid orthodoxy, vengeful judiciary, and general intolerance, was equally deadening to both culture and commerce. Many of the bourgeois leaders of trade were targets. Later, the Inquisition would virtually govern Portugal, usurping the authority of the monarchy during the union with Spain.

Left, detail from a portrait of João III by Christovão Lopes. Above, an engraving of the *auto-de-fé* processional; a festive affair for everyone, or almost everyone.

rocco in 1578. Sebastião was no better a military leader than administrator, madly dismissing stratagem and planning as cowardice. He refused, for example, to consider the possibility of retreat—and therefore had no plan for it. Outnumbered and outmaneuvered at the Battle of Alcacer-Quiber, his army of 18,000 men was destroyed. Some 8,000, including Sebastião and most of Portugal's young nobility, were slaughtered. Only 100 or so escaped death or capture. With this debilitating disaster, the way was open for Spain to step in. From 1578-1580, Cardinal Henrique was king, occupied primarily with raising the ruinous ransoms for the captured soldiers of Alcacer-Quiber. In 1580, Philip II of Spain invaded and within a year was installed as Philip I of Portugal.

THE CONQUERORS ARE CONQUERED

Throughout their rule over Portugal, the Spanish Habsburg kings faced many challenges to their authority. Not the least of their problems was that King Sebastião kept rising from the grave. After the massacre at Alcacer-Quiber, a devastating blow to national pride, there arose a popular belief that their lost king would rise again to restore all that was lost. Consequently, a number of false Sebastiãos tried to reclaim the throne. Though they satisfied the wild hopes of the lower classes, none of these rabble-mongers made a significant play for the crown.

At the root of both the accomplishment and the

continuation of the Iberian Union was the support provided by merchants and traders. The Dutch and other countries were strongly challenging Portuguese shipping, slicing into vital profits. It was supposed by the bourgeoisie that by combining Spanish and Portuguese interests, the maritime empire could be reclaimed; or at least what was left could be better protected. The "alliance" with Spain would also open up inland trade. At any rate, there were few options: Portugal's treasury was empty.

Politically, the union was accomplished by Philip II of Spain. After Alcacer-Quiber, a number of candidates aspired to take the Portuguese throne. Philip II, though his genealogical claim to the throne was more tenuous than his competitors', was a far more viable ruler than any of them.

He was the grandson of Manuel I, which proved adequate, given his political wiles and power. The majority of the populace was opposed to the Spanish king, but the relatively impoverished nobles, clergy, and upper bourgeoisie saw that Philip could provide fiscal and military stability. Ironically, the most powerful group to resist the union were the *Spanish* ruling classes, who saw the danger of untrammeled Portuguese trading within their traditional markets.

Part of Philip's appeal was that he promised to maintain Portugal's autonomy in many specific ways: no Spanish representation in Portuguese legislative and judicial bodies; no change in official language; the overseas empire would still be ruled by Portugal; no grants of Portuguese assets to non-Portuguese; and so forth. In fact, Philip would more or less fulfill these promises. On this platform, after chasing out a small army who supported the claims of António, Manuel's son, Philip took up residence in Lisbon. In 1581 he summoned the *cortes* to declare him king with the title Philip I.

After the years of mismanaged government, the efficient bureaucracy of the union provided relief for Portugal's uneasy finances. However, with the succession of Philip II (III of Spain), the Spanish began to press their powers too far. Lacking Philip I's diplomatic savvy, they bungled relations between the two countries, and tried to correct their mistakes through force. Resistance grew. Philip III managed to succeed to the throne in 1619, but the union continued to erode. Spain was weakened by its involvement in the Thirty Years' War with France. Portuguese troops were forced into battle and taxes were pressed upwards.

The 60 years of union with Spain did nothing to protect Portugal's empire. The Dutch and the English usurped one after another of their former strongholds. Naturally, Portugal tended to blame the Spanish administration for these defeats, rather than reacting constructively. Between 1620 and 1640, Ormuz, Baia, São Jorge da Mina and many more trade centers fell. In 1630 the Dutch established themselves in Brazil; in 1638 they took Ceylon. There were still ports and territories controlled by the Portuguese traders, but the "monopoly of the seas" was a dream quickly fading from memory. What's more, to a country once intent upon ridding the earth of the last vestige of the infidels, it was particularly devastating to surrender their missions to the Dutch, purveyors of the heretical Protestantism.

For the Portuguese, each of the three Philips who reigned over them was worse than the last.

The Spanish domination became less respectful and more grating on the populace. Philip II did not even deign to visit the country for years after his coronation. Philip III systematically breached all the guarantees put in place by his grandfather. The incipient revolution was aided by insurgents and secret diplomatic agents sent by the French, who were still embroiled with Spain in the Thirty Years' War.

The Bragança regime: On December 1, 1640, a coup in Lisbon capped the growing revolutionary fervor. The palace was attacked and the reigning Spanish governor, the Duchess of Mantua, was deposed and arrested while her strongman, Miguel de Vasconcelos, was fatally defenestrated. The Duke of Bragança, though he had been reluctant to lead the revolt, was declared king within a few days as João IV. So was ushered in Portugal's final royal period, as the House of Bragança would hold power until the 20th century and the First Republic.

Most of João IV's 16-year reign was occupied in hapless efforts to form diplomatic ties in Europe. France, England, Holland, and the Pope all refused to confirm Portuguese independence. Only Spain's preoccupation with other battles, some heroicPortuguese military stands along the frontier, and a well-organized national administration managed to hold their restored independence. One of João's most important long-term achievements, though he was at least partly forced into it, was turning emphasis away from trade with the Indies and toward Brazil.

On his ascension to the throne in 1656, Afonso VI was still a minor, though his youth was the least of his problems. Later, married off to a French princess, he behaved like a roustabout, associated with base criminal elements and, worst of all, proved to be impotent, a fact elicited from the scandalous public inquiry that was necessary to annul his marriage. Both his wife and his throne were eventually usurped by his brother, who ruled as Pedro II.

Until then, Queen-mother Luisa acted as Afonso's regent, and political control resided for the most part in the nobles who had been established in João IV's administration. War with Spain waxed and waned from 1640 until 1655. It was 1668 before the Spanish officially recognized Portugal's independence. During this period diplomatic efforts continued in the hopes of making vital alliances. In 1654 a treaty of friendship and cooperation was signed with England, a useful link, but also the first step down a primrose path that guaranteed Portugal's economic subservience to Britain for centuries to come. In 1661 a

treaty was also signed with Holland, and the alliance with England was sealed by the marriage of Princess Catarina to Charles II. Included in her dowry gifts to England were Tangier and Bombay. These moves sparked a new round of battles with Spain, but the two sides were quickly exhausted, both economically and politically. In 1665 a decisive Portuguese victory at Montes Claros ended the fighting.

Pedro II became prince-regent to his brother in 1668, was officially crowned king in 1683 and ruled until 1706. His long reign, though stable, was deeply marked by an unrelenting economic depression. The primary cause of this long decline was the dissipation of maritime commerce. The spice trade was almost entirely taken from out of their hands, while sugar and slaves went through periods of both competition and crisis

when Portugal could ill afford such instability. On the mainland, olive trees and grape vineyards offered good profits, but they were largely controlled by British interests, and they took up land that would have been better devoted to grain production. Grain shortages were common throughout the era.

Economists of that age who analyzed world trade patterns and studied the new doctrines of mercantilism dictated industry as Portugal's future. Two of Pedro's finance ministers, the Count of Ericeira and the Marquês of Fronteira helped plan numerous factories. Glass, textile, iron, tiles and pottery industries were all supported by the state in an effort to balance national trade deficits.

The mercantilist approach made some headway, but what finally dispelled the economic

Left, one of the movers and shakers of the Restoration, Antão de Almada. Above, Pedro II, a more potent leader than his brother Afonso VI

gloom was neither industrialization nor reorganization of any sort, but the discovery of gold in Brazil. With a constant stream pouring in, Portugal could once again rely on the exports of wine, olive oil and sugar. The infant industries sputtered and halted. The Count of Ericeira committed suicide, while Fronteira renounced his previous economic philosophy. Eventually, when Brazil began to hold onto its own mineral wealth, the various manufacturers started again, but it was only under Pombal, after mid-century, that they prospered.

Before the gold strikes of 1693-95, Brazil had been considered a second-rate colony. Portugal had hoped, given Spain's strikes in Peru and Mexico, that its piece of South American would yield the precious ore, but effort after effort came up empty. Despite these disappointments, when

Portugal had to retract the bounds of its empire, it wisely chose to defend Brazil and let the Asian trade go to the free market.

Even before gold, Brazil offered a number of valuable commodities: sugar, brazilwood, cotton, tobacco, and some spices and dyestuffs as well. The husbandry of cattle started slowly, but by the end of the 17th century, was providing lucrative exports of meat and leather.

The Jesuit missionaries were extremely influential in Brazil, as both explorers and settlers. Among other things they held the brazilwood monopoly for over two decades (1625-49). More importantly, they were successful in winning over the native populace to Christianity, and in large part, preventing their enslavement. The abundant colonial economy naturally had much

need for native labor, and the Jesuits were pressured to step aside, though they had the clear support of Rome in the form of a Papal bull (1639) that threatened excommunication for the trading of natives. Oddly enough, the Jesuit's humanitarianism did not extend to the African slaves, who were imported in great numbers to work the expanding sugar plantations.

In 1706, João V succeeded Pedro II, and began to spend the Brazilian gold with a vengeance. Taking his cue from other monarchs, particularly the French court of Louis XIV, he quickly earned the moniker "the Magnanimous." Palaces, churches and monasteries were erected, and support was granted to the arts and to education. Along with this extravagance came a moral profligacy. Convents around Lisbon were converted from religious houses into aristocratic brothels, while the inhabitants were still nuns, more or less. Among the royal constructions were palaces to house João's numerous bastard sons, born of various nuns. The instability of the monarch's life was in more or less inverse proportion to the economic and political stability of Portugal.

When João died in 1750 his son José succeeded him, but proved to be more interested in opera, a recent Italian import, than in matters of state. The full power of the crown was entrusted to a diplomat and member of the lower aristocracy, Sebastião José de Carvalho e Melo, who eventually earned the title by which he is better known, Marquês de Pombal.

Enlightened absolutism, as typified by the ministry of Pombal, represented both a beginning and an end. The enlightment ideal of rationalism meant a leap toward modernity, while the concomitant republican ideal of social equality meant that royal absolutism was on its last legs. Pombal's insistence on exercising royal prerogative sounded a death knell for the political power of nobles and clergy alike, and, quite unintentionally, allowed the bourgeoisie to take over administrative and economic control. His was an oppressive, dictatorial rule, though he was careful never to claim any personal power. The crown, which embodied all law, was omnipotent; he was merely its officer

The great earthquake: In 1755, on All Saints' Day—just as Mass was beginning—Lisbon was destroyed by a massive earthquake. Estimates vary, but at least 5,000 people were killed in the initial impact, many while attending morning services. Many more died of secondary and after-effects. Fallen church candles quickly ignited the wreckage around them. Survivors rushed from

Above, urban renewal in one fell swoop as Lisbon topples in the earthquake of 1755. Right, a 19th-century political cartoon satirizing Napoleon's deviltry

O DIABO COXO

O DIABO CORSO

41

the blaze toward the safety of the Tagus, only to be met by a massive tidal wave. In the weeks afterwards infected wounds, epidemics and famine also took their toll. The final count may have been as high as 40,000.

The Jesuits tried to fix the blame for this divine retribution upon Pombal's wayward and "athiestic" policies. (He had angered them by his hard line policies in Brazil, curbing their control over their native protégés.) He weathered both their criticism and their plot to assassinate him. The Jesuits' power throughout Europe was dissolving, and in 1759 they were officially disbanded and exiled from Portugal.

The catastrophe that shook the country's faith allowed Pombal's policies of secularization and rational government to take firm hold. He took absolute control, declaring "close the ports, bury

was first used, derisively as well, the word *estrangeirados* means "imitators of foreigners". It referred to Portuguese expatriates as well as those who had returned. Both groups were influential, particularly in defining a cultural identity for Portugal that was distinct from Spain. They undertook a conscious cultural split from Spanish influences, turning toward Europe and America. One *estrangeirado*, Correia da Serra, a diplomat and man of letters, became Portugal's first envoy to the United States, where Thomas Jefferson would later offer him the presidency of the University of Virginia.

As Pombal's sponsor-king José neared the end of his reign, the Marquês plotted to force the crown-princess Maria to renounce her rights so that her son José, a disciple of Pombal, could continue the policy of despotism. The efforts

the dead, feed the living," and setting the city to the task. José granted his minister emergency powers (which were not rescinded for some 20 years) and Pombal used them to rebuild Lisbon according to an eminently neoclassical plan, both neatly geometric and functionally sound. University reforms weakened religious elements. The social and legal distinction between old and "new Christians" (Jews) was abolished. Pombal's economic reforms helped Portugal remained stable when Brazilian gold production waned around 1760. And he managed to rebuild Lisbon without depleting the state treasury.

Pombal was one of the *estrangeirados*, a group of Portuguese who were educated in Europe, and looked toward Europe when planning their country's future course. Literally, and when it

failed and Maria, a pious, but somewhat imbalanced woman with no sympathy for Pombal's oppressive rule ascended in 1777. She immediately tried the former minister of various crimes against the state and found him guilty, confining him to his estate rather than prison, out of deference to his age. Though she revived religious elements of a government and culture that had been increasingly secular, she allowed most of Pombal's very necessary economic and administrative reforms to stay in place. Her reign was conservative in tenor, allowing the governmental underpinnings established by Pombal to provide steady, if slow, economic progress.

Both Maria's political and personal health were badly shaken by news of the French Revolution in 1789. In 1791 ong after her behavior had become an embarassment, she was declared insane. Her son João, an awkward and nervous man, took over the crown as regent, officially becoming king after Maria died in 1816 (his older brother José, had died in 1788).

The Portuguese monarchy and nobility feared that the French Revolution, and to a lesser extent, that of America, might be contagious. They were particularly wary about the possibility of democratic insurgency in Brazil. Though gold exports from that country were on the decline, they were quickly being supplanted by beef, cotton and tobacco. In 1793, Portugal sent troops to fight revolutionary France, further aligning itself with England and against French-controlled Spain. In 1801, Spain invaded in the War of the Oranges. Portugal ceded various political concessions, and forever lost the town of Olivença.

In July 1808, Britain came galloping to the rescue under the leadership of the master military tactician, Sir Arthur Wellesley, who was later dubbed the Duke of Wellington. The Peninsular War, sometimes called the War of National Liberation, lasted two years, expelling the French, but devastating the country. There were three waves of attacks set back by Portuguese victories at Roliça, Vimeiro, Buçaco, and the lines at Torres Vedras. The wars left the country in rocky shape. Portugal's capital was now located across the ocean in Rio de Janeiro and the nation's general weakness fostered Brazil's claims for autonomy. In 1815 Brazil was declared a kingdom on equal footing with Portugal.

The French (and English) had sacked many national treasures in Portugal, stealing paintings, sculptures, jewelry, books—all of which were

In 1807, Napoleon delivered an ultimatum to Portugal, a bad tiding to receive at a time when the Little Corporal was considered invincible. It was demanded that Portugal declare war on Britain, and, specifically, that it close its ports to British shipping. But Portugal could not possibly turn on its long-term allies. Napoleon was defied. While the royal family scooted off to Brazil for safety, the French General Junot marched into Lisbon. Initially, the Portuguese government offered no resistance.

Left, while Carlotta Joaquina led the debaucheries at Queluz, above, the citizens rallied in the streets, for the Liberal Revolution of 1820

especially lamentable losses for such a small country. The regency in Lisbon showed no intelligence in their rule, governing with uncoordinated despotism, ignoring the burgeoning democratic groundswell. The monarchy's blindness to contemporary political ideas fostered the revolution that would break in 1820.

The British military occupation, under the leadership of Marshal William Beresford, though necessary and sometimes appreciated, had further undermined Portuguese self-determination. British control, particularly in the economic realm had been growing throughout the 18th century. The Treaty of Methuen (1703) had established their dominance of the wine industry and generally served to stifle industrialization in Portugal. Various treaties continued this relationship, and in 1810, Portugal was forced to cede to Britain the right to trade directly with Brazil, eliminating its role as middleman, which had been an economic mainstay. Portugal was taking on all aspects of a British protectorate with Marshal Beresford wielding dictatorial control.

The roots of the liberal revolution of 1820 lay in the French influences, picked up by various military and secret societies, especially a Masonic lodge called Sinédrio. One of the primary events that coalesced the movement involved a plot by one of these clandestine groups against the British rule. A dozen conspirators were accused of plotting to assassinate Marshal Beresford in 1817. All of them, including the alleged leader, Lieutenant-General Gomes Freire de Andrade, were summarily tried and executed. This brutal reprisal heated Portuguese resentment and fos-

document was ahead of its time, with broad guarantees of individual liberties and no special perogatives for nobles or clergy. It lasted only two years, but did succeed in finally legally banning the Inquisition, which, though very nearly defunct, had lingered on and on.

Greedy for power: Portugal's profoundly conservative streak made the revolution not a time of competition among rival factions, but a simple split between republicans and absolutists. New charters and new efforts to restore full-bodied monarchy kept the country unsettled throughout the first half of the 19th century. In 1824, for example, João VI resisted a conspiracy of royalist extremists led by his own wife Carlotta and his son Miguel.

João's queen was the notorious Spanish princess Carlotta Joaquina, who had made herself an

tered support for the Liberal movement. The tyranny of the regime could no longer be denied, and it was becoming equally apparent that only violent means could force a change.

In 1820, the Spanish Liberal movement had won control of their government providing further inspiration, as well as political support for Portuguese Liberal forces. The moment arrived for Portugal when Beresford left the country to go to Brazil on a diplomatic mission to discuss the growing problem. His absence was the spark, and the Portuguese military revolved. The uprising began in Oporto, and eventually forced João VI to return from Brazil where he had been trying to ignore the turmoil at home. By the time he arrived, the new constitutional ideology was firmly in place. A constitution was adopted in 1822. The

epitome of the "old regime." She tried her best to make a Versailles of her palace at Queluz, surrounding herself with absolutists and engaging in outrageous royal decadence, begetting numerous children by various lovers from among her entourage. Her flamboyant leadership of the absolutist cause made her popular among a substantial following. However, the failure of her conspiracy to dethrone her husband in favor of her son, after which Miguel was banished to Brazil, marked the end of her influence.

The politics of the next 50 years were endlessly

Above, King Carlos and Prince Filipe, now honored in death, were reviled and assassinated by revolutionaries in 1910

complex, and this served to distract national attention and energies, which only further burdened Portugal's economic deceleration. In 1826 João VI died, leaving Pedro, his eldest son, who was still in Brazil, as heir to the throne. After failing to unite the two kingdoms through political maneuvers, he chose to stay in Brazil, abdicating the Portuguese throne to his seven-year-old daughter, who became Maria II. Pedro's plan was that the girl would marry her uncle, the exiled Miguel, who would rule as her regent under a moderate constitution.

Miguel had other ideas. Upon his return he abolished the constitution and invoked a counter-revolutionary *cortes* to name him king. There was considerable popular support for these moves, but still enough sympathy for constitutional ideas that Pedro could return and eventually defeat his brother in what were known as the Miguelist Wars. Pedro had abdicated his Brazilian empire so that he could defend his appointment of Maria II. Though this "War of Two Brothers" did little to resolve the deep conflict between absolutist and republican ideologies in Portugal, in fact it marked the last time that absolutism was ever in official power. Constitutional monarchy—though practically absolutist at times—would hold sway until 1910.

Pedro died in 1834 and his daughter, now 15, finally took the throne as Maria II. She reigned until 1853, during which time the first political parties developed. The liberals, victorious over absolutism, divided into conservatives and progressives. The *Septembrists*, given their name for their revolutionary victory in September of 1836, came into power first. They initially restored the constitution of 1822, but then adopted a more moderate constitution. They were opposed by *Chartists* who took their stand, and name, from the conservative charter of 1826.

In 1839, as the Septembrists were suffering from internal dissension, the Chartists came to the fore. Supported by the Queen, they were led by Costa Cabral and took power in 1839. Costa Cabral's government was authoritarian, and, though it provided stability, became more and more corrupt and autocratic. In 1846 the popular uprising known as the revolution of Maria da Fonte demanded his downfall. Maria II tried to replace him with the equally conservative Duke of Saldanha, a grandson of Pombal, and the country stood at the edge of civil war. English and Spanish intervention prevented mass violence, but resulted in Costa Cabral being returned to power. In 1851, without a war, Costa Cabral was ousted for good and Saldanha took his place.

The early period of Saldanha's rule was a period of transformation out of which came the political divisions that would exist throughout the century. Saldanha introduced a compromise to the constitutional debate that allowed his new party, *Regeneraçao*, to encompass both the old Chartists and the moderate progressives. The amendments to the constitution allowed for direct elections and an expanded electorate. Those who were still more radical, a small group at first, would become known as the *Históricos* and then *Progressistas*.

In 1853 Maria II died in childbirth. Her husband, the German Duke Ferdinand of Saxe-Coburg-Gotha, ruled as the regent until their son Pedro V, came of age in 1855. Pedro, a young but wise ruler, died in 1861 and was succeeded by his brother, Luís I. Constitutional monarchs tend to be judged best by those who stayed farthest from politics, and the change from the meddling Maria to the literary Luís was a clear victory for the republican government. Among his other accomplishments, King Luís translated Shakespeare into Portuguese.

The reign of Luís lasted until 1889 and was a period of relative peace. Conservatives and liberals alternated in controlling the legislature. Portugal's external affairs were more or less dictated by England, their protector under the Congress of Vienna's partitioning of smaller countries under major powers. Portugal was, however, tenacious in holding onto many of its colonial claims and territories in Africa. The high expense of maintaining those colonies was a burden to the rickety national economy, but it would stand them in good stead when the holdings finally did pay off during the 20th century. In the meantime, Portugal's finances were a muddle. The havoc wrought by the peninsular and Miguelite wars, on top of the loss of Brazil, was insurmountable. In 1889, Carlos I became king, setting African expansion as his primary goal, but his efforts were unsuccessful. In 1892, Portugal declared bankruptcy.

Carlos, still dreaming of restoring the empire, could do little to defuse the growing anti-monarchical sentiment. Socialism and trade unionism were growing influences. The legislative *cortes* had degenerated into a powerless assembly full of obstructive and self-promoting debate. Corruption and inefficiency were rampant.

In 1906, struggling to maintain some form of control, Carlos appointed João Franco as Prime Minister, endowing him with dictatorial powers. He quickly dissolved the useless legislature. In 1908 unknown parties, either members of a republican secret society or isolated anti-monarchical fanatics, assassinated Carlos as well as his son Luís Filipe, heir to the throne. In the assault upon the royal carriage, Manuel, the king's second son, was wounded but survived. In the next two years Manuel II tried to save the monarchy, offering various concessions, but the assassination had served to fortify the republican movement. The long-decrepit House of Bragança finally tumbled into dust.

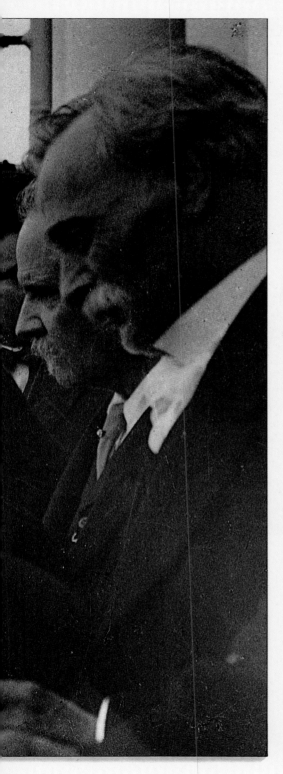

REVOLUTION AND EVOLUTION

The paths of Portuguese cultural development in the 19th century followed many of the same byways as the country's politics. The influence of the rest of Europe was both heavily felt and intermittently resisted. The slow turning from conservative romanticism to modern rationalism that seems so natural in retrospect was experienced as a series of shocks.

Arts and literature were greatly influenced by politics, even during the romantic period. The energies of both liberal and conservative intellectuals were turned outward; they were forever in the process of "rebuilding" their nation. Thus, the best Portuguese prose was in essay form, the best poetry and drama was in satire, and historical writing flourished. Among the celebrated literati of the era were Alexandre Herculano, who wrote both historical fiction and a monumental history of Portugal, and Almeida Garrett, who was best known for his drama, but also was a writer of political, legal, and critical essays.

The conflicts of the 19th century were encapsulated in the "Coimbra question." Two groups of university scholars stood divided. The older group, led by the blind poet Castilho, advocated the virtues of the status quo, while the "generation of 1870," as they became known, called for revision of both intellectual and spiritual values. They were rationalist, anticlerical, and antimonarchist. In their writing could be heard the first strains of emerging socialist thought. Their daring critiques, however, were suppressed by the government in 1871.

But the rising tide of republicanism could not be stymied forever. As the century drew to a close, the democratic ideal was combined with a nationalistic utopian vision, a shift that was hoped would raise Portugal to its long-lost glory. The national anthem that was adopted in 1910 echoed the theme of resurgence: *"Oh sea heroes, oh noble people...raise again the splendor of Portugal...may Europe claim to all the world that Portugal is not dead!"*

The assassination of Carlos sealed victory for Republicanism; but it took time for the various parties and coalitions to sort themselves into a workable government—practically speaking, they never did. Between 1910 and 1926 there were 45 different governments, with most of the changes being brought about by military intervention rather than parliamentary procedure. The

The First Republic is proclaimed in 1910 and Joaquim Teófilo Fernandes Braga forms an anti-clerical government

SALAZAR

António Oliveira worked as an overseer for absentee landlords around the small village of Santa Comba, halfway between Viseu and Coimbra. He was known for his austerity, strong faith and stringent supervision and was known as *O Manholas*—"The Crafty One." His first son, António de Oliveira Salazar, (born in 1889) took the conservative values of his father far beyond the small rural world that formed them: indeed, finally making the whole nation of Portugal into his image of what it should be.

Salazar, as a professor of economics at Coimbra, was an active polemicist for the right, expressing some pride in that mark of cultural purity. In the same way, Portugal steered through international affairs with neutrality wherever possible. His own conservative values of piety, economy, and fatalism were also imposed on his country, even where it meant that the technological and cultural advances of the 20th century passed by. He lived quietly, taking modest vacations by the shore or visiting farms around the countryside. He remained unmarried, though he had a close but apparently celibate relationship with his lifelong housekeeper, Dona Maria de Jesus Caetano, who raised his two adopted daughters.

pressing his political faith in the slogan "Nothing against the nation, all for the nation." Nonetheless, for years he resisted various invitations to political positions until 1928, when General Carmona, as Prime Minister, offered Salazar the role of Finance Minister with absolute power over national finance. In 1932, having founded the National Union party, Salazar became Prime Minister. Though there were periods of serious opposition, and various plots on the dictator's life, his pervasive influence on Portugal would not truly lift until the April revolution of 1974, six years after his retirement and four years after his death.

Salazar's character is best read in the character that he imposed upon the nation. An introvert, he seldom traveled out of Portugal, perhaps tak-

On September 6, 1968, at the seaside in Estoril, Salazar's deck chair collapsed. The Prime Minister hit his head, developing a stroke that left him an invalid. With little turmoil, Marcelo Caetano, a former loyal of the regime turned critic, was made Prime Minister.

For the duration of Salazar's life, less than two years, he lived with few visitors and little attention. Strangely, those close to him chose not to tell him the truth about his position and the succession of Caetano. Sparing him the harsh reality, they fabricated a Portugal still led by Salazar. When Dona Maria tried to convince him to retire during those final years, he refused and, in a last pathetic boast that displayed the egomania which had grown over the years, he said that he had no choice, for there was no one else.

early leadership pressed their radical antichurch and social reforms too hard, causing a reaction that revived the influence of the Catholic church. Labor movements sprang up with the best intentions, but often paralyzed industry. First and foremost, the republicans were unable to deliver promised financial reforms and stability, both through their own ineptitude and, later, because of the international depression of 1920s. It was their economic failure that most significantly eroded their popular support.

Afonso Costa rose to leadership of the Republican factions, but the hard stance of anticlericalism caused too much ill feeling to allow stability. The political structure was intransigent, so military coups became standard. General Pimenta de Castro grabbed control briefly, but democratic forces deposed him. Sidónio Pais formed a dicta-

until 1951, but it was not his leadership but that of his most influential appointee that made that stability possible. In 1928, Carmona named António de Oliveira Salazar to the post of Finance Minister, with wide-ranging powers. Salazar had made his first political impact as the youthful leader of the Centro Academico de Democracia Crista (Academic Center for Christian Democracy) a Catholic intellectual group that opposed the anticlerical and individualistic philosophy of the Republic. An economics professor, Salazar stayed out of the fray until his time was ripe. He resisted accepting any political position until he could be assured of what quickly amounted to complete control. By 1932, Salazar was made Prime Minister, a position he would retain until 1968.

Salazar's regime: Miraculously, Salazar imme-

torial government in 1917, but was assassinated in 1918.

Portugal, initially neutral, joined the Allies under Britain's influence in 1916, but World War I meant little to them except further financial upheaval. In 1926, the democratic government was overthrown by military forces and the constitution was suspended. Leadership passed through various hands and finally to General Oscar Carmona. He would remain as President

Left, Salazar delivers a public address. Above, shrine of Fátima, which gave the New State a foreign policy and encouraged domestic obedience.

diately straightened out the country's disastrous financial morass, mostly through an austerity that reflected his personal ideals. Having done what no leader had been able to do for a century, Salazar used his political capital to form what amounted to a dictatorship, taking Mussolini's Italy and Primo de Rivera's Spain as his models in the call for national order and discipline.

The "New State," as it was called, was a fascist regime, though nominally a corporative economic system under a republican government. The National Union was the only political party. It was authoritarian, pro-Catholic, and imperialist. A state police organization, the PIDE, were notorious and vigilant watchdogs against subversion. Censorship, rigid and effective, settled like a thick fog over all literature, journalism and art.

Nothing negative or critical could find its way into print. An example of the absurd extremity of the New State's repression was when a censor in Mozambique replaced the word "muddy" with "blue" in the sentence "...*the South African fleet had arrived in the muddy waters of the bay on a courtesy visit to Lourenço Marquês.*" The formerly lively national journalism withered away. And in blatant doublespeak, the government often referred to itself as a dictatorship without a dictator.

There was some resistance. In reaction to the powerful militaristic control of the country, there were numerous attempted coups and an underground Communist party that grew in power, leading the clandestine opposition. However, Salazar's leadership was never strongly challenged. Still essentially rural, relatively backward, and mostly conservative, Portugal accepted Salazar's fascism as a kind of defensive posture to the worldwide technological explosion of the 20th century. His conservative and at times reactionary attitudes toward industrialization, agricultural reform, education and religion kept Portugal out of the traumatic turbulence of the age. His attitude that Portugal was a naturally poor country—good for living but not for producing anything—was widely held. Catholic cults, like that of Our Lady of Fátima, were encouraged and turned into propaganda for the regime. Salazar also drew upon the romanticized history of the Portuguese exploration and trade, inculcating a generation of schoolchildren to the self-aggrandizing idea of Portugal's manifest destiny as an "empire." They turned inward, though still holding their colonies where possible, and tried to ignore the changing face of world politics. It was a comforting if finally debilitating attitude. Portugal, after all, would eventually have to catch up.

Putting self-preservation ahead of ideology, Salazar pretended to adhere to the League of Nations' nonintervention policy during the Spanish Civil War, because he could not afford international censure, but actually sent a great legion of soldiers—as many as 20,000—to aid Franco's Nationalist forces. The effort was well-conceived. Franco's victory served to validate the authority of Salazar's own regime.

The minor flourishing of culture of the republican era, when democratic ideals had encouraged efforts at mass education, a proliferation of journalism, and a few writers of modern fiction and poetry, was slowed by political upheavals, and effectively quelled with the advent of the New State. The greatest writer of the period, the poet Fernando Pessoa, was not "discovered" until after World War II, when most of his works were first published, posthumously. Few others transcended the romantic nationalism of the era, as formidable barriers to the larger currents of European culture were created. In any case, the censor-

ship of the New State slowed original thinking to a trickle, and most of that was devoted to political subversion. Of course, this was nothing new to a country that had been dominated by the Inquisition for so many years. In the whole 500-year history of Portuguese publishing, only 80 years have been free of oppressive censorship of one kind or another.

During World War II, the New State again sensibly concentrated on self-preservation. Though Salazar admired Hitler, Portugal's traditional political and economic ties with Britain demanded at least neutrality. However, Portugal did supply the Axis with much needed wolfram (the ingredient necessary to alloy tungsten steel) almost until the end of the war. On the other hand, the Allies were granted strategic bases in the Azores. In fact, the war's main effect—though it was not widely advertised—was to replenish Portugal's coffers as they did business with both sides. The defeat of the fascists did serve as a signal to Salazar, a warning to mute his totalitarianism, but he was by now firmly entrenched. The changes over the next decade served primarily to protect the dictatorship still further from democratic insurgency.

In the 1950s, opposition to the New State solidified into two blocs. The one, legal, took advantage of the relaxed censorship in the month preceding elections (the state's way of giving the impression of free elections) to run independent candidates. The other, furtive, organized various protest actions and engaged in what propaganda they could. These means kept resistance vital, forcing Salazar's hand. Their actions required new rounds of repression, deceit, and constitutional changes that eroded both Salazar's authority and popularity.

In 1958, General Humberto Delgado, a disenchanted member of the regime, ran for President, announcing among other things that he would use the constitutional power of that position to dismiss Prime Minister Salazar. Despite the mass demonstrations in his support, and his apparently successful campaign, the "official count" elected instead Admiral Américo Thomás, a Salazar loyal. Afterwards, further constitutional decrees were enacted to prevent the repetition of such an election, making the presidential election not by popular vote, but by an electoral college of the National Assembly, which was Salazar-controlled. Delgado was assassinated in 1965, while attempting to cross the Spanish border into Portugal, a murder generally attributed to PIDE operatives.

Portugal's entry into the United Nations had been prevented by the Soviet bloc and by oppo-

Right, the headline of April 25, 1974: Military strike—The Armed Forces Movement Takes Action at Dawn.

ANO VII ... Nº 2243 — 1974 — QUINTA-FEIRA, 25 DE ABRIL — PREÇO 2$50

A CAPITAL

EDIÇÃO ÀS 12 HORAS

Director: HENRIQUE MARTINS DE CARVALHO
Subdirector: JOSÉ JÚLIO GONÇALVES

PROPRIEDADE: S.G.C. - SOCIEDADE GRÁFICA DE «A CAPITAL» - R. JOAQUIM ANTÓNIO DE AGUIAR, 86 - LISBOA-1 · TELEFS. 686125/6/7 · END. TELEG. ACAPITAL · TELEX 12386

GOLPE MILITAR

"MOVIMENTO DAS FORÇAS ARMADAS" DESENCADEIA ACÇÃO DE MADRUGADA

(PÁGINA 2)

nents of Salazar imperial colonialism until 1955. Membership was finally granted not because of any real change, but by a successful diplomatic effort to whitewash his colonial despotism. Salazar would not actually alter his policies because despite the increasingly higher cost of maintaining military rule in the colonies, they were very profitable for the homeland. Subsistence crops were increasingly neglected in favor of crops like cotton, to feed the mills of Portugal while the native Africans went hungry. The policy of *assimilado*—claiming that the national goal was to assimilate the local culture into Western, Portuguese culture—allowed Portugal to exploit these "citizens" as virtually free labor. Despite international pressure, and increasing agitation within the colonies, the regime—steeped in the ancient idea of the glorious empire—fiercely resisted any incursions on its colonial outposts, to extreme and sometimes ridiculous lengths. For example, in 1961, the territory of São João de Ajudá consisted of a decrepit fortress and the governor's estate, a tiny enclave surrounded by the country of Dahomey. That year Dahomey had become independent from France, and had delivered an ultimatum to Lisbon to return Ajudá. Waiting until the last possible minute to surrender this tiny sliver of territory, the Portuguese governor spitefully burned down the buildings before departing.

Of course, Salazar's imperial intransigence had far more serious consequences elsewhere. An explosion of African nationalism was set off by a violent 1961 Angolan native uprising that had been brutally crushed by the Portuguese military and civilian reaction. Throughout the 1960s, the government was more and more economically and militarily involved in maintaining the colonies, which actually had been renamed "provinces" in a 1951 decree that semantically underscored the insistence on a permanent Portuguese settlement. Meanwhile, the stagnation of Portugal's home economy grew more oppressive. Hydroelectric power projects were successful, but industry and agriculture grew more and more backward compared with international standards. Emigration, mostly in search of employment, began to take a serious toll on the country's demographic resources.

Many young men were conscripted, and popular support for the wars in Africa waned quickly. Angola continued to be an economic boon, but the other colonies were a drain. Salazar, in response, trusted fewer and fewer members of the regime, taking on more direct responsibilities for continuing the wars. He also relaxed his former policy of fiscal austerity, and increasingly relied on foreign credit to finance the overseas operations.

Acting Prime Minister: In 1968, a deck chair collapsed under the 79-year-old Salazar. He suf-

fered an incapacitating stroke, and the long awaited succession had arrived. Because Salazar had made no provision for a successor—unwilling to face his own mortality—major upheavals were expected. But the transition to "acting" (while Salazar lived his final years in seclusion) Prime Minister Marcelo Caetano was relatively smooth.

Caetano, once a protégé of Salazar, had resigned seven years earlier over conflicts with his superior. Now called upon to resolve the national crisis, he saw the need for balanced change and stability. But he was not bold enough. Though many of the gravest injustices of the old regime were righted, other changes were superficial, and the colonial issue was not confronted. When his early efforts at liberalization failed to appease opposition unrest, Caetano returned to the oppressive hostility of the former regime.

Discontentment among all ranks of the military over the continual and ineffective wars in the colonies led to the formation of the Armed Forces Movement (MFA) in 1973. In 1974, General António de Spínola published *Portugal and the Future*, a stinging and comprehensive critique of the current state of affairs that recommended a military takeover to save the country. The book's messages had been heard before, but never from so high up the power structure. Though many factors had built toward the revolution, this famous publication lit the fuse. Caetano himself felt its importance, saying later that he began reading it in the late evening and "*did not stop until the last page, which I read in the small hours of the morning. And when I closed the book I understood that the military coup, which I could sense had been coming, was now inevitable.*" Like many revolutions, however, this one was as much a collapse of the old as it was a triumph of the new.

Two months later, on April 25, 1974, after a few premature uprisings, a nearly bloodless coup began in Lisbon. It was led in part by Spínola and fellow General Costa Gomes, and by all the "angry young captains" who commanded the 27 rebel units that seized key points throughout the city. One of the signals that was used to coordinate the coup's launch was the playing of a song on the radio. The song, "Grandola, Vila Morena," which was about a town where the people governed themselves, became an unofficial anthem of the movement. Caetano and other ranking government officials took refuge in the barracks of the National Republican Guard, a building that was once a convent. The formal surrender came after a young officer threatened to crash a tank through the gates. The rebel takeover was quickly accepted throughout the country. The revolution took the red carnation, then in season, as its symbol, and sparked nationwide celebration, including joyous mass demonstrations on the first of May.

The initial government was a National Salvation Board of military men, designed to give way to a constituent assembly as soon as it was practical. A provisional government was soon in place, and negotiations with African liberation movements went ahead. The government was divided over the new overseas policies, and an odd *coup* within the *coup* developed, with Spínola attempting to wrest control from his opponents. It was unsuccessful and liberal forces continued to divest colonies. Guinea-Bissau, Mozambique, the Cape Verde Islands, São Tomé and finally Angola were granted independence. One of the disastrous results of this sudden change was a mass immigration of Portuguese nationals back to their homeland. As many as 500,000 people flowed into Lisbon and other urban centers.

In 1976, with the economy in dire straits, a Pintassilgo. At the end of 1979, a coalition of the right took power.

In 1982 the long-awaited revision of the constitution finally arrived. The Democratic alliance and the far right were determined to quickly rid that document of its Marxist taint. They were partially successful after a period of nationwide demonstrations, strikes, and resignations. The Council of the Revolution, a powerful overseeing branch of the former arrangement was eliminated, but the hope for a classless society remained a signal goal, mentioned in Articles 1 and 2 of the document.

In the past few years, the country has witnessed a general conservative shift, away from socialism and toward capitalism. Though veteran socialist leader Mário Soares was elected President in 1986 (the first civilian to hold the post in over 60

socialist-influenced constitution was adopted, and Mário Soares, leader of the Socialist party, was appointed Prime Minister. The next decade brought little stabilization. The Socialists fell in 1977, then rose again as part of a coalition government with the Social Democratic Central Party. But it fell again the next year, replaced by a government of technocrats that lasted just 17 days. Small, powerful groups were ranged throughout the political gamut, keeping the government in turmoil. Among the various short-lived governments was an interim period led by the first woman Prime Minister, Maria de Lurdes

Above, Prime Minister Mário Soares signs and makes official the long-awaited entry of Portugal into the EEC in 1986.

years), the more capitalistic Social Democrats made Cavaco Silva prime minister in 1987

The political flux will never be completely over, but at least the variations are more contained. This relative stability, has allowed Portugal to emerge from its long financial doldrums. In 1986, it joined the European Economic Community (EEC). Among Silva's most successful programs has been the reprivatization of many companies and industries that had been nationalized under Communist pressure after the Revolution. These poorly managed national resources are regaining vitality as private enterprises.For a change, the Portuguese are looking within for economic viability—expanding industry, agriculture, education—putting their glorious but obsolete history of adventuring and colonizing behind them.

THE PORTUGUESE

Defining a national character is never simple, and Portugal presents no exception. Travelogues tend to portray the Portuguese as easy-going, smiling, patient, good-natured, but imbued with an inner *saudade*, a feeling variously defined as a nostalgia or melancholy. Certainly the Portuguese are perfectly suited to dealing with touring foreigners, whether the visitors are in search of sunny beaches, medieval architecture, or folklore. The native forbearance allows for cross-cultural missteps and halting phrase-book Portuguese. For the visitor, the only character flaw is the innate reluctance to consider time. Shopkeepers, gas station attendants, or postal clerks, no one is in a hurry, or even close.

The Portuguese have also faced more serious criticism. Writing in the 30s, the great modern poet Fernando Pessoa criticized their "provincialism", meaning their naively uncritical appreciation of all things "modern" and "civilized": big cities, new fashions, etc. Dr. Salazar, whose 50 years of oppressive rule still effect Portugal's character today, once commented bluntly, and unfairly, "The Portuguese are not a very intelligent people."

From childhood: Paul Descamps, a Frenchman writing earlier this century, isolated permissive childrearing as a key to understanding the national character. Though this may seem a specious argument, its conclusions make sense. Portugal is a matriarchal society and having been spoiled by mother, the Portuguese learn to operate by cajolery rather than diligence, to favor patience over perseverance. Raised permissively, they grow up without great self-discipline, with only the vaguest sense of time constraints, and generally with a streak of independence and an unsinkable self-esteem.

Generalities are great liars, however. It is, after all, 10 million individuals that make up this great country that is both ancient—the oldest national boundaries in Europe—and newborn—after the Carnation Revolution of 1974. And there may even be a prompt shopkeeper or two.

In the bucolic backways of Trás-os-Montes and the Beiras, it is possible to feel that one has stepped back in time. Indeed, ways of life from Europe's past are alive throughout Portugal. There are windmills on grassy knolls, cobbled roads from Roman times, and horse-drawn

farmer's carts—some with handmade wooden wheels—that look extremely picturesque when piled high with the grape harvest.

The people in rural areas generally distrust Lisbon and all that it stands for: political turmoil, taxes, police functions, bureaucratic regulation, centralized education, etc. They would rather keep their distance. Able to sustain themselves, if sometimes meagerly, by their harvests, they have no patience for worrying about the EEC, inflation, or trade deficits. They are self-reliant.

This is not to say that national pride is any less vigorous here. It seems that even the smallest

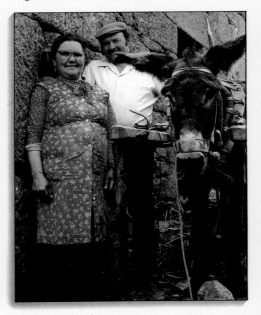

town will boast its own museum, scenic church, or historical monument, and the residents are anxious that you visit and appreciate them.

In both city and country, there are ingrained social classes, but there is also a broad sense of equality. Every man expects to be treated with dignity. Manners tend to be elaborate, especially in forms of address. "Your excellency" is a common tag. Handshakes are exchanged at every chance, in addition to a parting wave on turning out of sight.

The fairer sex: Women, on the other hand, are on a separate footing. Feminist ideas are only beginning to be heard. A ground-breaking feminist collection of poems letters and stories, *New Portuguese Letters* was written and attacked in 1972. Now there is more freedom of ideas, but a

Preceding pages, a Portuguese-French immigrant in the Upper Minho; Maria Lusa, Bruno, Marco, Eva and friend in Grandola; a lone traveler in Monsaraz. Left, a Braga resident. Above, a couple in Aldeia Solveira.

long way to go before attitudes change.

Throughout Portugal the general attitude—which English and Americans might consider cynical—is that there is no objective basis for laws or government. The assumption is that leaders and legislators are most dedicated to furthering their own interest. Anyway, history and current events dictate against forming strong attachments to current leaders—there have been 16 governments in the past 13 years. Change is all that can be depended upon. All this instability keeps politics lively and fills the daily papers.

Beneath the ever-shifting face of contemporary politics are the proud contours that are Portugal's history. Os Lusiads is hailed as the seminal Portuguese work not only for its beauty and literary influence, but for its paeans to the Discoveries and to national pride. In fact, this

agriculture, with 35 percent in industry. Naturally, many are employed at the ports all along the coast, especially Oporto and Lisbon, and fishing remains a strong vocation, as it has been for centuries (see page 191). The major agricultural products are olives, potatoes, and wine grapes among others. Trees provide numerous cork products, resins, and lumber (see page 164).

Portugal is still Europe's poorest country. The gross national product per capita in 1984 was US\$1,970. That of Spain, hardly a rich country, was \$4,440. However, the economic statistic that is more likely to be cited is growth rate, which is one of Europe's fastest. The natural optimism of the Portuguese is, for now, well founded.

Family ties: Home and family life is much more stable cultural framework than politics or economics. Kinship, in fact, can be a powerful

Portuguese identity—as explorers, colonizers, a world power—lent itself to dangerous illusions during Salazar's regime. The tendency to look overseas for answers to internal woes and weaknesses is only now being overcome as Portugal turns inward to develop.

Industries: The control of many industries was usurped by the state in 1974, and though the trend over the last few years has been toward reprivatization, many remain state-owned. Unemployment, rampant in the 1970s, is still high, particularly among young people seeking first jobs. Long-term emigration in search of steady work causes strange demographics; almost as in wartime, young and old are left behind as workers part from their families and send home wages. As of 1985, 31 percent of the workforce was in

influence in finding employment and aligning the many splintered political parties. The extended family is a common living situation, as grandparents help care for the children, and young adults—without any other housing option—often live at home until they are married.

Portugal is predominantly a Roman Catholic country (see page 68), with only a few Protestant communities, and a few Jews and Muslims, too. One interesting sub-group of the Catholics is the Marranos, the hereditary Jews who converted during the 16th-and 17th-century prosecutions, and who retain some Jewish rituals and practices in combination with their nominal Catholicism.

Television is a state monopoly called RTP (Radiotelevisão Portuguesa) offering two channels. However, within the past year there has been legislative activity towards allowing private broadcasting. The country owns 1.5 million TV sets (15 sets per 100 people; the US figure is 63 per 100.) The country counts a total of 31 daily newspapers and 379 movie theaters among its other distractions. Smoking is supposed to be on the decline, but it is still very evident and always accepted. Crime rates are relatively low and the prison population is a scant 6,000 or so. Capital punishment has been abolished.

Drive, baby, drive: The Portuguese may be easygoing by nature, but behind the wheel of a Mercedes, a BMW, or even a Morris Mini the locals are possessed by an irresistible urgency to get around that grape truck. Whether on winding mountain roads or the Lisbon-Oporto highway, the Portuguese drive with the bravado of immortals. Unfortunately, they are quite human and in

Pre-school is an option for three-to-six-year-olds, while basic mandatory education is six years during the ages six to 14. In the age group six to 12 enrollment is 97 percent. Secondary education is not compulsory. Numerous universities and polytechnic colleges offer higher education.

Illiteracy has been the scourge of progressive reformers, but recently the efforts of public education have made some headway. Over the last decade adult illiteracy has declined from 29 percent to just over 20 percent.

No portrait of the Portuguese would be complete without taking note of the differences between the South (Lisbon and below) and the North. First of all, the racial cast of the people is slightly different. In the North the basic Iberian strain—dark, thick-set—has been leavened with Celtic blood, while in the South, Jewish, Moorish

fact have the dismal distinction of one of the highest accident rates in Europe.

Military service is compulsory, for either 12-15 months in the army or 18-20 months in the navy or air force. The armed forces total 68,252. Though soldiers in uniform are certainly a common sight throughout Portugal, the defense budget is relatively small: 86 million e*scudos* in 1985, compared with 115 million spent on national health the same year.

Education has been thoroughly modernized.

Far left, a carrier in Caria. Left, time out for the latest gossip. Above, graduation day at the University of Coimbra. Following page, the Portuguese Cup Final packs the stadium

and African ancestors are evident.

The North is generally more conservative, both politically and culturally. It is the bastion of Portuguese Catholicism. The south has a tradition of liberalism and adaptation.

The two temperaments—the warm Mediterranean and cool Atlantic—wash over each other across Portugal. The people are as varied as the land that drinks at the banks of the Tagus and Douro rivers: bursting with verdure in Sintra, rippling with stark beauty in the Alentejo, and thundering up into the craggy Serra da Estrela. There is a folk saying that "Coimbra sings, Braga prays, Lisbon parades, and Oporto works." Nothing is that simple, but it is true that traveling here unveils not only a beautiful landscape but a beautiful panorama of character and humanity.

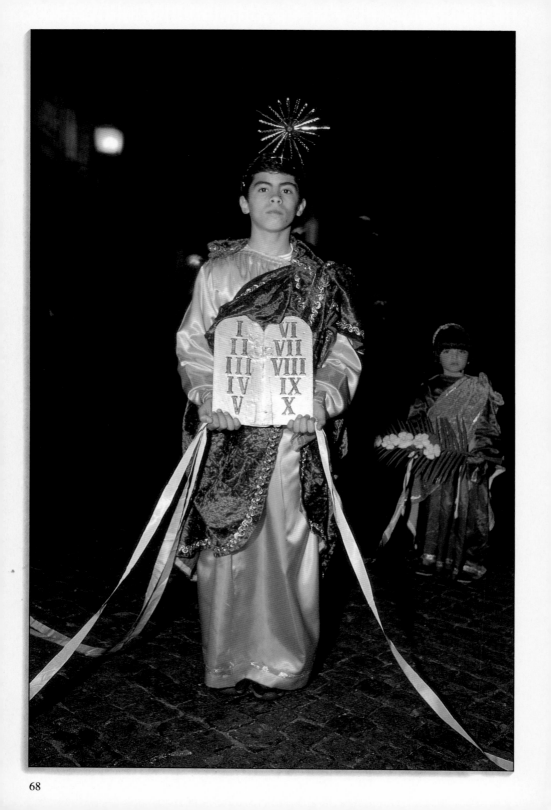

SAINTS, MIRACLES AND SHRINES

In the first decade of the 6th century, a young monk named Martin arrived in Braga. This former Roman capital was now the political and religious stronghold of the Suevi, the barbarian tribe that had adopted Arianism, a heretic form of Christianity. Martin, inspired at the shrine of St. Martin at Tours, was determined to convert these rulers to Catholicism.

Martin's parents came from Panonia (modern day Hungary), the original home of the Suevi, so he was well suited for this particular mission. And he succeeded. Martin founded an abbey at Dume, became a bishop, and, in 559, converted the Suevi king Theodomirus.

Martin found a further challenge, however, among the general population of the area. Although practicing Catholics since their conversion under the Roman Empire, the masses had incorporated many local beliefs and customs into their religion. To Martin, this amalgam was unacceptable, and in a written sermon entitled *De Correctione Rusticorum* (On the Correction of Peasants), he called for the cessation of the use of charms, auguries and divination, of the invocation of the Devil, of the cults of the dead, fountains and stars.

In this St. Martin of Dume did not succeed, nor have 14 centuries of similarly inclined zealots and reformers. All these elements are present to this day as an obstinate strain within the orthodox Catholic traditions in many areas of the country. The north, in general, is the most devout section of Portugal—over 40 percent of adults attend Sunday Mass as opposed to about ten percent in the south.

Naturally, there is still much wrestling over these issues between the church hierarchy and the practicing parishes—recently the bishops banned Padre Miguel, a priest from an isolated northern mountain parish who was supposed to have healing powers. Yet, though frowned upon by the orthodox Church, this spontaneous, independent Catholicism should not be seen as a form of pagan superstition or magic; rather, it is evidence of a vigorous religious tradition.

What are some of these still-current beliefs? When a newborn child proves healthy, it is said that it was conceived when the moon was waxing. The states of the moon are believed to be very influential in the way all vegetables, animals and humans grow. Similarly, certain fountains are reputed to have particular healing powers. And under many of these, beautiful Enchanted Mooresses are said to be hiding, watching over great treasures.

A variety of beliefs function to reassure people during the most frightening moments of the human life cycle. For instance, many practices have evolved that are meant to protect children as they gestate in their mothers' wombs, or just after they are born. Thus, a newborn should not be taken out of the house during certain hours, to protect it against the "evil air"; and its father's

trousers should be placed over the cot to frighten away witches; and the mother should not eat while breastfeeding, as the child may grow up to be greedy.

Midnight Baptism: One of the more dramatic folk practices is the Midnight Baptism. This happens when a pregnant woman is prone to miscarriages or when her previous child was stillborn. The "baptism" takes place at midnight in the middle of a bridge that divides two municipalities—a powerful place that is neither one place nor another, at the moment that is neither one day nor the next. Certain bridges, such as the Ponte da Barca in Minho, are famous for this and still secretly sought by hopeful parents. When all is ready, the father and a friend, armed with sticks, stand guard at the ends of the bridge. They are

Preceding page, the Fátima devout in a candlelit procession. Left, solemnity at Good Friday in Braga, while above, St. Anthony's festival rollicks in Lisbon

warding off cats and dogs—which may be witches or the Devil in disguise. The first person who passes after the church bells strike midnight must perform this rite. He (or less frequently, considering the late hour, she) pours river water over the expectant mother's belly and baptizes the child "in the name of the Father, the Son and the Holy Ghost…" but the final "Amen" must not be uttered. The child must wait to be born to be properly and completely baptized by the priest in church. Thus, the healing powers of baptism are extended to cover this dangerous period.

The church is the central meeting place of the whole parish, as most gather there on Sundays. At Easter, the cross that represents the resurrection of Christ is taken out of the church to visit successively all the households of the parish. The cross is kissed as it enters each house in the company

they have the power to hear or see a procession of the ghosts of those parishioners who have recently died. This procession is seen leaving the cemetery, with a coffin in its center. When it returns, the ghost of the parishioner who will be the next to die will be in the coffin. Thus these seers predict how many people are going to die soon—but they cannot reveal their names if they themselves want to remain alive.

The use of religion to establish a communal identity is most clearly shown by the celebration for the local patron saint. An organizing committee busies itself all year collecting money, planning decorations, arranging events. Whether it is a rural parish, a small village, or a middle-sized town, the importance of these celebrations is immense. They represent and solidify local pride. The *festa* is a joyful occasion heralded by fire-

of the priest and sacristan. This process may take days. When the cross returns to the church, it is a symbol of the new life shared by all in the community.

Similarly, on All Saints' Day and All Souls' Day (1st and 2nd of November), the celebrations at the parish cemetery are attended by all. Lamps are lit, tombs are cleaned and decorated with flowers. Friends and neighbors visit tombs. The whole parish celebrates this strongly felt sense of continuation with the past, praying together for "their" dead.

Perhaps the strongest evidence that the feeling of community extends beyond this life is the common belief in the "procession of the dead." This belief is found in the whole northwest section of the Iberian Peninsula. Certain people claim that

crackers—a familiar noise to those traveling the northern countryside in summer, when most of these occur—and by music blaring from loudspeakers placed on the church tower. The pivotal event is the procession after the Mass, when the image of the patron saint, along with other images, is carried with great pomp in a brightly decorated stand in a roughly circular, traditional path.

After that the lay celebrations begin. These usually involve a great deal of dancing to traditional brass bands, folk-dance groups, and nowadays, rock bands. Much wine is consumed and the occasion is indispensable for young people, who use these opportunities as social mixers. It is this section of the celebration that the priests have always opposed. For the people, however, the two aspects are deeply connected and cannot be disassociated. There is no sense of disrespect for the sacred part of the celebrations, simply that religion is fully integrated into their lives.

Popular attitudes to saints differ from Church doctrine not so much in content as in emphasis. The people place great importance on material benefits and personal, reciprocal relationships with saints. They pray to specific saints for specific problems—St. Lawrence for toothache, St. Bráz for sore throat, St. Christopher for traveling, Our Lady of the Conception for infertility, the Holy Family for family problems, and so on. Also, people will have unique devotions for particular saints that they have developed over time. If the believer's prayer has been answered, this proves that the particular image addressed is a singularly sacred one, a favored line of commu-

saint something in return. A wax heart might be given for a successful engagement or a wax pig if the pig has fully recovered. If the promise is not fulfilled, the saint may well aveng himself.

If one visits churches in northern Portugal, these kinds of offerings are often seen hanging on the walls of the sacristies alongside other gifts such as bride's dresses, photographs, written testimonies or women's braids. Shrines of great fame such as Bom Jesus and Sameiro, near Braga, or the Senhor de Matosinhos, near Oporto, have large displays of votive offerings. In Fátima (perhaps the most important shrine in the country), wax gifts accumulate so quickly that special furnaces have been installed to burn them.

Wax gifts are not the only kind of offering. Jewelry, money, flowers, and objects associated with the disease in question (crutches, glasses,

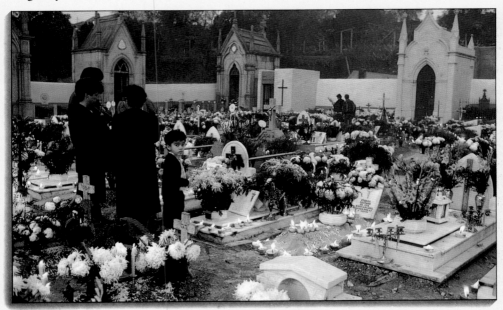

nication. In this way shrines develop, whether personal, family, or even national, with images famous for their miraculous powers.

The notion of the miracle in popular religion is also more loosely interpreted than in the Church. Essentially, a miracle is considered to have taken place every time a specific prayer is positively answered. The believer must then "pay" the saint whatever he or she had promised.

Wax Offerings: When a prayer to St. Anthony involves a loved one or a pig to recover from a bout of ill health, a promise is made to give the

wheelchairs, etc.) are also used. There is also another kind of gift: a personal sacrifice. Recently, the Church has been strongly critical of this, but until the late 1960s, it was strongly encouraged. If one visits the shrine of São Bento da Porta Aberta (St. Benedict of the Open Door), in the beautiful mountain landscape of Gerês near the dam of Caniçada on the 13th of August, one will find men and women laboriously circumambulating the church on their knees. There is a path especially laid out in cement for this, to avoid even more painful natural surfaces.

This scene is even more striking as these people are surrounded by others celebrating the day with song, dance, eating and drinking. It must be remembered that those on their knees are celebrating, too—because the saint answered their

Left, the much-kissed crucifix makes another stop on its Easter Sunday rounds. Above, cemetery candle-burning on All Saints' Day.

prayers. As São Bento da Porta Aberta often is called upon in cases of fatal disease, these people may have a great deal for which to be grateful.

Another shrine associated with such practices is Fátima, near the town of Leiria, in the center of Portugal. It deserves special mention, as it is one of the largest shrines in Western Europe. On May 13th, 1917, the Virgin is supposed to have appeared to three children on top of a tree (one of the children is, incidentally, still alive, an incarcerated Carmelite nun). This event is said to have been repeated on the 14th of each month until October of the same year, and each time, the Virgin spoke in a vague and allegorial way about peace in the world. Fátima soon became a rallying point for the revival of Catholicism in the 1930s and 1940s. Today, from May to October the roads around Leiria are lined with pilgrims,

many of whom have come on foot from great distances to "pay" the Virgin for her favors.

Another kind of "payment" to the saints has all but disappeared now due to strong Church opposition. In the parish of Senhora da Aparecida in Lousada, for example, before the main procession leaves the church, another procession takes place. This is the procession in which 20 or so open coffins are carried—containing live people, their faces covered with white handkerchiefs. Some coffins are dark brown and lined in white satin; some are tiny white coffins for children. Those who ride in the coffins are offering a false burial to the saint who saved them from having to participate in a real one. The occasion, therefore, is a joyful one. There are plenty of light-hearted comments, and the participants mingle

with the others afterward, drinking and dancing for the rest of the day.

The cult of the dead, another morbid religious tradition, and one of the targets of St. Martin of Dume during the 6th century, remains the object of popular fascination in the 20th. Occasionally, a body is buried but does not undergo the normal process of decay. Such people often are considered by the Northerners to be saints. There are a number of such grim shrines where the corpses are exposed. The Church nearly always opposes these cults at first, but eventually tolerates them as they grow in popularity—three such are the *Infanta Santa* in Arouca, the *São Torcato* near Guimarães, or the *Santinha de Arcozelo* near Oporto. Even in an unlikely spot like the small urban cemetery of the elegant neighborhood of Foz in Oporto, a shrine of one of these "saints" can be found.

Along rural roads one will frequently find pretty little shrines. These contain an image of Christ or the Virgin or a saint. At the bottom, little molded flames surround barely dressed figures who represent the souls of sinners suspended in Purgatory. These shrines are there to protect travelers.

Portuguese history is full of examples of the continuing conflict between the spontaneous and all-embracing religiosity of the less educated class and the more restrictive attitudes of the theologically learned. The tense embrace between these two traditions is an essential facet of the national character, and both the naive and the orthodox elements have often had a direct influence on politics. From the early days of the "Western Crusade" to the Knights Templar and their ilk to the dark days of the Inquisition, religion has vied with national authorities. Imperialism, like the early exploration, was seen as a form of religious crusade—each victory along the way was considered a miracle performed by the saints. Most extraordinarily of all, Salazar's regime presented its policy of neutrality during World War II as based on the reported sooth-sayings of the Virgin at Fátima.

Finally, it is important to realize that while Portugal is very much a Roman Catholic nation, there has always been opposition to the orthodox hegemony, from both within and without the Church, from both naive and sophisticated sources. These have ranged from the passive and popular forms that St. Martin campaigned against (and which still have their adherents) to the more active and intellectual rebellion of the victim's of the Inquisition and the anti-clerical forces of the 1910 and 1974 revolutions.

Above, the plaques are gifts from grateful supplicants. Right, a floral offering to the Virgin in Lamego's Cathedral

CENTRO SOCIAL JOÃO PA O I
(2ª FA)

"For me Lisbon was a very agreeable surprise," Evelyn Waugh wrote in his travel book *A Bachelor Abroad*. "There is no European capital of antiquity about which one hears so little." Without realizing it, Waugh was echoing the impressions of others before him, among them Dorothy Quillinan, daughter of the poet Wordsworth. In 1845, she had written, "There is, I believe, no country in Europe that is less thoroughly familiar to me."

The visitor to Portugal has always believed himself to be a discoverer of the one exotic land left in well-visited, well-described Europe. These revelations, however, have accumulated over the centuries; so frequently in fact that Portugal has developed from these preceptions a literary persona to complement—and occasionally contradict—her historical and geographical images. That is, a country that the rest of the world is just about to discover. And is it true? Is Portugal about to be discovered by the world? Yes, and it probably always will be.

Crusaders: Those ancient Greek and Roman sailors who made it to fair Lusitania left few written records of their impressions or opinions, noting only their belief that the sun off the Atlantic coast hissed when it set. In the centuries before Christ, the Greek historian Polybius remarked upon the fat tuna off the coast of Lusitania, and the geographer Strabo reported that the Cabo de São Vicente, the westernmost point of continental Europe, was shaped like a ship. Both these men were unknowing oracles of Portugal 's future maritime greatness. The 4th-century poet Avienus left us *Ora Maritime*, iambic verses in Latin about his sea journey along the Atlantic and Mediterranean coasts of Iberia. This poetic sea log would inspire the intrepid Englishwoman Rose Macaulay more than 1,500 years later to retrace part of his route in *Fabled Shore*, her book about Spain and Portugal.

The earliest full-scale account of travel to Portugal dates from the Crusades, reputedly jotted down by a British priest named Osbern. Before this bard ever set eyes upon Portugal, he had to make the crossing from Britain to the Iberian peninsula, a trip that was legendarily unpleasant. Frequently, on their way to the Holy Land, Crusaders would stop at Santiago, in western Spain, to visit the shrine of St. James of Campostella. The discomforting effect of the voyage on the constitutions of the pious through what Byron

Left, early tour group, like these Crusaders, did not have the luxury of buses and occasionally kicked up a fuss about accommodations

would later called "Biscay's sleepless bay," is depicted graphically by one unnamed medieval poet:

Men may leve all gamys,
That saylen to seynt Jamys!...
Thys mene whyle the pylgryms ly,
And have theyr bowlys fast theym by,
And cry aftyr hote maluesy,
"Thow helpe for to restore."

After the physically and spiritually restorative visit to the sacred bones of St. James, the pilgrims would continue south, eventually entering the Mediterranean through the strait of Gibraltar.

In 1147 a band of Crusaders—English, German and Flemish—broke their Atlantic journey in Oporto (they were shipwrecked, in fact) and were then persuaded by the new king of Portugal, Afonso Henriques, to join him on a sidetrip to seize Lisbon from the Moors. The chronicler Osbern sang the beauties of Lisbon first seen by the Britons—from the sea, of course. Her fertile countryside, lush with figs and vines, epitomized the seductive pleasures of the south. The 17-week siege led to victory for the Christians. A number of English settled along the Tagus: the first Bishop of Lisbon, Gilbert of Hastings, was an Englishman. This was neither the first nor the last of such stopovers for the Crusaders, but it was the most celebrated. It even became the subject of a poem written by the 18th-century-translator of Camões, William Mickle:

The hills and lawns to English valor given
What time the Arab Moors from Spain were driven,
Before the banners of the cross subdued,
When Lisboa's towers were bathed in Moorish blood
By Gloster's Lance—Romantic days that yield
Of gallant deeds a wide luxuriant field
Dear to the Muse that loves the fairy plains
Where ancient honor wild and ardent reigns.

The Portuguese themselves had less happy memories of the Crusaders from the north, whom they generally considered a loud drunken lot, given more to piracy than to piety. But the British, with their superior size and martial skills, would long feel a condescending pride in their Portuguese achievement, expecting gratitude and not a little obsequiousness from their allies to the south.

If the British Crusaders were given bad marks for their plundering and their fondness for the local wine, the Portuguese could not be praised for their later persecution of British "heretics." From its establishment in 1536 to its final dismantling under Pombal in the 18th century, the Inquisition got its unpleasant hands on a number of Englishmen. One of the first of these was the 16th-century Scottish humanist George Buchanan, who went to Portugal in 1547 to join the colony of educated men at the recently established University of Coimbra. The death of his protector, André de Gouveia, left Buchanan vulnerable to the attacks of his enemies. He was then made to suffer many months in a squalid prison, ignorant of both his accusers and his crimes. He was brought before the inquisitors and interrogated numerous times. His crimes, he finally discovered, were writing impious verses against Franciscans, eating flesh during Lent, and being critical of the monks. After a year and a half he was sentenced. In his autobiography (written in the third person) he sounds surprisingly forbearing about the whole affair: "They enclosed him

several months in a monastery, so that he could be taught by the monks, men indeed neither inhumane nor evil, but completely ignorant of religion."

Buchanan fared better at the hands of the Inquisition than others who were unwilling to deny their religion to escape the horrors of the torture chamber. The Roman Catholic church was not, after all, Buchanan's sworn enemy, as it would be for later visitors from Great Britain. While the Enlightenment, with its principles of reason and tolerance, lit up England, the fires of the *auto da fé* still raged in Portugal. In 1770, John Marchant compiled an anthology of monstrous experiences of the Inquisition in Spain and Portugal called *The Bloody Tribunal*, or *An Antidote Against Popery*. In it he states the rationalist view of the Inquisi-

tion: "Conviction can only be wrought by reason and argument; a convert by necessity is no better than a hypocrite."

Marchant includes the horrifying account of Mr. John Coustos, a British entrepreneur. Coustos came to Lisbon in 1743 to get a passage to Brazil, where he wanted to trade diamonds. His fierce loyalties to Protestantism and free-masonry inspired the wrath of the inquisitors. Coustos wrote:

"I considered that, being a Protestant, I should inevitably feel, in its utmost rigor, all that rage and barbarous zeal could infuse in the breast of monks; who cruelly gloried in committing to the flames great numbers of ill-fated victims, whose only crime was their differing from them in religious opinions; or rather who were obnoxious to those tygers, merely because they thought worthily of human nature."

Coustos, willing to die in the claws of these "tygers" rather than renounce his religion, managed to survive being tortured nine times.

For the most part Portugal was not a popular stopping place of the Grand Tourists of the 18th century. The modest list of ladies and gentlemen who published accounts of their travels in Portugal cannot compare with the massive catalog of writers offering narratives about France or Italy. Henry Fielding, who might have left a worthy literary tribute to the Portuguese, instead bequeathed only his grave to Lisbon. The novelist, who went to Portugal in 1754 in hopes that the mild climate would help his dropsy, survived only two months. His lengthy *Journal of a Voyage to Lisbon* is devoted to the journey itself and offers no impressions of the country, except to say that Lisbon was "the nastiest city in the world." Not very charitable, but then, he was dying. Nevertheless, his grave in the English Cemetery in Lisbon has been a pilgrimage spot for generation of travelers. The 19th-century missionary George Borrow wrote in his idiosyncratic and brilliant travel book *The Bible in Spain* that the cemetery was "Pere-le-chaise (the famous burying place of Paris) in miniature." He added that travelers, "if they be of England…may well be excused if they kiss the cold tomb, as I did, of the author of *Amelia*."

Beckford—The Grandest Tourist: Without a doubt, the most flamboyant of 18th-century visitors to Portugal was William Beckford, who set up sumptuous housekeeping in Ramalhoa near Sintra in 1787. He inspired Byron's Childe Harold, whose first stop on his pilgrimage to Portugal was to wander through Sintra conjuring Beckford's ghost and meditating on the brevity of life and pleasure:

"There thou too, Vathek! England's wealthiest son

Once formed thy Paradise, as not aware
When wanton Wealth her mightiest deeds had

done,
> Meek Peace voluptuous lures was ever wont to shun.
>
> Here didst thou dwell, here schemes of pleasure plan
>> Beneath yon mountain's ever beauteous brow:
>> But now, as if a thing unblest by man,
>> Thy fairy dwelling is as lone as thou!

Beckford first visited Iberia in 1787 shortly after the publication of his Gothic novel *Vathek*. The unorthodox Englishman, who had left England in the wake of a scandal over a homosexual affair, caught the fancy of the extremely pious Marquis of Marialva, who was convinced Beckford would convert to Catholicism. Beckford, meanwhile, as we learn from his diary, was desperate not for the salvation of his soul but for an introduction to the court of Queen Maria. England's ambassador Walpole had refused to perform this service for his disgraced countryman. The Marquis guaranteed an introduction if Beckford would become Catholic and abandon England. Beckford had no such intention and he left, petulant, without being presented to Queen Maria. By the time he was finally presented at court in 1795, Maria had long been insane. Beckford's *Sketches of Spain and Portugal, Recollections of An Excursion to the Monasteries of Alcobaça and Batalha*, and his diary give an idiosyncratic, slightly bitchy, aesthetically sensitive view of Portuguese art, music, nature and society. Beckford's Portugal is a land of the senses—he describes the haunting, erotic song called the *modinha* and the luxuriant beauty of the vegetation. (English plants he imported to his *quinta* in Ramalhoa grew strangely large and luxuriant in the southern clime.) Beckford's diaries and travel journals provided a brilliant, if haphazard guide to aspects of the art and climate of Portugal.

Byron: Beckford offers a pleasant alternative to the vitriolic portrait of Portugal left by the 19th century's greatest promoter of travel outside of Thomas Cook: George Gordon, Lord Byron. The poet left two accounts of Portugal, neither favorable: one in his letters home during his visit there in 1809, the other in *Childe Harold's* pilgrimage, *Canto I*. His hatred for the Portuguese has mystified and disturbed scholars and admirers of Portugal since it first appeared in print in 1812. There is no record of an encounter during his brief stay there that would have led to such dislike. Some of Byron's criticisms reveal a typical Anglo-Saxon ambivalence toward the South. Robert Southey, a romantic and the future English Poet Laureate, visiting Portugal 25 years earlier, had also been

torn between his disapproval of the filth of Lisbon, the discomfort of the country inns, and the corruption and superstition of the priests; and his delight in the sensual orange groves, long lazy days and lush, fertile fields. William Mickle, an unqualified admirer of Portugal's "genial clime" contrasted the "gloomy mists" of England to the "sun-basked scenes…where orange bowers invite." This view of Portugal differs little from reflections on other southern lands—Italy or Spain or the south of France. But while elsewhere Byron admires the southern spirit, his image of Lisbon is of a false and faithless harlot of a town, a southern siren who glitters beautifully from the water but who reveals, on closer contact, only filth and treachery:

> "But whoso entereth within this town,
> That, sheening far, celestial seems to be,

> Disconsolate will wander up and down,
> Mid many things unsightly to strange ee;
> For hut and palace show like filthily…
> Poor paltry slaves! yet born 'midst noblest scenes—"

Byron's summary of Portugal is that it is a fair land that has been peopled by beasts. The most likely explanation for his anger is that the Portuguese felt resentful rather than grateful towards the British for their help in expelling the French invader, "Gaul's locust host," from their country during Napoleon's Iberian campaign. Complicating emotions further, Byron probably, like many of his countrymen, felt shame that at the Congress of Cintra (Sintra), Arthur Wellesley (later the Duke of Wellington) allowed the defeated French to evacuate with their loot, many of

78

Portugal's treasures.

That the Portuguese felt resentment rather than gratitude toward their northern liberators is testified to by another Englishman, George Borrow. Traveling in 1835 he was miffed by the ingratitude of the Portuguese. Borrow, an eccentric itinerant minister, once left New Testaments and tracts next to the smouldering charcoal and broken liquor bottles of a bandit campsite in the wild back country of Portugal. His impatience with Portuguese hostility to the English is similar to the way many Americans felt after World War II about French criticism of the United States: "I could not command myself when I heard my own glorious land traduced in this unmerited manner. By whom? A Portuguese! A native of a country which has been twice liberated from horrid and detestable thraldom by the hands of Englishmen." He complains that the English "who have never been at war with Portugal, who have fought for its independence on land and sea, and always with success, who have forced themselves by a treaty of commerce to drink its coarse and filthy wines…are the most unpopular people who visit Portugal." But, unlike Byron, the pious if irascible Borrow attributed this not the Portuguese nature but to "corrupt and unregenerate man."

Borrow is a wonderfully comic traveler, especially in his belief that after just two weeks he could speak fluent Portuguese. His advice to novices speaking a foreign language is the sort of wrong-headed lesson that tourists of all times can never seem to forget. He advises, "Those who wish to make themselves understood by a foreigner in his own language should speak with much noise and vociferation, opening their mouths wide." Borrow's account of Portugal, less famous than the nasty stanzas from Byron, is a most original and evocative description. Borrow is a great reporter of human eccentricity and his account is extremely entertaining. He is also quite enthusiastic about the beauties of Portugal, comparing them favorably to other more visited countries. Lisbon, he claims, "is quite as much deserving the attention of the artist as even Rome itself." Sintra, praised lavishly even by the disagreeable Byron, is "a mingled scene of fairy beauty, artificial elegance, savage grandeur, domes, turrets, enormous trees, flowers, and waterfalls, such as is met with nowhere else under the sun." It is truly, Borrow writes, "Portuguese Paradise."

Byron's attacks on Portugal led predictably to a positive reaction. In 1845 Dorothy Quillinan, William Wordsworth's daughter, set out to contradict "Childe Harold's rash and unlordly sneer." Her *Journal of a Residence in Portugal*,

she had hoped, would "assist in removing prejudices which make Portugal an avoided land." Unfortunately her call was not heeded by many, and with the exception of the Danish Hans Christian Anderson's *A Visit to Portugal 1866*, which was never very popular in his time, none of the great 19th-century travel writers put down their thoughts about Portugal.

Mrs. Quillinan was hoping to inspire Americans to visit as well, but the closest any 19th-century American writers came was when Mark Twain visited the Azores Islands. Read today, *The Innocents Abroad* displays Twain's deep streak of jingoism and blustery intolerance. Every land he visited crumbled when compared to the United States. He also tends to look at the natives as if they were the foreigners. He comments upon the backwardness of the Portuguese islanders: "Oxen tread the wheat from the ear, after the fashion prevalent in the time of Methusalah." He continues with the real horror: "It is in communities like this that Jesuit humbuggery flourishes." The phony relics irk him. To Twain, backwardness is neither quaint nor romantic, but ignorant and un-American.

For 20th-century travelers, disenchanted with the progress which Twain htouted with such vehemence, Portugal has provided an escape from modernity. Close to a hundred years after Twain visited the Azores, the Irish writer Leonard Wibberly would also comment on the backwardness of the Portuguese agricultural methods, in his charming and funny account of a year in Portugal, *No Garlic in the Soup*. He found much wisdom in sticking to the old ways. For the 20th-century visitor, Portugal satisfies a nostalgia for the past. It is, after all, the last country in Western Europe to engage in full-scale modernization and industrialization. Wibberly devotes an entire chapter to "The Language of Oxen" in which he describes the mysterious way the farmers talk to their oxen when they're plowing the fields: "Here was one of the most ancient agricultural cries in the world . . . .It was a cry which Vasco da Gama, should he return to Portugal, would recognize immediately." The plow, he also notes, resembles those used by the Saxons in the dark ages. Wibberly cannot resist asking the farmer why he doesn't use a metal plow. His answer: "There must be work for the oxen to do."

What may seem charming and quaint to the traveler is often the source of hardship and poverty to the native. Portugal is fast modernizing. The traveler will have to look a little harder for the land where Moorish minarets inspired the blood lust of the Crusaders or where William Mickle wandered through orange groves that stretched to the horizon, or where Beckford "trifled away the whole morning, surrounded by fidalgos in flowered bee-gowns and musicians in violet-colored accoutrements. . ."

Left, invasion by the Crusaders

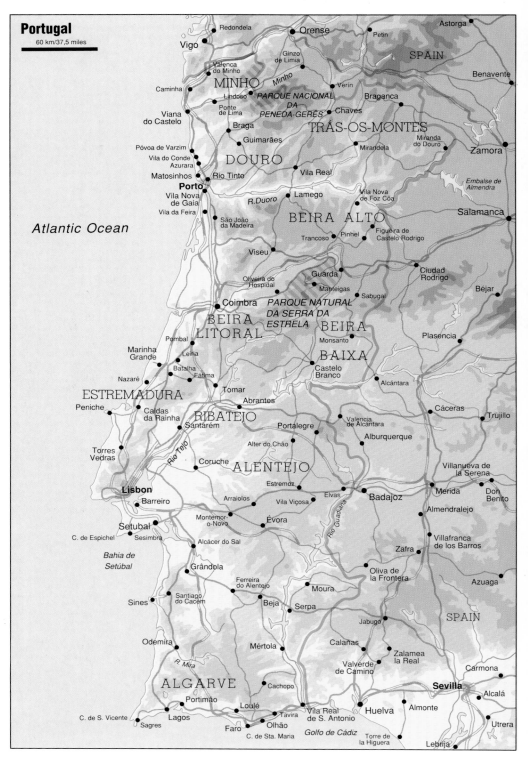

Portugal

60 km/37,5 miles

Atlantic Ocean

Astorga

Redondela
Orense
Petin

Vigo
Ginzo
de Limia

SPAIN

Benavente

Valença
do Minho
Minho
Verín

Caminha
MINHO
Lindoso
PARQUE NACIONAL
DA-
PENEDA-GERÊS

Braganca

Viana
do Castelo
Ponte
de Lima
Chaves

TRÁS-OS-MONTES

Braga
Guimarães

Póvoa de Varzim
DOURO
Mirandela
Miranda
do Douro

Zamora

Vila do Conde
Azurara
Mirandela

Matosinhos
Rio Tinto
Vila Real

Embalse de
Almendra

Porto
Vila Nova
de Gaia
R.Duero
Lamego
Vila Nova
de Foz Côa

Salamanca

Vila da Feira
São João
da Madeira
BEIRA ALTO

Figueira de
Castelo Rodrigo

Trancoso
Pinhel

Ciudad
Rodrigo

Viseu

Oliveira do
Hospital
Guarda
Manteigas

Béjar

Coimbra
PARQUE NATURAL
DA SERRA DA
ESTRELA
Sabugal

BEIRA
LITORAL
BEIRA

Pombal
Monsanto

BAIXA

Plasencia

Marinha
Grande
Leiria

Nazaré
Batalha
Fátima
Castelo
Branco

Alcántara

ESTREMADURA
Tomar
Abrantes

Cáceres

Peniche
Caldas
da Rainha
Santarém
RIBATEJO
Portalegre
Valencia
de Alcántara

Trujillo

Alter do Chão

Torres
Vedras
Coruche
ALENTEJO
Alburquerque

Estremoz

Villanueva de
la Serena

Lisbon
Barreiro
Arraiolos
Vila Viçosa
Elvas
Badajoz
Merida
Don
Benito

Montemor-
o-Novo
Évora
Almendralejo

Setúbal
Sesimbra
Alcácer do Sal
Villafranca
de los Barros

C. de Espichel
Zafra

Bahia de
Setúbal
Grândola
Oliva de
la Frontera

Azuaga

Ferreira
do Alentejo
Moura

Sines
Santiago
do Cacém
Beja
Serpa

SPAIN

Jabugo

Odemira
Calañas

Mértola
Valverde
de Camino
Zalamea
la Real

Carmona

ALGARVE
Cachopo

Sevilla

Alcalá

Portimão
Loulé
Huelva
Almonte

C. de S. Vicente
Lagos
Tavira
Vila Real
de S. Antonio

Sagres
Faro
Olhão
Utrera

C. de Sta. Maria
Golfo de Cádiz
Torre de
la Higuera
Lebrija

86

PLACES

There's no *wrong* way to explore Portugal—except to make too many plans in advance. A car is the handiest means because, although the trains are good and the buses adequate, they won't allow you the freedom to go just over the next hill…and the next, and the next. Portugal is wonderfully seductive, and if you give in to her, you'll never regret it.

There are surprisingly few roads in Portugal—a typical full-size road map shows virtually every tiny lane. In the mountains of the center and north, the roads are sometimes poorly maintained, and of course filled with curves as they wind up and down—another reason to take your time when traveling Portugal.

Lisbon (pg 95) and its environs are most certainly the best starting point for the traveler. Even just a few days there will give a good feel for this old European capital. From there, if the weather is fine, you may want to simply head south, a few hours on the very good highway, to the glorious beaches of the **Algarve** (pg 131), long an attraction for international beachlovers, and not far from some great golf courses as well. After relaxing here for a few days, you might begin meandering back up through the Portuguese countryside. Begin by exploring the expanse of the **Alentejo** (pg 147), spectacular plains with the charming ancient town of **Évora** in its midst.

Cutting back toward the Atlantic, still heading north, you can visit the old university town of **Coimbra** (pg 173) and some of the surrounding sights. You might also look in on some of the traditional fishing communities along the coast here. To the north is the Douro River and the **wine districts** (pg 200) of Douro and Minho. Here, world-famous port, the delightful *vinhos verdes* (pg 211), and other wines are produced—and shipped to the city of **Oporto** (pg 211) at the mouth of the Douro.

The far interior north of Portugal is called **Trás-os-Montes** (pg 221), a primitive, remote area that is hauntingly beautiful. And below Trás-os-Montes, still somewhat in the mountains, is the **Beira Alta**; below that, the plains of the Alentejo have crept up into the province of **Beira Baixa** (both, pg 235).

Now your tour is done. Are you lost? Don't worry, you've nearly come full circle. Lisbon is just a few hours to the west, and a little to the south.

Preceding pages, a traffic jam in the streets of Carvicais; the calvary parades in Belém on April 25th; the *cavaleiro* expertly plants the *farpa* mid-gallop

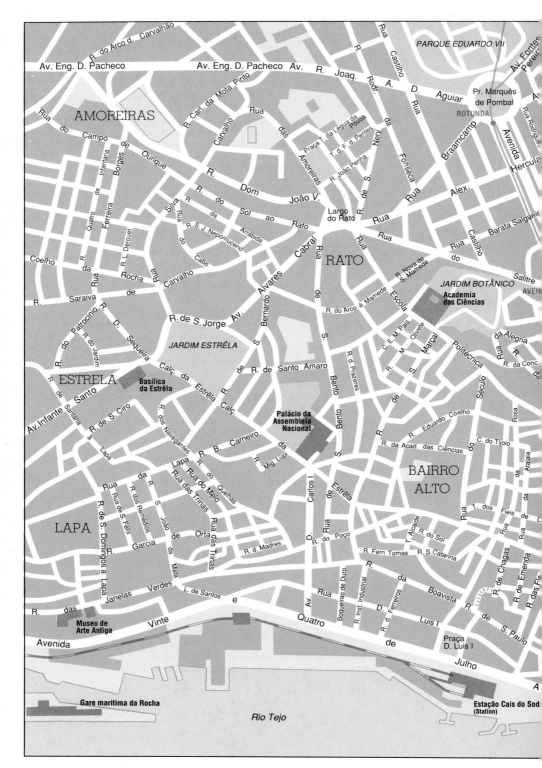

ROTUNDA

PARQUE EDUARDO VII

Av. Eng. D. Pacheco
Av. Eng. D. Pacheco
Av.

R. do Arco d. Carvalhão

Rua Castilho

R. Joaq. Rodr.
A. D. Aguiar

Pr. Marquês
de Pombal

Av. Fonte
Pereir

Av. Fonte Pereir

AMOREIRAS

Rua do Campo de Ourique

Rua Infantaria

R. Carl. da Mota Pinto

Rua Carvalho

Rua

das

Amoreiras

Praça T. da Légua da Póvoa

T. d. F. d. Pentes

R. João Penha

Rua da Nery

S. de

Rua da Fonseca

Braamcamp

Alex.

Rua Rodrigues

Avenida

Hercula

Borges

R. Dom

Dom

Silva

R. do Sol

ao

Rato

João V.

Largo
do Rato

Rua

Rua

RATO

Rua Castilho

Barata Salgueir

do

AVEN

Ferreira

Quatro

R. da Rocha

R. L. Derouet

R. S. J. Nepomuceno

Rua da Arrábida

do Cabo

Carvalho

Alvares

Cabral

de

R. Nova de S. Mamede

Escola

JARDIM BOTÂNICO
Academia
das Ciências

Salitre

Coelho

R.

R.

Saraiva

de

R. do Patrocinio

R. do Jardim

D. Sequeira

R. de S. Jorge

Av.

Bernardo

S.

R. do Arco à Mamede

C. E. M. Pais

Olivete

M.

Marçal

Politécnica

da Alegria

R. da Conc.

da

JARDIM ESTRÊLA

Sá

Rua de Santo Amaro

R. d. Prazeres

de

Século

R. da

ESTRELA

Santo

Basílica
da Estrêla

Calç. da Estrêla

Calç.

de

Bento

Eduardo Coelho

Rosa

Av. Infante Santana

R. de S. Ciro

R. dos Navegantes

S.

Palácio da
Assembleia
Nacional

S.

R. da Acad. das Ciências

C. do Tijolo

Atalaia

da

LAPA

Lapa

R. B. Carneiro

R. do Quelhas

R. Mig. Lúpi

da

Carlos I

de Estrêla

BAIRRO
ALTO

Rua

T. dos

Fieis

de

Rua

Rua

R. de S. Félix

Rua de S. Domingos a Lapa

Rua dos Remédios

João

de

Orta da

Mata

Rua do Meio

Rua das Trinas

Rua das Trinas

R. d. Madres

D. R. do Poço

R. Fern. Tomas

T. Alcade

R. do Sol

R. S. Catarina

R.

da

Boavista

C. de Chagas

R. de Emenda

R. das Fr

Garcia

Janelas

Verdes

L. de Santos

e

Av. Quatro

Boqueirão de Duro

R. Inst. Industrial

D. R. Ferreiros

Luis I

de

S. Paulo

R. das

das

Avenida

Vinte

de

Julho

Praça
D. Luis I

Museu de
Arte Antiga

Gare marítima da Rocha

Estação Cais do Sod
(Station)

Rio Tejo

A

88

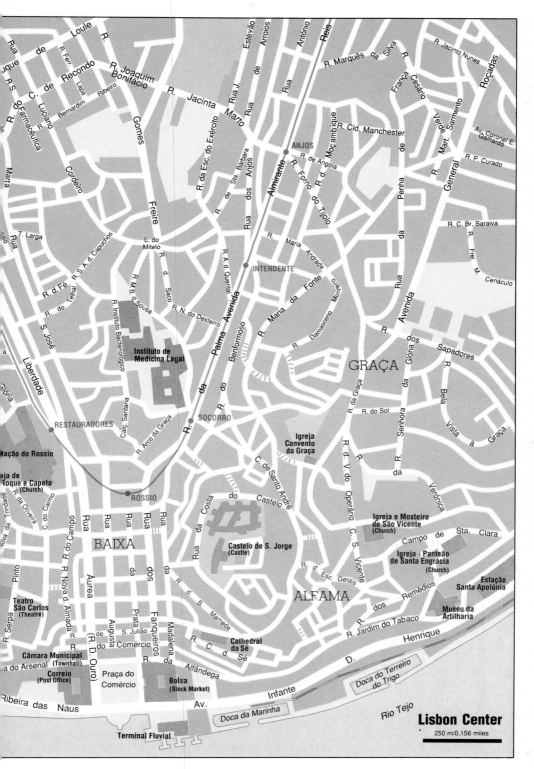

Lisbon Center

250 m/0,156 miles

89

LISB

93

LISBON

Lisbon, once the center of the world's last great colonial empire, nostalgically holds to the past as it tries to come to terms with Portugal's role as a new member of the European Economic Community (EEC).

A sense of history and tradition permeates downtown Lisbon, giving it a leisurely, old-world quality. The Portuguese still make pilgrimages to the monuments of Vasco da Gama and Prince Henry the Navigator. They still gather in the evenings in small wineshops in the Alfama quarter to sing of lost glories and lost loves. They browse for poetry in the dusty bookstores of Bairro Alto and pause for flowers and coffee on Rossio Square. They buy fresh fish at the Ribeira Market from *varinhas* imperiously wearing their wares like crowns. They bask in the shade of tropical gardens, stroll along the palm-lined mosaic sidewalks of Avenida da Liberdade and while away the time dreaming by the great olive-green Tagus River.

The Portuguese seem to have more time than most people to relax. Meals are a serious affair, and *siestas* are observed whenever possible. Shops tend to open at 9 a.m., take a long lunch break, and close at 6 p.m. Dining hours are reasonably early around 7:30 p.m. or 8 p.m., unlike the excesses of their Spanish neighbors. Weekends are sacred, perhaps a legacy of the British allies. The shops that do open Saturday generally close at 1 p.m. The only sure places to shop evenings and weekends are the shopping malls.

Lisboetans retain a certain formality that has long since disappeared from other European capitals. In business relations and even between friends and relatives, there is still much use of the third person. Titles of respect, such as *Senhor Doutor* or *Senhor Engenheiro*, *Excelentissimo Senhor* and *Vosa Excellencia* are used widely.

Appearances are very important. There's a popular expression, *"para Ingles ver,"* which loosely translated means "putting up a good front for the foreigners."

Contemporary heroes still tour the world, not as seafarers but as soccer players, cyclists and runners. The Portuguese characteristics of persistence and agility, which served the ancient explorers well, have made their descendants winners in modern international competitions.

Lisbon has felt the winds of change.

Many dilapidated palaces and mansions have been tastefully renovated and turned into elegant restaurants and bars, fashionable boutiques, art galleries and discotheques. Crumbling houses in the old quarters are beginning to be restored. In outlying neighborhoods, there are new hotels, a controversial shopping mall, office complex and a handsome modern museum. Beyond that is the inevitable monotony of satellite dormitories.

The first view of Portugal's capital should come from the great suspension bridge on the Tagus, one and-a-half miles long and clearly inspired by San Francisco's Golden Gate. It was originally called the Salazar Bridge after the late dictator António de Oliveira Salazar, under whose auspices it was completed in 1966. It has been rebaptized the **25th of April Bridge**, in honor of the bloodless 1974 revolution which restored democracy in all of Portugal.

Lisbon possess few architectural wonders, yet is a pleasing city to tour. The ensemble of buildings, with their faded elegance and harmonious arrangement on the hills and valleys along the northern shore of the Tagus, make it one of the loveliest capitals in the world. Located a few miles from the Atlantic Ocean, Lisbon is really a Mediterranean city: pastel and white buildings, orange tiled roofs, luminous sea and sky, mild winters and hot summers. But from time to time, the Atlantic prevails, bringing a dark opaque mist, chill rains and threatening waves.

With a population of about two million, Greater Lisbon has absorbed many Portuguese from rural areas, and many refugees from Portugal's former colonies, the last of which, with the exception of Macau and East Timor, gained independence in 1975 as a result of the Revolution. The influx of overseas Portuguese, Portuguese-Africans and Portuguese-Asians has made Lisbon a cosmopolitan and dynamic city.

History: According to Portuguese tradition, it was Ulysses who founded the city and gave it its original name, Olisipo. The Phoenicians, who occupied the area around 1200 B.C., are said to have called it Alis Ubbo, or "delightful shore." The Romans established the Lusitanian province by the end of the 1st century B.C. and named the site **Felicitas Julia**. Remains of their rule are seen in the **Castelo de São Jorge**, the castle that still overlooks the city, but the ramparts are essentially Visigoth, dating from the 5th century A.D.

The city became increasingly important under Moorish rule, from the 8th to the 12th centuries, when it was called **Al-Ushbuna**. The period of the Moslem-Christian wars of the 12th and 13th centuries was a time of great building. This is evident in many residential palaces.

It was only after 1255, when Afonso III drove the Moors out of the southernmost region of Portugal, that Lisbon became capital of the kingdom. Under the long reign of King Dinis (1279-1325), urban life flourished. But the Black Death, which is thought to have invaded Lisbon from the sea in 1348, decimated the capital.

In the 15th century, Lisbon became an important trading center and seat of a vast empire, rivaling Italy's Genoa and Venice. In 1497 Vasco da Gama opened the sea route to India, and Portuguese navigators began to establish trading posts around the world. By 1499, King Manuel I assumed the new title "Lord of the conquest, navigation and commerce of Ethiopia, Arabia, Persia and India."

Lisbon's golden age was the 16th century. She sent out countless ships to the colonies and many, although certainly not all, returned—ladened with riches to glorify the Portuguese court.

Although Portugal's fortunes declined with the costly colonial expansion, royal feuds and 60 years of Spanish rule, Lisbon's glory continued, reaching a new apogee from King João V's reign (1706-1750) through the first half of the 18th century, thanks to the gold and diamonds from the wealthy colony of Brazil.

Then came the terrible earthquake of 1755, followed by devastating fires. The total catastrophe took as many as 30,000 lives and left most of Lisbon in ruins. Voltaire's *Candide* bears witness to the devastation: *"The sea rises boiling in the port and shatters the vessels that are at anchor. Whirlwinds of flame and ashes cover the streets and public squares, the houses crumble, the roofs are tumbled down upon the foundations and the foundations disintegrate."* Lisboetans would not be happy with Candide's companion's consoling response: *"All this is for the very best. For if there is a volcano in Lisbon, it could not be anywhere else."*

An Enlightenment minister, the Marquês de Pombal, entirely rebuilt downtown Lisbon into, more or less, the form visitors see today: an imposing, cleanly designed 18th-century city. The grid design of the downtown quarter makes it easy to negotiate.

City center: Lisbon is a walking city of pleasant esplanades with kiosks, cafes,

Praça do Comércio seen from the southeast

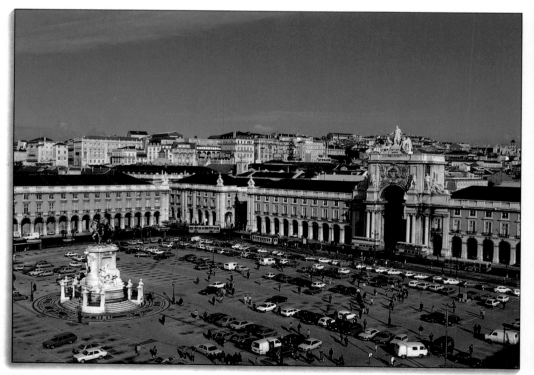

benches and belvederes. The black-and-white limestone mosaic sidewalks are decorative, if treacherous for high heels.

For handling the hills, there are plenty of reasonably priced, black-and-green taxis—except when it rains. A support network exists of bright yellow *eléctricos* or street cars, buses (some double-decker) and a modest subway.

The heart of the city is a vast square directly on the Tagus River called **Praça do Comércio**. This gracious space has been compared to Venice's Piazza di San Marco, but, unhappily, now is used as a parking lot. On the south, marble stairs lead down to a broad section of the river known as the *Mar de Palha* or Sea of Straw. Along the other three sides of the square are stately rose-colored 18th-century government buildings. Occasionally, English-speaking visitors refer to Praça do Comércio as "Black Horse Square" because of the large equestrian statue (now green because of its patina) in its center. The figure astride the horse is King José, the ruler at the time of the 1755 earthquake.

It was on the northwest corner of this square, opposite the main Post Office, that King Carlos and his oldest son and heir, Luís Felipe, were assassinated in 1908, leading to the abolishment of the monarchy two years later.

Praça do Comércio is also the center of Lisbon's port, a 15-mile (24-km) stretch of docks and warehouses. From a landing on the square, red ferryboats briskly ply back and forth. All kinds of sailing vessels are seen going up and down the river: long flat river barges loaded with coal or steel, container ships, the world's great cruise liners, as well as NATO gunships.

Unfortunately for the capital, there are no great promenades along the quay, no attractive riverside restaurants or cafes. It is clearly a working port. But from April to late October, there are daily afternoon boat excursions. These provide wonderful views of the city and the busy river life. Arrangements may be made at the main hotels or at the pier, on the southeast corner of Praça do Comércio.

Northwest of this square lies the **Praça do Municipio**, where the imposing 19th-century **City Hall** stands. In the center is a fine 18th-century pillory, which used to be symbol of authority. Atop the spiral is the Manueline sphere, a symbol from King Manuel I's reign seen frequently in Portuguese architecture (and on the country's flag). The banded globe recalls Portugal's

Moon rising over Castelo São Jorge.

conquests around the world.

A little further west, the **Cais do Sodré railroad station** is the starting point for the electric riverside train that goes to Estoril and other resorts. Here, too, is the **Ribeira**, the dock where fishing boats come in with their catch.

Across the road, the **Mercado de 24 Julho**, with its cathedral-like dome, has an overwhelming, lush display of fresh fish, fruits and vegetables. Lunch in the market's restaurant is a delightful experience, with tasty local swordfish, fresh grilled sardines or steamed bass, depending on the season and the catch.

Returning to Praça do Comércio, one goes through the triumphal arch on the north side of the square. This leads to **Rua Augusta**, which, like a number of side streets, has been closed to traffic and turned over to cafes, street vendors and shoppers.

This area is called the **Baixa,** or lower town, and forms part of Pombal's well-planned grid of streets. Pombaline architecture is relatively simple and graceful; the handsome color-washed buildings have carved corners and broad stone-framed windows. Now mainly an area of banks, offices and shops, the Baixa used to be divided into crafts. **Rua d'Ouro** and **Rua da Prata**, the streets of gold and silver respectively, still exist, and still claim quite a few jewelry shops, but they are now joined by a variety of other stores, including an inexplicable proliferation of shoe shops. On the eastern side of the Baixa, **Rua dos Fanqueiros**, which means "street of haberdashers," is now a street of textiles, yard goods and inexpensive clothing.

The Baixa leads into a square that everybody calls Rossio but is formally named the **Praça de Dom Pedro IV**. Once bullfights and executions were held in the Rossio; today it's a peaceful scene where old men feed pigeons, flower sellers preside over an elaborate display of seasonal blooms, and people of all ages congregate at the sidewalk cafes. The two fountains in the center were brought from Paris in 1890.

At the north end of the Rossio, the **National Theater of Dona Maria II**, built in the middle of the 19th century and restored in 1964, is a handsome rose building with arched windows and classic columns. The company generally gives quality performances of Portuguese and foreign plays in Portuguese. Standing to the west of the National Theater is a wonderful mock-rococo structure, the **Rossio railway station**. Trains leave from here for Sintra and

Roses, carnations, daisies and more for sale in the Rossio.

nearby towns.

Rossio is linked to another square called **Praça dos Restauradores**, with an obelisk in its center honoring the leaders of the 1640 movement against Spanish domination. Under the square there's a convenient underground parking lot.

On the eastern side of the Restauradores square is the post office. The street running behind this large pale pink building is **Rua das Portas de Santo Antão**, where shoeshine men practice their art with a flourish while their clients sit splendidly on thronelike chairs. This is an area of popular, cheap chicken-on-the-spit restaurants and some expensive seafood places.

Back across Restauradores, the Ministry of Tourism is located in the lovely rose-colored **Palácio Foz**. An office on the ground floor is open to visitors daily with maps, brochures and counsel.

To the north lies Lisbon's Champs Elysées, the **Avenida da Liberdade**, a broad boulevard lined with palm trees, pools and benches. This splendid thoroughfare was laid out in 1879. It terminates at the **Praça de Marquês de Pombal**, with a tall statue of the man who built new Lisbon.

About halfway up the avenue on the left, a secluded square called **Parque Mayer** has several pleasant, very Portuguese restaurants not aimed at tourists. Here, too, are several popular theaters that specialize in Portuguese musical comedy: known as *revista*, it is really a kind of political burlesque show with girlies, songs, comics and sharp satirical comments on current events, all unfortunately, only in Portuguese. During the dictatorship and press censorship, the *revista* was the only place where the regime was openly criticized.

The eastern hills: The best way to approach Alfama, the oldest quarter of Lisbon, is to take a taxi to its highest point, the **Castelo de São Jorge** and then wend one's way down on foot. On close view, the Moorish castle and medieval ramparts have been perhaps too perfectly restored; but it is a pleasant site, with a shady cobblestone terrace and peacocks and other colorful birds walking about. The view of Lisbon, the bay and the surrounding countryside is spectacular. Within the ramparts lies a small village with a shady square and a church.

Descending a little, one reaches the **Largo das Portas do Sol**, with another terrace providing a splendid vista over Alfama's orange-tiled rooftops, maze of television antennae and the river.

In a lovely 17th-century palace on the

The **Marquês de Pombal** surveys the **Avenida da Liberdade**

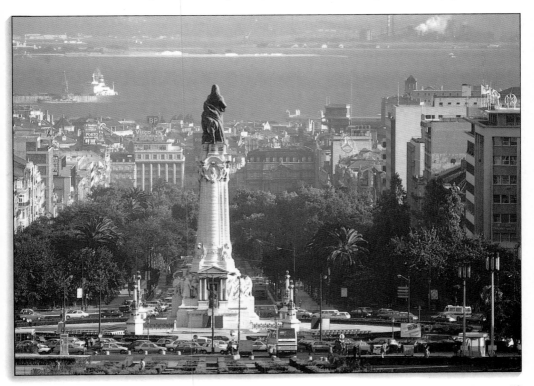

Largo is the **Espirito Santo Foundation** and **Museum of Decorative Arts**. Philanthropist and banker, Ricardo Espirito Santo established the foundation in 1953 to preserve the skills of Portugal's master craftsmen. Each Wednesday the workshops are open to the public, and visitors may see artisans working in leather, ceramics, wood, iron, bookbinding, carpet restoration and other crafts. The small church of **Santa Luzia** has some interesting old tiles, including a large panel outside depicting Martim Moniz, a soldier, helping to take Lisbon from the Moors. The *miradouro*, or lookout, is especially charming, with benches and trellised flowers. Portuguese often come here to meet friends or read.

Continuing downwards, the **Rua do Limoeiro** leads past the palace prisons of **Aljube** and **Limoeiro**, where many of Salazar's political opponents sojourned. They are now for common criminals. One should stop at the **Sé** or Cathedral, with its handsome Romanesque doorway, two square towers and rose window. The cloisters date back to the 13th century. They contain a variety of remnants, including some particularly interesting column fragments. The Sé was badly damaged by earthquakes in the 14th century and has been largely restored.

There are two other churches on the way down: **Santo António da Sé**, built in 1812 on the birthplace of Lisbon's unofficial patron saint, St. Anthony of Padua; and the **Church of Madalena**, built in 1783, with a fine Manueline doorway.

Another way to visit Alfama is to begin at the bottom, starting from the main square near the Tagus, **Largo do Chafariz de Dentro**. There's no particular way to go, just up: along the narrow winding alleys and stairs, past peeling facades and lines of well-scrubbed laundry, pausing in the shady cobblestone squares. **Rua de São Pedro** is a quintessential Alfama street, and it can lead one to the **Beco do Mexias**, a tiny alley with an inner court where women come to do their washing.

This aimless journey through Alfama can be a rewarding experience anytime for someone with a camera. But in summer, particularly June, every night seems to be a festival in Alfama. The street and squares are decorated with colored lights and streamers, and the air sparkles with fireworks. It seems that the whole city converges on Alfama to eat grilled sardines and sausages, drink wine and declaim poetry just for fun. The most important festival is

A much-needed shoeshine after a rough day on the cobbled walks

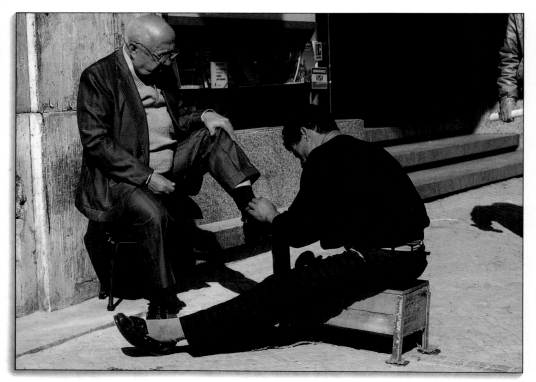

the nights of St. Anthony, June 12-13. Neighborhood groups parade down Avenida da Liberdade with colorful costumes and floats and end up singing and dancing in the squares of Alfama.

To the North of Alfama rises a hill called **Graça**, well worth the taxi ride up. The *miradouro* gives yet another magnificent view of the city. The Baroque church **Nossa Senora da Graça** has very fine tiles.

There are three other remarkable churches on the eastern heights, outside of what was, in the Middle Ages, the town walls of Lisbon. The churches are visible from the Alfama lookouts, but it is wise to take a taxi—the labyrinth of the ancient streets can tangle one's sense of direction. The 16th-century church of **São Vincente de Fora**, whose huge dome was restored after the 1755 earthquake, now serves as the Pantheon of the royal house of Bragança. Most of the members of Portugal's last royal family are buried there, including Dom Manuel II, who found exile in England in 1910 when the Portuguese monarchy was overthrown. King Carol of Rumania, who spent his last years in exile in Portugal, is also temporarily buried here, as is his morganatic wife, Madame Lupescu.

The National Pantheon is located in **Santa Engrácia**, nearby, and contains representative tombs of national heroes: Prince Henry the Navigator, Afonso de Albuquerque, Nuño Álvares Pereira, and Pedro Álvares Cabral, among others. The church was begun in the 16th century. According to popular legend, a merchant was wrongly accused of stealing the host from Santa Engrácia and put to death around 1630. It was said that he cast a spell whereby the construction of the church would never be completed. Whether due to a spell or not, the structure remained unfinished. Thus the Portuguese expression: *"obras de Santa Engrácia,"* meaning a task never done.

Salazar, however, took up the challenge and had the church restored in 1966. Some people wish he had not bothered, as it is not considered as one of Lisbon's loveliest monuments.

On the outskirts of town beyond the **Santa Apolónia railroad station**, the old monastery of **Madre de Deus** has been converted into the **Museu dos Azulejos**, the Tile Museum. Founded in 1509 by Queen Leonor, the monastery now boasts one of the best collections of Portuguese tiles of the 16th to 18th centuries. Among the most outstanding tile scenes are a panorama of Lisbon from 1730 and the life of St. An-

The ruined cloisters at the Cathedral

thony, about 1780. The church, connected to the museum, is decorated with rich gilded woodwork, huge panels of fine paintings, and, of course, tiles.

The western hills: The quickest way to get to **Bairro Alto**, or the high neighborhood, from the city center, is by using the **Santa Justa Lift**. This mini-Eiffel Tower on Rua Santa Justa, just off Rua d'Ouro, was built by the noted French engineer. For a small fee, one can ride to the top of the hill to the ruins of the 14th-century **Carmo Monastery**. The roof and other sections of this building were destroyed by the 1755 earthquake; what remains provides a dramatic setting for summertime concerts. The monastery serves as an archaeological museum as well, with marble bas reliefs, tombs from the 13th century and prehistoric pottery.

Then there's the slow approach, strolling up the **Chiado**, Lisbon's most fashionable shopping area. From Rossio, one takes **Rua do Carmo**, recently turned into a pedestrian mall, which leads into **Rua Garrett**. Here are the best boutiques, shoe shops, silver and porcelain shops and bookstores. Here too is the **Brasileira**, a venerated institution, the favorite cafe of Lisbon's artists and politicians.

On the south side of the Chiado is another great view of the city, the river and São Jorge, from the **Largo da Biblioteca Nacional**.

Nearby, the opulent **Teatro São Carlos**, built in 1792 and inspired by La Scala of Milan, has a rich season of international and Portuguese opera, ballet and concerts. Around the corner, the less ornate municipal theater of **São Luiz** also presents good concerts and the National Ballet Company.

At the top of the **Rua do Alecrim** is a small square with a romantic statue of Portugal's cosmopolitan 19th-century novelist Eça de Queirós embracing his scarcely clad muse.

Rua Garrett leads into the **Largo de Chiado**, with two churches of interest: 17th-century **Nossa Senhora de Loreto**, with some nice marble and wood sculptures, and **Nossa Senhora de Encarnação**, rebuilt in the 18th century with a lovely painted ceiling and an entire wall of blue tiles.

Adjoining the Chiado is the large **Praça de Camões** with shady elms and a monument to the great epic poet Luís de Camões, who died in obscure poverty in Lisbon in 1580. John Dos Passos compares Camões' monumental poem, *Os Lusíadas*, which glorifies the Discoveries, to the *Odyssey*: "An epic of the sea, full of the smell of pitch and creaking timbers and the spray screaming off the caps of the ocean waves ."

Nearby is another 16th-century church, **São Roque**. The facade, however, was largely destroyed in 1755 and has been restored without great ability. The interior is notable for its fine tiles, painted wood ceilings and beautiful marbles. One of its side chapels is the fabulous **Chapel of St. John the Baptist**, with columns made of lapis lazuli. Adjacent to this is the **Museum Of Sacred Art** with a very small collection of fine 17th- and 18th-century silver, paintings and embroidered altar pieces.

Moving up **Rua São Pedro de Alcântara**, noted mainly for its antique shops, one arrives at another shady terrace with an admirable view of the city and the São Jorge castle crowning the opposite hill. Just across the street is the **Port Wine Institute** located in an 18th-century palace. Its cozy bar offers an unbelievable selection of port wines.

Here on the left is Bairro Alto proper, a picturesque maze of cobblestone alleys and old tenements. This quarter was built on solid rock and generally withstood the great earthquake. Some of the buildings have peeling facades or worn blue tiles but are

Mass at the São Roque

decorated with fine wrought-iron balconies, flowerpots and birdcages.

In the old days, Bairro Alto was known for its good *fado* houses. There are basically two kinds of *fado* : the tragic epic song born in the former African colonies of hardship, full of *saudade* or bittersweet nostalgia; and the joyous *fado corrida* , sung usually after bullfights.

Fado is still a rite and visitors should obey the rules requiring dim lights and absolute silence during the performance. Most Portuguese go to *fado* houses after dinner (the food in *fado* houses is generally not outstanding), drink wine and lose themselves in nostalgic reflections for the rest of the evening. Today, many of the *fado* houses have become blatantly commercial, offering foreign guests songs like "*The Yellow Rose of Texas.*"

Some mansions in the Bairro Alto have been restored and turned into fashionable restaurants, discotheques and art galleries. Avant-garde Portuguese art can be seen and purchased—for a price, of course—in two recently converted elegant galleries, **Os Cómicos** and **Emi-Valentim Carvalho**. Another fine gallery is located in **São Mamede**, on **Rua da Escola Politécnica**.

The Portuguese are excellent gardeners so naturally Lisbon is laced with parks and gardens and other green spaces. Perhaps the finest of them all is the **Jardim Botánico**, one of the richest botanical gardens in Europe. Created in 1873, just off the Rua da Escola Politécnica, the garden has a magnificent wall of 100-year-old palm trees, banana trees, bamboo and water lilies and many exotic tropical plants.

Northwest of Bairro Alto is another hill with the charming **Estrêla Gardens** and splendid 18th-century **Basilica of Estrêla** with its great dome and pink, yellow and blue marble interior. Here can be found the remarkable room-sized crib carved by Machado de Castro. This neighborhood is a kind of Anglo-Saxon oasis. Close by is the British hospital, the little English **Church of St. George**, and the adjacent English cemetery where Henry Fielding, the author of *Tom Jones* is buried. Descending the hill on **Rua São Domingos á Lapa**, and turning to the right, one finds the **American Ambassador's Residence**, splendid old-rose palace and garden with a marvelous view of the river. Further down the hill is another rose palace housing the **British Embassy** and just beyond, the **British Ambassador's Residence** in a 17th-century convent.

Left, wedding music at São Roque. Right, the Estrêla Basilica

There are a number of ways to get to the **Palácio de São Bento**, where the national assembly is located. One may take the **Calçada Do Estrêla** downhill, or climb the **Avenida Dom Carlos I**, which begins on the riverfront road just west of the central market. Although special permission must be obtained to enter São Bento, visitors should take a look at it simply because so much of modern Portuguese history took place here. Originally built as a monastery, the palace was transformed into the parliament at the end of the 19th century. It was renovated in 1935 and decorated with rich sculptures and paintings.

This was the universe of former dictator António de Oliveira Salazar. He lived and worked in a small house behind the palace, hidden by a high wall. It was here in 1975 that Portugal's new leaders drafted their revolutionary constitution, which has since been amended. At São Bento political parties from the extreme left to the far right have painstakingly fashioned a dynamic European democracy.

Going back to the river road and continuing westward, one reaches the **National Museum of Ancient Art**, commonly called *Janelas Verdes* or the Green Windows. The museum is located in a fine 17th-century palace with a tasteful modern extension. On display are many fine pieces of 16th-century porcelain brought back by Portuguese sailors from India, Japan and Macão. Upstairs is the masterpiece attributed to the 15th-century Portuguese painter Nuno Gonçalves, a polyptych depicting St. Vincent, Lisbon's patron saint, and a select group of admirers including a figure presumed to be Prince Henry the Navigator, who wears a large black hat.

There are also fine wood and terra cotta figures by the great 18th-century sculptor, Machado de Castro. Foreign works include Pierro Della Francesca's *St. Augustine*, Hans Memling's *Virgin And Child*, Raphael's *St. Eusebius* , Bosch's dizzying *The Temptation of St. Anthony* and Durer's *St. Jerome*.

Leaving the museum one can move a short distance westward, and climb the Avenida do Infante Santo. There, on the left is a pre-earthquake royal palace, called the **Palácio das Necessidades**, originally a monastery. This fine building in Lisbon's ubiquitous rose-colored stone has a magnificent view and lovely gardens. It is now the Portuguese Ministry of Foreign Affairs. Although not open to the public it can be seen from the front courtyard.

Two views of Eduardo VII park

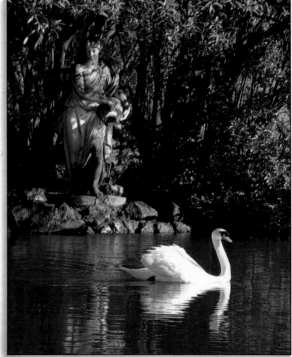

The
futuristic
Amoreiras
shopping
and office
complex

The northern hills: New Lisbon rises on the hills to the north of the city like a many-tiered fan. The Praça de Marquês de Pombal can be used as a point of reference for various tours.

Directly north of this circle rises the **Parque de Eduardo VII**, commemorating a visit by the British king to Lisbon in 1902. At the top of this grassy sloping lawn with box hedges in geometrical design is one of the finest views directly down to the city and the harbor. On the northwestern corner of the park lies the **Estufa Fria**, or Cold Greenhouse, a kind of tropical jungle, protected by bamboo slats and a joy to stroll in.

Overlooking the park on the west are residential apartments and several of the city's best hotels. Across the park stands the large **Pavilhão dos Esportes** with its elaborate yellow- and-blue tile scenes, where sports events, concerts and political rallies are held.

Driving in a northwesterly direction from the Marquês de Pombal Circle on Rua Joaquim António de Aguiar, (the road will run into the main highway towards Sintra.) One suddenly comes upon a group of startling pink- and-blue towers called **Amoreiras**. The vast complex of hotels, offices, apartments and shopping center looks like some futuristic fairyland. Architect Tomás Taveira's other shocking canary, black or multicolored edifices are increasingly disrupting the rows of drab conformist structures that characterize much of Lisbon's modern architecture.

On the hill at the northern end of Eduardo VII park stand the picturesque old penitentiary and the sleek new court building. Beyond lies the neighborhood of **Benfica**, known mainly for its stadium and as the home of Portugal's favorite soccer team. Even if one isn't a soccer enthusiast, it's worth trying to get into the **Benfica Luz stadium**, to see the fighting spirit of the fans when Benfica plays a foreign team, particularly the English or Spanish.

Here, too, is found the **Jardim Zoológico** which is not an ordinary zoo but rather a garden with animals. Founded in 1905 in the **Quinta das Laranjeiras**, the zoo is known for its magnificent rosebeds and flowers from around the world.

One area recently developed is the **Praça de Espanha**, slightly to the northeast of Pombal and the park. Here is the splendid new **American Embassy** in a renovated old palace.

Nearby is a conventionally handsome modern complex, the **Calouste Gulben-**

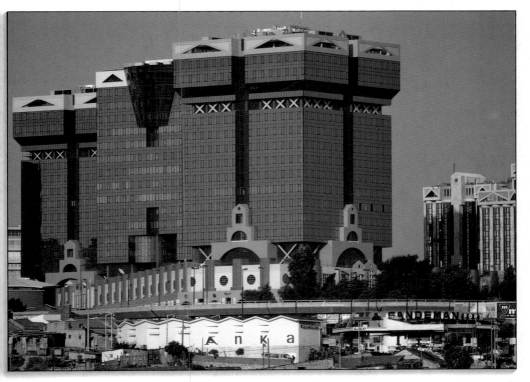

kian Foundation and Museum and the **Center of Modern Art**. Gulbenkian, an Armenian oil magnate from Turkey who personally owned five percent of Iraq Petroleum Company, spent the last 13 years of his life in Lisbon. He died in 1955. Besides supporting artists around the world, the Gulbenkian Foundation sponsors a comprehensive year-round program of lectures, ballet and concerts at its headquarters in Lisbon.

The Gulbenkian Museum contains what is said to be one of the richest formerly private collections in the world. Outstanding is the section of Middle Eastern and Islamic Art, which includes an alabaster bowl from Egypt's Old Kingdom (about 2,700 B.C.) and an Assyrian bas-relief representing the *Genius of Spring* in alabaster dating back to the 9th century B.C. There are Syrian mosque lamps and glass items from the 14th century, and many richly illuminated Armenian manuscripts from the 12th - 14th centuries.

The Greco-Roman section includes an outstanding collection of Greek gold and silver coins from the 6th century B.C. to the 1st century A.D. Among the Oriental pieces are fine Chinese porcelains of the 17th century, jades of the 18th century and Japanese prints and lacquers of the 18th and 19th centuries.

In the European collection, there are paintings by masters such as Carpaccio, Van Dyck, Ruysdael, Colbert, Rubens and Rembrandt. There are splendid 16th-century Italian tapestries and furniture by the finest French *ébénistes* of the 18th century. Also, there's an unusual display of the flamboyant jewelry and glass by the dean of Art Nouveau, René Lalique.

A well-tended park with ponds, paths with modern sculpture and an outdoor auditorium connect the Gulbenkian Museum with the newly built **Center of Modern Art**. Here are the works of many of Portugal's finest contemporary artists. There are several paintings by Maria Helena Vieira da Silva, who made her reputation in Paris. But other talented artists deserve to be better known abroad as well, such as the powerful first generation of modernists— José de Almada Negreiros, Eduardo Viana and Jorge Barradas—and the talented painters that followed, including Julio Pomar, Maria Ines Menez, Julion Rezend. There is Carlos Botelho who prints the soul of Lisbon; and sculptor João Cutileiro, creator of the slender frolicking women with big breasts and bushy hair that are increasingly

Lisbon's bullfights are in the Campo Pequeno

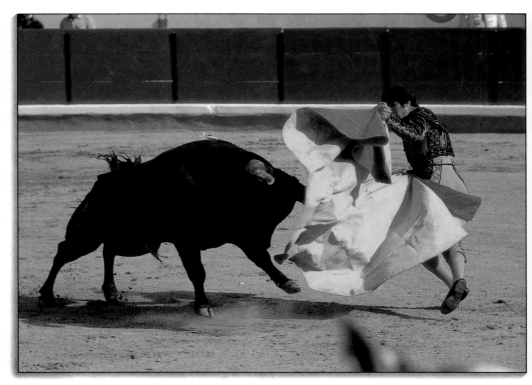

visible in the city's parks and gardens.

The easiest way to get to northeastern Lisbon and the "new avenues" is by taking Avenida Fontes Pereira de Melo again, from Pombal circle. On the left, the tall yellow tile Sheraton Hotel looks like the office building that it was originally meant to be.

Across the way, the large modern convention hall called **Picoas**, with a cafeteria, bookstore and bank, also has exhibition facilities.

Along Avenida da República, one cannot miss the large red bull ring, called **Campo Pequeno**, built in 1892. More sensitive visitors may enjoy Portuguese bullfights, called *touradas*, because unlike the Spanish, the Portuguese don't kill their bulls—at least not in public.

Across the street, the **Feira Popular** is essentially an amusement park, but it's a good place to get snails in butter and grilled sardines when they are in season (from June to October).

The avenue runs through **Campo Grande**, a shady promenade with a small lake. On the left stands **Cidade Universitária**, a group of pleasant if not spectacular modern buildings. The university campus is generally quiet and orderly these days although there was a time, just after the 1974 revolution, when the students to a large degree took the law into their own hands.

Attached to the campus is the **Biblioteca Nacional**. The National Library was founded in 1796, but moved to this huge new building in 1969. Its collection are extensive; visitors can get glimpses by viewing the two small exhibitions that change monthly.

At the end of Campo Grande, one may turn right to the airport, or visit two museums. In an 18th-century palace, the **Museu da Cidade**, or Municipal Museum, has an interesting collection of archaeological pieces and old engravings relating to Lisbon's past. About a mile down the road to Lumiar, the **Museu do Trajo**, or Costume Museum, located in an old manor with delightful gardens, is said to have one of the best collections of Portuguese costumes.

Belém: In a green, spacious zone by the river, on the western side of Lisbon, a number of monumental buildings stand as a reminder of Portugal's maritime and colonial past. This area is called **Belém**, which translated means Bethlehem in Portuguese. The name reflects the involvement of the Portuguese rulers and the religious orders with the crusades.

New State architecture: left, the Monument to the Discoveries; right, Christ in Majesty

Without doubt, Lisbon's most glorious monument is the **Monastery of Jerónimos**, built in memory of Vasco da Gama and his successful journey to India in 1499. King Manuel personally laid the cornerstone of the Hieronymite monastery in 1502 at Belém, on the site of a chapel founded by Prince Henry the Navigator. It was here in the cloisters of Jerónimos that the ceremony was held on January 1, 1986, that marked Portugal's entry into the European Economic Community.

This vast limestone building is a masterpiece of Manueline or Portuguese baroque architecture with its opulent decoration. Notable are: the two tiered cloisters completed in 1517, the southern door, with multiple carved statues and the Templar cross, and two windows with carved rope, anchors and other seafaring symbols. The grand interior has six great octagonal stone columns with ornate decoration which have withstood time and the earthquake of 1755. Also of special interest are the finely chiseled modern altars, brilliant stained glass windows, and monumental carved tombs. Here are the tombs of two national heroes, Vasco da Gama and Camões. Today the church is a favorite place for weddings and is open to all.

Some critics complain that Jerónimos has been too thoroughly cleaned because its golden patina is gone. Critics also lament the recent construction of a wing in rather poor Manueline imitation, obscuring a fine door. Built on the western side of the church in the latter part of the 19th century, this wing houses the **National Museum of Archaeology and Ethnology** with an interesting collection of folk art, dating to the Stone and Bronze Ages. On the other end of this wing, the **Museu da Marinha**, the Navy Museum, tells the story of Portugal's seafaring discoveries with paintings, models, sculpture and maps from the empire that stretched from China to Brazil.

Across the park and to the west on the river stands the **Torre de Belém**, on the site from where Vasco da Gama and other navigators set forth on their explorations. This exquisite little 16th-century fortress is another fine example of the unique Manueline style with its richly carved niches, towers and shields bearing the Templar cross.

Back a short way towards city center stands the modern **Monument to the Discoveries**, built in 1960 to honor Prince Henry the Navigator. It is a stylized caravel with figures representing the Portuguese who took part in the great adventure, standing on the prow, looking out to sea.

Across the way rises the ornate rose-colored **Palácio de Belém**, which once served as a royal retreat and is now the Presidential palace. Decorated with lavish Oriental and European furnishings, this palace is where the President of the Republic has his offices and gives official receptions. The palace and gardens, with an interesting blend of ancient and modern sculpture, are open to the public periodically.

Adjacent to Belém Palace in what was once the royal riding-school is the **National Coach Museum**, housing one of the finest collections of its kind in Europe. The museum contains a 16th-century coach that once belonged to King Philip II of Spain and a number of well preserved gilt carriages of the 17th and 18th centuries, royal litters and sedan chairs and an ecclesiastical throne.

Behind the palace is the wonderful but rather neglected **Colonial Garden**, with all kinds of exotic plants and shady walks.

On the eastern side of Belém Palace, up the Calçada da Ajuda hill is the immense **Palácio da Ajuda**, built after the earthquake as a royal palace but never completed. The palace is sometimes used for concerts, and some of the rooms with lovely unusual ceilings, fine tapestries and lavish furnishings are open to the public.

Left, south portal of Jerónimos Monastery; right, the now-serene Torre de Belém

CASCAIS AND ESTORIL

It is officially known as the Costa do Sol, but the locals simply call it the *Marginal*. It is a wonderful 18-mile drive along the northern bank of the Tagus River to the Atlantic.

A delightful way to make the trip is by the electric train that leaves from Lisbon's Cais do Sodré station and wends its way along the coast as far as Cascais. It's about a half-hour ride, with stops. Particularly in the spring the bank along the train track is filled with colorful wildflowers. A leisurely yellow tramway also runs from the **Praça do Comércio** as far out as the resort of Cruz Quebrada.

And there's the inland *autostrada* or superhighway, almost as lovely. It starts at Marquês de Pombal Circle, runs past the Amoreiras shopping complex, through the valley of Alcântara, parallel to the grandiose **Aqueduto das Águas Livres**. The 11-mile aqueduct was built in the 18th century as the main source of water for the capital, and it still supplies water for public parks and fountains. The highway goes through one of Salazar's finest legacies, the park of **Monsanto**, a vast area of eucalyptus trees and umbrella pines, pleasant winding roads and belvederes with magnificent views over Lisbon and the river. Beyond the park, the highway continues through gentle hilly countryside as far as Caxias, where it turns south to join the Marginal.

The river road starts out at the Praça do Comércio as the Avenida de 24 de Julho, changes its name to the Avenida da India and becomes the Marginal at the 25th of April Bridge.

As the road passes by the working quarter of **Alcântara**, some dramatic political art is visible. These murals are mostly the work of the Portuguese Communist Party and Marxist-Leninist groups, usually calling for peace and the ouster of whatever government happens to be in power. In the early days of Portugal's 1974 Revolution, there was more of this kind of political graffiti all over town. Some of Portugal's NATO allies and many tourists were quite alarmed at how aggressive the wall slogans appeared. But now the country has taken a more conservative line; many of the angry epithets have been cleaned up and what remains worries only visitors.

Further on, there is the **International**

Preceding pages, scenes from Cabo Espichel. Below, the beach at Estoril

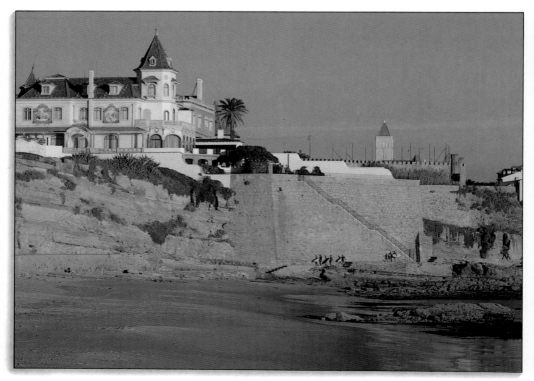

Fair Building, which frequently presents trade fairs and exhibitions. Then comes Belém with its historical monuments and parks.

Just beyond lies the elegant hillside neighborhood of **Restelo**, where many embassies and diplomatic residences are located. **Algés** is the first town outside the city limits, and it is here that taxi drivers turn off their meters and start counting the fare by kilometers.

A string of picturesque riverside towns follow. **Dáfundo** has several fine old mansions standing in sad contrast alongside dilapidated rent-controlled housing. It also boasts the **Vasco da Gama Aquarium**, with its fascinating world of sea turtles, eels, barnacles and all kinds of fish. **Cruz Quebrada** is the site of a lovely stone-seated stadium built for international soccer matches. **Caxias** is known for its flowering villas, 18th-century gazebos and an infamous hillside prison-fort. **Oeiras** has a fine 18th-century baroque **church**, lovely park, modern apartment blocks and an austere 16th-century fort. Just beyond lies the 17th-century fortress of **São Julião da Barra**, marking the point where the Tagus River meets the Atlantic. **Carcavelos** has several moderate hotels and a broad sandy beach.

Finally, **Estoril** is the first point of what has often been called the Golden Triangle and includes Cascais and Sintra. A flowering, palm-lined, pastel resort, Estoril first gained fame at the turn of the century for its therapeutic spring waters. During World War II, Estoril became known as hunting grounds for international spies. Later, this corner of the Atlantic, with its mild weather, gentle people and gracious lifestyle, became home-away-from-home for European royalty and other refugees fleeing the political upheavals after World War II. Among the Triangle's illustrious residents were former King Simeon of Bulgaria, former King Umberto of Italy, and Antenor Patiño of Bolivia. Others, like the Count of Paris, kept summer homes in the area.

With the changing times and passing royalty, local aristocrats are beginning to sell or rent their villas. More and more Portuguese, and foreign business and professional people come to the Triangle either to live, retire or keep summer homes. Estoril has now become a cosmopolitan playground with its celebrated casino, first-rate hotels, restaurants and international tennis and golf tournaments.

The **Casino** is a low white modern building with immaculately kept gardens. A

The gardens at Estoril Casino

passport or identity card is necessary to enter the casino as the minimum age limit is 18. There is everything in the way of games from slot-machines to blackjack, roulette and baccarat. Some people go to the Casino to see the show, usually a colorful international extravaganza. There is also an elegant dining room, an art gallery, a cinema and a bar.

Estoril has an active night life, with a variety of nightclubs, discotheques and very English bars. There are also several rather good *fado* houses in the area.

The **Estoril Music Festival** takes place from mid-July to mid-August. Concerts and recitals are held in the **Estoril Cathedral** and the **Cascais Citadel**, and also in the Jerónimos cloisters at Belém and the Lisbon Cathedral.

In recent times, the **Handicrafts Fair** has become a major production, lasting throughout the months of July and August. Located near the railroad station, the fair features arts, crafts, food, wine and folk music from all over the country. But a word of warning: Korean objects are showing up and are sometimes taken for local craft.

At this writing, the famed **Estoril Beach** and in fact all the beaches along the Costa do Sol are badly polluted, and crowded in summertime. Foreigners tend to swim in hotel pools on the coast and the Portuguese who can, go elsewhere: to **Guincho** nearby on the Atlantic; further north to **Praia Grande**; or to **Caparica** on the peninsula south of Lisbon. There's an ambitious program in the works to clean up all the beaches along the coast, but it will take a long time.

There is a lot to do in the way of sports in the Triangle. The **Estoril Golf Club**'s course, on the outskirts of town, is one of the loveliest in Europe. It was laid out by McKenzie Ross on a hillside dotted with pine and eucalyptus groves. The smaller **Estoril-Sol Golf Course** is located in a pine wood at **Linhó** near Sintra. Overlooking the Atlantic coast just beyond Cascais is the **Marinha Golf Club**, with swimming pools, tennis and riding facilities and a course designed by Robert Trent Jones. The **Estoril Autodromio** or automobile race track, located inland on the road to Sintra, draws large crowds for the Grand Prix Formula One races. It is also the site for the start and finish of the annual international Port Wine Rally.

Cascais has its own bull ring—the largest one in the country—but not many fights are scheduled. The main problem is that it is very windy: according to the locals, it would have made a better place for a windmill.

There's horseback riding at the **Escola da Equitação de Birre**, on the road to Sintra and at the **Hippodromio da Quinta da Marinha**, inland from the Guincho Beach. The Marinha Club also has mini-cruises of Cascais Bay. The **Cascais Naval Club** has facilities for water skiing, wind-surfing and sailing, and holds the Star Class Sailing World Championship.

Although it was once a royal resort, Cascais doesn't have the glitter of Estoril. In 1870, King Luís I established his summer residence in the 17th-century **Citadel** on the Bay of Cascais. Before that, it was known only as a fishing port. The locals claim that a fisherman from Cascais, Afonso Sanches, actually discovered America in 1482, and Christopher Columbus merely repeated the trip 10 years later and got all the glory. In 1580, the Duke of Alba attacked the village as part of Spain's claim to Portugal. And in 1589, the English arrived here as retaliation for the Spanish Armada's 1588 foray. But for the most part, Cascais has been as quiet as it is today, with the two principal attractions of the fishing village being the comings and goings of the colorful fishing boats in the bay and the noisy nightly **auction** at the central fish market.

There are several lovely old churches and chapels in Cascais, including the 17th-century **Church of the Assumption** with its plain facade, lovely tiles and marble nave. It houses several lovely paintings by Josefa de Óbidos. On the pedestrian mall, attractive shops and boutiques offer elegant fashions, jewelry and authentic fishermen's sweaters. A weekly market displays nice handicrafts as well as fresh fruits and vegetables.

A lovely hotel in the region is the **Albatroz**, built for the royal family in the 19th century. On the outskirts of town in an exotic garden, lies the **Castro Guimarães Museum** with a nice display of 17th-century Portuguese silver, tiles and furniture, and good 19th-century paintings.

Beyond Cascais lies the wooded rocky Atlantic coast. Lisboners flock here on weekends for the popular seafood restaurants, particularly at **Boca do Inferno**, where they can sit and watch the waves pound the rocky inlet and fish for their own lobsters. Some hardy people swim at the broad clean beach of Guincho, where the waves can be wild and the undertow fierce. Others come to shop in this unlikely spot where vendors often appear to sell colorful woven rugs, sheepskin carpets and craftwork. And some people simply like to take the long road to Sintra, through the pines and along the bleak rocky coast.

Right, windsurfing at Praia do Guincho

SINTRA

With its lush forests and gentle surrounding plain, Sintra has long been a favorite summer resort for Portuguese and foreign aristocrats and vacationers. People delight in the area because of its sheer natural beauty, in spite of man playing a few of his tasteless tricks.

Lord Byron, who could find little good to say about the Portuguese, was enamored with Sintra and likened it to "Elysium's gates." In *Childe Harold*, he wrote: "Lo! Cintra's glorious Eden intervenes in variegated maze of mount and glen."

Byron, Southey, Beckford and others who have written eloquently of the charms of Sintra would probably be horrified by some recent signs of "development." The most conspicuous mistake is the Tivoli Hotel, a huge graceless block, incongruously placed beside the imposing National Palace. The romantics would be dismayed by the recent growth of small, new, rainbow-colored houses below Sintra where there used to be large estates or wooded countryside.

Some 20 miles (32 km) to the northwest of Lisbon, Sintra is another world with its own special climate and almost bucolic way of life. The most practical way to go is by train from Rossio. If one drives, rush hour traffic should be avoided if at all possible. It seems that most of the inhabitants of Sintra commute to Lisbon on weekdays and vice-versa weekends. The road to Sintra from Lisbon starts at the Pombal Circle and is well marked. Avenida Duarte Pacheco runs into the *autostrada* or super highway that leads out of town, past the Aqueduto das Aguas Livres, up the hill through Monsanto Park, turning right to join the highway to Sintra.

A slight detour to visit **Queluz** is well worthwhile. The town has become a rather drab Lisbon dormitory. The **Palace**, however, is a marvelous rose-colored edifice with a monumental facade. It was first built as a simple manor for King Pedro in the mid-17th century and enlarged when the court moved there. Most of the palace is Baroque, but the courtyard and formal gardens were modeled after Versailles.

The palace is used as a government guesthouse for special visitors, such as Queen Elizabeth II and former President Dwight D. Eisenhower. In summer, concerts are sometimes held in the **Music Room**. At other times, the public may visit the lavishly decorated **Throne Room** with its fine painted wood ceiling, the **Hall of Mirrors, Ambassador's Room**, and others. The great kitchen, with its stone chimney and copperware, has been turned into a luxury restaurant called Cozinha Velha.

Back on the main road, one continues along rolling hills, past modest white-washed villages and rich *quintas*, or manors, to arrive at the **Serra de Sintra**. At the base of the mountain lies the village of **São Pedro de Sintra**, where on the second and fourth Sunday of each month, a wonderful country fair takes place. On display are all kinds of crafts from primitive wood carvings and ceramics to fine antique furniture, as well as the latest plastic utensils and polyester tablecloths. São Pedro is also known for its popular *tavernas*, with spicy sausages, hearty codfish and heady wines.

The road climbs slightly and curves around the mountain to reach the center of town. Here is the office of Turismo with permanent exhibition halls and a number of silver and craft shops. Also nearby, the **Estalagem dos Cavaleiros**, formerly called the Hotel Lawrence, where Lord Byron stayed in 1809. Despite official pressures, the owner, as of this writing, has still not been persuaded to open the building to the public.

Two 12th-century churches in town, **Santa Maria** and **São Martinho**, have both been much altered over time. There is also a **Municipal Museum**, which offers a pleasant way of getting acquainted with Sintra's history.

The centerpiece of Sintra is the former royal palace, now called the **Palácio Nacional**, parts of which date back to the 14th century. Broad stairs lead up to the stately building with Gothic arches, Moorish windows and two extraordinary chimney cones. Of special interest on the guided tour of the palace are: the **Sala dos Brasões**, with its remarkable ceiling panels painted in 1515, which show the coat-of arms of 72 Portuguese noble families. (Note that actually only 71 exist; that of the Távoras was removed after the conspiracy against King José in 1758); the **Sala dos Arabes**, with marble fountain and 15th-century Moorish tiles; the **Sala dos Cisnes**, an enormous reception hall with swans painted on the paneled ceiling; the **Sala das Pegas**, whose ceiling is covered with magpies brandishing banners reading "*Por Bem.*" It is said that when Queen Philippa caught King João I courting a lady-in-waiting, he claimed it

Preceding page, the eccentric Pena Palace. Below, Queluz, Portugal's Versailles

was an innocent kiss. "*Por Bem,*" he said, which loosely translated means: "All for the good."

Sintra's other palace-museum, the **Castelo da Pena**, dominates the town from the top of the mountain and is best visited by taxi or horse-and-carriage. The road winds up steep rocky slopes through thick woods to the castle, built on the site of a 16th-century monastery. For many visitors, Pena is better viewed from afar, where it gives the impression of some medieval stronghold. Close at hand, the castle is an architectural monstrosity, a potpourri of various styles and influences. Arabic minarets, Gothic towers, Renaissance cupolas, Manueline windows. It was commissioned by Prince Ferdinand of Saxe-Coburg-Gotha, husband of Queen Maria II, and built by German architect Baron von Eschwege around 1840. At the entrance of the castle, a tunnel leads to the ruins of the original monastery. The old chapel walls are decorated with fine 17th-century tiles and there is a splendid altar of alabaster and black marble by 16th-century French sculptor Nicolas Chanterene. But the best thing about the castle is the view. Below lies **Pena Park**, with lakes and black swans, tangled forest and tile fountains. When Richard Strauss visited the

park, he supposedly said: "*I know Italy, Sicily, Greece, Egypt, but I have never seen anything equal to Pena.*"

Across the way, another mountain-top castle, the **Castelo dos Mouros**, is now only ruins of a Moorish fortress, dating to perhaps the 11th century. The fortifications visible along the mountain ridge were restored in the middle of the 19th century. To the southwest rises the highest peak called **Cruz Alta**, 540 meters (1,772 feet) high and marked by a lovely stone cross.

The mountainside is a luxuriant mass of vegetation—subtropical plants, boulders covered with moss, giant ferns, walnut, chestnut and pine trees, and rhododendron bushes.

One of the strangest sights on the mountain is the **Convento dos Capuchos**, a 16th-century monastery built entirely out of rocks and cork. Some say the monks lined their cells with cork to obtain absolute silence—but there is little noise in the forest other than bird sounds. More likely, the cork helped the monks bear the long and humid winters.

On the outskirts of town stands the **Palácio de Seteais**, which means "The palace of the seven sighs" clearly a reference to the great beauty of the surroundings. Built

The Throne Room at Queluz

by a Dutch diamond merchant in the 18th century, Seteais is remembered as the site where Generals Junot and Dalrymphe signed the Convention of Sintra in 1809, after the defeat of Napoleon's forces by British and Portuguese forces. The palace was restored and turned into a luxury hotel and restaurant in 1955 and should be seen, if only for tea or a drink. The parlors are decorated with crystal chandeliers, wall-hangings, murals and antique furnishings. From the gardens, with sculpted hedges and lemon trees, one has a magnificent view of the countryside. At the *quinta* of *Penha Verde*, not far from here, João de Castro planted the first orange trees in Portugal after retiring as viceroy of India in 1542.

Nearby is the **Quinta da Monserrate**, a strange Moorish-type villa built in the 19th century by Sir Francis Cook. The property is now owned by the State but poorly maintained. The villa is closed but the exotic garden and greenhouse are worth seeing. The wild jungle includes trees and plants from all over the world: palm trees, bamboo, cedars, magnolia trees, cork-oaks, pines and giant ferns.

Once part of the Monserrate gardens, the **Quinta de São Thiago** is a 16th-century manor owned by a retired Englishman and his Spanish wife. It has a lovely chapel, majestic kitchen, cell-like bedrooms, garden and pool. Like other gentry, the Braddells found taxes and utilities prohibitive and, in 1979, opened the *quinta* to paying guests.

The main cultural event of the area is the annual **Festival of Sintra**, generally running three weeks in July. First class recitals, concerts and ballet are presented in the National Palace, Queluz Palace and some of the great *quintas* of the region. And all summer long, there is a "Sound and Light" program presented on weekend evenings at the National Palace.

For a delightful excursion, the **Colares** Road leads through vineyards, white-washed hamlets and stone walls to the sea. Enroute, it is possible to visit the **Adega Regional**, a traditional winery. Colares grapes grow in sandy soil with humid maritime climate. The wines are dark ruby and very smooth.

Cabo da Roca is a wild desolate cape, known as the westernmost point of continental Europe. Visitors receive a certificate for their trouble. Camões described it as the place *"where the land ends and the sea commences."* Heading north, there are several beaches frequented mainly by Portu-

Left, the conical chimneys of the Royal Palace. Right, the Seteais.

120

guese: broad, sandy **Praia Grande** and **Praia das Maças**. The fishing village of **Azenhas do Mar** has natural rocky swimming pools.

Another excursion goes to **Mafra**, the immense palace-convent which is almost as large as Spain's Escorial. One follows the road for **Ericeira**, a beach resort and fishing village, and then drives inland for six miles.

Mafra rises just like some dark mirage across the plain from the modest low-lying houses that make up the village of the same name.

Originally a Capuchin monastery stood on the site. João V erected the new collection of buildings, on quite a different scale, in fulfillment of a vow he made in hopes of having an heir. Work began on the palace in 1717 and ended 18 years later. Estimates of the total of the project vary, but it is said that more than 50,000 workers and 1,000 oxen were employed. Planned to house 13 friars, the final result could easily fit 280—and many novices as well.

Mafra's construction drew so many artists from so many countries that João decided to found the School of Mafra, utilizing these talented artisans as masters to local apprentices. The most famous teacher was probably Joaquim Machado de Castro.

The Limestone facade is massive, 220 meters long. From its center is the **church**, with two tall towers and an Italianate portico. The interior of the church is decorated with the finest Portuguese marbles of different colors. The 14 large statues of saints, located in the vestibule, are carved from Carrara marble—they were made by Italian sculptors. The church contains a generous supply of organs—six.

Part of the monastery is off-limits, being used by the military, but many sections can be visited. The most impressive room is the **library**, full of Baroque magnificence and light. Among its 35,000 volumes are first editions of *Os Lusíadas* by Camões and the earliest edition of Homer in Greek.

Other areas open to the public include the **hospital**, with original decorations and fittings, the **pharmacy**, the **audience room**, painted with a *tromp l'oeil*, and the oval **chapterhouse**. There are three cloisters. The north tower can be climbed, and the two **towers** together contain more than 100 bells, some of which were cast in Belgium.

The town of Mafra is also the site of the church of **Santo André**, which contains the tomb of Diago de Sousa. Pedro Hispano was priest here before he was elected Poe John XXI in 1276.

The library at Mafra

SETÚBAL AND THE ARRÁBIDA PENINSULA

Lisboetans call it *Outra Banda*, the other shore, meaning the southern bank of the Tagus River, long neglected because of the sheer inconvenience of getting there. This all changed after 1966 with the completion of what was then Europe's longest suspension bridge, the 25th of April Bridge. The region, known as the **Arrábida Peninsula**, has developed rapidly, and not always wisely.

Directly across the river is the unassuming ferryboat port of **Cacilhas**. Its main charm is a string of riverfront fish restaurants with a great view of Lisbon. About five km west of the bridge is **Trafaria**, the whole town, since rebuilt, that was burned to the ground on the harsh orders of Pombal in 1777, official punishment for resisting press gangs. Most visitors tend to drive through the neighboring industrial town of **Almada**, except those who want to examine the **Christ the King** monument close at hand. Christ seems dwarfed by his pedestal—irreverent Portuguese say some priest must have dipped into the till before the statue

was completed. Visitors may go up to the top of the pedestal by elevator and stairs for a magnificent view of Lisbon. Almada also contains the monastery of **São Paulo**, founded in 1568.

Most people avoid the Outra Banda dormitory district by taking the superhighway leading directly from the bridge. After a few miles, a turnoff leads to **Costa da Caparica**, a series of broad Atlantic beaches with moderately priced hotels and restaurants. This popular resort is cleaner than the Costa do Sol, and the currents are safer than those of the Atlantic north of the Tagus.

Continuing south on the highway, one passes new factories where there used to be only fields, pine forests and vineyards. The road marked **Palmela** leads to a small town with a great **medieval castle**. This has been restored and converted into a luxury *pousada*, with a lounge in the cloisters, elegant dining room in the old refectory, and antique furnishings. The attached **church** is a beautiful, simple Romanesque structure. The walls are covered with 16th- and 18th-century tiles. The church contains the tomb of Jorge de Lencastre (1431-1550) natural son of João II.

Built by the Moors, the castle was reconstructed in 1147 as a monastery and the seat

The Igreja de Jesús

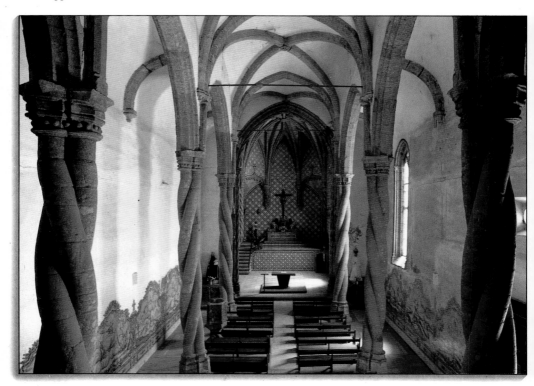

of the Knights of the Order of Saint James. In 1484, the bishop of Évora, Garcia de Meneses, was imprisoned in the dungeon here for his role in conspiring against the king, João II. He died a few days later, probably of poison. Palmela castle was badly damaged by the 1755 earthquake, but the monks rebuilt and remained until the abolition of religious orders in 1834. It is said that much of the town of Palmela was built from pieces of the old castle. At the foot of the castle stands the church of **São Pedro**; its interior is lined with tiles showing the life of the saint.

Just outside of **Setúbal** rises another great castle-turned-pousada, **São Filipe**, with a magnificent view of the **Sado River** estuary. Philip II of Spain ordered the construction of the strategic castle in 1590 to keep a watch over the area—Portugal was under Spanish rule at the time. Starting in 1766, the fortress-castle was used as a prison until its conversion into a pousada in 1965. The castle's **chapel** is decorated with tiles that recount the life of Saint Philip (not Philip of Spain), signed by the master painter Policarpo de Oliveira Bernardes and dated 1736.

According to local legend, Setúbal was founded by Tubal, the son of Cain. It is said that Phoenicians and Greeks, finding the climate and soil of Arrábida similar to their Mediterranean homelands, brought their grapes and started vineyards. Setúbal is known to have been an important fishing port since Roman times.

Today Setúbal is an industrial town, a center of ship-building, fish-canning, and the production of fertilizers, cement, salt and moscatel wine. Nevertheless, there are a number of interesting sights in town and in the region. Setúbal's pride is the **Church of Jesus**, a spectacular monument dating back to 1491. The church was designed by Diogo Boytac, known as the founding master of the Manueline style of architecture. It is considered one of his finest works. The narrow building has a high arched ceiling supported by six great stone pillars that look like coils of rope; its apse is etched with stone and lined with tiles. Arrábida marble was used, and the pebbled, multi-colored stone gives the whole a distinct appearance. There are also lovely tile panels along the walls. The **cloister** has been turned into a museum with an exhibition of rare 16th-century Portuguese and Flemish primitives, numismatics, jewelry and archaeological discoveries from the region.

Nearby is the **Praça do Bocage**, with palm trees and a statue honoring one of the town's illustrious sons, 18th-century sonneteer, Manuel Barbasa du Bocage. Off the square stands the church of **São Julião** with a handsome Manueline doorway built in 1513. The inside walls are decorated with 18th-century tiles showing the life of the saint and popular fishing scenes. Also of interest is the **Ethnographical Museum**, with models depicting the city's main industries: fishing, farming and textiles. The church of **Santa Maria de Graça**, at the east end of town has 17th-century paintings.

One of the great scenes is **Setúbal Harbor**, particularly in the morning with the arrival of brightly painted trawlers loaded with fish. Then there's the continual show of fishermen mending nets and working on their boats. Best of all is the lively fish auction.

Setúbal is the main point of departure for the peninsula of **Troia**. From Setúbal's dock, ferryboats make the 20-minute crossing frequently in season; there is also a hovercraft service. Troia, a long narrow spit jutting out into the Sado estuary, is said to be the site of the Roman town of **Cetóbriga**, buried by a tidal wave in the 5th century. Substantial ruins have been found but little has been excavated besides a temple and tombs. Underwater, one may see the walls of Roman houses. On the northern end of the peninsula, there is a rather unattractive modern beach resort with large apartment blocks, hotels and villas. The **Troia Golf Club** has an 18-hole course designed by Robert Trent Jones. On the southern end of the peninsula, however, there are still miles of pine forest and fine empty beaches and dunes.

Many Portuguese and foreigners regret that the Portuguese authorities did not see fit to protect this City of the Dead in its natural state, as the Greeks have done with Delos.

At the mouth of the Sado, about three miles (five km) southwest of Setúbal, is the **Torre do Outão**, originally a Roman temple to Neptune, which offers a great view. Another delightful excursion from Setúbal goes along the ridge of the **Serra da Arrábida** which rises to 2,000 feet (606 meters). As one leaves the city, the only sight that mars the natural beauty of the coast is the cement factory, usually spitting out black smoke. From the belvederes, there are majestic views of the mountain slopes. A cluster of whitewashed hermitages and chapels, built around 1542, lie almost lost in the dense mass of greenery, oaks and pines, ferns and wildflowers. Far below, ochre cliffs drop into the turquoise sea.

A road descends to **Portinho da**

Arrábida, a popular bathing beach with transparent waters, white sand and the splendid **Grotto of Santa Margarida**. Hans Christian Andersen, who visited the region in 1834, marveled in his diaries at this cave with its imposing stalactites. Scuba diving is popular here.

But it was Robert Southey, a young traveler who was very difficult to please, who consecrated Arrábida for English readers, calling it "a glorious spot." In his letters, he recounts going swimming at the base of the mountain and writes: "I have no idea of sublimity exceeding it."

Regaining the ridge, one continues along the skyline drive, which is reminiscent of the Amalfi coast. The next turnoff leads to **Sesimbra**, a lovely fishing village and resort with several notable sights. The castle above the village, although known as Moorish, has been entirely rebuilt since that time. Afonso Henriques captured it in 1165, but the Moors utterly razed the structure in 1191, following a scorched earth policy. King Dinis almost certainly helped with the rebuilding, and King João IV again added and repaired in the 17th century. Inside the walls are ruins of a Romanesque church, Santa Maria, and the old town hall. King João IV also ordered the fort of São Teodo-sio built, to protect the port from pirates.

In town is the Misericórdia, constructed in the 15th century, with a painting attributed to Gregório Lopes. The 16th-century parish church contains a noteworthy 18th-century gilded wood alterpiece.

But the most fascinating sight is the port with its fishermen, always busy either going out to sea, coming back, or selling their catch. There are several simple bistros near the port where one may eat fresh fish—swordfish is the local specialty—and enjoy the show.

Going westward about seven miles (11 km), the road ends at **Cabo Espichel**. This promontory with the shrine of **Nossa Senhora do Cabo** used to be an important pilgrimage site, as shown by the long rows of dilapidated pilgrims' quarters on either side of the church. There is still a fishermen's festival here each October. On the edge of the high cliff is the small fisherman's **Chapel of Senhor de Bomfim**, in a rather desolate state but with a breathtaking view of the Atlantic coast.

The road back to Lisbon goes through **Vila Nogueira de Azeitão**, sometimes simply called Azeitão, which means large olive tree. In the center of this charming village is the stately **Távora Palace**, where

The endless beach at Troia Peninsula

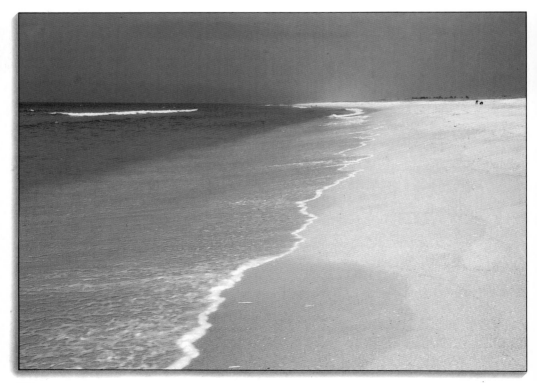

the Duke of Aveiro and his friends are said to have plotted to overthrow King José. The Duke, and his friends, were burned at the stake for their troubles, in Belém in 1759. Townspeople plan to restore the palace and turn it into a museum. Lovely Baroque fountains border the town's main street. The **Church of São Lourenco** has been restored and boasts of beautiful 18th-century altars, paintings and tile panels.

The **Azeitão fair**, held in the central square on the first Sunday of the month, became so popular that it caused havoc and had to be moved to the outskirts of town. Less picturesque now, it is still a major attraction with stands offering everything from shoes and pottery to furniture. There is also a large section devoted to livestock and poultry.

In the village, stands the original **José Maria da Fonseca winery**, founded in 1834. The old family residence, which now houses a small museum, stands nearby. The winery still produces one of Portugal's best red table wines, the soft rich Periquita, as well as Setúbal's popular moscatel wines. Moscatel is a sweet aperitif wine, topaz in color with 18 to 20 percent alcohol.

Da Fonseca also coproduces **Lancers**, one of Portugal's best known table wines, in new modern installations on the outskirts of town. Visitors are welcome to tour the factory and see its assembly-line production.

Not far from town stands one of the oldest inhabited manors in the country, the **Quinta da Bacalhoa**, built in 1480. It had fallen into ruins and was saved by an American woman from Connecticut, Mrs. Herbert Scoville, who bought it in 1936 and restored it scrupulously. The gardens, which are open to the public, are admirable with their clipped boxwood in geometric design, orange and lemon groves, and pavilion with beautiful tile panels. One of these scenes, showing Susanna and the Elders is dated 1565, and said to be the earliest known dated panel in Portugal.

Another attractive manor, the **Quinta das Torres**, stands just outside the neighboring village of **Vila Fresca de Azeitão.** This 16th-century *quinta*, decorated with tile panels and set in a romantic garden, has been converted into a cozy inn and restaurant and is an ideal spot for tea.

In the village, there is yet another charming church, **São Simão**, with more ancient tile walls and polychrome panels.

The easiest route back to Lisbon is to take the old national highway, N10, which runs into the superhighway.

Cabo Espichel sweeps into the Atlantic

ALGARVE

Separated from the rest of Portugal by smooth rolling hills, the Algarve, a southernmost province, seduced the ancient Phoenicians with its abundance of sardines and tuna, which they salt-cured for export almost 3,000 years ago. Four centuries later, around 600 B.C., the Carthaginians and Celts arrived, which in turn attracted the Romans.

The Romans adopted the Phoenician practice of curing and exporting fish—the precursor to Portugal's large tinned sardine industry. They built roads, bridges, and spas, such as that in Milreu. They also enjoyed the springs of Monchique.

But the Algarve really blossomed under Moorish rule, which began in the early 8th century. Its name comes from the Moorish **Al-Gharb** meaning "The West".

The Moorish period was one of vivacious culture and great strides forward in science. Moorish poets sang of the beauty of Silves, while the more practical settlers introduced orange crops, and perfected the technique of extracting olive oil, still very much an important Portuguese product. The blossoming almond trees in February remains one of the most beautiful sights to behold in the Algarve thanks to the passion a Moorish king once held for a northern princess.

Legend has it that the princess, pining for the snows of her homeland, slowly began to waste away. Distraught, the king ordered thousands of almond trees to be planted across the region, then one February morning carried her to the window where she saw swirling white "snow flakes" carpeting the ground—the white almond blossoms. She quickly recuperated, and the two as you might guessed, lived happily ever after.

King Afonso Henriques led the Portuguese conquest of the Algarve in the 12th century, and later his son Sancho I was to lead the siege against Silves and its estimated population of 20,000 people with the help of the Crusaders. It took 49 days before the Moors of Silves surrendered. In 1192 they reconquered the city and remained there for another 47 years. It was Sancho II who, supported by military religious orders headed by Paio Peres Correia, finally crushed the Moors. The last major city to fall was Faro in January 1249.

But the Arabic influence is visible even today: town names, words beginning with the "al" prefix, and Tunisian blue is still used in trimming the whitewashed homes, terraces atop houses used for the drying of fruit, and the white-domed buildings still popular in many towns. The Algarvian sweets made of figs, almonds, eggs and sugar called *Morgados* or *Dom Rodrigos* are yet another reminder of the area's ancient heritage.

For centuries almond, fig, olive and carob trees represented a major part of the Algarve's agriculture, as they are suited to the dry inland areas. Recently, citrus fruit has taken on greater importance, changing the region's typical agricultural cycles.

Thanks to the area's different climates—coastal, inland and mountain—the Algarve also produces pears, apples, quince, loquats, damask plums, pomegranates, tomatos, melons, strawberries, watermelon, peas, lima beans and green beans.

The export of wine from the Algarve—began during the Muslim occupation and reached its peak in the 14th and 15th centuries. Lagos, Portimao, Lagoa and Tavira are the primary wine centers. The Lagos *Algar Seco* is a very dry aperitif wine, served chilled. The region's dry and sweet *Moscatel* wines are both aged in oak barrels for at least seven years and have an alcohol gradient of 18 to 19 percent. The dry wine should be served chilled as an aperitif, while the sweet is essentially served as a dessert wine.

Afonso III is a very dry wine from Lagos, served chilled, while the *Cruz de Portugal* is a sweet red wine, normally aged eight to 10 years, that should be served at room temperature with desserts. From Tavira comes the sweet, dark and fruity *Licoroso de Tavira* which should be served at room temperature in a port glass.

Medronho is a clear brandy-type of drink made out of wild strawberry of the same name and is famous throughout the Algarve. It has an alcohol gradient similar to the kick of a mule, and is available everywhere, but especially in the roadside *tascas*, or bars, where it is served in small Port glasses. The best Medronho is homemade. In the tiny village of Cachopo lost in the inland eastern part of the Algarve, a tiny pixie-like old widow soberly dressed in the obligatory black will be quite happy to usher you into the back of her house (if you can find her) and tip herself almost upside down into her huge medronho barrels to fill your empty bottles with her own special make. Another favorite in the Algarve is *Brandymel*, a type of honey-brandy

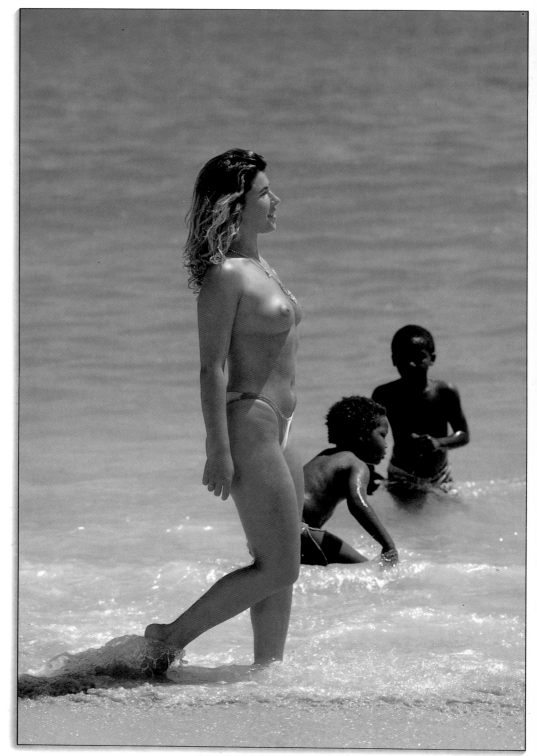

Typical handicrafts are fading fast, but you can still find soft yellow *esparto* or matgrass baskets, hats, mats and hampers and so on in Loulé. This is traditionally made by women who pick and dry the *esparto* in May, then shred it into thin strips which are soaked before worked.

Lovely *esparto* rugs are also made in Albufeira, Monchique and Vila Real de Santo Antonio. Cane basketry is almost exclusively made by men and is most popular in Alcoutim, Castro Marim, Odeleite, São Brás and Aljezur. These stiff baskets are used to carry eggs, or are sometimes transformed into fish traps.

Lagor, Loulé, Tavira and Martinlongo are reknowned for pottery, including the two-handled big-bellied water pitchers that resemble Roman amphoras, as well as various bowls, plates and tiles, and the famous white lace-like chimney tops that embellish the Algarve's skyline. Dark wrought-iron railings are the work of ironsmiths from Silves, Portimao, Loule and Tavira, while the art of beaten copper, similar to that of Northern Africa, is most seen in Lagos and Loulé. An excellent example of this is the *cataplana*—grandmother of the modern pressure cooker.

The copper *cataplana* is a wok-like cooking dish with a hinged lid which has become a symbol of the Algarve. Originally used by hunters, it is now used to make a series of seafood dishes like *Ameijoas na Cataplana*: a delicious dish of fresh steamed clams mixed with chopped onion, pork, parsley, green peppers and oil. One warning: Pollution has increased drastically in the past few years due to the tourist boom, and this with the heat has affected clams and mussels, so only eat them in reputable restaurants in the summer, and never eat one that has not opened.

Other handicrafts include woodwork, such as the wooden spoons of Aljezue, or the colorfully painted mule-drawn wagons. Beautiful hand-made bobbin-lace is on sale in Olhão, Fuzeta, Castro Marim and Azinhal. Wool-weaving is more typical in the mountainous regions, and some flax-weaving is still practiced in Monchique. Driving south of Monchique you can also see stoneworkers hand-cutting blue and white stone squares used to make the striking mosaic-like pavements seen around Portugal.

There are various ways of getting to the Algarve. The most direct is to fly to the Faro International Airport, a half-hour hop from Lisbon. Faro is the Algarve's capital, thought to have been founded by the Phoe-

nicians, then used by Greeks and Romans as a trading post before it became a flourishing Moorish town. It was largely demolished by the violent 1755 earthquakes, and its architecture reveals a hodge-podge of styles and eras.

Faro: The city surrounds an attractive yacht basin. Off to one side is the beautiful Renaissance **Arco da Vila** archway that leads to the old part of town and the Renaissance-Baroque **cathedral**. The second chapel in this cathedral has a lovely panelled depiction of the Biblical flight to Egypt in Dutch tiles. Another 15th century chapel, dedicated to Our Lady of Conceiçao, also has a lovely collection of 17th century tiles. The red Chinoserie organ in the main part of the church dates from the 15th century.

A most bizarre and macabre sight can be found in the **Carmelite Church**. Within this 18th century structure is the **Chapel of Bones**, built entirely out of skeletons and lined with grinning skulls, said to have been created out of a nearby over-crowded cemetery.

The museum in the former **Clarissas Convent** has a good selection of Roman artifacts from Faro and the ancient Roman site of Milreu to the north. The **Ethnographic Musem** in the Praça Alexandre Herculano is also interesting, with detailed replicas of a typical Algarvian home as well as handicrafts from all over the province. The **Nautical Museum** in the Port Authority building is worth a quick visit for the history of Algarve fishing, complete with models of ancient fishing boats.

The rest of town is divided into different quarters with one quieter 18th century section and other scattered historical features, but overall Faro has lost some of its old-fashion charm in growing into a bustling resort town. However, a number of lovely villages are within driving distance from here.

Estói, for example, is a tiny place where archaeologists have found artifacts dating from Paleolithic times down to the Bronze and Copper Ages. Not far are the remains of the Roman settlement of **Milreu**. There is usually a guide to show you around the ruins of baths believed to have belonged to an important Roman noble. Some of the original mosaics depicting leaping blue dolphins and fish are still visible, and the walls of an old Roman temple, presumably built to honor the god or goddess of the baths, still stand.

North of Estói is **São Brás de Alportel**, founded by the Moors, and topped by a large hill that has a great view of the lower

A late-20th-century ideal of beauty on the Algarve coast

Algarve. Some eight miles (13 km) west is **Loulé**, a charming white washed town whose old quarter, the *almedina* (like the *medinas* or *casbahs* of north Africa) is a maze-like array of streets full of shops selling regional handicrafts. The old **parish church** here was built by King Dinis (1279-1325). Worth a visit is the *Mae Soverana* or **Sovereign Mother shrine** built in the early 16th century—today overshadowed by a modern dome-shaped cathedral—whose interior is covered in 17th century tiles and frescoes.

North again and off the beaten track is the **Serra do Caldeirão**. This range of hills, reaching 1,800 feet (545 meters), has been left largely untouched by the tourist explosion; areas of it are still home to some not very friendly wild boars. Walks through these mountains can be wonderfully peaceful after the summer bustle of the coastal resorts, and it is a great place for picnics under the cork trees, holm oaks and pink and white blossoming oleanders. Sheep, goats, and their shepherds are the only inhabitants of this area. The plain white houses with their small windows and simple tiled roofs reveal the hardworking and gentle character of the shepherds.

Another route into the Algarve is to drive from Lisbon, through the Alentejo. The main road passes through the lovely mountain village of **São Marcos da Serra**. There is a terrific roadside restaurant here—ignore the rough edges on the outside and go inside where they serve fresh fish, chicken and meat grilled on a wood fire.

The road then leads to **São Bartolomeu de Messines**, whose small 15th century red sandstone **church** is filled with 17th century tiles. Drive on then to the coastal resort town of **Albufeira**. Once a small fishing village favored by the Romans and Moors, Albufeira today is a populous tourist spot with an active nightlife, hundreds of bars crushed next to each other blasting rock music, plenty of restaurants ranging from La Pizza to more typical regional fare, and late-night discos.

The old part of town is still very attractive, as are the rock-protected beaches where the fishermen keep their boats, gaily painted with large eyes (to ward off evil), as well as stars and animals. There is a bustling seafood market near the fishermen's beach and a fruit, meat and vegetable market in the main town square held daily except Mondays.

The distance between towns east or west of Albufeira is negligible, the roads being

Mixing business and pleasure on the beach of Albufeira

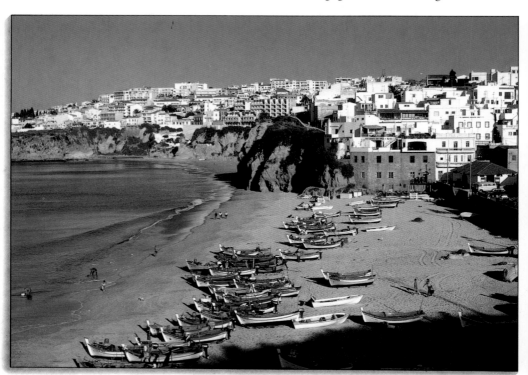

boring but easy to drive; and the relentless tourist industry has built so much in between that it is hard to tell when you have left one town and entered another. Unfortunately, much of this area has been ruined with massive billboard advertising and bad urban planning.

However, veering off to the shore you can still find some uncrowded beaches. One good alternative is to hire a boat (and a fisherman) for the day, fill the boat up with food and drink, and go exploring the coast for the deserted beaches and grottoes that dot this rocky coastline that can only be reached by sea.

Most of the well-known golf courses lie east of Albufeira, such as Quinta do **Lago**, a 27-hole course, **Vale do Lobo**, and **Vilamoura**, which was originally designed by Frank Pennink and is part of a 4,000 acre (1,600 hectares) tourist development. Penina, designed by three-time British Open champion Henry Cotton, is west of Albufeira, closer to Portimão. More than 120,000 golfers visit Algarve's six courses every year.

Northeast of Albufeira is Alte, a naturally elegant village lying at the foot of woolly hills huddled around its parish church. The church of **Nossa Senhora da Assunção** dates from the 16th century and has magnificent 18th-century tile panels. Within, the tiles in the **Our Lady of Lurdes Chapel**, considered the best in the Algarve, are of 16th century Sevillian origin. Alte is perhaps one of the most typical villages of the province with its delicate laced white chimneys, simple white houses and timeless serenity.

A nearby brook (to which people come from miles around to gather water) has transformed the area into an oasis amid the region's sometimes scrubby landscape. It's a lush garden of oleanders, fig and loquat trees and rose bushes. The blue- and white tile panels around the **Fonte da Bicas** or fountain, contain poems by Candido Guerreiro. This area is perfect for long walks or picnics, or a donkey ride up the Pena hill where you can visit the **Moors' Cave** (*Buraco dos Mouros*). Further up the mountain is **Rocha dos Soidos**, a cave filled with intricate stalactite and stalagmite formations.

Northwest of Albufeira is **Silves**, the oldest town in the Algarve, settled in the 4th century B.C. Although the city was important in Roman times, it reached its greatest splendor under the Moors, who made it the capital of the Algarve. You can

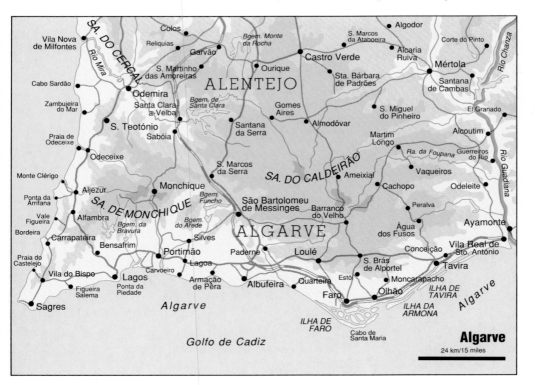

Algarve
24 km/15 miles

drive to Silves, or sail up the Arade River from Portimão—the same route used by the crusaders centuries ago—stopping on the way to see the **Ibne Ammar** and **Algar** caves, or the famous grottoes near the **Our Lady of Rosario** islet, or just to watch the old watermills turning creakily on the river banks.

In its glory days Silves was the home of some the greatest Arab poets. They recorded its ruin when the city fell to Portugal's King Sancho I in 1189: "*Silves, my Silves, once you were a paradise. But tyrants turned you into the blaze of hell. They were wrong not to fear God's punishment. But Allah leaves no deed unheeded,* " wrote Assilbia. His call may have been heard because in 1192 the Moors occupied Silves once more before it was finally re-conquered by the Portuguese.

Yemenite Arabs built the walled city, but the **castle** (on top of a Roman citadel, itself on top of neolithic foundations) and the defensive Albarra towers were heavily restored in the later Almohad period of the 12th and 13th centuries. The Moorish castle and Christian Sé (cathedral) dominate the city, the dark-red sandstone contrasting with the soft pinks and faded blues of the older surrounding houses. A sense of an-cient history and poetry still permeates Silves and the castle—except in June when an international beer festival held within its walls considerably changes the atmosphere.

The Moorish cistern to the north surmounted by four seven-meter-high arches once supplied the city's water, and is architecturally similar to 13th century cisterns found in Palestine and in Cacares, Spain. These enormous systems, built both by Romans and Moors, were part of the advanced irrigation technology that transformed the Algarve into the garden of Portugal.

The Sé is originally of 13th-century Gothic, restored in the 14th century and almost destroyed by the earthquake of 1755. Its apse is decorated with square arches, pyramid-shaped battlements and fanciful gargoyles. The inner chapel of **João de Rego** dates from the 15th century. Various tombs here are said to be of crusaders who helped capture Silves from the Moors in 1244. One of the most interesting sights on leaving Silves on the road to São Bartolomeu de Messines is the Cross of Portugal, which is a 19 feet (six meter) crucifix thought to have been sculpted in the early 16th century. It pictures Christ nailed to the Cross on one side and His descent

The coast of Aljezur

from the Cross on the other.

Tourist delights: Once an important cork-curing center, today Silves depends more on tourism. In addition, barges on the Arade river bring citrus fruit, olive oil, almonds, figs and various grains. The town is known for its almond and fig sweets, as well as its cork and wrought-iron work.

South of Silves is **Lagoa**, where growers from around the area take their grapes to the central cooperative wine cellar. It's a great place to stop for a glass of wine after a cool walk through the town's parks. East of here is **Porches**, famous for its painted pottery, and to the south, through the almond groves, is **Cape Carvoeiro**, a craggy coastline of isolated beaches, like that of Algar Seco. Carvoeiro itself is a lively tourist spot.

Portimão lies west of Carvoeiro, and although its has no ancient monuments, it is a pleasant shopping town built right onto the ocean with a number of sidewalk cafes and a good fish market. Portimao is famous for its grilled sardines and pastry shops. Just outside the city is **Praia da Rocha**, a beach with amazing yellow-brown rock formations standing in the blue-green sea, its soft stone sculpted into freakish shapes by centuries of wind and water erosion.

Driving west you will come to **Lagos**, which some believe was founded by a Carthaginian chieftain, and later taken by the Romans in the 5th century B.C., when it was called *"Laccobriga"* or "fortified lake." The moors took it over in the 8th century and renamed it *"Zawaia,"* or "lake." The city finally fell to the Portuguese during the reign of Afonso III.

In 1434 Gil Eanes left Lagos and became the first person to round Cape Bojador of northwest Africa, south of the Canary Islands—then the limit of the known world. Most of the city was rebuilt in the 18th century. Some evidence of the town's darker past still stands such as the columns and semicircular arches of Portugal's first slave market in the **Praça da Republica**. (Portugal brought slaves in from Guinea and Senegal), or the modern **monument** by Portuguese artiest João Cutileiro making King Sebastião's departure to the disastrous battle of Alcacer-Quibir.

Take a walk through the city's winding streets and this will lead you to the **Church of Santo Antonio**, a sober-looking church on the outside. But, inside, however, is an extraordinary and beautiful example of gilded carving. The nave has an impressive painted wood barrel-vault with an 18th century shield in the middle, and Baroque

The cathedral in Silves

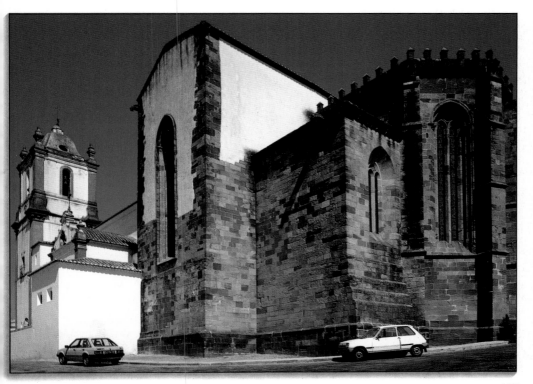

paintings on the side walls.

From Lagos you can walk along the shoreline's many beaches to Ponte **da Piedade**, which has a stunning view over the ocean. Try to hire a boat from local fishermen to explore the grottoes with their cathedral-like natural skylights.

The countryside changes drastically towards the west, particularly from **Salema** and **Figueira**, moving from coastal plateaus and tree-covered hills to a rockier and more undulating horizon. The trees, usually the hardier carob, fig and almond, get smaller and squatter, permanently bent from the unrelenting southwest wind.

The western Algarve is divided into two parts: the Atlantic coast and the Monchique mountains, known as the garden of the Algarve. In spring Monchique is covered in mimosa, narcisi, freesia, azeleas. Hundreds of wildflowers bloom in the deep green valleys between the **Foia** and **Picota** peaks. Foia is the highest point of the Algarve reaching 2,950 feet (900 meters) above sea level, but for the most breathtaking view go to Picota. Although its summit rises a more modest 2,500 feet (770 meters). The town of Monchique is rather disappointing if you merely drive through, but park the car and walk about the steep streets to get a better feel for the place.

The Monchique spas (*caldas*) are off to the right heading south, and are surrounded by chestnut, cork, pine, orange and eucalyptus trees. The spa has been in use since Roman times and the waters are believed to cure a number of ailments ranging from convulsions to rheumatism. There are eight springs, four of which are medicinal, that pour out an estimated 20 million liters (about four million gallons) of water a year.

The Algarve's dramatic coastline begins at **Odeceixe** and sweeps all the way down to Cape St. Vincent and Sagres, and is as yet unexploited. Odeceixe is a small Moorish-style village that reaches out to long sandy beaches and looming high cliffs. Further south is **Aljezur**, comfortably sprawled over the hills—and the last town to be taken from the Moors. Directly west are the **Monte Clerigos**, **Arrifana**, **Popa** and **Atalaia** beaches. At **Saiceira** there are large caverns and underground galleries to be explored, once the hide-out of pirates, now a refuge for many species of marine birds.

From Aljezur the road bumps down to the wild and windswept forked promontory of **Sagres** and **Cape St. Vincent**, the latter once believed to be a sacred meeting place **A house in Sagres**

of the gods, as it stood teetering on the edge of the known world. Here, even on a calm day, waves crash against the dramatic cliffs with a violence that sends spray everywhere. In spring the smell of cistus fills the air, a bush with a perfumed oil on its leaves which the Egyptians had once used for embalming.

In Sagres, Henry the Navigator gathered the most renowned cartographers, astronomers and sailors of his day and founded the famous Navigation School in the 15th century. Although much of what stood then has been destroyed, a huge rose compass (*Rosa dos Ventos*) still lies on the stone floor of the fortress, stretching 130 feet (39 meters) in diameter. Today Sagres is a small fishing town that uses the **Baleeira Bay** as its fishing port. While here, make a point of seeing the **Torre of Aspa**, a natural rock formation that soars some 500 feet (150 meters) above sea level and is the area's highest point.

Sacred ravens: Sitting atop the impressive cliffs of Cape St. Vincent is a tall red lighthouse whose warning beams can reach ships as far as 50 miles (90 kilometers) away. Legend has it that in medieval times Christian followers of the martyr St. Vincent defied the Moors and buried his body somewhere on the cape, building a small shrine in his honor. Ten sacred ravens were said to have kept a permanent swooping vigil over the spot, and they can still be seen circling the skies today.

From here you can drive north to beaches with curious names like **Cor do Homem** (Color of the Man), **Barriga** (Belly), and **Cara da Teira** (Teira's Face). The area is wild—lynxes and birds of prey prowl here. Further north and inland is **Vila do Bispo**, an unspoiled town where rust-colored oxen still have the right-of-way, windmills are in use, and chattering women gather around the communal washing places to do the family's laundry.

Try to see **Castelejo**, a fabulous beach just north of here where the full force of the Atlantic crashes onto white-veined rocks. Back down again and going towards Lagos is **Salema**, a booming tourist town with a pre-13th century chapel of **Our Lady of Guadelupe**, believed to have been built by the Templars.

Perhaps the least traveled way to the Algarve is on the eastern edge of Portugal, on the road alongside the **Guadiana River** on the Spanish border which meanders through abandoned golden furze-covered hills dotted with corks, olive and fig trees.

The best part of traveling on this road is that it gives you a chance to branch off into as-yet-unspoiled Algarvian villages on either side of it. For example, just south of the Alentejo the road cuts off east to **Alcoutim**, one of the most serene and lovely towns on this side of the Algarve. Time seems to have stopped here. The only sounds are that of a donkey braying or a turkey gobbling. Sunning dogs in the only square in town have priority, so you'll have to park around them.

From the promenade built on the edge of the Guadiana River you can see the Spanish town of San Lucar de Guadiana settled in its nook of windmill-topped hills, reflected in the slow-moving water. The **village church**, also by the riverside, has interesting bas-relief carving on the baptismal font dating from the 16th century. Signs to the "castle" lead to an empty shell of walls—but the view from here is worth the short walk.

On down to the **Castro Marim** near the mouth of the Guadiana River, one of the oldest and historically most important areas of the Algarve. Once a major Phoenician settlement, it was also host to the Greeks and Carthaginians before the Moors and Romans invaded. Portugal's kings later used it as a natural point from which to fight the Moors to the east. The city was largely reconstructed after the 1755 earthquake, but the **castle** built by King Afonso III is still standing, overlooking the surrounding valley.

Surrounding the town is the **Castro Marim fen** or marsh, home of many migratory birds including storks and flamingoes, and hundreds of different species of plant life. Try the local *Servico de Parques e Reservas* for a guided tour and information. Next to the fen is the popular **São Bartolomeu** fair that sells local basketry and other handicrafts.

Further south, sitting right on the border with Spain is **Vila Real de Santo Antonio**, a city carefully laid out in geometric streets—the mark of the famous Marquês de Pombal who was responsible for re-designing old Lisbon. Pombal intended this town as an administrative, industrial and fishing model and he founded the Royal Fisheries Company here. But he lost favor with the court, and his plans never really took off until the Genoese arrived to take advantage of the fishing trade in the 1800s. However, constant fishing and modernization has depleted the supply of fish and today tourism is the main money-maker.

Left, a Tavira belltower. Right, Fortaleza in Sagres

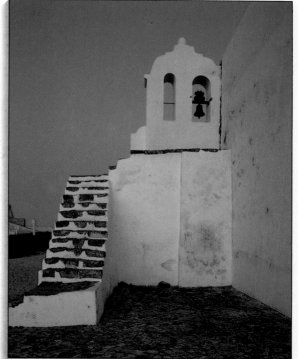

Traveling west past the popular beach resort towns of **Monte Gordo, Praia Verde, Alagoas** and **Cacela** you will come to **Tavira**, known as the Venice of the Algarve. Tavira lies elegantly on both sides of the Sequa River, which becomes the Gilão as it slides under the seven-arched Roman-style bridge towards the sea. Mainly an estuary town, Tavira flourished in the 16th century because of its location. But trade rapidly dwindled as the fish disappeared, and this lovely town of narrow streets, palatial houses, miniature towers, domes, unusual four-sided roofs and minarets today stands strangely silent.

There are 15 churches and six monasteries in Tavira, of which the most interesting being **Senhora da Ajuda**, the **Igreja da Misericórdia** and the church of **Santa Maria** rebuilt on the site of the town's old mosque. (Guides are not always available, but detailed pamphlets of these monuments should be on hand either at the tourist center or town hall.)

From Tavira is a brief drive through **Fuzeta** to **Olhão**, a 17th century town built in the Moorish style, famous for its crowded indoor fish market. Get there early and be prepared to use your elbows to get to the slithery hills of fish which the women hawk at the top of their voices, poking them to prove their freshness. The best buys are gilt-head bream (*dourada*) bass (*robalo*) and sole (*linguado*). Nearby there is a fruit, vegetable and live fowl market.

With a basket full of fresh food, head back towards Tavira but veer off at the little fishing port of Fuzet. There, you can get a ferry to **Fuzeta Island** with its long strip of beach, and have a barbecue. Or alternatively, you can get a simple lunch from the only local *tasca*.

Fuzeta lies practically in the middle of the **Ria Formosa** a huge undeveloped wild life area that stretches some 30 miles (50 m) from Anciao in the west to Cancela in the east, hitting a width of some four miles (six km) around Faro.

This natural lagoon system, protected from the sea by a network of sand bars, is crucial, as it provides for 90 percent of Portugal's total harvest of clams and oysters. The Ria is also an important bird sanctuary, especially for waders like egrets, black-winged stilts, oyster catchers, and rare species like the purple gallinule. Tragically, the uncontrolled and heavy influx of people in this area and the absence of the necessary governmental infrastructures to deal with it today threaten the entire area.

A church at Boliqueime

ÉVORA AND
THE ALENTEJO

Alentejo, literally "beyond the Tejo" (the Tagus River), has a distinctive character and beauty unlike that of any other Portuguese province. Its vast plains, colored burnt ochre in summer, are freckled with cork oaks and olive trees which are the only shade for the small flocks of sheep and herds of black pigs.

Nicknamed "terra do pão" (land of bread) because of field upon field of wheat, oats and rice, the visitor will pass by acres of grapevines, tomatoes and other vegetable plantations.

The Alentejo is the largest and flattest of the Portuguese provinces; about the size of Belgium, it occupies one-third of Portugal's total land area. It stretches from the west coast eastward to the Spanish border and separates Ribatejo and Beira Beixa in the central regions from the Algarve in the south. The open countryside is punctuated by picturesque whitewashed towns and villages, many of which were built on the low hills which dot the horizon.

The Alentejo is rich in handicrafts. Rustic pottery with naive, colorful designs can be found everywhere. In addition, certain towns specialize in particular crafts or products: handstitched rugs from Arraiolos; loom-woven carpets from Reguengos; cheese from Serpa; tapestries from Portalegre; sugar plums from Elvas. All these can be purchased, of course, elsewhere in the Alentejo, or in Lisbon or Oporto, but for price, selection, freshness and adventure, isn't it more satisfying to go to the source?

By Portuguese standards, the roads which connect the towns are excellent. Most of the traffic is local and slow moving. You will need to equip yourself with a reliable road map—signposting is limited, and without a map you could drive miles before discovering you've taken a wrong turn.

The Portuguese in general are not renowned for their tidiness but the Alentejanos are the exception. The towns are litter free and there is always a *dona de casa* in view whitewashing her already pristine home. Cool and simple is the theme for the Alentejo architecture; low, single-story buildings are painted white to deflect the sun's glare, with a traditional blue skirting to reflect the sky. Large domed chimneys indicate chilly winters. This practical style is followed from the humblest cottage to the large hacienda-style homes of the wealthy

landowners; ornate and impressive architecture is reserved for cathedrals and churches.

Inland from the coastline, Alentejo temperature in the summer can reach inferno level: what little wind there is blows hot and dry from the continental land mass—no cooling sea breezes here. As you would expect from this dry, flat terrain, temperatures drop dramatically in winter, resulting in some bitter cold nights.

Geographically the province is split into two regions, Upper (A*lto*) and Lower (*Baixo*) Alentejo. Portalegre is the capital of the former and Beja of the latter. To the east are two low mountain ranges, the Serras of **São Mamede** and **Ossa**. Some of the towns in these ranges, particularly Marvão, have breathtaking, even precipitous settings. Portugal's third longest river, the Guadiana, flows through the province and in places provides a border between Portugal and Spain. This is by no means the only waterway. The region is crisscrossed by a network of small rivers and dams.

The Alentejo is steeped in history which goes back to the days of Roman colonization. Later, it was the seat of the great landed estates of the Portuguese nobility and home to former kings. Even as late as 1828 Évora—capital of the Alentejo—was considered the second major Portuguese city, an honor first bestowed on it by King João I (1385-1433).

Estremoz, whose ancient castle has been converted into a comfortable *pousada* (state-run hotel) was a nerve center to medieval Portugal. Vila Viçosa has a history which began in the Middle Ages and continued up to the early 20th century. It was the seat of the Dukes of Bragança, whose royal dynasty began in 1640 with the coronation of João IV and ended in 1910 with the fall of the monarchy.

Political change: Nowadays, modern Alentejo is a far cry from the days of aristocratic domination, although farming techniques of the smallholdings have changed little over the centuries. The greatest change is a political one: since the restoration of democracy in 1974 the Alentejo has been the heart of Portuguese communism.

Many of the great estates—so vast that they included villages, a school and even small hospitals—were taken over by the farmworkers during the Revolution. Some of the land-owning families were forcibly ejected, but the majority lived away from the farms for most of the year anyway, in other properties nearer Lisbon or Oporto. Unfortunately, lack of management skills has led many of the cooperative-run farms to near-bankruptcy, but others flourish. Government legislation is attempting to ensure that the former owners have their lands—or parts of them—reinstated and/or that they receive compensation for their losses. There is also a new land-owning generation that has a modern approach to agriculture and is skilled at effective farm management.

Farming, is the pulse of Alentejo, and the lives of its people revolve around the seasons. Aside from Évora the towns are small and the rest of the population is scattered in hamlets linked to farms. Secondary schools are restricted to the larger towns; in the more remote areas the general practice among young people is to leave school early to work in the fields.

Throughout the year, but particularly at harvest time, you will see the fieldworkers making their way to and from work on foot, by bicycle or crammed into open-topped trucks. Most rural *Alentejanos* adopt the traditional dress: black wide-brimmed hats for both men and women, black trousers, waistcoats, jackets and white collarless shirts for men, black shawls and thick black skirts for women under which are worn layers of petticoats. Neckerchiefs for extra

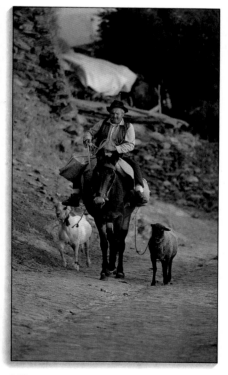

protection against sun and dust are loosely knotted around the men's necks, while women favor head-squares worn under their hats. The faces of the old *Alentejanos* are extraordinary—leathery skins baked a deep brown, furrowed like tree bark and colored like walnuts.

One of the traditional pastimes for the menfolk is a wild boar hunt. These animals are most populous near the Spanish border. It really is a case of out of the frying pan and into the fire for the poor creatures. They cross the border from Spain to flee the Spanish hunters, only to find themselves hunted here, although to a less extent. Hunting is especially popular in the open Alentejo terrain, and during the season (October-February), one will inevitably see men out with their shotguns, pouches and a gaggle of dogs.

Singing and dancing is popular across the length and breadth of Portugal, and the Alentejo does its share. Here, the folk songs are the domain of the men. The songs are slow, rather melancholic, but of a completely different style than the haunting *fado* heard elsewhere. A slow tempo is set by the stamping of the men's feet as they sing in chorus, swaying to the rhythm by the time they reach the end of the song. A performance is well worth listening to; ask at an Alentejo tourist office about where to hear one.

Évora is the largest and most important of all the Alentejo towns. It is a superb city, full of fascinating sights, all of which are in a good state of preservation. They are likely to remain so as the entire city has been proclaimed a historical monument by the international preservation organization World Patrimony, therefore qualifying for its financial aid.

It takes about two and a half hours to drive from Lisbon to Évora, and a tour could be comfortably managed as a day trip. But that would not leave time to see the lovely towns and villages along the way, nor those within striking distance of the city. To base yourself in Évora is easy; there are plenty of small guest houses and hotels.

To reach Évora leave Lisbon via the April 25th Bridge and head down towards the *autostrada* for Setúbal, and then turn eastwards on the N4 for Évora. You will not need a welcome billboard to tell you that you have just reached the Alentejo; suddenly the roads are wider and less potholed, and you will find yourself at the edge of the rolling plains. Look for the jumbles of twigs on top of the high walls and buildings— homes to the storks that flourish in the

Roadside attractions in Monsaraz

province. As you drive further inland you will also notice the waning breeze and the increase in temperature.

Pegóes is the first small Alentejo town on the route. It's a rather dry, dusty and deserted town nowadays, all of which you observe if you're delayed at the railway crossing there. It once must have been a thriving market town but it appears quite depressed today. A little further along the road is **Vendas Novas**. About the same size as Pegóes, it makes a great contrast. Shady, neat and with an air of affluence, it is not really worth a stop, but it is attractive to view from the car.

Montemor-o-Novo can be seen from quite a distant approach, its ruined medieval castle crowning its low *monte* (hill). The castle ramparts are thought to date back to Roman times. The town is divided into the upper old town and lower new town. As you might expect the old town is the one more interesting to stroll through. It was here that St. John of God (São João de Deus) was born in 1495. He was baptized in the ruined parish church, the only of part of which is still intact is the granite Manueline portal. In the square outside the church is a statue commemorating the saint, a Franciscan monk of great charity and humility. Accord-

ing to legend, he carried a beggar to the hospital one stormy night. Although they hardly boast the population to support them all, the town's religious significance has resulted in the building of five churches, three convents and two monasteries.

Évora: As you enter Évora on the main Lisbon road, there is a small tourist office just before the town's Roman walls. There is a larger tourist office in the center, but at this one you can pick up a street map with suggested walks marked to take in the most important sights. The best place to park is the center of the city at the **Praça do Giraldo**, a large square with arcades on two sides and a 16th-century **church** and fountain at the top end. From this central parking area you can explore the inner city with ease.

The history of Évora can be traced back to the earliest civilizations on the Iberian Peninsula. It derives its name from *Ebora Cerealis*, as it was called during the Luso-Celtic colonization. The Romans later fortified the city and renamed it *Liberalitas Julia*. It thrived under the Romans, who elevated it to the status of *municipium*, which gave it the right to mint its own currency. Its prosperity declined somewhat when it was conquered by the Visigoths, but rekindled

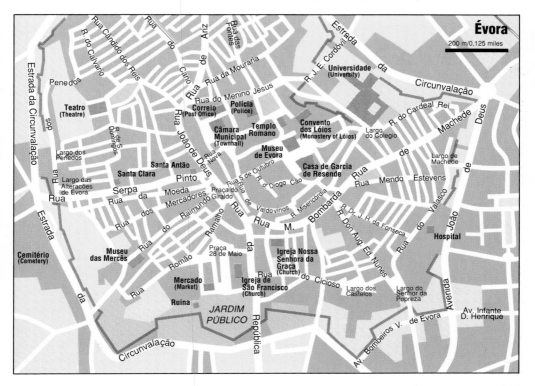

under the long Moorish rule (early 8th century to 1165). Much of the architecture reflects the Moorish presence with arched, twisting alleyways, tiled patios and potted plants filling terraces.

Évora was liberated from the Moors by a Christian knight, Geraldo Sem-Pavor (Gerald the Fearless), in 1165. He did so in the name of King Afonso I, the first king of Portugal.

For the next 400 years Évora enjoyed great importance and wealth. It was the preferred residence of the kings of the Burgundy and Avis dynasties. During these centuries the courts attracted famed artists, dramatists, humanists and academics to Évora. Great churches, monasteries, houses and convents were built. The splendor culminated in 1559 when the last of the Avis kings, Henrique—who was also the Archbishop of Évora—founded a Jesuit university there. In 1580, following the annexation of Portugal by Spain, Évora's glory waned. The Castilians paid little attention to it, except as an agricultural and trading center. Even after Portuguese independence was restored in 1640, Évora did not regain its former brilliance.

The oldest sight in Évora is the so-called **Temple of Diana**, which dates back to the 2nd or 3rd century A.D. To reach it walk down Rua 5 de Outobro, off Praça do Giraldo. The temple is presumed to have been built as a place of imperial worship, dedicated, perhaps, to the goddess Diana. The Corinthian columns are granite, their bases and capitals hewn from local marble. The facade and mosaic floor have disappeared completely, but the six rear columns and those at either side are still intact. The temple was converted into a fortress during the Middle Ages and then used as a slaughterhouse until 1870. Although not an elegant role, this use saved the temple from being torn down; its brick walls helped preserve the columns as well. Until recently, you could actually wander among the columns, but sensibly the temple has been roped off to prevent further wear and tear.

There is a lovely viewpoint just across from the rear of the temple in the shady garden. From here you can look down over the lower town and across the plains: the tiny village of Évoramonte is just visible on the horizon to the northeast.

To the right of the temple is the **Monastery of Lóios** (also known as the church of John the Evangelist). The conventual buildings have been converted into an elegant

A prospect of Évora

pousada but the church is still a public one. Founded in 1485, its style is Romano-Gothic, although all but the doorway in the facade was remodeled after the earthquake in 1755. The nave has an ornate vaulted ceiling and walls lined with beautiful tiles depicting the life of St. Laurence Justinian, dated 1771 and signed by António de Oliveira Bernandes. Guided tours of the church, cloisters and chapterhouse can be taken.

Nearby the temple is **Cathedral** (*Sé*), dedicated to the Virgin Mary. An imposing, austere building, its granite facade was built in the 12th century, also in Romano-Gothic style. Its main portal is flanked by two grand conical towers. These towers are unusual in that they are asymmetric—the glittering blue tiled one is particularly lovely. Both were added in the 16th century.

Before going into the cathedral, take a close look at the main entrance. It is decorated with magnificent 14th-century sculptures of the apostles. The vast broken barrel vaulted ceiling inside is quite stunning; suspended from it are huge chandeliers, their supports appearing to be of interminable length. The cathedral has the most capacious interior in Portugal: its three naves stretch for 70 meters.

Once you've seen the cathedral, it really is worthwhile to pay the nominal sum to see its cloisters, choir stalls and Museum of Sacred Art lodged in the treasury. They are open at the usual visiting times (9 a.m. to midday and from 2 p.m. to 5 p.m., closed Mondays and public holidays).

A short climb up a staircase will take you to the **museum** which contains a beautiful collection of ecclesiastical gold, silver and bejewelled plate, ornaments, chalices and crosses. The Renaissance-style choir stalls, tucked high in the gallery, are fashioned with a delightful series of wooden carvings whose motifs are of both sacred and secular design. Particularly charming are those of day-to-day life: wine pressing, wheat threshing, singing and feasting. From the choir stalls you get a good birds-eye view of the cathedral.

The **cloisters** are 14th-century Gothic—large and imposing in their granite plainness, more awe-inspiring than encouraging of meditative contemplation. Next door to the cathedral is the **Regional Museum**, formerly the Bishop's Palace and now home to a fine collection of paintings, both Portuguese Primitives and Flemish. There is also interesting sculpture, furniture and decoration from local buildings.

14th-century Apostles greet visitors to Évora's Cathedral

More elegant and graceful cloisters are visible at the old **Jesuit University**. You have to follow a short road down to the east of the city to reach it. The marble of the broad **students' cloisters** seems to have aged not at all since the 16th century. The cloisters still maintain the peaceful atmosphere of the serious academic: it's the sort of place that makes you involuntarily drop your voice to a hushed whisper.

The classroom entrances at the far end of the cloister gallery are decorated with *azulejos* representing each of the subjects taught within. If you take a slow walk back up the hill and head for the church of St. Francis (São Francisco), you'll pass by another church—the **Misericórdia**, noted for its 18th-century tiled panels and Baroque relief work. Behind it stands the **Soure Mansion**, a 15th-century Manuline house formerly part of the Palace of Infante D. Luis.

As you walk, take notice of the houses. Nearly all have attractive, narrow, wrought-iron balconies at the base of tall rectangular windows. A rather odd tradition in Évora is that visiting dignitaries are welcomed by a vivid display of brightly colored bedspreads hung from these balconies. A forerunner to bunting, perhaps?

When you reach the Misericórdia Church, take a brief detour of the **Portas de Moura Square**. The gates there mark the fortified northern entrance to the city, the delimitation of construction and safety as it was in medieval times. This picturesque square is dominated by a Renaissance fountain, built in 1556.

Back on the road again, keep an eye out for the church of **Nossa Senhora da Graca** (Our Lady of Grace), just off the Rua Miguel Bombarda. Built in granite, it is a far cry from the austerity of the cathedral. A later church (16th century), its influence is strongly Italian Renaissance. Note the four huge figures supporting globes which represent the children of grace.

A mother's curse: The church of **São Francisco**—from the late 15th or early 16th century, has a remarkable chapel, the **Casa dos Ossos**. This bizarre and macabre room is entirely lined and decorated with bones of some 5,000 people. It was "created" in the 16th century by a Franciscan monk. At the entrance lies the inviting Latin inscription: *"We bones lie here waiting for yours."*

The skulls and bones have not merely been placed in a random fashion; a lot of creative thought has gone into their placement! Hung at the far end of the chapel are

One of the indignities of being a statue in Évora's public gardens

the corpses of a man and a small child. These centuries-old bodies are said to be the victims of a dying wife and mother's curse. Father and son were supposed to have made her life a misery—their ill treatment killed her. On her death bed she cursed them, swearing that their flesh would never fall from their bones. The corpses are far from fleshy, but there is plenty of leathery substance attached to their bones.

Braids of human hair dating to the last century are hung at the entrance of the chapel, *ex-votos* put there by young brides. The **chapterhouse** that links the chapel to the church is lined with *azulejos* depicting scenes from the Passion and contains an *altar dos promessas* (altar of promises) on which are laid wax effigies of parts of the body, particularly arms, legs, and feet. The ailing, or their friends and relatives, go to the altar and pray for a cure. If it comes, then an effigy of the cured part is placed in thanks on the altar.

Évora's **public gardens** near the church provide a very pleasant walk; if you're lucky you may catch the band playing on the park's old-fashioned wrought-iron bandstand. A delightful **palace** stands in the park, that of King Manuel (1495-1521). Luso-Moorish in style, it has typical paired

windows in horseshoe arches. Exhibitions are held quite regularly in the long Ladies' Gallery.

During the last week of June, Évora is filled with visitors who come to enjoy the annual **Feira de São João**. This huge fair fills the grounds opposite the public gardens. If you don't mind the crowd then you'll enjoy what is offered: a local handicraft market, an agricultural hall, a display of local light industry, the general hodge-podge of open-air stalls selling everything, folk singing and dancing, and special restaurants serving typical cuisine.

If you're visiting Évora during the summer and want to cool off, go to one of the local swimming pools on the edge of town. Although well-patronized because they are inexpensive, they are spotlessly clean, with plenty of lawn on which to stretch out and dry. A cafe serves all kinds of snacks and drinks.

If you're not intent on going inside Évora's monuments, a night stroll displays its exterior architecture admirably. Nearly all the monuments are floodlit until midnight, and the winding narrow streets are very inviting on a balmy evening.

The Alentejo has a number of megalithic monuments scattered across its plains, and some of the most important are just outside Évora. The best preserved and most significant stone circle, or cromlech, on the Iberian Peninsula is seven miles (12 km) west of the city, close to the hill of Herdade dos Almendres. **Cromoleque de Almendres** has 95 standing stones.

Next to the Agricultural Department of the University of Évora in Valverde, which neighbors Évora, stands the largest dolmen on the peninsula. The **Zambujeiro Dolmen** stands some 17 feet (5 meters) high with a 10 feet (three meter) diameter and is dated about 3,000 B.C.

Estremoz is a lovely town steeped in a history which goes back to the Middle Ages. Although much smaller than Évora, it has its own fascinating monuments worth a few hours' visit.

The old part of this sleepy town, crowned by a castle now converted into a *pousada*, was founded by King Afonso III in 1258. The monument was a residence of King Dinis in the 1300s and it is with him that it is most often associated. His wife, the sainted Queen Isabel of Aragon is honored by a statue in the main square, and a **chapel** dedicated to her can be seen in one of the castle towers. To view this chapel ask either at the *pousada* or at the museum on the main square.

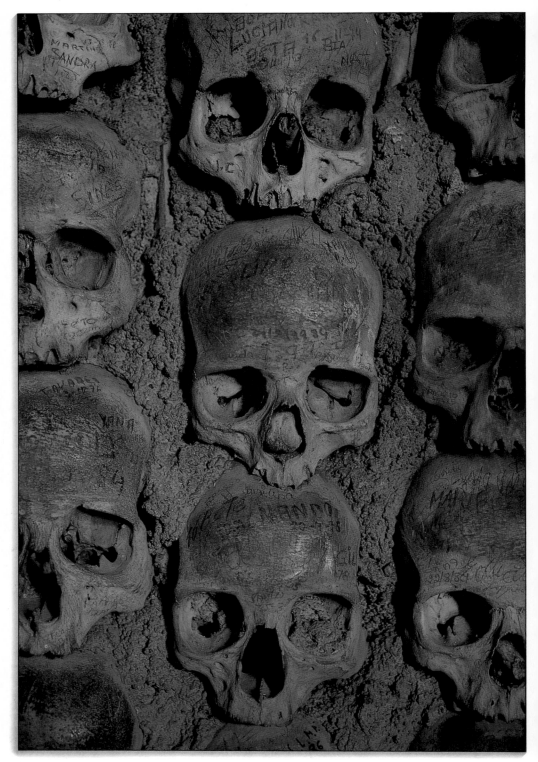

154

The chapel is at the top of a narrow staircase; small, and highly decorated, it is where she is said to have died. (Mind you, she is said to have died in the nearby **King's Audience Chamber** as well.) The chapel walls are adorned with 18th century *azulejos* and paintings depicting scenes from the Queen's life. The most famous incident, represented here, is the "miracle of the roses." Isabel was a very charitable woman, sometimes more so than her husband might have wished. Once when Isabel was distributing alms to the poor King Dinis came upon her. She hastily hid the coins in the folds of her skirts, but the king demanded to see what the gown held. When Isabel spread her skirt, the gold miraculously had turned to roses. Behind the altar is a tiny, plain room bearing a smaller altar on which the Estremoz faithful have placed their *ex votos*.

The most impressive part of the castle is the wonderful 13th-century **keep** which is entered via the *pousada*. To get to the top you need to be fairly fit—or make a slow and steady ascent. The second floor has an octagonal room with trefoil windows. From the top platform there is a breathtaking view. The red rooftops contrast beautifully with the whitewashed houses and the green plains beyond, much of which are planted with rows of olive trees.

Across the square from the *pousada* is the **Royal Palace of D. Dinis**. It must have been a beautiful palace, but all that remains standing after a gun-powder explosion in the palace arsenal in 1698 is the Gothic colonnade and star-vaulted chamber (D. Dinis' Audience Chamber). It is used nowadays for exhibitions by local artists. Having survived the narrow roads and hairpin bends on the drive up to the castle, the descent should seem easier. The upper town is connected to the lower town by 14th-century ramparts and fairly modern buildings: the wrought-iron balconies here are decorated with colored tiles.

Estremoz is famed for its pottery jugs and figurines, which can be bought throughout the town, but they are perhaps most attractively displayed at the Saturday markets **main square** of the lower town. If you're a lover of Portuguese wines then you're likely to be familiar with the name **Borba**, a co-operative wine company which produces a good red wine. The wines take their name from the ancient village of Borba, said to date back to the Gauls and Celts. There is not much to see there now except for a splendid fountain, **Fonte das Bicas**, built in 1781 from local white marble.

Just down the road from Borba is **Vila Viçosa**, the previously mentioned seat of the Dukes of Bragança. Vila Viçosa comes as quite a surprise after the Moorish-influenced towns perched on the top of hills. The town is cool and shady, its large main square (**Praça da República**) is filled with orange trees, and elsewhere there are lemon trees and lots of flowers. *Viçosa* means shade, and its elegant boulevards are a pleasure to walk through.

A lovely, if rather overgrown medieval **castle** overlooks the town square. It is very peaceful there, the only sound is the cooing of the white fan-tail doves which nest in the ramparts. The drawbridge is lowered across the moat (now dry), and the first floor has been converted into a modest archaeological **museum**.

Vila Viçosa is best known for the **Ducal Palace**, an enormous and elegant building which is open to the public for guided tours. Its furniture, painting and tapestries are very fine, and worth an hour or so. The palace also contains an excellent collection of 17th- to 19th-century coaches.

The palace overlooks a square in which stands a bronze statue of João IV, the first king of the Bragança dynasty. To the north of the square—on the Lisbon road—is a curious edifice, the **Knot Gate**, part of the

Left, the macabre **Casa dos Ossos**, embellished by Évora's teens. Right, the 16th-century **Porta dos Nos** at Vila Viçosa

16th-century town walls. It is so called after its design: the stone archway appears to be roped together.

Between Évora and Estremoz stands **Évoramonte**, a village at the foot of a recently renovated **castle**. It was in this village that the convention ending the civil war was signed on May 26, 1834. A plaque commemorating the event is placed over the house where the historic signing took place.

Évoramonte is a particularly high hill and the views from there are quite remarkable: well worth the detour and the clamber up to the top of the somewhat bland, if well-kempt castle. From there you can see for miles and miles.

Close to the Spanish border, about 30 miles (50 km) from Estremoz, is the strongly fortified town of **Elvas**. Founded by the Romans, it was long occupied by the Moors and finally liberated from them in 1230—nearly 100 years later than Lisbon.

The town was of great strategic importance during the wars of independence with Spain in the mid-17th century. The fortress of **Santa Luzia**, south of town, was built by a German, Count Lippe, for the purpose of repelling the Spanish. The older **castle**, above the town, was originally a Roman fortress, rebuilt by the Moors and enlarged in the 15th century.

If you walk around the ramparts you cannot fail to be impressed by the effective engineering which completely encircled the town. The town itself is particularly attractive, from the triangular "square" of Santa Clara, with its 16th-century marble pillory, to the main square, **Praça da República**, with its geometrically patterned mosaic paving.

Elvas has a nice *pousada* which used to have one of the most famous restaurants in the country. One of its specialties nowadays is a *Bacalhau Dourado*—slivers of salted cod fried with thinly-chipped potatoes, onions, olives and scrambled egg.

An interesting history surrounds the **Amoreira Aquaduct**, designed by a great 15th-century architect, Francisco de Arruda. It took nearly 200 years to complete, all five miles (7.5 km) and 843 arches of it. Its cost was borne by the people of Elvas under a special tax named the *Real de Agua*.

Handwoven rugs used to be manufactured throughout the Alentejo, but nowadays the small town of **Reguengos** is the only place where they are still made, in a factory that has been using the same looms for the past 150 years. Reguengos is another nucleus of megalithic stones and dolmens,

A sleepy afternoon in Vila Viçosa

156

found in several sites near the town.

Up the road from Reguengos is the delightful walled town of **Monsaraz**, so small it can easily be seen on foot—leave the car at the fortified gate. Its proximity to the Spanish border combined with its height made it of strategic importance. Once the threat from Spain had gone, however, Reguengos became gradually more influential. Monsaraz relaxed into a charming, peaceful village. Its main street, **Rua Direita,** is all 16th- and 17th-century architecture, yet, the town maintains a distinctly medieval feel.

The countryside surrounding the capital of the Upper Alentejo, **Portalegre**, is rather different from that in the lower lands. This area is in foothills of the Serra de São Mamede, and the cooler and slightly more humid climate makes it much greener.

Quite a large town by Alentejo standards, Portalegre is unusual in that it is not built on top of a hill. It is built on the site of an ancient ruined settlement called Ammaia. In the mid-13th century, King Afonso III instructed that a new city was to be built and called Portus Alacer: Portus for the customs gate which was to process Spanish trade and Alacer (which meant joy) because of its pleasing setting.

King Dinis ensured that the town was fortified in 1290 (although only a few of those ruins can be seen today) and João III gave it the status of the city in 1550.

The lofty 16th-century interior of the **cathedral** (*Sé*) is late-Renaissance style. The side altars have fine wooden retables and 16th-and 17th-century paintings of Italian style. The sacristy contains lovely blue-and- white *azulejo* panels from the 18th century depicting the life of the Virgin Mary and the flight to Egypt. The cathedral's facade is 18th-century, dominated by marble columns, granite pilasters and wrought iron balconies.

Portalegre's affluence began in the 16th century, when its tapestries were in great demand. Continued prosperity followed in the next century with the establishment of silk mills. Don't miss the opportunity to see the tapestry workshops in the former Jesuit Monastery. The looms are still worked by hand, following modern as well as traditional designs.

Portalegre was home to one of Portugal's most famous poets: José Régio (1901 - 1969). His house has been opened as a museum. Of particular interest is his collection of regional folk and religious art.

Also of note is the 17th-century "Yellow

Silhouettes in Monsaraz

Palace," formally called the **Palácio dos Albrancalhas.** The ornate ironwork is remarkable.

Marvão must be one of the most spectacular sights of the Alentejo. About 15 miles (25 km) north of Portalegre, it is a medieval fortified town perched on one of the São Mamede peaks. Its altitude (2,830 feet/862 meters) affords it an uninterrupted view across the Spanish frontier. The precipitous drop on one side made it inaccessible to invaders and an ideal defensive situation.

At this height the land is barren and craggy. The seemingly impenetrable **castle** was built in the 13th century from the local gray granite.

Clinging to the foot of the castle is the tiny village, a few twisting alleyways flanked by red-roofed whitewashed houses. Close by the church of **Espirito Santo**, on the street of the same name, is an austere Baroque granite **fountain**. On the same street is the sober-looking **Governor's House**: its only decoration is two magnificent 17th-century wrought-iron balconies.

On the road to Castelo de Vide are the ruins of the Roman settlement of **Medobriga.** Many artifacts have been found here, although most were removed to Lisbon. Completing the triangle of noteworthy upper Alentejo towns is **Castelo de Vide**, a delightful town built under the shade of an elongated medieval castle. The whole is situated on the summit of a foothill on the northern *serra*.

Castelo de Vide is a spa town. You can drink its curative waters from the plastic bottles in which it is sold in the supermarkets, or sip from one of the 300 fountains located in the town and environs. Perhaps its prettiest outlet is the quadrangled, covered fountain (**Fonte da Vila**) set in the small square below the Jewish Quarter. The Barque fountain has a pyramid roof supported by six marble columns. The central urn is carved with figures of boys and the water spills from four spouts.

Near Castelo de Vide you will find still more megalithic stones: these *Pedras Talhas* are everywhere, standing in fields, open scrubland or in local villages. The town itself was first a Roman settlement. Alongside it ran the major Roman road which traversed the Iberian Peninsula. The settlement was sacked by the Vandals at the beginning of the 4th century; occupied by the Moors during their domination of the southern part of the peninsula; and fortified by the Portuguese in 1180.

The rooftops of Marvão

As in nearly all fortified Alentejo towns, Castelo de Vide has two very distinct faces. The first is the older one, situated next to the castle. The most interesting and picturesque is the medieval **Jewish Quarter** (Judiaria). This host of back alleys, cobbled streets and whitewashed houses is splashed with green, as potted plants sprout their tendrils from every available niche, windowsill and step. Notice the doors: this section of Castelo de Vide has the most and best-preserved stone Gothic doorways in Portugal.

You don't see many young people here; the majority of the inhabitants appear to be old people who sit in the doorways of their homes calmly watching the world go by. Further down the hill is the newer part of town: essentially 17th- and 18th-century buildings with wider, less steep streets, more space, more order and more elegance. On the main square (**Praça D. Pedro V**) stands the grandiose 18th-century **parish church** and the old town hall (**Paços de Concelho**), remarkable for the huge 18th-century wrought-iron gate securing the main entrance.

Nisa is a small, rather spacious, town slightly north of Castelo de Vide. It has the mandatory medieval **castle**, walls and an unusual squat, round-towered **chapel**.

Homemade cheese is Nisa's speciality.

Some 15 miles (26 km) south of Nisa on the road to Estremoz is **Crato**, best known for the Brotherhood of Hospitaler—later known as the Knights of St. John—who were installed there. The main square is dominated by a splendid 15th-century stone veranda (**Varanda do Grão-Prior**), which is all that survives of the former priors' residence. Two royal marriages took place in this town. The first was that of Manuel I, who married Leonor of Spain in 1518 (his third marriage). The second was seven years later when King João III married Catarina of Spain.

Further south, in countryside filled with olive groves stands **Alter do Chão**, a medieval town interesting for its equine traditions. It is from here that the Alter Real horse takes its name. Based on Andalusian stock, the Alter stud was founded in the mid-1700s by the Bragança family. The horse thrived until the Napoleonic Wars when the best horses were stolen and the royal stables abolished.

Unspoiled beaches: An area of the Alentejo overlooked by most tourists is its coastline. If you like unspoiled cliffs and beaches, quiet roads and sleepy villages, then you'll love the area and hope that no

one else discovers it. However, with the Algarve becoming more built up and crowded it probably is only a matter of time before the property developers creep up the coast. It borders on the open Atlantic and the ocean is therefore much rougher than on the south coast. But there are plenty of sheltered bays for swimming, although the water is chilly. And it's wonderful just to watch the waves crashing against the cliffs.

The Alentejo coast is not renowned for its nightlife. Bars, discos, and fancy restaurants simply do not exist; nor do large hotels, except at Vila Nova de Milfontes. There are campsites, however, and all the villages have at least one *pensão*. You'd better bring along your phrase book. Where tourists are rare, so are natives who speak English.

Access to the coast is easy; in fact, the coastal highway was the main north-south route until the faster inland road was built. Keep on the main Algarve road until you reach Grandola, then take the turn for the quaint town of **Santiago do Cacém**, which is crowned by a castle built long ago by the Knights Templar. From there it's just a short hop to the Alentejo's largest coastal town, **Sines**.

Sines is not what you'd call a beauty spot,

but you may find it interesting as an exercise in misguided expansionist idealism. For centuries Sines was a pretty fishing village, known for being the birthplace of Vasco da Gama. The old part is still picturesque; but what surrounds it is horrible.

During the Caetano regime it was decided to build a massive oil refinery to process the oil from the hundreds of tankers which were expected to port there. They didn't. Sines was left with an ugly white elephant which dominates the town. It functions, as does a large power station on the northbound approach, but between them they produce pervasive smells of gas and chemicals and make the area look like some futuristic industrial forest.

To forget the ugliness of Sines, go and clear your lungs at the lovely village of **Porto Corvo**. The road which takes you there is tree-lined and virtually traffic-free. Several tracks lead from the main road down to shingly beaches. Porto Corvo is a tiny little village, with cobbled streets swept scrupulously clean. The main square, grandly named **Largo Marquês de Pombal**, is very small, bordered by homes and the tiny parish church. A few small trees and plentiful benches surround the square. Down by the sea you can find shops, cafes

Cork trees on the Alentejo plain

and a restaurant.

Just off the coast of Porto Corvo is the fortified **Ilha do Pessageiro** (Peach Tree Island), which in bygone days provided protection from raids by Dutch and Algerian pirates.

Some nine miles (15 km) down the road from Porto Corvo is the little village of Cercal, and here is the turn for **Vila Nova de Milfontes**, the busiest of the coast's resorts. If ever there was a perfect seaside town then Vila Nova de Milfontes is it. The only time it gets really busy is in high summer when many *Alentejanos* and *Lisboners* come for their annual holiday at the large campsite there.

Again, there is little nightlife but there are a few more seafood restaurants and a small beautifully kept hotel which overlooks the sea. This is converted from an ivy-clad fortress—drawbridge and all, its only drawback being that you have to pay a steep price for room and three full meals.

Vila Nova de Milfontes is set at the mouth of the Mira River, and this provides miles of golden beaches and calm sea. There is beach around the mouth which then opens out onto the Atlantic proper. Park out at the headland overlooking the ocean, and you can turn back to see the quaint town to your left, the winding river and the hills beyond—all very idyllic. If you are planning a day or two on this coast, then here is the place to stay as you can rent an apartment or stay at a guest house, the campsite, the castle/hotel, or a more modern, larger hotel complex just outside the town at Moinho Asneira.

Almograve and **Zambujeira** offer more stunning, deserted beaches and some fine clifftop viewpoints across the basalt cliffs to the sea. Between these two beaches is another one, **Cabo do Girão**. But it is naval property and access is prohibited.

If you have some extra time and feel like moving inland from here, in the lower Alentejo is the pretty village of **Odemira**, set on the banks of the Mira River for which it's named. It is a verdant town full of flowers and trees, so green that you are apt to forget that it is in the Alentejo. Water, water everywhere can also be found up at the nearby **Barragem de Santa Clara**, a huge dam which feeds the Mira as well as the local water supply. You might take some time and indulge in water sports here.

Ourique is a charming little agricultural town north of the dam. On its surrounding fields (**Campo do Ourique**) are grown fruit, olive and cork trees. These fields, however, have seen far more than just farm-

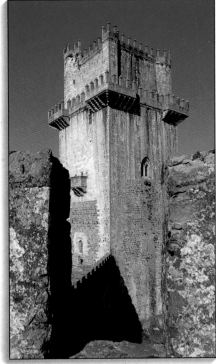

ing. In the hamlet of **Atalaia**, archaeologists excavated an extraordinary Bronze Age burial mound, and it was on those fields, thousands of years later in 1139, that a significant battle was fought between the Portuguese and the Moors. Afonso Henriques had just been crowned the first King of Portugal. The victory on this battlefield strengthened his determination to rout the Moors from Portuguese soil, and gave a tremendous boost to his army's morale.

The capital of lower Alentejo, **Beja**, is possibly the hottest town (in air temperature terms) in Portugal during the height of summer. It takes about three hours by car from Lisbon and an hour or so from Évora. A town existed on the present-day site as early as 48 B.C. and when Julius Caesar made peace with the Lusitanians the settlement was named after this event, *Pax Julia*. During the 400-year Moorish occupation, the name was adulterated to Baju, then Baja, until it finally became known as Beja.

Beja is now a fairly prosperous town, its income derived from trade in olive oil and wheat. It has a large German Air Force base where fighter pilots are trained. Beja is not a beautiful town overall, but it does have some interesting sights. The 15th century Convent of Conception (**Convento da Conceição**) is a beautiful building and a fine example of the transition between Gothic and Manueline architecture. The Baroque chapel is lined with carved, gilded woodwork. The chapterhouse which leads to the cloisters is tiled with superb Hispanic-arabic *azulejos* dating back to the 1500s. Their quality is rivalled only by those in the Royal Palace at Sintra. The convent also houses the **regional museum**.

The small and modest **Santo Amaro** is the oldest church in Beja. It is thought to date back to the 7th century and is a rare example of Visigothic architecture. Beja's 13th-century castle still stands, and its castellated walls run around the town perimeter. At one corner is the tall keep which contains a **military museum**, and a narrow balcony on each side from which you can enjoy a remarkable view across the plains.

Driving in to **Serpa** is—as with so many small Alentejo towns—like driving into a time warp. The **castle** and fortified walls were built at the command of King Dinis. A difference here from other 13th-century walls is that these have an aqueduct built into them.

A well-preserved gate is the **Portas de Beja**, which, along with the rest of the walls, were almost sold by the town council in the latter half of the 19th century. Cooler heads prevailed and the walls were saved, though a great part of them had been destroyed in 1707 when the Duke of Ossuna and his army occupied the town during the War of the Spanish Succession.

There are several churches worth seeing, as well as the delightfully cool and elegant palace belonging to the Count of Ficalho. The **Paços dos Condes de Ficalho** was built in the 16th century. It has a majestic staircase and lovely tiles. The present Marquise, incidentally, is the granddaughter of Portugal's great 19th-century novelist Eça de Queiroz.

The **Guadiana** is a lovely river. It's the most peaceful of Portugal's three big rivers (the others being the Tagus and Douro), but an exception is at Pulo do Lobo near **Mértola**. This is a stretch of high and wild rapids, which can be reached by road and is worth a visit if you're in the area. Mértola, an ancient fortified town, is also worth a brief stop, set in the confluence between the Guadiana and the Oeiras Rivers. The **parish church** was originally a mosque. To see it ask at the house nearby. It is one of the few mosques in Portugal to have survived virtually intact.

The Alentejo's culinary specialities should not be missed. Try *sopa alentejana*—a filling soup of bread, lots of coriander (a herb used a great deal in Alentejo cooking), garlic and poached eggs; or *sopa da cação*, which is a rich fish soup. One of the classic meat dishes is *carne de porco à alentejana*—chunks of pork seasoned in wine, coriander and onions and served with clams. Two much heavier but delicious stewed dishes are *ensopada de cabrito*—kid boiled with potatoes and bread until the meat is just about falling off the bone, and *favada de caça*, a game stew of hare, rabbit, partridge or pigeon with broad beans. The best Alentejo cheese comes from Serpa. Made from sheep and goat milk it has a creamy texture and a strong, slightly piquant flavor. Évora has its own goat, cheese which is hard, salty and slightly acid. It is preserved in jars filled with olive oil.

Alentejo is a demarcated wine region. Its reds are full-bodied and mature well in the bottle. Most towns have their own cooperative winery from which you can buy stocks at rock-bottom prices. Most restaurants have a modestly priced cooperative house wine. To appreciate really good Alentejo wines, try the reds from the Reguengos cooperative or those from Quinta do Carmo in Estremoz (Borba region). White wines from the Vidigueira cooperative are far superior to any other Alentejo whites.

Capela de São Gens in Serpa

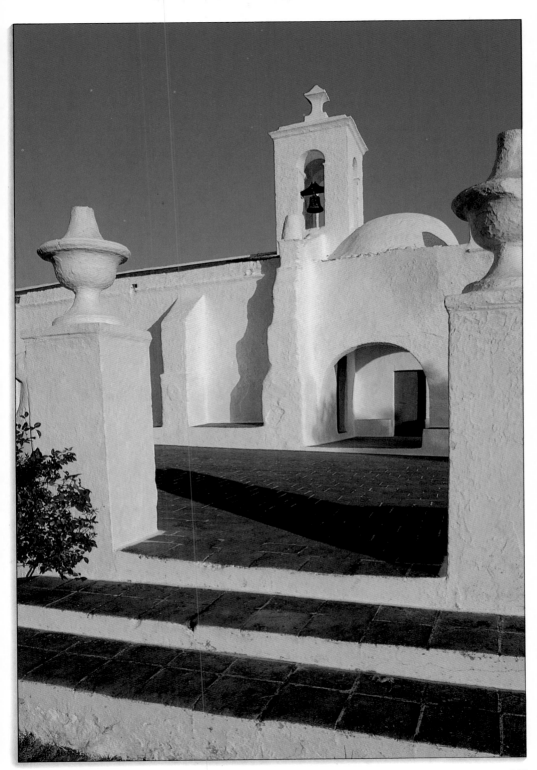

TREES OF THE ALENTEJO

The Portuguese are a people of the earth: they describe their country as garden sown on the edge of the sea; they weave their ancient legends around roses and almond blossoms; and a flower—the red carnation—is the symbol for the 1974 Revolution, which restored democracy.Many people still cherish the flowers, now pressed and dried.

But the land that the Portuguese have inherited does not make cultivation easy. Nowhere in the country is this more true than in the toilsome soil of the large, parched plains and craggy coastline of the Alentejo.

argue that the labor expended on raising sparse crops from barren soil could be turned to more productive account by using the land in a different way. The agronomists' answer to Portugal's farming problems is a return to the country's historic wealth—forests.

Centuries ago dense oak woods covered most of Portugal. They have largely disappeared. One third of the country, about 7.5 million acres, is now forested. Some experts believe the Portuguese economy would benefit greatly if the extension of forest was almost doubled so that trees covered 59 percent of the country. Massive

Alentejo balconies brim with hydrangeas and the white walls of houses are cloaked with purple bougainvillea in the late summer. But Portugal must work its land to produce useful crops, not decorative blossoms.

Almost a third of Portuguese workers are engaged in farming, three times the European average. But poor soil, a difficult climate and out-moded methods mean that most crops yield less than half the average per acre in Western and Eastern Europe. Struggling farmers have to culti-vate every square inch of land to earn their live-lihoods.

About half the surface of Portugal is devoted to farming. But experts estimate that because of the poor quality of the soil only half of that land is really suited to agriculture. Economic planners

planting projects are underway to achieve this aim, such as a plan funded by the World Bank to reforest a huge area of central Portugal north of the Tagus River. Similar plans will surely be instituted in the Alentejo before long.

Even now trees big business. The forestry industry employs some 100,000 workers in a sector that earns $1 billion a year in export reve-nue. Pine, said in Portugal to be of use to man from cradle to coffin, is used to produce timber for furniture and construction, as well as resin for pitch and turpentine. Pine accounts for about 40 percent of the country's wooded land. Driving through pine forests, you will see metal cups strapped below holes to collect sap. The openings are cut in the trunk with a special long-bladed axe. Each mature tree is tapped for resin once or twice in each of the last two years before it is felled and each tapping takes about a month, during which the resin is collected three times.

The main product of Portuguese forests is pulp used for manufacturing paper and cardboard. Pine has lost its place as the mainstay of the pulp, industry as demand grows for the short fiber pulp produced by the eucalyptus. The Australian eucalyptus, whose distinctive aroma fills the air, was introduced into Portugal in 1856. Today it accounts for 10 percent of all forested land. Eucalyptus oil also is used for various pharmaceutical products.

Pines and eucalyptus are found in many parts of Portugal, including, of course, the Alentejo. But other products are more specifically characteristic of this province. Perhaps most distinctive of all are sprawling cork-oak trees with their raw, stripped trunks spread over the grasslands in thousands.

More than half the cork in the world, from stoppers in bottles of the finest champagne to the linings of spacecraft, is supplied from these fields where pigs, turkeys and sheep amble between the trees, feeding on the acorns as the bark slowly matures to readiness over the decades.

Pulp manufacturers are lobbying to extend the cultivation of the eucalyptus, or gum tree. Their main concern is expediency, as the eucalyptus grows to maturity in 12 to 15 years, compared with 40 to 50 years for pine, and is hardy enough to grow on poor, sandy soil.

But some farmers oppose the spread of eucalyptus groves that they claim rapaciously draw up water needed for other crops if not managed correctly. The anti-eucalyptus lobby currently holds sway, with official planting programs for the tree amounting to about half those of pine.

Left, some of the groves that produce the piquant Portuguese olive oil. Above, the distinctively twisted and knotted cork trees

Cultivating cork is not a trade for the impatient. From the acorn, the spreading tree with its heavy, twisted branches grows for about 25 years before it is ready to yield its bark. The branches of shiny dark-green evergreen leaves with a grayish underside are carefully pruned to admit the sunlight and make the bark accessible to the cutters. What underbrush there is on the plains is periodically burned away.

At the height of summer, when the trunk has shrunk away from the gnarled, dull-gray outer skin, workmen skillfully begin the stripping. Using special axes ground to razor sharpness, they first make horizontal cuts around the circumference of the trunk and the lower branches. These are linked with vertical incisions and the roll of bark is stripped off, leaving the rich red, bare trunk beneath. Machines cannot replace the expertise of the strippers, who cut the bark with such skill that the tender trunk below is left undamaged.

The first stripping yields virgin cork that is used for specialized purposes such as life-jackets. Each tree gives between 60 and 100 pounds of cork at a cutting. It will be another nine years before a sufficiently thick layer of bark has grown back for another crop. A tree is usually stripped 12 to 15 times in a life of around 200 years. After sorting, the cork strips are piled high on trucks and transported to one of the 700 processing plants across the country. They are dried for up to a year to remove any viscous residue that might remain in the millions of minute, air-filled cells that make cork so light. An improperly dried cork could doom a vintage port! The strips are then

boiled in water for a day in huge copper vats to bond the cells and make the cork more flexible. The strips are smoothed out into flat sheets and dried again in the sun.

Cork is graded into almost 50 different categories that mark them for a huge variety of uses including heat insulation, floats, tiles, soundproofing, containers for radioactive materials, badminton shuttlecocks, table tennis bats and, of course, corks—or bottle stoppers as they are known in the cork trade. Workmen who manually punch out thousands of stoppers a day from strips of cork are now being replaced by machines. But mechanization cannot match their skills for crafting the perfect fits that are needed to cork fine wines and champagnes. Nor are artificial materials,which do not allow wine to breathe,

ever likely to replace bottle corks.

The Alentejo produces around 2,000 tons of cork a year but the tree, a *sobreiro* in Portuguese, also grows in the Algarve and parts of the Ribatejo. Portugal earns more than $200 million dollars a year in exports from this constantly expanding sector.

Older still than the cork oaks of the Alentejo are many of the olive trees found mainly in the Alentejo but also across all of southern and central Portugal and along the Douro Valley in the north. Experts believe some Portuguese olives are as old as the trees in the Garden of Gethsemane, shown by carbon-14 tests to date from the time of Christ. Whatever their age, the lovely groves of evergreen olives rising on gentle, grassy slopes with their gnarled trunks, tangled branches and dark-green silvery leaves are one of

the strongest visual bonds between Portugal and its Mediterranean neighbors from Spain to the Middle East.

Olive oil, called "the thread of life," is as basic to Portuguese cooking as salt and pepper in other countries. The starting point of most dishes is a *refogado*, or base of chopped onions and garlic browned in olive oil. The oil is also poured onto boiled fish, potatoes and vegetables and into some soups. Much of the olive oil produced in Portugal, which has a slightly more tangy taste than in other countries, is used in the canning of sardines and tuna.

A great deal of labor goes into producing the oil. The tree, which reaches between 10 and 40 feet in height, does not bear fruit during its first 25 years of life, sometimes longer if frost affects its growth. The olives are picked in November, just before they ripen fully, between six and eight months after the tree flowers. Crops are erratic, varying from heavy one year to sparse the next. A white sheet, that was once made of linen but is more often of cotton or plastic today, is spread beneath the tree. The pickers shake the fruit onto the sheet with long poles, then climb into the tree to glean the rest. Today, some farmers use machines that grip the tree trunk in a large clamp and shake it mechanically.

Some olives are preserved in salt water and served as an appetizer or a garnish. Between 20 and 30 percent of the weight of the fresh fruit is oil. Traditionally, this was extracted by grinding the oil between two large stone wheels onto a granite slab. The pulp was then drained through a stack of rope baskets that are pressed so that the

oil most commonly used for cooking. Third pressings are usually refined for industrial uses. Complex methods of repressing and processing are used to produce other grades of oil.

Though the trees of the Alentejo are perhaps not as strikingly exotic as the lovely almond and carob of the Algarve to the south, the landscape is given its unmistakable texture by its own particular trees. The cork and olive lend character—scrappy, smallish, but indomitable—to the land. And there are other native beauties to be found. The *loquat*, another southern tree, is an evergreen of the rose family that originated in China and Japan. You can tell the tree by its stiff leaves and small, fragrant white flowers. The oval yellow, plum-like fruits grow between one and three inches long in large, loose clusters. Eaten raw, the juicy white flesh has a tart but pleasing taste.

oil drips into metal containers of water beneath. The oil was poured off, leaving the impurities in the water. These traditional methods are still used on small farms in many parts of the country, but most farmers today sell their olive crops to cooperatives who use modern, mechanical presses to produce and refine industrial quantities of oil.

Lightweight, dark-green virgin oil of the highest quality is produced from the first pressing. The second pressing delivers a heavier oil, also of excellent quality, that is blended to make the olive

There are other crops, of course, although their roles are minor when compared to the great trees that do so much for the country as a whole. Only vineyards compare in importance nationally, and they are cultivated in every province, including a modest offering from the Alentejo. Vines take three years to bear grapes, and another three to produce mature fruit. Alentejo wines—Redondo, Borba, Beja and Vidigueira—are good. Dark fruity reds and pale, sharp whites, they are generally high in alcohol content. In the alluvial plains, as the Alentejo's rivers near the Atlantic, a fair crop of rice is produced.

Far left, the imposing and aromatic eucalyptus trees. Left, a half-naked cork trunk shorn of its valued bark. Above, Robinson's Cork Factory in Portalegre

The ubiquitous forests of carefully cultivated trees along with the irrepressible wildflowers combine to make the Alentejo a verdant, vibrant province.

COIMBRA

Perched on a hill overlooking the Mondego River, Coimbra is surrounded by breathtakingly beautiful countryside. The city itself is a mixture of ancient and new, rural and urban—a combination that is sometimes jarring but always interesting.

While there are few traces of the Roman occupation, vestiges of the Middle Ages still abound. Turning into some parts of old city is like stepping back in time.

The University is the most stalwart guardian of the past. Students clad in black capes, the traditional academic dress, resemble oversized bats as they flit around town. Note that the bottoms of the capes are slit: the number of slits depends on either academic or romantic prowess, depending on whose story you believe. These capes, by the way, have only recently come back into style, since for a time they were associated with Salazar's New State, and therefore not worn in the years after the Revolution.

In the spring of every year, the University celebrates the *Queima das Fitas*, the "burning of the ribbons," during which graduating students burn the ribbons that they have been wearing on their sleeves. The color of the ribbons depends on which department the students are in. The various celebrations last a week. The grand finale is a large, drunken parade of students that floats through the center of the city. It is the most elaborate academic festival in the country.

Another Coimbran tradition is *fado*. The music is the more serious and intellectual cousin of Lisbon *fado*. The somber tradition of Coimbra *fado*, in fact, requires one to clear one's throat in approval after a rendition, and not applaud. This type of *fado* has a slow, rhythmic beat and is performed only by men, usually graduates of the University.

Although the University has been and remains a great influence on Coimbra life, don't imagine that there's nothing else here. As the country's third-largest city, Coimbra has grown prosperous under the shadow of its ivory tower. It is the center of an agricultural region and has a large market. The students, by the way, are not the only ones in black: it is the traditional dress of many of the rural women who come in to town as well. Coimbra also has its share of manufacturing—fabrics, beer—and a lively handicrafts industry as well.

Roman roots: Coimbra traces its roots to the Roman municipality of *Aeminium*. The city gained in importance as the city of Conimbriga, a few miles south, proved vulnerable to invasion. Convulsions in the empire and various invasions brought an end to Roman rule in the city, and throughout Portugal. The Moors took over in 711, ushering in 300 years of Islamic rule, with a few interruptions. One such interruption occurred in 878 when Afonso III of Asturias and Léon captured the city. But Coimbra was not permanently taken by Christians until 1064.

Coimbra then became a base for the reconquest of other parts of Portugal from the Moors. It was about this time—the 11th century—that the city was originally walled. In the 12th and 13th centuries, Coimbra became the capital of Portugal.

The 12th century was an age of great progress for Coimbra, including plans for a bridge over the Mondego River, and construction of the city's most important monastery, Santa Cruz, which still stands. Both projects were started in 1131. The city was a lively commercial center and included both Jewish and Moorish quarters. Division was not only by religion, but by class as well. Nobles and clergy lived inside the walls; merchants and craft workers lived outside in what is today called the Baixa, the

Preceding pages, a Lusitanian stallion on proud display; a mural in Moita. Left, a Coimbra University student sports the red ribbons of the law school. Right, tomes from Coimbra's library

downtown area.

The University was founded in 1290—not in Coimbra, however, but in Lisbon. In 1308 the University moved to Coimbra, only to return to Lisbon in 1377. These shifts were the result of continual political conflict between the monarchy and the academic leaders. It was not until 1537 that the university settled permanently in Coimbra. A few years later, it moved to its present site at the top of the hill. Since then, the University and its students have been a continual influence on the character and growth of the city.

Most areas of touristic interest are easily reached on foot—that is, if you're willing to do some uphill walking. There is an extensive bus system, although the bus maps are difficult to read. It's probably more trouble than it's worth to have a car within the city, as streets become one-way at frustrating times, and parking is difficult. The old city and the University crown Coimbra's central hill. The Baixa, which is the main shopping district and also quite old, lies at the foot of the hill along the Mondego River. Santa Clara lies across the river.

Old city: Once located inside the city walls, the old city is a tangle of narrow streets and alleys, lined by ancient buildings and filled with squares and patios. If you can ignore the cars, you can look back in time as the historical vistas spread before you. Shortly after the University moved to Coimbra, King João III offered his royal residence to house it, and there, in the heart of the city, it has stayed. Buildings have, of course, been remodeled and added, but the University has preserved its dignified air.

The modern center of the university is the statue of Dom Dinis, founder of the University. Around it are the buildings that house the **Faculties**, as the schools are called, of **Science and Technology, Medicine and Letters,** and the **new library**.

Of more historical interest than these rather stolidly functional buildings is the **Patio das Escolas**, Patio of the Schools. To enter the patio, pass through the 17th-century **Porta Férrea**, a large portal decorated in the Mannerist style. This doorway leads to a large, rather dusty courtyard, which unfortunately now is used as a parking lot. Here are some of the oldest and stateliest buildings of the University.

The figure of João III, who installed the University in Coimbra, still reigns from the center of the patio. Behind him, there is a magnificent view of the river below.

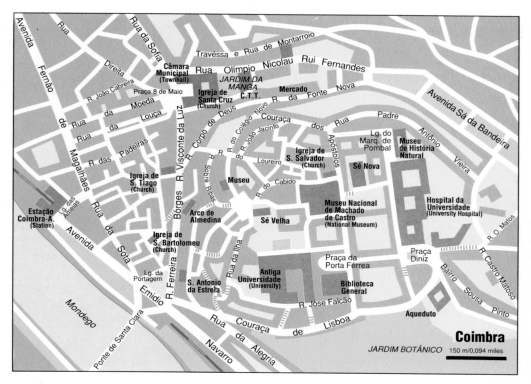

The building in the farthest corner from the Porta Férrea is the old **Library**, the most beautiful of all the university buildings. To enter, knock or ring and wait for the caretaker to open the door (closed for lunch, 12:00 p.m.-2:00 p.m.). The three 18th-century Baroque rooms were built during the reign of João V, whose portrait hangs at the far end. Bookcases, decorated in gilded wood and oriental motifs, reach gracefully to the second floor. Even the ladders are intricately decorated. Note the frescoes on the ceilings. The rare books that fill the cases make up a venerable and quite valuable collection that still is consulted by resident and visiting scholars.

Next door is **St. Michael's Chapel**, begun in 1517, and remodeled in both the 17th and 18th centuries. The chapel is notable for its "carpet" style tiles, the painted ceilings, the altar, and the Baroque organ. There is also a **museum of sacred art**.

The long terraced building to the right of the Porta Férrea houses several interesting rooms. The **Sala dos Capelos**, where many academic ceremonies take place, was probably a reception room in the royal residence. Portraits of the kings of Portugal hang from its walls. Other rooms into which the visitor should wander are the **Rectory** and the **Private Exam Room**.

To the left of the Porta Férrea is São Pedro College, a 16th-century building that has been remodeled several times.

Leaving the University grounds, one finds the nearby **Sé Nova** (new cathedral) whose sand-colored facade presides over an uninteresting square. Built for the Jesuits in 1554, it became a cathedral in 1772. Inside, the altar is of lavish gilded wood. Fourteen of the 16 paintings around the altar are copies of Italian masters.

The **Machado de Castro Museum**, open 10 a.m. to 12 p.m. and 2 pm. to 4:45 p.m., is housed in the old Episcopal Palace and the church of **São João de Almedina,** both 12th-century constructions. The former was the home of the city's early bishops. The museum is built over the ruins of a Roman crypt. It has an excellent collection, both extensive and varied. Unfortunately, much of it is unlabeled, which can be quite frustrating or quite liberating—every artifact can become a source of speculation. What labels there are, are all in Portuguese, and there is no complete catalog in either Portuguese or English. Still, the museum is certainly worth a visit for its collection of Roman artifacts, medieval Portuguese sculpture, a large collection of Portuguese

Coimbra at night

painting from the 15th century onward, gold work, ceramics, tapestries, furniture, and even two coaches. There is also a great view of the Sé Velha (old cathedral) and the roofs of the old city from the courtyard.

The Sé Velha, renovated this century, was built between 1162 and 1184. It served as cathedral until 1772, when the episcopal see was moved to the Sé Nova. The fortress-like exterior is relieved by an arched door and an arched window directly above. The intricate Gothic altar within is of gilded wood, created by two Flemish masters in the 15th and 16th centuries. On the left side, a 16th-century door sports a beautiful sculptured medallion. The door, unfortunately, is in somewhat decrepit condition. There are several **tombs** in the church, including those of 13th-century Bishop Dom Egas Fafes (left of the altar) and Dona Vetaca, a Byzantine princess who lived in the Coimbran court in the 14th century. The **cloister** is early Gothic; construction began in 1218.

Construction on the **Colégio de São Agostino**, on Rua Colégio Novo, began in 1593. The ecclesiastical scholars and monks who first occupied it would be shocked by the goings-on here today, for this pleasant building, lined with pretty *azulejos*, is now home to the University's Psychology Department.

Nearby, on Rua Sub-Ripas, the medieval **Torre** (Tower) **do Anto** was once part of the 12th-century walls of the city. Much later it was the home of poet António Nobre during his undergraduate days. Today it displays and sells traditional crafts from the Coimbra area, sponsored by the city council. The enthusiastic and knowledgeable manager will tell you all about the works in any one of seven languages, including English.

The **Casa de Sub-Ripas**, also on Rua Sub-Ripas, is an aristocratic mansion from the 16th century. Note the archetypal Manueline door and window, but don't bother knocking, it's still a private residence. Here, according to tradition, Maria Teles was murdered by her husband João, eldest son of the tragic Inês de Castro. João had been convinced by Queen Leonor Teles, who was jealous of Maria, that his wife—the queen's sister—was unfaithful.

The **Arco de Almedina**, an entrance to the old city just off of Rua Ferreira Borges (the main downtown street) was also part of the Coimbra walls.

The Baixa is the busy shopping district. **Rua Ferreira Borges**, with many fashionable shops, is the principal street. Other winding streets lead off toward the river. Although this district lay outside the walls of the old city, it dates back to nearly the same time.

The **Santa Cruz Monastery**, in Praça 8 de Maio, off Rua Ferreira Borges, was founded in 1131 by Portugal's first king, Afonso Henriques. The facade and portal date from the 16th century, when the church was restored. Inside, although the church is small, it is light and spacious. Eighteenth-century *azulejos* adorn either wall: the right side depicts the life of Saint Augustine, the left scenes related to the Holy Cross. The prize piece of the church is the exquisite **pulpit** on the left wall, an intricately carved work by sculptor Nicolau Chanterene.

The sacristy is open from 9 a.m. to noon and from 2 p.m. to 5 p.m., and contains several paintings (the largest is the *Descent from the Cross*, by Andre Gonçalves), a silverwork collection, and some vestments. You can visit the **tombs** of the first two kings of Portugal, Afonso Henriques, and Sancho I, who are ensconced in truly regal monuments. You may also see the **Chapterhouse** and the lovely **Cloister of Silence**.

The Rua da Sofia, off Praça 8 de Maio, a 16th-century street, was extraordinarily wide for its time. It was the original home of several colleges of the University before they were moved to their present location on the hill.

Praça do Comércio, off Rua Ferreira Borges, is an oddly shaped square lined with 17th- and 18th-century buildings. At the north end stands the sturdy **Santiago Church**, dating from the end of the 12th century. The capitals are decorated with animal and bird motifs. At the south end is the church of **São Bartolomeu**, built in the 18th century.

The Santa Clara section of town lies across the river. **Santa Clara a Nova** (New Santa Clara) **Monastery** is worth a visit if only for the view of Coimbra from the praça in front of it. Inside, in a wildly Baroque setting, stands the **tomb of the Queen Saint Isabel**, the patron saint of Coimbra.

Closer to the river, too close for its own comfort in fact, is **Santa Clara a Velha**, the old Santa Clara Monastery, which is now partially submerged. This 12th-century edifice is simpler and lovelier than its replacement, for which it was abandoned in 1677.

Nearby, **Portugal dos Pequenitos** is an outdoor museum of small-scale reproductions of traditional Portuguese houses and famous monuments.

In other areas of the city, the **Celas Monastery** is notable for its cloister and the pretty church of **Santo António dos Olivais** was an old Franciscan convent.

There is a lot of sightseeing to do in Coimbra—perhaps too much; church after church becomes wearing. However, there are other ways to enjoy the city as well.

One is shopping in the Baixa. Shops range from the fashionable to the hole-in-the-wall, and it's always an adventure to let yourself get lost in the meandering and illogical streets of the shopping district. For those interested in traditional Coimbran ceramics and handicrafts, the city runs a showcase shop in the **Torre de Anto**, in the old city. For a different shopping experience, go to the **covered market** on Rua Olimpio Nicolau, not far from the Baixa, which is open every morning but best on Saturdays. The market vendors hawk fish, bread, fruit, vegetables, flowers, even live animals (chickens and rabbits). You'll get a real taste of Coimbra life.

Coimbra's many parks make delicious resting places. The **Botanical Garden**, on Alameda Dr. Julio Henriques, next to the aqueduct, is a lovely garden filled with a wide range of plant life. Unfortunately, not all the grounds are open to the public—but enough for a pleasant visit. Other nice parks are **Santa Cruz**, off the Praça da República, and **Choupal**, west of the city—a larger park good for walks and bike rides. The very small **Penedo da Saudade** has a nice view over the city.

Canoing in Coimbra: For those who want physical exercise, one option is to rent canoes from the municipal boat club near the **Santa Clara Bridge**, on the far side of the river. Another possibility is to walk on some of the smaller roads to or between the villages outside Coimbra—the countryside is beautiful and easily accessible.

Outlying districts accessible by bus or by car include **Penacova**, a village with a strikingly beautiful view—try lunch there at the Panorâmica Restaurant, which lives up to its name. The drive/bus ride there runs along the lovely Mondego River valley. There are windmills—somehow, always a surprising sight—on hilltops in the surrounding countryside. Or visit **Penela**, a village with a Moorish castle overlooking the area; or **Lousã**, a mountain town.

Coimbra is located 118 miles (188 km) north of Lisbon and 74 miles (118 km) south of Oporto on the Lisbon-Oporto highway and the Lisbon-Oporto train line. It takes an hour and 20 minutes to and from Oporto by fast train, and two hours 10 minutes from Lisbon. The tourist office is located in the center of town in **Largo de Portagem**. They will provide you with a good map of the city.

Alumni of the Medical School gather at the Old University

A Walking Tour Of Conimbriga

The largest excavated Roman ruins in Portugal, complemented by one of the country's finest museums, lies not far from Coimbra, near the town of Condeixa. Conimbriga (pronounced with the stress on the second syllable: Co-NIM-briga) is a fascinating site that includes the remains of a Roman wall, several public buildings and private houses, and beautifully preserved mosaics which alone would be worth the visit.

Of an estimated 32-acre site, only a few hundred yards have been excavated. A glance out onto the hot, dusty field that is still off-limits to tourists reveals signs of further ruins, and, happily, the beginnings of more excavation. In fact, the site stretches much further than is obvious; archaeologists believe remains may be found as far away as the main highway and even under the homes of people in the nearby village of Condeixa-a-Velha.

Conimbriga probably was settled as early as the Iron Age (800-500 B.C.). The name Conimbriga itself suggests Celtic habitation, as *briga* is a Celtic suffix. The site was likely chosen for its natural defenses: it is protected on two sides by deep gorges.

It was not until the last part of the second century B.C. that Romans came to Conimbriga. Perhaps they first arrived as part of a campaign to subdue Lusitania, the Roman name for this part of the Iberian Peninsula. Two hundred years of conflict eventually ended, and the people of the area were gradually Romanized, their names Latinized and they adopted Roman gods. The local Romans, in kind, adopted some of the native deities and cults.

Prosperity accompanied peace. Conimbriga profited from its location along the Roman road between *Olisipo* (present-day Lisbon) and *Bracara Augusta* (now Braga). Some time around 70 A.D., the Roman Empire designated Conimbriga a *municipium* and bestowed the name of Flavia on it.

In the year 391, Christianity became the official religion of the Roman Empire. The earliest evidence of Christianity's spread to Conimbriga is a tombstone from 522.

Great Wall of Conimbriga: Conimbriga's prosperity was not to last. Crises in the Empire and Barbarian incursions into Iberia prompted the construction of the defensive wall still prominent today. The wall was built of bits and pieces of everything, including stone, remnants of old houses, and brick. To take advantage of the natural defensive position of the area, and to concentrate the area of defense, the inhabited area of Conimbriga was reduced and some parts of the

town were left outside the wall. Despite the new wall, in 464 Suevi successfully attacked the city; of this early raid we know that they captured the wife and children of the nobleman Cantaber, whose home, next to the wall, has been excavated. They returned four years later and overran the city, destroying much of the population.

Conimbriga continued to be inhabited, but it lost its status as an important center to its neighbor, the more easily defensible *Aeminium*. The population of Conimbriga decreased, and little or no new buildings were constructed. It is likely that the Episcopal see of the region was moved to

Aeminium during the 6th century. *Aeminium* even absconded with Conimbriga's name, which eventually was shortened to Coimbra.

As you enter the site, you are walking down the very road that gave Conimbriga its original importance—the highway between *Olisipo* and *Bracara Augusta*. In front of you is the enormous wall, built later, that cut off parts of the city.

Before the wall, and to your right, lie the ruins—still not entirely excavated—of a large house. The house was partially destroyed by the construction of the wall, which went right through the front of it. Indeed, pieces of this house were used to make the wall.

At the front of the house, the part closest to the wall, is the main entrance which leads into a small courtyard and atrium. Small service rooms lie on either side. Just beyond is the peristyle—a central courtyard with sculptured pool, which the Romans kept stocked with fish. Thick walls and central pools helped keep Roman houses cool even on the hottest of days—something you'll understand as you simmer among the ruins of Conimbriga in the middle of summer.

Several mosaics line the peristyle. Among them are a scene of Perseus and the sea monster; a man returning from the hunt with a rabbit; and a very small minotaur and a very large labyrinth. Mosaic scenes such as these served not only for decoration but also as a means of keeping mythical traditions alive among the part of the population that was illiterate.

The family's private quarters are on the side of the house closest to the road. There are bedrooms here, as well as a courtyard and an *impluvium* for catching rainwater. Here are other noteworthy mosaics, including one of stag-hunting and another of Silenus riding a donkey.

Opposite, on the north side of the house, is a lavatory. Overflow from the central pool may have been used for the flushing system. The rooms to this side served unknown purposes; there is another hunting mosaic in one of these. Finally, on the east side of the house, opposite the main entrance, is the main reception area and dining room.

Passing through the main entrance in the wall, and continuing along the path through to the right, you'll come to the arch of the aqueduct (rebuilt); parts of the aqueduct, and the remains of several buildings which might have been small shops.

Back to the main entrance, Cantaber's house stretches to the south (left, with your back to the entrance). The house is full of ornamental pools. The first is just beyond the entrance to the house; there are more flanking a reception room just further south. In the middle section of the house, up against the city wall, is a suite of rooms (which you can view by climbing a small staircase). These too have a pool; note the trident symbol of Neptune at the entrance to the suite.

Roman baths: Perhaps the most interesting part of the house is the baths, which lie at the extreme south end. They are easily recognizable by their hexagonal and round shapes, and by the heating system (of pipes) visible through the stone grid covering the floors. The *frigidarium* is the square room; this was the room for cold baths.

The *tepidarium* held warm water, and the *caldarium* hot. The Romans believed it was healthful to progress through all three temperatures during a bath. Beyond the house, on the south side of the ruins, are tombs and skeletons from a much later period.

Back around the other side of the wall, we can see more baths: the public ones, this time. The stacks of tiles piled on the ground indicate that these baths ran on a different, less expensive, system than the baths at Cantaber's home. While Cantaber's baths used a system of piped hot water, in the public baths the floor was raised off the ground by means of stacked tiles. A slave would stoke a furnace and pump bellows to push the hot air under the floor, which thus heated the room above.

The public baths were an important part of Roman life, and wealthy Roman men would spend hours daily bathing. It was both a health ritual and a place to discuss politics and other subjects. The Romans were particularly convinced of the salutary effects of bathing, and took great care in covering themselves with olive oil after a bath and then scraping their skins clean with a curved blade, to remove impurities.

Beyond the baths is an area of marvelously patterned mosaics. The colors were once much brighter than the pleasing pastels to which they have mellowed today. Note the delicate shading of the reds and yellows in some of the mosaics.

The museum is small but thoughtfully designed. A long case displays artifacts relating to ceramics, weaving, agriculture, lighting, writing, health and hygiene, jewelry, and other areas. There is also statuary and a very good model of the forum and temple, buildings that date from around 70 A.D. when Conimbriga became a *municipium*.

The room devoted to superstition and belief is especially interesting. A shelf of tombstones dominates the room; the inscriptions are translated to Portuguese, and include such dedications as "Aviro and Rufina dedicated this monument to their son Vegeto, dead at 18, hoping that the earth lie light upon him." A display case shows amulets that were used to ward off bad fortune and the disfavor of the gods. Another case is dedicated to the specific gods Conimbrigans worshipped. The final case illustrates the coming of Christianity to Conimbriga.

Conimbriga lies about 9 miles (15 km) south of Coimbra. The drive is easy; there is also a bus service. The site and museum are open 9 a.m. to 1 p.m. and 2 to 5 p.m. daily; the museum is closed on Mondays and holidays.

Left, a Roman mosaic from Conimbriga's House of the Fountains depicts Perseus holding out the head of Medusa to a sea serpent

SIDETRIPS FROM COIMBRA

Coimbra is the largest city in the province of Beira Litoral, which lies above the provinces of Estremadura and Ribatejo. All three are lush, green and laced with waterways. The Beira Litoral has a very ragged coastline, as the Atlantic constantly pushes in with greedy fingers, both at the Ria and south of it. Ricefields are planted in this low coastal area, which is sometimes known as "Costa da Prata," the Silver Coast. There are patches of pine trees that have been planted in some spots in an effort to stabilize the sand dunes. Inland, the ground begins to rise very gradually, and fruit trees and grain fields flourish.

Estremadura stretches below the coastal part of Beira Litoral like an arm reaching down to touch Lisbon and Setúbal. It was once the southern extremity of Portugal, a fact confirmed by its name, which means "farthest land on the Douro." It continues the beaches of the "Costa da Prata," and, indeed, the inland agriculture of its northern neighbor. Ribatejo, "bank of the Tejo (Tagus)," is a small strip to the east of

Estremadura. It is an alluvial plain, again planted with grains. Wherever flooding allows, ricefields are sown. But most important are the large meadows on which graze the horses and bulls bred to participate in the grand sport of bullfighting. These beautiful animals are used all over Portugal, and the Festival of the Red Waistcoats, held each July in **Vila Franca de Xira**, is five days of bull running and celebration.

Fátima: There are many other colorful festivals in these provinces, but the most important celebration—indeed, one of the most populous Catholic events in the world, is the pilgrimage at **Fátima**. In 1917, three peasant girls here had a vision of the Virgin of the Rosary on May 13th. Thereafter, she appeared before the three children, and the townspeople that gathered with them on the 13th of every month until October, asking for peace in the world. The processions that now take place each year draw thousands from around the world. Two of the original girls died shortly after the miracle, but one, Lucia, is still alive, a nun in a convent near Coimbra. Today, the town has capitalized on its sacred history with ubiquitous merchandizing of religious souvenirs. Furthermore, unlike a few decades ago, when making the pilgramage was a genuine hardship

Batalha Monastery

because of scarce lodgings, today motels have proliferated.

Beira Litoral, Estremadura, and Ribatejo are pleasant for casual meandering, but they are full of historical points of interest as well—Batalha, Alcobaça and Tomar being the best known of these.

The largest town in these provinces, apart from Coimbra, is **Aveiro**. It is likely to be described as "the Venice of Portugal," a claim some of its inhabitants make. Don't be disappointed: Aveiro, although pleasant enough, is nothing like the Italian city.

The comparison with Venice stems from the canals that traverse the city and the boats that ply them. There is, in fact, only one main canal with two smaller canals along the edges of town; only a few boats harbor here. These canals lead to the real attraction of the area: the **Ria**, the lagoon that extends 29 miles (47 km) just inland of the coast.

As might be guessed, the Ria plays a large part in Aveiro's economy. The colorful boats with large, graceful prows, the *moliceiros*, are used to gather *moliço*, seaweed, for fertilizer. Next to the canals are large saltpans, another local industry. Other important industries are fishing, wood, cork, and ceramics from nearby Vista Alegre.

It is believed that Aveiro, then known by the Roman name Talabriga, once lay directly on the ocean. Later, a strip of sediment built up, creating the Ria and a perfect sheltered harbor.

Aveiro was a small settlement during the Middle Ages. In the 13th century it became a town, later encircled by fortified walls (1418) at the suggestion of Infante Prince Pedro (after whom the city park is named). Shortly after this, the king granted Aveiro the concession of a town fair, and the March Fair still goes on to this day. In 1472, the king's daughter, Joana, entered the convent of Jesus in Aveiro against her father's will. Today the convent is a museum, and the princess, Santa Joana Princesa, has several miracles attributed to her locally.

The 16th century was a time of growth and expansion for the town. With its easy access to the sea and the interior, Aveiro became a mercantile and trade center from which products of the entire Beira region were exported to the world.

The city makes an interesting study in geographic destiny. A fluke of nature cut short Aveiro's prosperity. In 1575 a violent storm shifted the sandbanks in the lagoon, blocking the canal to the sea. A dramatic decrease in population (to about one-third of the original number) accompanied the inevitable decline in Aveiro's importance as a maritime center.

In 1808, another storm opened up the passage to the sea again, but it was not until the last half of the 19th century that Aveiro's fortunes picked up. A key figure in this economic redevelopment was José Estevão, whose statue stands in the **Praça da República.**

As well as serving as a base for a trip on the Ria, Aveiro itself holds some interest, and is worth a few hours' exploration. The city is divided into two parts by the principal canal. The southern part of the city is where the aristocracy once lived; the northern half is the old fishermen's section.

The southern half centers around the Praça da República. In the simple square, the nicest building is the solid and prim **town hall**, which stands directly opposite the tourist office. Its large clock tower presides over the statue of José Estevão in the middle of the square. On the east side of the square, the 16th- and 17th-century **Misericórdia** church boasts a lovely Renaissance portal and 19th-century tiles on its facade.

In a square further south the 17th-century **Carmelite Convent** housed the barefoot Carmelite order. Note the paintings on the ceiling which depict the life of Saint Teresa.

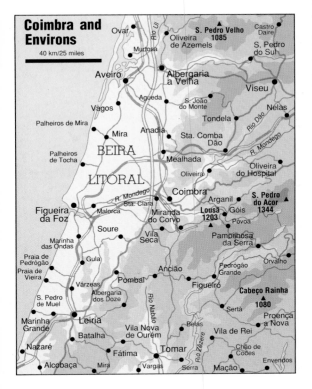

Coimbra and Environs

40 km/25 miles

Ovar · Rio U? · S. Pedro Velho 1085 · Castro Daire
Oliveira de Azemeis · S. Pedro do Sul
Murtosa
Aveiro · Albergaria a Velha · Viseu
Agueda · S. João do Monte
Vagos · Nelas
Palheiros de Mira · Anadia · S. Comba Dão · Tondela · Rio Dão
Mira
BEIRA · Sta. Comba Dão · R. Mondego
Palheiros de Tocha · Mealhada · Oliveira do Hospital
LITORAL · Oliveira
R. Mondego · Coimbra · S. Pedro do Acor 1344
Figueira da Foz · Sta. Clara · Arganil
Malorca · Miranda do Corvo · Lousã 1203 · Góis · Póvoa
Soure · Vila Seca · Pampilhosa da Serra
Marinha das Ondas
Praia de Pedrógão · Gula · Orvalho
Praia de Vieira · Anção · Pedrógão Grande
Várzeas · Pombal · Figueiró
S. Pedro de Muel · Albergaria dos Doze · Rio Nabão · Cabeço Rainha 1080
Marinha Grande · Leiria · Sertã · Proença a Nova
Nazaré · Batalha · Vila Nova de Ourém · Belas · Vila de Rei
Alcobaça · Fátima · Mira · Tomar · Rio Zêzere · Chão de Codes
Vargas · Serra · Mação · Envendos

Although the **museum** of Aveiro is not well-labeled, guides will take you through and answer questions. The museum is housed in the 15th-century **Convento de Jesús**. The **church** of the convent is a riot of gilded wood. Arching over the choir are lovely hand-painted ceilings, and off the choir is a chapel with beautiful tiles. Just outside the church is Santa Joana Princesa's **tomb**, done in intricately carved colored marble with statues supporting and crowning it. The tomb took 12 years to construct. The walls are also of marble.

The rest of the convent holds pieces of varying interest: many ornate altars, painted biblical scenes, a gruesome Christ covered in graphic sores. Perhaps the most interesting pieces are those that illuminate the life of the convent: the choir music stands, the Mother Superior's chair, the old convent pharmacy, where a bookcase holds containers for opium, belladonna, and cocaine extracts; drawers labeled for various herbs, scales to weigh the medicine, and books on pharmacology.

The **São Domingos Cathedral** is near the museum. Its Baroque facade has twisted columns and sculpted figures of Faith, Hope and Charity. Inside, an enormous skylight over the altar lends the church an airiness that many Baroque churches lack. The enormous blue altar rises strikingly in the all-white interior. The **tomb of Catarina de Atalíde** is here, a woman honored, under the name Natércia, by the poet Camões in his sonnets. The church was founded in 1423 and remodeled during the 16th and 17th centuries.

Several blocks away is the refreshing **Dom Infante Pedro Park**, on the grounds of the old **Franciscan Monastery**. Colorful flowers, lush trees, fountains, and a small lake where you can rent paddle boats make this a nice spot for a break.

North of the canal lies the fishermen's section, where narrow one- and two-story houses support facades that sometimes rise beyond roof levels. The arches and curves on the tops of these false fronts are reminiscent of the fishing boats themselves and their curved prows. The **fish market**, where the catch is sold each morning, is in this area. There is also the bright white, oddly shaped chapel of **São Goncalinho** and the church of **São Goncalo**. Inside this 17th- and 18th-century church gleam a gilt altar and newly placed tiles.

The beautiful Ria is the real reason for coming to Aveiro. You can tour its length by boat, car, or bus, although boat is by far the

One of the *moliceiros* of Aveiro

most rewarding. The Ria and its subsidiary canals extend as far south as Mira and as far north as Ovar. There are many camping areas around. You will see the traditional *moliceiros,* shorelines dotted with saltpans, forests and villages, glorious sea fowl plummeting into the water after fish, and the sandbar which protects the city's access to the sea.

There is regular bus and boat service along the Ria. The tourist office runs a boat tour to the area twice daily in summer. In addition, you may rent tour boats on an hourly basis from the tourist office; there are several itineraries from which to select.

Tomar, about 75 miles southeast of Aveiro and about 40 miles south of Coimbra, is a beautiful town that also happens to be the site of an important historical monument, the castle/church of the Knights Templar and the Order of Christ. The town population of about 15,000 is settled between the banks of the Rio Nabão and the woods which overlook the town from low hills. In the old part of Tomar, narrow stone-paved streets are lined with whitewashed buildings from which bloom exuberant flowers. Whether for its gentle ambience or for a chance to learn a little of Portugal's history, Tomar is worth exploring.

Tomar was the home of the Knights Templar in Portugal, an order which was formed in 1119, during the Crusades. The order spread quickly through Europe, gaining extraordinary wealth, including properties throughout the continent. They also made powerful enemies, and in the early 1300s, with accusations of heresy and foul practices, and finally the suppression of the order altogether, they took refuge at their property in Tomar. They re-emerged in 1320, though under royal, as opposed to independent or papal control, as the Order of Christ. They played an important role in the exploration of other continents later, in the age of Portuguese discoveries.

In Tomar they left behind the marvelous ruins of the old Templar castle and the still intact church and cloisters on the site. The **castle** is located on a hill above the city, and the 10-minute walk up commands a view of the roofs of the old town. The castle is set alongside a forest, and the grounds are extensive and tranquil.

The castle itself is a maze of staircases, passages, nooks and crannies. The seven cloisters (only four are open to the public) have been added at irregular angles, leaving eccentric spaces between. Even the main entrance is oddly tucked into a corner.

Another scene of Aveiro's canal

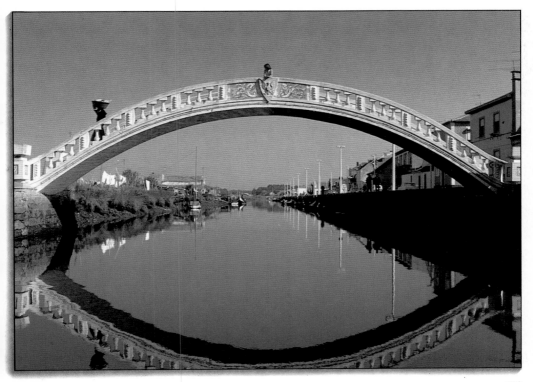

Inside the entrance, the original **Templar church** lies to the right. Begun in 1162, the octagonal temple was modeled on the Church of the Holy Sepulchre in Jerusalem. Here the knights would hear services while seated on their horses and pray for victory in battle. Despite its faded colors, the gilt painting on the walls still retains its majesty.

The **choir loft**, added much later, provides a sharp contrast to the original temple. Lighter, emptier and airier, this loft is an example of the Manueline style in full bloom.

Adjoining the original church is a 16th-century cloister with 17th-century tiles. Some of the tombs of the knights are found here. From here there is access to the upper level of the choir loft, then into the other cloisters. From the terrace of the small **Claustro de Santa Bárbara**, there is a view of the amazing, ornate, Manueline window structured around two deep relief carvings of ships' masts and decorated with knots, cork, coral, and seaweed. The whole is topped by a shield, crown and cross, symbol of the union of church and king.

From the opposite side of the building, there is a view of the surrounding forest and the castle yard where knights trained their horses and spent their free time. Also on this side lies an unfinished chapel, which was to be a copy of the entrance. Bad luck during construction led the superstitious knights to abandon it.

Tomar's **synagogue** is at Rua Joaquim Jacinto, 73. Although up to 70 percent of Portuguese have Jewish ancestry and Tomar was once the home of a thriving Jewish community, there are very few Jews left in Tomar or in Portugal. When in 1497 the Portuguese king married Isabella of Castile, part of the marriage contract was to expel the Jews from Portugal. Instead, Jews were allowed to remain if they converted, although practices were not closely monitored. Later, the Inquisition would brutally enforce these laws.

The synagogue/museum is simple and moving, decorated with gifts from all over the world. The director of the site will explain the synagogue's history and tell you about recent excavations and the ambitious plans for a bigger museum and library.

The church of **São João Baptista** has a dark wood ceiling and sombre atmosphere. There are 16th-century wood panel paintings on the walls depicting scenes including *The Last Supper* and *The Decapitation of John the Baptist*. On the left is a delicately carved pulpit.

Standing incongruously on an empty lot in the new part of town, **Santa Maria do Olival** is a lovely simple church dating from the 12th century. It was later remodeled.

The tourist office is located on Avenida Dr. Cándido Madureira, near the road to the castle.

The Martyred St. Irene: **Santarém**, the central town of Ribatejo, lies 30 miles down the Tagus River from Tomar. It was named for St. Irene, a young nun who was accused of being unchaste and so killed in 653 near Tomar. Her body, thrown into the river, washed ashore here, where apparitions attested to her innocence. The Romanesque-Gothic church of **São João de Alporão** contains a fine archaeological museum, as well as the beautifully carved tomb of Duarte, a son of Pedro I who died in the Battle of Alcacer-Quiber in 1458. It contains only one of Duarte's teeth, the sole relic retained by his wife.

Also in Santarém is the church of **Santa Clara**, originally part of a 13th-century convent. There are two tombs of Dona Leonor, the original and, below a lovely rose window, another from the 17th century. The church of **Nossa Senhora da Graça**, a bold Gothic structure with a beautiful nave, contains several tombs, among them that of Pedro Alvares Cabral, discoverer of Brazil.

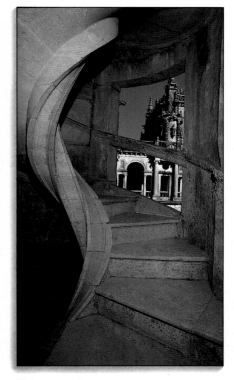

Detail of the Convent of Christ

Batalha's monastery perches like a wedding cake on one side of the Lisbon-Oporto highway. This incongruous sight rises suddenly around a bend in the road, and it's well worth getting off the highway to have a look. In fact, it's worth planning a special trip—by car or by bus—to one of Portugal's most beautiful monuments.

The **Santa Maria da Vitória Monastery** (the full name of Batalha's Abbey) traces its origins to Portugal's struggle to maintain its independence from Castile. One of the decisive battles for independence was fought at Aljubarrota, not far from Batalha. The Castilian king, Juan, based his claim to the Portuguese throne on his marriage to a Portuguese princess; he invaded Portugal to enforce the claim in 1385. The 20-year-old Dom João, Master of the order of Avis, illegitimate son of Pedro I, promised to raise a church to the Virgin Mary if the Portuguese won. With his young general, Nuño Álvares Pereira, João defeated Juan and became João I. Construction of the church began in 1388, and was completed—or, more accurately, was last worked on—in 1533.

The **front portal**, though large, is smaller than those of most Gothic churches. The arches sweep upward to a sculpture of figures representing the hierarchy in the heavenly court—as it was perceived in the Middle Ages. In the center is Christ surrounded by Matthew, Mark, Luke, and John.

Though the outside of the church is ornate, the interior is endowed with a simple Gothic elegance and dignity. The vaulted ceiling arches above a slender nave lighted by colorful stained glass. A feeling of light and spirit fill this room, intensified if you're fortunate enough to witness the organist playing.

The room to the right is the **Founder's Chapel** (Dom João's Pantheon), built around 1426 by João I. In the center are the tombs of João and his English queen, Philippa; the lovely carving on the top shows the pair holding hands. Other tombs, including that of Prince Henry the Navigator, are set into the walls under regal arches. The room is topped by a dome supported by star-shaped ribbing.

On the other side of the church you may enter **Dom João's Cloister**. Arches filled with Manueline ornamentation surround a pretty manicured courtyard. The arches are patterned with intricate, rope-like weavings decorated with vegetable motifs.

The **chapterhouse** is the first room off

the cloister. It has an unusual and beautiful ceiling with no support other than the walls. This seems to pull the whole room together to a central point. The impression is of precarious balance. The window is filled with a stained-glass scene of Christ on the Cross, remarkably rich in color. This room houses the tomb of two unknown soldiers, whose remains were returned to Portugal in 1921 from France and Mozambique. Above them, the sculpture of "Christ of the Trenches" was given by the French government in 1958. The lamp on the top burns Portuguese olive oil. The three armed soldiers guarding the tombs seem out of place in this otherwise peaceful setting.

Other rooms off the cloister house a **military museum** and temporary exhibits.

Another cloister abuts Dom João's: this is **Dom Afonso's**, a much simpler, austere construction with a lovely central garden. This cloister was built in the 15th century.

To reach Dom Duarte's Pantheon, or, as it is more commonly known, the **Unfinished Chapels**, it is necessary to exit the cloisters and walk along the outside of the monastery. This octagonal structure is attached to the outside wall of the church and, as it is abruptly roofless, it seems awkward. Ordered by Dom Duarte to house the tombs

of himself and his family, the chapel was begun in the 1430s but never finished. No one is quite certain why, but it is likely that the building funds were redirected by the king to a project that interested him more.

The building contains simple chapels in each of seven walls. The chapel opposite the door holds the tomb of the king and Dona Leonor, his wife. The eighth wall is a massive door of limestone, with endless layers of beautifully detailed ornamentation carved in Manueline style.

There is little else to see in the village of Batalha. There is a shopping mall next to the monastery filled with tourist-oriented "handicraft" shops. The tourist office is located in the shopping mall.

About eight miles (12 km) south of Batalha lies the town of **Alcobaça**, named after two small rivers, the Alcoa and the Baça. At its center, and looking, oddly enough, right at home, is the huge, magnificent **Cistercian Abbey**. The first king of Portugal, Afonso Henriques, founded the monastery as thanks to St. Bernard for the capture of the town of Santarém from the Moors. Afonso laid the foundation stone himself, in 1148. There has been much alteration since, and now some sections are shut off for a variety of uses, including a home for the elderly.

The Unfinished Chapels of Batalha

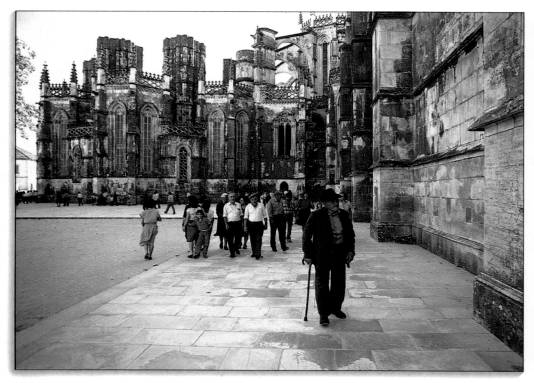

The Cistercian monks were a productive, vivacious bunch. Numbering, it is said 999 ("one less than a thousand"), they tilled the land around the abbey, making it to this day Portugal's greatest source of fruit. In Sebastião's reign, the exceedingly wealthy and powerful Alcobaça Abbey, or Santa Maria Abbey as it is also known, was declared by the Pope the seat of the entire Cistercian order. The monks were known for their lively spirits and lavish hospitality. They ran a school, perhaps the first public school in Portugal, at the abbey, and a sanctuary and hospice as well. In 1810, however, the abbey was sacked by French troops. In the Liberal Revolution of 1834, when all religious orders were expelled from Portugal, the abbey was again pillaged.

The long Baroque facade of the abbey, added in the 18th century, has twin towers in the center, below which are a Gothic doorway and rose window, the only part of the original facade left. Directly inside is the astonishingly serene and austere **church**. It is the largest church in Portugal, and the three equally tall aisles give a wonderful light to the clean lines. In the transepts are the justly famous, richly carved **tombs of Pedro I and Inês de Castro**, whose story is one of Portugal's most romantic (see page 17). Much of the damage to the carvings was caused by the French.

Off the south transept are several royal tombs, including those of Afonso II and Afonso III, and a sadly mutilated 17th-century terra-cotta of the Death of St. Bernard. To the east of the ambulatory, there are two fine Manuline doorways that were designed by João de Castilho.

An entrance in the north wall of the church leads to the **Cloister of Silence**. Several rooms branch off from the cloister, including the chapterhouse and, upstairs, a dormitory. There is a large but narrow **kitchen**, with an enormous center chimney and a remarkable basin—a rivulet runs through it which once provided the monks with not only water but a constant supply of fresh fish! Next door to the kitchen is the **refectory**, with steps built into one wall leading to a pulpit.

One other room of note is the **Sala dos Reis**, with statues, probably carved by monks, of many of the kings of Portugal. The panel in the same room, which tells the history of the abbey, is a rare example of a manuscript *azulejo* panel.

Also in Alcobaça is a ruined Moorish **castle**, which provides a fine view of the surrounding area.

Left, inside Batalha. Right, the beautiful lines of Alcobaça

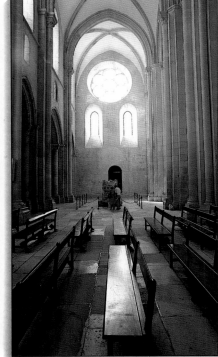

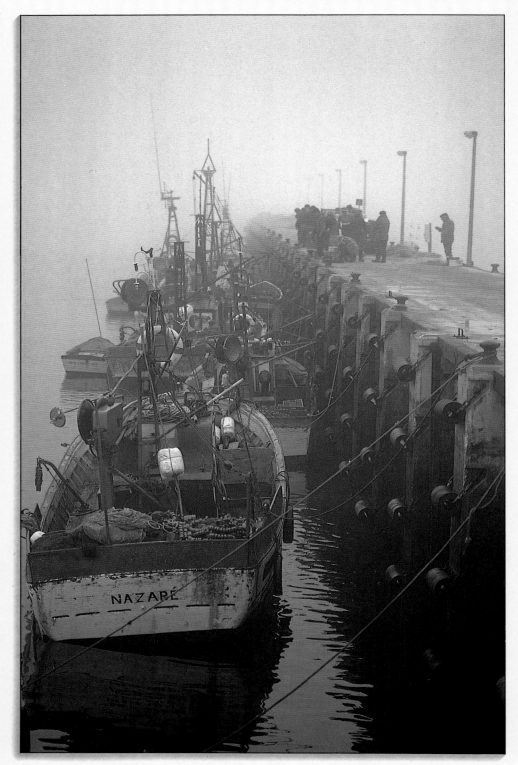

FISHING
COMMUNITIES

Women still gaze out over the sea along Portugal's Atlantic coast as they have since the rocky edge of western Europe was first settled by Phoenician sailors 3,000 years ago. Some wait anxiously for the fishing boats to return with their husbands, brothers, fathers and sons. Others, dressed in black, stare into waters that have claimed their menfolk for ever.

In a country whose character as well as its coastline has been shaped by crashing Atlantic breakers, fishing remains the trade most emblematic of the Portuguese soul. Skill in handling tides and winds, pioneering ship-building and navigational techniques, and the courage to explore the unknown took Portuguese navigators around the uncharted globe in the 15th and 16th centuries to discover new worlds.

Similar prowess and bravery—though toward humbler ends—is shown today by the hardy Portuguese fishermen who trawl for cod in the North Atlantic, harpoon whales off the Azores islands, or set sail in small boats into the treacherous Atlantic swell from the fishing communities that edge westernmost Europe.

A 90-minute journey northwest of Lisbon takes you to the port of **Peniche** and into the heart of the age-old Portuguese fishing industry. Like most of Portugal's coastal towns, Peniche has no natural harbor, only a bay sheltered by the rocky promontory of Cabo Carvoeiro, the second most westerly point in Europe. The town has built a seawall to protect the bay from the fury of Atlantic storms.

Peniche is an uncompromising town of some 15,000 people. Here, the waves beat against dramatic crags of black rock, and the spare white houses cling to the slopes for shelter from the sweeping northwesterly winds. Too stark and exposed for tourism to have taken hold, the town typifies life in Portuguese fishing communities, where the people labor to subsist from the sea in a daily struggle with the weather and the limitations of outdated equipment.

The **Fortaleza Prison** physically dominates the town. The veteran leader of Portugal's communist Party, Alvaro Cunhal, and others, who had been held there by the pre-1974 authoritarian regime, escaped in 1960. They climbed down the cliffs to a waiting boat that reportedly took them to a Soviet-bloc submarine. Later, Fortaleza served the nobler purpose of a refugee camp for

the *retournados*, who arrived after the colonies were declared independent. Today, the building serves as a museum, containing an interesting hodge-podge of local artifacts, crafts and natural history.

Most of the boats that work out of Peniche are small trawlers, or *traineiras*, about 80-feet (24-meters) long, powered by diesel engines with a cabin enclosing the wheel andequipped with a basic VHF radio of limited range. They are wooden-hulled with high, broad bows and, characteristic of all Portuguese fishing boats, painted in bright yellows, blues, reds and greens. These colors and designs, that lend such gaiety to fishing villages are not just an aesthetic whimsy. The unique creations, serve the eminently practical purpose of enabling skippers to recognize individual boats at a distance.

Traineiras, old and battered though many of them are, stand in the front rank of Portuguese fishing. Of the country's 11,000 working boats, only a small number are more than 40-feet (12-meters) long and two-thirds are powered by oar or sail. Most vessels are 20 years old or more, and little more than 100 are designed to fish in deep waters.

Peniche bustles with activity when the boats return, usually early in the morning, low in the water laden with their catch, the sea birds wheeling hungrily behind. The men hurl plastic crates packed with gleaming fish from the decks high up onto the quay where the women sort the catch before it is taken to the auction building, known as the *lota*, to be sold.

The catch varies, but the bulk of it is usually

Preceding page, Mira beach. Left, dawn at Nazaré. Above, mariner's workhorse at rest

sardines, the fish that accounts for more than a third of the 250,000 metric tons of fish harvested by Portugal each year. The other main catches are cod from Newfoundland and Greenland, accounting for about 10,000 metric tons, and some 8,000 metric tons of tuna from around the islands of Madeira and the Azores. Much of the sardine and tuna is canned for both export and domestic use, in factories such as the one in Peniche, using another of the country's main products, olive oil.

A good night's fishing could land a catch worth $5,000. The owner's share is usually a little more than half, out of which he has to meet high running and maintenance costs, particularly fuel. The remainder is divided between the crew of around 25 in decreasing sums depending on position. These would be high earnings in Portugal if they were consistent. But many nights at sea

force as you dip and rise across to the red granite outcroppings that loom 300 feet (90 meters) above the sea. The trip is nevetheless well worth taking. A 17th-century **fortress**, now converted to an inn, the **lighthouse** and a few fishermen's cottages are the only buildings. The entire island has been demarcated a national bird sanctuary, and seagulls and eider are everywhere. Officials patrol the make-shift paths to ensure that visitors don't wander into forbidden territory and distrub the birds. Rabbits and flowers abound, but the greatest excitement lies in taking a boat trip around the reefs, caves and smaller islands, past a breathtaking sea tunnel called the **Furado Grande**. The ferry runs from June to September; the trip takes one hour.

Sport fisherman often choose the Berlengas as a home base. It is a simple matter to catch more

yield catches of very little value or nothing at all; often the weather prevents boats leaving harbor for days on end.

Some 40,000 men are employed in the fishing industry, some spending long months in the freezing North Atlantic fishing for cod, others facing fire from Polisario guerrillas off North Africa and many plying Portugal's difficult coastal waters. Small open boats, age-old methods and obsolescent equipment put the mariner's safety constantly at risk.

A sense of the Atlantic swell that is the fisherman's constant companion and nemesis can be felt by taking the ferry from Peniche to the **Berlengas Islands**, seven miles (four km) offshore. Once out of the shelter of the peninsula, the powerful current rocks the boat with unexpected

mackerel and sardines than you want, and with a little expertise and experience you can land a 100 lb. (45 kg) swordfish. Most off-shore fishing does not require a license. It is available all year (inland the season is limited to April through November). Complete fishing trips—including bait, tackle, and a professional craft—are available at Peniche, Ericeira and Nazaré.

The hazards faced by Portuguese fishermen are reflected in their strong Roman Catholic faith and the many religious festivals along the coast dedicated to blessing their vessels and praying for their safety. On the first Sunday in August, the people of Peniche hold a typical celebration in the festival of Our Lady of Safe Voyages (**A Nossa Senhora da Boa Viagem**).

The image of the Virgin, the fishermen's patroness, is carried by night from its shrine on the rocky cape to the harbor in a procession of boats gaily decorated with colored paper and lit by lanterns. Carrying candles, the townspeople gather on the quay beside the twinkling vessels as a priest, in a fishing boat moored alongside, blesses the small fleet.

For several days after this stirring convocation ceremony Peniche gives itself over to the *festa*. A fair fills the streets, brass bands play, fireworks burst over the harbor and the town dances into the early hours under the stars.

The daily labors of the Peniche fishermen and their seasonal celebrations are part of the general rhythm of life along the Portuguese coast. But every community has its unique character and traditions.

Thirty miles (48 km) north, the fishing port of

abound. But the life of the hardy fishermen goes on as it has for centuries, almost indifferent to the crowds of holiday-makers.

Because they had no natural harbor, the fishermen used to launch their boats from the beach. They managed this by pushing their craft down log rollers into the sea then clambering aboard and rowing furiously till they overrode the incoming breakers. When they arrived home again, the boats were winched ashore by oxen and later by tractors. The building of a modern anchorage at the south of the beach has relieved the fishermen of this arduous labor.

Similarly the traditional dress for which the Nazaré fisherfolk are famed—having become one of the most photographed populations in all of Portugal—is today seen more in souvenir shops than on the townspeople. But some women

Nazaré nestles along a sweeping mile-long bay, a brightly-colored, gay and bustling town in striking contrast to the severity of Peniche. In summer, thousands of holiday-makers pack the beach in rows of peaked, striped canvas tents that create the rather romantic atmosphere of a Moorish battle camp.

The abundance of tourists vitiates some of Nazaré's charm, but it also assures that all the visitor's desires will be catered to. Pleasant seafood restaurants and small hotels line the sandy bay; esplanade cafes, bars and souvenir shops

Left, the "Good Voyage" promises many more. Above, winching the boats ashore at the end of a long day, the old-fashioned way

still wear the seven colored petticoats under a wide black skirt and cover their head with a black scarf or shawl; the men still favor woolen shirts in traditional plaids, but few wear the distinctive black stocking bonnets whose tops fall down to the shoulder.

The Nazaré fishing boat is traditionally about 18-feet (five-meters) long with a flat-bottomed hull and high bow rising in a spiked crescent. These boats with distinguishing eyes, stars and other symbols painted on the prow can still be seen at the south of the bay. But motorized *traineira* today account for the bulk of the fisher's catch. The yield is mainly sardines along with whiting, blue mackerel, sole and perch, and is sold at the *lota* or canned in a local factory.

Nazaré named from a statue of the Virgin that

a 4th-century monk brought to the town from Nazareth, lives literally on two levels. In the lower part of town, small, white-walled fishermen's cottages line the narrow alleyways. High above on the cliff that towers 360 feet (109 meters) above the old town is the quarter known as **Sítio**. Reached by a funicular that climbs the tallest cliffside in Portugal, Sítio is dominated by a large square and on its edge the tiny **chapel** built to commemorate a miracle in 1182 when Our Lady of Nazaré saved the local lord by stopping his horse from plunging off the cliff as he pursued a deer.

The 17th-century **Church of Our Lady of Nazaré** on the other side of the square is the focus for the annual religious festivities during the second week of September that include processions and bullfights in the Sítio ring. The steep,

narrow pathway and steps from the **lighthouse** west of the church affords stirring views of Atlantic breakers crashing against the rocks.

One of the most enjoyable aspects of becoming acquainted with Portugal's fishing communities is sampling the freshest of fish. Peniche and Nazaré are both ideal venues.

For excellent grilled fish, usually served with boiled potatoes, vegetables and a butter sauce, choose between *robalo* (bass), *cherne* (turbot), *salmonettes* (red mullet), *garoupa* (merou) and *peixe espada* (scabbard fish). *Espadarte* (sword fish), either grilled or smoked as an hors d'ouevre, is a delicacy worth paying a little extra for. Other delights probably less familiar to visitors include *tamboril* (monkfish) with a texture similar to shellfish, *lulas* (cuttlefish), *chocos*

(squid), *polvo* (octupus) and *safio* (conger eels).

Shellfish has grown expensive in Portugal as much of it is imported. But a visitor who can splash out a little on a local crayfish (*logosta*) or lobster (*lavagante*) is unlikely to regret it. An excellent setting is the picturesque fishing village of **Ericeira**, 30 miles (48 km) outside Lisbon and south of Peniche.

The village, which takes its name from the abundance of sea hedgehogs, or *ouriços,* found there, is on the clifftops looking down onto the rocky beaches. A winding path leads down to the tiny fishing beach protected by a jetty and concrete boulders piled into the sea to break the Atlantic current. From the wall high up above the small harbor, you can watch the fishermen unload their catch, mend their nets and repaint their boats.

The tiny chapel of **Santo António** above the harbor is the center of the summer festa. The chapel—and a replica of a fishing boat holding a statue of the Virgin—are filled with hundreds of candles lit by the townspeople as a prayer for the safety of the fishermen. The Virgin is carried at night in a procession down to the harbor where the priest blesses the brightly decorated boats.

A tiled plaque on the side of the chapel records the flight of King Manuel II and his family from the beach here in October, 1910, after the monarchy was overthrown and Portugal became a republic. The king sailed via Gibraltar to Britain where he lived the rest of his life in exile, devoting himself to amassing an important collection of early Portuguese books. Documents including British newspaper reports on the escape can be seen in Ericeira's small but interesting **municipal museum**. Ericeira becomes a bustling resort in the summer not least of all sought for its seafood, much of it raised in tanks on the rocky shore.

Ericeira, Nazaré and Peniche are similar in spirit to the many other fishing communities that have struggled for centuries to earn a living from the sea on the frontier where Europe meets the Atlantic. Each is unique; others that will reward a visit include **Sesimbra** nestled beneath the beautiful Arrábida Hills south of Lisbon; the beautiful bay of **São Martinho do Porto;** and **São Pedro de Moel** surrounded by Pine forest close to Nazaré.

In the north, **Vila do Conde** at the mouth of the Ave River is renowned for its lacemakers' procession in the third week of June, which winds across the candle-lit town to the beach. **Viana do Castelo** has prospered since the 16th century as the home of fishermen who brave the distant and icy Atlantic waters to fish for cod off Newfoundland.

Above, amateur fisherman still hoping to land dinner as the day nears its end. Right, a successful day's catch of sardines, destined for the *lota*

THE WINE DISTRICTS

Northern Portugal is wine country par excellence. Fine vineyards flourish throughout the land, but the best known wines, dating back to Roman times, come from the districts of Minho and Douro.

The two provinces make up an area shaped like a large L: From the Minho River on the northern border with Spain, south to the Douro, then along the river valley eastward to Spain again. Grapes are grown everywhere. They hang from trees, pergolas and porches, and climb along slopes and terraces. They grow in rocky, poor soil where little else flourishes.

There are still great old grape-growing estates but most grapes are produced on small farms and then sold either to cooperatives or to large companies. The *vindimia,* or grape harvest, is still done by hand and is a wonderful sight to behold. Harvesting occurs in September and October and lasts until early November. It is often a hazardous task, requiring towering 30-rung ladders to get at the elusive treetop grapes. In the hilly country, men still carry on their backs huge baskets of grapes weighing as much as 150 pounds (70 kilograms). On some back roads, squeaky oxcarts still transport the grapes to wine-presses. In these modern times, however, the fruit is generally transported in trucks.

While harvest is a festive occasion, it is no longer the unbridled merry-making of yore. In the old days, workers used to perform a kind of bacchanal dance, their arms linked and stamping on the grapes with their bare feet. It was said that this was the only way to crush the fruit without smashing the pips and spoiling the flavor of the wine. This was often accompanied by music and clapping, glasses of spirits and a good deal of sweat. Nowadays, mechanical presses are generally used to crush the grapes, although treading still takes place on some of the small farms. (For more information on Portugal's wines, see article "Moscatels, Ports and *Vinhos Verdes*" found on page 255)

The Douro: The name means "of gold" and the river, on certain glowing days, does resemble a twisting golden chain as it winds through the narrow valley between the steep hills and terraced vineyards. The countryside is exceptionally beautiful, particularly in spring and fall. To explore the Douro Valley, the point of departure is the city of

Oporto. The river wends its way for about 130 miles (210 km) in Portugal and then another 70 miles (110 km) along the border with Spain. One option is a bus tour to the port wine estates, offered by several travel agencies in Porto. The N108 road runs along the northern bank as far as Regua and the N222 follows the southern shores of the river, sometimes high above, sometimes along the water's edge. There is also a train that runs along the northern bank of the river, crossing at **Saõ João da Pesqueiro** and continuing along the southern bank until the Spanish border at **Barco d'Alva.** The ride takes about six hours.

The **Lower Douro** is technically *vinho verde* country although farther north, the Minho, is more closely associated with the "green" or young wines. The main town is **Penafiel**, between the Sousa and the Tâmega Rivers. There are some lovely old granite houses with gargoyles and wooden balconies and a 16th-century **parish church.**

A few miles to the northeast lies the charming town of **Amarante**, on the bank of the Rio Tâmega. The three-arched **bridge** was built in 1790. It leads to the convent of **São Gonçalo**, named after the local patron saint, protector of marriages. The festival held in the Saint's honor every June is a particularly raucous one—and distinctly phallic cakes are served during it.

The convent, however, is much more somber. It was begun in 1540 but not completed until 1620. Inside is the tomb of São Gonçalo, who died about 1260, and some lush gilded carved woodwork. There are two cloisters; above the rear one is the **Museu de Albano Sardoeira**, which includes some modern Portuguese painting—Sardoeira, was a cubist artist from Amarante.

Nearby is the **Quinta da Aveleda**, seat of one of Portugal's main wine empires and leading exporter of *vinho verde*. The Quinta is included on some wine-tasting tours. Individual visitors are welcome but advised to make prior arrangements at the company's office in Oporto. A tour of the 500 acre (200 hectares) Aveleda estate includes a visit to the **family chapel**, which was built in 1671. The luxurious gardens contain a ruin from Prince Henry the Navigator's Palace in Oporto. One can also observe contemporary *vinho verde* production: miles upon miles of grapes; climbing poles, trellises and crosses; and mechanical crushers, modern concrete storage vats and mechanized bottling and labeling.

Preceding pages, the Rio Tâmega near Amarante; a round of cards in Gerês; a regional fair. Below, the Sandeman Port House

202

At the wine lodge visitors are invited to taste different types of *vinho verde*. Those who wish to purchase a bottle or a case may do so in the old distillery, now converted into a store.

Beyond, the road turns abruptly south, running parallel to the Douro. From **Mesão Frio**, on a steep hillside, there is a sweeping view of the Upper Douro twisting through the gorges and port wine country.

Portugal's authoritarian Marquês de Pombal staked out the Douro in 1756, making it the first officially designated wine-producing region in the world. Subsequent legislation designated the Upper Douro as the Port Wine Region. The area stretches along the Douro River Valley from **Barqueiros**, south of Mesão Frio, to **Barca d'Alva** on the Spanish border. It includes the valleys of tributaries.

The port wine vineyards grow on neatly terraced hillside farms along the Douro. Seignorial manors and whitewashed cottages perch among the vineyards and olive groves. The climate is cold, wet and foggy in winter. Summers are hot, and made hotter by the direct rays of the sun reflected on the schist, or crystalline rock.

Regua is a busy river port and headquarters of the Port Wine Institute, founded in 1932 to establish quality control. In the area lie some of the oldest British and Portuguese estates. Here the road crosses the Douro and runs along the southern bank, recrossing the river at **Pinhão**, another wine center.

Nearby lies the **Quinta Do Infantado**, an ancient wine estate that had once belonged to Prince Pedro. The Roseira family, which has owned the property since the turn of the century, recently began selling a drier "Estate Bottled" port directly, without going through the normal channels of shippers of Vila Nova Da Gaia. Other locally bottled wines, that have challenged the Gaia monopoly are Quinta Cotto and Roma Nera. A grape growers' association has since been established to stand up to the shippers.

At Pinhão, the traveler should make a side trip north to **Sabrosa,** the birthplace of Fernão de Magalhães, better known as Magellan, the man who led the first tour around the world in 1522—under the Spanish flag.

A couple of miles northwest is the village of **Mateus,** with its celebrated **palace** and **gardens.** It was built by Nicolau Nasoni in 1739-43 for António José Botelho Mourão. Today, an illustration of the palace graces the distinctive label of the less-than-distinctive rosé wine from this area. The handsome

Terraced vineyards and a port house on the Douro

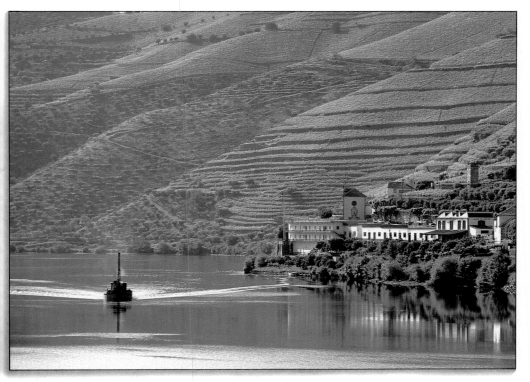

building with whitewashed facade, double stairway, and huge coat of arms has been restored and is open for visits.

To break the journey, a road leads southeast to the valley of the **Tua** with its orange groves, and crossing the Douro again, climbs along the terraced hills to São João da Pesqueira, on a plateau. Winding along the contours of the hills, past quaint churches and the ruins of a castle, one comes to **Vila Nova de Fozcôa** and the valley of the **Côa.** Then the road moves away from the Douro, heading either north or south. The railroad, however, continues along the Douro, with spectacular views of the steep vineyard. It ends in Barca d'Alva, at the Spanish border—which is also the end of port wine country.

The Minho: Nowadays the Minho is generally called Costa Verde, or the Green Coast, a reference to the vineyards and thick pine forests along the shore. It is beautiful countryside, with joyous fairs, festivals and pilgrimages. Foreigners do not often travel here. The Minhotos are naturally good-tempered and hard-working; they seem to enjoy life.

With Oporto as a starting point again, the best way to visit the Minho is to drive up the coast and return by an inland route. The

Atlantic beaches are generally broad with fine sand, but the sea is cold and rough. A fishing town and resort, **Vila do Conde**, is the site of the vast **Convent of Santa Clara**, which was founded in 1318, the 16th-century parish church of **São João Baptista** and a lovely 17th-century **fortress**. Travelers are welcome to watch how fishing boats are made and visit the lace-making school. Nearby, **Póvoa de Varzim** is another popular fishing port-resort, with an 18th-century **fort** and a **parish church**. There's also a casino and a modern luxury hotel, the Vermar dom Pedro, with heated pools and tennis courts. Further north, **Ofir** is a delightful sea and pine forest resort. Just across the **Cávado** River is the town of **Esposende** with the remains of an 18th-century **fortress**. There are many new, often garishly-painted houses in towns and villages along the way; many of these have been built by remittances from Portuguese workers in France and Germany.

A lively fishing and ship-building port, **Viana do Castelo** was called *Diana* by the Romans. This was the center of Portugal's wine trade until the port declined in the 18th century and Oporto took preeminence. There is a good deal to see in Viana, starting with the 18th-century **Palace of Távoras**,

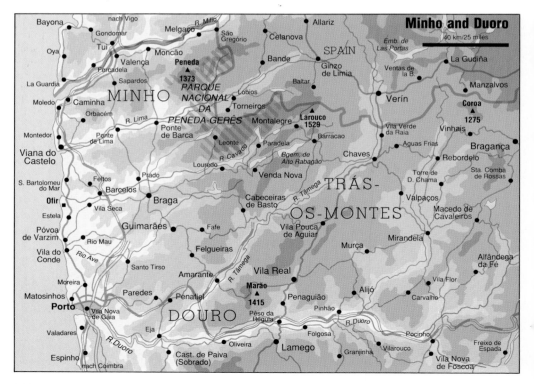

now the main Tourist Office. On the central **Praça da República**, there's a beautiful 16th-century fountain and the remarkable **Misericórdia Hospital**, with its three-tiered facade supported by caryatids. Nearby stands the handsome 15th-century **parish church** with a Gothic portal and Romanesque towers. The town is dominated by **Monte Santa Luzia,** with a rather ungainly modern basilica. To the west, in a large field, the baroque **Nossa Senhora da Agonia** church is the site of a popular pilgrimage every August. Dancers, musicians, and other celebrants, wearing red- and white traditional costumes, come from all over Minho to take part in the three-day festival.

Continuing north, the road leads to **Caminha**, an attractive town with echoes of its past as a busy trading port. The parish church, dating from the 15th century, has a beautiful carved-wood ceiling. There are a number of lovely 15th- and 16th-century buildings near the main square.

At the estuary of the **Minho River**, the road turns inland and follows the river, which forms the border with Spain. **Valença do Minho** is a bustling border town with shops and markets. Spaniards come here regularly to purchase items that include coffee, cigarettes and crystal chandeliers. The Portuguese, on the other hand, cross the border frequently to Tuy or Vigo to buy canned goods such as asparagus and artichokes, and ready-made clothing. The old town of Valença is still fairly intact with cobbled streets and stone houses with iron balconies. It is surrounded by 17th-century granite ramparts. The ancient **convent**, with a splendid view of the Minho River and Spain, that has been since converted into a *pousada.*

From **Monção,** a fortified town famous for its spring water as well as its wines, one takes the road south through the heart of the Minho province: lush green countryside, crisscrossed by rivers with medieval stone bridges; simple white churches with elaborate granite doorways and windows; and, of course, unending vineyards. Because of the high population density, the land has been divided and sub-divided for generations, so the average property is an acre or two. To get the most out of the land, the Minhotos train their vines to grow up, on trees, houses and hedges, leaving ground-space for cabbages, onions and potatoes. This free-wheeling system has made it difficult to modernize grape production, but in recent years, the larger farms have begun to use a system of crosses called *cruzetas.*

The road passes **Arcos de Valdevez,** a charming hillside town built on the two banks of the **Vez River**, with a magnificent view of the valley. Just a few miles south, **Ponte de Barca** on the left bank of the **Lima River**, has a lovely 15th-century **parish church** and an old **town square**, but the principal attraction is the fine stone **bridge** with arches, built in 1543 and restored on several occasions.

Here the traveler should turn westward, along the beautiful valley of the Lima River, which the Romans believed was the Lethe, the mythological river of oblivion. Situated here are great estates or *solares*, a tangible reminder of the glories of the old empire. Some are now guesthouses, and arrangements to visit these manors should be made beforehand in the Portuguese tourist office in Lisbon or Viana do Castelo.

Generally the owners or family members live in the *solares* and welcome visitors to share their way of life. This might mean hunting and fishing, taking part in the grape harvest, or simply holding long conversations by the fireplace. Each *solar* has its own history and charm. On the outskirts of **Ponte de Lima,** the original tower of the **Quinta de Sabadão** was built in the 16th century, and the house has been in the Abreu

Vila do Conde's aqueduct (1705-14) peers above the rooftops

Lima family since the beginning of the 17th century. The lady of the manor proudly shows visitors the family portraits, antiques and her great-grandfather's diary from the war against Napoleon.

Ponte de Lima is one of the loveliest towns in Portugal, mainly because of its location on the south bank of the Lima River. The town faces a magnificent long **Roman Bridge** with low arches. Remains from the old city wall still stand. A 15th-century **palace** with crenellated facade is now used as a hospital. Across the river, stand the 15th-century **São António convent** has beautiful woodwork, including two Baroque shrines.

Continuing towards Viana do Castelo, there are more *solares*, such as the **Casa de Cortegaça**, with its great stone tower dating back to the 15th century. This is a working manor, with wine cellars, flour mill and stable. Guests are welcome to take part in the farm life.

South of Viana, another inland road leads to the charming market town of **Barcelos**, on the northern bank of the **Cávado River**. Barcelos boasts 15th-century **fortifications**, a 13th-century **church** and a 16th-century **palace**, but more than that, it has one of the best handicraft fairs in the coun-try. Every Thursday, merchants and artisans display their folk art and other wares at the fairgrounds in the center of town. It was here that the late Rosa Ramalho, Portugal's Grandma Moses, created her world of fanciful ceramic animals and people. These can be seen in the **Ceramic Art Museum**, which is connected to the parish church. Other popular items include copperware, hand-made rugs, wooden toys, bright cotton tableware, and of course the Barcelos cock, now the national emblem.

According to the medieval legend, a pilgrim from Galicia was suspected of committing murder and condemned to death. Protesting his innocence, the Galician pointed to a roast chicken on the magistrate's table, and declared, "As surely as I stand innocent, so will that cock crow when I am hanged." The cock obligingly crowed *before* the sentence was carried; the prisoner was set free and a monument built to mark the miracle.

Guimarães: A busy manufacturing town noted mainly for textiles, shoes and cutlery, Guimarães still possesses many reminders of its past glory as birthplace of the Portuguese nation.

In the year 1128, an 18-year-old boy named Afonso Henriques proclaimed inde-

The serenity and beauty of Ponte de Lima

pendence for the county of Portucale from the kingdom of León and Castille. It was in the field of **São Mamede**, near Guimarães, that the young Afonso Henriques defeated his mother's army, which was battling on behalf of Alfonso VII, king of León and Castile.

The city's Festival of Saint Walter, the *Festas Gualterianas,* dates from the middle of the 15th century. This three-day celebration, held on the first weekend in August, includes a torchlight procession, a fair with traditional dances and a medieval parade.

Guimarães has long been the center of the Portuguese linen industry. It still produces high quality, coarse linen from home-grown flax naturally bleached by the sun. The region is also known for its hand embroidery on linen. This, unfortunately, is gradually being replaced by machine.

A visit should begin at the 10th-century **castelo** on the northern side of town. It is believed that Afonso Henriques was born here in 1110, the son of Henri of Burgundy, count of Portucale, and his wife Teresa. The castle is a large mass of walls and towers on a rocky hill with magnificent view of the mountains. The dungeon and fortifications were restored many times. Early in the 19th century, the castle was used as a debtors' prison; it was restored again in 1940. At the entrance stands the small Romanesque chapel of **São Miguel do Castelo** with the original font where Afonso Henriques was baptized in 1111.

Heading into town, one passes the 15th-century Gothic **Palace of the Dukes of Bragança,** now occasionally used as an official residence by the President of the Republic. Otherwise, it is open to the public. This massive granite construction consists of four buildings around a cloister and has been completely restored. Outside is a fine statue of Afonso Henriques by Soares dos Reis. Visitors may also view the splendid wood ceiling of the Banquet Hall, the Persian carpets, French tapestries, ancient portraits and documents.

The **Rua de Santa Maria**, with its cobblestones and 14th- and 15th-century houses with wrought-iron balconies leads to the center of town. On the left lies the **Convento de Santa Clara**, built in the 17th century and now used as the Town Hall.

Nossa Senhora de Oliveira, originally of the 10th century, was rebuilt by Count Henri in the 12th century; it has since undergone several restorations. Still visible are the 16th-century watchtower and 14th-century western portal and window.

According to a 7th-century legend, an old Visigoth warrior named Wamba was tilling his field near Guimarães when a delegation came to tell him he had been elected king. He refused to take the office. Driving his staff into the ground, Wamba declared that not until it bore leaves would he become king. As these things happen, the staff turned into an olive tree. The church was named in honor of the miracle.

Adjacent to the church of Oliveira, the Romanesque cloisters have been converted into the **Museu de Alberto Sampaio**. This includes the church's rich **treasury** of 12th-century silver chalices and Gothic and Renaissance silver crucifixes as well as 15th- and 16th-century statues, paintings and ceramics.

The busiest square in Guimarães is the **Largo do Toural**. Just beyond, the church of **São Domingoes** was built in the 14th century and still has the original transept, rose window over the portal, and lovely Gothic cloister. The **Museu Martins Sarmento** is located in the cloister, built in 1271 and enlarged early in the 20th century. Here are artifacts and objects from Briteiros and other citânais—ancient Iberian fortified villages—of northern Portugal; statues, Roman votives, inscriptions, ceramics and coins.

Continuing along the broad garden called the **Almeda da Liberdade**, one reaches the church of **São Francisco**, founded in the 13th century. There is little left of the original Gothic structure. However, the sacristy is very fine with its 17th-century gilt woodwork and ceiling.

High on the outskirts of the city stands a most interesting building. **Santa Marinha da Costa** was founded as a monastery in the 12th century and rebuilt in the 18th century. The church functions regularly and may be visited. The cells of the monastery, which were badly damaged by fire in 1951, have recently been restored with great care and turned into a luxury *pousada*. Visible in the **cloisters** are a 10th-century Mozarab arch and vestiges of a 7th-century Visigoth structure. The veranda is decorated with magnificent 18th-century tile scenes and a fountain.

After seeing the Briteiros exhibit at the Martins Sarmento Museum, the traveler must visit the original site, only six miles north toward Braga. At first, the **Citânia de Briteiros** appears to be nothing more than piles of stones on a hillside, but is in fact one of Portugal's most important archaeological sites. Here are the remains of a prehistoric fortified village said to have been inhabited by Celts. It was discovered in 1874 by archaeologist Francisco Martins

Sarmento. At the summit, a small chapel and two round houses have been restored. Also visible are the remains of triple defensive walls, ancient flagstones and foundation walls of some 150 houses. Most houses were circular with stone benches running around the wall. A large rock in the center supported a pole that in turn held up a thatched roof. Several houses are larger, with two or more rectangular rooms. The town seems to have been well organized with a water system: spring water flowed from the top of the hill down gutters carved in the paving stones to a cistern and a public fountain.

Braga: Some people still refer to the Braga somewhat wistfully as "the Portuguese Rome." They point out that in Roman times, it was known as *Bracara Augusta* and was the center of communications in North Lusitania. In the 6th century, two synods were held here. Under Moorish occupation, Braga was sacked and the cathedral badly damaged. But in the 11th century, the city was largely restored to its former eminence by Bishop Dom Pedro and Archbishop São Geraldo. The Archbishop claimed authority over all the churches of the Iberian Peninsula, and his successors retained the title of Primate of the Spains for six centuries. Like a Renaissance prince, Archbishop Dom Diogo de Sousa in the 16th century encouraged the construction of the many handsome Italian-style churches, fountains and palaces. Zealous prelates restored many of these works in the 17th and 18th centuries, but often with unfortunate results.

Braga lost its title as ecclesiastical capital in 1716, when the Patriarchate was established in Lisbon. Even so, Braga is still an important religious center, the site of the most elaborate Holy Week procession in the country, with torches, floats, folk-dancing and fireworks.

Any visit to Braga begins at the **Sé**, built in the 11th century on the site of an earlier structure destroyed by the Moors. Of the original Romanesque building, there remains only the southern portal and the sculpted cornice of the transept. Although it has been greatly modified by various restorations, the cathedral is still an imposing edifice, with its great facade, twin towers, transept and dome. The interior contains a fine granite sculpture of the Virgin, an 18th-century choirloft and organ case and richly decorated chapels and cloister. The cathedral treasury is now a **Museum of Religious Art** with a fine collection of vestments

The gardens at Bom Jesús do Monte

going back to the 15th century, and silver chalices and crucifixes of the 10th and 12th centuries.

Nearby, in a garden with an 18th-century fountain, is the **Palace of the Archbishop,** built in the 14th century. It, too, has been reconstructed several times. The palace now houses the **Public Library,** with city archives dating to the 9th century, 300,000 volumes and 10,000 manuscripts.

On the other side of the **Agrolongo Square** stands one of the Rome-inspired churches, **Nossa Senhora do Pópulo,** built in the 17th century and remodeled at the end of the 18th century. It is decorated with tiles showing the life of St. Augustine.

The **Casa dos Biscainhos,** across the way, is a 17th-century mansion with lovely garden and fountains. Now a museum, the collection includes 18th-century tiles, ceramics, jewelry and furniture. Part of the museum has been set aside for artifacts from the recent excavations at **Colina de Maximinos.** Long known as the original site of *Bracara Augusta,* a protected zone finally was finally established in 1977—after some damage from modern construction. The university of Minho is directing the excavations, which have uncovered **Roman Baths**, a sanctuary called "**Fonte do Idilio**"

and the remains of a house called "**Domus de Santiago.**" These may be visited.

On the northern side of the city, the church of **São João de Souto** was completely rebuilt in the late 18th century. But here is the superb **Chapel of Conceição,** built in 1525, with crenellated walls, lovely windows and splendid statues of St. Anthony and St. Paul.

There are many other churches and chapels of interest in the religious center, but the best known is **Bom Jesús**, on the wooded **Monte Espinho,** just outside the city. This popular pilgrimage center is remarkable, not so much for the building but for its grandiose stairway and the view from its terrace of the Cávado River valley and mountains in the distance. The double flight of stairs is flanked by chapels, fountains and terra-cotta figures at each level, representing the Stations of the Cross. If a visitor is not up to making the climb, there's a funicular and a winding road to the top. There, in a park of huge oak trees, eucalyptus, camelias and mimosa, stands the 15th-century church, rebuilt in the 18th century. In its **Chapel of Miracles,** there are many votives and pictures left by past pilgrims. Several hotels, souvenir shops and restaurants are also located near the sanctuary.

Thousands gather at the sanctuary of Bom Jesús do Monte each Pentacost

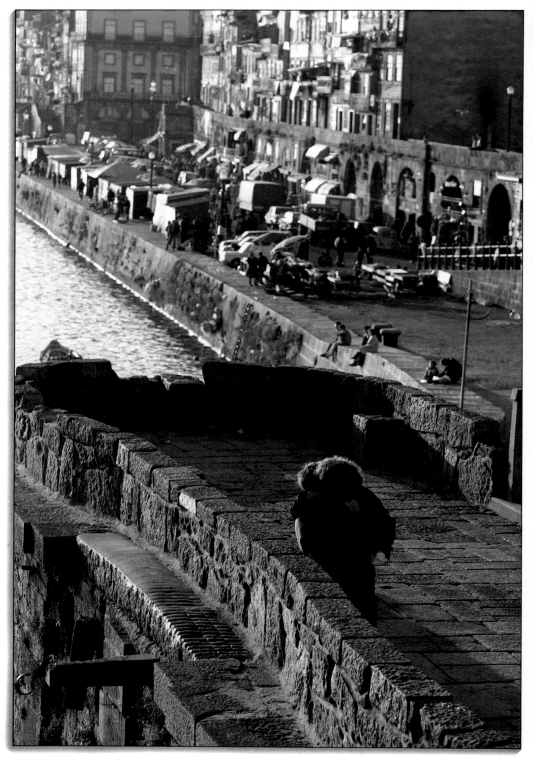

OPORTO

As its name implies, Oporto is the commercial center of northern Portugal and is the hub of the lucrative port wine trade. (The Potuguese spelling, by the way, is simply *Porto*.) Like Lisbon, Oporto is clustered on hills overlooking a river. But unlike the pastel walls and Mediterranean light of Lisbon. Oporto is a northern European city with granite church towers, stolid dark buildings, narrow streets and hidden Baroque treasures.

Posed majestically on the rocky cliffs overlooking the Douro River, Oporto is linked by three bridges to Vila Nova de Gaia, an industrial area where most of the wine lodges are located. Large ships often dock at the seaport of Leixões because of frequent silting of the Douro estuary; but coal barges, fishing trawlers and other small vessels still sail up the river.

The climate is temperate and the *Portuenses,* as the inhabitants are called, are traditionally industrious. The population of Greater Oporto is about one million.

In Roman times, the twin cities at the mouth of the Douro were known as Portus on the right bank and Cale on the left bank. During the Moorish occupation, the entire region between the Minho and Douro rivers was called Portucale. When Afonso Henriques founded the new kingdom in the 12th century, he took the name of his home province and called it Portucalia.

Closely linked to Portugal's golden epoch of the Discoveries, Oporto prospered from the seafaring exploits. Its shipyards produced the caravels that sailed around the world. Prince Henry, who founded the country's school of navigation, was born in Oporto. Also proudly numbered among the *Portueses* are the poet Almeida Garrett and novelist Julio Dinis.

The city's close English connections developed with the wine trade. According to some Portuguese accounts, it was actually the English who discovered port wine. They say that in 1678, two sons of a wealthy English merchant stayed for awhile in a monastery on the Upper Douro. They discovered that by adding a little brandy to the sweet wine of the Douro, it was sufficiently fortified to withstand temperature changes and long sea voyages. When the brothers returned to England, they reportedly took back large quantities of this fortified wine, which came to be known as port.

Pasquale Iocca, a wine authority with the Portuguese Trade Commission in New York, gives a different story. He notes that in the 17th and 18th centuries, the wines of the Upper Douro were robust table wines. Then in 1820, a "climatic accident" occurred, with very warm weather producing unusually sweet grapes and a wine appreciated by the British. In the following years, amid much controversy, the wine companies added *aguardente,* or brandy, to stop the fermentation and fix the sugar content. This was the beginning of the sweet fortified nectar as it is known today.

Whatever the history is, the Methuen Treaty of 1703 opened English markets to Portuguese wines, and the British shippers of Oporto became increasingly rich and powerful. In 1727 they established a Shippers Association, which regulated the trade and controlled prices paid to Portuguese growers. To combat the English monopoly, the dictator Pombal founded the Alto Douro Wine Company in 1757, which restored a measure of Portuguese control.

Rose Macaulay describes whimsically how British port wine shippers virtually "captured and occupied" Oporto in her delightful book, *They Went to Portugal.* She notes that the "Oporto families, some of

Left, plenty of activity along the Douro in Oporto. Right, constructing port barrels at Vila Novo de Gaia

them established in Oporto or Viana do Castelo since the 17th century, have the air of owning the city, so Britanically, so unconsciously arrogantly." The British presence still can be felt, although it is, most would agree, less overbearing.

Portugal's liberal revolution began in 1820 at Oporto. The severest fighting took place against absolutist King Miguel in 1832-3, leading to his exile and the restoration of liberalism.

In modern times, the city was the center of liberal opposition to Salazar's right-wing dictatorship. After the 1974 revolution, the city served as a bastion against the spread of Communism to the north.

Oporto today is a relatively prosperous commercial city, where people like to eat and drink well. Regional specialties include roast pork, fresh salmon, lamprey, trout and tripe.

Generally Oporto is a sober city. Apart from dining, there's not much nightlife. Visitors may hear *fado* at some restaurants such as Mal Cozinhado or Taverna de São Jorge. The Portuguese usually make a trip out of town for some entertainment. The younger set frequents discotheques at the suburb of **Foz do Douro,** while their elders prefer the nearby coastal resort of **Espinho**

with its casino and night club.

The city's main festival is that of Saint John the Baptist on June 23 and 24. This coincides with the ancient celebration of the summer solstice, so the Christian feast is laced with pagan traditions. People take to the streets and slap one another teasingly with bundles of leeks, feathers and nowadays, plastic hammers. The most popular festivities occur at the **Alameda das Fontainhas,** a square overlooking the **Dom Luís I Bridge,** where people sing and dance around bonfires, drink *vinho verde* and feast on roast kid and grilled sardines.

The heart of the city is the **Praça da Liberdade,** with an equestrian statue of Pedro IV in the center. On the north side of the square is the broad **Avenida dos Aliados,** with bright flowerbeds and mosaic walks, leading uphill to the **Town Hall.** Here stands the modern stone statue of native son Almeida Garrett, liberal poet and novelist.

"From here, where it got its name, Old Portugal, the name will again rise up with distinction," Garrett wrote in 1819. "The brilliance, the honor, the healthy customs, pure love of native land, the sincere frankness, the noble independence of other epochs will resurge once more from here…"

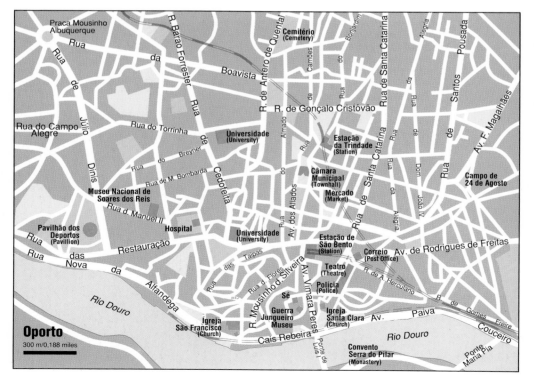

To the southeast of Praça da Liberdade lies the **Praça de Almeida Garrett**, where the **São Bento Railroad Station** has a fine entrance hall, decorated with tiles showing historical scenes.

Heading south up the hill, one arrives at the **Sé**, or cathedral, with its square towers and small domes, dating back to the 12th century but greatly modified since. Here King João I wed the English Queen Philippa of Lancaster in 1387. The Gothic **cloister** is decorated with fine tiles. Nearby on **Pena Ventosa**, the site of an ancient citadel, stands the impressive 18th-century **Bishop's Palace**. Just beyond, the **House of Guerra Junqueiro**, a poet who died in 1923, is a museum with his memorabilia and furnishings.

Across the avenue stands the 15th-century church of **Santa Clara**, next to one of the best preserved parts of the old city wall. Santa Clara has been rebuilt several times but is noted for its splendid gilt-wood choirstalls and altars. Sacheverell Sitwell writes: "After it, every other building in Porto, even São Francisco, is drab and dull."

To the west, the church of São Lourenço better known as Grilos (for the crickets that lodge there), is one of the earliest examples of Portuguese Baroque, built in 1570.

At the end of Rua dos Ingleses stands the bastion of English life, the **Feitoria Inglesa** or the Factory House. Here the old British port wine shippers do their business, play billiards or cards, read English newspapers and enjoy English cuisine, as they have for the past 200 years. Outsiders must obtain special authorization from the British Port Wine Shippers Association to visit.

Around the corner, on Rua da Alfândega, stands the much restored **palace** where Prince Henry the Navigator was born in 1394. For a time it served as the customs house; it is now a museum.

Going by the **Praça do Infante Dom Henrique**, one reaches the **Church of São Francisco**, founded by King Sancho II in 1233 and rebuilt in the 14th century. The interior glitters in Baroque splendor with gilded columns, arches and statues. On the site of the convent, which burnt down in 1832, is the **Bolsa**, seat of the Commercial Association of Oporto and the stock exchange. It is noted for its opulent neo-Moorish reception hall.

Up the hill is the Port Wine Institute, a government agency established in 1932 to control the quality of port. Every year, the Institute establishes specific quotas for port production. About 40 percent of the

The Douro snakes through Oporto

region's grapes go into port; the rest are used for ordinary table wines.

Following the Rua Belmonte past lovely old homes with balconies and tiled walls, one arrives at the church of **São João Novo**, built in 1592. Across the way, stands the 18th-century **Palace of São João Novo,** a whitewash and granite building that houses the **Museum of Ethnography and History.** The collection includes archaeological finds going back to the Paleolithic Age, old wine presses and wine boats, fishing equipment, pharmacy, vases, ceramics, costumes, jewelry and folk art.

The road leads to the graceful **Torre dos Clerigos**, a six-story granite tower built in the 18th century as a landmark for ships coming up the Douro. It is worth climbing the 225 stairs for a spectacular view of the city.

Outside the city center, there are various sites that will interest visitors. To the east lies the busy square called **Praça da Batalha**, with a statue of Pedro V in the middle. On the square stands the imposing 18th-century church of **São Idlefonso** with a fine granite facade decorated with blue-and-white tiles.

The main shopping street is **Rua Santa Catarina**, where one may find good buys in a variety of local products from shoes and clothing to pottery. **Rua das Flores** has the best gold and silver shops.

Northwest of the center lies the main **university** building, a handsome granite structure built in 1807 as the Polytechnical Academy. Further north, stands the 12th-century **São Martinho de Cedofeita** church. "Cedofeita" means "done too soon;" the church was hastily built to honor the patron St. Martin of Tours.

On the western side of the city, in the old royal **Palácio dos Carrancas** where Wellington once slept, is a museum that should not be overlooked. The **Soares dos Reis Museu**, named after the important 19th-century sculptor, has a fine collection of archaeological articles, religious art, regional costumes, ceramics and contemporary paintings, as well as sculpture. A number of paintings by Grão Vasco are on display, among them *St. Catherine* and *St. Lucy.*

Past the modern **Sports Pavilion** is the **Solar do Vinho do Porto**, where one may test a wide variety of port wines.

Nearby lies the **Quinta da Macierinha**, where the former King Charles Albert died in 1849, after abdicating the throne of Sardinia. Called the **Romantic Museum**, this

Left, portrait of King Carlos, in the Stock Exchange. Right, the ebullient gilded woodwork at São Francisco

mansion is set in a rose garden and it contains most of its original furnishings and paintings.

Returning to the river, one should spend some time just strolling along the river bank, called **Cais da Ribeira**, the liveliest part of the city. Many small shops and restaurants are built right into what remains of the old city wall.

The splendid steel arch farther up river is a railroad bridge, **Ponte de Dona Maria Pia**, built in 1876 on a plan by the ubiquitous Alexandre Gustave Eiffel. On the Western side of the city, the modern concrete span called **Ponte da Arrábida**, is used mostly by the north-south travelers, wishing to avoid Oporto.

From the center of Oporto, travelers generally take the picturesque **Ponte de Dom Luís I**, built in 1886, which provides splendid views. This two-story iron bridge leads directly to **Vila Nova de Gaia**, an industrial zone that is rather black, with ceramic, glass, soap and other factories. But above all, Gaia is the real seat of the port wine industry, where most of the warehouses or lodges are found.

In springtime, the new wine is brought down from the Upper Douro by truck—less picturesque but considerably more practical than by *barcos rabelos*, the flat-bottomed sailboats that used to sail the Douro. In the Gaia lodges, the wine is left to mature in 139-gallon (534-liter) oak casks called pipes. Here the blending takes place for most ports, with wines from different vineyards and years blended to produce the correct taste and color. Then the wine is bottled and again left to continue maturation until its time has come, depending on the type of wine.

Like museum pieces, a few *barcos rabelos* are kept docked at Gaia near the Dom Luís I bridge. Once a year, during the feast of São João on June 24, the boats participate in races on the Douro.

Visitors, however, may take a short launch cruise on the Douro, with fine views of Oporto and the three bridges. The excursion lasts 50 minutes and leaves hourly from a dock near the **Ferreira Lodge.**

There are about 60 port wine lodges located in Gaia. Many of them welcome visitors who wish to tour the installations and taste the wines. The **Sandeman**, **Ferreira** and **Ramos Pinto** companies have full-time guides for visitors. A French expert once calculated that a normal human being can only go through three such tasting visits in one day and remain lucid.

The Stock Exchange's Salon de Arabe, built in 1862

TRAS-OS-MONTES

The English translation of Trás-os-Montes sounds rather awkward—"Back of the Mountains," or "Behind the Mountains." But the meaning suits this remote northeast corner of Portugal. To most Portuguese the province of Trás-os-Montes could be on the other side of the moon. Most Lisboners are inclined to look at it with that distance—albeit with fierce affection as well. It is a province for the more adventurous traveler, for when journeying here, one occasionally has to do without modern comforts.

The word "trás"—"back" or "behind"—fits the region like a glove, for it is certainly "backward" in almost every aspect, cut off from the rest of the country by mountains, poor road and rail systems, and a grinding poverty which has driven the workforce of almost every village into migration to the larger urban areas, or emigration up into the more advanced economies of northern Europe, or overseas. It's quite possible that this ancient historic area is the single most "backward" pocket of civilized Europe—on par, perhaps, with the remoter areas and islands of Greece, and the hinterlands of Sardinia, Sicily or Yugoslavia.

The Portuguese, however, are proud of Trás-os-Montes. Those who come from there, or who go there to spend their holidays—or visit with relatives and childhood friends, unanimously praise the area. The place has its share of regional stories, anecdotes and ethnic jokes. But about the venerable if underdeveloped Trás-os-Montes there is a universal affection that comes across in every conversation one will have on the subject.

"You think we are poor?" queried a village priest from a tiny village in the Barroso district. He was seated on a stone slab inside the stone structure of the communal bake oven, the broiling sun outside the open doorway cooking the dust and dung that "paved" the village street. Against a far wall is an ox-cart with wooden wheels, a design used in the Middle Ages. A hand-held wooden plough, also designed for ox-power—a type used in pre-Roman times—leaned against the ox-cart, its metal digging tip freshly hammered into place by a local smith readying it for work the next day.

"Well, we are poor up here," he said with a broad smile, "but if you look around you—anywhere you go in Trás-os-Montes—you will not see people begging the way you see them in the streets of Lisbon or Oporto. We grow enough food up here to feed everybody. We eat well. Our wine is the best. Others should come and learn from our example..."

There is much higher emigration from the north of Portugal than from the South, and one of the principle reasons is due to the division of lands. The south is an area of *latifundios*—large landholdings, while the north has *minifundios*—small holdings. A farmer's land in the north is simply not sufficient to provide him and his family with a living. The northern people are conservative, and resist any form of cooperative farming venture such as those widely used in the southern province of Alentejo. Another reason for the *minifundios* is the terrain—high mountains and steep-sided valleys have made it difficult to organize farming on a large scale.

A more subtle factor affecting Portugal's conservative north is the Church. While all of Portugal might be viewed as Roman Catholic, the sheer remoteness of the northeast corner of the country has meant that national government has little impact, while native religion predominates. This has affected education, particularly; until recent years, often the only educated man in a village was the priest, whose wisdom and opinion would be sought on every matter ranging from the spirit to advice on crop harvesting.

One may enter the region, which is often overlapped with the Alta Douro, the upper valley of the Douro River, from a number of directions. Border crossings from Spain are at Vila Verde da Raia, on the road leading south to Chaves (this is a historical invasion route—employed by the armies of Napoleon in the early 1800s); at Portelo, in the Parque Natural de Montezinho; at Quintanilha, east of Bragança; and at Miranda do Douro and Bemposta, where the River Douro forms the frontier. From inside Portugal, the main routes into the region would be from Oporto via Vila Real; and from the south, from Lamego via Vila Real; or from Guarda via either Torre de Moncorvo or Freixo de Espada à Cinta. The region is split into two administrative districts, with capitals at Vila Real in the southwest and Bragança in the northeast.

Heading north, one is still in port wine country when one crosses the Douro from the direction of Lamego and enters Regua. There are two bridges crossing the river here—one a road bridge, the other a railway bridge that has never been used, but some 50 years ago was intended for a spur line connecting Regua with Lamego. Of greater curiosity is the tiny rail-link between Regua, Vila Real and Chaves, a south-north route built in 1890 which still uses original rolling stock—toy-sized carriages with wood-slat seats and a humorously primitive toilet system aboard. A conversation with Stationmaster Agostinho Bernardo dos Santos would be enlightening for any railroading buff. He has spent nearly 30 years as chief at Regua—and is particularly proud of the running record of the tiny Regua-Chaves line.

The original steam engine stands proudly displayed on a rusted old section of the narrow-gauge track behind the station—replaced by a specially-built diesel locomotive only five years ago. The train leaves, more or less on time, five times a day—and manages an average speed of 16 miles (27 km) an hour as it wends its way north. Some passengers, when in season, take along empty baskets on their journey; the blackberries one can pick off the bushes en route are delicious.

Driving north out of Regua, you can make a stop at Martha's port wine house in **S. João de Lobrigos**. Try a sweet port, at any time of the day. The trip to **Vila Real** gives one a first glimpse of the terraced vineyards of this province, where more than half of the working population is employed in agriculture.

Vila Real: An ancient settlement in the Terra de Panóais, Vila Real was founded and renamed by Dom Dinis, the sixth king of Portugal, in 1289. Its name literally means "royal town"—fittingly, as Vila Real boasts more noble families than any city other than the capital, and has ever since King Dinis first patronized it. Walking in the ancient streets, one will see many residences marked, often above the main entrance, with the original owners' coat of arms. Like as not, the same family is still living there. The famous 19th-century writer Camilo Castelo Branco lived in Vila Real, and wrote many of his most enduring works using the town as a backdrop.

"In what century are we on this mountain?" asks one of his characters.

"In what century?" comes the reply. "Why, it is the same 18th century here as it is in Lisbon."

"Oh!" says the first. "I thought time here had stopped in the 12th century."

Vila Real became a city proper only in 1925, but the importance of the region dates from 1768 when the vineyards were first developed commercially. The first of

The Corgo railway line, which runs from Chaves to Régua

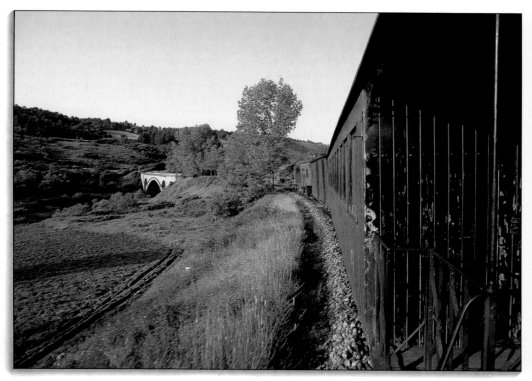

Portugal's port wines were blended here, and most of the region's red and white wines are labelled *reserva* to mark their excellence. The wines of Vila Real are exported to more than 150 countries.

Panóais, the original name given to the pre-King Dinis settlement, is also the name of a strange pagan sanctuary about three miles (six km) out of town in the **Vale de Nogueiras**, where a series of enormous carved stones rest, which are believed to have been used as altars of human sacrifice. Inscriptions in Latin invoke the ancient god Serapis, known to both Greek and Egyptian mythology. It is believed that an early Roman settlement existed here—dating to a time not very long after the birth of Christ, and possibly even earlier. It is known that Christianity had taken a firm foothold in this region by the second century A.D., and it is likely that the inscriptions predate the Christian era of the settlement.

The **Sé**, or cathedral, was originally the church of a Dominican convent. Although much of the present building dates from the 14th century, still remaining are Romanesque columns from and earlier structure.

Vila Real's oldest church is the ancient **Capela de São Nicolau** on a promontory of high land behind the municipal hall, over-looking the valley of the **Rio Corgo**. Other churches of note are the baroque **São Pedro**, built in 1528, with a lovely coffered ceiling, and the Gothic cathedral of **São Domingos**.

There are also a number of fine houses dating from the 15th to the 18th centuries. An example is the **Casa de Diogo Cão**, an Italian Renaissance-style house that was, according to tradition, the birthplace of the navigator who discovered the mouth of the Congo River.

In the area of handicrafts, the Vila Real region is particularly noted for the black pottery of Bisalhães, and the woolen goods of d'Agarez, Caldas do Alvão and Marão.

Addressing modern interests, Vila Real has become known as the motorcycling capital of the country, with a circuit that runs within the city's limits. International motorcycle meets and races are held in June and July.

Serra de Alvão: Two scenic routes lead north out of this capital city, one on each side of the high Serra da Padrela—to Chaves in the north, and Bragança in the northeast. But the adventurous traveler may strike northwest into the rugged Serra de Alvão, and be treated to one of the most lavish mountain vistas the country has to offer. The road leads through a small natural park and across the **Rio Olo** to **Mondim de Basto** on the banks of the **Rio Tâmega**. There it forms the border between Trás-os-Montes and Minho.

Granite gives way to slate—many of the houses are roofed by it—and in the high passes, one can hear the rushing of mountain waters, the tinkle of goat bells, or the calling of a herder to his dogs. In the winter there is snow here, but at other times of the year one is likely to encounter a profusion of wild flowers—whole mountainsides of purples or yellows—and everywhere the smell of pine forest. Pine resin, used in making paints and turpentine, is a major product of this area.

A side trip of some eight miles (12 kilometers) from Mondim de Basto will take one to **Atei**, a delightful little village containing numerous archaeological remnants of Roman occupation. From here a curious subterranean road of either Roman or Arab construction leads down to Furaco on the banks of the Tâmega.

Leaving Mondim de Basto, the road winds northwards to **Cabeceiras de Basto**, which is actually in the Minho province, at the head of a small "peninsula" that juts up into Trás-os-Montes. Stop at the imposing baroque **Refojos Monastery** before heading into the high Serra de Cabeceira and

A stork busy with nest repairs, near Bragança

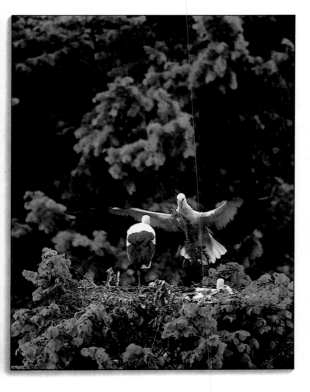

back into Trás-os-Montes at **Póvoa**.

Barroso District: One soon joins the main Braga-Chaves road that runs beside **Barragem do Rabagão**, a gigantic expanse of lake formed behind a dam, but here again another side trip is called for—to Mont'alegre, the towering Serra do Larouco, and the primitive villages of the Barroso district.

In truth, one could spend weeks or more in this area; anthropologists and sociologists have spent lifetimes studying this extraordinary corner of Portugal, for the region lends some understanding to life in medieval Europe.

As the largest town in the area, **Mont'alegre** might be considered the "capital" of Barroso. Given a charter in 1273 by King Afonso III, and restored and expanded in turn by King Dinis and King Manuel I, Mont'alegre (*monte* meaning hill, *alegre* meaning happy or cheerful) is thought to have possibly enjoyed its villa status from a much earlier time, for the pillory in the center of town carries the coat-of-arms of King Sancho I, who was on the throne of Portugal from 1185 until 1211.

The hill on which the town stands commands a view over a wide area, so it is hardly surprising that it has been a military center for some dozens of centuries. Mont'alegre is rich in archaeological finds. It was a center for the ancient Lusitanians, the Romans, Suevi and Visigoths. There have been no finds of Moorish occupation, although they did play an important role in the history of nearby Chaves. At **Outeiro Lesenho**, near Mont'alegre, in the 18th century were found two gigantic granite statues of warriors. They are thought to be from the Iron Age, and have been attributed to Celtic influence. Both are to be found today in the Ethnology Museum of Belém in Lisbon.

A magnificent four-towered **castle** stands at Mont'alegre and was in constant use during the many wars that Portugal fought against Spain. North of the region rises the mass of the **Serra do Larouco**, second highest range of mountains in the country (after the Serra da Estrêla), with a number of passes leading into Spanish Galicia.

The district of Barroso stretches from the foothills of the Serra do Larouco to some nine or 12 miles (15 or 20 km) northwest of the city of Chaves. There is no absolute boundary, but it would include such villages as Meixide, Padornelos and Tourem Pitões, to name a few. If one can shut out the "emigrant architecture" that blights the vil-

Archaic building methods survived until recently in Barroso

lages in northern Portugal—uncontrolled modern housing that is built with money saved by the Portuguese who work abroad—one will find in these settlements vestiges of a bygone era, a sense of history utterly remote in time.

The ancient houses are built of enormous granite or slate blocks. Doors, windows, balconies are of weathered antique wood. Until recently, many houses were thatched, although tiled roofs are now more the rule. Streets are dirt, or simple bare rock. In many villages, electricity was installed only within the past decade. Almost every church is in Romanesque style—early Middle Ages—with the typical facade rising to a twin-columned peak to house the church bell. Ox-carts are still standard transport between the villages and the surrounding arable fields. It is rare to see a tractor; most ploughs are hand-held, wooden-stocked and pulled by oxen.

For centuries the people of Barroso lived out their lives cut off from the outside world. They developed their own customs, songs, festivals and habits. In many corners of the world under similar circumstances, local people may treat outsiders with suspicion or alarm. This is certainly not the case in Barroso. It is hard to imagine a more warm-hearted, hospitable people, eager to share the peculiarities of their daily lives with others who come to visit them. By tradition, the bread oven, which is fired up once a week, is both meeting place for each village, and local hostel for travelers seeking shelter for a night or two. Winter or summer, the bread ovens are never cold—but they are housing at its most primitive—residents must supply their own sleeping bags!

Local cultural groups keep alive the ancient customs and folklore. Along with the recognized need to modernize there is, happily, a proud awareness of the area's link with the past.

One of the region's most colorful festivals is the annual *Chega dos Toiros*, an intervillage competition which means "The Arrival of the Bulls." Each village takes enormous pride in its bull, a communal animal bred especially for the purpose of covering the various cows owned by the individual farmers. This bull, by both tradition and breeding, is the biggest and most ferocious animal imaginable—one feels that his breeding is as much to gain the honors at the annual competition as it is for stock purposes.

Held in June, July and August, the *Chega* is essentially a bullfight, where the bull of

Basic farming in Rio de Onor, where wooden-wheeled carts are still in use

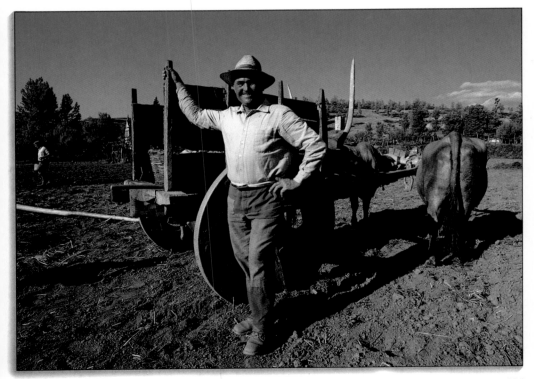

one village is pitted against another in a duel. Each animal is decorated and feted by his villagers, and paraded with bands and crowds with much color and hoopla.

The fight itself is deadly earnest, with the champions of each bull shouting and goading their animal into battle. The fight continues until one animal is killed, or turns and runs away. The victor is lead away by his villagers with much celebration to be prepared for the next fight.

At the end of the season there will be a regional champion—and this is the lucky animal who'll be put out to pasture with the region's cows. He is a source of great pride to the residents of the village from which he comes.

Chaves: Chaves, just a few kilometers down the road from Barroso, seems a world away. Itself an ancient city (the fortified Lusitanian village of the present site was captured by the Romans in the year 78 A.D.—the Emperor Flavius founded the city of *Aqua Flaviae* there, inaugurating the still popular hot springs and baths), Chaves is a bustling center with a population of about 15,000. It is an agricultural and textile center, famous for its ham, and boasts the largest *taverna* or *tasca* in Portugal.

Situated on the Rio Tâmega, Chaves commands a strategic position in a wide valley that extends from the Spanish frontier into the heart of Trás-os-Montes. Just about every invader who set his heart on Portugal, or chunks of it, routed his armies through this channel. Thus, at one time or another, Chaves has hosted Celts, Lusitanians, Romans, Vandals, Suevi, Moors, Spanish and French.

In addition to fortifications and the baths, the Romans built here the largest of their bridges ever to be built in the Iberian Peninsula. Completed in 104 A.D., it has 20 arches, is 150 yards (140 meters) in length—and is still very much in daily use. In the middle of the bridge are two inscribed Roman milestones.

Chaves means "keys" in Portuguese, but actually this is not the derivation of the name of the city. The ancient *Aqua Flaviae* was much later shortened to *Flavias*, and local mispronunciation eventually produced the current name.

Sights include the **parish church**, originally rebuilt in the 16th century; and the Baroque **São João de Deus**, a church near the bridge.

Prior to the formation of Portugal, the fortified city was made a part of the original County of Portucale. Various of Portugal's

Scythe-seeing near Aldeia Santo Andre in Barroso

early kings added significantly to its **castle**, one of the most important in the land. A second castle, in its day also an integral part of the defenses of this strategic valley, still stands at **Monforte de Rio Livre**, about eight miles (12 kilometers) east of Chaves.

Heading eastwards towards Bragança one will pass the old town of **Vinhais** high in the **Serra de Montesinho**, on the south flank of the natural park of the same name. There was a castle long since destroyed at Vinhais, and it is known that there was a significant population here long before the formation of Portugal as a country. For lovers of nature, the high parkland is well worth a visit of at least several days. And, like Barroso farther to the west, the villages of this region are steeped in ancient history, the customs and culture of centuries past.

The area is famous for its agriculture, particularly vines. Fine woodwork, weaving and basket-making are traditional handicrafts throughout Montesinho.

A mountain, **Ciradela**, rises behind Vinhais. Over it passed the Roman road that led from Braga to Astorga; today this ancient route is rich in archaeological discoveries.

In the 11th and 12th centuries there was a general movement of the population of this area towards the more fertile farm lands of the south. To prevent this, various monasteries were founded and encouraged by the early rulers of the region to develop their own agriculture and cottage industries. One of the most important of these monasteries was the magnificent **Mosteiro de Castro de Avelãs**, a few miles west of Bragança. Parts of the church of the Benedictine abbey have been incorporated into the present-day parish church.

A visitor to the region is well advised to stop at the tourist office in Bragança and ask specifically for the book available on the Parque Natural de Montesinho. In it one will find a detailed map of the park area—and it would be of value to spend a few minutes studying it before heading out on the intricate road system through the park. Many of the roads are paved—but many are not. Whichever direction one takes, one is guaranteed a journey through spectacular countryside. But be sure your car is up to it, and that you carry plenty of fuel. There are no gas stations.

Bragança: Bragança is, at least to many travelers, the most fascinating spot in all of the province. With a current population of some 30,000, it is the administrative capital of the province. A university town, it is also an agricultural trade center (livestock, vine-

A "novelty store" in Chaves

yards, olive oil, grains), a thriving textile industry, and has been famous for its ceramics since prehistoric times (in a nearby cave at **Dine**, archaeologists have found bits and pieces of pottery dating well into the Paleolithic Period).

Known as *Brigantia* to the Celts and *Juliobriga* to the Romans, Bragança received its first *foral* (royal franchise) from King Sancho I in 1187—the same year that the family of the Dukes of Bragança started building their feudal castle there.

The Braganças—still pretenders to the throne of Portugal—provided the land's kings and queens consistently from 1640 until the formation of the republic in 1910, and the emperors of Brazil from 1822 to 1889. The title of Duke of Bragança was traditionally held by the heir to the throne. In 1661, Catherine of Bragança became Queen Consort to Charles II of England, thus renewing the age-old friendship between the two nations.

Traditionally, the possessions of the Bragança family support the *Fundação da Casa de Bragança*, a foundation of the Portuguese state. Its headquarters, a library, a museum and a lecture center, are all based at the family's 16th-century residence in Vila Viçosa, in the Alentejo province.

Bragança's ancient **castle** still stands,—with a **Princess's Tower** full of tragic ghosts. The keep of the castle houses a very fine **military museum**. Nearby, still within the castle walls, one will find the 12th-century five-sided **Domus Municipalis**, the oldest municipal hall in the land. The town walls with their 18 watch towers are still largely intact, and the city boasts a particularly fine Renaissance **cathedral**.

Basing oneself in this historic city, it is relatively easy to make short day trips out into the surrounding region—north into the Montesinho, or south into the center of the district where there are a number of villages that have been specially built, it would seem, to boggle the mind of the latter-day Childe Harold.

Firstly, to the north, in the farthest corner of Portugal, there is **Rio de Onor**, a tiny village that actually straddles the border.

"Bragança has forgotten us up here," complains one of the locals, in reference to the nonexistent bus service. "As for Lisbon—well, the president made a big show of coming up here once, but he didn't arrive by public transport!"

Cut off from civilization for so many centuries, the people of Rio de Onor have actually developed their own dialect. In

Bragança's medieval mien

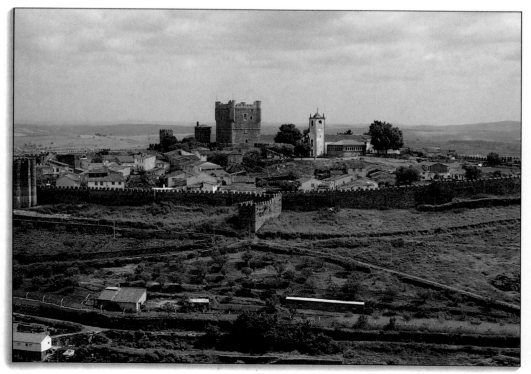

their music and folk dances a common instrument is the *gaiteiro*—a bagpipe, which although more commonly associated with Scotland, Ireland and parts of northern England, is more accurately associated with the Celts.

A good time to visit many of the villages that reach in an arc from Vinhais, across Bragança, and down as far as Miranda do Douro and Freixo de Espada-a-Cinta, would be between Christmas Day and Epiphany (January 6th), when the local population celebrate a number of feasts connected with the Christian calendar. The "Christian" element is really a modern addition to celebrations, complete with ferocious masks and unearthly costumes, which date back to the dawn of time when the simple agrarian people of these pastoral regions practiced fertility rites and paid more than passing attentions to strange magical forces that emanated from the bowels of the earth.

Carnival, of course, is another good time to visit. Forty days before Easter the masks come out again, and one cannot be sure if it is the Christian spirit or the bogeyman that dominates the season.

South of Bragança one may head towards the Spanish frontier at **Miranda do Douro**

where the Douro River has cut a deep gorge into the rock. This charming village is the site of a former **cathedral**, a 16th-century granite building with a series of gilded wood altarpieces.

The river flows southwesterly towards **Freixo de Espada-a-Cinta** in the bottom corner of the province. There are five dams built along the Douro here, jointly operated by Spain and Portugal. This route will lead one through the area inhabited by the Mirandês—a word that denotes both the people living in the villages of this zone and the language they speak. In fact, this language, close to Vulgar Latin, is considered such a valued relic of Portugal's cultural past that it is currently being revived and taught as a subject in the region's schools.

Freixo, as it was first known, is one of the oldest towns in the province, and had initially been fortified by Lusitanians, then Romans, Visigoths and Moors—though nothing now remains of their works. However, an important **castle** was built there when Dom Afonso Henriques first granted the town its charter. The castle's beautiful seven-sided tower, known as the **Cock's Tower**, and remnants of its walls remain.

To promote settlement in a town lying so near—only two and a half miles (four kilometers)—to Spain, Freixo was granted the status of sanctuary for fugitives. Here selected condemned people might receive their freedom once again, although certainly none who had committed treason.

Freixo's Manueline **parish church** was built over a very long period and concluded only in the 17th century. It has a fine Gothic doorway, and, inside, a notable carved chancel.

Taking a more interior route south from Bragança, one may visit such beautiful villages as **Chacim**, in the **Serra de Bornes**, or **Vila Flor**, a little farther south.

Lovers of castles will want to see the impressive ruins at **Algoso**, south of Vimioso. Since the 12th century, this fortress has guarded the area surrounding its lofty perch—a hill called **Cabeco da Penenciada**—while 1,650 feet (500 meters) below, the **Rio Angueira** flows westward until it joins the **Rio Maçãs**.

And in the south center of the province, the castle of **Ansiães**, lonely atop its craggy peak, deserves special mention. As a fortification, the castle and its village grew in importance during the reign of Dom João I. In the 18th century most of the families living there drifted away; now this imposing fortress guards only a sleepy little village—and a realm of silence.

Fernando, the Duke of Bragança and Governor of Ceuta, in a 20th-century statue

BEIRA ALTA AND
BEIRA BAIXA

The provinces of Beira Alta and Beira Baixa, the Upper and Lower Beiras, constitute a large rural section of eastern Portugal—reputedly the poorest geographical region in a country already considered the "poor boy" of western Europe. But it is a richly historical area, because it was for centuries riddled with invasion routes for both the Spanish and Moors: the many castles and remnants of fortresses in these provinces clearly illustrate that. The area has its natural attractions as well: whether the dramatic mountains of the Alta or the stark plains and plateaus of the Baixa here are some of the most beautiful natural landmarks in Portugal.

The region is bounded by the Spanish frontier in the east, the Douro River in the north, and the Tagus River in the south. The western boundary is a ragged line that starts at the Rio Douro some 38 miles (60 km) east of Oporto.

Guarda is the principal city and administrative capital of the Beira Alta's eastern district. The charter of Guarda was granted by Sancho I, Portugal's second king, in 1199. It was already established by 80 B.C., though, when it had a role in the attempted secession from Rome.

Roman gates: There are still traces of Roman occupation. Ruins of the period can be found just outside of town, near the Romanesque chapel of **Póvoa de Mileu**, notable itself for a small rose window and nicely carved capitals. Three town gates, the **Torre de Ferreiros** (Blacksmith's Tower), the **Porta da Estrêla** (Star Gate), and the **Porta do Rei** (King's Gate), still stand from the 12th- and 13th- century castle and town walls, along with the castle **keep**. From the top there is a magnificent view of the mountains, and the broad plains to the north.

The **Sé** (cathedral) was built of granite cut from the surrounding area. An earlier cathedral, close to the city's original walls, was destroyed before this one was begun; it was believed to be in an unsafe position. Work on this "new" edifice started in 1390 and was not completed until 1540, so that there were many Renaissance and Baroque elements added to the original Gothic architecture. The renowned builder Boytac worked on the cathedral, which bears some resemblance to Batalha. The exterior boasts flying buttresses and fanciful gargoyles. Inside, the 16th-century stone **retable**, later

highlighted with gilt, represents scenes in the lives of the Virgin and Christ. A beautiful Renaissance doorway, off the north aisle, leads to the **Capela dos Pinas**, which contains a late Gothic bishop's tomb.

Local people from Guarda call it "the city of four F's—*feia, forte, farta e fria*," which means roughly, "ugly, strong, plentiful and cold." Ugly would be a matter of taste: perhaps the predominance of heavy gray granite makes it look dull, but the old parts of the city are charming. Strong alludes to Guarda's history as a defense point against the Moors and Castile. Plentiful refers, no doubt, to the rich land surrounding the town, noted particularly for its wine and sheep farming. Cold it certainly is, in winter. Situated some 3,500 feet above sea level, Guarda in Portugal's highest city—high enough to ensure abundant snowfall during winter months, a rarity in this southern country.

South of Guarda is a ring of majestic Crags of such disturbing shapes that the town in its midst, entered through massive Gothic gates, is called **Sortelha**, "magic ring." This area has long been the legendary home of witches and werewolves. Ancient civilizations may have shaped some of the rocks, and they certainly mined in the

Preceding pages, the village of Monsanto; the Palace Hotel in Buçaco. Left, in the Serra da Estrêla. Right, sanctuary of Nossa Senhora de Boa Estrêla

area—there are entrances that have been closed for countless centuries.

Stretching southwest of here is the **Serra da Estrêla**, the highest mountain range in Portugal and the source of Portugal's most delicious cheese. Its tallest peak, the Torre or **Malhão da Estrêla**, is 1,993 meters (6,537 feet). Near the Torre is a pilgrimage site, a huge statue of the Virgin carved into the rock, to which the faithful journey on the second Sunday of August. Dramatic crags and ravines make this area a stunningly beautiful drive or hike.

Covilhã, an ancient Roman town on the eastern side of the range, is Portugal's only winter resort. This picturesque town also have several churches of interest, including the 15th-century **Santa Maria** fronted with *azulejos*, and the 16th-century **Chapel of Santa Cruz**.

Covilhã is low enough that it seldom receives snow itself, but it is the principle gateway to the high *serra*, and from there it is a short drive to the ski area at **Penhas da Saúde**. The skiing, mind you, is not to be compared with Kitzbühel, but skiing there is, with a lodge, school facilities and equipment to be rented. The season runs from January through May—although the snow in May may be disappointing.

Edging the Serra on its western side, actually in the Beira Litoral province, is the beautiful **Buçac Forest**. For many centuries this area has been protected, and the 400 native and 300 exotic species of trees have flourished. Various springs and flower-lined walks make the forest a joy to visit.

Benedictine monks established a *hermitage* here in the 6th century, and later Augustine canons took over and guarded the area vigorously. Beginning in 1622 women were forbidden by Pope Gregory to enter. The Carmelites, who built a monastery in 1628, began thorough-going cultivation, planting species brought back from the Portuguese discovery voyages. Species include Himalayan pines, monkey-puzzles, Japanese camphor trees, huge Lebanese cedars, and ginkgoes. In 1643 the pope promised excommunication to anyone harming the trees of Buçaco.

In September 1810, Wellington routed Napoleon's army here, as the French attempted for the third time to conquer Portugal. There is a military museum devoted primarily to the battle.

A **royal palace** was built in Neo-Manueline style at the end of the 19th century next to what remained of the convent. It became a spectacular hotel in 1907, when

The exotic Buçaco Forest

the monarchy was abolished. The hotel is well worth a visit, preferably a stay if possible. There is a small **church**, the **cloister**, and several **monks' cells** remaining from the monastery. In one of these small cells, Wellington spent the night before the Battle of Buçaco.

Near Buçaco is the village of **Luso**, famed for its water which flows freely here from fountains and is available bottled throughout Portugal.

The eastern district of Beira Alta is governed by the city of **Viseu**, which, at a population of 20,000, is a third again larger than Guarda. In the 2nd century B.C., the Romans built a fortified settlement here—some of their road system can still be seen, along with a number of Latin-inscribed stones and signs from the same period.

A thorn in the side of the Romans was a rebel Lusitanian chieftain named Viriathus, who harassed local Roman legions until he was finally betrayed and killed. A monument to this hero has been erected in a park here—the **Cava de Viriato**. It is on the site of a Lusitanian and Roman military encampment. Here one can still see the old earthworks used by the Romans after the campaign of Brutus Calaicus in 138 B.C.

Viseu was made a bishopric during the time of the Suevian-Visigothic kingdom, and a record still exists in the form of a signature of th Bishop of Viseu, dating from 569 A.D.

The city suffered alternating invasions of Moors and Christians from the 8th until the 11th centuries. Fernando the Great of Castile and León captured it for good, and for the Christians, in 1057. Teresa, mother of the first king of Portugal, granted the city its first charter in 1123.

From the 14th to the 16th centuries, building in Viseu seems to have been concentrated in the upper part of town. About this time also an active Jewish colony evolved here. In 1411 the Infante Dom Henrique (Prince Henry the Navigator) became Duke of Viseu, and toward the end of that century the town walls were completed. But the area was becoming a center for the vigorous agricultural activity in the surrounding area, and by the 16th century, much of the town was outside the walls, and there were empty spaces inside.

Perhaps this was fortunate, because over the next two centuries, many of these spaces were filled with a lavish assortment of barque churches, chapels, mansions and fountains. Today the architectural richness lends a dignified air to the enclosed city.

The pure Baroque facade of the Church of the Misericórdia

Pure Baroque: Of the specific sights, the 13th-century cathedral would be one stop worth making. The ribbed vaulting overhead is beautifully carved to look like knotted cables, and the ceiling of the **sacristy** is extravagantly filled with numerous carvings of lively satyrs, animals and plants. The twin-towered **Misericórdia church** is up the hill from the cathedral. This whitewashed building is pure Baroque. The hill it crowns may have once been a Celtiberian settlement.

One should also take in the **Grão Vasco Museum**, many of the works being representative of the fine school of Portuguese Primitive painting that flourished here in the 16th century. The museum's name comes from the nickname of the school's most famous member, Vasco Fernandes. There are also modern Portuguese works and other attractions.

The São Mateus Fair, held annually in August and September, is a major event; the Festival of St. John the Baptist is another, held each June 24th. A Tuesday market is held throughout the year, with plenty of fresh produce, bolts of cloth, pots and pans, and handicrafts. Viseu is well known for its lace, carpets, and black pottery.

Some 25 miles (30 km) west of Viseu, on the main road toward Aveiro on the coast, one enters the valley of the Vouga River, a beautiful river which divides the mountain ranges of the **Serra de Arada** and the **Serra do Caramulo**. The town of **Caramulo**, a spa, has a notable **museum**, with medieval decorative arts, and impressive collection of 19th- and 20th- century European paintings. There is also an exhibit of more than 50 antique cars and motorcycles, including an 1898 Peugeot and a 1902 Darracq.

Nearby is the small town of **São Pedro do Sul** and, a few kilometers farther on, the **Termas de São Pedro do Sul**—possibly the best known and most frequented hot springs in the country. Sinus, rheumatism, hangover or foul temper, the springs are said to cure them all and more.

To the south is the **Barragem de Aquieira**, a gorgeous lake—especially considering it is man-made. Its shores provide popular retreats for campers and boat enthusiasts. A few kilometers away is the charming village of **Mortagua**.

A short hop will land one in the town of **Santa Comba Dão**, which, though a very pleasant spot, is known principally for being the birthplace of Portugal's notorious former dictator, António de Oliveira Salazar. His humble home, now abandoned, belies

Azulejos panels brighten Viseu's streets

the station he ultimately achieved in life. Political divisions within the old town are marked. Following the Revolution of 1974, zealots in opposition to the dictator's legacy decapitated a bronze statue of Salazar outside the local courthouse. Angry and outraged Salazarists immediately ordered a new head founded. But the opposition had the final say. Within days, a bomb exploded at the foot of the offending statue; it and the courthouse windows were blown to smithereens. To date the little town is still without a statue of its most famous son.

There are several other delightful little villages to visit in this region. Just south of São Pedro do Sul is Vouzela, in the valley of the Vouga River, with a lovely 13th-century **parish church**. Vouzela also has the Rococo **São Gil** chapel. Not far from here is the village of **Cambra**, clustered around the remnants of its **castle**. Just to the south is another Celtiberian site, **Cova de Lobishomem** (Werewolf's Cave). And near Caramulo is the pretty village of **Tondela**. South of Viseu, on the way to Nelas is the village of **Santar**, a gem of a place once known as the "court of the Beiras." On the western side of the Serra is the town of **Oliveira do Hospital**. It once belonged to the Hospitalers. Tombs of the Ferreiros, in

the **parish church**, are crowned on the wall above by a carving of an equestrian knight. There is also a beautiful 14th-century **altarpiece** showing the Virgin Mary with St. Joachim and St. Anne. In the village of **Lourosa** is an extremely old **church**. In 911, Ordoño II ordered the Mozárab building begun. In the shape of a basilica, it uses Roman columns and has elegant, typically Visigothic windows.

Returning to the Vouga River and journeying northeasternly from São Pedro do Sul, the traveller will find a particularly lovely stretch of road that runs between the **Serra de Montemuro** and the **Serra De Leomil** toward Lamego, and passes through the high town of **Castro Daire**. The Romans used this site as a garrison and built an important bridge here, the **Ponte Pedrinha**, over the **Paiva River**. A recently discovered stone says the bridge was built during the governorship of Caius Julius Caesar.

Lamego itself is a city of considerable historical importance. Although the Lusitanians had finally been subjugated by the Romans (after nearly two centuries of fighting), the tribes people of this area arose in revolt, refusing to pay the heavy taxation. In retaliation, the Romans—never much for diplomacy—burned the town to the ground.

But it was an important defensive location, so Emperor Trajan ordered it rebuilt.

By the 4th century A.D., the town had turned to Christianity, and was granted the status *civitas*, the Roman equivalent of city franchise. Then came the invasions of the Suevi and Visigoths—and then the Moors. For years Christians and Moslems fought over Lamego. One side would pull down the walls, then the other. Finally, in the same sweep that won him Viseu, Fernando of Léon and Castile took the city, aided, in fact, by the legendary mercenary El Cid. Fernando allowed the Moslem *wali* to continue to govern Lamego—as long as he converted, and paid tribute to the king.

Perhaps the city's most significant role in Portugal's history was as the site where, in 1143, the *cortes* met for the very first time. At this meeting, the nobles declared Afonso Henriques to be Afonso I, first king of Portugal.

Lamego's 12th-century **castle**, on one of the city's two hills, preserves a fine 13th-century **keep**, with windows that were added later, and an unusual vaulted **cistern**, very old, possibly Moorish, with monograms of master masons.

Atop Lamego's other hill is perhaps its most important building, the pilgrimage church of **Nossa Senhora dos Remédios**. The first chapel of this sanctuary was founded by Durando, Bishop of Lamego, in 1361, and dedicated to Saint Stephen. In 1564, it was pulled down, and a new one built. From that time, there has been a steady steam of the faithful seeking cures. The present sanctuary was started in 1750, and was consecrated 11 years later—but the magnificent Baroque-style **staircase** leading up to it, started in the 19th century, was not completed until the 1960s. Fountains, statues and pavilions marking the 14 Stations of the Cross dot the 600 steps.

The **Cathedral**, a Gothic structure, was built by Afonso Henriques in 1129. Only the Romanesque **tower** is left from the original building. The city **museum**, housed in the 18th-century Bishop's palace, has a fairly good collection, which includes 16th-century Flemish tapestries and works by Grão Vasco. Also to be seen in Lamego are several 17th- and 18th- century **mansions**.

Near Lamego, the village of **Tarouca** has a former monastery, the first Cistercian one to be built in Portugal. It contains lovely **Choir stalls** and the impressive **tomb** of Conde Pedro de Barcelos, illegitimate son of King Dinis, who assemble *Livro das Linhagens*, an early register of the country's nobility.

North of Lamego, in the valley of the **Balsemão River**, stands **São Pedro de Balsemão**, a Visigothic church that is believed to be the oldest in Portugal.

There is a fine **castle** at **Penedono**, a particularly graceful structure with two lovely detailed towers and a well-designed arch between them. The castle, which is known to have existed before 960, is thought to be the birthplace of Alvaro Gonçalves Coutinho, known as *O Magrico* (The Paladin). He was immortalized for his bravery and gallantry by Portugal's national poet-hero, Luis Vaz de Camões, in Canto VI of *The Lusiads*.

Miracle legend: Traveling in the Viseu district, one should also keep an eye open for **Sernancelhe**, a little south of Fonte Arcada. There is a miracle legend associated with the sanctuary here, that the Virgin Mary appeared before a mute shepherd girl and gave her the power of speech.

Other villages of special interest—there are many—might be **Ermida do Paiva**, where there is a 12th-century **church** built by the Augustinians, and **Carvalhal**, where there are **thermal springs**. Both of these villages are close to the town of Castro Daire. **Vila Nova de Paiva** and villages near it have been dubbed the **Terras do Demo**,

Strange denizens of the pilgramage church of Nossa Senhora dos Remédios

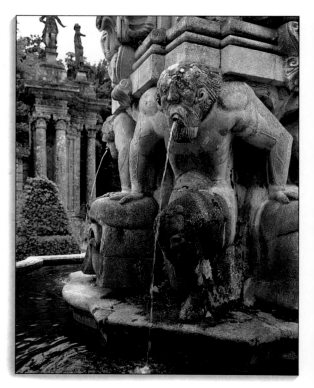

Lands of the Devil, made famous by a number of Portuguese literary figures—notably Aquilino Ribeiro in his 19th-century romance *Malhadinhas.*

Aguiar da Beira lies very near Vila Nova de Paiva. An exquisitely preserved example of a medieval town, the largely granite site includes a **town square** with an ancient **keep** and an unusual **council chamber**, atop a squat structure and open to the sky. Also here is a small **castle**, built entirely without mortar, and believed, therefore, to possibly date from the Iron Age.

Traveling south toward the Beira Baixa, one encounters the **Zêzere River**, which forms the northwest border of the province. In recent years, this river has become a favorite for canoeists looking for a little rough and tumble. The river flows most swiftly from early April through June. There are other water sports to be had in the **Barragem de Castelo do Bode**, a long, many-armed lake that runs south into the province of Ribatejo. Both the river and the lake have rather fine fishing.

Another dam, on the **Tagus River** at **Fretel**, marks the southern limit of Beira Baixa. Upstream the Tagus reaches and crosses into Spain. Here, on both the Portuguese and Spanish sides, is desolate scrub country. The gorge formed by the river is steep-sided and virtually inaccessible to vehicles other than four-wheel-drive jeeps. It is, nonetheless, an extraordinary part of the Rio Tejo. On the Portuguese side along much of the river here runs an **ancient road** built by the Romans. Originally it was the route from **Vila Velha de Rodão** to the Spanish town of Alcántara. Water now conceals large chunks of the work, but where the road rises above the surface, one can see a formidable engineering structure: instead of building the road with flat stones, the entire way is paved with local slate stood on edge, its upper surface rutted by centuries of cart traffic. Twisting in and out of all the gullies and indentures along the river bank, it is an impressive sight.

Both Beira Alta and Beira Baixa have a notable number of castles, not surprising when one considers the geographic development of Portugal's tumultuous history. There are dozens of stories associated with every castle, but a fitting choice to discuss would be that of the village of **Monsanto** in Beira Baixa, once declared "the most typical Portuguese village."

Built around and atop a steep rocky mass in the center of a broad valley some 30 miles (50 km) northeast of the city of Castelo Branco, Monsanto is located bang in the middle of what was major invasion route of the country. The Castle commands a superlative view in every direction and, being close to the Spanish frontier, it has been the scene of many a battle.

It is thought that this *monte* has been fortified since Neolithic times, and in fact the castle is so well-integrated into the natural rock that it looks like it simply grew here.

Rice-filled calf: Some say it was during the Roman invasion in the 2nd century B.C., others claim it was some 1,400 years later during a Moorish invasion, that the people of Monsanto, under a long siege and nearly out of food, showed their spirit to their attackers by killing a calf, filling its belly with rice, and hurling it off the ramparts to the soldiers below. The attackers were so impressed, the story goes, that they packed up and left. Today one of the biggest feast days is May 3, when young villagers, singing and celebrating, tramp up to the battlements and toss down pitchers filled with flowers.

Much of the castle was destroyed at the beginning of the 19th century. One Christmas Eve, there was a tremendous thunderstorm, and a bolt of lightning hit the castle's gunpowder magazine. Divine retribution, the people of the village believed, for that

Working in the vineyards near the village of Carapito, near Lamego

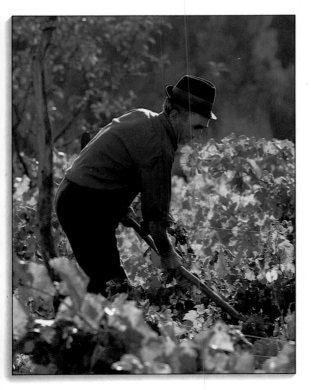

year the unpopular governor had forbidden the traditional burning of a cork oak tree trunk in front of the parish church. Instead, he had ordered the ceremonial log to be carried into his own home, and set alight in his hearth. At that point, however, the gunpowder exploded, and the and irons flew from the hearth and struck the governor dead.

The ruins of the Romanesque **chapel of Sao Miguel**, outside Monsanto's walls, lie in the midst of the original village. Nearby are several **tombs**. There is another ruined **chapel** inside the castle.

The folk music of Monsanto is charming if strange. Half chanted, half sung, there is nothing quite like it in the country. Its rhythm (one cannot really call it a melody) is beaten out with the assistance of a square tambourin-like instrument known as an *adufe*.

The great **Idanha Plain** stretches all the way south to Castelo Branco and beyond— a vast area of cattle-raising country, bitterly cold in winter, scorching in the summer. Near Castelo Branco, there are large areas of pine and a eucalyptus trees.

Castelo Branco, with 25,000 inhabitants, is an ancient city the origins of which, like so many communities in Portugal, are lost in time. It dates its "modern" history back to 1182 when it and the surrounding area—then called Vila Franca de Cardosa—were given as a gift to the Knights Templar by Dom Fernmão Sanches. It received a charter in 1213, and became a city in 1771, in the reign of José I.

The battlements of the old Templar **castle**—the "white castle" of the city's name, provides a fine view, though the castle itself is not noteworthy. The old town is delightful, with narrow winding streets. Points of interest include two churches, **Santa Maria do Castelo** and **Misericórdia Velha**, the latter a 16th-century structure with a particularly nice doorway; and the **Praça Velha**, also known as the Praça de Camões—a fine medieval square off which one can find the ancient **municipal library**.

Certainly the most important thing to see in Castelo Branco is the splendid **Episcopal Palace**, built on the order of Dom Nuno de Norunha, Bishop of Guarda, in 1596. It served as the winter residence of the bishops of the diocese. It now houses the **Museu de Francisco Tavares Proenca Júnior**, with prehistoric pieces from the area and Portuguese art.

In 1725 Bishop João de Mendonca commissioned the building of a garden at

The ruined fortifications at Monsanto

the side of the palace—the **Bishop's Garden**, today considered to be one of Portugal's most treasured national monuments. It is not a particularly large garden; one can walk around it in a matter of minutes. But certainly it is an extraordinary sight, if only for the multitude of statues erected along the course of every pathway and at every corner.

These statues are all named, and have been placed in homage to just about everybody and everything the bishops thought important: the kings of Portugal, of course (it is amusing to note that the two hated Spanish rulers of Portugal, Felipe I and II, are represented here, but by smaller figures); the saints, apostles and evangelists, along with the virtues of the religious; but also the seasons of the year, the signs of the zodiac, and the elements of the firmament. It is hard to believe that there once were even m*ore* statues, but apparently the invading French armies of 1807 carted off the best of the works—some in bronze, some in granite—as spoils of the war. The plinths of the stolen statues have been left standing in their places, in many cases with the name of the missing item clearly engraved. Frenchmen are thus encouraged to look on with shame. Their invasion of Portugal is not remembered too kindly.

If you are looking for your own spoils to cart off, you might consider a bedspread made in Castelo Branco. Since the 17th century it has been the custom for brides-to-be to painstakingly had-embroider their wedding bedspreads. From this tradition and skill a cottage industry was born. Traditionally the spreads are white, but in recent years, they have become available in interwoven colors. Earlier patterns were extremely geometric, echoing Persian carpets, but other decorative themes have since become popular as well.

Northeast of the city, **Idanha-a-Velha** was an episcopal see until 1199, when it was moved to Guarda. There remains here a strange, ancient **basilica** with dozens of Roman inscriptions inside. It is said that Wamba, the legendary king of the Goths, was born here. There is a Roman **bridge** in the village, still in use, and various coins, pottery and bones have been found.

Other charming villages in the Beira Baixa include **Proenca-a-Velha, São Miguel d'Acha, Bemposta, São Vincente da Beira, Castelo Novo**, and **Alpedrinha**. There is a tourist office in the center of Castelo Branco, and it is worthwhile calling in to obtain literature about the district.

The garden of the Episcopal Palace, Castelo Branco

THE LUSTY FOOD OF PORTUGAL

To dine in Portugal is to taste the presence of other countries, other cuisines. It is to conjure up images of empire. Brazil, Angola, Mozambique, Goa—these and others all belonged to Portugal once; in a manner of speaking, each helped to stir the pot.

The period of Portuguese Empire, when this nation smaller than the state of Alabama reached out across the terrifying "Green Sea of Gloom," as the Atlantic was called, has long passed. Yet Portugal, left with only Macão, the Azores, and Madeira, has preserved the flavors of other cultures in its cooking.

Prince Henry the Navigator, less than 30 years old when he started his School of Navigation, was a true scientist in an age of superstition. He ordered his 15th-century explorers to bring back from new lands not just riches and wild tales, but fruits, nuts and plants as well. In 1420, Prince Henry sent settlers to colonize the newly discovered island of Madeira. With them went plants he believed would thrive in Madeira's volcanic soil and subtropical climate—including grapevines from Crete and sugar cane from Sicily, both are indispensable today. Even more significant for Portuguese cooking, was Vasco da Gama's discovery of the water route to the East in 1497-98, five years after Columbus's aborted attempt and accidental discovery of the West Indies.

Black pepper was what Vasco da Gama sought, but cinnamon, which he also found in Calicut, would soon become equally precious to Portuguese cooks. Indeed, one boatload of cinnamon sticks, history tells us, fetched enough money to pay for an entire expedition to India. Cinnamon is perhaps the most beloved spice in Portugal today, certainly for the famous egg sweets (*doces de ovos*), which may not only contain the heady brown powder but also be decorated with it. Spaniards, on the other hand, prefer vanilla for their puddings and flans. There's good reason for this. It was the Spaniards who found Montezuma sipping vanilla-spiked hot chocolate in Mexico and learned the trick of curing vanilla beans, the seed pods of a wild orchid. Perhaps this is why chocolate, too, is more popular in Spain than in Portugal.

More surprising than the Portuguese appetite for cinnamon, however, is their fondness for curry powder (another bonus of Vasco da Gama's voyages). In the beginning, only the rich and the royal could afford the precious yellow stuff, which pepped up the blandest dish—and also retarded spoilage.

Today, packets of curry powder can be found in *supermercados* everywhere. Its function,

rather than to set food afire, is to mellow and marry the other ingredients, and add a mysterious muskiness to a large repertoire of soups and stews. The spiciest Portuguese dishes, incidentally, are not found on the mainland but in the Azores and Madeira. These islands were ports-of-call for the navigators, who would barter with the natives—offering spices in exchange for fresh fruits, vegetables and meats (and no doubt the local brew, too).

New Food for the Old: During Portugal's lavish Age of Empire, Portuguese navigators became couriers, bringing New World foods to the Old and vice-versa. Mediterranean sugar cane, for example, was cultivated in Brazil. Brazilian pineapples were introduced to the Azores, a colony established under Prince Henry. They still flourish there in hot houses, ripening under waftings of woodsmoke. Azorean pineapples, chunky, honey-sweet and tender to the core, are teamed today with rosettes of Portugal's mahogany-hued, air-cured *presunto* (prosciutto-like ham) and served as an elegant appetizer in fashionable Lisbon restaurants.

Tiny, incendiary Brazilian chili pepper took root in Angola early on, another important Portuguese colony, and became so essential to cooks there that today they're known by their African name, *piri-piri* . Since the collapse of Angola as a Portuguese colony in the mid-1970s and the subsequent influx to Lisbon of thousands of Angolan refugees, *piri-piri* sauce (an oil and vinegar mixture strewn with minced chilies) is as popular a table condiment in mainland Portugal as salt and pepper. Other exchanges thanks to the Portuguese: African coffee was transplanted in Brazil, which today produces about half of the world's supply; Brazilian cashews landed in both Africa and India; and Oriental tea plants arrived in the Azores (interestingly enough, the Portuguese word for tea—*chá*—is almost identical to the Cantonese one—ch'a).

All of this fetching and toting of seeds, leaves, barks, roots, stems, stalks and cuttings by Portuguese explorers across oceans and continents dramatically affected Portuguese cooking.

New World tomatoes and potatoes came to Portugal about as early as they did to Spain—in the 16th century. But Portuguese cooks, unlike the Spanish, might drop a few garlic cloves into the soup or stew along with the tomatoes and potatoes, or tuck in a stick of cinnamon.

It's unlikely that anyone grows nuttier, *earthier* potatoes today than the Portuguese. Indeed, along the New England coast in the U.S., where so many Portuguese families have settled, there's an old saying: "*If you want your potatoes to grow, you must speak to them in Portuguese* ."

Tomatos respond to the Portuguese touch, too, and those harvested in the vast Alentejo province, east of Lisbon, are as juicy, red and deeply flavorful as any on earth. Not for nothing does that French menu phrase, "*á la Portugaise*," mean richly sauced with tomatoes.

Onions and garlic, indispensable to any respectable Portuguese cook, were probably introduced by the Romans, who established colonies in Portugal. The Romans are believed to have brought wheat to Portugal, too. They aimed to

and the Moors is found. It is seen in the snow-white cubistic villages that spill down red sandstone cliffs to embrace beaches, in the filigreed chimney pots (the Algarve status symbol), even in the paintbox-bright fishing boats of Albufeira, Lagos and Portimão, whose turned-up prows and lateen rigs clearly smack of the Arab dhow.

It was the Arabs who set up the water wheel in Portugal, who dug irrigation ditches there, who first planted rice (it now grows up and down the west coast), and who covered the Algarve slopes with almond trees. The Algarve's almonds were ground into paste, sweetened, and shaped into

make Iberia the granary of Rome. They also probably introduced olives (a major source of income today), and grapes as well. From shards found in the Alentejo, it's known that the Romans were making wine there as early as the 2nd century A. D.

The Moors, who occupied a large chunk of Portugal from the early 8th to the mid-13th centuries, enriched the pot even more than the Romans. The southern provinces were the Moorish stronghold—the Algarve and Alentejo, in particular—it is here that the look of North Africa

Preceding pages, snacking at Cascais; more elegant dining in Pousada ds Almeida Nossa Senhora da Oliveira in Guimarães. Above, *carne de porco á alentejana*

miniature fruits, birds and flowers of intricate detail. To this day the sculpting and painting of marzipan is an art that requires years to perfect.

The Moors also introduced figs and apricots to the Algarve together with the tricks of drying them under the relentless sun. They planted groves of lemons and oranges and, as it was their custom, they combined fish with fruits and fruits with meats.

Innovative Cooks: Finally, it was the Arabs who invented the *cataplana*, a hinged metal pan, a sort of primitive pressure cooker shaped like an oversize clam shell that can be clamped shut and set on a quick fire. The food inside—fish, shellfish, chicken, vegetables or a medley of them all—steam to supreme succulence. What goes into a *cataplana* depends upon the whims of the cook (and on what's available), but the most famous cataplana recipe is *amêijoas na cataplana*, clams tossed with rounds of sausage and cubes of ham in an intensely garlicky tomato sauce.

It's been said that this unlikely pork and shellfish combination was created at the time of the Inquisition to test one's Christian zeal. Pork and shellfish, of course, were forbidden to Jews and Moslems alike. What the *cataplana* does prove is the Portuguese cook's uncanny gift for combining unlikely ingredients.

There is no shortage of examples that attest to this culinary ingenuity. No one but a thrifty Portuguese cook with an eye on her *escudos* would have made bread a main course by layering yeast dough into a pan with snippets of chicken and sausage and two kinds of ham (this classic from the remote northern Trás-os-Montes is *folar*).

The cod-fishing continues today, with the men putting to sea in spring and not returning until fall. Sometimes, of course, the men do not return and to see their widows dressed in black, some of them barely 20 years old, is to understand why so many of Portugal's poems, stories, folk sayings, even *fado* songs focus upon the nation's proud but bittersweet seafaring tradition:

"O Waves from the salty sea,
From whence comes your salt?
From the tears shed on the
Beaches of Portugal."

It was as early as the 16th century, that Portuguese fishermen learned to salt cod at sea to last the long voyage home, to sun-dry it into board-stiff slabs that could be kept for months, later to be soaked in cool water before cooking.

Cod is still sun-dried on racks the old way on

Or who would have thought to crumble yesterday's bread into shrimp cooking water and come up with another favorite, this is an Estremadura classic known as *açorda de mariscos*. Or to braise duck with bacon and rice as it's done in the Serra da Estrêla, or to smother red mullet the Setúbal way with tiny tart oranges, or to scramble flakes of salt cod with eggs and shoestring potatoes as it's done all over the country?

Cod Country: Dried salt cod, or *bacalhau* (pronounced bockle-YOW), is a purely Portuguese invention. António M. Bello, first president of Portugal's gastronomic society, wrote in his *Culinária Portuguesa* published in Lisbon in 1936, that the Portuguese were fishing Newfoundland's Grand Banks for cod within just a few years of Columbus's discovery of America.

the beach at Nazaré, although much less of it now than in past decades. The Grand Banks have become so overfished that the Portuguese have taken to importing *bacalhau* from Norway just to be able to meet their annual demands. This, puts the price of salt cod beyond the reach of the very people it sustained for centuries—the poor.

Someone once said that the Portuguese lived on dreams and subsist on salt cod. Not quite, although they do claim to know 365 ways to prepare it, one for each day of the year. The best and most famous bacalhau dishes are *bacalhau á gomes de sá* (cooked in a casserole with thinly sliced potatoes and onions, then garnished with hard-boiled eggs and black olives), *bacalhau à brás* and *bacalhau dourado* (two quite similar recipes composed of scrambled eggs, onions and shoe-string potatoes), *bacalhau á conde de guarda* (salt cod creamed with mashed potatoes) and *bolinhos de bacalhau* (cod fish balls, a particularly popular *hors d' oeuvre*). All of these once-humble recipes are served with pride today in the most expensive restaurants of Lisbon.

Very nearly as popular as salt cod are the sardines netted off the Portuguese coast. These are what the tartan-clad fishermen of Nazaré go out for day after day in their gaily colored boats decorated with mermaids, stars and "eyes of God." Portuguese sardines are considered the sweetest and fattest in the world and Portuguese women grill them right on the streets in every town and village, using little terra cotta braziers. But only in spring, summer and early fall—the unofficial "sardine season." As every Portuguese knows, sardines are too bony to eat between November and April.

If salt cod and sardines share top billing as the favorite fish in Portugal, pork reigns supreme as the king of *carne* (meat). With good reason— Portuguese pork is incomparably sweet and tender because of its life of leisure and diet of acorns, truffles and chestnuts.

In the northerly Trás-os-Montes province, they say if you want good pork in the autumn you must feed your hogs twice a day in August. Some farm women even go as far as to cook potatoes for their hogs. Small wonder the hams (*presunto*) and sausages (*salsicha*) are so highly prized here. (the best of all are said to come from Chaves). Small wonder, too, that *charcuterie* figures so prominently in the lusty regional soups and stews. Cooks here even wrap freshly caught brook trout in slices of presunto, then bounce them in and out of a skillet so hot the ham is transformed to a crisp, deeply smoky sort of "pastry."

But Portugal's most famous pork dish comes from the Alentejo in the nation's midriff where hogs are no less pampered. It's *porco à alentejana* for which cubes of pork are marinated in a paste of sweet red peppers and garlic, browned in the very fruity local olive oil, then covered and braised with baby clams, still in the shell. The clams open slowly under the gentle heat, spilling their briny juices into the ambrosial red muddle. What accounts for the distinctive nut-like flavor of Alentejo pork is that the hogs are turned loose each autumn to forage in the cork orchards. Here they nibble upon acorns, wild herbs, and yes, the occasional truffle, too.

Sausage-making is as great a culinary art in the Alentejo as it is in the Trás-os-Montes, and this region's garlicky *chouriços, linguiças, farinheiras* (porridgey sausages plumped up with cereal) and chunky, smoky *paios* are without peer. As

Bacalhau a gomes de sa, one of the 365 receipes that keep Portuguese eating salted cod all year round

Portugal's food authority, Maria de Lourdes Modesto, writes in her masterwork, *Cozinha Tradicional Portuguesa*, "The grand destiny of the pig in the Alentejo is to become sausage."

Here, every part of the pig is used—ears, snouts, tails, feet, even it would seem, the squeal. At Carnival time, for example, the centerpiece of each Feast Day (*Mardi Gras*) banquet is *pezinhos de porco de coentrada*, dainty pig's feet braised with onions, garlic and gobs of fresh coriander.

Another province famous for its pork is the seaside Beira Litoral, particularly the little town of Mealhada, nothing more, really, than a wide place in the road about 12 miles (20 km) north of Coimbra. Here both sides of the highway are lined with restaurants that make suckling pig (*leitão assado*) specialty. The piglets are rubbed with secret their blends of oil and herbs, skewered from head to tail, then spit-roasted over white-hot hardwood coals until their skin is as crisply brittle as an onion's and their milk-white flesh so meltingly tender it falls from the bones at the touch of a fork.

Cabbage Patch: The Portuguese national dish, ironically, is built neither upon salt cod nor pork. It's key ingredient is cabbage, specifically a richly emerald, non-heading, tender-leafed variety (*couve gallego*) much like the collards of the American South. The dish, itself, is *caldo verde* , a bracing, jade-green soup brimming with potatoes, onion, garlic and filament-thin shreds of green cabbage. Sometimes it's fortified with slices of *chouriço* or *linguiça* although in the humblest Minho versions (it's here that the recipe originated), it often contains nothing more than water, potatoes, onion, garlic, cabbage and perhaps a tablespoon or two of robust olive oil.

To some people, "robust" may seem a kind euphemism. Portuguese olive oil, *azeite*, is richly aromatics—to critics, "*rank*." The distinctive flavor comes from harvesting methods. The festive December olive harvest is a casual event. The olives, beaten down from their branches, are left to age on the ground, only gathered after a week or so. That in addition to the hot-water pressing methods, accounts for their intense flavor.

Every Portuguese province now calls *caldo verde* its own, and it's not unusual to find kettles of it steaming on the backs of stoves. Indeed, *caldo verde* is such a staple in the Portuguese diet that plastic bags of minutely shredded *couve gallego*, ready to drop into the pots of potato broth bubbling back home, can be bought at Lisbon's rollicking **Mercado da Ribeira** (city market)— the ultimate in convenience food.

Country women, whether they grow their own cabbage or buy it at the local market, must cope with the whole head. A purely Portuguese sight is a small, ramrod-straight woman balancing cabbages on her head, sometimes six or eight at a time, as she goes about her shopping or chats with friends, completely oblivious to the burden she carries. Anyone who drives the back roads of Portugal will be awed by the inventory of items that Portuguese women balance atop their heads: crates of squawking chickens, wicker baskets of laundry, terra cotta water jugs, tables, chairs, even, incredible as it seems, sewing machines!

As for the preparation of *couve gallego* , every country girl learns, by the time she's head-high to the kitchen table, to shred it with the speed of light. It is not difficult once this technique is mastered. The leaves are stacked, perhaps five or six deep, rolled into a fat cigar, then literally shaved as a razor-sharp knife is whisked back and forth across the end of the cabbage roll so fast the movements are scarcely visible. The fineness of the cut is what makes a bowl of *caldo verde* resemble molten jade, also the cabbage is tossed

into the pot just minutes before serving so that its color intensifies but does not "turn."

The food of Portugal has often been refered to as the food of farmers and fishermen. And nowhere is this more evident than in the making of soups and stews. Fishermen brew giant drums of *caldeirada* (literally, "kettle of fish") on the beaches at Sesimbra, Nazaré, Albufeira and Sagres, beginning with water (sometimes sea water), adding tomatos, onions and garlic, then lean and oily fish in roughly equal proportion, and if their catch has been especially good, squid and/or octopus, too.

No two *caldeiradas* are ever alike, indeed they vary from day to day depending upon whatever the fishermen's nets have fetched up. One of the pleasures of visiting a deserted *praia* (beach) in

Portugal is the chance of running into a group of fishermen boiling up their latest catch. They're always willing to share.

Farmer's soups and stews are ever-changing, too, as country women constantly improvise with odds and ends—a bit of chicken from the Sunday dinner, a few *favas* (beans) left over from lunch, a handful of carrots, a dab of rice, some crumbles of yesterday's bread, and maybe some freshly minced mint or coriander. This is the way many of Portugal's great classic recipes were created.

Next to *caldo verde*, Portugal's most famous soup is probably *açorda á alentejana* , a coriander-strewn, bread-thickened, egg-drop soup seasoned, as someone once quipped, "with enough garlic to blow a safe." The soups and stews of Portugal—whether they're made of chick peas and spinach (another Alentejo classic), of tomatoes and eggs (a Madeira specialty), of pumpkins and onions (a Trás-os-Montes staple), or of dried white beans and sausages (the universally beloved *feijoadas*)—are frugal and filling, nourishing and soul-satisfying. All they need for accompaniment are a glass of wine, a chunk of cheese and a crust of bread.

Does any country bake better bread than the Portuguese? Not likely. The simple country breads usually contain only four ingredients—flour milled from hard wheat, water, yeast and salt—but they're kneaded until their dough fairly springs to life. And because they're baked in wood-stoked brick or stone ovens, they have a faintly smoky flavor. There are fancier breads, to be sure, notably the sweet festival breads (*pão doce* of Easter and fruit-studded *bolo rei* of Christmas). There are huskier breads, too, the rough round barley breads and most famous of all, the *broas*—yeast-raised corn-breads of the Minho that are sold by the truckload at the merry market in the river town of Barcelos.

This country market is Portugal's biggest and best. Held every Thursday in a vast tree-shaded square, it's divided into quadrants: one for breads, cakes and other baked goods; one for fresh produce (everything from potatoes to poultry); one for farm and wine-making equipment, and the fourth for the lace tablecloths, fancifully painted brown pottery and exuberantly decorated ceramic roosters of the region (these have become a national symbol).

Cheeses can also be bought here, too, as they can at country markets everywhere. The queen of them all is the ivory-hued *queijo da serra*, a cheese so strictly demarcated it can be made only from the milk of sheep grazing on the wild mountain herbs of the Serra da Estrêla. At the peak of its season—winter—a properly ripened "*serra* " is as biting, buttery and runny as the finest Brie.

Portugal also produces a number of other cheeses that are a match for the world's best: the nutty, semi-dry *serpa* from the Alentejo town of the same name, which connoisseurs rank as the nation's second best (it's cured in caves and brushed regularly with paprika-laced olive oil); *beja*, a buttery semi-hard cheese from Beja, near Serpa; *azeitão*, lovely little rounds of gold, tangy and creamy, that come from the village of Azeitão on the Arrábida Peninsula just across the Tagus River from Lisbon. Finally, there are the *queijos frescos*, snowy, uncured cheese much like cottage cheese, which calorie-conscious Portuguese sprinkle with cinnamon and eat in place of the country's devastating egg sweets.

The Moors are thought to have introduced egg sweets to Portugal during their 500-year occupation. It may be so. What is known, however, is that the 17th- and 18th-century nuns of Portugal glorified them—one reason, no doubt, why so many egg sweets bear such amusing names as "bacon

every Portuguese restaurant, no matter how simple or sophisticated the presentation, is at the pastry cart, a glittering double-decker trolley laden with *doces de ovos* (egg sweets) brought round at the meal's end.

Usually there are five or six choices—sunny little hillocks bathed in clear sugar syrup, flans decorated with siftings of cinnamon, individual goblets of rice pudding (*arroz doce*) as radiant as molten gold, flat yellow sponge cakes twirled up around orange or lemon custard fillings, tiny translucent tarts (*queijadas*) reminiscent of the American South's chess pies, and snowy poached meringue ring known as *pudim molotov* (one of the few egg sweets made out of the whites).

The egg sweets of Portugal look irresistible, even to the most resolute dieter. And they should be tried. But most of them, alas, are excruciat-

from heaven" (*toucinho do céu*), "nun's tummies" (*barriga-de-freira*) and "angel's cheeks" (*papos de anjo*).

Regardless of their names, what the dozens of different egg sweets share in common is a prodigious use of egg yolks and sugar. Many are flavored with cinnamon, others with lemon or orange or almonds. Each, moreover, is shaped in its own traditional way—like little bundles of straw, for example, or miniature haystacks, even like lamprey eel. The Portuguese so love this ugly river fish they make golden egg effigies of it for festive occasions. A ritual practiced at nearly

Portuguese cooks demand fresh food, which keeps the markets hopping. Left, Ribeira Market in Lisbon, and above, the fish market in Setúbal

ingly sweet and too rich for non-Portuguese palates. The Portuguese, on the other hand, whose sweet tooth is legendary, find that nothing complements—or follows—an egg sweet like a silky, syrupy wine. A vintage port, or a madeira.

When you do choose a *doce* from the cart, you can at least be assured of good cup of coffee to cut the sweetness. Coffee houses are a national institution, a gathering place morning, noon and night. It's actually not surprising for a country whose former colonies—Brazil, Angola, Timor—produce some of the world's finest coffee. The native choice is usually a*bica*, a powerful espresso-like brew. *Café* is closer to American standards, but if you really miss your morning coffee, order *carioca*: half-café, half-hot water; it will still be plenty strong and, very good.

The wines of Portugal have only begun to gain popularity in the United States. Except for port, the famous fortified wine of the Upper Douro Valley, fine Portuguese wines are mostly unknown. Two immensely popular and inexpensive rosé wines, Mateus and Lancers, come from Portugal, but they give no hint of the diverse, unique, world-class wines that flow from this ruggedly handsome country.

Grape vines are cultivated in Portugal as far south as the Algarve. Eight of the best and most distinctive areas, all with long histories of winemaking, are given attention in this article. Starting from the north, they are: the Minho, the Upper Douro, the Dão Bairrada, and the environs of Lisbon—Carcavelos, Bucelas, Colares and Setúbal. Through their wine, each region offers the receptive traveler the unabashed flavor of their countryside—sometimes eccentric, sometimes sublime, yet always with the gregarious pride that typifies this inviting corner of the continent.

Portuguese wines may be divided into two basic categories: *vinho verde* and *vinho maduro*. The wine lists of Portugal's restaurants often show them this way. *Vinhos maduros* translates as "mature wines," wine that is made for aging and maturing in the bottle. *Vinhos verdes*, or "green wines," which demand less patience, are unique to Portugal.

The Minho: From the northwest corner of Portugal, in a province called the Minho, come these most distinctive wines. They can be either red or white; they are "green" only in figurative sense. Their youthful, stimulating acidity and charged effervescence take credit for the title.

Along with the four Lisbon regions and the Dão area, the Minho wine region was officially demarcated by the government in the early 1900s. The decree defined not only the boundaries of region, but also the characteristics of *vinho verde*, the types of grapes to be used and the viticultural techniques for making it.

The Minho encompasses an area of over two million acres of which some three percent are planted in vines. Within the Minho, six official subzones have been created: Amarante, Braga, Basto, Lima, Monção and Penafiel. They acknowledge the difference of each area's climate, which makes the wines distinctive.

The terrain of the Minho is green, lushly for-

Left, a vintage in the making? Young grapes ripening on the vines of the Estremadura province

ested with oaks, pines and chestnuts. The *vinho verde* vines are allowed to grow practically everywhere, climbing around trees and trained up high to create oases of shade. The look of the land is one of verdure and fecundity. The height above the ground at which these vines grow serves to produce grapes that are lower in natural sugar and higher in malic acid—characteristics of unripe grapes. In the fall, they are harvested by ladder-toting pickers, who bring the relatively immature grapes to the *quintas* (estates) for vinification. First, they are fermented to convert their natural sugars into alcohol. Then a secondary fermentation, called the malolactic, takes place, induced by naturally occurring bacteria. As you might guess from its name, this process converts malic acid to lactic; a harsher, more unpleasant acid into a milder, more palatable one. While this secondary fermentation is common to wines made in many countries, the *vinhos verdes* are distinguished by their retention of the fermentation's by-product: carbon dioxide. Hence, a sparkle or light fizz in the wine, which can vary—depending upon age, technique and storage—from a light tingle on the tongue to a spritely carbonation. This is the hallmark of *vinhos verdes*.

The *vinhos verdes* comprise almost a quarter of the production of wines in Portugal. There are some 80,000 growers of grapes in the Minho region, most quite small operations. Over half of them produce no more than two pipes (about 110 cases) each of wine. This is a clear indication of the endless varieties of the wine. Moreover, there are many grape types allowed in the region. Amongst the whites are the Azal Branco, Dourado, Trajadura, Avalrinho, and Loureiro; the red varietals include the Azal, Padeiro, Borracal and Vinhão. The attributes of a typical white *vinho verde* will be low alcohol (8-11 percent) a straw yellow color, and a bright and fragrant bouquet. To taste, it will display alacritous zest and crisp finish. In the warm local weather, they can be marvelously thirst-quenching.

It is curious that the white *vinhos verdes* that are acknowledged as being the best depart from the features with which the wine is so identified. These are the wines from Monção, where the rare Avalrinho grape is grown. Paradoxically, it most resembles a *vinho maduro*, in that its carbonation is far more subtle, its alcohol content slightly higher, and its capacity to improve with age a proven fact. To acquaint yourself with the wines of Monção, try the "Cepa Velha," produced by Vinhos de Monção Lta. It has won many awards in international competitions and is definitely worth seeking out.

In white wine, an effervescence is not entirely unexpected. Many young white wines, upon their uncorking, will temporarily exhibit a light "spritz," or tingle. Unlike that of champagne, this feature "blows off" or vanishes after several minutes of exposure to air. In red wine, however, the presence of this verve can be disconcerting.

For the uninitiated, the first taste of red *vinho verde* may produce contorted facial expressions as one struggles to gain some gustatory equilibrium. Lightly fruity, effervescent, firmly tannic, the melange of sensations are like no other. Appropriately, Portuguese cuisine provides some compelling partners for this wine. Grilled sardines, for example, with their dense oily flesh, help the wine reveal its logic. My own memories of this lunch in the fishing village of Nazaré always recall the flavors of that uniquely sensible wine with the charred, delectable fish.

Red *vinho verde* makes up almost 70 percent of the entire Minho production. It is an important wine locally, but has made few inroads on international markets. The whites, however, have begun to appear in the United States. Two factors have contributed to this. First, improved shipping conditions preserve the wine's charm and freshness. Secondly, and rather ironically, the marvelous petillance, or sparkle, for which the U.S. government levies a stiff protective tariff has been stifled in the wines for export—to make the proposition economically feasible. Which is why they must be tasted here!

Port: The wines of Portugal are best known around the world by their eminent ambassador, port. With a long and fascinating history, port has earned its place beside the other great dessert wines: Sauternes, Tokai and Madeira. It is a fortified wine, the grapes for which are grown in the rugged, mountainous terrain of the Upper Douro River. The wine can be red or white, though it is from the red that port has gained its fame. To be fortified means that the natural conversion of grape sugars into alcohol has been arrested at a calculated time by the addition of Portuguese grape brandy. This bolstering brings the wine's alcoholic content up between 15-24 percent by volume, and makes for a medium sweet, hearty product.

Port as we know it today, has been made since the 1830s. It developed by dint of the historic commercial alliances between the British and Portuguese. The British invested considerably in both the research and development of port, thus controlling the industry. Needless to say, the British populace acquired a healthy thirst for these wines and for hundreds of years were the primary bottlers and consumers of the product. Today, among the port lodges of Vila Nova de Gaia, the blending and storing place for these wines, one still finds a high percentage of British names representing Portugal's finest wine.

Port wine begins its life in a region called the Upper Douro, an officially demarcated region whose boundaries cling to the banks of the Douro and its tributaries. A number of approved grape types grow here. The reds include Tinta Roriz, Tinta Francesa (a descendant of the French Pinot Noir), Touriga Nacional and Bastardo; among the whites, Malvasia, Esgana Cão and Rabigato.

The earth of the Upper Douro is the slate and granite "soil" of the river's banks, a craggy terrain that often approaches a slope of 60 degrees. Into this unabiding territory countless hours of manual labor have been spent to create the terraced grounds in which the vine can prosper. The slate and granite had to first be broken up. Support walls were then built with the shattered stone to harbor the vine from erosion. Driving along the river, one sees thousands of these walls, many of

them nearly 300 years old. A haunting sense of timelessness pervades the area. Day-to-day maintenance of vineyards in such an area is onerous. One must climb from terrace to terrace. At harvest time, the work becomes ever more arduous: the harvested grapes are carried up and down the steep paths in baskets on the backs of men and women. This is how it has been for hundreds of years. At harvest time, the Upper Douro breathes of cultural richness. Ancient songs, the primitive music of pipe and drum, the night-long treading of the grapes with the feet (still done to a considerable degree here), all contribute to a sense of strange, romantic ritual.

As new vineyards are planted, modern techniques—bulldozing and dynamiting—have made expansion economically feasible. In turn, the port wine area has grown tremendously since its inception, increasing to almost 20 times its original size. Virtually all of the new area has been forged upriver, in the valleys of the Douro and its tributaries: the Pinhão, Tua, Torto and Távora Areas which comprised the region through the 18th and 19th centuries, around the town of Régua and the Rio Corgo, are now thought of as lesser wines. The regions producing the finest ports presently center around Pinhão, some 14 miles east of Régua, and extend to the Spanish border.

The famous shipping houses have their *quintas* in the hills of the Douro. These are spacious white houses, often clad in vines, that offer sanctuary from the heat and glare of the region. They can generally be visited if arrangements are made in advance. It is here in autumn that the fermentation process takes place. It is of course interrupted by the addition of grape brandy, creating the raw, fortified wine. Young port then spends the winter at the *quinta*. In springtime, it is transported to the port lodges in Vila Nova de Gaia, by train or truck, where it is blended and matured into a variety of styles. In times past, the port was shipped to the lodges by boat, in the lovely "Barcos Rabelos," narrow ships with large, square riggings. A retired "Barcos" can still be seen moored at the docks in Vila Nova de Gaia.

Vila Nova de Gaia is the town at the mouth of the Douro, on its south bank, facing Oporto. It has more than 80 port lodges, most of which have regular visiting hours—many with English-speaking guides. It is here that one can be instructed in the basic differences of port styles, aided, delightfully, by sampling the product itself. What follows are brief descriptions of the varied styles of port that one may encounter.

Vintage Port: The most famous and most expensive of the ports is vintage port. Representing only two percent of the entire annual port production, it is the crown jewel of Portuguese wines. It is produced from a single harvest's grapes and is "declared" only in years when the quality is deemed extraordinary. This decision—to declare a vintage—comes only after much testing, sampling and deliberation. With minor exceptions, one finds that the shippers declare vintages as a group, the regions' climate affecting the grapes more or less uniformly. Vintage port is bottled after two or three years in wood. For example, the great 1963 vintage must, by law, have been bottled between July 1, 1965, and June 30, 1966. This is what distinguishes vintage from all other ports: the majority of its aging takes place in glass, not wood. From a legal standpoint, vintage

port must identify itself as such, stating the name of its maker, the year of the vintage and carrying the governmental seal of approval, the "selo di origem."

As bottle aging progresses, vintage port "throws" a heavy sediment, the simple phenomenon of heavier particles in the wine succumbing to gravity. In appreciation of this, it is important that the wine be stored correctly: horizontally, yet at a slight incline, wine in contact with the cork. This measure will permit the bulk of the sediment to settle into the punt, or base, of the bottle. When vintage port—or any aging red wine, for that matter—is then opened, its contents will be disposed to decanting. Decanting is a simple procedure whereby the clear wine is poured away from the accumulated dregs. A properly stored bottle will facilitate this procedure.

Vintage port can be drunk as soon as 10 years after its vintage date, but most would agree that the wines hit their stride after 15 to 20 years. Vintage ports which I have enjoyed over the years have come from Taylor-Fladgate, Graham and Croft for the English houses, Fonseca and Quinta do Noval for the Portuguese.

Crusted Port: Crusted port differs from vintage port in that it needn't be from a single year, or vintage. It is mostly created from two or three different harvests. Crusted port spends extra time in wood, accelerating the wine's maturation. This extended aging makes for a lighter-bodied wine. Like vintage port, however, crusted port throws a sediment and needs to be decanted.

Late Bottled Vintage: Late bottled vintage (LBV) sees even more time in wood—from four to six years—than the aforementioned wines. As its name implies, the wine comes from a single year's harvest, but is much lighter in color than vintage port and need not be decanted. To comply with the law, both the date of the vintage and the date of bottling must appear on the label. Those who are exploring the world of port should be advised that ordering a glass of "vintage" port does not always yield true vintage port; late bottled vintage is sometimes served in its place. As an aid, it is thus worth remembering that the shipper's generally do not offer late bottled vintage in the same years as real vintage port. Knowing the more recent vintage declarations can help to avoid any misunderstandings. With minor exceptions, most of the port houses declared vintage wine in: 1985 (declaration made in early 1987), 1983, 1982, 1980, 1977, 1975, 1970, 1966, 1963 and 1960. Thus one tends to see late bottled vintage dates of 1981, 1978 and 1974.

Port with a Date of Vintage: A confounding offshoot of the vintage-dated wines is "Port of the Vintage" or "Port with Date of Vintage." Not to be confused with late bottled vintage, port with a date of vintage will come from a single year, but will have been aged in wood for no less than seven

Left, tawny port, so called because of its relatively light coloration, a result of being kept in the cask for seven years or longer

years. The bottle will often say *Colheitas* (which means "vintage")19xx, will have the date of bottling and some indication that the wine has been aged in wood. Port with a date of vintage can be found dating back to the early 1900s. The house of Nierport has a wonderful stock of these *Colheitas* wines. For all intents and purposes, these wines are the first step into tawny ports; that they are from a single vintage, however, prevents them from legally being so titled.

Wood Ports: Wood ports are the bread and butter of port trade. They are blended wines— from several harvests—that are matured in cask until they are ready for drinking. Because they are blended, it is the goal of the shipper to define his style through this wine so that year after year the customer can expect a consistent product. Three main types are: ruby, white and tawny.

Normally, white ports are sweet and served after the meal, but they are no competition for the reds. In response, winemakers have sought to popularize them by fermenting out the sugar, then adding brandy, and marketing them as dry, aperitif wines. These, however, are no competition for a good Fine Sherry. So they have yet to find their market. My first taste of the white port in the lodge of Villa Nova de Gaia was shortly accompanied by the hurling of the balance of my glass over my shoulder onto the sawdusted floors of the caves! Yet where there is wine there is hope: white port has became a viable accessory in the cuisine of today's chefs. More than once have I tasted dishes whose subtleties were enhanced by the addition of white port.

Last, but by no means least, there is tawny port, a special blend of port wine from different vin-

Ruby is young and hearty, not complex and not expensive. To a port drinker, it is the staple wine, attractive for its full, overt flavor. It is aged for two or three years in cask before bottling. One offshoot of ruby port is called "Vintage Character" port. This wine will have the same general features of ruby, but will be of a higher quality, usually older, and certainly more expensive. Unfortunately, such an appellation can only help to blur the distinctions between the several ports which appropriate the word "vintage." Vintage Character, however, will show no date.

White ports are also matured in wood. They can come from either red or white grapes. A white or clear color can be gotten from red grapes by separating the juice from the skins during fermentation before the color has been extracted.

tages which sees many years in cask. Through the more rapid oxidization process within a barrel, this wine matures rather quickly, evolving its tawny color and fabulously scented bouquet. Tawny port is thus more mellow in style than the "vintage-dated" ports, but it is refined, pensive and self-esteeming. True, old tawnies are rather expensive, priced in correlation to the long years the wine has spent aging in barrel. They should not be confused with the cheap tawny port so readily available in the United States. Cheap tawny port owes its existence to the strong world demand for a less concentrated, eminently drinkable port wine. The port shippers have handled this demand by concocting inexpensive tawny port, a blend of ruby and white port. The product is a simple wine of pinkish hue, in contrast to the fading russet of a true tawny. It will have none of the complexity that real tawny port gains through long aging. Since the name "tawny" can apply to either wine, the consumer must rely on color and price to distinguish between the two. Real tawny is not cheap; cheap tawny should never be expensive! True tawny port is a wonderful wine. I have always found the Taylor 10, 20 and 30-year-olds to be fine examples of tawny port. Only the "real thing" will reveal why this is the wine which many port houses most prize.

Dão Wines: The Dão region is the primary producer of Portugal's *vinhos maduros*, or aged wines. It is a mid-altitude area in central Portugal, delineated by no fewer than six mountain ranges. It is shaped and irrigated by a number of rivers including the Rio Dão, from which the area takes its name. This network of rivers, along which

grape quality. While there is little geological differentiation within the area—the soil consists primarily of granite—informed opinion will have it that the wine made between the rivers Mondego and Dão, around the towns of Nelas and Mangualde, are the best products.

In the past, the wines of the Dão were made by many small winemakers, who didn't trouble to make the fine distinction between the grapes that fared best in the environment and lesser varietals. To some extent this is still true today, despite the diligent prodding of the area's wine administration, the Federacão dos Vinicultores do Dão. The goal is to convince farmers of the relative superiority of certain varietals and encourage the eradication of the inferior species. Needless to say, change in the old country takes time.

The primary approved varieties producing the

much of the best planting is done, runs in a general southwest direction, and has by the time it reaches Coimbra converged with the Mondego, the region's main river.

The Dão covers approximately 1,000 square miles, only five percent of which are under vines. Driving through the territory, one is struck by its minimal composition: green geometries of vine, tortuous bands of pine forest, stark expanses of raw granite. It is divided into three main subregions, based upon the general consensus on

Left, the older the better: vintage 1863 botles of Ferreira Port Wine. Right, the barrels of port await their judgment

best Dão reds are the Tourigo, Tinta Pinheira, Tinta Carvalha, and the Avarelhão. More successful white varieties include the Dona Branca, Arinto and Barcelo. Reds are traditionally fermented in large granite tanks, then transferred to wood barrels where a slower fermentation continues under cooler conditions. This retarding and extending of the fermentation process graces the Dão reds with the trait for which they are most appreciated: a glyceral, velvetly feel on the palate. The reds then spend three years aging in wood; the *reservas* even longer. The whites must age in cask for at least 10 months before bottling. They comprise a very small percentage of total production, some three percent. White Dãos mature in a relatively short time—two to three years— and when good have a clean, rather nutty bouquet, and a dry, medium-bodied weight in the mouth.

As Portugal has modernized, the wine industry, which accounts for some 20 percent of its export revenues, has benefited from government incentives. In the Dão region, tremendous cooperatives, like the one located at Mangualde, have been built in the past 20 years. The local landholding growers have accepted the facilities and increasingly bring their grapes there to be processed into wine. After fermentation in the fall, their wine generally remains at the cooperative no later than summer, at which time it is brought to the *adega* (cellar) of the purchaser to age.

The larger growers, whose wine is rarely sold in its entirety, use an unusual interim storage facility: the concrete balloon. This bizarre construction is made by inflating an enormous rubber

Standard Dão reds see about three years of wood aging. This is where the wine evolves, appropriating the attributes of the barrel, slowly oxidizing through the wood's porousness and developing complexity during this introspective stage. The *Reservas* spend even more time in wood and the *Garafeiras*—loosely, "private cellar selection"—are often kept in wood for as long as seven years.

The acceptance and use of the new facilities have unquestionably taken Dão wines to a higher level of quality from the wines of years past. They give the consumer the sought-after balance of price and quality. Concurrently, however, one is obliged to acknowledge a certain homogeneity, that slights the Dão wines of their charismatic individuality.

While French and Italian wines are recogniz-

balloon and enclosing it with a dense grid of curving steel rods. Cement is then sprayed over the monstrosity. When the insides are sealed with a suitable resin, these huge white balls become halfway houses for wines in transit. They have capacities up to 96,000 gallons and can be seen all over Portugal. In the Dão they serve a function beyond mere storage. Each balloon frequently stores a different kind of wine: some will have been made with extended skin contact and thus be colorful and quite tannic; another may contain soft, fruity, free-run wine.

To the winemaker, each offers its own virtues to blending, so that an established flavor and house "signature" can be designed and maintained. When the "assemblage" is complete, the wine is channelled into wooden barrels to age.

able by any of a number of factors—estate, grape type, producer, etc.—many Dão wines lack the cult of personality that would encourage a worldwide popularity. On the other hand, Dão wines have one compelling advantage over their Continental counterparts. They can be enjoyed at the peak of their development at prices that would make any traveler relax. While it would be irresponsible to give any hard and fast data regarding the vintages of Dão wines (so hard to do anywhere, really) the 1954, 1957, 1964, 1970, 1973 and 1978 years are fairly safe bets.

As the producers go, the cooperative facilities have narrowed the gaps in quality between most producers. The following are wines I have regularly found rather pleasing: "Conde de Santar" from Carvalho, Ribeira & Ferreira. "Grão Vasco" from the Vinicola do Vale do Dão, "Terras Altas" from Jose Maria da Fonseca, "Dalva" from the Caves da Silva, "Porto dos Cavaleiros" from the Caves São João.

Don't let this list deter you from sampling the other Dão wines. Do remember that the notations *Reservas* and the *Garrafeiras* usually mean far better wine at a mildly higher price.

Bairrada: To the west of the Dão, stretching southward from Oporto to the university town of Coimbra, is the recently designated wine region called Bairrada. An area which has produced wine as long as any other in Portugal, Bairrada was nonetheless overlooked during the demarcation of 1906. Finally, as a result of concerted pressure from the local lobby, this legitimately estimable area was formally sanctioned in 1979. It is not an area frequently visited by tourists, but it does offer the renowned Buçaco Forest.

Both red and white wines are made here, the bulk of the white being used to make rather good sparkling wine by the "méthode champenoise." It is the red wine, though, that deserves attention. Made from the Baga grape, which dominates the region's acreage, the Bairrada reds require years of aging to reach their peak.

While somewhat tannic in its youth, the Baga repays patience with the elegance of its maturity. Deep, brilliant ruby in color, with the fine, cedary fragrances of an old Bordeaux from the St. Julien area, Baga wines unfurl layers of fruit and flavor on the palate. Its tannins, so prevalent in the wine's youth, faithfully endure, but adapt and give balance and structure in the wine's maturity. Such are my memories of a 1958 Buçaco that confirmed my beliefs in the fine wines of Portugal. But you will not find these wines in many city shops. Why not venture up into the "Green Cathedral," as Buçaco is known?

With a lunch in Sintra, an afternoon coffee in Coimbra among the students at the university, Buçaco and its Palace Hotel can be leisurely reached from Lisbon before nightfall. As you drive, the ground becomes higher, the vegetation greener, darker and taller. The dense, fairytale forest, thickened with exotic species, is broken by lonely, winding footpaths. Up you go, until you arrive at an absolutely eccentric palace. Begun as a monastery in the early 14th century; built into a Neo-Manueline palace in the 16th century; converted to a royal hunting lodge in the 18th century; "The Palace Hotel" is a quixotic amalgam, with remarkable first-class quarters. The rooms are ornate and furnished with antiques.

Dining proves to be an exercise in old-world leisure and elegance. Five to six-course meals are the norm, served by attentive, accommodating waiters. Yet the biggest thrill comes as you open the wine list and discover the treasured cellars of Buçaco.

Available only through the properties of Mr. Alexandre d'Almeida (at the Metropole in Lisbon; Das Thermas in Curia; the Astoria in Coimbra and the Praia-Mar in Carcavelos), the wines of Buçaco are not available for export. These wines are made on the premises at Buçaco in the old method of foot-stomping fermentation. The cellars, which contain over 200,000 bottles, are readily displayed to anyone interested. Both a red and a white are produced and selections can be made from vintages dating back into the 1920s. Invariably, a wine-lover's vacation slows down here. One can luxuriate for days in this wine list, sampling 30-year-old whites and 40-year-old reds! Reasons to visit this unusual palace are numerous—the forests are enchanting—but none better than to taste the finest red table wines this country has to offer.

Lisbon: In the environs of Lisbon, there are four officially demarcated wine regions, two on the verge of extinction and two eking out a living despite the onslaught on modernity. While none of the four are of great commercial importance, they are each quite distinct, with long traditions of wine-making.

To the west of Lisbon, just north of Estoril, lies the vanishing area of Carcavelos. Swinging northwest onto the actual shores of the Atlantic is the remarkable, yet endangered region known as Colares. Almost due north of Lisbon, the Bucelas zone maintains most of its original shape, producing some of the country's best whites. And to the south, one can explore the vineyards of the famous sweet Muscat wine: the Moscatel de Setúbal.

Carcavelos, like many Portuguese wines, gained a reputation through the Anglo-Portuguese economic alliances of earlier centuries. Its proximity to Lisbon—about 15 miles (25 km)—was once a boon to its popularity. Today, however, real estate developments in the resort towns of Estoril and Cascais, have reduced production of this wine to a mere trickle. When you can find it (your best chance of doing so is in the better Lisbon restaurants) Carcavelos is a nutty-flavored, fortified wine. On the sugar scale, it will vary from moderately dry to medium-sweet. For those eager to seek out this endangered species, the best lead that can be offered is the name Quinta do Barão, the sole remaining property, owned by Raul Ferreira & Sons Ltd.

Colares makes some of the most unusual red wine in the world. The town itself sits between the hills of Sintra to the east and the beaches of the Atlantic Ocean to its west. The best Colares vines are planted in the sand of the Atlantic shoreline through exceedingly labor-intensive methods.

Left, they grow in every single province of Portugal. Here, vineyards in the Ribatejo

The varietal used in winemaking is called the Ramisco, a small, dark blue grape.

Planting the vine in sand is no mean feat. A trench must first be dug down to the layer of Mesozoic clay below. Into the clay the roots of the plant are laid. During this work, the laborers often place baskets atop their head to ensure a channel of oxygen if and when the walls of sand cave in. The work is so physically difficult that rather than plant individual vines, the vine is cropped in such a way as to have one "mother" plant course through the ground. The final visual effect is of many seemingly individual plants sprouting upward; thus a row of vines is created.

The single most fascinating fact of the Colares vines is that their original root stocks have survived intact. Those who know their viticultural history will recall that Europe was plagued in the 1870s by the invasion of a parasite named the phylloxera aphid. The louse had arrived from the United States during viticultural exchanges with the Continent. It ravaged the vineyards of Europe by burrowing into the soil and chewing the roots of the vine for sustenance. In several years, virtually all of the vine-growing areas of the continent had been attacked. Many inventive cures were tried, yet nothing seemed to help. Eventually, the crisis was remedied, in an ironic manner. Root stocks from grape vines of the United States, huskier and largely immune to the phylloxera, were shipped to Europe, where the European vines were grafted onto its new root host with a kind of jigsaw fitting. This surgery was successful and today even the great classified growths of Bordeaux—no doubt to the chagrin of the French—have American rootstocks.

Not so with Colares. What saved their roots was the extremely dense soil—packed sand—into which the phylloxera could not burrow. So the plants and thus their wines remain much as they were over a hundred years ago. The red, which are the wines of note, are rather astringent in their youth, with firmly entrenched tannis. They become approachable after six or seven years, as the wine improves distinctly with age. When the wine is at its best, Colares tannins have relinquished their hold on the wine: the bouquet is fully fruited and bright. In flavor, Colares is medium-bodied, somewhat briary, with a concentrated, impressive finish. When dining, take the advice that I did: order, if possible, the "Colares Chita," produced by Antonio Bernadino Paolo Da Silva. In this case, the older, the better.

Some 15 miles (25 km) northwest of Lisbon lies the tiny wine-making region of Bucelas. Encompassing a mere 450 acres, production of Bucelas rarely exceeds 75,000 cases. The vines are grown both on the gentle slopes and the valley floor of the Trançao River, in soil that is predominantly clay. There are only two grapes—both white—grown in the region, the Arinto and the Esgana Cão. Like other wine regions surrounding Lisbon, wine-making in Bucelas—or Bucellas, as one sometimes sees on wine labels—has declined to practically one main producer: Camillio Alves, which bottles its wine under the label Caves Velhas.

In its youth, Bucelas wine is pale greenish-yellow. The bouquet is fine and fragrant, the taste, clean and dry, with a light but marked acidity. The young Bucelas spends very little time developing in wood. Despite the miniscule production, these young wines are geared for export and can be found in several of the EEC nations. The traveler's mission then becomes to locate an older Bucelas, or a "garrafeira." Mature Bucelas, which can spend years in Brazilian oak before bottling, will show far more exotic fruit flavors, and a dry, nutty finish. The older ones are some of Portugal's best white wines.

Setúbal: Moscatel de Setúbal is a fabulous dessert wine whose description has coaxed poetry out of all but the most perfunctory of oenophiles. Moscatel de Setúbal is sweet, perfumed, ethereal. Grown in an area south of Lisbon, across the bridge on the Arrábida Peninsula, the wine takes its name from the nearby port of Setúbal. Moscatel de Setúbal earned its "selo de origem," or governmental sanction, back in 1907. The area is presently being rezoned so that a distinct region for the local red wine will be recognized. Moscatel de Setúbal may be red or white, the majority being white. The small amount of red Moscatel, made with the Moscatel Roxo and rarely seen outside of Portugal, is worth the search if one is adventurously inclined.

Moscatel de Setúbal is fortified wine whose grapes grow rather wildly around the villages of Palmela and Azeitão. The grape "must"—crushed grapes—is vinified in cement vats and the fermentation is arrested by the addition of grape brandy at a specific sugar level. The vinified wine is then transferred to large cement containers, where lightly crushed grapes and skins are added to the must. The added contents are allowed to steep in the original concoction and their marvelous effect is to impart the signature aroma of the Moscatel grape at its freshest. After a single pressing, the wine is held, spending some time in cask, until ready for bottling and sale.

The two white wines commercially available are the six-year-old and the 25-year-old Moscatel de Setúbal. Both are intensely sweet and quite alluring as a finale to a summer's meal. The younger wine exhibits the intense varietal beauty of the grape; the fully mature 25-year-old does the same, with the added complexity and smoothness of age, as well as a dark, cosmetic brilliance.

Right, wine casks must be tended with great care; blends are added at specific times over the years

POUSADAS AND MANOR HOUSES

If waking up in a bed that once belonged to a Portuguese queen, or staying in an opulent remodeled convent, or even eating homemade bread and cheese in a shepherd's cottage sounds like an exciting change of pace from standard hotels, try the government-run *pousadas* (inns) or the privately-owned *turismo de habitacão* (tourist lodging) networks. The *pousadas*, now numbering more than 30, have justly earned a good reputation for comfort, luxury and service, and are easily located by abundant road signs. The quality of the tourist lodging varies widely, as these are private homes now open to the public.

If you happen to be traveling in the lush green and thick-forested northwestern corner of Portugal, you will come to the town of **Valença do Minho** and the **Pousada de São Teotonio**. This elegant *pousada* sits on a high point inside the ancient walled city and has a spectacular view of the Minho river across to Spain and the Galician mountains. It is also perfectly located for walks around the medieval town of tiny winding streets and stone houses.

The **Pousada D. Diniz**, named after the 14th-century Portuguese king, is in **Vila Nova da Cerveira**, just west of Valença, and also overlooks the Minho river. The inn is actually built into the town's ancient castle and has a small 18th-century chapel around the corner. The rooms, housed in several separate buildings, are large and feature lovely carved beds.

To the east is the **Pousada de São Bento**, a comfortable ivy-covered stone building on a hill inside the **Peneda-Gerês National Park**, a beautiful dense forest veined with cool streams. Its floor-to-ceiling windows overlook the Caniçada Dam and the surrounding countryside. This inn has a swimming pool and tennis court.

The **Pousada de Santa Marinha da Costa** is further south, in **Guimarães**, the town known as the "cradle of Portugal"—the first king of the country was born here. Do not confuse this *pousada* (some three miles outside of town) with the more modest but charming **Santa Maria** in Guimarães proper. The Santa Marinha is a beautiful converted 12th-century monastery, luxurious with all its original stone walls and windows—including the large center hall where the last owner is rumored to have exercised his horses! Some of the small rooms here used to be monks' cells but don't think you will feel incarcerated; many have balconies with a view of a charming courtyard that saves them from feeling cramped.

The north of Portugal is the birthplace of the tourist lodging plan, which was created as a

means of conserving some of the country's most beautiful private manor homes and palaces. The owners of these magnificent homes can no longer afford the expensive maintenance and have opened them up to tourists. One of the most pleasant aspects of these lodgings is that visitors are usually treated as guests of the family and are expected to respond as graciously.

One of the most impressive examples of tourist lodging in the northwestern tip of the country is **Paço de Calheiros**, a three-century-old manor house and chapel. The house has been the home of the Count of Calheiros since 1336, and the

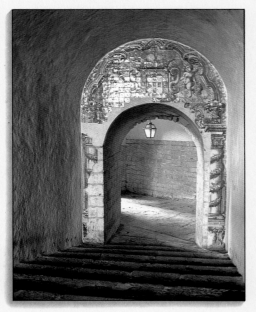

present count now lives here with his mother and family.

There are 10 rooms here, all restored with antiques and, where possible, with original materials, and all done in impeccable taste. Be sure to sample the homemade jams as you dine using the family's heirloom silverware.

The bedrooms are all wonderful, but perhaps the most romantic experience is to sleep on Portugal's Queen Carlotta Joaquina's original bed, a precious antique decorated with wood carved legs in the shape of dolphins crowned with flowers.

Another breathtaking home in the north is **Paço da Gloria** in **Arcos de Valdevez**, just northeast of Calheiros. This 17th-century stone palace, which once belonged to the Count of

Santa Eulalia, is now owned by an Englishman, Colin Clark. The house, with its large book-end towers, sits on a hill surrounded by vineyards and a garden. The interior has been decorated with a hospitable international sophistication—note the highly-polished entry-hall floor of black basalt and orange brick relecting the busts on their pedestals.

The bedrooms here have spacious bathrooms. One of the loveliest features of the house is its arched veranda. Have a seat and gaze out at the ice-blue pool and the tailored green lawns.

Further south, the **Viana do Castelo** and **Ponte de Lima** areas offer a wide range of lodging homes. North to Meadela on the road to Ponte de Lima stop at **Casa do Ameal**, a gracious shell-shaped building with a flower-framed pool. The house has three double rooms, four apartments,

sitting rooms and an attractive garden.

In Ponte de Lima itself, try **Casa do Outeiro**, a large, comfortable 18th-century house framed by large shade trees and well-kept grounds. It is fitted with all the modern conveniences, yet has lost none of its original charm. Not far away is **Casa do Antepaço**, tucked away in a lovely *quinta*, or estate. This house has been carefully restored, and guests can stay in the one private apartment or in one of the four double rooms

Preceding page, the Pousada da Santa Marinha in Guimarães. Left, an outside stairway at Pousada de São Filipe in Setúbal. Above, the hall down which the former owner ran horses at Pousada da Santa Marinha

available, and enjoy the comfortable living room complete with fireplace, the library, or the terrace which overlooks the garden and Lima River.

In the same area, near Facha, rising suddenly out of a curve in the road, is **Casa das Torres**, a magnificent example of King João V (1706-1750) architecture, with stone-framed windows, thick white-washed stone walls and gracefully tiled tower roof-tops. There is one double room in the main house and a separate annex apartment. Visitors are welcome to make full use of the swimming pool and gardens.

For those who prefer a more rural setting and more privacy, **Quinta da Aldeia** in Crasto-Ribeira is a lovely if small *quinta* with an ivy-covered entrance. It offers an entire apartment complete with kitchen, bathroom and living room, all furnished with rustic wood furniture.

Your own watermill: Minho de Estoroes, also near Ponte de Lima, is a delightful small, old stone watermill sitting on the banks of the Esteroes brook that has been carefully refurbished to fit one family. Don't be surprised if you share the brook with a group of local women who kneel at the rocks to wash their family's clothing.

These are just a few of the 50 or so different houses dotted around this area, known as the *Costa Verde* or "Green Coast." Every house is very different, and every owner will receive you in his or her own personal way.

In the Douro Valley there are a few Tourist Lodging houses, two of the most interesting being the **Villa Hostilina** in Lamego and **Casa dos Varais** in Cambres. The villa overlooks the old city of Lamego and has been totally refurbished to include a gym, sauna, massage room, tennis courts and a swimming pool. In the Casa dos Varais you can enjoy the full beauty of the Douro, for its large stone house, terraces and gardens overlook the river and nearby hillsides. This house has only two double rooms and a separate sitting room for guests.

Deep in the heart of the **Serra da Estrêla** is the town of Manteigas and the **Pousada São Lourenço**, a modest building of stone with a red-tiled roof. The rooms are plain but comfortable with wooden four-poster twin beds. Rooms on the second floor have little verandas with dramatic views of the mountains and the town below. The inn has a lounge and snug television room, and a fireplace warms up the dining room. Regional specialities, such as the famous Serra da Estrêla sheeps' milk cheese, is served here. You should also try the local *gerupiga* wine, usually served in unmarked bottles.

One of the best spots in the Serra is **Sabugueiro**, a tiny mountain village of narrow cobblestone and mud streets and granite houses. Any villager can show you the way to the **Casa do Sabugueiro** run by Dona Teresa da Graça Trinidade, who also happens to run the local tavern, selling shot-glasses of red wine to tired shepherds wearing brown felt hats and overcoats. Staying here gives you a real taste of rural Portugal (although with considerably more comfort than in the houses around you). Expect to wake up to the tinkle of sheeps' bells and the low calls of the shepherds before sunrise.

Dona Teresa has remodeled the inside of two granite houses into charming white-walled bedrooms, neat bathrooms and sitting rooms with small corner fireplaces. She has also set up a small dining room where she serves homemade rye bread, cheese and heaping platefuls of the meal of the day. One of her nieces makes cheese by hand over a wood fire, as well as fresh cottage cheese. This is a dying art, so ask if you can watch the process—but be prepared to wake up at 5:30 a.m. to do so.

vent of Christ, and a little way out of town, in **Castelo do Bode**, is a *pousada* perched above a large blue-water dam on the Zêzere River. This inn is surrounded by olive and pine trees. The bedrooms are smallish but very comfortable with plain wood furniture and floral print curtains. The breakfast room is full of sunlight in the morning and looks out over the dam.

Just south of Batalha is **Porto de Mós**, with its massive castle. The rambling **Quinta do Rio Alcaide**, recently remodeled, is set in the side of the mountains, with columned terraces and red-tiled roofs overlooking the wide gardens. The quinta has four sections: the main house, the "middle" house, the old "bread-oven" house, which has been transformed into a self-contained apartment, as has the "windmill" house that sits on a hill overlooking the *quinta*.

At the foot of the Serra is **Alpedrinha**, a small town huddled under the mountainside. Turn right off the main street and you will come to a 19th-century-style house called **Casa do Barreiro**. Here you will be ushered through several rooms full of overstuffed chairs, pianos, thick carpets, and numerous knick-knacks and antiques. The walls of the houses are decorated with antique fans, tapestries and tiny crowded vitrines. If you come in winter be prepared for the cold. A glimpse underneath those floor-length tablecloths reveal small pans filled with coal—heating the old-fashioned way. The bedroom has a 19th-century-style canopy bed, chaise lounge and small eating table, for breakfast served in your room in the morning.

The town of **Tomar** boasts the intriguing Con-

Southwest of here and just north of Lisbon is the graceful walled town of **Óbidos**. The **Pousada do Castelo**, which is built into a section of the old castle, is very small and popular, and therefore difficult to reserve. If you miss out on a room, it's still more than worthwhile to stop in and have a drink.

Closer to Lisbon is **Torres Vedras** and **Quinta do Hespanhol**, a 16th-century manor which still has much of its original Manueline detail. The house, has four double rooms and various sitting rooms, is bordered by large shady trees and has a lovely columned veranda on the top floor. Some three miles (five km) outside of Torres Vedras, in **S. Mamede de Mertola**, is the **Moinho do Loural**, an old windmill converted to a tiny two-bedroom apartment, complete with kitchen, bathroom and sitting room with fireplace.

Following the Tagus River north, the traveler comes to **Santarém** where two families have opened up their homes to guests. **Casal da Torre** is the more modest of the two, a small house on the edge of a cobblestone street with flowering bushes covering its front and plants sprouting from its roof. The house has three bedrooms, sitting rooms, and a small garden where you can share an open-air barbecue.

Quinta da Sobreira is larger and more elegant, with an arched entranceway and tower on one side. This early-19th-century home has a swimming pool and riding facilities, Santarém being famous for its horses. There are only three bedrooms here, each with a private bathroom.

A view to Spain: If you head east from here, you will arrive at the border town of **Marvão**, a 14th-

hostess will provide large logs in winter) in the open sitting room, a cozy loft bedroom with white-on-white bedspreads and a lovely arched window seat and kitchenette. There are two more bedrooms downstairs, so the house is big enough for three couples or a family.

A few of the houses in the greater Lisbon area live up to the beauty and grace of the houses in the north of the country. One example of this is the **Quinta da Capela** in Sintra, an exquisite place that fits in perfectly with the Byronesque setting of the Sintra hills. The palace belongs to the Marchioness de Cadaval and is arranged in perfect taste with fresh orchids on the windowsills; the dining room in soft shell-pink tones; and the extensive gardens carefully tended. The *quinta* has one suite, with four double rooms in the main house. Two apartments large enough for four

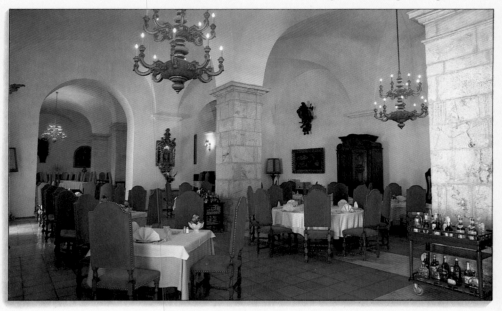

century whitewashed walled town perched like an eagle's nest at the top of the mountain. Inside the medieval walls is the **Pousada Santa Maria**, simply decorated with red tile floors, wood-beamed ceilings and fireplaces, and a glassed-in terrace with a panoramic view into neighboring Spain. The bedrooms are comfortable but small, and the restaurant's menu includes local game.

If you prefer to have a house of your own here, for a few days or a few weeks, try **Travessa do Terreirinho**, owned by Margarida Leite Rio. The house is typical, with a huge fireplace (the

Left, the vaulted ceilings of Pousada dos Lóios in Évora. Above, the dining room of Pousada da Rainha Santa Isabel in Estremoz

people each have been set up on the grounds.

Also in Sintra is **Quinta de São Thiago**, close to the **Seteais Palace**. The seven double rooms here are all luxuriously fitted, as are the various lounges, the bar and the sitting room. The *quinta* also has a large garden with magnificent shade trees that surround the modern swimming pool and tennis court.

Directly south of Lisbon is **Palmela** and the impressive **Pousada Castelo de Palmela**. This *pousada* is part of a 15th-century monastery built in the reign of King João I and faces the Palmela Castle. All the large airy bedrooms have sweeping views over the countryside, and there is also a gorgeous sun-filled cloister in the center, protected by a series of stone arches.

Not far away is Setúbal, whose **Pousada de**

São Filipe is actually inside the walls of the São Filipe Castle. Most of the high-ceilinged rooms have a view of the bay, as does the restaurant, which specializes in regional dishes. There is a pleasant outdoor lounge on the old stone terrace for a drink before dinner.

Traveling toward Spain you will come to **Elvas** and **Estremoz**. The **Pousada de Santa Luzia** in Elvas is best known for its cuisine and lavish servings of food. Many people just stop in for lunch. The rooms, however, are perfectly adequate.

You should make a point of staying in the fantastic **Pousada Rainha Santa Isabel** in Estremoz, which sits elegantly above the small town. This inn has been brilliantly restored with 17th- and 18th-century antiques. A majestic marble staircase leads to the bedrooms upstairs, all ro-

tions of the ancient castle. Today completely refurbished, it is a fabulous inn with high ceilings and granite and marble arches. A carved marble staircase leads upstairs to the bedrooms. The sitting room here is all hand-painted and decorated with antiques, and the dining room has been set around the glassed-in interior garden and fountain.

The tourist lodging in Évora is also exceptional. The towers that formed the original gates to the city dating from Moorish times now form one of the walls of the **Casa do Conde da Serra**, owned by Sra. Sousa Cabral. The house came into the hands of the first Count da Serra da Tourega in the mid-1600s, and his coat of arms is still displayed on the front of the house.

Inside, the house is filled with precious furniture and artful decor. An impressive 17th-century

mantically furnished in deep rich colors, and all with good views. The dining room is made up of a series of low arches and huge stone pillars which are softly lit in the evening, and the menu branches out from local specialities to include Steak Diane and Crepes Suzette, cooked at your table.

In between Estremoz and Elvas, slightly past Borba, is **Vila Viçosa** and the elegant **Casa dos Arcos**, named after the slender arches that embellish its entrance. The grandest features of this 16th-century home are the original frescoes that cover the walls of the sitting room. The rooms are not as inspiring, but they are pleasant, airy and private.

In Évora, the **Pousada dos Loios** was originally a 15th-century mansion built on the founda-

oil painting depicting Christ's cruxifiction on four arched wooden panels adorns a huge stairway. Some of the bedrooms have their own gracefully tiled fireplaces and Arraiolos rugs on the floor. Breakfast is served in the main dining room, which is furnished with 18th-century commodes, a vitrine of *lignum vitae* dating from the reign of King João V, and a Dutch cupboard that dates from 1625.

Not far from Évora and just a few kilometers from the village of Redondo is the magnificent **Convento da Serra D'Ossa** which has been in the family of Sr. Henrique Leotte for over 150 years. Originally built by monks of the Order of Saint Paul around 1070, other sections were added in the 14th and 18th centuries. The surrounding countryside is covered in olive, pine and eucalyptus trees. The rooms are converted monks' cells which branch off a main corridor, itself a work of art, with panels of blue- and -white tiles dating from the 18th century.

A wonderful outdoor patio, also decorated in original tiles, faces a Florentine fountain with archways overhead. The original chapel, which is open to guests, displays frescoes dating from the 17th and 18th centuries and tiles depicting biblical scenes, which have the rare feature of being signed.

On the west side of the Alentejo, not far from the Roman ruins of Mirobriga, is **Santiago do Cacém** and the **Pousada de São Tiago**, a small ivy-covered building with a garden full of flowers and a swimming pool. There are four bedrooms in the original part of the inn, all with a pleasant rustic flavor, with wood floors and whitewashed

absolutely perfect for hours of star-gazing.

And finally to the Algarve, Portugal's southernmost province. The **Pousada São Brás** is a peaceful whitewashed inn located some two miles (three kilometers) above the town of **São Brás de Alportel**. The rooms are plain, but have a view over the valley below and beyond to the coast. The glassed-in semicircular dining room also has a panoramic view, and the lounge is comfortably decorated with leather furniture and throw rugs on the floor.

Pousada do Infante, named after Prince Henry the Navigator, is on the Atlantic edge of the Algarve in Sagres. It is a sprawling modern building with pleasant, airy rooms that overlook the coast. With the dining room fireplace, thoughtfully selected art and amenities, and the carefully tended, lush green lawn that reaches out to the

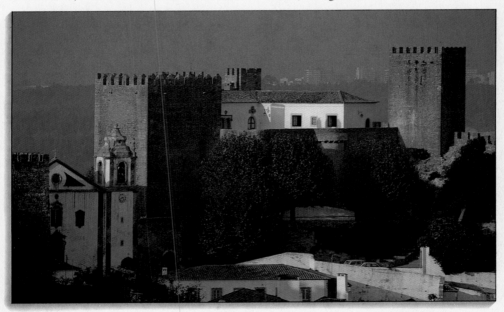

walls, and there are additional bedrooms in the annex. This *pousada* has a calm and welcoming feeling about it.

Seeing stars: Heading south, almost on the border with the Algarve, is **Pousada Santa Clara** overlooking the vast blue waters of the **Santa Clara Dam**. This *pousada* is a little hard to get to, as it is off the main road, but it is worth the extra drive. The dining room looks out onto a stone terrace and a sloping garden planted with orange trees. During the day you can go for long walks around the lake, and the darkness at night is

Left, exterior of Pousada de Santa Marinha da Costa outside Guimarães. Above, Pousada do Castelo in the walled town of Obidos

cliff's edge, these comfortable lodgings are reminiscent of an American country club.

Tourist lodging is not as developed here as it is in the north, but there is one place worth staying, the **Quinta do Caraçol** just at the entrance of **Tavira** on the east side of the Algarve. The owner recently converted the quinta and did a lovely job, picking up on the Tunisian blues and soft yellows traditional for this region. The house is sparkling white and low, covered in occasional splashes of purple bougainvillea, reflected in the crisp blue water of the mini-pool tucked into the back of the house. There is also a tennis court and small bar open to guests, who are made to feel comfortable in this gem of a home. (For information about reservations, see "Where To Stay" in the Travel Tips section)

ART AND ARCHITECTURE

Portugal's unique geographical position, cut off from Europe by Spain on one border, facing out toward the New World on the other, is reflected in its art and architecture. In order to counter the natural tendency toward isolation, Portuguese artists and architects have for centuries looked outside for influence and affirmation. Even today, a kind of magical aura surrounds cultural events that occur *lá fora*—literally "out there," meaning abroad, overseas. Simultaneously, because it serves as a bridge, Portugal has attracted numerous foreign artists, as will be seen below. Thus, a kind of filtering process has occurred, where local traditions have blended with imported ideas. At its best, Portuguese art has forged out of foreign influences powerful and original stylistic languages.

Romanesque

In Europe, the reiteration of Christianity in the face of encroaching Moslem faith was represented not only by the Crusades, but also by the reforms introduced by the new religious orders, especially those of Cluny and Cister, whose influence spread far and wide.

In Portuguese art, a discussion of the Romanesque period, the period that began with the 12th century is essentially a discussion of religious architecture. Other than a few illustrated manuscripts, very little except architecture has survived from that time. The predominance of religious architecture is hardly incidental: the founding of the kingdom corresponds to the reconquest of Portugal from the Moors; and hence, to a period in which Christianity was strongly felt. The construction of cathedrals during this period followed the path of reconquest from Braga to Oporto, southwards to Coimbra, Lamego (reconstructed in the 18th century), Lisbon and Évora.

The man who, enlisting the aid of the Crusaders, led this sweep of Portugal and became its first king was Afonso Henriques. His father, Henri, had arrived from Burgundy in the late 11th century. These Burgundian roots of the kingdom were instrumental in the development of Portuguese Romanesque architecture. The close relations of the duchy of Burgundy with the Order of Cluny meant that this order became especially influential—numerous monks from Cluny and Moissac became bishops of Oporto and Braga. Portuguese Romanesque cathedrals, especially those in the west of the country along the route to the pilgrimage church of Santiago de Compostela (in what today is Spanish Galicia), have an affinity with the Clunian churches of Auvergne and Languedoc.

The building of Romanesque churches in Portugal continued into the 14th century in the north, at which time the Gothic style was already spreading throughout the rest of the country. Portuguese Romanesque is an architecture of simple, often dramatically stark forms, whose sturdiness is frequently explained by the need for fortification against the continued threat of Moorish or Castilian invasion. This fortified appearance is enhanced in the cathedrals of Lisbon and Coimbra by the crenellated facade towers which seem to balk against intrusion.

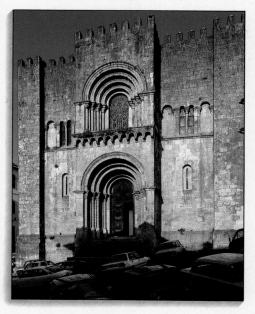

Portuguese Romanesque is largely an architecture of granite. This stone abounds in the northern regions, where numerous monasteries were built—of which usually nothing more than the churches have survived. The hardness of granite renders detailed carving impossible, thus favoring a simplicity of form. Absent, therefore, are the ornately carved tympana of French and Spanish Romanesque churches. In areas where the softer limestone abounds, such as the central belt of the country (including Coimbra, Tomar and Lisbon), carved decorations are more common.

Although there are regional variations, these Romanesque churches share a certain robustness; a method of construction based on semi-circular arches and barrel vaults; a cruciform plan; and a solid, almost sculptural sense of form in the interior which allows for a play of light and shade. All these features serve to enhance a sense of mystery, indeed of Divine Mystery. This sobriety is accentuated by the paucity of decoration, which is frequently reduced to the capitals of columns and the archivolts surrounding the portals. When the tympana are not bare, the simplified carvings are usually stylized depictions of Christ in Majesty, or the *Agnus Dei* (Lamb of God) or simply of a cross. In some cases, animals and serpents climb up the granite columns, as in the *Sé Velha* (Old Cathedral) of Coimbra or in the unusually richly decorated principal portal of the early 13th-century Church of São Salvador in Bravães in Minho.

Gothic

In France, new methods of construction involving pointed arches and ribbed vaults allowed for lighter, taller architectural forms. As the main weight of the building was now borne outside at fixed points by flying buttresses, the walls could be pierced at frequent intervals. The light filtering into these Gothic interiors became a metaphor for Divine Light, replacing the Romanesque emphasis on Mystery.

The first building in Portugal to use these new construction methods was the majestic church at the Abbey of Alcobaça, commissioned by Afonso Henriques. With its great height and elegant, unadorned white interior bathed in a milky light, Alcobaça is one of the most serene and beautiful churches in Portugal. Begun in 1178 and consecrated in 1222, it is almost purely French in inspiration: its plan echoes that of Clairvaux, the seat of the Cistercian Order in Burgundy—a nave and two side aisles of almost the same height, a two-aisled transept, and an apse whose ambulatory fans out into various chapels. Other Portuguese churches at this time did not employ this Cistercian plan and usually followed the scheme of a nave and two side aisles, a salient well-lit transept, and an apse consisting of three or five chapels, without ambulatory.

The true affirmation of the national Gothic style came after the Portuguese armies defeated the invading Castilians at the Battle of Aljubarrota. In fulfillment of a religious vow made prior to the battle, King João I commissioned the construction of a magnificent monastery. In 1388 work began on the now famous Dominican Monastery of *Santa Maria da Vitória* (St. Mary of the Victory), better known as Batalha, which means "battle."

The stylistic heterogeneity of Batalha is due to the many years it took to build. Its construction can be divided into three stages. The first, lasting until 1438, was initially supervised by architect Afonso Domingues, who died in 1402, and then by a figure known as Huguet, whose nationality is unknown. Domingues' plan was entirely Portuguese in inspiration, following the general scheme of the churches of the Mendicant Orders (Franciscans and Dominicans), which were now gaining ascendance. The central nave is illuminated by clerestory windows; simple ribbing supports the vault; and the chancel gives on to two pairs of chapels, without ambulatory.

Offset by Domingues' scheme, Huguet's contributions, which include the Founder's Chapel and the famous chapterhouse vault, have a greater refinement and elegance, influenced by English Gothic architecture. Indeed, similarities have been noted between Batalha and the Cathedrals of York and Canterbury. Contact with England was close at this time as João I's wife, Philippa of Lancaster, was the daughter of John of Gaunt. But these and other foreign influences were subject to modifications, especially in the relatively low proportions of the nave, in a certain oriental flavor in the Founder's Chapel, and in the large, airy cloister characteristic of Portuguese Gothic churches. With Huguet's sudden death in 1438, the chapels of the octagonal pantheon remained incomplete.

The second stage, under Martim Vasques and Fernão de Évora, lasted until 1481, during which time a second cloister was built. The third stage was supervised by Mateus Fernandes and Diogo Boytac, and corresponded to the Manueline (see below) phase of the building, culminating in the arcade of the incomplete chapels and the Royal Cloister.

The stylistic influence of Batalha is felt in various churches throughout the country, examples being the Cathedral at Guarda and the ruined Church of Carmo in Lisbon, which were both begun at the end of the 14th century. The state of ruin in which the latter stands today is a poetic if somber commemoration of the Lisbon Earthquake of 1755.

In general, the austerity imposed by the Mendicant Orders meant that the national Gothic style leaned toward temperance rather than flamboyance. Soaring pinnacles and the dissolution of form into light did not suit either the religious orders or the national temperament.

If Portuguese Gothic architecture retains something of Romanesque sobriety, this is not the case with its Gothic sculpture. In addition to the decoration of capitals and columns, three-dimensional sculpture became increasingly common. In free-standing pieces in both wood and stone, the image of the Virgin presides. Emphasis is given to those aspects of her relationship with her Son that are most human and tender—from preg-

Preceding pages, detail from the six-paneled masterpiece, *Veneração a São Vicente* by Nuno Gonçalves. Left, the Romanesque Old Cathedral at Coimbra

nancy in the *Senhora do O* (such as the beautiful example by the renowned Master Pero, now at the Machado de Castro Museum in Coimbra, to suckling (sometimes while caressing the Child's foot), or carrying the Infant on her raised hip, as at the cathedrals of Braga and Évora. The hieratic sternness of Romanesque carvings is replaced by the humanization of Christ and his Mother. The handling of the drapes also becomes less stylized: now ample, they follow the curves of the body they clothe.

By far the most important category of sculpture in the 14th and 15th centuries was that of tombs, often carved with representations of their inhabitants. Previously, burial within the church walls was not practiced, and exterior tombs were seldom extensively carved. It was only well into the 13th century that sculpted sarcophagi began to

proliferate. Coimbra was the most important focus for this tradition, as a result of the abundance of soft limestone there. While the sarcophagi of Lisbon and Évora are generally archaizing, the tomb (1330) at the Church of Santa Clara-a-Nova in Coimbra of the *Rainha Santa* (Holy Queen) lying serenely, clothed in the Franciscan habit of the Order of St. Clare, is a moving example of early Gothic naturalism. The sculpture has no Portuguese precedents. It is thought that it was inspired by the School of Aragon, which was then the most important center for sculpture in the Iberian Peninsula.

The two tombs that together emerge as the crowning glory of Portuguese 14th-century funerary sculpture are those of King Pedro and his lover Inês de Castro in Alcobaça. The illicit,

passionate love affair, the brutal murder of Inês, Pedro's unmitigated sorrow and horrible revenge—this sad and beautiful story has been sung by the nation's greatest writers and poets. (see page 26) The sarcophagi do justice to the dramatic tale. Of unknown authorship and hybrid influence, they outshine all preceding funerary sculpture in their monumentality, plasticity, refinement of naturalistic detail, and richness of symbolism. With the tombs facing each other in opposite transepts, come the Day of Judgment, the lovers, as Pedro planned, will rise gazing into each other's eyes.

Inês lies calmly, surrounded by angels and crowned at last, in earth as never in life, as Pedro's queen. The sides of her tomb are carved with scenes from the life of Christ and the Virgin, while the head and foot depict scenes of Calvary and the Last Judgment respectively. The latter, a favored theme of European portal sculpture, is especially interesting for being the only one of its kind in Portugal.

The sides of Pedro's sarcophagus display incidents from the life of St. Bartholemew. Carved on the head of this tomb is a magnificent rosette—two concentric circles, the themes of which have been controversial. Some scholars see in them the narration of the story of Pedro's love for Inês; more frequently, the rosette is considered to be a wheel of fortune, representing life's vicissitudes. The masterful grace in the carving of these twin tombs brilliantly executes both symbolic and narrative detail.

Of a later date (ca. 1433) is the double tomb in the Founder's Chapel at Batalha of King João I and Philippa of Lancaster. The tomb itself is unadorned but for a Gothic inscription. The King clasps the sword of Aljubarrota, and his armor bears the crest of the House of Avis, the dynasty he founded. The crowned couple lie open-eyed and hand in hand. Although common in England, this type of double tomb was rare in the Peninsula; it seems possible that it was made by English sculptors who came to work at Batalha at the request of the queen.

The 15th century was the first great age of Portuguese painting. Almost no paintings of the 12th through 14th centuries have survived, although frescos were certainly painted in churches. One fragment of an early 15th-century fresco is an interesting, rare example of secular painting—the allegory of justice entitled *O Bom e o Mau Juiz* (The Good and the Bad Judge) in a Gothic house that was probably a court of law, in the town of Monsaraz. The most notable surviving religious fresco of the same period is the *Senhora da Rosa* in the sumptuous Church of São Francisco in Porto. It has been attributed to an Italian painter, António Florentino, who, it is thought, may also have painted the portrait of João I now at the Museu Nacional de Arte Antiga in Lisbon.

By far the most brilliant contribution to painting during this period was the introduction of *retábulos*—painted panels, or altarpieces. The importance of Flemish art to this development has often been noted and is undeniable. In 1428, the celebrated Flemish master Jan Van Eyck was invited to the court of João I to paint the portrait of the Infanta D. Isabel, future wife of Philip the Good (1396-1467), Duke of Burgundy. The Netherlands were, at the time, under the control of the dukes of Burgundy who were renowned for their excellent taste in art. When the Flemish artists turned from illumination to the painting of altarpieces, they added to their own love of realistic detail the Burgundian passion for gemlike decoration. To aid them in these pursuits, they developed and perfected the heretofore little-used medium of oil painting.

The most outstanding 15th-century Portuguese *retábulo* is the polyptych of St. Vincent attributed to Nuno Gonçalves, in Lisbon's Museu Nacional de Arte Antiga. The mystery that enshrouds this work has increased its aura. The panels were "lost" for some centuries, and there are various conflicting accounts of their reappearance at the end of the 19th century. No sooner were they cleaned and hung publicly than an angry polemic arose as to the identity of their author as well as of the figures therein depicted. Scholarly arguments have raged ever since. A touch of drama was added when one eminent scholar committed suicide after a dispute concerning two documents which radically altered the direction of the research. The documents were later proved false by a commission of inquiry.

The eminent Portuguese art historian José de Figueiredo, who was responsible for hanging the polyptych at the Lisbon Museum in 1910, was also primarily responsible for its attribution to Gonçalves. He based his argument on the 16th-century *Treatise on Ancient Art* by Francisco de Holanda, which mentioned that a great Portuguese artist had painted the altar at the Church of St. Vincent, then the patriarchal see in Lisbon. Holanda later praises one Nuno Gonçalves, royal painter at the court of Afonso V, for his panels depicting St. Vincent. Figueiredo was convinced that the polyptych he installed in the Lisbon Museum and the St. Vincent altarpiece mentioned by Holanda were one and the same. Later research supported these findings through detailed comparisons of the dates of known events in the life of Gonçalves, with the dating of styles in dress and arms. The panels thus could not date before 1467, and were probably painted around

1467-70. The work includes a portrait of King Afonso V, and it is known that in 1471 Gonçalves was still a favorite royal painter. In light of these clues, Nuno Gonçalves is generally regarded as the author of these famous panels.

The theme of the polyptych has also given rise to dispute. Some see in it the veneration of the *Infante Santo*—D. Fernando, uncle of Afonso V, who died at the hands of the Moors. But nowadays, it is generally thought to represent the adoration of St. Vincent, patron saint of the kingdom and of the city of Lisbon. While many of the figures have still to be identified, the important point of departure was the identification of the Infante D. Henrique (Prince Henry the Navigator) to the left of the saint in the third panel from the left. This identification was based upon the similarity of this depiction with a portrait of the

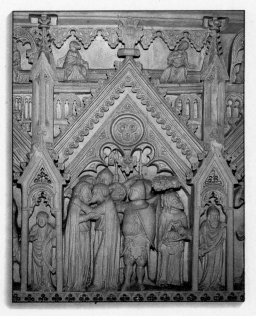

Prince in an illuminated chronicle. A snag: Henrique had died in 1461. The dating of the work, however, is still plausible, as the prince's haircut and Burgundian hat were somewhat out-of-date for 1467-70. His portrait in the polyptych is thus assumed to be posthumous, although possibly based on an earlier one by the same painter.

The panels, from left to right, are known as the Panel of the Monks (the white-robed monks of the Cistercian Order), the Fishermen, the Infante, the Archbishop, the Cavalry and finally, the Relic Panel. Among the characters identified are the king himself in profile beneath the Infante D. Henrique in the Infante Panel; his brother D. Fernando along with the Archbishop in the Archbishop Panel; the Archbishop (D. Jorge da Costa), the chronicler Gomes Eanes de Azurara

Left, detail from the great polyptych showing Prince Henry the Navigator and the future João II. Above, detail from the sepulchre of Inês de Castro

ESCOLA do MESTRE de TOMAR

holding an open book in the Relic Panel; and the second Duke of Bragança and his children in the Cavalry Panel. The panels are thought to have originally flanked a central votive sculpture.

The polyptych uses neither the linear perspective of the Italians nor the aerial perspective of the Flemish, who often included landscapes in their altarpieces. Instead, the composition of figures filling up the format echoes tapestry design. While the chromatic richness and exquisiteness of handling seem of Flemish influence, the drawing of the heads and the almost sculptural drapes is Italianate—broader and more synthetic than that of the northern masters.

While arguments may continue about influence, the work's real genius and originality lie in the fineness of the portraiture—its masterful attention to realistic detail as well as its psychological dimension. The work is monumental, heroic. Without actually portraying any historic events, it reads like an epic poem of King Afonso's dreams of conquest and of the magical world of the Infante D. Henrique's navigations—blessed, as it were, by the patron saint of the kingdom.

Manueline

In the 15th and 16th centuries, the Portuguese rulers were forerunners in supporting the navigation of the Atlantic. The exhilaration resulting from their discoveries had a marked effect on art, architecture and literature. The term "Manueline" was first used in the 19th century to refer to the reign of Manuel I (1495-1521) during which Vasco da Gama reached the coast of India (1498), Afonso de Albuquerque conquered the Indian city of Goa (1510), and the art of the Discoveries reached its zenith. The term is now used more broadly to refer to certain stylistic features predominant during the Avis dynasty (1383-1580), especially in architecture.

Manueline architecture does not have major innovative structural features—the twisted columns, such as those at the Church of Jesus in Setúbal, perform the same function as do plain ones. Rather, Manueline can be seen as a heterogenous late Gothic, its real innovation lying in its stone decoration, the exuberance of which reflects the optimism and wealth of the period. Inspired by the voyages to the New World, it is ornate and imposing, uniting naturalistic maritime themes with Moorish elements and heraldic motifs: during the reign of Manuel I, the king's own emblems are usually included—his military sphere or coat of arms, or the cross of the Order of Christ. These emblems were also used in the

churches built in the newly "discovered" overseas territories.

The Monastery of Santa Maria de Belém in Lisbon, better known as Jerónimos, is one of the great *hallenkirchen* of the period—that is, a church whose aisles are as high as its nave. The construction was at first supervised by Diogo Boytac who, as mentioned was also responsible for the Royal Cloister at Batalha, as well as for the Church of Jesus at Setúbal. The apse of Jerónimos was rebuilt along more classical lines after an earthquake destroyed the original one in 1571, and the happy marriage of Manueline and Renaissance features account for the extraordinary interior space of this church.

Perhaps the most notable feature of Manueline architecture is the copious carving surrounding portals and windows. These are often contained

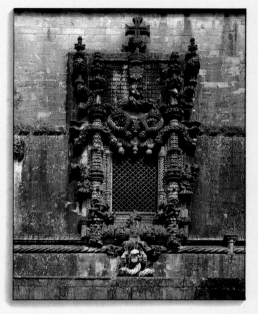

in semi-circular arches rather than the pointed Gothic ones. The imposing southern portal of Jerónimos and the window of the chapterhouse at the Convent of Christ in Tomar well deserve the acclaim they receive. Construction on the latter began in the 12th century with the famous Templar *Charola*—a chapel with the circular floor plan. When the Order of the Templars was dissolved in 1314, the convent became the seat of the Order of Christ. During the 16th century, the conventual buildings, including four cloisters, were added. The lavish Manueline decoration of the church culminates in the famous window, which is designed with two great ship's masts on either side, covered with carvings, topped, like the southern portal at Jerónimos, by the cross of the Order of Christ.

Left, *Calvario* by Gregório Lopes, from the School of the Master of Tomar. Above, the fantastically ornate Manuline window at the Convent of Christ at Tomar

Cloisters were now also richly ornamented, and there are many fine examples: Batalha's Royal Cloister, the Cloister of Silence at the Santa Cruz Monastery in Coimbra, and the cloisters of Jerónimos, as well as those of the churches of Jesus at Setúbal and Lóios at Évora.

Manueline architecture also adopted and modified certain Moorish features, known as *morisco*. At the Palácio Nacional at Sintra, for instance, restored during Manuel's reign, *morisco* features include the use of tiles, merlons, and windows divided into two lights by columns reaching the parapet. Another *morisco* feature is the horseshoe arch, as in the chapterhouse at the Convent of Lóios in Évora. In the Alentejo province, especially around Évora and Beja, numerous palaces are strongly *morisco* in their decoration, which includes flat lattice-worked ceilings.

During the reign of João II (1481-1495), when the navigations occupied the energies of the nation, there was a lull in painting activity. However, with the discovery of the sea-route to India and the consequent prosperity, painted *retábulos* again became a dominant form of expression. At the end of the 15th century, Portugal was one of the largest importers of Flemish paintings. Many of the altarpieces in Portuguese churches were Flemish, and some can still be seen today, such as the *Fons Vitae* at the Misericórida Church in Oporto, and the magnificent altarpiece originally at the Cathedral of Évora (now in the Évora Museum). Furthermore, like Afonso V before him, Manuel I invited Flemish masters to come and work in Portugal. Some—including Francisco Henriques and Frei Carlos—then settled there.

The visiting Flemish artists attracted local disciples and had a marked influence on national painting. Nevertheless, Portuguese painting maintained local features, giving rise to the "Luso-Flemish" style. Manueline painting has thus been characterized by the following features: monumentality, a fine sense of portraiture, brilliant gem-like colors, a growing interest in the naturalistic depiction of architectural and landscape backgrounds and an increasing preoccupation with expressive detail.

It is essential to remember that at this time, painting was not the expression of an individual sensibility, but more often the collaborative effort of a master and his assistants. Attribution, then, is extremely difficult, and often paintings are known as the products of particular workshops rather than individual artists. The two principal Portuguese workshops were that of Vasco Fernandes in Viseu and that of Jorge Afonso in Lisbon.

Vasco Fernandes, better known as Grão Vasco, is doubtless the most celebrated regional Manueline painter. For many years, the myth of "Grão Vasco" obscured his real work in a plethora of attributions—Gothic and Renaissance paintings alike were thought to be of his authorship, although a single lifetime would not have sufficed for so large an output. Since the 19th century, a clearer and more historical image of Vasco Fernandes has emerged. It has now been established that he was responsible for the altarpiece originally at the Lamego Cathedral (now in the Lamego Museum), dating 1506-1511, as well as the one for the Viseu Cathedral (Grão Vasco Museum, Viseu) of a slightly earlier date. The stylistic differences between the two works befuddled scholars for some time, but it is now assumed that Flemish assistants at Lamego account for the differences. The panels for the chapels of the Viseu Cathedral (also in the Grão Vasco Museum), of which those of the *Calvary* and *St. Peter* are the most renowned, are also attributed to him, although dating to his mature phase (1530-1542).

Noteworthy for their emotional strength and drama, these works are also characterized by a denser application of paint than that of the Flemish masters. Furthermore, the faces of the Portuguese works tend to be less stylized, more expressive, and, it would seem, often drawn from specific local models, just as the landscape backgrounds are drawn from the Beja region rather than being imaginary or purely symbolic.

The Lisbon workshop was under the aegis of Jorge Afonso, royal painter from 1508. Many artists are known to have worked there, including Grão Vasco himself, Francisco Henriques, Cristovão de Figueiredo, and Gregório Lopes, whose works can be seen in churches and museums in various parts of the country. As for Jorge Afonso himself, documents from the reign of Manuel I show that he was involved in various royal projects, but none has helped to identify which works were actually by him. It is possible that he painted the "anonymous" panels at the Tomar *Charola*.

Two of the most important artists to emerge from Jorge Afonso's workshop were his son-in-law Gregório Lopes, royal painter to Manuel I and João III, and Cristovão de Figueiredo. Of all the works attributed to the former, the one that is in the best state of repair is the *Martyrdom of St. Sebastian* (Museu Nacional de Arte Antiga) painted for the Tomar *Charola*. As for the latter, little is known about his life except that between 1515 and 1540 he was extremely prolific and exercised great influence on Portuguese painting. One of his most impressive works is the *Deposition* (also in the Museu Nacional. de Arte Antiga in Lisbon). This work is remarkable for its emotional power and its portraiture, especially that of the two donor figures on the right.

The discussion of Manueline painting would not be complete without mention of the *Santa Auta* altarpiece, whose panels now hang separately in the Museu de Arte Antiga. This work was commissioned by Queen Leonor; a case has been made for the authorship of Cristovão de Figueiredo, who is known to have been a favorite painter of the queen's, but this is not certain. The central panel represents the martyrdom of eleven thousand virgins pierced by the arrows of the Huns, and includes a shrimpnet, which was Leonor's emblem. One of the side panels depicts the arrival at church of the saint's body and includes what is assumed to be a portrait of the queen. The Manueline portal with Leonor's coat of arms and the Della Robbia medallion identify this as the Church of Madre de Deus in Lisbon, which indeed is where the work originally hung.

Renaissance and Mannerism

The Renaissance has been described as a narrow bridge crossed the moment it was reached; this was certainly the case in Portugal. In their art and architecture, the Portuguese shied away from the Renaissance rationalism, instead inclining toward naturalism or toward the drama of the Romanesque—and later the Baroque. The Renaissance in Portugal, then, was best represented by foreign artists. Foreign sculptors were frequently invited to decorate the portals and facades of Manueline buildings, introducing elements of Renaissance harmony and order within the general flamboyance of the Manueline decorative

Above, a 16th-century portrait of the reckless and ill-fated King Sebastião by Cristavão de Morais

scheme. The temporal coincidence of Manueline and Renaissance and later of Renaissance and Mannerist forms explains the hybrid style prevalent during this period.

Mannerism uses elements of Renaissance classicism but the sense of an ordered, harmonious whole—intrinsic to the Renaissance style—gives way to an exaggeration of these elements. Applied to painting, this often means a certain elongation, which is considered the most characteristic feature of Mannerism. It can also mean unexpected highlighting of a seemingly incidental section of the work, rather than the typically Renaissance orientation towards a central incident. In architecture, Mannerism is characterized by a stress on detail, a shift away from the basic classical proportions and Greco-Roman vocabulary.

To the drama of the art of the Discoveries, the French sculptors Nicolas de Chanteréne and João de Ruão added a touch of Mediterranean rationalism and sobriety. The heraldic motifs and abundant foliage of the former were transformed into the plaques, medallions, and symmetrical foliate arabesques typical of the latter. Chanteréne's work includes the portal sculptures of Manuel I and his second wife, Queen Maria, on the western portal of Jerónimos. The pulpit at the Church of Santa Cruz in Coimbra has been variously attributed to both Chanteréne and João de Ruão. The latter was most prolific and introduced classicizing elements to Portuguese carving, especially in the region around Coimbra, in works such as the altarpiece at Varziela.

Architects, too, immersed themselves in an Italianate vocabulary. The Spaniard Diogo de Torralva is thought to have designed one of the finest examples of Renaissance construction in the Peninsula—the Chapel of *Nossa Senhora da Conceicão* (Our Lady of the Conception) in Tomar (ca.1530-40), with its simple exterior and diffusely lit, barrel-vaulted interior. Also in Tomar, Torralva's Great Cloister at the Convent of Christ evokes the balance and harmony of Palladian classicism. After Torralva's death in 1566, this majestic cloister was completed by the prestigious Italian architect Filipo Terzi.

Terzi, a specialist in military architecture, had been invited to Portugal by Philip II of Spain, who ascended the Portuguese throne in 1580 after the tragic battle of Alcacer-Quiber, which lost Portugal its king—the young Sebastião—and its independence. Terzi also designed some of the most imposing works of the period, such as the Castle of St. Philip in Setúbal and the fortress in Viana do Castelo.

The imposing Church of St. Vincent in Lisbon, previously attributed to Terzi, is now thought to be by Herrera, architect of the Escorial. The plan is in the shape of a Latin cross, with intercommunicating chapels. The huge central nave is spanned by a barrel vault. The exterior, dominated by two towers and three equally sized portals, is divided into two stories, the bottom with Doric arcades the top with Ionic, in the manner of an Italian *loggia*. This facade became a prototype for many Portuguese churches, especially of the Benedictine and Carmelite Orders, which, however, were frequently more ornate, thus being considered Mannerist rather than typically Renaissance.

From the late 16th through the 17th centuries, the spirit of the Counter-Reformation was pervasive, and another type of church became predominant. The Jesuit Order of St. Ignatius Loyola insisted that the interiors of its churches should be ample, and that the pulpit should be clearly visible from all parts of the church. This, in effect, meant a broadening of the central nave, disposing of the side aisles and giving rise to a centralized plan with ambulant chapels. The first church to be built along these lines in Portugal was that of *Espírito Santo* (Holy Ghost) in Évora, whose construction began in 1567, one year before that of the Church of Gésu in Rome, long thought to be the first of its type.

The magnificent Jesuit Church of São Roque in Lisbon, which unfortunately suffered much damage during the 1755 earthquake, was begun in the late 16th century, following a plan by Terzi. Simple and austere on the exterior, the interior is richly decorated with tiles and gilded woodwork. It is, nevertheless, extremely spacious and sober, in keeping with the Jesuit tradition.

With the death of Gregório Lopes (ca.1550), the great age of the Manueline *retábulo* had come to an end. During the reign of João III, many artists went to Rome, and Italian influence replaced that of Flanders. Altarpieces, for instance that at the Cathedral of Portalegre, became overtly Italianate, with their emphasis on modeling and *chiaroscuro*. This was also the period in which portrait painting came into its own. The fine, aristocratically elongated portrait of King Sebastião (Museu de Arte Antiga), attributed to Cristovão de Morais, is but one example.

Baroque and Rococo

The Baroque is considered to be that stylistic range which, although it uses a basic classical vocabulary, strives for dissolution of form rather than definition. Emphasis is given to motion, to the state of becoming rather than being. This obliteration of clear contours—whether by brushstrokes or as an optical illusion in sculpture and architecture—is further enhanced by a preference for depth over plane. These features all stress the grand, the dynamic and the dramatic.

The first truly Baroque Portuguese church is Santa Engrácia in Lisbon with its dome and undulating interior walls. This building was not

actually completed until 1966. The octagonal plan, like the oval used in Italy, dispenses with axiality: instead of being oriented in one direction, one is engulfed by a more fluid space. The richness of the colored marble lining the walls and floor, the dynamic interior space, and the general sumptuousness of the edifice are typical of construction during the reign of João V (1706-1750).

The wealth from Brazil and the munificence of João V rendered the early 18th century a period of great opulence. It was this king who commissioned the Chapel of St. John the Baptist at the Church of São Roque in Lisbon. The entire chapel was built in Rome, blessed by the Pope, shipped to Lisbon in three ships and reassembled in the church, where it shines with bronzes, mosaics, rare marble and precious stones.

The most extravagant project that was launched by João V was the construction of the huge complex of church, palace, and convent at Mafra, near Sintra. The king commissioned the German silversmith-turned-architect, Johann Friedrich Ludwig, frequently known by the Latinized name Ludovice, and construction began in 1717. The plan of the complex is a huge square; the church is at the center of the principal facade, flanked by wings belonging to the palace, with a monumental turret abutting at each end. Hybrid influences are evident in the imposing Italianate facade and the Germanic bulbous domes; local features are, on the whole, absent.

While the construction of Mafra dominated the south, in the north the major centers for the development of the Baroque were Oporto and

Braga. Here, the influence of the Tuscan architect-decorator Nicolau Nasoni, who reached Portugal in 1725, predominated. He introduced a greater buoyancy and elegance, and rich contrasts of light and shade. Unlike Ludwig, he incorporated local characteristics as well. His elliptical-naved Church of Clérigos in Oporto was without successor. But his secular buildings, such as the Freixo Palace in the same city, with their interplay of whitewash and granite, established a large following.

The Chapel of Santa Madalena in Falperra and the Casa do Mexicano in Braga, although following Nasoni, are already Rococo—drama is replaced by fantasy and a love of flourish and ornament. In the former, the portal is bordered by exuberant granite volutes playing against the white wall; this sense of contrast is less effective in the latter, whose facade is dressed in tiles. In addition to the love of fanciful, sensuous ornament, the Rococo was also marked by a growing interest in landscaping. The type of church represented by Bom Jesus in Braga became popular: surrounded by gardens, it sits atop a hill, and is reached by a sweeping succession of stairways which at a distance seem to cascade downward from the twin-towered facade.

In Lisbon the Rococo was more sober than in the north. The architect Carlos Mardel designed many of the city's public fountains, including those of Rua do Século and Largo da Esperança. he was also responsible for a section of the Aguas Livres Aqueduct, which was commissioned by João V and has been for over two centuries a handsome and familiar part of the Lisbon cityscape. Mardel was one of the architects involved in the Pombaline reconstruction of downtown Libson after the 1755 earthquake. Much of what characterizes the Lisbon of today dates to this period. The masterpiece of the reconstruction of the city was Praça do Comércio, the majestically proportioned, arcaded square giving onto the mouth of the Tagus River. As the point of contact between the city—indeed the Portuguese kingdom itself—and the ocean much traversed by Portuguese navigators, the square is a kind of symbol of the nation itself. From its center, mounted on his horse, King José, immortalized in bronze, casts his eye towards the horizon. The square is more commonly known as Terreiro do Paço—the Palace Square—for the royal palace was here, on the square's prototype, until destroyed by that fateful earthquake.

One of the truly singular features of this period was the use of azulejos—ceramic tiles. Any visitor to Portugal cannot fail to be amazed at their abundance and variety. They were first used in

the mid-15th century, gained importance in the mid-16th century, and by the 17th century they were nearly indispensable. Impressive examples are in the Church of Marvila at Santarém or that of São Lourenço in Almansil in the Algarve. At the end of the 17th century, the improved economic conditions allowed for much restoration and reconstruction of older buildings, and many azulejo panels date from this period. Both Oriental and Dutch porcelain, in blue- and- white, temporarily substituted the local polychrome tradition. While vast decorative schemes of azulejo panels filled churches and palaces alike—a notable instance of the latter is the Palace of the Marquês de Fronteira in Lisbon—the tile also enjoyed humbler use in settings such as kitchens and stairways. In addition to the murals, the use of small floral panels, or single tiles, in the Dutch manner, adorned with motifs such as flowers, birds or human figures were also popular. In the 18th century, decorative azulejo panels sumptuously adorned gardens such as those of the Palace of Queluz or of the Quinta dos Azulejos at the Lumíar Palace in Lisbon.

In religious architecture, exteriors continued to be quite austere until relatively late. Interiors, however, became increasingly ornate: the use of azulejos was often accompanied by that of carved and gilded woodwork known as talha dourada. Used first mainly on altars, this carving soon came to invade the entire interior space. This was particularly, although not uniquely, the case in the north. The Convent of Tibães near Braga, for example, and the smaller Church of São Francisco in Oporto, have walls encrusted with an overwhelming confection of gilded putti and floral arabesques.

The reign of João V saw another influx of foreign artists. The first of these was the French sculptor Claudio Laprade. His tomb of Bishop D. Manuel de Moura at the Chapel of Nossa Senhora da Penha (Our Lady of the Cliff) in Vista Alegre, with its angels securing a billowing drape, is the most Baroque of Portuguese funerary monuments. The bishop, founder of the Chapel, is depicted not serene in death but propped up on his elbow, gazing upwards.

Laprade spent his last years at Mafra, where João V had also commissioned numerous works from Italian sculptors, all in the tradition of Bernini—swirling drapes and suspended motion were the order of the day. Alessandro Giusti, who came to Lisbon from Rome in 1747 in order to reassemble the St. John the Baptist Chapel at São Roque, was commissioned to carve a marble altarpiece at Mafra; there he formed a school which attracted a large following. Undoubtedly the most gifted Portuguese sculptor to emerge from Giusti's school was Joaquim Machado de Castro who was the author of the first Portuguese equestrian statue, which we have already encountered—King José at the Praça do Comércio. He also made polychrome clay figures—a national popular tradition which flourished in the 17th and 18th centuries—such as those at the Regional Museum of Aveiro, where the arabesques formed by the drapes, their intricate gilded patterns, the rosy luster of lip and cheek, were already typically Rococo.

While the 17th and 18th centuries were particularly rich with regard to architecture, carving, and the *azulejo*, painting receded in importance. Nevertheless, this period saw the flourishing of portrait painting, in Portugal as indeed elsewhere in Europe. Perhaps the most celebrated 17th-century portraitist was Domingos Vieira (1600-1678), known as "the Dark" to distinguish him from his contemporary Domingos Vieira Serrão. His nickname stemmed from his predilection, in works such as the Portrait of D. Isabel de Moura (in Museu de Arte Antiga in Lisbon), which dramatically contrast the deep, velvety backgrounds and the rich, creamy whites of ruffs and headgear.

Neoclassicism and Romanticism

The Pombaline style of the reconstruction of Lisbon is closer in many ways to classical models than to the contemporaneous Rococo constructions in the north of Portugal. The Neoclassical style proper, with its interest in Greco-Roman colonnades, entablatures and porticoes, was introduced in Lisbon in the last decade of the 18th century. It was given court approval when used for the Royal Palace of Ajuda which was begun in 1802 (and never actually completed) after a fire destroyed the wooden building that had been the residence of the royal family since the 1755 earthquake.

The Basilica of Estrêla in Lisbon (1789) was the last church to be built in the Baroque Grand Style. With the dissolution of the monastic orders in 1834, religious architecture lost its privileged position in Portugal. This had a negative effect on the development of large-scale public architecture. In Lisbon, after the Palace of Ajuda, perhaps the only noteworthy public building to be built in the first half of the 19th century was the Theatre of D. Maria II (1843), with its white Greco-Roman facade.

In the north, the middle-class ambience of Oporto proved fertile ground for conservative Neoclassicism to take root. The large English community connected to the port-wine industry favored this style, perhaps because of its affinities to the architecture of Richard Adam. It was the British Consul John Whitehead who commissioned not only the *Feitoria Inglesa* (literally English Trading Depot, actually more of a club) in Oporto, but also the Hospital of Santo António—perhaps the finest Neoclassical build-

ing in the entire country.

The return to the Greco-Roman aesthetic principles of Neoclassicism is also evident in such works as João José de Aguiar's statue of Queen Maria I, flanked by allegorical figures representing the four known continents, now presiding over the driveway at the Palace of Queluz, itself an example of Neoclassical architecture.

At this time, two painters emerged as especially outstanding: Francisco Vieira, known as Vieira Portuense (1765-1805), and Domingos António Sequeira (1768-1837). The two met in Rome, which was the essential venue for any serious artist. Vieira Portuense also spent some time in London, where the classicizing Roman influence was tempered by that of Sir Joshua Reynolds, as is evident in the elegant *Portrait of an Unknown...*, which is in the Museu Nacional de Arte Antiga in Lisbon.

The work of Sequeira offers an ideal study in the transition from Neoclassicism to Romanticism, a rare example when a single life can encapsulate two eras. He was nominated court painter in 1802 by João VI, and was thus charged with executing paintings for the rebuilt Palace of Ajuda. Political turbulence forced Sequeira to emigrate to France and then Italy, where he died. Thus, his work can be divided into three stages: the first, largely academic and Neoclassical in inspiration, corresponds to his first sojourn in Rome and to his work as a court painter; the second stage (1807-1823) which includes the *Alegoria de Junot* (Soares dos Reis Museum, Oporto), is stylistically freer and more individualistically inspired, with Goyaesque contrasts of dark and light, rapid brushstrokes and sudden bursts of luminous white; the last phase corresponds to his visits to Paris, where he won a gold medal at the Salon for his *Death of Camões*, since lost, and Rome. The late works show great painterliness and luminosity. The four cartoons for paintings in the Palmela collections, again in the Museu Nacional de Arte Antiga in Lisbon, are some of his most inspired, mystical works.

If Neoclassical art and architecture represented an escape from the turmoils of the present into a restrained, harmonious classical ideal, another form of escapism became an important ingredient in Romanticism. The flight into the past (medievalism) or into other cultures (orientalism), or into other states—the dream, madness, trance—are all forms of escape. The most extraordinary architectural manifestation of this was the Pena Palace in Sintra, commissioned by the Prince Fernando of Saxe-Coburg-Gotha (consort of Maria II). The building is a strange agglomeration of medieval and orientalizing forms, includ-

Right, the work of Domingos António Sequeira offers an ideal study in the transition from Neoclassicism to Romanticism.

ing Manueline, Moorish, Renaissance, Baroque, and incorporating parts of the site's original structure, a 16th-century monastery. The whole is a rather overwhelming pastiche of English Neo-Gothic revivalism.

While the importance of sculpture receded yet again in this confused period of ideological tumult, painting styles echoed the architecture. Alongside the slackening of religious interests came the dissolution of the "Grand Style." Heroic, religious and ceremonial works gave way to more intimate and personal pieces. This also corresponded, in Portugal as elsewhere in Europe, to the rise of the middle-class. Courtly art had breathed its last. The liberal revolutions questioned the long upheld notion of history as the unfolding of a predetermined order, in favor of a relativism which heralded our modern times.

also gave increasing emphasis to the sitter's inner life. In Miguel Lupi's *Sousa Martins' Mother*, in Lisbon's Museu Nacional de Arte Contemporanea, the illuminated areas correspond to the face and hands—the most expressive parts of the body—and convey a sense of dignified pensiveness tinged with a certain restrained melancholy.

The foundation of the Artistic Center in Oporto (1879) and of the Lion Group in Lisbon (1880) were of seminal importance, especially as contact was established between them and the artistic milieu in Paris. Individuals, as well as these groups, admired the "City of Lights." Whether settling in as members of the vivacious emigré culture, or simply sampling the new ideas bursting everywhere in the newly recrowned capital of artistic innovation, the Portuguese joined the rest of the world in turning toward France. Paris was

Similarly, the idea that art expresses timelessly valid principles gradually gave way to the subjectivist and individualist notions which continue to hold sway in art today.

Sequeira represented the mystical, religious side of early Romanticism. With his death, Romanticism took a turn: nature became the new religion. The humbling of man before the larger, inscrutable forces of nature was a contemporaneous theme of English Romanticism, in both painting and literature. In Portugal, Tomás da Anunciação became the foremost romantic landscapist of this generation, along with Cristino da Silva.

Not surprisingly, the portrait, too, continued to enjoy popularity. Portraiture not only became the art form of the bourgeoisie par excellence, but

to remain the focus for the next generations of Portuguese artists. The individualism which colored the late 19th century makes any stylistic generalization difficult; this is true again in the 20th century. As in France, in landscapes and portraits, romanticism gave way to naturalism: the difference between them is often merely one of emphasis. While the former stresses the perceiving subject through whose eyes the landscape or sitter is seen, the latter stresses the objects of the artist's perception.

At the end of the 19th century, Silva Porto, José Malhoa, and Henrique Posão were the foremost naturalists. As opposed to their loose, painterly,luminous outdoor scenes, Columbano Bordalo Pinheiro (1857-1929) continued in the tradition of studio painting. Columbano, as he is known, is considered the Grand Master of Portuguese 19th-century art. He studied under Miguel Lupi at the Academy of Fine Arts (founded in 1836) and then spent three years in Paris. There, in 1882, he painted the renowned *Concert of Amateurs* (in Lisbon's Museu Nacional de Arte Contemporanea) where the dramatic illumination in no way conflicts with the naturalistic observation. On his return to Portugal, he joined the Lion Group, and painted a group portrait of its members in 1885, also in the Museu Nacional de Arte Contemporanea. His later portraits especially reveal him as a colorist; they are lighter, airier, with a masterly quick touch.

Columbano's brother, Rafael Bordalo Pinheiro, was perhaps a figure of even greater popularity in his day. A celebrated ceramicist working within popular caricatural traditions, he founded a porcelain factory in 1884 which became a veritable school for ceramicists. He was also a sketch artist known for his biting political caricatures.

Modernism

The first few decades of the 20th century saw an unprecedented ferment of artistic activity and invention, first in Europe and then in America. In Portugal, the political turmoil that resulted in the end of the monarchy (1910) did not provide a propitious context for this artistic revolution. Not long thereafter, the absolutist regime, which governed the country from 1926 to 1974, closed the doors to external cultural influence. For these reasons, many of the modern movements arrived late or in diluted form to Portugal. Indeed in architecture, the most interesting works were those which reappraised local traditions such as the Pombaline style. Expectably, this was a period not only of reappraisal of what constitutes "Portugueseness" but also of urban expansion and extensive renovation to public buildings.

For painters, 1911 was a turning point, for it saw the founding of the Museu Nacional de Arte Contemporanea in Lisbon, the transformation of the Academies into Schools of Fine Arts, and the establishment of the first Salon of Humorists in Lisbon—a turning away from conventional salon painting. Paris remained an important venue for forward-looking artists, and the point of contact with the Modernist avant-garde. Many painters of the first generation of Portuguese Modernists were, however, forced to leave Paris at the outbreak of World War I. Of this generation, the most daring and interesting were Santa-Rita and Amadeo Souza-Cardoso. The premature deaths of both these artists within six months of each

other in 1918 signalled the end of that generation. Santa-Rita was an eccentric personality who brought Futurism, with its talk of speed and dynamism and progress, to Portugal. Almost none of his work survives, as it was destroyed by his family, according to his wishes, after his death. Amadeo, many of whose works are in the collection of the Center for Modern Art at the Calouste Gulbenkian Foundation in Lisbon, was deeply influenced by Cubism, and by Robert and Sonia Delaunay, whom he met in Paris. In his works of 1913-14 this is particularly clear, as the figures delineated are merely a pretext for interplay of the brightly colored arcs.

One of the brightest lights of the 1911 exhibition of Humorists was José Almada Negreiros (1893-1970), who was to become one of the most fascinating, charismatic and energetic cultural figures in Portugal in the 20th century. Painter, draftsman, poet, and playwright, he also flirted with choreography and dance. He was a polemicist and theoretician of some import, and wrote, among other texts, an explication of the 15th-century Polyptych of St. Vincent, with which he was obsessed. His early caricatures drew the attention of the poet Fernando Pessoa, who became a friend and whose celebrated posthumous portrait he painted in 1954 (in Lisbon's City Musuem) and again in replica in 1964 (now in the Calouste Gulbenkian Foundation). One of his most important commissions was that for the frescoes for the port of Lisbon in 1943-48. He also designed stained-glass windows, ceramic tiles and tapestry cartoons. His last major project was the mural for the lobby of the Calouste Gulbenkian Foundation in Lisbon. While for most of his life Almada painted the world he saw about him, he turned in his later years to abstraction based on complex geometrical and metaphysical precepts. The title of this last work—*Comecar* (Beginning)—indicates a sense of spiritual rebirth at the end of his life.

Although all the major modern movements found expression in Portugal, Salazar's regime closed the doors to outside stimulus and meant effectively that forward-thinking, confrontational intellectual and artistic exchange was either clandestine or short-circuited. The military coup which initiated Portugal's democracy in April 1974 breathed new life into the arts, which had become invested with a great exploratory energy. The fervent activity bespoke the sense of exhilaration after years of repression and censorship. With access to external artistic events, Portuguese artists have been able to enter the contemporary artistic discourse, often modestly, sometimes boldly. The conflict between the relative value of imported and indigenous ideas—the conflict between "in here" and "out there" is now, as it has been for centuries, one of the central concerns of Portuguese art. This tension is perhaps also its most interesting feature.

Left, portrait of the poet Fernando Pessoa, painted by Almada Negreiros, originally commissioned for the Cafe Irmãos Unidos

TRAVEL TIPS

GETTING THERE

BY AIR

Portugal's national airline, TAP Air Portugal, has daily flights in summer between the United States (New York or Boston) and Portugal. There are less frequent flights in winter. All flights land at Lisbon's Portela Airport, where you can make connections to other parts of the country.

TWA also flies daily in summer and less often in winter, with all flights flying to and from New York's Kennedy Airport.

TAP, British Airways and DANAIR fly the Portugal-London route. There are direct flights to and from Lisbon, Oporto and Faro. Also available are frequent charter and package deals that can be surprisingly inexpensive. Between the three regular airlines and charter companies, there are quite a few weekly flights.

BY RAIL

A daily train makes the Paris-Lisbon run; another runs from Paris to Oporto. (Actually it's the same route from Paris to the French-Spanish border). The Lisbon branch passes through Coimbra as well. This grueling 24-hour trip is made on the well-worn *Sud Express*, and should be avoided if possible. Most connections for parts of Europe outside Iberia are made from Paris – even southern destinations, as it's usually faster to head north, then south again. If you hire a *couchette*, you can make the journey directly; otherwise, you must change at the French-Spanish border.

Two daily trains make the 10-hour Madrid-Lisbon and Lisbon-Madrid journey. Other connections are from northern Spain – Galicia to Oporto; and from southern Spain – Seville to Ayamonte to the Algarve. The latter is very time-consuming, involving three poorly coordinated trains and a boat.

TRAVEL ESSENTIALS

VISAS & PASSPORTS

All non-European Community visitors must show a valid passport to enter Portugal. On arrival, your passport will be stamped with a 60-day tourist visa. No one with a tourist visa is permitted to work in Portugal.

European Community citizens may enter Portugal with a national identity card. Citizens of Great Britain, which issues no national card, must use a passport.

MONEY MATTERS

CURRENCY

The *escudo*, which is divided into 100 *centavos*, is the basic unit of currency. The coin with the smallest denomination is the 50-*centavo* piece; the largest is the new 50-*escudo* coin. 1,000 *escudos* is usually called a *conto*. Don't accept any 20 *escudo* notes, or any of the older 1,000 *escudo* notes (they are larger, more colorful and don't have a picture of Dom Pedro V); these were removed from circulation.

The symbol for the *escudo* is the same as for the dollar sign, but is written after the number of *escudos* (and before the number of *centavos*). Thus, 75$00 is 75 *escudos*; 75$50 is 75 *escudos* and 50 *centavos*. In numerals, a period is used instead of a comma (and vice-versa). For example, 1.000 means one thousand; 1,000 means one.

CHANGING MONEY

There is neither a minimum nor a maximum for buying Portuguese currency. While you may want to buy a small amount of *escudos* before you leave home, you'll get a much better exchange rate if you wait until you're in Portugal. Once you have bought *escudos*, however, it may be difficult to re-exchange them for foreign currency. The best policy is not to change large amount and risk having lots of money left over, but to change money as you need it.

Money is best exchanged at banks (rather than hotels or travel agencies). Outside of banking hours, there are currency exchanges at Santa Apolónia train station as well as at the airport.

TRAVELER'S CHECKS & CREDIT CARDS

Traveler's checks are accepted in all banks; it is best not to spend them in stores, where, if they are accepted at all, you can be certain that they're being changed at a rate disadvantageous to you. Major credit cards can be used in the more expensive hotels, restaurants and shops.

WHAT TO BRING

Bring enough prescription medication to last through your stay, if only to avoid confusion with brand names and/or language. Toiletries and personal effects are all available locally, and are often much cheaper than in other countries. The exception is newer or less common articles, such as contact lens solution, which are more expensive. Common methods of contraception are available with the exception of contraceptive cream specifically for use with diaphragms.

Bring batteries with you: they'll be of better quality and longer lasting. Film and photographic equipment are cheaper outside the country.

EXTENSION OF STAY

To obtain an extension, contact the *Serviço de Extrangeiros* (Foreigner's Service). In Lisbon this is located at Rua Consilheiro José Silvestre, 1º, tel: 714-1027.

GETTING ACQUAINTED

GEOGRAPHY

Portugal is roughly the shape of a rectangle, bordered on the east and north by Spain and the west and south by the Atlantic Ocean. It is about 360 miles (560 km) north-south and 130 miles (220 km) east-west – approximately the size of the state of Indiana. A 500-mile (830 km) coastline borders the country.

The mountainous northern half of the country is more populated. The intense greens of the northern valleys, the winding riverbeds, and the mountain peaks (the highest of which is the Serra da Estrêla, at 6,500 feet (2,000 meters), make central and northern Portugal extraordinarily beautiful. Northern Portugal can be divided into several regions: the Douro Valley, the rich wine country of the northern coast; Tras-os-Montes, literally "Behind the Mountains" in the northeast corner; and the Beira Alta and Beira Baixa, in the north central Portugal.

The southern half of Portugal contrasts strongly with the north, and has an unusual beauty of its own. Dry, flat and less populous than the north, the southern plains (the Alentejo) are sprinkled with bright villages surrounded by fields of wheat. The far south – the Algarve – is mountainous, and boasts long stretches of beautiful beaches, most of which has been discovered by vacationers.

CLIMATE

Spring and summer are definitely the best times of year to visit Portugal. Especially in the north and central regions, including Lisbon, winters are rainy, and while not frigid, are surprisingly chilly. Furthermore, few homes, restaurants and inexpensive hotels are heated or insulated, so to keep warm, you must have an adequate supply of sweaters. In the mountains it's even colder, and quite a lot of snow falls on the Serra da

Estrêla between November and February. (There is enough for ski enthusiasts, although conditions are far from ideal.) Winters are short, beginning in November or December and ending in February or March. The weather starts getting warm in May and June and usually stays so through September. The weather is changeable and difficult to predict from year to year: winters can be considerably shorter or longer; the rainy season heavy or light.

Nights can be cool even in summer, especially along the coast of north Lisbon. Along the western coast, the Atlantic tends to be cool until July. It warms up earlier along the southern coast. Summers in the Alentejo are extremely hot. The Algarve is moderate year-round, with a generous share of sun even in winter. It is far from hot, however, between November and April.

CULTURE & CUSTOMS

The Portuguese are extremely polite. A few minutes to learn the basics, and liberal use of these thereafter, will serve you well. "*Obrigado*" (if you're a man) or "*obrigada*" (if you're a woman) is "thank you". "Please" is "*por favor*". To get someone's attention when you want service, say "*faz favor*" (pronounced "fash fuhVOOR"). Greet people with "*bon dia*" in the morning, "*boa tarde*" in the afternoon, and "*boa noite*" at night. Take leave in the same way.

Other hints: If you are invited to someone's house, it is polite to bring flowers for the hostess or a small toy if there are young children. Don't bring wine.

There are always orderly lines at bus stops. Be certain to respect them.

For some reason, stretching in public – on the street or at the table – is considered rude. Otherwise, use common sense and a smile.

TIPPING

A tip of 10 percent is sufficient in restaurants and for taxi drivers. Barbers and hairdressers receive the same or a little less. Theater ushers get a tip of five or 10 *escudos*.

WEIGHTS & MEASURES

Portugal uses the metric system of weights and measures. While conversions are given below, here are a few tips:

– 100 grams of cheese or cold cuts is more than enough for a sandwich.

– Shellfish in restaurants is usually sold by the gram. About 300 grams is sufficient for one person.

– To convert Celsius temperatures to Farenheit (roughly), multiply the Celsius temperature by 2 and add 32. Thus, 20°C x 2 + 32 = 72°F.

CONVERSION CHART

1 meter = 1.09 yards
1 yard = 0.92 meters
1 km = about 5/8 miles
1 mile = 1.6 km
1 kilo = 2.2 pounds
1 pound = about 0.46 kilo
1 liter = 1.76 pints
1 pint = about 0.57 liter
1 cm = about 0.3 inch
1 inch = 2.56 cm

ELECTRICITY

The electrical current in Portugal is 220 volts AC, with a Continental (round-prong) plug. If you plan to bring electrical appliances on you trip, bring a voltage converter as well.

BUSINESS HOURS

Most stores open for business Monday through Friday 9 a.m. to around 1 p.m., and from about 3 p.m. until 7 p.m. Stores are open on Saturdays from 9 a.m.-1 p.m., and are closed Sundays and holidays. Banking hours are Monday through Friday 8:30 a.m.-11:45 a.m. and 1 p.m.-2:45p.m., closed Saturday, Sunday and holidays.

HOLIDAYS

The following is a list of public holidays in Portugal. All banks and most stores are closed on these days.

January 1   New Year's Day
April 25   Anniversary of the
                Revolution

June 10	Portugal and Camões Day
June 13	Saint Anthony's Day (Lisbon only)
June 24	Saint John's Day (especially in Oporto)
August 15	Day of the Assumption
October 5	Republic Day
November 1	All Saints' Day
December 1	Independence Day
December 8	Day of the Immaculate Conception
December 25	Christmas Day

Other holidays are Mardi Gras (February or March), Good Friday (in April), and Corpus Christi (in June).

COMMUNICATIONS

POSTAL SERVICES

Post offices open Monday through Friday 9 a.m. to 6 p.m.; smaller branches close for lunch from 12:30 p.m. to 2:30 p.m. In larger cities, the main branch may be open on weekends. Mail is delivered Monday through Friday; in the central business districts in the larger cities, it is delivered twice a day.

To buy stamps, stand in any line marked *selos*. To mail or receive packages, go to the line marked *encomendas*. Postage rates are as follows:

– letters and postcards inside Portugal cost 25$00 for the first 20 grams, and usually take one to two days to arrive.

– letters to Europe cost 57$00 for the first 20 grams; postcards cost 51$00. These can take anywhere from two days to two weeks, depending on destination.

– letters to North America cost 74$50 for 20 grams; postcards cost 68$50. Letters take a week or so to the East Coast of the US and two to three days more to other parts of the country.

Be certain to write *Via Aerea* on all airmail items. To send large packages home, consider less expensive sea mail, which takes two to six months to cross the Atlantic.

The post office also provides services such as express mail (*expreso*), postal money orders (*vales*), general delivery (*posta restante*), registered mail (*registos*), insurance on packages (*seguro*), and telegraph and telephone services (see below).

TELEPHONE

There are plenty of pay phones in most cities; the problem is finding newer phones, which are easiest to use. Newer phones equipped for international calls are located in city centers. Instructions are written in English. The older phones are close to incomprehensible no matter what language you speak. They cannot be used for international calls; even for local calls, you'll need patience and good luck, as well as a large supply of small coins.

If you lack the proper change, you can make calls – both international and local – from the post offices. Go to the window for a cabin assignment and pay when the call is finished. In Lisbon there is also a phone office in the Rossio, open everyday from 9 a.m.-11 p.m.; in Oporto, there is one in Praça da Liberdade (same hours).

Most bars have telephones. Phone first, pay later, but be prepared to pay more than double the rate for pay phone or post office calls. This also applies to calls made from hotels.

To reach an English-speaking international operator, dial 098 (intercontinental service) or 099 (European service). To call direct to the US or Canada, dial 097-1, plus the area code and phone number. For the UK, dial 00-44 plus the full phone number. Dial slowly.

TELEGRAM

You may place telegrams by phone (tel: 10) or from the post office. The following are telegram rates:

– To the US: 1.045$00 plus 68$00 per word.

– To Europe: 1.045$00 plus 43$00 per word.

– In Portugal: 82$50 plus 3$00 per word. The cheapest way to send a quick message outside of Portugal is to use the Telecopy service available only in the Praça dos Restauradores post office in Lisbon. For a little over 1.000$00 *escudos*, you can write (or even draw) as much as you want within a given space. The copy reaches its destination within a few hours.

GETTING AROUND

DOMESTIC TRAVEL

BY AIR

TAP Air Portugal is the national airline. There is daily service between Lisbon and Oporto, Faro and Covilhã. Flights run several times weekly between Lisbon and Bragança, and Lisbon and Portimão.

BY RAIL

Trains in Portugal range from the comfortable and speedy *rápidos* to the painfully slow *regionais*. Generally the most efficient routes are the Lisbon-Coimbra-Porto and the Lisbon-Algarve lines.

Rápidos, which run only on the two routes mentioned above, are quick and punctual and cost more to ride. Some *rápidos* have first-class carriages only; others have a very comfortable second-class as well. Next in line are the *directos*, which make more stops and travel more slowly. These have both first- and second-class compartments; second-class here is likely to be less comfortable than in the *rápidos*. Finally, the *semi-directos* and especially the *regionais* seem to stop every few feet and take longer than one could have believed possible. On *directos*, *semi-directos*, and *regionais*, second-class seats are not assigned, and CP (Caminhos de Ferro Portugueses, the train company) has no qualms about issuing more tickets than seats, if the need arises. If you want to be certain of a seat, board early.

On rural routes, trains are almost always regional. Furthermore, to reach more remote – or even not-so-remote – destinations, it may be necessary to change trains, and schedules are seldom coordinated. Except for the *rápidos*, which are punctual, leave yourself plenty of time between transfers, as trains are regularly late.

There are four train stations in Lisbon. Cais do Sodré and Rossio are commuter stations. International and long distance trains with northern and eastern destinations leave from Santa Apolónia Station, about a mile and a half to the east of Praça do Comércio. For trains to the Alentejo and the Algarve, catch a boat at the Terreiro do Paco station (across from the Praça do Comércio). The price of the boat is included in the train ticket, which you can buy at the boat station. Just be certain to buy the right one; there are two boat stations next to each other. For the train link-up, use the eastern station, i.e., the one to the left as you face the river.

Oporto and Coimbra each have two train stations. Porto's São Bento and Coimbra A are located in the respective town centers. Most long-distance trains, however, arrive and leave from Oporto's Campanhã station and Coimbra B station, outside the cities. There is frequent shuttle service between São Bento and Campanhã and between Coimbra A and B.

BY ROAD

Buses: Rodoviária Nacional (RN) is the national bus company. RN runs direct and regional service between most cities and towns. Outside the routes between major cities, the bus is often faster than the train, and the bus system is certainly more extensive. This is particularly true in the north and between the smaller towns in the Algarve and Alentejo.

RN is not your only choice; there are dozens of private bus lines which tend to specialize in particular routes or areas of the country. Often, they have more direct routes to smaller towns. Many travel agencies can book tickets on a private line, or may even run their own.

LISBON

Trains: There are four train stations in Lisbon. Commuter trains to Cascais (stopping in Oeiras, Carcavelos, Estoril and other towns along the western coast) depart from Cais do Sodré, located along the riverfront. Depending on the day of the week and the time of day, trains depart every 15 to 20 minutes; they arrive in Cascais (the end of the line) between 33-40 minutes later (again depending on the time of day).

Trains to the northwestern suburbs, including Sintra, leave from the Rossio station at 15-minute intervals. The trip to Sintra takes about 45 minutes. This station houses an information center which can inform you about trains all over the country. For more information about long distance trains, see the section on "Domestic Transport".

Buses/Trams: CARRIS, the city bus company, maintains an extensive system of buses, trams (*eléctricos*) and funiculars. Bus stops are clearly marked by signposts or shelters. All stops display a diagrammatical map of the bus route; many have a map of the entire city system.

The orange and white CARRIS information kiosks scattered throughout the city provide information about buses and trams and sell tickets and passes. If you're lucky, they may even have city bus maps in stock. Two of the most convenient kiosks are located in Praça da Figueira, near the Rossio, and near Eduardo VII park (the Marquês de Pombal statue).

An alternative for tourists is to buy a three-day or seven-day tourist pass, which gives unlimited access during the period of validity. If you have no pass, you may pay a flat rate when you board. Less expensive are the pre-paid *modules* that you can buy in packs of 20 from the kiosks (405$00). It is unwise to board the bus without paying, ticket inspectors appear from time to time, and the fine is steep.

The pre-World War I trams often ply the smaller, steeper streets where buses are unable to navigate the narrow passages. Some of them are quite beautiful, inside and out; they are slower and cheaper than the buses and are a good way to see the city.

CARRIS also runs two funiculars and an elevator. The Santa Justa elevator, located near the Rossio, leads to the Bairro Alto. One funicular climbs and descends the steep Calçada da Gloria from Praça dos Restauradores; the other is in São Bento. Pay the driver only after boarding the funicular.

Metro: The Metro, with 20 stops, is quite limited and principally useful for travel in the central zone of the city. The line is V-shaped, with the point of the "V" in the Rossio, and the two arms stretching up Avenida da Liberdade and Avenida Almirante Reis. Though limited, the system is easy to use.

A tourist pass is valid on the Metro. You can also buy books of 10 tickets or single tickets. You must validate your ticket at the machines next to the ticket booths. As with buses, it is inadvisable to try to ride for free.

OPORTO & COIMBRA

Buses/Trams: Oporto's public transportation is limited to buses and trams, and Coimbra's to electric buses. Both these systems run on the same principal as Lisbon's system: you may either pay the driver a flat fee, or buy prepaid modules and validate the number required by the length of the journey. You may buy modules and get information from bus company kiosks in both Oporto and Coimbra.

Taxis: In all of Portugal's cities, taxis are plentiful and cheap. The great majority of them are black with green roofs. In the city, they charge a standard meter fare, with no additions for extra passengers. (They carry as many as four people.) Outside city limits, the driver may run on the meter or charge a flat rate, and he or she is entitled to charge for the return fare (even if you don't take it). Tip taxi drivers about 10 percent.

PRIVATE TRANSPORT

Car Rentals: Portugal is a trying place for drivers. In the cities, traffic is heavy, road construction hinders movement, parking is close to impossible, and cars and pedestrians regularly ignore both the rules of the road and plain common sense.

Outside cities, conditions are not much better. Highways are all too often in poor condition. Many are very narrow, making it difficult to pass slow-moving rural trucks and tractors. On winding mountain roads, driving takes great skill and concentration. Portuguese drivers are medium macho: relatively safe, but occasionally frightening when they pass at the last minute on the ubiquitous two-lane highways. And wherever you are, gasoline is expensive.

If you're still determined to drive, the Yellow Pages are full of car rental firms. The big two – Hertz and Avis – are there, along with many other smaller and lesser-known (and often cheaper) companies. With Hertz and Avis, you can rent before leaving home and this, inexplicably, is often less expensive.

It's advisable to shop around, as costs vary and many agencies offer special packages from time to time. There are various options to choose from, including having a driver or not. The type of car you can hire ranges from the tiny Mini to much larger machines. To get more information and to compare prices, look up car rentals in the local Yellow Pages under *Automóveis – Aluger com e sem Condutor*. Most companies employ staff that speak English.

To rent a car in Portugal, most agencies require you to be at least 21 years old and to have had a valid driver's license for a minimum of one year. An international license is not necessary.

WHERE TO STAY

HOTELS

The Portuguese tourist office divides accommodations into several categories: hotels, residentials and pensions are the most popular.

Hotels are usually bigger than other types of accommodation, and offer amenities such as restaurants and room service. All rooms have bathrooms. Hotels are rated from one to five stars: five stars denote a luxury hotel; four stars, while not luxury, is pretty close; three-star hotels are typically clean but slightly run-down; one- and two-star hotels are sometimes depressing.

The list below includes a small sample of places to stay in Portugal. You'll find many others by walking down any street: most towns in Portugal are crowded with them. Remember, however, that you'll have difficulty finding a decent room in July and August if you haven't made a reservation. The following are listed by area, beginning from the north and moving south.

GUIMARÃES

Estalagem São Pedro (Four-star)
Riba de Ave
tel: (053) 931-338

Hotel Fundador Dom Pedro (Four-star)
Avenida Dom Afonso Henriques, 274
tel: (053) 931-338

BRAGANÇA

Albergaria Santa Isabel (Four-star)
Rua Alexandre Herculano, 67
tel: (073) 224-27

Hotel Bragança (Three-star)
Avenida Arantes Oliveira
tel: (073) 222-42

OPORTO

Five-star Hotels

Hotel Infante de Sagres
Praça Filipa Lencastre, 62
4000 Porto
tel: (02) 281-01
Near the central square.

Hotel Meridien
Avenida da Boavista, 1466
4100 Porto
tel: (02) 668-863
A little bit farther out than the above.

Hotel Porto Atlantico
Rua Afonso Lopes Viera, 66
4100 Porto
tel: (02) 694-941

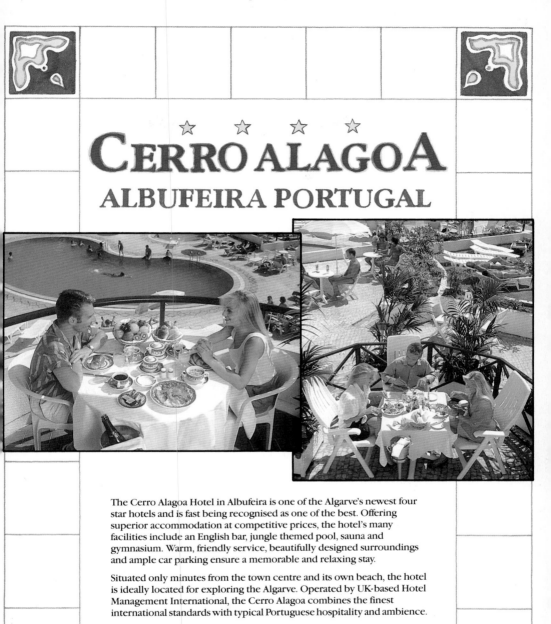

★ ★ ★ ★
CERRO ALAGOA
ALBUFEIRA PORTUGAL

The Cerro Alagoa Hotel in Albufeira is one of the Algarve's newest four star hotels and is fast being recognised as one of the best. Offering superior accommodation at competitive prices, the hotel's many facilities include an English bar, jungle themed pool, sauna and gymnasium. Warm, friendly service, beautifully designed surroundings and ample car parking ensure a memorable and relaxing stay.

Situated only minutes from the town centre and its own beach, the hotel is ideally located for exploring the Algarve. Operated by UK-based Hotel Management International, the Cerro Alagoa combines the finest international standards with typical Portuguese hospitality and ambience.

Reservations can be made with HMI, UK—tel 081 908 3348, through UTELL International offices worldwide or with the hotel direct on 089 588261. Apartado 2155, 8200 Albufeira, Portugal.

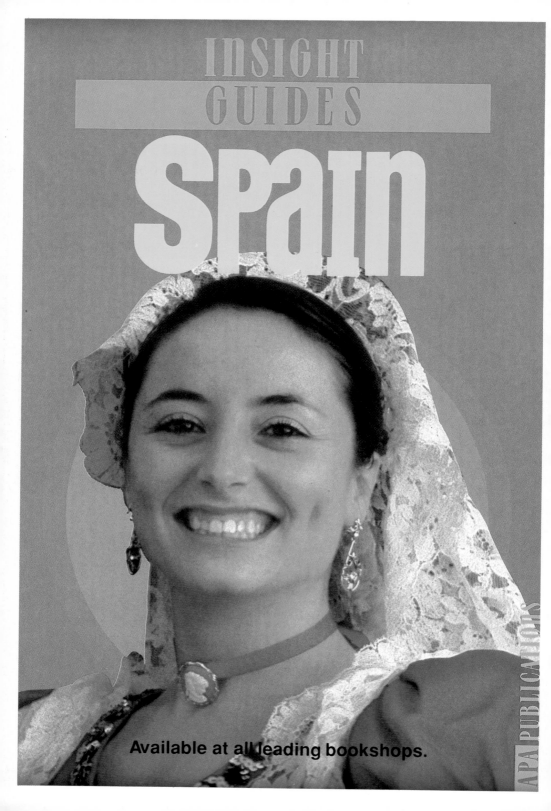

INSIGHT
GUIDES
Spain

Available at all leading bookshops.

APA PUBLICATIONS

Hotel Porto Sheraton
Avenida da Boavista, 1269
4100 Porto
tel. (02) 668-822

Four-star Hotels

Grande Hotel da Batalha
Praça da Batalha, 116
4000 Porto
tel: (02) 205-71
Near the center.

Hotel Castor
Rua Doze Casas, 17
4000 Porto
tel: (02) 384-151

Hotel Dom Henrique
Rua Guedes Azevedo, 179
4000 Porto
tel: (02) 257-55

Hotel Inca
Praça Coronel Pacheco, 50
4000 Porto
tel: (02) 384-151

Hotel Ipanema
Rua do Campo Alegre, 156/174
4100 Porto
tel: 668-061

Hotel Porto Boega
Rua do Amial, 607
4200 Porto
tel: (02) 825-270

Three-star Hotels

Grande Hotel do Porto
Rua Santa Catarina, 197
4000 Porto
tel: (02) 281-76
A few blocks east of the central square.

Hotel Corcel
Rua de Camões, 135
4000 Porto
tel: (02) 380-268
Just north of the town center.

Hotel do Império
Praça da Batalha, 127
4000 Porto

tel: (02) 268-61
In the center of town.

Hotel Tuela
Arq. Marques da Silva, 200
4100 Porto
tel. (02) 667-161

Others

Pensaõ-Residencial Pão de Açúcar
(Three-star)
Rua do Almada, 262
4000 Porto
tel: (02) 224-25
A large, clean, standard place right in the middle of town.

Residencial Castelo Santa Catarina
(Four-star)
Rua Santa Catarina, 1347
4000 Porto
tel: (02) 495-599

Residencial Rex (Four-star)
Praça da Republica, 117
4000 Porto
tel: (02) 245-48
In the center of town.

AVEIRO

Hotel Afonso V (Three-star)
Rua Dr. Manuel das Neves, 65
3800 Aveiro
tel: (034) 251-91
A few blocks from the center.

Hotel Arcada (Two-star)
Rua Viana do Castelo, 4
3800 Aveiro
tel: (034) 230-01
A bit drab, but very centrally located along the canal.

Hotel Imperial (Three-star)
Rua Dr. Nascimento Leitão
3800 Aveiro
tel: (034) 221-41
Very modern and central.

Pensão Residencial Estrêla (Three-star)
Rua José Estevão, 4
3800 Aveiro
Across from the Arcada Hotel.

Residencial Paloma Blanca (Four-star)
Rua Luis Gomes de Carvalho
A sweet place with a lovely courtyard/garden. Near the train station, a few blocks from the center.

COIMBRA

The four best hotels in Coimbra all have three-star ratings.

Hotel Astoria
Avenida Emídio Navarro, 21
3000 Coimbra
tel: (039) 220-55
Across from tourist office.

Hotel Bragança
Largo das Ameias, 10
3000 Coimbra
tel: (039) 221-71
Near Coimbra A Train Station.

Hotel Oslo
Avenida Fernão de Magalhães, 23
3000 Coimbra
tel: (039) 290-71
Behind the Bragança.

Pensão Rivoli
Praça do Comércio, 27
3000 Coimbra
tel: (039) 255-50
Centrally located. A beautiful courtyard, friendly management; slightly run-down.

LISBON

Five-Star Hotels

Most hotels are located in the newer part of town.

Hotel Alfa Lisboa
Avenida Columbano Bordalo Pinheiro
1200 Lisboa
tel: 726-2728
A bit out of the way.

Hotel Altis
Rua Castilho, 149
1200 Lisboa
tel: 522-496

Hotel Avenida Palace
Rua Primeiro de Dezembro, 123
1200 Lisboa
tel: 360-151
Smack in the old center of town, between the Rossio and Praça dos Restauradores. The most centrally located of the luxury hotels.

Hotel Lisboa Sheraton
Rua Latino Coelho, 1
1000 Lisboa
tel: 563-911
Good for short stays and business trips. Else, there are better hotels for the price.

Hotel Meridien
Rua Castilho, 149
1200 Lisboa
tel: 690-900
Elegant. Overlooking the park.

Hotel Ritz
Rua Rodrigo Fonseca, 88
1000 Lisboa
tel: 657-523
High-quality rooms and service. Overlooking Eduardo VII Park. The top of the luxury hotels.

Hotel Tivoli
Avenida da Liberdade, 185
1200 Lisboa
tel: 530-181
Big and beautiful, between the old and new parts of town. Friendly service.

Four-Star Hotels

Hotel Diplomatico
Rua Castilho, 74
1200 Lisboa
tel: 562-041

Hotel Florida
Avenida Duque de Palmela, 32
1200 Lisboa
tel: 576-145
Near the Marquês de Pombal Square. Standard, clean rooms.

Hotel Lisboa Plaza
Traversa do Salitre, 7
1200 Lisboa
tel: 370-331
Just off Avenida da Liberdade.

Hotel Principe Real
Rua da Alegria, 53
1200 Lisboa
tel: 360-116
Beautiful, small and quiet; a few blocks from Avenida da Liberdade in an interesting residential area near the Bairro Alto.

Hotel Tivoli Garden
Rua Julio C. Machado, 7
1200 Lisboa
tel: 539-971
Run by the same people in charge of the five-star Tivoli, right next door.

Three-Star Hotels

Hotel Britania
Rua Rodrigues Sampaio, 17
1100 Lisboa
tel: 575-016
Clean, if slightly shabby, and on a nice street near Avenida da Liberdade but far from the noise.

Hotel Dom Carlos
Avenida Duque de Loulé, 121
1000 Lisboa
tel: 539-769
On an unattractive but centrally-located street.

Hotel Eduardo VII
Avenida Fontes Pereira de Melo, 5-C
1000 Lisboa
tel: 530-141
Right next to the park of the same name. A beautiful view from the restaurant and the front rooms. Slightly dark, but clean.

Hotel Flamingo
Rua Castilho, 41
1200 Lisboa
tel: 532-191
Near the Marquês de Pombal, but on a quieter street.

Hotel Miraparque
Avenida Sidónio Pais, 12
1000 Lisboa
tel: 575-070
Decent rooms; poor service; a good location on a quiet street overlooking the park.

Hotel Rex
Rua Castilho, 169
1000 Lisboa
tel: 682-161
For those who can't afford the Ritz or the Meridian, the Rex is a nice place next door.

RESIDENTIALS & PENSIONS

Residentials offer fewer amenities than hotels, and are rated from one to four stars. Pensions, usually smaller than residentials, are also rated from one to four stars. Despite being less expensive and "lower" on the scale than hotels, many residentials and pensions are lovely and clean and offer a more personal atmosphere than the larger hotels.

LISBON

York House – Residencia Inglesa
(Four-star)
Rua Janelas Verdes, 32
1200 Lisboa
tel: 6624-35
In a class by itself: comfort and charm combined. This place draws raves. In an old and interesting neighborhood, about 15 minutes by bus from the Rossio. Reserve well in advance. The annex is down the street at number 47 (tel: 668-143).

Albergaria Senhora do Monte (Four-star)
Calçada do Monte, 39
1100 Lisboa
tel: 862-846
Beautiful views overlooking Lisbon, not far from the Alfama.

Residencia Roma (Four-star)
Travessa da Gloria, 22-A
1200 Lisboa
tel: 360-557
The size and amenities of a hotel: private baths and TVs in every room. Don't let the shabby exterior faze you; the inside is well kept and very clean.

Pensão Ninho das Aguias (Three-star)
Costa do Castelo, 74
1100 Lisboa
tel: 860-391
One of the few pensions in the Alfama. Come for the charm, if not the comfort.

Some rooms have great views; others none at all. Some people love it; others don't.

Residencia Dom João (Three-star)
Rua José Estevão, 43
1100 Lisboa
tel: 543-064
In quiet, residential neighborhood, a bit off the beaten track, but only a 15-minute walk to the Marquês de Pombal Square.

Residencia Florescente (Two-star)
Rua das Portas de Santo Antão, 99
1100 Lisboa
tel: 326-609
Simple, lovely and inexpensive. Tiled hall-ways and bright, clean rooms, some with full baths. Very centrally located, near Restaura-dores Square.

ÉVORA

Évora is small enough so that nothing is more than a few blocks from the center. The *pousada* (see following list) has the best location, right between the Cathedral and the Temple of Diana.

Albergaria Vitória (Four-star)
Rua Diana de Liz
7000 Évora
tel: (066) 271-74

Estalagem Monte das Flores (Four-star)
Monte das Flores
7000 Évora
tel: (066) 125-018

Hotel Planicie (Three-star)
Largo de Àlvaro Velho, 40
7000 Évora
tel: (066) 240-26

Residencia Diana (Three-star)
Rua Diogo Cão, 2
7000 Évora
tel: (066) 220-08
A nice little place near the Cathedral.

Residencia O Eborense (Three-star)
Largo da Misericórdia, 1
7000 Évora
tel: (066) 220-31
In a converted mansion.

Residencia Riviera (Four-star)
Rua 5 de Outubro
7000 Évora
tel: (066) 233-04

THE ALGARVE

• Faro and Surrounding Areas

Hotel Atlantis Vilamoura (Five-star)
Vilamoura, Quarteira
8100 Loulé
tel: (089) 347-01

Hotel Dom Pedro Vilamoura (Four-star)
Vilamoura, Quarteira
8100 Loulé
tel: (089) 347-01

Hotel Dona Filipa (Five-star)
Vale do Lobo
Almansil
tel: (089) 568-48

Hotel Eva Dom Pedro (Four-star)
Avenida da República
7000 Faro
tel: (089) 240-54
Highest class hotel in the city.

Hotel Faro (Three-star)
Praça Dom Francisco Gomes
8000 Faro
tel: (089) 220-76

Estalagem Aeromar (Four-star)
Praia de Faro
8000 Faro
tel: (089) 235-42
On the beach.

Pensão O Farão (Three-star)
4 Largo da Madalena
8000 Faro

Residencial Samé (Three-star)
Rua do Bocage, 66
8000 Faro
In the center of town.

• Lagos and Surrounding Area

Albergaria Casa Sao Gonçalo (Four-star)
Rua Cándido dos Reis
8600 Lagos

tel: (082) 621-71

Albergaria Cidade Velha (Four-star)
Rua Dr. Joaquin Telo, 7
8600 Lagos
tel: (082) 620-41

Hotel de Lagos (Four-star)
Rua Nova da Aldeia, 83
8600 Lagos
tel: (082) 620-11

Hotel Golfinho (Four-star)
Praia Dona Ana
8600 Lagos
tel: (082) 620-81
On the beach.

Hotel Meia Praia (Three-star)
Meia Praia
8600 Lagos
tel: (082) 620-01
On the beach.

Hotel Riomar (Three-star)
Rua Cándido dos Reis
8600 Lagos
tel: (082) 630-91

• Sagres
There are many private rooms to let in
Sagres – just look for the signs in the windows. Aside from these and the *pousada*,
there's the three-star **Hotel da Baleeira**,
Baleeira, 8650 Sagres, Vila do Bispo, tel:
(082) 642-12.

POUSADAS

As an alternative to hotels, residentials or
pensions, the Portuguese tourist office
maintains a list of private houses converted
for guest use. Most of these are old, renovated mansions; some are owner-occupied,
some not. For reservations and information
on the Tourist Lodging (except for the Costa
Verde region) in manor houses and other
private homes, visit the local tourist office,
or contact the Direção-Geral de Turismo,
Turismo de Habitacão, Rua Alexandre Herculano 51-3º, Direito, 1200 Lisboa, Portugal, tel: (1) 681-713. For reservations in the
Costa Verde, contact: Delegacao de Turismo de Ponte de Lima, 4990 Ponte de Lima,
Portugal, tel: (58) 942-335, telex: 32618.

Either office will supply you with a complete list of the houses available.

Finally, an expensive but worthwhile
option is the government-run network of
pousadas, first-class accommodation in
historic castles, palaces and monasteries, or
in specially built sites. The following is a
complete list of *pousadas* and manor houses
by area. For reservations, contact a travel
agent or Empresa Nacional de Turismo,
Central de Reservas, Avenida Santa Joana
Princesa, 10, 1700 Lisboa, tel: 881-221.

NORTHERN PORTUGAL

**• The Douro, the Minho,
& Tras-os-Montes**

Pousada Barão Forrester
Alijó
tel: (059) 954-67
Near Vila Real.

Pousada Dom Dinis
Vila Nova da Cerveira
tel: (051) 956-01
North of Viana do Castelo. Inside the walls
of the village's old castle.

Pousada Santa Catarina
Miranda do Douro
tel: (073) 422-55

Pousada Santa Maria Oliveira
Guimarães
tel: (053) 412-157

Pousada Santa Marinha
Guimarães
tel: (053) 418-453
Area showcase *pousada*, in an exquisitely
renovated monastery.

Pousada São Bartolomeu
Bragança
tel: (073) 224-93

Pousada São Bento
Canicada
tel: (053) 571-90

Pousada São Gonçalo
Amarante
tel: (055) 461-113
East of Oporto.

Pousada São Teotónio
Valença do Minho
tel: (051) 222-42
North of Viana do Castelo, on the border with Galicia.

NORTH-CENTRAL PORTUGAL

Pousada Castelo
Obidos
tel: (062) 951-05
Tiny but lovely, part of the original castle.

Pousada Mestre Afonso Domingues
Batalha
tel: (044) 962-60
Right next to the famous abbey.

Pousada Ria
Murtosa
tel: (034) 483-32
Near Aveiro, right on the lagoon.

Pousada Santa Barbara
Oliveira do Hospital
tel: (038) 522-52
Between Coimbra and the Serra da Estrêla.

Pousada Santa Maria
Marvão
tel: (045) 932-01
Near Portalegre.

Pousada Santo António
Serem
tel: (034) 521-1230
Near Aveiro.

Pousada São Jeronimo
Caramulo
tel: (032) 862-91
Between Viseu and Aveiro.

Pousada São Lourenço
Manteigas
tel: (075) 471-50
In the Serra da Estrêla.

Pousada São Pedro
Castelo do Bode
tel: (049) 381-75
Near Tomar.

Pousada Senhora das Neves
Almeida
tel: (071) 542-83
East of the Serra da Estrêla.

SOUTHERN PORTUGAL

Pousada de Palmela
Palmela
tel: (065) 235-0410
Near Setúbal. Very well designed, inside castle walls.

Pousada dos Loios
Évora
tel: (066) 240-51

Pousada Infante
Sagres
tel: (082) 642-22
Each room has a small balcony overlooking the ocean.

Pousada Santa Clara
Santa Clara-a-Velha
tel: (083) 982-50
Between Sines and Portimão.

Pousada Santa Isabel
Estremoz
tel: (068) 226-18

Pousada Santa Luzia
Elvas
tel: (068) 621-94

Pousada São Bras
São Bras de Alportel
tel: (089) 423-05
North of Faro.

Pousada São Felipe
Setubal
(tel. 065 238-44)
In an old fortress, overlooking the harbor.

Pousada São Gens
Serpa
tel: (084) 903-27
East of Beja.

Pousada São Tiago
Santiago do Cacem
tel: (069) 224-59
Just east of Sines.

Pousada Vale do Gaio
Alcacer do Sal
tel: (065) 661-00
Southeast of Setúbal.

FOOD DIGEST

WHAT TO EAT

Portuguese food is simple and fresh, abundant and filling. There is not an overwhelming variety in a country that can afford to import little. Portuguese rely on hearty basics; no complicated sauces, but broad flavors and lots of garlic, olive oil and salt. Canned and frozen foods are almost unknown, or if known, scorned. Portions are more than filling, and you'll have to work hard to clean your plate in most cases.

Soup is made especially well in Portugal. Perhaps the best – certainly the most famous – is the traditional *caldo verde*, a kale and potato puree with a piece of *chouriço* (sausage) in every bowl (some claim that the *chouriço* is required by law). For garlic lovers, there's *açorda á alentejana*, a bread-thickened garlic broth with egg. *Canja* is chicken soup; *sopa de mariscos* is seafood chowder; both are mouth-watering.

Fish, of course, is abundant. *Bacalhau* (codfish) is a national obsession. There are, supposedly, 365 ways to prepare it, and almost every restaurant features at least one of the ways. Shellfish ranges from the miniature clam-like *conquilhas*, to lobster and everything in between including snails, squid and octopus.

Carne de porco à alentejana (clams and pork with coriander) is a favorite meat dish. So is *cozida à portuguesa*, a stew. Other popular meats are goat, rabbit, suckling pig and chicken.

The Portuguese make wonderful regional cheese. Try *queijo da serra*, from Serra da Estrêla, in northern Portugal. While the real stuff is difficult to get in Lisbon, there is no shortage of *queijo tipo serra*, its imitation.

Other desserts are sweet. They include *arroz doce* (rice pudding), flan (custard), mousse (at its best, homemade and thicker than the French variety), and a wide selection of pastries and cakes.

Portuguese meal times are slightly later than what the Americans are accustomed to. Lunch is anywhere between 1 p.m. and 3 p.m.; dinner can start anywhere between 8 p.m. and 9:30 p.m. The following is a list of regional specialties.

IN THE NORTH

Coimbra and Aveiro
Chanfana (kid stew); *leitão* (roast suckling pig); *pasteis de Tentugal* and *pasteis de Santa Clara* (pastries).

The Douro and the Minho
Port and green wines (including red "green" wine); *caldo verde*; *Tripas a moda do porta* (tripe with butter beans)

Serra da Estrêla
Queijo da serra (serra cheese); Dão wines; roasted kid; varieties of sausage.

Tras-os-Montes
Alheiras (flour sausage); *chouriços de sangue* (blood sausage); *feijoada* (bean stew); veal; goat; rabbit; trout; lamprey.

IN THE SOUTH

Alentejo
Açorda de alhos or de coentros (a bread stuffing heavily spiced with garlic and/or coriander); *carne de porco à alentejana* (clams and pork with coriander); lamb dishes.

Algarve
Ameijoas na cataplana (clams with ham and sausage, spiced with parsley and pepper); fried sardines; snails; seafood in general.

WHERE TO EAT

Restaurants are rated on a scale of one to four, depending on expense, decor and service. The quality of food does not necessarily relate to the rating; there are plenty of great one and two-star neighborhood places. The list has a few recommended restaurants in several cities. There are, of course, many more. Throughout the country, the *pousada* dining rooms are of consistently high quality (and are usually expensive).

NORTHERN PORTUGAL

• Braga

A Narcisa
Largo do Monte de Arcos
tel: 229-48
Charming, moderately priced restaurant.

Retiro do Cacador
Nogueira
tel: 265-50
Serves good, inexpensive Portuguese and regional cuisine.

• Bragança

Arca de Noe
Avenida do Savor
tel: 227-59
For less expensive fare.

Hotel Bragança
tel: 225-79
A high-class restaurant.

• Chaves

O Arado
Rua Ribeira Pinheiro
tel: 219-96
A noteworthy restaurant with a panoramic view.

• Oporto
You'll find a number of homey restaurants in the Ribeira area:

Casa Filha da Mae Preta
Cais da Ribeira, 40
tel: 315-515
A local favorite for traditional entree; inexpensive. Nearby is the slightly more expensive **Bebobos**, also very good.

Mal Cozinhado
Rua Outeirinho
tel: 381-319
A somewhat expensive *fado* house.

Mamuda
Rua do Campinho, 30
tel: 233-51
A very good restaurant officially known as "Montenegro". Expensive.

Portucale
Rua da Alegria, 598
tel: 570-717
A high-class restaurant with a panoramic view.

• Viana do Castelo

Os 3 Potes
Rua Beco dos Fornos, 9
tel: 234-32
Offers regional dishes in a traditional atmosphere; moderately priced.

The restaurant at the **Hotel Santa Luzzia**, on the top of the hill overlooking the city, is more expensive and very good.

• Viseu

O Cortiço
Rua Augusto Hilario, 47
tel: 238-53
An excellent restaurant specializing in regional dishes. Moderate to expensive.

• Aveiro

A Cozinha do Rei
Rua Dr. Manuel das Neves, 65
in the Hotel Afonso V
Serves Portuguese and international food. Expensive.

Avenida
Avenida Dr. Lourenco Peixinho
Moderate.

Centenário
Praça do Mercado
Regional specialties. Moderate.

Galo d'Ouro
Travessa do Mercado, 2
Moderately priced Portuguese specialties.

Imperial
Rua Dr. Nascimento Leitao in the hotel of the same name.
A first-class restaurant. Expensive.

Sheik
Largo da Praça do Peixe, 3
Near the fish market. Large portions at low prices.

COIMBRA

Adega Paço de Conde
Rua Adelino Veiga, off the Praça do Comércio in the Baixa.
Has a nice atmosphere; offers grill specialties. Inexpensive.

Big Ben
Avenida Emídio Navarro, opposite park.
Expensive.

O Alfredo
Avenida João das Regras, on the far side of the bridge.
Seafood. Moderate.

O Patio
Patio da Inquisicão, near Praça 8 de Maio.
Good food; modest and inexpensive.

O Ticino
Rua Bernardo Albuquerque, in Olivais section of town.
Swiss-Italian specialties. Moderate.

Piscinas
Over the municipal swimming pool on Rua General Humberto Delgado.
Expensive.

Praça Velha
Praça do Comércio.
Good food outdoors. Moderate.

Real das Canas
Antiga Estrada de Lisboa
(on the old road to Lisbon).
Excellent view. Moderate.

Sereia
Rua Dr. Henriques Seco, near Santa Cruz Park.
Counter service downstairs, restaurant upstairs. Friendly service. Inexpensive.

• **Outside Coimbra**

Conde de Marialva
In Cantonhede, about 21 km northwest of Coimbra.
Expensive.

O Escondidinho
In Figueira da Foz.
Goanese cooking. Moderate.

O Verde Moinho
Casal do Lobo, near Vale das Canas, 5-6 km (3-4 miles) outside of Coimbra.
Unusual specialties in an atmospheric setting. Moderate.

Panorâmica
Penacova, about 23km (14 miles) northeast of Coimbra.
Beautiful view of the Mondego valley. The drive there is also scenic. Moderate.

IN & AROUND SERRA DA ESTRÊLA

• **Seia**

O Camelo
On the main street. A large restaurant with pleasant atmosphere, good service and good food. Moderate.

• **Oliveira do Hospital**

A Onda
Small, friendly and bright. Limited menu but the food is good. Inexpensive.

LISBON

It is wise to make reservations at the more expensive restaurants, especially if you are planning to go on weekends.

Expensive

Avis
Rua Serpa Pinto, 12-B
tel: 328-391
Chic atmosphere, international menu.

Bachus
Largo da Trinidade, 9
tel: 322-828
Sophisticated atmosphere.

Casa da Comida
Travessa das Amoreinas, 1
tel: 685-376

Casa do Leão
In St. George's Castle
tel: 875-962
Elegant decor, and the best view in town.
Open daily for lunch only.

Escorial
Rua das Portas de Santo Antão, 47,
near Restauradores Square
tel: 363-758
Shellfish specialties.

Gambrinus
Rua das Portas de Santo Antão, 25,
near Restauradores Square
tel: 321-466
A popular splurge for Lisboners. Noted for
its fish and seafood.

Pabe
Rua Duque de Palmela, 27-A
near Marquês de Pombal Square
tel: 535-675
Portuguese and international dishes.

Tavares Rico
Rua da Misericórdia, 37
tel: 321-112
Best-known luxury restaurant in town.
Beautiful gilt and mirrored dining room.

Moderate

Adega da Tia Matilde
Rua de Benificencia, 77
tel: 772-172
Regional Portuguese dishes.

Casa Transmontana
Calçada do Duque, 39
tel: 320-300
Portuguese specialties.

Mercado de Santa Clara
Campo de Santa Clara, where the Feira da
Ladra flea market takes place.
tel: 873-986

Michel
Largo de Santa Cruz do Castelo, 5,
just outside São Jorge's castle
tel: 864-338

Pap' Acorda
Rua da Atalaia, 57, in the Bairro Alto
tel: 364-811
In a remodeled bakery. Extremely popular;
difficult to get a table on a Friday or Saturday
night.

Porto de Abrigo
Rua dos Remolares, 18
tel: 360-873
An excellent seafood restaurant near the
waterfront. Try the *pera doce* (sweet pear)
for dessert.

Xele Bananas
Praça das Flores, 29
tel: 670-515
Popular with the Portuguese.

Inexpensive

Antigua Casa Faz Frio
Rua Dom Pedro V, 96
tel: 361-860
Excellent *paelha* (rice with seafood).

Bomjardin
Travessa de Santo Antão, 11,
near Restauradores Square
tel: 324-389
Three annexes on the same street. The best
roast chicken in town.

Bota Alta
Travessa da Queimada, 35
tel: 327-959
A nice, popular restaurant in the Bairro Alto.

Casa do Alentejo
Rua das Portas de Santo Antão, 58
tel: 328-011
Alentejano specialties in a lavishly tiled
interior with several dining rooms.

Cervejaria da Trindade
Rua Nova da Trindade, 20-C
tel: 323-506
A beautiful converted convent with lovely
tiles and a garden. Although it's large, it fills
up on Friday and Saturday nights. Get there
early.

O Bichano
Rua Atalaia, 78
tel: 372-546
A tiny place in the Bairro Alto with good
food.

Os Anarquistas
Largo da Trindade, 14
tel: 323-510
Another Bairro Alto favorite.

Portugalia
Rua Almirante Reis, 117
tel: 520-002
Well-known for its steak sauce. A large,
spacious interior.

ÉVORA

Two excellent and very elegant places to eat
are **A Cozinha de Santo Humberto**, Rua da
Moeda, 39 (tel: 242-51); and **Fialho**,
Travessa das Mascarenhas, 14 (tel: 230-79).
Other good, but more moderate choices are
Lagoa, Rua Cándido dos Reis, 19 (tel: 268-
82) and **O Taco**, Largo Luis de Camões, 19
(tel: 233-01). For very good food at very
reasonable prices, the best deal in town is O
Sobreiro, Rua do Torres, 8.

THE ALGARVE

Faro offer lots of good splurges, but perhaps
the best is **Cidade Velha**, Largo da Sé (tel:
227-45); very expensive. The **Hotel de Faro**
has a larger restaurant (tel: 220-76); very
expensive. The **Clube Naval**, (tel: 234-34)
next to the dock, serves less expensive seafood dishes.

Nearby Olhão has several good and inexpensive places, including **O Escondidinho**,
Rua Leonardo (tel: 726-74).

In Lagos, try **Marafado**, on the highway
to Lisbon (tel: 638-39), with a panoramic
view; moderate. Sagres offers several seafood restaurants. The **Mar A Vista** is moderately priced and has a lovely view.

DRINKING NOTES

Portuguese wine is delicious. There are three
basic types: red, white and green, the last
being young and slightly sparkling, and not
green in color. Port, for after dinner, comes
in both red and white. Most wines are inexpensive, and a low price does not indicate
low quality. It's generally safe to stick with
the house brand. Wine is drunk at both lunch
and dinner.

Beer (*cerveja*) is ordered by the bottle
(*garrafa*), the mug (*caneca*) or the glass
(*imperial* or *fino*).

A small, strong cup of coffee is *bica*; this
same portion in a large glass filled with milk
is a *galão*. If you want less milk and more
coffee, order a *meio de leite* (may-oh duh
late).

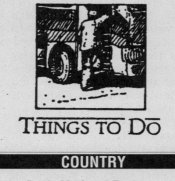

THINGS TO DO

COUNTRY

Peneda-Gerês National Park
Portugal's only official national park is
Peneda-Gerês, which extends over some
50,000 acres (20,000 hectares) and is located in the far north of the country. The park
is bordered by Spain, and encompasses parts
of the Peneda and Gerês mountain ranges,
the Lima River, a branch of the Cavado river,
and countless streams and dams. The highest
peak on the Peneda-Gerês measures 5,095
feet (1,544 meters) with a view of the Minho,
Tras-os-Montes, and across the border into
Galicia.

The lush plant life is fed by heavy rainfall.
The park is the home of 17 species of plants
to be found nowhere else, as well as extensive forests of oak and pine. Wild ponies,
deer, wolf, golden eagles, wild boars and
badgers, as well as many other animals, live
within the boundaries.

You may fish, ride horseback, hike and
mountain climb amid the breathtaking scenery in the park. You can also visit picturesque villages including Castro Laboreiro
and Cidadelhe, probably of prehistoric origin; Soajo, probably Roman; and Lindoso,
medieval. There are also dolmens perhaps
5,000 years old, and milestones that once
marked the old Roman road to Braga.

Entrance to the Peneda half of the park – the northern section – is from Melgaço, just at the Galician border. To Gerês, there are entrances from Ponte da Barca and from the Braga-Chaves road (follow the turn off to Caniçada). There is a *pousada* at the edge of the park, in Caniçada.

Tourist offices in the Minho, especially Braga, can provide information about the park.

Montesinho Park

Resting in the far northeastern corner of Portugal, Montesinho lies between Bragança, Vinhais, and the Spanish border. Like Peneda-Gerês, varieties of flora and fauna abound. There is not only breathtaking scenery but also ancient villages. These villages preserve age-old customs, and a few even speak their own dialect. Entrance is from Bragança or Vinhais.

Serra da Estréla

Granite peaks, glacial valleys, and streams and lakes are all part of the Serra da Estréla. The highest peaks in Portugal are also among the most beautiful, winter or summer; and they are quite accessible by car as well (though in wintertime roads may be blocked). In winter, this is the place for the little that Portugal has to offer in the way of winter sports. Visitors ski here, despite poor facilities, but mostly they scu. (Scu is a combination of the words ski and *cu*, which means rear end in Portuguese. To scu, grab a plastic bag, sit on it, and slide downhill.)

There are places to stay in the larger towns in or near the Serra, which include Gouveia, Seia, Covilhã and Guarda. There is a *pousada* in Manteigas. The Serra is about two hours by car from Coimbra.

Serra da Arrábida

Just south of Lisbon, the Serra da Arrábida's natural beauty is accessible to anyone with a car. The peaks are modest, but beautiful nonetheless, as are the preglacial forests and the beaches. The Serra da Arrábida lies along Highway 379-1, which runs west from Setúbal.

CULTURE PLUS

MUSEUMS

Lisbon overflows with museums, Oporto has several, and any self-respecting town in Portugal has at least one. You won't be overwhelmed by the size of any museum in Portugal; they are all small enough to be manageable. Some of the most interesting are the local handicrafts museums, which are not museums in the purest sense, but rather showcases where works on display are sold. Most museums are open from 10 a.m.-noon. and 2 p.m.-5 p.m., and closed Mondays. Generally, a small admission fee is charge.

The following is a list of museums in several cities and regions in Portugal.

THE ALGARVE

• **Faro**

Infante Dom Henrique
Archaeological Museum
(in the Convento de Nossa Senhora da Assunção)
Exhibits Roman and Arabic artifacts, tiles and ceramics.

Regional Ethnographic Museum
Praça da Liberdade, 2
Models of Algarvian life are put up, as well as handicrafts and photographs.

• **Lagos**

Regional Museum of Lagos
(in the annex of Santo António Church)
Archaeology, religious art and handicrafts.

THE ALENTEJO

• Beja

Queen Leonor Museum
(in the Convento da Conceição)
Archaeology, ceramics and religious art.

• Évora

Handicrafts Museum
Rua da Republica, across from São Francisco Church
Display and sale of local crafts.

Museum of Évora
(between the Cathedral and the Temple of Diana)
Archaeology, Roman sculpture, good Portuguese Primitives.

Sacred Art Museum
(in the Cathedral)
Old costumes, intricate embroidery, silver pieces, sculpture.

COIMBRA & SURROUNDING AREAS

• Aveiro

Museum of Aveiro
Convento de Jesus, Rua Santa Joana Princesa

• Coimbra

Machado de Castro National Museum
Largo de Dr. José Rodrigues
Important collection of sculpture; Roman galleries.

Museum of Conimbriga
Archaeological Site
Pieces from and explanation of the Roman ruins.

• Tomar

Abraham Zacuto Luso-Hebraic Museum
(in the old synagogue)

THE MOUNTAINS & TRAS-OS-MONTES

• Guarda

Regional Museum
(in the old Paço Episcopal)
Archaeology, painting, sculpture.

• Viseu

Grão-Vasco Museum
(next to the Cathedral)
A collection of 16th-century paintings.

• Bragança

Regional Museum
Rua Abílio Beca

THE MINHO & THE DOURO

• Braga

Dom Diogo de Sousa Museum
Roman Archaeology.

Museum of Regional Art and History
Palácio dos Biscainhos

Sacred Art Museum
(in the Cathedral)
Beautiful tiles, sculpture, religious costume, jewelry and other objects in rather musty rooms.

• Guimarães

Alberto Sampaio Museum
(in the annex to the Church of Nossa Senhora da Oliveira)
14th-19th century art.

Martins Sarmento Museum
(in the Convento de São Somingos)
Archaeology; modern and contemporary art.

Sacred Art Museum
(in the old Convento das Dominicas)

OPORTO

Guerra-Junqueira Museum
Rua D. Hugo, 32
Collection of art objects and furniture from the 16th-19th century.

Museum of Archaeology and Prehistory
Praça Parador Leitão

Museum of History and Ethnography
Largo São João Novo, 11

Sacred Art and Archaeology Museum
(in the old College of São Lorenzo)

Soares dos Reis Museum
Rua D. Manuel II, in the Palácio das Carrancas
Art from prehistory to the 19th century, including the sculptures of Soares dos Reis.

• **Viana do Castelo**

Municipal Museum
(in the old Solar dos Macieis)
Holds exhibits of pottery, furniture, archaeology, anthropology.

LISBON

Archaeological Museum
Largo do Carmo, at the top of the Santa Justa Elevator
In the ruins of the old Carmo Convent. Roman and medieval artifacts. Open 11 a.m.-6 p.m.

Calouste Gulbenkian Museum
Avenida de Berna, 45
tel: 735-131
The city's largest museum houses a permanent collection of Egyptian, Oriental, Greek/Roman and European art. The museum's Modern Art Center is next door, on Rua Nicolau Bettencourt. Usually one or two excellent special exhibitions in addition to the regular collection. Open Tuesday, Thursday, Friday and Sunday, 10 a.m.-5 p.m. (both museums). The Gulbenkian opens Wednesday and Saturday, 2 p.m.-8 p.m. The Modern Art Center, 10 a.m.-7 p.m.

Calouste Gulbenkian Planetarium
Praça do Império, Belém, next to Jerónimos Monastery
tel: 610-192
Open Wednesday, Saturday and Sunday with sessions at 3:30 p.m. and 4:45 p.m.

City Museum
Campo Grande 245, in Pimenta Palace
tel: 759-1617
Traces Lisbon's past and present. Open 10 a.m.-1 p.m. and 2 p.m.-6 p.m.

Costume Museum
Estrada do Lumiar, 2
tel: 759-0318
A lovely museum of antique dress and toys. A section detailing spinning and weaving processes. A good restaurant on the grounds. Open 10 a.m.-1 p.m. and 2:30 p.m.-5 p.m.

Decorative Art Museum
Largo das Portas do Sol, in the Alfama
tel: 862-183
In an 18th century palace. Furniture, tapestries, and an interesting mix of other articles. Open Monday through Saturday between 10 a.m.-1 p.m. and 2 p.m.-5 p.m.; Opening hours on Sundays are 1 p.m.-5 p.m. Workshops on decorative arts open Wednesdays.

Ethnological Museum
Avenida Ilha da Madeira
Artifacts from all over the world, principally from former Portuguese colonies in Africa. Open 10 a.m.-12:30 p.m. and 2 p.m.-5 p.m.

Maritime Museum
Praça do Império, Belém, next to Jerónimos Monastery
tel: 612-541
Maps, instruments and detailed models of ships. Open 10 a.m.-5 p.m.

Military Museum
Largo do Museu de Artilharia, near Santa Apolónia station
tel: 867-135
Weapons and armor from the 15th century to the present. Open 11 a.m.-5 p.m.

Museum of Sacred Art
Largo da Trindade, in the Bairro Alto
tel: 360-361
A small museum in São Roque church. Open

10 a.m.-5 p.m.

National Art Gallery (Museum Nacional de Arte Antigua)
Rua das Janelas Verdes, 95
tel: 676-001
The most important national collection of European painting; worth a visit. Cafeteria and garden on the premises. Open 10 a.m.-1 p.m. and 2:30 p.m.-5 p.m.

National Coach Museum
Praça Afonso de Albequerque, in Belém
tel: 638-022
A collection of antique carriages, one of the most complete of its kind. The oldest is from 1619. Open 10 a.m.-5 p.m.

National Museum of Contemporary Art
Rua Serpa Pinto, 6
tel: 368-028
Open 10 a.m.-12:30 p.m. and 2 p.m.-5 p.m.

National Tile Museum
Rua Madre de Deus, 4, in the Convento de Madre de Deus
tel: 824-132
Lovely museum of antique and modern tiles. Open 10 a.m.-12:30 p.m. and 2 p.m.-5 p.m.

Popular Art Museum
Avenida de Brasilia on the docks in Belém
tel: 611-282
Folk and popular art: filigree, porcelain, embroidery. Open 10 a.m.-12:30 p.m. and 2 p.m.-5 p.m.

Rafael Bordalo Pinheiro Museum
Campo Grande 382
tel: 759-0816
Pottery and drawings by the 19th-century artist. Open 11 a.m.-5:30 p.m.

Vasco da Gama Aquarium
Dáfundo, near Algés, on the Cascais train line
tel: 419-6337
Open every day 10 a.m.-5:30 p.m.

MOVIES

Movies in Portugal are subtitled, not dubbed, so they're accessible to non-Portuguese speakers. Seats are assigned, and the usher should be tipped 5 or 10 *escudos*.

NIGHTLIFE

Nightlife in Portugal is different things to different people. For some, it's a jug of wine and a night of *fado*. For others, it's a flashy disco, or a night at the neighborhood cafe.

Much of Portugal's nightlife takes place in Lisbon, and much of Lisbon's nightlife – from *fado* to disco – takes place in the Bairro Alto, an odd mix of the historical and the trendy. Towns and smaller cities – anything smaller than Oporto, tend to get very sleepy at about 10 p.m. or 11 p.m., and you'll find very little to do besides going to an odd disco or two. There are two exceptions: the tourist centers in the Algarve, where summer visitors like to stay up late; and any town, village, or city on the night of a festival.

For a list of just about everything going on and everywhere it's happening, consult the weekly newspaper *Sete*, which comes out on Wednesday. Even if you can't read Portuguese, the listings are comprehensible.

MUSIC

The Portuguese musical tradition is much broader than simply *fado*. Folk music, very different from *fado*, is a surprisingly vibrant current. Portuguese rock music, born after the Revolution, ranges from the mediocre to the superb. Below are some of the better musicians that play in Lisbon or that have albums available.

FADO

Amália Rodrigues, of course. Her two-volume *Greatest Hits* was released in 1986, and covers a wide range of her work. Other well-known *fadistas* include Carlos do Carmo, João Braga, and Manuel de Almeida.

FOLK/POPULAR

Vitorino. Folksy, traditional ballads, many from the Alentejo.

Janita Salome. Vitorino's brother sings folk music with an Arabic influence. Brigada Vitor Jara. This Açorian group collects folk songs from all over Portugal.

Carlos Paredes. Traditional Portuguese guitar. Beautiful instrumentals.

Julio Pereira. Portugal's best *cavaquinho* player; the *cavaquinho* looks like a baby guitar and is the ancestor of the ukelele.

Popular balladeers include **Fausto** and **Paulo de Carvalho**.

ROCK

Rui Veloso. The "father" of Portuguese rock music, influenced by soul and blues. His first album, from 1980, is *Ar de Rock* and his most recent is *Rui Veloso*. Both are excellent.

GNR. An energetic band whose latest album is *Psicopatria*.

Other bands include: **Radio Macau**, **Trouvante**, and **Xutos and Pontapes**.

DISCO/BOITES

Music – in *fado* houses, concert halls, and nightclubs alike – tends to start fairly late, perhaps around 10 p.m. Bars with live music – and often dancing – are called "boites" or "dancings". Discos occasionally have live music as well.

• Lisbon
In or near the Bairro Alto, Rato, and São Bento three areas located just west and up the hill from Avenida da Liberdade.

A Lontra
Rua São Bento, 157
tel: 661-083
A bar with small dance floor; people usually end up dancing all over the place, anyway. Live African music.

Clave di Nos
Rua do Norte, 100
tel: 368-420
Live music.

Copo do Tres
Rua Marcos Portugal, 1
(in Praça das Flores)
tel: 670-230
Live music ranging from string quartets to jazz to Brazilian bands.

Fragil
Rua da Atalaia, 128
tel: 369-528
The trendiest disco in town. Good music.

Gafiera
Calçada de Tijolo, in the Bairro Alto
tel: 325-953
A lively Brazilian bar; exotic drinks, Brazilian bands, lots of sambaing and lots of fun.

India a Noite É Uma Crianca
Praça das Flores, 8
tel: 663-545
Portuguese, Brazilian and Latin American folk music, live. Nice and cozy, but it gets crowded.

Longas Noites
Largo do Conde Baráo, 50
(in Casa Pia Athletic Club)
Open on Fridays, just about all night. The name means "long nights", and if you've made it to this place, you've probably had one – it's the place to be at about 4 a.m., after everything else has closed. Unpretentious; lots of room, lots of people.

• Elsewhere in Lisbon

Hot Clube de Portugal
Praça de Alegria, 39
tel: 367-369
The place for jazz.

Jamaica
Rua Nova do Carvalho, 6
(near Cais do Sodré train station)
tel: 321-859
DJ'd American music and dancing. In the city's red-light district.

Primorosa de Alvalade
Avenida dos Estados
Unidos da America, 128-D
tel: 771-913
Disco.

Rock RendezVous
Rua Beneficencia 175
tel: 774-402
Live rock music in a nice setting.

FADO HOUSES

Fado is a nostalgic – though not necessarily unhappy – music, a popular art which goes back several hundred years. Long associated with traditional, working-class neighborhoods, it is now more of a province for tourists. The *fadista*, a powerfully-voiced singer, is usually backed by *guitarras* – the twelve-stringed Portuguese version, and *violas* – what we would call a guitar. The Portuguese say it takes more than a good voice to become a *fadista* – it takes a lot of soul as well.

Many *fado* houses are located in the Bairro Alto. There are others in the older neighborhoods – the Alfama, Alcântara and Lapa. The houses usually serve dinner (optional) and often charge a fairly steep entrance or minimum consumption charge. Singing starts around 9:30 p.m. or 10 p.m. It's best to reserve in advance.

A Cesária
Rua Gilberto Rola, 20
tel: 665-745

A Sévera
Rua das Gáveas, 5
tel: 364-006

Adega Machado
Rua do Norte, 91
tel: 360-095

Lisboa À Noite
Rua das Gáveas, 69
tel: 368-557

Mascote de Atalaia
Rua da Atalaia.
Traditional *fado*, for the neighborhood, not the tourists. The local *fadistas* come to sing the night away in a small tavern. No food, no fancy decor – only wine and *fado*.

• **Oporto**

D. Uracca
Rua Padre Luis Cabral

1090 in Foz Velha
"Medieval" decoration and modern music.

Flying Dutchman
Centro Comercial Dallas
Avenida da Boavista, 1588
Attracts a more sedate crowd. The organist plays old favorites.

Griffon's
Rua Julio Dinis
Centro Comercial Brasília
Downstairs, a disco; upstairs, relative peace and quiet, and tables for resting.

Luis Armastrondo
Rua dos Mercadores 132, in the Ribeira
Live music, some of it jazz.

Postigo do Carvão
Rua Fonte Taurina, 26/34, in the Ribeira
A bar with a piano if you feel like playing.

Splash
Centro Comercial Dallas
Avenida da Boavista, 1588
Live music.

• **Coimbra**
There are two interesting places to be on a Friday or Saturday night in Coimbra. In the **Diligência**, off Rua da Sofia, there's usually a group who pick up the restaurant's guitars and sing *fado* and folk songs. If you're lucky, the music will be good. If not, just enjoy the *sangria*. Music starts around 10 p.m.; the Diligência closes at midnight.

The other place to be is the **Agora**, which starts and ends much later than the Diligência. The Agora has a variety of live music, much of it a simple setting.

Check also the **Gil Vicente Theater**, which usually has a weekly program of concerts, dance groups or movies. Keep an eye out for posters of other events – there is usually a concert or two. The tourist office also keeps a list of events.

SHOPPING

WHAT TO BUY

Portuguese handicrafts range from hand-carved toothpicks to wicker furniture to blankets and rugs. The most famous Portuguese handicrafts include ceramic tiles (*azulejos*) and pottery, Arraiolos rugs, and embroidery and lace work. Different varieties of ceramic work are produced all over the country; in the Alentejo, for example, you'll find examples of barro pottery, a simple brown clay, sometimes decorated, sometimes glazed. Decorations on ceramics tend to be paintings of fruit or flowers, or sometimes scenes of rural life. Fine pottery from around Coimbra often carries animal motifs, and looks quite intricate in comparison with the simple Alentejano decorations. Farther north, blue-and-white glazed pottery appears.

Arraiolos rugs, by contrast, come from only one place: Arraiolos, in the Alentejo. (They are, however, sold in other parts of the country, especially Lisbon.) The art of designing and stitching these rugs probably goes back to the Middle Ages.

SHOPPING AREAS

While many regional crafts are sold in Lisbon, there is usually a wider and more authentic selection in the provinces. The following is a list of traditional crafts by area.

• Alentejo
Cane and wicker work, cork products (baskets, coasters, sculpture), wool blankets, Arraiolos rugs, ceramics (barro), traditional hand-painted furniture, copper goods and lace.

• Algarve
Palm and wicker work, copper and brass articles, candles.

• Coimbra and the Beiras (including Aveiro)
Ceramics (colorful animal motifs from near Coimbra; elegant Vista Alegre ceramics from the Aveiro region; black clay pottery from the Viseu region); woven rag quilts (from the Serra da Estréla); as well as lace and embroidery.

• Douro and Minho
Ceramics, wickerwork, straw baskets and hats; embroidery, crochet, and regional costumes (especially from the Viana do Castelo area), religious art (from Braga). The Thursday market in Barcelos, north of Oporto, has lots of handicrafts for sale.

• Tras-os-Montes
Blankets; weaving and tapestries; black pottery from Bisalhões (near Vila Real).

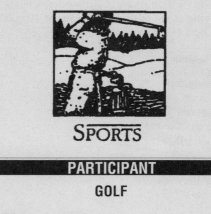

SPORTS

PARTICIPANT
GOLF

• Lisbon
All golf facilities are located outside the city proper.

Estoril Golf Club
Avenida da República
Estoril
tel: 268-0176

Estoril-Sol Golf Club
Estrada da Lagoa Azul, 3
Linho, near Sintra
tel: 923-2461

Lisboa Country Club
Quinta da Aroeira
Monte de Caparica
tel: 226-3244

Lisbon Sports Club
Casal da Carregueira
Belas, near Queluz
tel: 431-0077

Marinha Golf Club
Quinta da Marinha,
near Cascais
tel: 226-3244

• **Setúbal**

Troia Golf Club
Torralta, Troia
tel: (065) 441-51 or 442-36

• **Costa de Prata**

Vimeiro Golf Club
Praia do Porto Novo
Vimeiro, about 65km north of Lisbon
tel: (061) 981-57

• **Northern Portugal**

Miramar Golf Club
Praia de Miramar
Avenida Sacudura Cabral
Valadares, near Porto
tel: (02) 762-2067

Oporto Golf Club
Pedreira, Silvada, near Espinho
tel: (02) 720-008

Vidago Golf Club
Vidago, about two hours from Porto
tel: (076) 971-06

• **Algarve**

Palmares Golf Club
Meia Praia, near Lagos
tel: (082) 629-53 or 629-61

Penina Golf Club
Penina, near Portimao
tel: (082) 220-51 or 220-58

Quinta do Lago Golf Club
Almancil, near Loulé and Faro
tel: (089) 945-29

Vale do Lobo Golf Club
Vale de Lobo, near Loulé
tel: (089) 941-45

Vilamoura-1 and Vilamoura-2 Golf Clubs
Vilamoura, near Loulé
tel: (089) 336-52 or 336-53

TENNIS

In Lisbon, the **Marinha Golf Club**, **Lisboa Country Club**, and **Lisbon Sports Club**, listed above, have tennis courts. Try also the **Clube Ténis Estoril**, in Estoril, near the Casino (tel; 268-1675). There are two municipal courts in the city – one in **Monsanto Park**, the other in **Campo Grande** (tel: 638-073 or 648-741).

In Oporto, the **Miramar Golf Club** has facilities. There are also municipal courts at the **Clube de Tenis do Porto**, Rua Damala Góis (tel: 488-506).

In the Algarve, there are courts at the **Penina**, **Quinta do Lago**, **Vale do Lobo**, and **Vilamoura-1** Golf Clubs.

WATER SPORTS

There are very few rental facilities outside of the Algarve. In the Lisbon are, try **John David Snack Bar**, on the beach in Cascais, near the Palm Beach Disco. They rent waterskis, windsurf boards and paddleboats. In Porto, the **Oporto Golf Club** (see above) has skindiving facilities. Try the **Leca de Palmeira Beach** (to the north) for sailing.

In the Algarve, most of the larger tourist beaches and towns have some facilities. Near Lagos, there are windsurfing and waterskiing facilities at **Luz, São Roque** (Meia Praia) and **Alvor** beaches; the latter two also have sailing facilities. **Praia da Rocha** has sailing, windsurfing and waterskiing facilities; sailing and windsurfing are practiced at **Armacão de Pera**, near Albufeira. **Vilamoura** has extensive watersports facilities, as does **Vale de Lobo**.

FOOTBALL

Football (what Americans call soccer) dominates Portuguese sports life. From the 10-year-olds playing in the street to the hundreds of professional, semi-pro and amateur teams, to the massive coverage the sport is given on TV and in the papers, football in Portugal is inescapable. The three most important teams in the country are F.C. Porto, from Porto (the 1987 European champions), Benfica, and Sporting, both from Lisbon. Every Portuguese, no matter where he's from, is a loyal fan of one of the three.

The football season stretches from September or October to July. Tickets for the big three are difficult to get, as there are many season-ticket holders. In Lisbon, try the ABEP ticket kiosk located in Restauradores Square; elsewhere, try the stadiums themselves. Games are usually held on Sunday afternoons.

BULLFIGHTING

Portuguese bullfighting is different from the Spanish. It is considered less violent because the bull is not killed inside the ring (but later outside). Nonetheless, it is not for those with weak stomachs, as the bull is poked and prodded and stabbed until it is quite bloody. Unlike Spanish bullfighters, the Portuguese are on horseback; the horses are beautifully bedecked and highly trained.

Bullfighting is popular primarily in the Ribatejo (just outside Lisbon) and in Lisbon itself. The season begins in the spring and ends in the fall. In Lisbon, fights are held in the Campo Pequeno bullring. There is also a ring in Cascais. The most famous bullfights, however, are held in Vila Franca da Xira, a Ribatejana suburb of Lisbon. (Take the train from Santa Apolónia.)

Ribatejana festivals, which are frequent during the summer, almost always feature bullfighting and the freeing of bulls in the streets.

FURTHER READING

Although the Portuguese have a long and rich literary tradition, few books have been translated into English; fewer are still in print. The following is a partial list of works available in English.

Antunes, Antonio Lobo. *South of Nowhere* (*Os Cus de Judas*). Lobo Antunes writes psychological novels of great intensity.

De Camões, Luis. *The Lusiads*. An epic poem, written in 1572, celebrating the Portuguese Era of Discoveries. Written by Portugal's premier poet and national hero.

De Castro, Ferreira. *The Emigrants* and *The Mission*. Another modern Portuguese author of interest.

De Queiroz, Eça. *The Maias*, *The Illustrious House of Ramires*, *The Mandarin and Other Stories*, *The Relic*, and *The Sin of Father Amaro*. One of Portugal's best-known and most enjoyable authors. Eça wrote in the latter half of the 19th century.

Garrett, Almeida. *Brother Luis de Sousa*. Almeida Garrett was an important 19th-century poet and playwright.

Namora, Fernando. *Mountain Doctor*. One of the Portuguese "neo-realists" who tried to capture the ordinary texture of life. Another good neo-realist is Mario Braga, who wrote short stories.

Pessoa, Fernando. This early 20th-century poet is second only to Camões in the long list of illustrious Portuguese writers. Many of his poems have been translated into English; others were originally written in English. Pessoa wrote under the names of Alberto Caeiro, Ricardo Reis and Alvaro de Campos; not simply changing from pseudonym to pseudonym, but transforming his style with each persona as well.

Again, the selection in English is not wide, and sometimes hard to find. The following is a short compilation of historical, anthropological, and sociological books about Portugal, listed in rough chronological order according to the time periods they cover.

Boxer, C.R. *The Portuguese Seaborne Empire 1415-1825*. Harmondsworth, 1973.

Buneau, Thomas C. *Politics and Nationhood: Post Revolutionary Portugal*. Eastbourne Praeger, 1984.

Cutileiro, José. *A Portuguese Rural Society*. Clarendon Press, 1971. A study of Portuguese village life.

De Figueiredo, Antonio. *Portugal: 50 Years Of Dictatorship*. Harmondsworth, 1975. A general survey by a former political exile. Also, *Portugal and Its Empire: The Truth*. Gollancz, 1961.

De Oliveira Marques, A.H. *History of Portugal, Vol. I, From Lusitania to Empire*, and *Vol. II, From Empire to Corporate State*. Columbia University Press, 1972. The best general history of Portugal.

Gallop, Rodney. *Portugal, A Book of Folkways*. Cambridge University Press, 1936. A fascinating collection of Portuguese folklore.

Graham, Lawrence S. and Harry M. Makler. (eds.) *Contemporary Portugal, The Revolution and Its Antecedents*. University of Texas Press, 1979.

Graham, Lawrence S. and Douglas L. Wheeler. (eds.) *In Search of Modern Portugal, the Revolution and Its Consequences*. University of Wisconsin Press, 1983.

Harvey, Robert. *Portugal: Birth of a Democracy*. Macmillan, 1978.

Livermore, H.V. *Portugal, A Short History*, Edinburgh University Press, 1973. Also, *A New History of Portugal*, Cambridge University Press, 1976.

Mailer, Phil. *Portugal: The Impossible Revolution?* London, 1977.

Nowell, Charles E. *Portugal*. Prentice-Hall, 1973. Also, *A History of Portugal*, Van Nostrand Co., 1952.

Robinson, Richard Alan Hodgson. *Contemporary Portugal*. Allen and Unwin, 1979.

Soares, Mario. *Portugal's Struggle for Liberty*. Allen and Unwin, Ltd., 1975. By Portugal's current president, one of the key figures in the Revolution.

Sunday Times. *Insight on Portugal: The Year of the Captains*. Andre Deutsch, 1975. A journalistic survey of the events of the Revolution.

USEFUL ADDRESSES

Aveiro
Praça da Rebublica
tel: (034) 236-80

Beja
Rua Capitão João Francisco Sousa, 25
tel: (084) 236-93

Braga
Casa dos Crivos, Rua São Marcos
tel: (053) 769-24

Bragança
Avenida 25 de Abril
tel: (073) 222-72

Cascais
Arcada do Parque
tel: (01) 268-0113

Coimbra
Largo da Portagem
tel: (039) 237-99

Elvas
Praça da Republica
tel: (068) 622-36

Évora
Praça de Geraldo
tel: (066) 226-71

Faro
Rua Ataide de Oliveira, 100
tel: (089) 240-67

Guimarães
Al. Resistência Fascismo, 83
tel: (053) 412-450

Lagos
Praça Marquês de Pombal
tel: (082) 630-31

Lisbon
Praça dos Restauradores
tel: (01) 363-314

Oporto
Praça Dom João, 25
tel: (02) 258-05

Tomar
Avenida Dr. Candido Madureira
tel: (049) 330-95

Viana do Castelo
Avenida Candido dos Reis
tel: (058) 226-20

Viseu
Avenida Gulbenkian
tel: (032) 222-94

EMBASSIES

• **Lisbon**

Australia
Avenida da Liberdade, 244
tel: 523-350

Canada
Rua Rosa Araujo, 2
tel: 563-821

Great Britain
Rua São Domingos, 37
tel: 661-191

Ireland
Rua da Imprensa, 1
tel: 661-569

United States
Avenida Forças Armadas
tel: 726-6600

• **Porto**

Great Britain
Avenida Boavista, 3072
4100 Porto
tel: (02) 684-789

United States
Rua Júlio Dinis 826-3º
4000 Porto
tel: (02) 630-94

ART/PHOTO CREDITS

INDEX

C